QUEST
FOR
THE
PAST

READER'S DIGEST

QUEST FOR THE PAST

The Reader's Digest Association, Inc.
Pleasantville, New York/Montreal

Edited and designed by Dorling Kindersley Ltd

Project editors Ann Kramer, Lindy Newton
Art editor Flo Henfield
Designer Julia Harris
Text editors Donald Berwick, Keith Lye
Assistant editor Simon Adams
Managing editor Jackie Douglas
Editorial director Christopher Davis
Art director Roger Bristow
Contributing writers Nicholas Best, Alan Blackwood,
Tim Healey, Richard Humble, Margaret Mulvihill,
Theodore Rowland-Entwistle, Nigel Rodgers, Tony Scott
Researchers Janet Abbott, Brenda Clarke, Phyllis Hunt,
Fiona Lindsay, Miren Lopategui
Picture researchers Jenny de Gex, Caroline Lucas
Major illustrations Giovanni Caselli
Historical advisors Neil Ardley BSc FRSA, Iris Barry MA,
M.Bierbrier BA MA PhD, David Braund MA PhD,
F.D.Harvey MA, J.G.Taylor BSc BA MA PhD FInstP FRAS,
Bruce Welsh BA MA

Reader's Digest staff Jane Polley, *Editor*
Vincent L.Perry, *Art Director*

Library of Congress Cataloging in Publication Data
Main entry under title:

Quest for the past.

At head of title: Reader's digest.
1. History—Miscellanea.   2.   Curiosities and wonders.
I.   Reader's Digest Association.   II.   Reader's digest.
D21.3.Q83 1984   909   83–60795
ISBN 0–89577–170–5

The credits and acknowledgments that appear on page 320 are
hereby made a part of this copyright page.

Title page – *Detail of gold gilt shrine from the tomb of
Tutankhamon, depicting the pharaoh and his consort in a
ritual hunting scene, 14th century BC.*
Title page inset – *Detail of handle mount of a bucket found
in the Oseberg Viking burial ship, 9th century AD.*
Contents page – *Detail of stone relief from Sargon II's
palace at Khorsabad, Mesopotamia, 8th century BC.*

INTRODUCTION

The 19th-century poet Henry Wadsworth Longfellow suggested that people who make history leave "footprints on the sands of time." Footprints in the sand may blow away, but this does not necessarily erase their significance. To be sure, much of the past is cloaked in mystery and is likely to remain so. For hundreds of centuries our ancestors left no written records; for many more centuries they recorded events haphazardly, if at all. Yet their "footprints" have seldom been fully obliterated. Clues to the past keep turning up everywhere. The sudden finding of long-buried artifacts in America can indicate the existence of a forgotten Indian village. The discovery of a portrait in a tomb may reveal the countenance of an ancient Macedonian king. Modern scholars are constantly broadening our historical horizons by means of increasingly sophisticated archeological methods, technological advances, and sheer persistence.

There are facts behind every legend, truths at the heart of every fanciful anecdote, whether about Cleopatra, the first Japanese emperor, King Arthur, the ruins of Zimbabwe, or any of the countless people and places that once loomed large in history. And wherever the reality can be unearthed, today's historians and archeologists are gradually revealing it. The purpose of this book is to give you a rich sampling of their work.

In the following pages you will find a series of brief, illustrated true stories, each of which poses and seeks to answer a provocative question about a person, a society, or an incident from the past. They date from the shadowy beginnings of man up to the moment when the European discovery of the New World signaled the start of our modern age. These stories – many might be aptly called mystery stories – are arranged in roughly chronological order and grouped in four sections: *Early Man* (around 100,000–4000 BC); *The Ancient World* (up to about 600 BC); *The Classical World* (up to AD 500); and *The Medieval World* (up to AD 1500). They need not be read consecutively; each story is self-contained. And each presents a highly readable summary of the facts as we now know them.

The scholars who planned and wrote this book have not tried to cover all the events of a given time or place. Instead, they have chosen a wide selection of fascinating moments in a journey backward through time. Occasionally, of course, an article can be understood only if read in historical context; in such cases background material appears side by side with the main story. And charts at the beginning of each section offer a general view of the history of the period.

Quest for the Past, then, is not a conventional history book. Though it will doubtless increase your store of knowledge about the behavior (and misbehavior) of our remote ancestors, you should, above all, find it enjoyable.

CONTENTS

EARLY MAN 8
100,000 BC–4000 BC

What became of Neanderthal man? 10   Stone Age Venuses 11   Hands across the centuries 13
The first flower children 15   The incredible Polynesian navigators 16
The first technological revolution 19   Big-game hunters 20   The boomerang 23
Brain surgery in the Stone Age 24

THE ANCIENT WORLD 26
4000 BC–600 BC

Who were the first metal-workers? 28   Daily life in Copper Age Europe 30   No broken reeds 32
Wheels within wheels 34   A rose by any other name? 36   The earliest literates 38
A Neolithic Venice? 40   Loyalty in ancient Ur 42   The miracle of the Nile 44
Pinpointing the trouble 46   The cult of the dead 47   Dentistry – an ancient skill 49
Rats, rice, peanuts, and jade 51   Translating the past 53   Tomb or temple? 54
The puzzling labyrinth 56   Planning a family 57   An early lawbook 59
How India acquired the caste system 60   One way to belittle a foe 62   The Thira eruption 63
The mystery of the Basques 66   Egypt's bearded queen 67   The message of the "dragon bones" 69
The strange disappearance of Queen Nefertiti 71   Bearers of the purple 73   A dive into the past 75
The mysteries of Eleusis 76   Desert strikers 78   The mysterious mound builders 80
The Assyrian came down like a wolf on the fold 82

THE CLASSICAL WORLD 84
800 BC – AD 500

Who was – or were – Homer? 86   Professionalism in ancient Greece 88
Were the Vestal Virgins pure? 90   The Delphic oracle 92   The elusive Etruscans 93
Life and death 95   World-class engineering 97   How the Spartans learned to be spartan 98
America's first gold rush 99   Women's lib in ancient Greece 101   Frozen tombs 103
A lucky find 105   The history of Herodotus 107   Theatre-going in ancient Greece 109
The four elements 110   Sacrilege in Athens 112   Symposiums 113
The other side of Aristotle 115   Ancient secrets 117   The work of years gone in hours 119
Butser Farm 121   The greatest scientist in the ancient world 124
The Seven Wonders of the World 125   The terracotta army 127   Burnt offerings to Baal 129
Death in the Alps 130   War by proxy 133   Farming in republican Rome 135   Imperial travel 138
Bacchus defeated 140   The Antikythera mechanism 142   What sort of woman was Cleopatra? 143
The talking Colossus 145   The mystery of the Bog people 146   Celtic "barbarism" 148
Danebury: A Celtic hillfort 150   Buried treasure 152   Traitor or patriot? 154
Roman comforts 156   Bath: A Roman leisure center 158   Boudica 160
The truth about Nero 162   The lost treasure of Jerusalem 165   The day disaster struck 166
Animals for the Colosseum 169   Early Christianity's biggest battle 172
The battle that made this book possible 174   Indians who loved deformity 176
Japan's imperial family 178   Claudius Ptolemy: Genius or fraud? 180   Christianity in Africa 182
Inflation: An ancient woe 183   "In this sign conquer!" 184   Keeping fit in the imperial army 186
Simeon Stylites 187   The end of an empire 189   "The Scourge of God" 191

THE MEDIEVAL WORLD 194
AD 450 – AD 1500

King Arthur and the Round Table 196   Empress with a purple past 198
The pilgrimage of Hsuan Tsang 200   The Vikings: Destroyers or creators? 203
A knorr: Cargo vessel of the Vikings 206   Making the most of horsepower 208
Charlemagne: Emperor of the Romans 209   The Arabian Nights 212   Sindbad the sailor 214
Daily life in a monastery 217   The medieval monastery: A masterplan 220   Cave bandits 222
The most restless of royal minds 224   The "mad" scientist of Cairo 226   Lines in the desert 228
The mystery of Murasaki 230   The Bayeux Tapestry 232   England's total wealth: $100,000 234
The untamable Tafurs 236   Prester John: A king who never was? 238   Home-made gold 239
Warriors of feudal Japan 240   Love in the Middle Ages 243   New Jerusalem in Ethiopia 245
Of gunpowder and guns 247   The death of William Rufus 248   The greatest Christian relic 250
Sporting knights played for keeps 252   The Wonder of the World 255
Who built Great Zimbabwe? 257   Repent or burn 259   An empire held together with string 261
Chan-Chan: Desert capital of the Chimu 264   The galloping hordes of Genghis Khan 266
The unknown cathedral builders 268   Egypt's slave-kings 270   The Sicilian vespers 271
The longbow 273   Marco Polo's amanuensis 276   Food for the gods 278
The splendor of ancient Mali 280   When knighthood was in flower 282   The Black Death 284
The equals of kings and princes 287   The Peasants' Revolt of 1381 289
The fake bequest that devastated Europe 291   Pompeii, American style 293
Tamerlane the Terrible 295   The flames of Rouen 297   Prototype of Dracula 299
The magnificent Medici 301   Pretender to the throne 303   Leonardo's "Last Supper" 305
Lucrezia Borgia 308   The reconquest of Spain 310   The discoverer of the New World 312

Index 314   Picture Credits and Acknowledgments 320

EARLY MAN

100,000 BC   Period of time covered by this chart

AD 1500

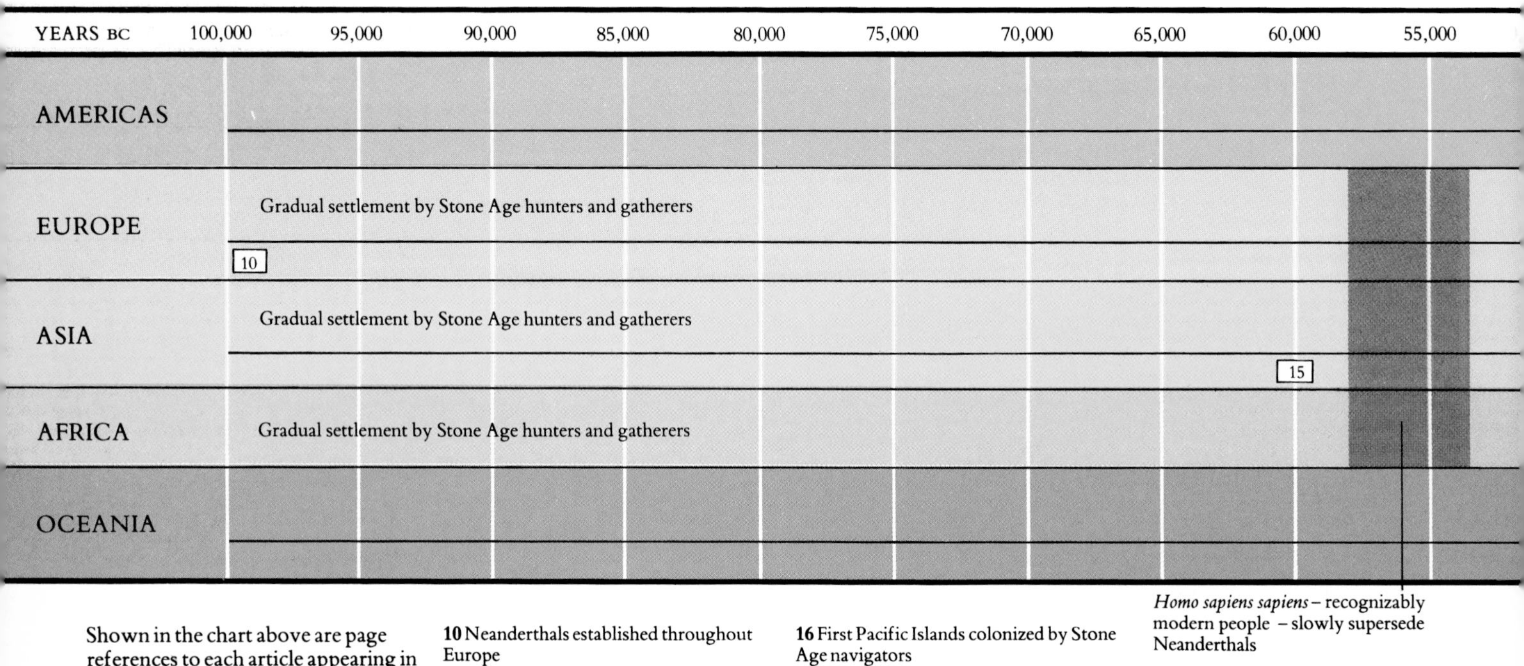

YEARS BC	100,000	95,000	90,000	85,000	80,000	75,000	70,000	65,000	60,000	55,000
AMERICAS										
EUROPE	Gradual settlement by Stone Age hunters and gatherers									
	10									
ASIA	Gradual settlement by Stone Age hunters and gatherers								15	
AFRICA	Gradual settlement by Stone Age hunters and gatherers									
OCEANIA										

Homo sapiens sapiens – recognizably modern people – slowly supersede Neanderthals

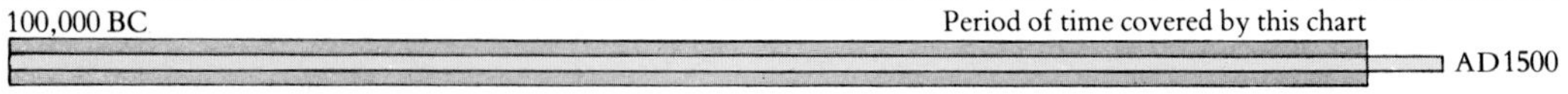

Shown in the chart above are page references to each article appearing in this section of the book. The subject of each article is listed here.

10 Neanderthals established throughout Europe
11 Venus figurines carved by Stone Age peoples
13 Hands painted on walls of Gargas caves by Cro-Magnon people
15 Shanidar man buried with flowers by fellow Neanderthals

16 First Pacific Islands colonized by Stone Age navigators
19 Technological revolution gets underway
20 Paleo-Indians hunt big game
23 American-Indian boomerang lost in Little Salt Spring, Florida
24 Brain surgery practiced by Stone Age brain surgeons

The first foundations of history were laid during an extremely long period of time. By about 100,000 years ago human beings like us were populating Africa, Asia, and Europe, sharing the Eastern hemisphere with their close but doomed kin, Neanderthal man. The first immigrants to the Americas did not arrive until around 40,000 years ago. And it was some time thereafter that the Pacific Islands were slowly settled by early voyagers. Gradually mankind began to make an impact upon the world. With no written records, we cannot, of course, name individuals or tell anyone's life story, but many poignant details about our early ancestors' lives have been revealed by the painstaking work of archeologists. These early people depended entirely on Nature's provision of animal and plant food. Though at first they could exploit the environment only by means of crude stone axes, they slowly developed a specialized tool kit, and invented clever techniques for hunting the roaming herds of mammoth, bison, and reindeer.

The retreat of the glaciers heralded the end of this earliest affluent society, for the population grew and game supplies diminished as climate and vegetation changed. By 4000 BC animals were being domesticated and plants cultivated to ensure a more reliable food supply. And so a vast change in the life style of mankind had taken place. No longer nomadic hunters and gatherers, people now settled in permanent villages, and it was from these that the world's great civilizations would spring.

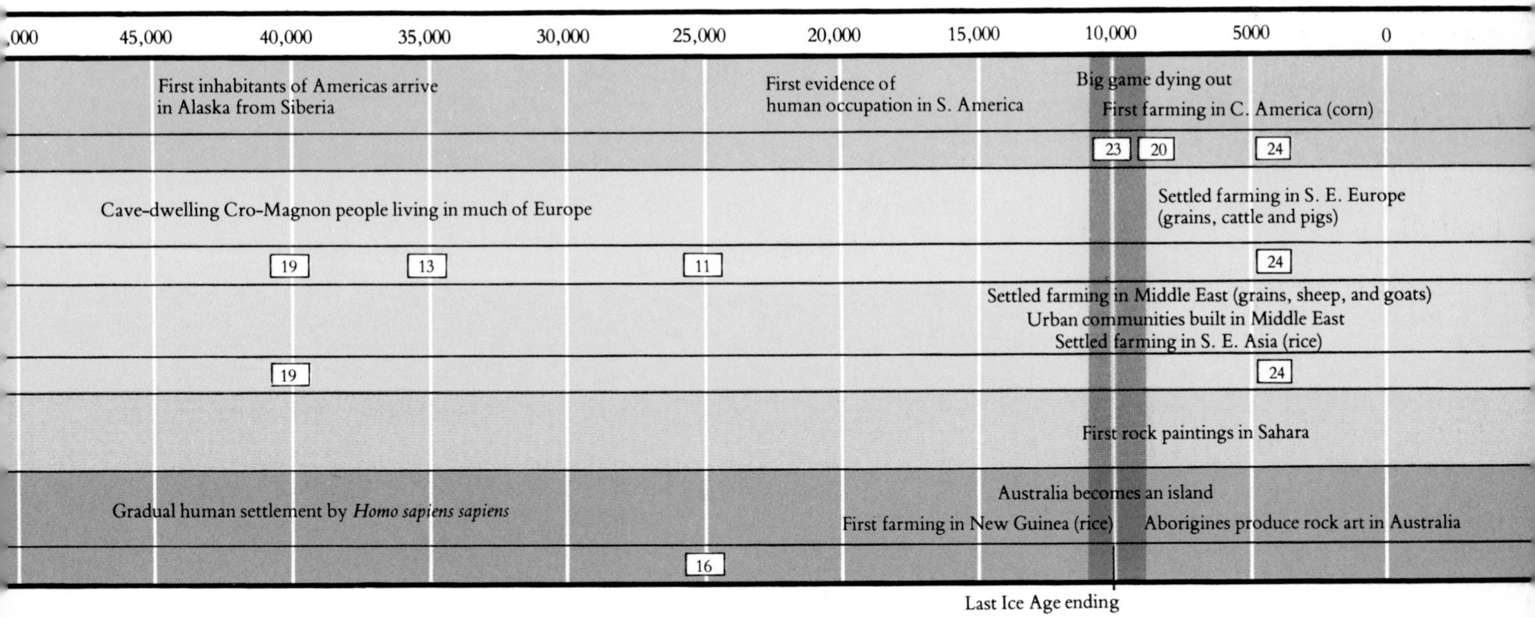

,000	45,000	40,000	35,000	30,000	25,000	20,000	15,000	10,000	5000	0

First inhabitants of Americas arrive in Alaska from Siberia

First evidence of human occupation in S. America

Big game dying out

First farming in C. America (corn)

[23] [20] [24]

Cave-dwelling Cro-Magnon people living in much of Europe

Settled farming in S. E. Europe (grains, cattle and pigs)

[19] [13] [11] [24]

Settled farming in Middle East (grains, sheep, and goats)
Urban communities built in Middle East
Settled farming in S. E. Asia (rice)

[19] [24]

First rock paintings in Sahara

Gradual human settlement by *Homo sapiens sapiens*

Australia becomes an island

First farming in New Guinea (rice)   Aborigines produce rock art in Australia

[16]

Last Ice Age ending

What became of Neanderthal man?

Why is he so misunderstood?

THE TERM "prehistoric caveman" evokes an image of a shambling brute clad in a bearskin loincloth, brandishing a club and tugging his mate along by her hair. This popular notion stems largely from the study in the 19th century of an early Neanderthal skeleton, which seemed to indicate that he was a lumbering, stooped creature with a heavy, brutish jaw. Recent re-examination of that skeleton, however, has shown that it belonged to an old man, crippled by arthritis, and so is scarcely typical of its kind. Assessment of other evidence about Neanderthals suggests that there are many popular misconceptions about them.

In the long time-span of Man's evolution, *Homo erectus* (upright man) probably emerged about 1.5 million years ago. *Homo sapiens* (wise or thinking man) evolved about a million years

later. Most anthropologists place Neanderthal man among the subspecies of *Homo sapiens*, giving him the scientific name *Homo sapiens neanderthalensis*. Neanderthals existed as a recognizable group between about 100,000 and 30,000 years ago. They were named for the first important archeological discovery, in 1856, of part of a skull and other bones at a site in the Neander valley, near the German Rhineland town of Düsseldorf. Subsequently, more Neanderthal remains have been unearthed at other sites in Europe, North Africa, and the Middle East.

The most significant feature of Neanderthal anatomy, as with all other hominids (manlike beings), is the skull. Specimens vary, but typical features include a wide, vaulted cranium, heavy "beetle brow" ridges above the eyes, a big jaw, and large teeth. Neanderthals may have looked

Neanderthals hunted and killed wild animals, such as ibex and reindeer, using their meat for food and their skins for clothing. Armed with wooden spears tipped with flakes of flint or sharp stone, the hunters would corner their prey before killing it, then drag the carcass back to their cave or camp site.

faintly apelike, but their brain capacity was as large as, and in some cases larger than, that of modern human beings. As a whole, Neanderthals seem to have been tough and stocky individuals, with about the same build and height as modern Eskimos.

Some but not all Neanderthals lived in caves. Others established camp sites, digging holes or trenches for shelter, or gathering stones to build simple walls. They often chose sites near animal migration routes, to ensure a good supply of meat. They also snared birds and caught fish. Neanderthals had the knowledge to make fire. They used stone tools to skin, clean, and cut up animal furs and hides for clothing. Other objects found on Neanderthal sites included polished teeth and stones; and natural color pigments indicate that they practiced some kind of decorative art. The remains of Neanderthals indicate that, on average, they lived longer than members of the earlier *Homo erectus* species. They cared for their sick and infirm and, most important, they buried their dead. They may, therefore, have had a form of religious belief.

Despite their skills and social organization, the Neanderthals died out. Did they fail to adapt to the changing environment when the Ice Age entered its final phase about 40,000 years ago? Were they outclassed by even more skillful races? Or did they interbreed with more modern species, becoming absorbed in the continuing evolutionary process? Some experts have suggested that the increasing size of Neanderthal crania made childbirth more and more difficult. Any or all of these factors may have contributed to their extinction.

But has Neanderthal man really disappeared? Could there be pockets of his descendants living in remote areas at the present time? Such a possibility owes nothing to improbable stories about the Yeti or the Abominable Snowman of the Himalayas, or Sasquatch or Big Foot of North America. The notion of Neanderthal survival is based largely on the work of Soviet and Mongolian scholars, including Professor Boris Porchnev who published papers on the subject in the 1970s. These papers have reawakened the debate about the accumulated reports of "wild men" living in parts of Asia.

One such group, known as the *Chuchunaa* (outcasts or fugitives), was reported by a branch of the Soviet Academy of Science as recently as the 1950s in the bitterly cold and forbidding region of northeast Siberia. These people are said to have an extremely limited range of oral sound. This may have been a genetic mutation – or is it an indication of the people's Neanderthal origin? More recent reports suggest that these people have withdrawn to even more remote areas away from encroaching civilization.

Most sitings of groups of "wild men," however, come from a vast stretch of Central Asia, extending from the Caucasus Mountains to the Gobi Desert. These "wild men" have been given the collective name of *Almas* (plural *Almati*). This Mongolian word can mean either a cross between ape and man, or a hunter. From the 15th century, local tribesmen and explorers have reported sightings of these mysterious and elusive beings. In the 20th century, a Red Army official serving in the Pamir Mountains at the time of the Russian Revolution actually claimed that his men had tracked down and shot such a creature. In descriptions, the same phrases recur: "slanting forehead . . . eyebrows very powerful . . . nose very flat . . . heavy protruding jaw . . . medium height." These features conform closely to what we already know about Neanderthal man. So perhaps the soldiers were actually killing the last remaining Neanderthals.

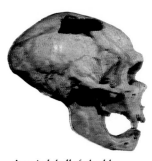

A typical skull of a healthy Neanderthal, with its characteristic protruding jaw. A comparison with the skull of one of the "wild men" of Asia might well prove that descendants of Neanderthal man still exist.

Stone Age Venuses
The first statues

MOST OF US know something about the remarkable paintings of Stone Age artists in the caves of southwestern France and Spain – those magical, still-fresh-seeming representations of hunted beasts that date back 30,000 years. Equally amazing, but much less well-known, are three-dimensional, shaped figures sometimes given the rather inappropriate name, "Stone Age Venuses." Often ugly and always small – only a few inches high – these have been found in the Old World wherever the hunting-gathering peoples of the Stone Age settled. Examples have turned up throughout Europe, in a great arc all the way from the Iberian Peninsula to southern Russia. Tiny and ugly they may be, but they are the earliest sculptures ever found; and they may well have seemed beautiful to their creators.

ICE AGE HUMANITY

The world that the hunter-gatherers of the last glacial epoch (from 35,000 to 10,000 years ago) knew was very different from ours. Much of the northern hemisphere was covered by a great ice-sheet. Sea levels globally were 300 feet (about 100 meters) lower than today's – so that, for example, the British Isles and Sicily were attached to the continent of Europe, the northern Adriatic was dry land, the Black Sea was landlocked, and North America and Asia joined where the Bering Strait now separates them. All land areas were considerably drier as well as colder than they are today, and this discouraged dense woodlands but favored rich grasslands.

Now-fertile regions such as northern Europe were bleak subarctic wastelands, but Mediterranean areas like southwest France, so rich in archeological finds, had a milder climate not unlike that of Sweden or parts of Canada today. The great prairies of Europe supported an abundance of game; bison, woolly rhinoceros, woolly mammoths, and giant elk were among the species then numerous but now extinct, and reindeer and the silver arctic fox roamed as far south as the Pyrenees. So – in Europe, at least – Stone Age people had all the meat, furs, bone, and ivory they needed.

Across this vast territory teeming with wild life roamed nomadic bands no more than 25 to 30 strong, each band settling for months or years in one site, then moving on. Though at times the climate was bitterly cold, they had animal skins and furs which they had discovered how to tailor with needles of bone into snug-fitting clothes. They could also now construct permanent dwellings, beneath overhanging cliffs, in the entrance to caves, or even in open places where necessary. Some of these dwellings were quite extensive tent-like structures, with sunken floors, stone bases to their hide walls, and cunningly corrugated fireplaces that produced great heat when tested by modern archeologists. In Russia, evidence suggests that some may have been joined together like a series of interconnecting igloos made of fur. Food supplies were probably easy to come by except in very cold weather, with roots, nuts, berries, and leaves supplementing the regular diet of meat. But theirs was no Garden of Eden. Mortality rates, especially among children and women of childbearing age, were very high. These early people, however, were apparently free of one modern scourge: Archeologists have found no sign of dental decay in any of their skeletons.

Their achievements in sculpture were made possible by the development of better and better flint tools. Flint heads were also added to the arrows that the invention of the bow – so useful in hunting – demanded. And so life went on with only gradual changes for thousands of years. With the end of the Ice Age 10,000 years ago, humanity was ready for its next leap forward – into a settled rather than nomadic existence.

In Stone Age sculpture, breasts and buttocks were often greatly emphasized at the expense of the face, arms, and legs. The ivory Venus of Lespugue (above) from France and the stone Venus of Willendorf (at right) from Austria are typical.

Made of bone, ivory, or soft stone, the figurines are mainly images of the human figure. Almost all of them, in fact, are of women, especially women with massive thighs, huge breasts, and monstrous buttocks. What purpose did these fat, diminutive figures, sometimes with the merest suggestion of head, arms, or feet, serve? Were they religious emblems of a mother-goddess, or fertility figures, or simply Stone Age man's pin-up, realizations of his bloated ideal of female beauty?

A possible reason for the extreme obesity is that the statues were created sometime between 35,000 and 10,000 years ago, during the last glacial epoch, when the human body could survive throughout the long and fierce wintertime only by storing a hefty supply of fat in the summer, when game and fruit, leaves and roots, were abundant. It was in the later part of the Stone Age that anatomically "modern" people first evolved, and many human traits, from building shelters to burying the dead, developed. Above all, human beings acquired the ability to think conceptually and even creatively. Crouched around the fires that warmed them and cooked their food, these hunter-gatherers may have used sculpture as a means of keeping idle hands active when poor weather made outdoor activities impossible. (It seems strange, though, considering the cold, that the bodies are generally portrayed naked!)

Most of the little "Venuses" are either faceless or have no distinctive facial features, but there are a few notable exceptions. One, found in France, is an exquisite ivory miniature of a woman with an elaborate hairstyle. Another is an ivory carving from Czechoslovakia; the face is sculpted with the kind of crooked mouth that could have resulted from damage to a facial nerve. Archeologists think it may be an actual portrait of a woman whose skull, damaged on the left-hand side, was dug up nearby. Could she have been an important personage? Artifacts created by modern hunter-gatherers in Australia provide evidence of an extremely long tradition of creating and preserving the likenesses of individuals who were considered to be of particular importance by the rest of the tribe.

To modern eyes the Stone Age sculptures tend to look gross, suggesting that they are the products of fertility cults; but this could easily be a misconception rooted in our standards of good taste and beauty. Even if the theory that Ice Age people *wanted* to get fat in order to survive the cold is invalid, the figurines may reflect a general tendency toward steatopygia (fatty degeneration that causes immense accumulations of fat around the buttocks). Among the present-day hunting tribes of the Kalahari Desert, women especially suffer from steatopygia – and they do not consider such fatness ugly.

We shall probably never know the exact purpose of these early sculptures, but the great similarity among finds in sites from the mountain ranges of the Pyrenees to the Russian River Don indicates some sort of cultural unity. Whatever their purpose, they remain the earliest representations of humankind ever found.

One of the few Stone Age Venuses with a recognizable face, the ivory lady from Brassempouy, France.

Hands across the centuries

150 mysterious 35,000-year-old handprints

DID OUR STONE AGE forefathers mutilate their hands by chopping off their fingers during some sort of religious rite? This is a fascinating and as yet unanswered question that has been suggested by observers of images on the walls of the Gargas cave in southwestern France – a cave whose walls pose questions as challenging in their way as those suggested by such better-known and artistically superior caves as Altamira in Spain and Lascaux in France. Gargas, which lies in the Pyrenees not far from Lourdes, is known as the Cave of the Hands. On its black walls the hands glow with a freshness 350 centuries cannot dim – some are black, stenciled in a framework of red, other hands are red. And most of them have portions of two or more fingers missing.

The hands of Gargas are probably the oldest surviving form of cave art. They were painted about 35,000 years ago, during the last part of the Ice Age, by the direct ancestors of today's Europeans, the Cro-Magnons (a name that comes from the site in France where their skeletons were first found). The Cro-Magnons, one of the later cave-dwelling peoples of the Old Stone Age, were not the first living creatures to leave marks upon the walls of Gargas. They were preceded by the great bears that once roamed through Western Europe. Stropping

their claws on the soft stone of the cave walls, much as domestic cats sharpen their claws on furniture, the bears left scratch marks, known as *griffes* (the French word for scratches). And interspersed among the *griffes* are *meanders* – sinuous lines grooved in the clay – which were made by people, perhaps in imitation of the bears; the meanders may be even older than the hands.

There are more than 150 stenciled or painted hands on the walls of Gargas, and most of them are left hands rather than right. The coloring, whether of the hand itself or of the stenciled framework around a black hand, is mostly red ocher (pigmented earth). Whether red or black, the hands glow in the light of a flashlight or lamp

ACCIDENTS OF THE ROCK
Cave artists were quick to take advantage of what French cave experts call *accidents de la roche*, contours or outcroppings of rock suggesting shapes that can be "improved" into images.

There are few human figures in cave art. Some of those that do exist were drawn around accidents of the rock suggesting certain parts of the human anatomy. The cave at Gargas contains one delightful accident of the rock: a projecting boss of stone which a few strokes by some Ice Age cartoonist transformed into a convincing likeness of a wild boar's head.

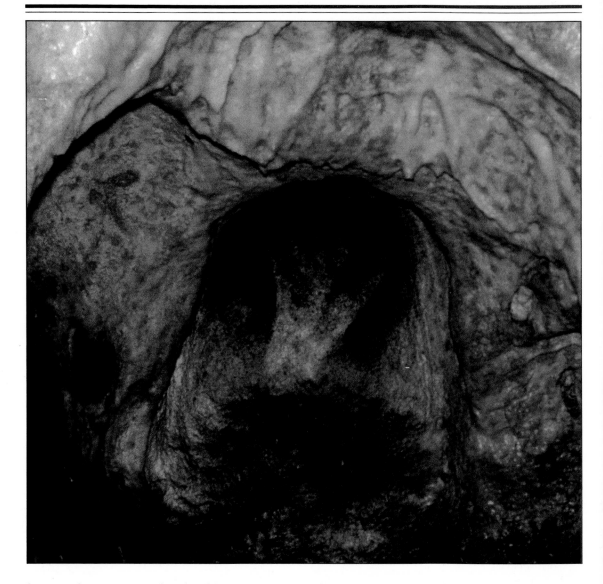

A left hand outlined on the cave wall at Gargas, with all four fingers mutilated above the knuckle.

because they are covered with a thin, transparent layer of limestone, the same substance that creates stalagmites and stalactites. This deposit is still building up, for Gargas is a damp cave.

Comparisons with more recent primitive societies, such as the Aborigines of Australia and certain African tribes, suggest that the imprint of a hand on a cave wall might have been an extension of body-painting. An ocher-covered palm pressed onto smooth stone would have left its impression there. The stencil effect was probably achieved by blowing coloring matter, either as a liquid or a fine powder, onto the hand when it was held against the wall. Perhaps the color was held in the mouth and sprayed out between the lips, but the prevalence of left hands at Gargas suggests that the ocher is more likely to have been blown through a tube that was held in the right hand.

But why the almost universal mutilation of fingers? The top two joints of at least two fingers are usually missing; sometimes four fingers are affected, sometimes all but the forefinger, sometimes the second and third fingers, sometimes the third and fourth – but never the thumb. Careful study of the paintings indicates that the fingers were probably truncated, not just bent over. It has been suggested that, since the Cro-Magnons lived during the latter part of the Ice Age, frostbite may have played a part. Some anthropologists believe, though, that the lopping off of finger joints may have been a deliberate ritual, but what the ritual might have been or what its implications were are still not known. We do know, however, that a similar type of mutilation, was practiced by Bushmen in Africa and by North American Indians, either as a good-luck birth ritual or as a means of propitiating the gods of hunting.

A large number of the Gargas hands are to be found in one small section of the vast hillside cave. As an obvious tribute to the religious-rite theory, that section is now known as the Sanctuary of the Hands.

The first flower children

Honoring the dead

FLOWER POWER may well have died in the San Francisco streets of Haight–Ashbury, but it was not born there. The first flower children may well have lived, not on the edge of the New World, but in the heartlands of the Old … and at least 60,000 years ago. At that time the world was dominated by Neanderthals (the Stone Age people whose name derives from the Neander Valley in Germany, where skeletal evidence of their existence first came to light).

In the Neanderthal world, love and gentleness must have been rare commodities. Life "in a state of nature," as the 17th-century British philosopher Thomas Hobbes put it, was "nasty, brutish, and short." Every day was a struggle for survival, every hunt a mortal risk, every injury a potential killer, every change of camp site a voyage into the unknown. Examination of Neanderthal skeletons indicates that few Neanderthals died peacefully, and that most died before the age of 20.

Yet, despite the harshness of their daily existence, they were capable of compassion for the weak and reverence for the dead. Evidence of such tenderness was unearthed, a few years ago, by Ralph S. Solecki of the Smithsonian Institution while excavating a cave near the village of Shanidar in the remote Zagros Mountains of northeastern Iraq. In nearly 10 years of patient work, during which Solecki's team uncovered layers of human habitation reaching back into the last Ice Age, their most fascinating find was a grave in which flowers had been placed along with the corpse. More extraordinary still, the buried man was a cripple. Analysis of his fossilized bones shows that he lost his right arm as a child and suffered from severe arthritis.

Despite their tough and dangerous existence, Neanderthals both cared for their sick and infirm and honored their dead. Rather than leaving the dead where they fell, they dug individual graves. The bodies were sometimes buried with flowers, as at Shanidar, indicating perhaps a belief in the afterlife.

In most primitive societies, so handicapped an individual would not have been allowed to survive childhood; societies close to the margin of survival can ill afford to feed and protect unproductive members. Yet this disabled man, who would have been unable to do his share of the hunting, was cared for by his tribe for about 40 years – more than twice the average life expectancy – until he was killed, apparently by a chance fall of rock from the roof of the cave. And he was laid to rest in a bed of picked flowers.

Although the flowers have long since rotted away, botanists know they had been there because the microscopic pollen grains they contained were so well preserved in the humid soil that even the precise plant species from which they were picked 60,000 years ago can be identified. Altogether, there were eight types of flower: yarrow, cornflowers, hollyhocks, groundsel, grape hyacinths, a centaurea known as St.-Barnaby's-thistle, woody horsetail, and a kind of mallow. The grape hyacinths, cornflowers, and mallow seem to have been laid in the grave purely as ornaments, and the woody horsetail as bedding. But because several of the others are known to have been widely used since ancient times for herbal remedies, it seems at least possible that the unsophisticated Neanderthal – who must have collected the flowers from a wide area around the cave, since not all grow nearby – had already, at this early stage in human development, acquired an understanding of the healing properties of plants. If so, some of the flowers might have been laid in the grave not merely as a gentle gesture but to help ensure the dead man's health in the afterlife. The pollen analysis, one of the first ever carried out on a prehistoric burial place, has even enabled botanists to determine the precise season of the burial. The flowers found in the grave bloom in the Zagros Mountain region during early summer, between the end of May and the beginning of July. Thus we know that the elderly flower child of the Shanidar died sometime around June all those years ago.

Because so little soil analysis has been carried out on prehistoric graves, nobody knows when it was that human creatures first thought of paying respect to the dead with flowers. But just the basic practice of digging individual graves – instead of leaving dead bodies where they fall – implies a degree of sensitivity and feeling on the part of the survivors.

Indeed, the custom of burying the dead is an exceedingly ancient one. The earliest grave yet found is in China, in a limestone cave at the village of Chou-k'ou-tien, just north of Beijing (Peking), and it dates back an astounding 400,000 years! This is significant not only because it marks a very early stage in humanity's development, but because, like the medicinal flowers in the Shanidar grave, it provides powerful evidence of our species' enduring belief in life after death. Deliberate burial could not have been a simple matter of hygiene for early man; human populations were small and scattered, and scavenging animals would quickly have disposed of abandoned corpses. The consideration that drove our prehistoric ancestors to the laborious task of digging out large holes with their inefficient tools was, most scholars agree, a belief in some sort of spirit world beyond death – a wistful faith in immortality that is probably as ancient as the mind of man.

The incredible Polynesian navigators
Stone Age island-hoppers

WHEN EUROPEANS first probed the Pacific Ocean in the 1500s they made an astonishing discovery: Without navigation instruments of any kind, Stone Age peoples, some at least 26,000 years ago, had already found their way to scores of the islands scattered over this immense body of water. Local traditions told of purposeful voyages of sea-going canoes across hundreds – even thousands – of miles. In this way three groups of islands seem to have been deliberately populated. Archeologists have firm evidence that black people settled one group (the Europeans named it Melanesia, from the Greek words for "black islands") stretching eastward from New Guinea to Fiji. People with light-brown skins colonized Micronesia ("little islands") north of Melanesia. Tall people with pale skins settled Polynesia ("many islands"), a vast eastern triangle embracing Hawaii, New Zealand (colonized by AD 1000), and Easter Island.

Many Europeans refused to believe that these primitive people could have found distant islands unaided by any instruments to help plot

position and keep course. In 1595 the Portuguese navigator Pedro Fernandes de Queirós pointed out that even experienced Europeans could "neither know nor determine their situation" once they had lost sight of land for more than a couple of days. And skepticism about prehistoric navigational skills persisted into our own time – until, in fact, the late 1960s, when the skeptics were proved wrong by the exploits of a New Zealand-born yachtsman, David Lewis, who discovered that islanders in traditional catamarans and other craft were still making long-distance fishing and trading trips without modern instruments.

Because the old navigational skills were fast vanishing as Western tools and techniques supplanted native lore, Lewis decided to learn all he could about that lore before it was forgotten. And so, assisted by a fellowship from the Australian National University at Canberra, he spent nine months of 1968–69 in a criss-cross journey over the West Pacific, sometimes piloted by native navigators in ocean-going canoes, sometimes aboard a 39-foot (12 meters) auxiliary gaff ketch stripped of compass and other instruments. His skillful (and illiterate) companions included Tevake, an old Polynesian from the Santa Cruz Islands, and a young Micronesian, Hipour, from the Carolines. He also talked at length with, among others, members of a clan on Tonga, where navigational skills were once looked upon as hereditary secrets.

Lewis's book *We, the Navigators* not only tells the story of his nine-month-long voyage of

discovery but sheds light upon the quality of seamanship found among islanders whose directional aids differed little from those of their Stone Age ancestors. For example, they used stars as nocturnal guides to tiny islands far beyond the horizon, simply steering toward a star known to stand above a given destination. Each guiding star was a useful pointer, of course, only when low in the sky – just risen if you were sailing east; about to set if you were heading west. But the islanders followed a "star

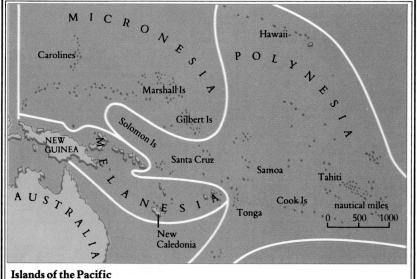

Islands of the Pacific
Map of the Western Pacific Ocean, showing the main island divisions of Melanesia, Micronesia, and Polynesia. How Stone Age people could have found their way to and from thousands of islands in the region without navigational instruments perplexed the first Europeans to probe the area. Today we know that they had developed highly sophisticated skills to enable them to journey through this immense ocean.

path." After one star had risen too high or had sunk below the horizon, they would guide themselves by another that rose or set in the same position. During one night-time voyage Lewis and his companions, sailing down a pathway of nine successive stars, were able to reach an objective 70 miles (112 kilometers) away.

Some islanders also used a star "compass" – a natural direction-finder based on the positions of 32 stars rising and setting around the horizon at unequal distances apart – as a virtually infallible guide to scores of destinations. Lewis learned that certain islands were called *etak* (reference) islands because of the known shift in their apparent position from below one star to another during a voyage. Thus, sailing from island 1 to island 2, you might start by choosing island 3 under star A as your *etak*. As you sailed on, the bearing of island 3 would change until it lay under star B, the next point in the star compass. And so on. It had taken Lewis's companions years of hard study to memorize the various astronomical guides to specific islands. By means of traditional land-based training methods such as the placement of stones in positions representing star placements, they had become astonishingly adept at interpreting the night sky. Young Hipour, for example, could pinpoint a boat's position when just a few stars glimmered briefly through the overcast sky.

By day the seamen could obviously guide themselves by the position of the sun. But they were far from being dependent on stars and sun, for they had a thorough understanding of the behavior of wind, waves, currents, and other natural phenomena. In one storm the old Polynesian, Tevake, navigating at night for more than 40 miles (64 kilometers), brought the boat safely between two islands only half a mile (less than a kilometer) apart. Even when blown off course or unaided by stars, sun, or familiar wind and wave factors, men like Hipour and Tevake had ingenious techniques for sailing in the right direction. For instance, they could guide themselves toward an invisible island 10 miles (16 kilometers) away by scanning clouds, which look subtly different in color and tone depending on the kind of land or depth of water over which they are drifting. Similarly, the islanders could interpret such clues as the flight of birds, floating branches, or the "land waves" that can sometimes cause a boat to pitch when it is as much as 50 miles (80 kilometers) away from the island whose surf creates them. Perhaps most interesting of such signposts is an unexplained phenomenon called in different parts of Polynesia *te lapa*, *te mata*, or *ulo aetahi* ("glory of the seas"). This "glory" is a deep-level phosphorescence – flashing streaks of light several feet below the surface. The streaks are aligned with land up to 100 miles away. And Stone Age navigators must have found them as helpful for deliberately peopling the islands of the Pacific as David Lewis's companions did for their purposes only a few years ago.

So it seems highly probable that Stone Age navigators were able to people the Pacific islands deliberately and with precision.

A Fijian ndrua, *or double canoe, a highly maneuverable craft despite its hulls of unequal length. In all the many different designs for the great canoes of the Pacific, a recurring feature is the "claw" sail, set here at an angle of 45° to the masts.*

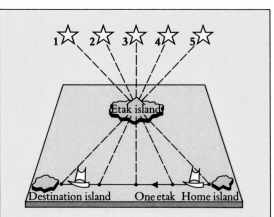

Navigating by the stars

To sail from one island to another, navigators make use of an etak *or reference island. In this example, when the voyage begins the* etak *island appears to be under star 1; as the voyage progresses the* etak *island moves toward the sailor, becomes parallel, and then recedes. He must, therefore, change his directional guide from star 1 to star 2 and so on. Thus, when he sees that the* etak *island aligns with star 2 he knows how far he has traveled in* etaks.

The first technological revolution

Cold comforts

RAPID TECHNOLOGICAL progress is often thought of as being an exclusively 20th-century phenomenon. Yet the biggest such explosion happened during the latter part of the Old Stone Age – between 40,000 and 12,000 years ago – when the last Ice Age was reaching its climax.

For hundreds of thousands of years man's ancestors had used the crudest of tools, making clubs and chopping blocks out of broken animal bones, chipping pieces of stone into primitive choppers and axes, and using simple wooden spears with fire-hardened points. Then, at some time in the last few thousand years of the Old Stone Age, tool-making techniques took a giant leap forward.

The vast expansion and increased sophistication of the contents of humanity's tool kit was generated by *Homo sapiens sapiens* (sometimes known as Cro-Magnon Man because of remains first found in the Cro-Magnon cave in the Dordogne region of France), who spread across the warmer parts of Europe and Asia as the last Ice Age gradually chilled the world, reaching its frigid peak about 20,000 years ago. These astonishingly inventive people devised the bow and arrow, made tents and clothing out of animal skin, learned how to fish with hooks and with harpoons that had detachable heads, and carved

spear-throwers, of the kind still used by Australian Aborigines and South American Indians, to enable hunters to hurl their weapons farther and with more force. They greatly exploited the crucial technique of using one tool to make another – a concept vital to the development of complex and specialized equipment.

Two important examples of tool-making tools are a doughnut-shaped piece of bone with a handle, used for straightening the wooden shafts of spears after they had been softened in water or steam; and burins (chisel-like points made of flint). Many types of burin have been found on Stone Age sites, each type designed to chip or cut different shapes from flint, wood, and especially bone. As a result of the invention of tool-making tools, particularly the burin, craftsmen at last were able to produce more tools for an increasing variety of jobs. Using specially designed scrapers, they could also clean animal skins before softening them with oils and sewing them into tents and clothing with leather or gut.

The new technologists learned to seek different materials for different purposes. For example, flints found at a prehistoric site at Kostienki in the USSR are known to have come from high-quality deposits 80 miles (130 kilometers) away – evidence that hunters or traders were prepared to travel considerable distances to get

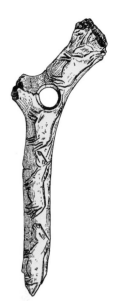

A section of reindeer antler decorated with engravings of wild animals and used to straighten the wooden shafts of spears. It was found in a cave in the Dordogne region of France.

HOW THE TOOLS WERE MADE

Before the discovery of tin-and-copper alloy ushered in the Bronze Age (around 4000 BC), flint was the most durable material for manufacturing tools and weapons. Bone, antler, and ivory, which are more flexible than stone, were increasingly used for making more delicate tools such as harpoon heads and needles.

Craftsmen had several techniques for turning flint into sharp-edged tools. The earliest-known method involved striking the edge of a rock with a less brittle hammerstone so as to break off a piece along one of the rock's natural planes of cleavage. The cloven face of the "core" rock could then be shaped further by splitting off smaller pieces with a wooden or bone hammer. Alternatively, the craftsman might shape a rock into a rough cylinder or cone, then break thin two-edged blades off the sides. Often the blades were worked further – either to blunt one edge so that a hunter could apply finger pressure without getting cut, or to realign the edges (for a spearhead, say). This delicate chipping was usually carried out not by

striking the stone but by pressing downward on its edge with a pointed tool of wood, bone, or stone. The unfinished blade was held in the hand or against an anvil stone, and pressure was applied until a flake broke off the lower face. By adjusting the angle and position of the tool and supporting the blade with their fingers, tool-makers could control sizes and shapes of flakes with remarkable precision. Sometimes a Stone Age tool-maker would work on and discard dozens of blades before achieving a satisfactory result; hundreds of these unfinished fragments have been excavated over the years at sites known to be Stone Age quarries and work shops.

Needles and awls (tools for making small holes in wood, hide, and bone) were usually made by gouging converging grooves into a length of bone with a burin (stone chisel). Once the burin had cut through into the spongy central tissue in the marrow, the hard splinter between the grooves would be prised out, then rubbed on a sandstone block to round it off.

A Stone Age tool-maker would fashion flint pieces by striking them with a harder hammerstone, then shaping them further with a wooden or bone hammer.

THE REINDEER SPECIALISTS

As the last Ice Age drew to a close about 10,000 years ago, the new tool-makers were flourishing across Europe. In present-day Germany and France some of the most advanced peoples specialized in hunting reindeer; in fact, animal bones found in northern Germany near what is now the city of Hamburg suggest that Stone Age hunters of the region got most of their meat from reindeer. They used the bow and arrow for hunting, and they made strong pointed clubs from reindeer antlers to finish off wounded animals.

Perhaps the most outstanding reindeer-based culture was the Magdalenian (named after a site at La Madeleine in France). The Magdalenians, who lived between about 15000 and 9000 BC, dominated much of France and spread as far south as Valencia in Spain and as far east as Poland. Although they also hunted horses, oxen, and deer, they lived mainly off reindeer, using wandering herds as both a walking larder and a storehouse of raw materials.

Reindeer skins were used as blankets, leather tents, and clothes; sinews became thongs for sewing or for binding spearheads onto wooden shafts; teeth became ornaments strung onto thongs; and bones and antlers were turned into barbed harpoons and spear-throwers.

The Magdalenians decorated their spear-throwers with elaborate naturalistic carvings of horses, ibex (a type of goat), birds, and fish. These throwing devices were essentially long rods with a handle at one end and a notch at the other for engaging the base of a spear. In effect, they lengthened the hunter's arm by the distance between handle and notch and so increased the power of the throw.

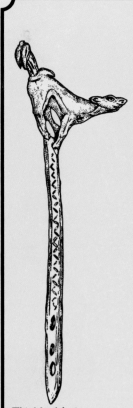

This Magdalenian spear-thrower has been carved from a reindeer antler in the shape of a young ibex. The hook at the top of the thrower engages the base of the spear-shaft.

the best flint for their tools. They discovered how to utilize antlers (from the reindeer that then roamed across Europe as far south as Spain) and ivory (from the herds of mammoths farther north). They found a way to polish the blades of bone and stone by rubbing them on abrasive sandstone. They even invented ivory ladles and spoons as eating utensils.

Archeologists at a Siberian site known as Kokorevo 1 have found a bone spearhead with its tip grooved so as to encourage the wound it made to bleed freely, thus hastening the end of a fleeing animal. At some European sites there are the remains of fireplaces with small ditches leading out from the central hearth – a design that makes the fire burn more fiercely by drawing in more air. And the discovery of clay figurines at the Czech site of Dolni Věstonice 27,000 years ago indicates that people had already discovered that soft clay could be made more durable by heating it, thereby paving the way for the development of pottery.

The impetus for much of this progress was, of course, the dropping temperature. The cold drove people to shelter in tent-like structures in places where there were no caves, to cover themselves with fur and leather, and to look for ways and means of making hunting quicker and more efficient. And the sophistication of the new tool kit suggests that something still more far-reaching also came into being: the beginnings of a complex language for passing information from one place to another and from one generation of craftsmen to the next.

Big-game hunters
The Paleo stalkers

ON A SPRING afternoon in 1925 George McJunkin, a cowboy, relaxed in the saddle as his horse followed the edge of a dry gully near Folsom, New Mexico. He was tracking a lost cow, his eyes moving back and forth across the gully, when he caught a glimpse of something that seemed to be glittering on the sun-drenched bank of the dried-up stream bed. Dismounting, he walked over for a look at what he took to be a small heap of bleached cattle bones. When he examined them closely, however, he realized that the bones were too big to be those of ordinary cattle; and as he lifted a few pieces of bone, he uncovered what seemed to be a carefully worked flint blade, which was quite

unlike any modern Indian arrowhead he had ever seen. McJunkin's interesting but apparently insignificant discovery turned out, in fact, to be the forerunner to a uniquely important find in the field of North American prehistory. The flint blade and samples of the Folsom bones were soon brought to the attention of New Mexico's Director of Natural History, J. D. Figgins, who eventually identified the bones as those of a species of bison that became extinct around 10,000 years ago. (In honor of Figgins, zoologists now call it the *Bison antiquus figginsi*.) More importantly, however, Figgins became convinced that the strange-looking spearhead that McJunkin had found among the bones was a prehistoric flint projectile point. Increasingly he felt that this suggested the possibility that a big-game hunting society might have existed in North America at least 10,000 to 12,000 years ago – a supposition for which no evidence had previously been found.

It was still only a theory, though, and many archeologists doubted its validity for a long time after the Folsom find. For one thing, no human remains of prehistoric big-game hunters had ever been discovered. For another, it was possible that the stone projectile point was simply an unusual but relatively modern weapon that had somehow been washed into the pile of prehistoric bones. Not until 1967, after long years of digging at the Folsom site, did Figgins and his colleagues find what seemed to be certain proof. This time they found a stone spearhead embedded between two ribs of the skeleton of a *Bison antiquus figginsi*. There could be no doubt of it: This great beast had been deliberately killed by a man-made weapon.

Archeological detective work since 1967 has revealed that these Old Stone Age Americans – now generally known as Paleo-Indians – were expert, methodical hunters. Toward the end of the Ice Age, ice sheets still dominated the northern part of North America, but farther south, where there are now arid deserts, fertile grasslands provided food for great numbers of animal species, and the animals were huge compared with their modern counterparts. In the New Mexico canyon where George McJunkin made his discovery there must once have been a body of water surrounded by long, thick grass; and some of the bison that went there to drink were doubtless killed quickly and efficiently by the skillful Paleo-Indians' finely wrought spearheads, now known as Folsom points (after the place where they were found).

The prehistoric big-game hunters left traces of their activities not only at the Folsom site but elsewhere in southwestern America, as archeologists have discovered in recent years. The site of one fascinating find is a ravine near Kit Carson, Colorado, where the positioning of bones indicates a mass slaughter of bison. It seems certain from the evidence that Paleo-Indians forced a herd of nearly 200 bison to stampede and that more than half of the frightened animals leaped into the ravine, only to be trampled to death by those following or killed by hunters standing on the rim. And in and among all the skeletons were a number of weapon points.

From the fact that the bones of 16 calves, some appearing to be only a few days old, were

THE EXTINCTION OF ICE AGE ANIMALS IN NORTH AMERICA

Before the end of the Ice Age (around 8000 BC) mammoth, bison, giant sloths, tapir, and other huge animals of the great plains were the principal food source for prehistoric North Americans. By 5000 BC most of the ancient species had completely disappeared. Why? Was extinction the result of natural forces, was it man's fault, or did it result from a combination of these factors?

Some scientists believe that a tremendous earthquake and volcanic eruptions may have wiped out a number of species. It is possible that some succumbed to disease of one kind or another. The end of the glacial period may also have brought about or hastened the extinction of non-adaptable species since, among other things, it led to a drying out of the land along with drastic alterations in the weather and the composition of the forests. The Paleo-Indians nonetheless, may have played an important role in the final tragedy. The big, ponderous animals, must have been physically unprepared to withstand such a cunning predator. For example, although the giant sloth – huge, yellowish, and lumbering, with claws as long as daggers – may have looked fiercely unapproachable to other beasts, it was a harmless vegetarian and easy prey for the early hunter, to whom every sloth captured and killed represented a good 1,500 pounds (680 kilograms) of meat.

We know also that Stone Age hunters used fire as a means of cornering their quarry, and fires may sometimes have gotten out of control and killed thousands of animals.

An elkhide robe, painted by a member of the Shoshone tribe late in the 19th century, depicting the Indian pursuit of bison-hunting.

found among the rest, archeologists have deduced that the stampede was caused on a late May or early June day. It must have been a particularly successful day's work for the hunters. They would have gained enough food from this one hunt to last for many weeks, not to mention hides for clothing and bone and horn for implements.

From all the evidence it seems clear that these Stone Age Indian tribes were as proficient at butchering their prey and utilizing the products as they were at organizing and carrying out hunting procedures. After skinning a bison, they divided it into "butchering units." Individual groups cut up several bison simultaneously, and, as the meat was removed from each unit, the bones were piled up into separate heaps of various types of bone; thus, in the Colorado ravine many skulls were piled together at one end. The hunters obviously ate certain parts while they worked; tongue bones, for example, have been discovered scattered throughout kill sites. About 75 per cent of the bison killed at the Colorado site appear to have been butchered. This, it has been calculated, would have given the tribe about 56,640 pounds (25,690 kilograms) of meat, 5,400 pounds (2,450 kilograms) of fat, and 4,000 pounds (1,800 kilograms) of internal organs. About 100 men would have needed only half a day to do the job. Some of the meat was probably eaten fresh, some dried for future consumption.

Conjecture plays a large part, of course, in drawing tentative conclusions about the life style of the Paleo-Indians. It is thought that they were free-roaming nomads, who never had a chance to accumulate material possessions (which may account for the meat left unbutchered and implements such as spearheads often left behind). But we really know nothing more than that they were enormously capable big-game hunters. They left numerous signs of their existence – weapons, bones of the enormous animals they killed, hearths on which they roasted their meat – but they themselves remain, for the present at least, mysterious.

Paleo-Indian spearheads, blunt at one end and sharp at the other, were fitted to short wooden shafts. A throwing stick might be used to project the spear farther and faster. The spearheads were designed to penetrate deeply and fall out easily, so that they could be retrieved and used to finish off the prey.

WHY DID THEY LEAVE THEIR WEAPONS BEHIND?

The tools of North America's Paleo-Indians are the only evidence on which we can form some idea of their life style. Though they lived at the end of the Ice Age 10,000 or more years ago, the points of their weapons, often delicately chipped and gracefully fashioned, indicate that their stone-chipping technology was remarkably advanced. Some excavation sites have yielded what look like hunters' kits, complete with weapon points, scrapers for processing animal skins, and implements apparently designed for sharpening, scraping, cutting, perforating, and even for engraving materials such as stone.

Since so much care seems to have gone into their manufacture, why did the Paleo-Indians leave so many of these weapons lying around at the kill site? The answer to this question came indirectly from the work of an American archeologist Halvor L. Skavlem who had spent many years collecting early Indian relics. One day in 1912, it suddenly occurred to him to put himself in an Indian's shoes: "How," he asked himself, "would *I* make stone weapons? How would *I* produce and use stone tools?"

Skavlem found that it was possible to break away flakes from flint by pressing with rounded bones or sticks of wood. Finally, he became so skilled, that he could make an arrowhead in a few minutes and a stone ax in a few hours. No wonder the early hunter casually left his weapon behind him. He knew it would only take him a few minutes to make another.

The dry ravine near Kit Carson, Colorado, scene of a mass bison kill, with the bones lying in a long row down the center of the gully. Separate piles of skulls, limbs, and other bones indicate a systematic process of stripping off the meat from each part of the carcass in turn.

The boomerang

An American first?

THINK OF A boomerang and you will probably think of an Australian aboriginal invention: After all the word "boomerang" itself comes from "bumarin," which is what Australian aborigines call the curved stick that can sometimes soar gracefully back to the thrower after being hurled at a distant target. But although the modern use of the boomerang, both as weapon and plaything, is certainly an Australian specialty, recent finds now suggest that the boomerang may well have originated elsewhere.

Boomerangs have been used throughout the world, the remains of ancient boomerangs having been found, for instance, in Europe, Egypt, and India. But the oldest boomerang ever found was dredged up in Florida only a few years ago. It dates back to about 10,000 BC, and its discovery gives rise to the intriguing possibility that boomerangs were first invented in America rather than in Australia.

The Florida boomerang had been preserved in the mud of a ledge 85 feet (26 meters) below the surface of Little Salt Spring, a deep lake near the Gulf Coast north of the Everglades. Part of the longer wing of the boomerang, which was made of oak, is missing, but enough of the weapon remains to permit us to determine what it was like. Most interestingly it has been established that it was a non-returning, or straight-flying, boomerang; in other words, it was built to hit its target and stay there, not to return to the distant thrower.

That may seem a contradiction in terms, since most people believe that a chief characteristic of boomerangs is that they turn around in mid-air and come "home." Though this is a common assumption, it is a wrong one. In Australia and elsewhere, there are both returning and non-returning boomerangs, and the non-returning type is often preferred – though it may be less fun as a plaything – because it can be thrown farther and with more accuracy (the circular path of the other sort naturally shortens its range). Models based on the design of the 12,000-year-old Florida non-returner have been thrown with a fair degree of accuracy for distances of nearly 200 feet (65 meters), but modern straight-flying boomerangs can reach targets as much as 650 feet (200 meters) away from a skillful hurler.

The differences between the returning and non-returning boomerang are not always clear.

Usually the returning type, which is more a sophisticated toy than a hunting weapon, has wings of roughly equal length, forming a wide angle or curve, whereas the non-returning type has wings of unequal length, forming an angle closer to 90 degrees. Also they tend to be larger and heavier than returning ones. But a returning boomerang can sometimes be converted into a straight-flying one – and vice versa – by heating and twisting the wings slightly. Very subtle differences in a boomerang's shape will make significant differences in its flight path.

The Florida boomerang was just one of many prehistoric objects preserved in the waters of Little Salt Spring, a site which has recently yielded some remarkable evidence of the life style of Stone Age Americans. Before 1979, when a partial account of the finds was published, the earliest known example of a wooden boomerang was one dug up in Jutland (a north European peninsula now forming parts of Germany and Denmark) dating from about 5000 BC. Like the Florida boomerang, it was not designed to return to the thrower. Such discoveries have led some observers to believe, despite much expert opinion to the contrary, that the more fascinating returning type is a relatively recent development on the non-returners, which have until recently been considered "inferior" models.

The ancient art of making boomerangs still continues in parts of Australia, where they are produced largely for the tourist trade.

FLORIDA'S "NATURAL TIME CAPSULE"

Human remains, fossils, and other artifacts of Paleo-Indian origin, dating back 12,000 years, have been preserved in the layers of sediment that have accumulated on the ledges of a sinkhole in Little Salt Spring, Florida. This cross-section shows how the sinkhole, which is 150 feet (48 meters) deep by about 75 feet (25 meters) in diameter, is hidden beneath a much broader lake.

Little Salt Spring was once thought to be just a shallow lake. In 1959, however, divers discovered that a deep sinkhole with nearly vertical sides lies beneath the broader surface waters of this Florida lake. Some 12,000 years ago the water level was much lower. At that time therefore the sinkhole (known locally as a cenote) probably provided drinking water for human beings; also it offered good hunting, and animals that tumbled over the cenote's sharply dropping walls were likely to be trapped or drowned. Since 1959, but more especially since the early 1970s, exploration of layers of sediment that accumulated in ledges of the cenote as water levels rose and fell during the course of thousands of years has yielded extraordinarily well-preserved evidence of ancient societies. Research under the water and in the vicinity of Little Salt Spring is still going on, and the array of human remains and artifacts is so rich that the investigative team of scientists have called the cenote a "natural time capsule." Apart from the dramatic recovery of the world's oldest surviving boomerang, divers have brought up many other interesting objects. On the uppermost edge of the cenote (at the point where the lake now widens into a shallow basin), for instance, there were a number of wooden stakes driven into the sediment in such a way as to suggest that they formed part of a trap. Lower down, on the ledge where the boomerang was found, was the collapsed shell of an extinct type of giant turtle; embedded in the enormous shell, which was about four feet (over 1 meter) long, were fragments of a wooden stake and bits of fire-hardened clay. Evidently the animal was trapped, killed by a sharp-pointed stake driven into its body, then cooked and eaten. Such evidence that Stone Age Floridians hunted this species of tortoise suggests that they may even have caused its extinction.

Beginning 9,000 years ago, the water table in the region rose, and, with the greater availability of fresh surface water in other places, Little Salt Spring was gradually deserted. Then, nearly 7,000 years ago, the water level fell again, and the area once more attracted settlers. In a nearby swamp the scientists have found a 6,000-year-old burial ground containing around 1,000 bodies, one of the biggest cemeteries of prehistoric Indians ever found in North America. Some of the corpses are exceptionally well preserved in the moist peat surrounding them; one skull contains part of a brain, its convoluted structure still discernible. The bodies were partially wrapped in grass, and beside them were buried leafy branches and numerous artifacts.

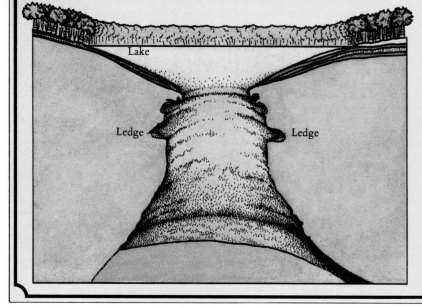

Lake

Ledge   Ledge

Brain surgery in the Stone Age
Motives and techniques

IN THE 1860s, Ephraim Squier, an American diplomat and anthropologist whose hobby was searching for relics of prehistoric man, made an amazing discovery in Peru. He unearthed the skull of a Stone Age man, through which, with great precision, two thin, parallel grooves had been cut. The grooves were crossed by two more and between them, a neat central section of bone had been removed evidently to expose the brain.

Squier had stumbled on a case of prehistoric brain surgery, a bone-cutting procedure known today as *trepanning*. He sent the skull to a Frenchman, Dr. Paul Broca, the leading contemporary expert in physical anthropology and Broca confirmed that the skull had been trepanned while its owner was still alive. Broca went even further: he claimed that the bone around the trepanation showed signs of infection, indicating that the patient had lived for perhaps 15 days after the operation.

Over the next 20 years examination of European Stone Age skulls confirmed that trepanning had not been confined to the Americas. Stone, Bronze, and Iron Age trepannings were identified at sites from western Russia to the Atlantic coast. The finds revealed skull openings of many shapes and sizes. The most common were circles, ovals, diamonds, and squares. In 1936, two trepanned skulls in Palestine were even found to have exactly the same crosscut pattern as had the hole in Squier's original skull from distant Peru.

Trepanning was still practiced in the Pacific Islands well into the 20th century, enabling anthropologists to ask the modern "Stone Age" trepanners some questions. What were they trying to do? How did they manage to cope with the bleeding and pain?

The answers gave clues to the motives and techniques of the Stone Age surgeons. Like prehistoric trepanners these Pacific Islanders were ignorant of the brain's functions and as a result lacked inhibitions concerning drastic skull operations. If they saw someone in a coma caused by a head injury, they wanted to tidy up the wound and remove inward-pressing skull fragments. Further, they believed that fits, chronic headaches, lethargy, and depression indicated that the skull contained something that would be better released. Evil spirits must be let out, and good spirits let in.

Brain surgery was not restricted to warriors with head wounds from battle, the men on whom the survival of the community depended. Stone Age patients from Poland to Portugal and from Peru to Alaska included men, women, and children, from six to 60. Moreover, Stone Age patients often underwent more than one operation. A skull found at Cuzco, Peru, had no less than seven circular openings. All showed unmistakably healthy new bone, evidence that the operations had been successful.

Judged by the proportion of skull openings revealing post-operative healing, the success rate of Stone Age trepannings was surprisingly high. In one study, more than 80 per cent of a group of skulls from Poland and Czechoslovakia displayed signs of healing. And out of 214 trepanning wounds identified on skulls found in the Americas, nearly 56 per cent showed complete healing and 16 per cent partial healing. Considering that the success rate of trepanning operations in World War I was 25 per cent at best, the Stone Age operations, the earliest-known surgical operations of any kind, are all the more remarkable.

How could men working with chipped or even polished stone blades make such neat incisions? Examination of Stone Age trepannings has revealed that a combination of techniques was used. The commonest method seems to have been repeated scraping, rather than sawing, along the same line of pressure. Such an operation must have been protracted, because excessive pressure with a thin stone flake would easily have broken the blade leaving it in the wound.

Modern surgery depends on the use of anesthetics to kill pain and antiseptics to check infection. It seems, from the survival rates of these operations, that prehistoric peoples had far higher pain thresholds and resistance to infection than people have today. Indeed, in prehistoric times, people had to be extremely hardy simply to survive infancy. Nevertheless, Stone Age surgeons must have taken great care in stopping and dressing wounds, because evidence of infection is rare. Anthropologists have found that primitive peoples have effective folk medicines and pain-killers made from herbs and plants. And archeologists have discovered that Stone Age Peru possessed a particularly powerful drug, coca, from which we get cocaine and which they took by chewing the leaves of the coca plant. Peru has yielded more trepanned skulls than the rest of the world combined, although there were other trepanning centers in France – in the Paris region and the Massif Central – and in Czechoslovakia, especially near the city of Prague.

As the Stone Age gave way to the Bronze and Iron Ages, superstitions rather than the wish to heal played an increasing part in the motives for skull surgery. Skulls were certainly trepanned, but generally after death, so that discs of bone could be removed, polished, drilled, and worn as amulets. And throughout the Middle Ages in Eastern Europe, the accepted method of saving the dead from possession by vampires was the piercing of a corpse's skull. Such grim customs contrasted sadly with the energy and confidence of the first Stone Age skull surgeons.

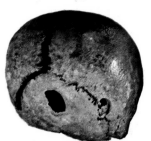

Found on the northwest coast of South America, this 2,000-year-old trepanned skull bears the scars of two operations.

In the 1930s, an English doctor, Wilson Parry, carried out trepanning operations using Stone Age methods and tools. Three of the instruments he made for this purpose are shown above (with wooden handles). The items without wooden handles are original Neolithic knife blades.

With the aid of a brain scanner, which uses X-rays to scan a cross-section of the brain (shown at left), investigation and diagnosis of brain injury is now possible without having to resort to surgery.

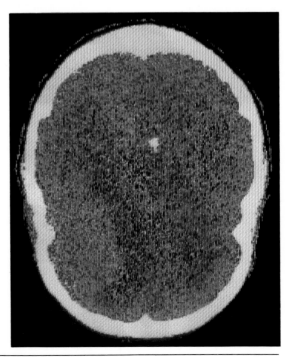

4000 BC-600 BC

THE ANCIENT WORLD

100,000 BC   Period of time covered by this chart

■ AD 1500

YEARS BC		4000	3900	3800	3700	3600	3500	3400	3300	3200	3100	3000	2900	2800	2700	2600	2500
AMERICAS		COPPER AGE — Copper tools made by Indians around Great Lakes										Pottery made in Ecuador and Columbia — Settled farming communities in N. America (gra						
							51										
EUROPE		COPPER AGE — Copper-working skills spread slowly through Europe from Balkans										BRONZE AGE — First civilizations in Aegean area						
		30										40					
ASIA	MIDDLE EAST	COPPER AGE			BRONZE AGE						First major Mesopotamian state, based in Sumer, at its peak						
	FAR EAST	BRONZE AGE — Bronze-working in S. E. Asia			First Chinese city built						Growth of civilization in Indus valley — Bronze-working in Ch						
		28					34				32 38 51						42
AFRICA	EGYPT	BRONZE AGE									Unification of Upper and Lower Egypt				Pyramids built		
		STONE AGE									Arable farming in C. Africa						
											36 44					47	
OCEANIA		Gradual colonization of Pacific Islands by Stone Age peoples						STONE AGE									

Shown in the chart above are page references to each article appearing in this section of the book. The subject of each article is listed here.

28 Bronze-working in Ban Chiang, Thailand
30 Copper-working communities well established in Danube valley
32 Trading contracts thriving between Ur, Dilmun, and Indus valley
34 Invention of wheel in Mesopotamia

36 Egyptians using perfume
38 Sumerians writing in a cuneiform script on clay tablets
40 Lakeside settlements built in Europe by fishing and farming communities
42 Mass suicide at Ur's Royal Cemetery?
44 Nile flood utilized in agriculture by Egyptians

46 Use of acupuncture recorded in China
47 Egyptians embalm their dead
49 Egyptians practicing dentistry
51 Chinese first visit America?
53 Ebla sacked by Akkadians
54 Hypogeum constructed by Stone Age temple-builders of Malta

The three and a half millennia stretching from 4000 to 600 BC saw a rapid acceleration in the advance of cultural achievement in many parts of the world. At the beginning of the period only a few settled communities existed; by the end great cities and civilizations had risen and fallen, and the stage was set for the flowering of such advanced societies as those of Greece, Rome, China, and Mexico.

Technological progress was astonishing (though it must be noted that some civilizations of this period did not yet know about such vital developments as writing and the use of the wheel). In all settled societies, craft specialization began, and skilled potters, weavers, masons, and goldsmiths flourished. Perhaps the most important group to emerge was the priesthood, often the sole masters of the skill of writing among more advanced civilizations. Although artifacts and buildings can tell us much about the past, it is the survival of written documents that really keeps a long-vanished people "alive."

It would be misleading, however, to give the impression that the whole world became civilized during these few thousand years. At best there were centers of high culture – chiefly in the Middle and Far East – surrounded by extensive regions whose populations had much less advanced life styles. Throughout most of Europe, sub-Saharan Africa, the Americas, and Oceania, stone continued to be the primary material for making tools and weapons long after other societies had learned the use of copper, bronze, and iron. Such divergencies exemplify the uneven spread of technology and innovation in the world.

2300	2200	2100	2000	1900	1800	1700	1600	1500	1400	1300	1200	1100	1000	900	800	700	600

Metal-working in Peru

Americas' first urban civilization established by Olmecs in Mexico

62   80

Mycenaean civilization in Greece
Minoan civilization on Crete

I R O N   A G E
Iron-working in S. E. Europe

56   76   66   63   73   75

Sagan rules powerful Akkadian empire – the first great empire known to history

Assyrian empire

I R O N   A G E
Babylon major power in Mesopotamia

Phoenicians trading throughout Mediterranean world

Fall of Assyrian empire

I R O N   A G E
Use of iron in S. E. Asia

Urban civilization in China under Shang dynasty develops writing

Aryans fully occupy Indian sub-continent

Iron technology spreading throughout China

53   59   46   69   73   60   82

New Kingdom inaugurated after expulsion of invaders

I R O N   A G E

Foundation of Carthage by Phoenicians
Tribal kingdoms established in W. Africa

49   57   67   71   73   78

Melanesia settled from Indonesia   Fiji colonized   Easter Island colonized

56 Palace of Knossos built by Minoans on Crete
57 Contraception practiced in Egypt
59 Hammurabi, King of Babylon, codifies the law
60 Aryans invading Indian sub-continent
62 Head-shrinking practiced in S. America

63 Thira eruption shakes the Mediterranean world
66 Basques – ancient Egyptians or Paleolithic hunters?
67 Hatshepsut on throne of Egypt
69 Oracle bones consulted by Shang dynasty Chinese

71 Akhenaton and Nefertiti overthrow traditional Egyptian gods
73 Phoenician merchants supplying luxuries to the Mediterranean world
75 Antikythera mechanism sinks in Aegean
76 Eleusinian mysteries celebrated in Greece

78 First recorded strike in history takes place in Egypt
80 Adena Indians building temple and burial mounds
82 Ashurnasirpal, King of Assyria, boasts of his cruelty

Who were the first metal-workers?

Rewriting the history books

This bronze spearhead found at Ban Chiang may eventually prove that Thailand was the birthplace of the Bronze Age.

FOR DECADES historians have placed the cradle of civilization in just one part of the world. Sophisticated writing techniques, the first true cities, the wheel, the first use of bronze – all, the experts have held, began around 3500 BC in Mesopotamia, the valley between the Tigris and Euphrates Rivers that flow through modern Iraq down to the Persian Gulf. But this consensus has now been challenged by the discovery of an age-pitted bronze spearhead in Thailand, thousands of miles east of Mesopotamia. The spearhead, along with other artifacts, was found in the mid-1970s at Ban Chiang, a village in northeastern Thailand, and the find has thrown ordinarily sedate scholars into a frenzy of debate. For it apparently dates back to about 3600 BC – as early as the Mesopotamian Bronze Age, and a full 1,000 years before the nearby Chinese are first known to have used bronze.

The reason for the frenzy is not merely a question of dates; the find raises a number of basic questions. For instance, most accounts of world history used to proceed on the assumption that major steps in human development started at a single geographical point, then spread outward through the agencies of trade and war – rather like the ripples from a stone tossed into a pond. Thus Mesopotamian advances could be traced, century by century, as they spread eastward to India and westward to Europe. Chinese initiatives could be followed in the same way: westward into Central Asia, southward into Southeast Asia, eastward into Korea and Japan. But the Ban Chiang spearhead has thrown this tidy ripple theory of history into disarray. Thailand may well represent a new stone and a new pond.

Will the Mesopotamian and hence the European Bronze Age turn out to have been triggered from Thailand? Was tin – the metal which turns soft copper into harder bronze – exported from Southeast Asia, where it was widely available, to Mesopotamia, where it was extremely rare? Could bronze have been invented *independently* in both Thailand and the Middle East? Did news of the Thai discovery spread to China (instead of the other way round) in the same way that news of the Mesopotamian discovery spread to Europe? If so, how can the 1,000-year gap between the Thai and Chinese Bronze Ages be explained? If not, why not? After all, similar developments elsewhere always had an early impact on neighboring cultures. Nobody is sure of the answers to any of these questions. But the implications of the Ban Chiang find are staggering since they may eventually lead archeologists to make a wholesale revision of pre-recorded history in both the Far East and the West.

The archeologists who sparked off the current debate are an American, Dr. Chester Gorman of the University of Pennsylvania, and a Thai, Dr. Pisit Charoenwongsa of the National Museum in Bangkok. They headed an expedition organized a few years after some bronze artifacts were found in ancient grave mounds in Ban Chiang and nearby Non Nok Tha in the late 1960s, along with some pottery dating from between about 4000 and 3500 BC. In 1974 Gorman and Charoenwongsa began digging at the Ban Chiang site, where within two years, they unearthed 126 human skeletons and 18 tons of artifacts. The pair identified seven separate layers of remains at Ban Chiang. The lowest, reaching back to about 3600 BC, was some 16 feet (5 meters) below ground level; and it was here that the diggers found their historical bombshell: not only a bronze spearhead lying beside a skeleton but also a second skeleton that was wearing bronze anklets and a third with bronze bracelets.

In addition, the expedition turned up iron knives and axes on higher, later-period levels; and these objects, indicating that Ban Chiang's metallurgical sophistication lasted through to sometime between 1600 and 1200 BC, are themselves something of a bombshell. They predate by at least a century the Hittite culture of the Middle East that was previously thought to be the first to make extensive use of iron. So an obscure little village in Thailand has been catapulted in the past few years to worldwide fame as the presumptive founder not only of the Bronze Age but of the Iron Age as well.

A number of archeologists, however, have serious doubts about the validity of the Ban Chiang claims. They contend that Gorman and Charoenwongsa derived their only unquestionable dates from analysis of fragments of wood found close to the skeletons and artifacts. Since the mound that was excavated at Ban Chiang had been used for centuries as a burial ground, they argue, such fragments of wood are an unreliable guide to the age of the objects. Each new burial must have disturbed the fragments and soil layers, and penetration by plant roots has moved the earth still further. A more reliable guide to the age of the bronzes, say the doubters, is the age of the skeletons themselves – and analysis of some of the bones suggests that they date from sometime between 750 and 50 BC. In that case, the Ban Chiang culture would have been an offshoot of China's Bronze Age, rather than its predecessor.

For now, both sets of dates – the one reaching back to 3600, the other no further than 750 BC – remain fiercely defended and apparently irreconcilable. Other sites in Thailand have yielded pottery of a similar age (4000 to 3500 BC) to that at Ban Chiang, but no very early bronze. It may be that the Ban Chiang culture was limited to the Khorat plateau of northeastern Thailand, which is notably rich in both copper and tin, the two metals essential to bronze. Cut off from China and more southerly civilizations in Southeast Asia by hills and jungle, the metalworkers of Ban Chiang may have developed their pioneering technology in isolation, and their techniques may later have been duplicated by other, more expansive cultures that never even heard about the remote unsung inventors.

Nobody yet knows for certain. Meanwhile, the hunt goes on for more evidence to confirm or undermine the Ban Chiang findings – and to piece together the full story of that enigmatic bronze spearhead.

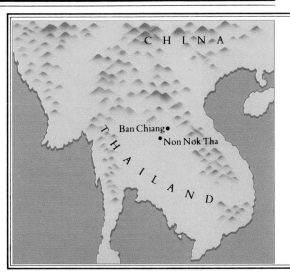

The extraordinary discoveries of ancient bronze objects at Ban Chiang in Thailand have led some archeologists to consider for the first time the possibility that the Bronze Age may in fact have originated in Thailand, and then spread to China, and not vice versa, as was generally believed.

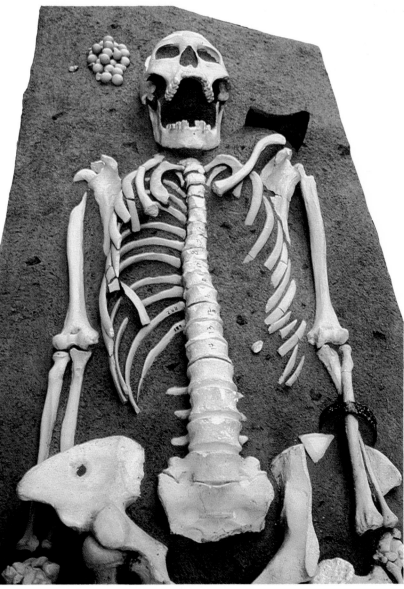

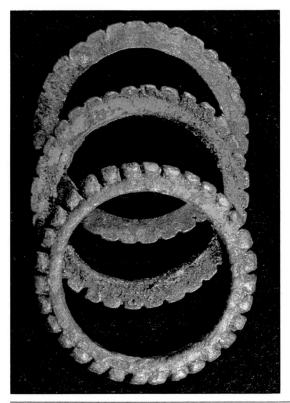

One of the greatest finds at Ban Chiang – a skeleton (above) wearing bronze bracelets (at left) – was discovered in the same layer of remains as the bronze spearhead shown opposite.

Daily life in Copper Age Europe

Six thousand years ago, the first farmers of Europe were cultivating the Danube valley and the Ukraine. They grew cereals, kept horses, sheep, and cattle, and hunted wild animals. Living off the land, these hunters and farmers developed an astonishingly rich and sophisticated culture, which archeologists have learned about from the remains of their villages, and from such objects as the clay altar built in the form of a house gable. A typical village contained up to 50 houses, built with elaborately decorated walls of thick clay on a framework of wooden posts and wattle. A central row of heavier posts supported a thatched roof which was daubed with clay and grooved for drainage. The houses served as workplaces as well as providing living and sleeping accommodation. These early farmers also learned how to work the locally found copper. They discovered that copper can be separated from its ore by heating, and that at still higher temperatures it becomes liquid. Using open molds, they cast tools and weapons, which, though sharp, could not have had the durability of the stone tools they also used. Later Bronze Age people who inhabited this area did not display the same creativity, and archeologists have still to discover what caused the disappearance of these Copper Age communities.

Tools

Copper Age people used a wide range of tools. Shown below are: (1) a bone fishing-point and hook; (2) a sickle with a flint blade; (3) two copper awls and a borer; (4) copper fishhooks; (5) two copper ornamental plates; (6) a pipe for bellows (shown in the reconstruction at right); (7) a crucible; and (8) two copper ax-adzes.

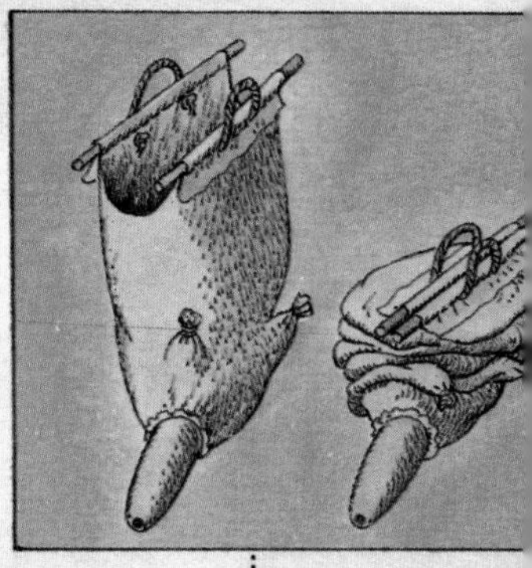

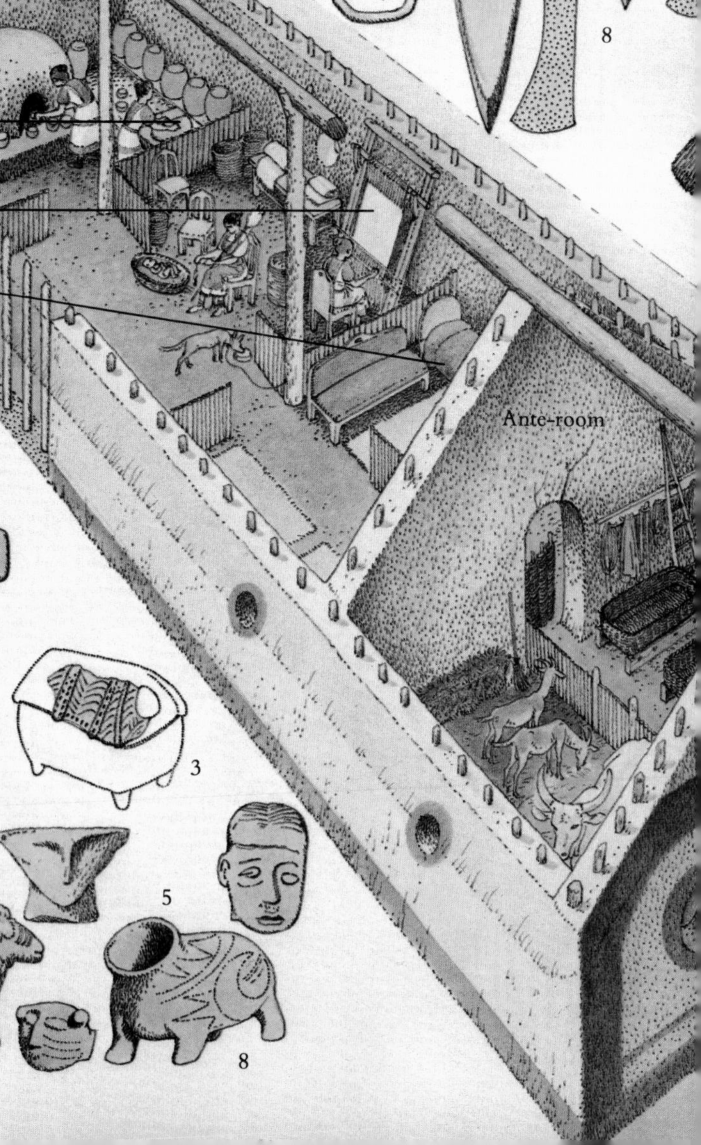

Oven built of clay-daubed wattle or reeds
Quern for grinding corn
Cooking platform
Loom
Sleeping accommodation

Ante-room

Artifacts

Many miniature clay models and figurines have been uncovered from Copper Age sites throughout southeast Europe. Probably made for religious purposes, they depict everyday objects, animals, and people, particularly women. Some are shown at right: (1) five pieces of furniture; (2) two sledges; (3) a fragment of a house; (4) a goat's head; (5) two human heads; and (6) two female idols. Clay was also used for making such items as the ritual lamp (7), and the animal-shaped container for liquids (8).

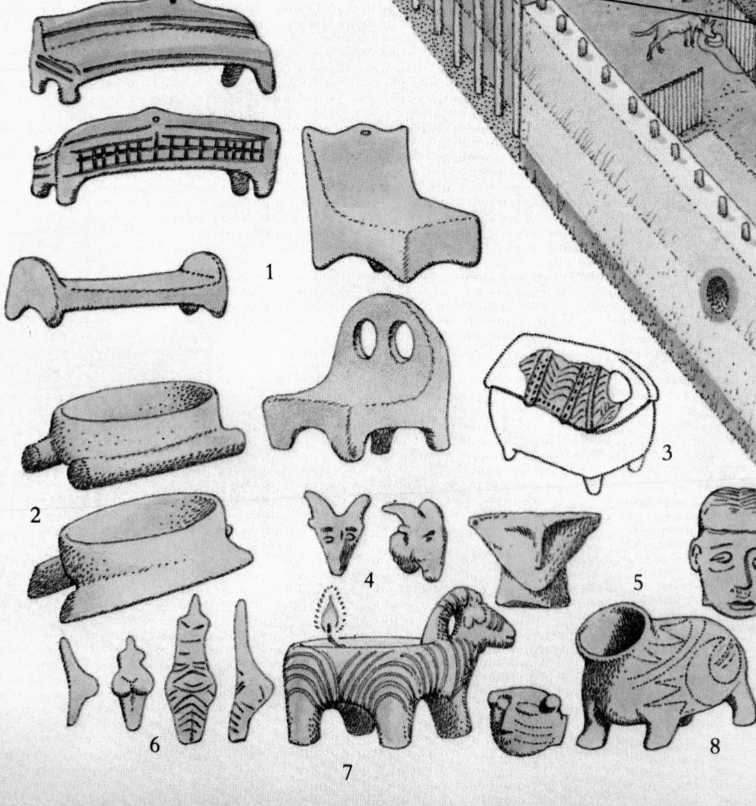

7

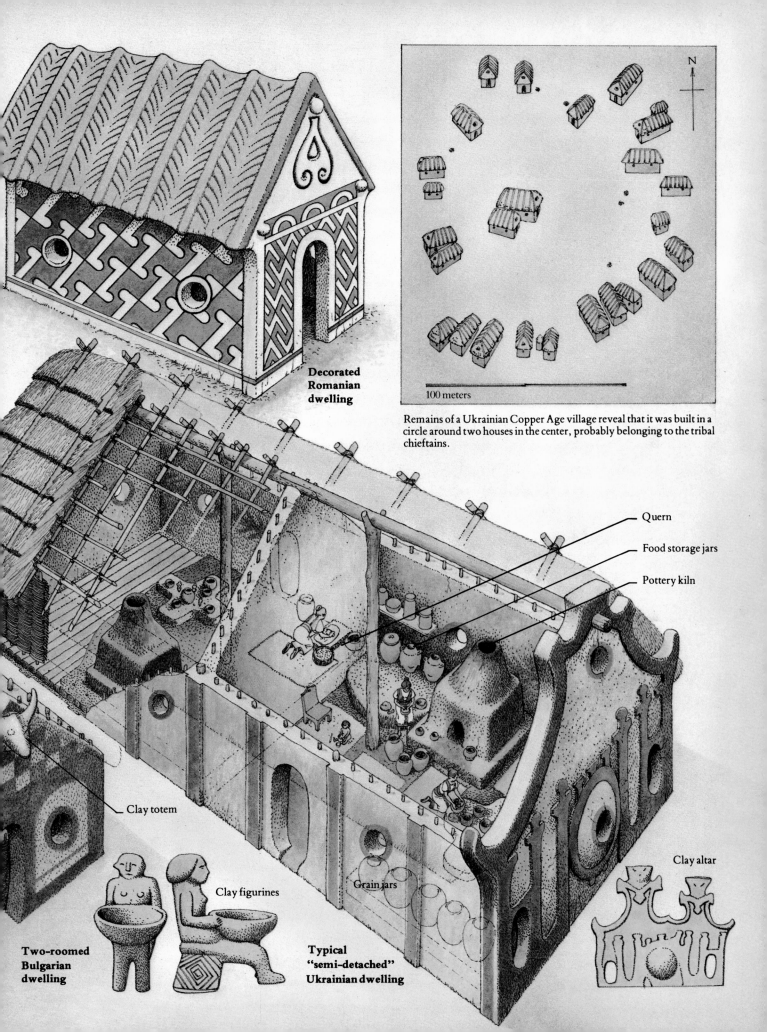

Decorated Romanian dwelling

Remains of a Ukrainian Copper Age village reveal that it was built in a circle around two houses in the center, probably belonging to the tribal chieftains.

100 meters

Quern

Food storage jars

Pottery kiln

Clay totem

Clay figurines

Grain jars

Clay altar

Two-roomed Bulgarian dwelling

Typical "semi-detached" Ukrainian dwelling

No broken reeds

Distributing the wealth

MAX MALLOWAN, the British archeologist, was intrigued. In his hand he held a little shell, of a species known as *Cypraea vitellus*, which is found in the Indian Ocean. Yet Mallowan had just unearthed it in the buried ruins of a 6,000-year-old settlement at Chagar Bazar, in landlocked northern Syria. It was a clue to a mystery as fascinating as any contrived by Mallowan's wife, detective-story writer Agatha Christie – a mystery that was eventually to be solved by a hazardous sea-voyage in a boat built of reeds. How did the shell come to be found so many miles away from its place of origin, and how was it brought there?

Professor Mallowan made his discovery in the mid-1930s. More than half a century of excavations in Mesopotamia, that rich and fertile land which lies between the Tigris and Euphrates Rivers, have now produced artifacts and written records to show that a large, organized trading network was flourishing in the area 4,000 years ago. One of the most important trading centers was "Ur of the Chaldees," from which the Hebrew patriarch Abraham set out on his travels. Ur lay on the Euphrates, not many miles from the head of the Persian Gulf. Its traders kept their accounts on clay tablets, many of which have survived to give a vivid if incomplete picture of life in this prosperous city. Ur was a busy, bustling port through which many prized commodities passed. Trade was in the hands of the *alik-Dilmun*, a group of seafaring merchants, who took the manufactured products of Ur, particularly cloth and readymade clothes, to a city they called Dilmun (or Telmun), where they bartered them in exchange for much-needed copper. A tablet found in the house of a merchant of Ur named Ea-Nasir gives the weight of a cargo of copper received from Dilmun and subsequently sold off in smaller

Thor Heyerdahl built his boat Tigris in 1977 along the lines of ancient Mesopotamian reed boats such as the one shown (inset), which is taken from a cylinder-seal dating from 2300 BC. Used successfully by Heyerdahl to retrace the trade routes of the merchants of Ur and Dilmun, Tigris provided positive proof that reed boats could have been used as long-distance cargo ships.

lots. And not only copper was traded: other clay tablets found in Ur record a whole shopping list of luxury goods, including red gold, lapis lazuli, ivory and items made from it, eye paint, timber, and "fish-eyes," which were probably pearls. None of these is native to Ur or its vicinity, indicating that trading contacts between Ur and Dilmun were considerable and far-reaching. But where was the city of Dilmun, the other end of this lucrative trade?

For a long time archeologists have suspected Dilmun to be on the island of Bahrain in the Persian Gulf, now famous for its oil production. Proof of this was finally found by the British archeologist Geoffrey Bibby, who spent many years excavating on the island, where he discovered the remains of an ancient port on the north coast. Among the many artifacts uncovered there were soapstone stamping seals used to register the contents of a cargo or shipment of goods. Bibby sent a description of the seals back to an expert on classical archeology in Aarhus, in Denmark, who replied with a suggestion that these seals were identical to some found during the excavations in the 1930s at Ur. Here indeed was proof that trade was transacted between Ur and Dilmun across the Persian Gulf.

But even more remarkable was the discovery of similar seals found amid the ruins of the city of Mohenjo-Daro in the Indus valley in Pakistan, many hundreds of miles to the east, through the Persian Gulf and across the Indian Ocean.

So did the traders of Ur and Dilmun reach as far as the Indian sub-continent? Further clues exist which suggest they did. Trade records found at Ur mention two places, Magan and Meluhha, whose location is not known for certain. It is thought likely that Magan was on the north shore of the Persian Gulf, in present-day Iran, and that Meluhha, from where Ur received its shells and ivory, is farther away on the coast of the Indian Ocean in the Indus valley. Could Meluhha in fact be the city of Mohenjo-Daro? Five small stone weights, made of polished chert, a flint-like quartz, found in Dilmun were identical in type and weight to those known to have been used in Mohenjo-Daro and its sister-city of Harappa. Other items found in the city link it with Dilmun and Ur, suggesting that Mohenjo-Daro is indeed the city known to the people of Ur and Dilmun as Meluhha, their partner in an extensive trading network operating over thousands of miles of sea.

But there remained one obvious question still to be solved before the existence of such a network could be established. What kind of boat was used that could both sail up the relatively

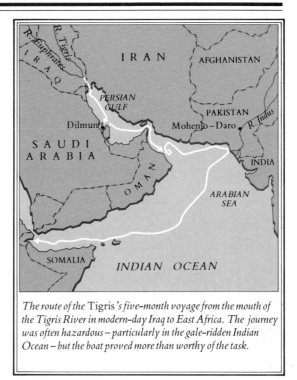

The route of the Tigris's five-month voyage from the mouth of the Tigris River in modern-day Iraq to East Africa. The journey was often hazardous – particularly in the gale-ridden Indian Ocean – but the boat proved more than worthy of the task.

shallow Euphrates to Ur, yet venture across the sea to Dilmun, Magan, and Meluhha?

An expert on early boats is the Norwegian anthropologist Thor Heyerdahl. Heyerdahl had built and sailed a papyrus reed boat across the Atlantic in 1970 and knew about their method of construction and their seaworthiness. He noticed that the seals found in Ur showed pictures of reed boats, and thought it likely that such boats could have been the cargo ships of the *alik-Dilmun*. The Marsh Arabs living in the marshy delta of the Tigris and Euphrates Rivers still use reeds to build their houses, and the fishermen of Bahrain still make reed boats. So in 1977 Heyerdahl built a large raft-like reed boat on the banks of the Tigris near to the city of Ur. In a five-month voyage, Heyerdahl sailed his ship, appropriately named *Tigris*, down the river to the Persian Gulf and over to the ancient port of Dilmun, from there to Mohenjo-Daro on the Indus River and, finally, to Djibouti in East Africa. *Tigris* drew only three feet (1 meter), shallow enough for both the river section of the journey and the shallows off Dilmun. Yet the ship also proved adequately seaworthy to withstand the gales of the Indian Ocean, and carry a cargo. On reaching the Indus River, Heyerdahl found that great stands of reeds, similar to those used in the making of his boat, grew along the banks, suggesting that reed boats might well have been built there as well as in ancient Mesopotamia. He had proved that reed boats could have been used by the Dilmun merchants for their trading activities.

Wheels within wheels

The invention that makes the world go round

O F ALL THE discoveries that have made human progress possible, none exceeds the wheel in importance. The invention of the wheel not only revolutionized transport but ushered in the age of machinery. Almost everything inside and outside the 20th-century home depends to some extent on the wheel. Modern plastics, for example, are extruded from rollers, which are themselves shaped on spinning lathes. The motor in a washing machine is, in fact, just a sophisticated wheel, powered by the current generated by other wheels in electric turbines. Most modern textiles, from carpets to clothes, are made by machines that rely on the rotary principle. So are the pages of this book, and the letters you see printed on each page.

The wheel is so much the hub of our civilization that it is hard to believe that intelligent human beings could ever have managed without it. Yet for thousands of years after man first learned to grow crops and build cities, the wheel was unknown. And, curiously, despite its obvious usefulness for transport, the earliest known wheel was the potter's wheel, which was probably invented in Mesopotamia about 5,500 years ago. The first potter's wheels were flat discs, usually of stone or wood, with a central hollow on the underside that fitted over a stone or hardwood dome set in the ground. At first these were simply turntables, useful only for bringing different sections of the pot within easy reach of the potter but the technique of forming pots on a constantly spinning wheel soon followed. Part of one such wheel, made of clay, has been found at the ancient Mesopotamian city of Ur (possible

birthplace of Abraham). Dating from about 3250 BC, it has a series of holes around the circumference. The holes would have made it easier for the potter to grip the wheel when he or she set it spinning.

Archeologists have been able to trace the evolution of the potter's wheel in some detail by studying the telltale finger grooves and the direction of the particles in the clay walls of wheel-thrown pots. When and where the principle of the wheel was first applied to transport remains unknown, however, since very few examples of early wheeled vehicles have survived. It is generally agreed that the first wheeled vehicle was probably a four-wheeled cart, which must have come into use shortly after the invention of the potter's wheel; and scholars have suggested two regions as possible sources of this revolutionary device: the city-states of Mesopotamia or the steppes of Central Asia. Most of the available evidence points to Mesopotamia as the likely place, but some scholars argue that no evidence has been found on the steppes only because the nomads who lived there built no cities for modern-day archeologists to explore. In support of this argument they point out that the flat, open land of the Asian steppes was more suited to wheeled transport than the soft sand of Mesopotamia. Moreover the Mesopotamian cities moved most of their freight by river – a far more efficient method of transport in the roadless conditions of the time – and so had no pressing need to invent the wheeled vehicle though they must have been quick to perceive its advantages once it came along. Although the claims for both regions as inventor of the wheel

The Royal Standard of Ur, dating from around 2500 BC, depicts an early chariot with soldiers, the two-piece wheels held together by brackets. A picture book of Sumerian life, the standard is worked with mother-of-pearl and lapis lazuli embedded in asphalt on a wood base.

remain tantalizingly plausible, most archeologists believe that the wheel was invented only once, not in several places independently. They base this conviction on the remarkable uniformity of design among ancient carts that have been discovered in places as far apart as Western Europe, Egypt, India, and China. Almost all have two important – and not obvious – features in common: a shaft designed for yoking two animals and a spokeless wheel made up of three distinct pieces of wood held together by cross-struts. Had wheeled vehicles been invented in more than one region, the experts say, there would surely be differences in the way they were pulled and the construction of the wheels.

At first the carts were usually drawn by oxen, just as plows had been for thousands of years, and they were used mostly to move goods over short distances – from a farm to a nearby market, say – or to carry dignitaries in ceremonial processions. But two later developments turned these relatively clumsy and largely agricultural vehicles into the world's first war machines. The two developments, which appeared more or less

simultaneously in about 2000 BC, were the taming of horses and the development of the spoked wheel. The result was a light, fast chariot that could outrun even the best infantry.

Because they were mounted on such chariots, the archers of the Hyksos, a tribe of desert nomads, were able to invade and conquer the mighty Egyptian empire in the 17th century BC. The oldest extant pictures of horse-drawn chariots with spoked wheels are found on cylinder-seals – the stone or clay stamps with which

The development of the wheel slowly affected every aspect of daily life. For example, hunting, shown here on a ninth-century-BC Hittite limestone relief, was transformed by the increased mobility afforded by wheeled vehicles such as the chariot.

THE HEMISPHERE THAT IGNORED THE WHEEL

Why did the wheel, which was in almost universal use across the Old World by 1000 BC, remain unused in the New World for a further 2,500 years? The principle must have been known in the Americas as early as the time of Christ, for wheeled clay models of animals have been found in Mexican tombs dating from the first century AD. But the knowledge was not put to practical use until after the arrival of the Spanish *conquistadores* 1,500 years later.

Scholars have speculated that there were two major reasons for this extraordinary oversight. First, at a time when the wheel was being invented the pre-Columbian New World had no draft animals such as oxen or horses; and secondly, much of the terrain – especially the dense jungles of Central and South America and the precipitous mountains of both North and South America – was unsuitable for wheeled traffic. But neither argument is free of objections. After all, the Maya of Mexico and the Incas of Peru built superbly engineered roads between their cities. Indeed, the Incas made their stone-paved network remarkably level as well by throwing stout bridges across the Andean chasms and tunneling, where necessary, through the solid rock of the peaks. And the absence of draft animals would not have prevented the development of versatile hand-carts and wheelbarrows; yet no evidence of either has been found. Nor is there any evidence that pre-Columbian craftsmen used the potter's wheel.

Instead, the peoples of Central and South America, if not of the north, built highly sophisticated civilizations entirely without the wheel – and did so with conspicuous success.

While land journeys in medieval Europe were still a nightmare of axle-clutching mud and unreliable inns, relays of Inca couriers were capable of carrying royal messages and commands from one end of the empire to the other along a well maintained network of roads punctuated at regular intervals by food-stocked rest houses. And they did it all on foot.

None of this, though, explains the existence of miniature wheeled animals that were unearthed in the 1940s from graves at the town of Panuco (near Tampico on Mexico's east coast) and at Tres Zapotes, farther south in the province of Veracruz. Scholars are still sharply divided on the function of the 2,000-year-old models' origin and purpose. Some claim that the little clay wheels were an American invention, though it seems odd that a designer imaginative enough to conceive of wheeled clay animals should not also have grasped the practical possibilities for a larger version of the wheel. Other scholars, by contrast, have drawn attention to similarities of design between the models and similar wheeled objects from China – which raises the intriguing possibility of Chinese contact with the New World more than 1,000 years before Columbus.

As for the purpose of the animals, it may be that they were merely toys. But the fact that they were placed in tombs and that toys seem to be unlikely gifts for the dead suggests that they had some more solemn ceremonial function in Indian religions. In any event, the very existence of wheeled miniatures is baffling. They are archeological oddities posing unanswered questions in the otherwise wheel-less Western hemisphere.

Two of the wheeled clay models found in tombs in Mexico, dating from the first century AD and proving that the New World was aware of the wheel, if not of its practical uses.

merchants identified their goods. Seals bearing such pictures and dating from between 2200 and 1900 BC have been found in northeastern Iran and Turkey. Many archeologists believe, however, that the earliest chariots were developed farther north, on the plains of Central Asia where horses were first tamed by the nomads.

Whatever its origin, the new invention brought dramatic changes in its wake as it spread across the ancient world, reaching Western Europe by 1550 BC and eastern China by 1300. The mere existence of efficient wheeled vehicles created a need for a network of better roads; better roads speeded up the development of trade; and traders, administrators, and armies could travel farther and faster than ever before, making it possible for aggressive peoples to conquer ever-larger territories. Archeologists have argued that without the spoked wheel, it is probable that the Hittite warriors from Central Asia could never have conquered the Anatolian plateau of central Turkey as they did in about 1850 BC, the Assyrians could not have brought all mainland Greece under their control, and the Shang dynasty could not have founded the first major Chinese empire.

A rose by any other name?

The ancient custom of anointing the body

Among the most exquisite of objects found in the royal tombs of Egypt are the little jars and boxes that once held perfumes and oils. Many of these containers were fashioned in the shape of birds and fishes, and were tinted blue and amber – colors that were thought to prevent perfume from losing its potency. Only the wealthy could afford such beautiful containers. Poorer people simply rubbed their bodies with palm oil, which was available in large quantities. The priests who made the perfume kept it in delicate boxes of alabaster and onyx or in hand-blown glass flasks, such as the opaque flask illustrated above, made with narrow necks (as they are now) to stop the perfume evaporating quickly.

PERFUME: Men have been seduced by it and women have risked their lives for it. In fact, man's bizarre obsession with perfume has continually colored the pages of history books. One king loved it so much that it literally brought about his downfall.

Of all the ancient kings, none could have been a more ardent admirer of perfume than Antiochus Epiphanes, King of Syria from 175 BC to 163 BC, who, at the games in Daphne, had all his guests sprayed with rose water from golden watering cans and anointed with perfume from golden dishes.

On another occasion, King Antiochus ordered a ewer of perfumed oil to be poured over one of his subjects. This generous gesture backfired when in full view of an admiring crowd, who had gathered to watch, the king slipped in the oily pool and fell flat on his back.

The earliest records of perfume and its uses date back much farther than that – to the Egypt of 5,000 years ago, where it also had social importance: the pharaohs gave it as official gifts, and by 1500 BC it was already an important trading commodity. Since then, its popularity has, if anything, grown and spread worldwide. Perfume is still associated with ideas of glamour and sophistication, and vast amounts of money have been poured into what is today one of the most lucrative and thriving industries of all time. Why should it have assumed such importance and popularity over the years?

Vanity is an age-old preoccupation. Humanity has always been obsessed with making the body more attractive, especially to the opposite sex, and this was no less true in the time of the Egyptians than it is today. The Egyptians seem, in general, to have been a vain race, and were probably the first people to concoct recipes for perfume, and a primitive form of deodorant.

The connection of perfume with enhanced sexual attraction was not confined to the Egyptians. The beautiful Queen of Sheba traveled 2,000 miles (over 3,000 kilometers) across a desert to maintain the perfume trade, and beguiled Solomon with her beauty and wiles. Men were warned about the danger of giving in to the charms and perfume-induced attractions of women. Writing about the ancient Greeks, the British anatomist, Robert Burton, tells us: "Philocharus, a gallant in Aristoenetus, advised his friend Polyaenus to take heed of such enticements, for it was the sweet sound and motion of his mistress's spangles and bracelets, the smell of her ointments, that captivated him first."

The love of perfume was certainly strong among the Greeks, who believed that different perfumes should be used on different parts of the body. Even the Romans, who in their early history had shown no interest in it, were gripped by the perfume fever, so much so that by the first and second centuries AD their use of perfumes and spices had reached ridiculous proportions. Nothing was ignored. Everything was perfumed – not just the body or clothing. The Emperor Nero was reputed to have slept on a bed of rose petals (it was said that he suffered from insomnia if even one of them was curled) and once, on returning from Greece, he found the streets of Rome sprinkled with aromatic oil in his honor. At his wife's funeral, it was recorded that he burned more oil and incense than the Arabs could produce in 10 years. His palace was built with concealed pipes from which guests were sprinkled with a fine mist of exotic smells. In fact, during his reign perfume was so widely used that it was considered unfashionable for a soldier to go into battle without it.

Personal use of perfume was not all self-indulgent, however, since it also formed part of important cleansing and health rituals. The effects on the body of the arid climate of the Middle East was probably one reason for the Egyptian love of oily lotions and heavily scented perfumes (it seems that the Egyptians also invented the bath). The oily creams were used to protect the skin from burning and drying out – as were many of their cosmetics.

There are many other instances of the medicinal uses of perfume. The Greeks, for example, believed that wearing sweet-scented flowers such as the rose or myrtle around the head relieved headaches – particularly those caused by the after-effects of drink. The soothing qualities of rose water are still well-known today.

Perhaps the most important use of perfume in ancient times, however, was its contribution to religious ritual. The word "perfume" itself evolved from the Latin *per fumum*, meaning "through smoke" – reminiscent of perfume's earliest use as incense, which was essential to many ancient rites of worship. Ancient peoples believed that by burning sweet-smelling woods and aromatic gums, so that their prayers would be wafted upward through the smoke, they would be looked on more favorably by the gods. Even the sacrificed animals were stuffed with incense to make them smell sweeter.

The ancient Egyptians used perfumes in the process of mummification and embalming to preserve the corpse and, it was thought, help it travel to a new life. And the Egyptians were not alone in believing that perfumed cedarwood contained the essence of immortality. The Arabs, Indians, and the Jews all used perfumed woods when building their religious temples.

When the Jews returned from exile in Egypt, they brought with them the hygiene habits of the Egyptians, including the use of oils and perfume. These, in turn, eventually became an intrinsic part of the Jewish religion. The Bible is packed with references to the religious use of perfume. Moses was told by God to build an altar of incense and to mix holy oil and perfume. The oil was used to anoint the tabernacle, the ark of the covenant, altars, and sacred vessels. From this Jewish rite is derived the ceremony of anointing which today still forms the basis of coronation services.

IS BEAUTY MERELY IN THE EYE OF THE BEHOLDER?

"Gall of ox, powder of ostrich egg, germinated speld are mixed, made into a dough and pounded with viscous fluid . . ."

You could easily be forgiven for thinking that this was the recipe for a rather nauseating dish, or even some sort of magic potion, but it is, in fact, an Egyptian recipe for a face pack, designed (according to the Ebers Papyrus, a medical manuscript written in 1550 BC) to "expel wrinkles from the face." It seems that then, as now, people were anxious to look younger than their age, and there are many other such recipes recorded for beautifying the skin. They were supposed to work miracles – one, for example, claiming to transform an old man into a youth. Honey and milk – two ingredients which are still widely used today in "natural" cosmetics – were among the many favorite remedies for skin complaints.

In many tomb paintings, Egyptian women are shown with peculiar, cone-shaped objects perched on their heads. These were pomades, made by steeping flowers in fat, and molding the resulting mass into a cone. During the evening, as the atmosphere grew warmer, the fat would trickle down their faces and necks, soaking into the skin, to give them their beautiful, highly praised necklines.

The most perfected beauty techniques were those used in eye cosmetics. Eye shadows of different colors were popular, as was antimony-based kohl – the latter still a basic ingredient of mascara. As well as beautifying their user, cosmetics were meant to be practical. Eye paints originally evolved in Egypt as a protection against the sun and eye diseases. Gradually, health began to take second place, and more importance was attached to the effect of different colors.

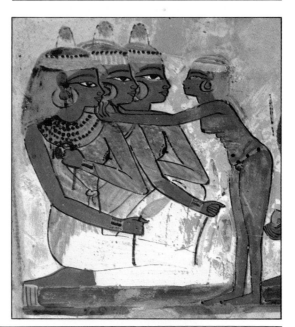

Wealthy Egyptian ladies employed slave girls to help them with their dress and their make-up.

The earliest literates

The discovery of a language unearthed a civilization

WHEN EUROPEAN travelers began exploring ruins in Persia and Mesopotamia (present-day Iran and Iraq) in the 16th century, they found a number of strange-looking inscriptions composed of wedge-shaped characters, some impressed on clay tablets and cylinders, others carved in stone alongside relief sculptures depicting the glories of ancient empires. Were the inscriptions – eventually dubbed "cuneiform," after the Latin word for "wedge," – merely decoration, the Europeans wondered, or were they a form of writing? If they were meant to be read, what was the language?

It took hundreds of years to find answers to these questions, but the answers were well worth waiting for. Because cuneiform was a meaningful script, its eventual decipherment not only increased our store of knowledge about civilizations such as the Assyrian and Babylonian, but also revealed the existence of an ancient civilization never before guessed at: that of Sumer. This discovery also brought to light the earliest known heroic poem, the *Epic of Gilgamesh*, which even antedates Homer's *Iliad* by about 1,500 years.

The deciphering of cuneiform really got underway in the 1830s when a young English army officer, Henry Rawlinson, who happened to be stationed in Persia, became fascinated by the wedge-shaped carvings. Most of those found at Persepolis, the ancient capital of the Persian empire, had already been studied, and it was generally agreed that they represented three distinct dead languages, arbitrarily identified as Class I, Class II, and Class III. Because Class III had the largest number and greatest variety of

The Epic of Gilgamesh, *dating from the third millennium BC, recorded the heroic deeds of the renowned god-king, Gilgamesh (above). One of the most popular and enduring tales throughout Mesopotamia, in later years it came to be illustrated on many objects such as the Assyrian cylinder-seal (shown at right), dating from 1350 to 1000 BC.*

distinguishable symbols, 19th-century linguists correctly assumed that its language was the most ancient of the three, for the normal pattern in the development of writing is from the pictorial (requiring hundreds of symbols) to the alphabetic (requiring relatively few symbols, representing sounds). Class I, with only 32 symbols, was evidently alphabetic and more recent than the others; and it was assumed that this must be Old Persian, the language spoken at Persepolis in the sixth and seventh centuries BC. Since this dead language was partially known, scholars had a basis on which to work, but they were still squabbling about dates and meanings when Rawlinson, temporarily relieved of military duties, set himself the task of achieving a convincing translation of all three classes of script.

To do this, he realized he needed to find parallel cuneiform texts containing a larger vocabulary than anything so far available – something like the Rosetta Stone, which had enabled Champollion to decipher Egyptian hieroglyphics a few years earlier. He began a determined search and finally found what he was looking for at Behistun Rock in western Persia, where the high cliff face was covered with relief sculpture and some 400 carved lines of Class I text, along with what appeared to be parallel versions in Classes II and III. Perched precariously on a ladder 300 feet (100 meters) above a sheer drop, Rawlinson began the arduous task of copying the inscriptions by pressing wet sheets of paper over the stone to take impressions of them. For two years he labored at the task in temperatures that sometimes reached 120°F (49°C). At night, sitting in a hut cooled by water poured over the roof by his Persian assistants, he worked on the translations.

The work was interrupted for nine years by a recall to active military service, but in 1844 he returned to the rock and finished translating the Class I text, which proved to be an account in Old Persian of the exploits of King Darius (521–486 BC). He now had the key to the Class II and Class III inscriptions, but it took him several more years to complete the work. The language of Class II, which we now call Elamite, was that of a people who had flourished around 1000 BC and had been subjugated and eventually assimilated by the Persians. And Class III, the oldest language, turned out to be that of the Babylonians, and of the Assyrians before them. We call this tongue Akkadian, and thousands of Akkadian inscriptions in addition to those of the Behistun Rock and Persepolis had already been found by Rawlinson's time.

Akkadian is a Semitic language; but, as Rawlinson and other scholars studied quantities of extant inscriptions, many excavated from King Ashurbanipal's library in Nineveh, they became increasingly puzzled by the fact that there were many words – especially proper names – that were not Semitic and did not relate to either the Babylonians or Assyrians. In particular, there were frequent references to a "King of Sumer." It became more and more apparent that there had probably been an even earlier Mesopotamian society than that of the Assyrians.

This hypothesis was confirmed in the 1870s when archeologists uncovered the city of Lagash, 100 miles (160 kilometers) east of Babylon. Here they found ample evidence of a very ancient civilization with a language strikingly different from the Akkadian – the very language, in fact, of which traces had been seen in clay tablets already studied. Cuneiform writing, it became clear, had been invented – or, at least, first inscribed on clay – by the Sumerians, whose civilization had reached a peak sometime around 3000 BC. The language, which belongs to no known linguistic family, was difficult to decipher, but archeologists soon managed to piece together a picture of what was possibly the first civilization on earth.

Most Sumerian writings are of a mundane character – such things as inventories and agricultural records. But a few literary works, poems that convey the Sumerian view of the world, have survived. The most important of these is the *Epic of Gilgamesh*, extensive fragments of which have been found. The story tells of the heroic deeds of Gilgamesh, fabulous god-king ("strong as a savage bull") of a city called Uruk, capital of Sumer, and of his friend Enkidu. In one of the episodes, there is an account of a great flood, which resembles the story of Noah in many respects. The discovery of this passage kindled new efforts to find traces of such a flood – efforts which have as yet been unsuccessful. But, most important of all, the whole epic reveals many aspects of the Sumerian religion and way of life.

A CIVILIZATION BUILT ON CLAY

The land inhabited by the civilized Sumerians about 5,000 years ago is an unlikely place for a society to thrive. Flat, arid, poor in minerals, it would seem to offer only a subsistence living – as it does for the few people who live there today. But the Sumerians were a resourceful, inventive people. They developed a sophisticated system of irrigation, channeling the waters of the Tigris and Euphrates Rivers into their lands to make them fertile. And they organized themselves into city-states and formulated systems of laws to facilitate the smooth functioning of society.

Despite their high degree of organization, the Sumerians realized that their prosperity was precarious. Because floods and other abnormal weather conditions could inflict severe damage on the system that sustained them, they felt they were ultimately dependent on superhuman forces; and this feeling found expression in the faith that a god ruled over each city. (The human ruler derived his authority from an assembly, but was considered, in effect, the steward of the god.) The temple in which the god was believed to reside was usually constructed on top of a great stepped pyramid (ziggurat). Since there was little stone in southern Mesopotamia, the Sumerians built this ziggurat, as well as their houses, of sun-dried brick.

The brick mold was but one of many Sumerian developments. Others included the potter's wheel, the plow, the sailboat, the water clock, casing in copper and bronze, engraving, and inlay work. Sumerian jewelers produced elegant work in gold, silver, and semi-precious stones, and sculptors carved delicate objects in wood and ivory. Stone

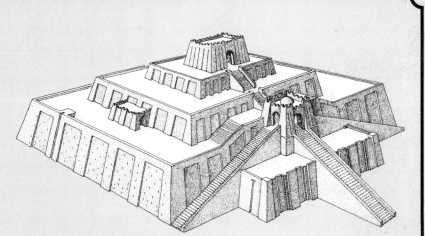

was used for cylinder-seals, on which representations of people, animals, and other subjects were incised. When a seal was rolled over the damp clay on which all documents were written, the result was a design in low relief.

Clay determined the form of the Sumerians' most distinctive achievement. Their first writing consisted of pictographs (stylized drawings) scratched on bits of stone. But clay was far more abundant than stone and could easily be marked with a reed stylus, then left to dry. The only problem was that stiff reed cutting into clay could not easily reproduce the curved lines necessary for "readable" pictographs. So, in time, the symbols became so stylized as to be unrecognizable; the resultant short, straight, wedge-shaped characters are what we now call cuneiform.

The ancient Sumerians believed that different gods ruled each city, and they built temples for these city gods on the top of ziggurats, which were stepped pyramids made from sun-dried bricks. Above is an artist's impression of one of the best preserved – the ziggurat of Ur-Nammu, Ur, built in the 21st century BC.

A Neolithic Venice?

The stilt villages of prehistoric Europe

DURING THE exceptionally dry winter of 1853–54, the level of many European lakes fell. At Lake Zurich in Switzerland, a number of upright piles were seen sticking up, like so many woody excaliburs, through the unusually shallow water. Since it was already known that this region had attracted prehistoric communities, an eminent archeologist called Ferdinand Keller was summoned to the scene. After studying the piles, he announced that they were the remains of platforms on which houses had been constructed over the lake some 4,000 years ago.

Keller's interpretation was inspired by the pictures he had seen of the modern platform dwellings of certain preliterate Pacific Islanders. It seemed natural to assume from the evidence that dwellings had been built over Lake Zurich and other Alpine lakes in a similar way. Keller's vision of a Neolithic Venice aroused tremendous popular enthusiasm and, before long, Alpine fishermen, who had often damaged their nets on the piles, had abandoned the fish in favor of the far more exciting and sought-after catch of ancient ornaments and pots that they dredged up from the lake bed. But Ferdinand Keller was only guessing. A hundred years were to go by before archeologists would have the facilities to investigate the evidence buried in the soil, sediment, and rubble in which the piles were fixed.

Neolithic villages, built some 4,000 years ago on marshy ground by the sides of lakes, supported a population living off the lake and the land. The houses were constructed of wood on foundations of long piles driven into the swampy ground.

A BALANCED DIET – NEOLITHIC STYLE

Even by modern nutritional standards, it seems that the people who lived on the shores of Lake Paladru enjoyed a healthy and varied diet. From their main food crops – wheat and barley – they milled the coarse flour with which they baked flat cakes on their clay hearths. In addition, they gathered numerous wild food-plants. From the bountiful forest came blackberries, plums, and apples, as well as mushrooms and nuts. There is evidence to suggest that, though they tended to fell trees fairly indiscriminately for their log dwellings, these people left oak trees standing. They valued the acorns for themselves or, more likely, for their pigs – it is still said today that the best hams grow on oak trees. They also protected other nut-yielding trees, clearing away any nearby growth so that the maximum sunlight could reach them. The resulting harvest of nuts would have rewarded such efforts by being at least twice as big as the harvest yielded by unprotected trees.

Though the Lake Paladru people were stock-breeders who enjoyed beef, mutton, pork, and goat meat, they also regularly hunted deer and even, on occasion, bears. Stone net weights and bits of netting suggest that they liked fish too. The meat was probably broiled over an open fire, but the many fragments of quartzite littering the hearths of Lake Paladru suggest that stone boiling was a favored cooking method of these Neolithic lakeside dwellers.

Stones were placed in the fire until they were red hot. Then the hot rocks and the food to be cooked were placed in a pot which was partly filled with water; the water came to a boil, but there is abundant evidence to suggest that the sudden drenching often caused the stones to shatter.

Held fast in the wet debris of the lake bottom were other wooden objects, textiles, and tools – even plant and animal remains – all of which would have weathered and decayed if they had remained dry. It was the invention of practical free-diving gear in the 1940s, and the development of sophisticated underwater salvaging techniques in the 1950s, that made it possible to know what these ancient Alpine lake homesteads really looked like.

Once further investigations were underway archeologists realized that the picture painted by Keller of a Neolithic village built on stilts emerging from the water was completely wrong. In fact, the villages had been built beside the lakes, not over them; and the piles formed part of the foundations of houses that had been built on very swampy ground. Hundreds of years after the houses were first erected, the water levels rose and the remains of these lakeside villages – by then deserted – were consequently submerged at some considerable distance away from the new shorelines.

Why did the pioneering farmers of northern Europe build their homes on such damp ground? The answer probably lies in the natural distribution of vegetation at the time. Since the Alpine valleys were covered with dense forests, it made sense for the settlers to use the readymade clearings around lakes as sites for their houses. It was also convenient – as any modern camper knows – to have their households near fresh water. Once established by the lakeside, the settlers could start winning land from the forest.

As hunters and gatherers, fishers and farmers, these early Europeans were on intimate terms with their environment. Just how good they were at tapping its resources has been shown from discoveries made at Lake Paladru in France where, in the 1970s a painstaking underwater salvage operation was begun. The people who lived alongside Lake Paladru 5,000 years ago used flint axes to fell the lumber for their houses. The frames were made of fir-trunks, and chinks between the walls of hazel and fir poles were filled in with moss and reeds. The roofs covering these sturdy frames were probably thatched with reeds, and their foundations were supported by piles. The Lake Paladru people slept in beds made of fir boughs and in the evening they gathered around clay hearths.

Like the pioneering families who trekked across America, they were hardy, self-sufficient folk. The fragments of textiles found – along with wooden loom combs and spindles – show that they made their own cloth, while for storage they used clay pots and woven baskets. In addition to crops of barley and wheat, they grew flax, which was probably valued on account of its nutritious seeds as well as for its fiber. A small palisade fence on the landside of their settlement kept their cattle enclosed when they were not foraging in the forest or in nearby meadows.

The development of agriculture during the Neolithic period meant that food supplies were more reliable, and the population of Europe was still tiny enough to ensure that there was plenty of land to go around. After about 15 years, when their cabins began to show signs of irreversible wear and tear, and their crops had exhausted their fields, these early settlers would move on and colonize another lake shore. Lake Paladru may have been a backwater – while its people were going about their daily chores, the pyramids were being raised in faraway Egypt – but the picture conjured up by what remains of the settlement is of a peaceful way of life.

Loyalty in ancient Ur

Followers through death's door

A BELIEF IN LIFE after death, say the anthropologists, is one of the things that distinguish human beings from animals. This belief may have inspired "mass suicides" that occurred nearly 5,000 years ago in the ancient Sumerian city of Ur.

Ur of the Chaldees, as it is called in the Book of Genesis, is known as the birthplace of Abraham. By Abraham's time – about 2000 BC – it was already a flourishing city, sited on a bank of the River Euphrates, not far from the Persian Gulf. In common with other cities of ancient Mesopotamia, its most imposing building was the ziggurat, or temple, rising above neighboring structures like a small mountain. It was close to the site of this ziggurat that, in the late 1920s, the British archeologist Sir Leonard Woolley found what he himself called the "death pits" of Ur, which later scholars have identified as the city's Royal Cemetery.

The burial ground that Woolley opened up dates from about 2500 BC. Among its many individual graves, which are of only limited interest to archeologists, were several larger tombs strewn with startlingly well-wrought artifacts such as gold cups and amulets, necklaces

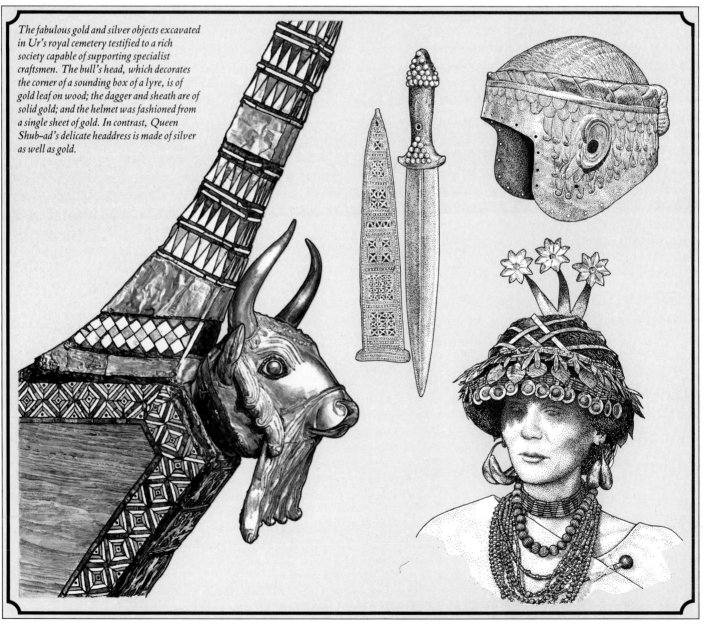

The fabulous gold and silver objects excavated in Ur's royal cemetery testified to a rich society capable of supporting specialist craftsmen. The bull's head, which decorates the corner of a sounding box of a lyre, is of gold leaf on wood; the dagger and sheath are of solid gold; and the helmet was fashioned from a single sheet of gold. In contrast, Queen Shub-ad's delicate headdress is made of silver as well as gold.

of semi-precious stones, the frames of harps and lyres inlaid with mosaics, sculptured animal figures, the remains of a chariot decorated with semi-precious stones and metals, and even an exquisitely inlaid gaming board with a set of dice or counters. Clearly, each of these large tombs was the final resting place of an important person, whose body was laid out in a central position. But the striking fact about them was that a number of other bodies lay in proximity, obviously in what might be deemed "subordinate" positions – sometimes within the tomb itself, sometimes congregated in groups of up to 70 in adjoining anterooms.

A careful examination of the remains convinced Woolley and his colleagues that violence had played no part in the multiple deaths. Bodies lay in orderly rows, each on its right side, knees drawn up, hands folded over chest, in peaceful attitudes of sleep. They were of both sexes; and all, especially the women, had been splendidly groomed and attired, as if for a great occasion. Chemical traces on skulls indicated that the ladies had dressed their hair in silver ribbons. And there was some evidence that voluntary death had come swiftly to these people. For instance, Woolley found a roll of silver ribbon lying near the skeleton of one woman, who must have taken it into the tomb and not had time enough to weave it through her tresses. Scattered among the bodies, moreover, there lay many little cups, which might well have held the poison that they drank in order to follow their masters or mistresses into the hereafter.

Woolley believed that the tombs were those of kings and queens of Ur, one of whom he identified as Queen Shub-ad (or Puabi). The head and face of another, better-preserved, female skull were later reconstructed by Woolley's wife in plaster and wax and crowned with the gorgeous headdress of silver and gold found on the queen's bier. In Woolley's opinion the accompanying bodies were members of the royal household such as guards, grooms, ladies-in-waiting, and musicians who willingly joined their monarchs in death. Other experts, pointing out that the cemetery lies in the shadow of a great ziggurat, have suggested that the occupants of the tombs may have been priests and priestesses accompanied by acolytes, all of whom went to ceremonial death after the celebration of some sort of religious rite. Whoever they were, we can only marvel at the dignity with which they faced death.

Entrance to the king's tomb at Ur, excavated by the English archeologist Sir Leonard Woolley in the 1920s.

HIGH AND DRY
"Mesopotamia" derives from a Greek word meaning "land between the rivers" – the Tigris and the Euphrates. Parts of Mesopotamia were first settled about 10,000 BC; this – the world's earliest known civilization – is known to us today as the land of the Sumerians.

The city of Ur existed almost from the start of Sumerian civilization. Rival city-states rose to challenge the supremacy of Ur, and at one time in its long history it was all but razed to the ground by enemies. But it was Nature that finally brought about its end, in or around the fourth century BC, when, for some reason, the channel of the Euphrates delta on which Ur stood silted up, leaving the city high and dry.

Excavations during this century have revealed a walled city and suburbs with an area of about four square miles (7 square kilometers), with an estimated population of something over half a million.

The miracle of the Nile

The foundation of Egyptian civilization

LIKE MOST early peoples, the ancient Egyptians regarded all manifestations of nature with awe. But nothing could match the inundation of the Nile valley each summer, when the swollen river spread fertile silt over the land. And in the fall, the re-emergence of the land as the floodwaters subsided was nothing short of miraculous. For Egypt was then reborn and refreshed by the Nile's fertilizing waters.

Ancient Egypt's brilliant civilization represented a successful adaptation to the Nile's changing seasons. In the Nile valley scattered groups of people learned the enormous benefits of communal cooperation. Leaders emerged to direct their effort, making possible the development of a thriving farming culture ultimately controlled by dynasties of pharaohs.

The importance of registering the rise and fall of the river was recognized from early times. Nilometers – stone gauges scored with lines to measure the depth of water – were installed along the 800-mile (1,300 kilometers) stretch of water between Aswan, Egypt's southern frontier, and the sea. References in Egyptian records show that a system of measuring the flood level was in operation around 3000 BC. Such records enabled the authorities to forecast the likely extent of the following season's flood and, therefore, the probable size of the harvest – knowledge that gave them enormous power.

As information accumulated about the endless annual cycle of flood, cultivation, and drought, an ingenious taxation system evolved, which was used to determine the value of real estate. People who owned land that was never flooded paid the lowest taxes, while landowners whose fields were inundated annually paid the highest taxes. Further, the annual obliteration of field boundaries by the flood forced the Egyptians to become surveyors, so laying the foundations of their mathematical knowledge. Another important science was engineering, because flood control underlay the economy. Dikes were built to prevent the countless villages in the Nile valley being submerged, while catch basins retained floodwater for irrigating the fields when the level of the Nile went down.

Visitors to ancient Egypt must have envied the advantages enjoyed by the people. They would have been impressed by the fact that the narrow Nile valley was enclosed and protected by burning-hot desert. The desert barriers offered security which, in turn, promoted stability and a sense of national identity. It is no wonder that this spectacular civilization lasted virtually intact for 2,500 years.

Egypt, as the Greek historian Herodotus observed, was "the gift of the Nile," and inevitably the Egyptians regarded the river as an object of wonder and worship. The actual inundation, honored by the name of Hapi, was worshiped as a god. In sculpture, Hapi was usually depicted as a bearded man, wearing the narrow belt of Nile boatmen and fishermen and holding the riches provided by the fertilizing waters. But his pendulous female breasts and bulging stomach suggested that, above all, he was a fertility deity. His strength, the driving force of the flood, was thought to come from underground sources, namely a primordial ocean, called Nun. Hapi was worshiped in mid-June as the level of the Nile started to rise, but he was not part of any theological system. However, he later became so intimately associated with Osiris, the corn god, that he was called "the soul of Osiris." The Egyptians believed that Osiris died in early spring, when drought prevailed and harvesting started, only to be reborn in the fall, when the flood subsided and planting began anew.

Osiris represented the fertile properties of the Nile. He also personified the ruler of the world of the dead. As such he was one of the most important of all Egyptian deities, because he gave his devotees hope of eternal life.

The shadoof (above) has been an essential device for irrigating land in the Middle East for thousands of years, as can be seen in the carving from Sennacherib's palace (at right) dating from the sixth century BC. The weight at one end of the pivoting pole balances the bucket on the other, allowing the bucket to be filled with river water, lifted, and swung around with relatively little effort, to be emptied into the high-level irrigation ditches.

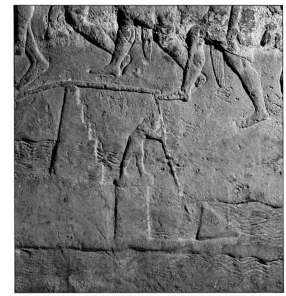

THE WATER OF LIFE

The world's longest river, the Nile, has two major sources, the White Nile and the Blue Nile. The White Nile flows from Lake Victoria, south of the equator in Uganda, northward for more than 4,000 miles (6,437 kilometers) to the Mediterranean Sea. Halfway along its journey, at Khartoum in Sudan, it is joined by the Blue Nile, which rises in Lake Tana, in Ethiopia, about 6,000 feet (1,830 meters) above sea level. The Blue Nile erodes and carries away vast amounts of sediment, which have been deposited along the Nile valley and in the Nile delta for thousands of years. This silt suspended in the water gives the Blue Nile its name. When it meets the White Nile, the river becomes milky-green, which is said to be the origin of the color Nile green. Summer rains in Ethiopia swell the Blue Nile, making it the chief source of floodwater in Sudan and Egypt. At the height of the flood in late August and early September, it provides three-quarters of the river's total volume. In May, when the drought is most severe, it accounts for less than one-fifth.

The behavior of the Nile divided the Egyptian year into three seasons and so gave rise to the first practicable calendar. New Year began when the bright star Sirius first appeared at dawn on the eastern horizon. This occurrence coincided approximately with the beginning of the flood in mid-June. By the end of July, muddy silt started to arrive in lower Egypt. The water was green at first, but it later took on a reddish tinge, associated with the blood of the dying god Osiris, from whom new life would spring. As the waters continued to rise, the dikes were breached and water spread over the Nile valley to a depth of three to six feet (0.9 to 1.8 meters).

By mid-September, the Nile valley was a broad, shallow river flowing through the desert. Villages located on the higher ground stood out like islands. By early October, the river level had fallen, but water was trapped in large, manmade basins. By late November to early December, the silt dried out and was moist enough for plowing and planting. As time passed, grains germinated and soon the valley was verdant, while the river continued to dwindle.

By mid-February, the drought was absolute. In March or April, the peasants began to harvest the crops. By the end of May, the Nile had shrunk to a narrow river composed largely of water from the White Nile. The valley turned brown and the Egyptians awaited signs of the next flood, so that the cycle could start again.

Today, however, the Nile is controlled by a series of dams and irrigation systems. There are no more annual floods and much of the fertile silt that once enriched the Nile valley in Egypt now ends up on the floor of Lake Nasser.

Pinpointing the trouble

An ancient craft

RETURNING from the dead in time for your own funeral must be an unnerving experience. For the ancient Chinese prince of Kuo, whose death was mourned by thousands, it was a major public event as well. The prince apparently dropped dead one morning about 2,500 years ago. When news of the prince's death was announced, an itinerant doctor named Pien Chueh set off for the palace where he asked to see the body. A tiny flutter of breath and the warmth of the inner thighs – both evidently unnoticed by the court physicians – told him all he needed to know. The prince was not dead; he was in a coma. Pien Chueh signaled to his assistant Tzu Yang, who produced a set of needles that were kept for just such an emergency. One by one the needles were carefully inserted into parts of the prince's body specified by Pien Chueh. Before long the patient began to stir; then he opened his eyes and sat up. The funeral was canceled, and within less than a month the prince had completely recovered.

When the people heard that their ruler was alive, many of them assumed that he had been brought back, not from death's door but from death itself, and that Pien Chueh must therefore be a magician. As he himself explained, however, no magic was involved. The prince had been unconscious, not dead, and he had been revived by acupuncture – an extremely old and trusted technique for treating sick people.

According to one legend, the benefits of acupuncture were first discovered when a hunter who had been accidentally shot by an arrow in the bridge of his nose noticed that the headache from which he had been suffering suddenly cleared up. Be that as it may, the origins of the technique certainly go back to the Stone Age; sharp stone tools for puncturing the skin have been discovered in many different places. Although the practice is associated mainly with China, similar techniques were also used by Eskimos, ancient Egyptians, and the rural Bantu in Africa, who lacerated certain parts of the body in order to cure specific diseases. A tribe of cannibals in Brazil are known, too, to have used blowpipes for injecting arrows into points in the body corresponding to acupuncture points.

The first written evidence for the use of acupuncture comes from a remarkable book, the *Huang Ti Nei Ching Su Wen* ("The Yellow Emperor's Classic of Internal Medicine"), which took about 1,500 years to write and was probably completed in about the second century BC. This, the Bible of ancient Chinese medicine, deals with acupuncture in considerable detail. It recommends nine different types of needle ranging in length from, roughly, $1\frac{1}{4}$ to $9\frac{1}{2}$ inches (3 to 24 centimeters), and it names a total of 365 potential needling points on the surface of the body, all grouped according to suitability for the relief of specified pains and diseases. Of the various kinds of material from which needles could be made, the book indicates that gold, in spite of its cost, proved highly useful for treating certain diseases because it stimulates bodily functions, and that silver needles had a pronounced sedative effect.

Although the *Huang Ti Nei Ching Su Wen* project seems to have been initiated under the patronage of a monarch known as the Yellow Emperor, he was only one of many Chinese rulers to take an active interest in physiology, with particular emphasis on the nervous system (an understanding of which is considered essential for the efficient use of acupuncture in medical and surgical procedures). In the first century AD, the Emperor Wang Mang, aided by his doctor and a palace butcher, is said to have gone so far as to carve up a political rival and trace the nerves of the body with a bamboo stick. A

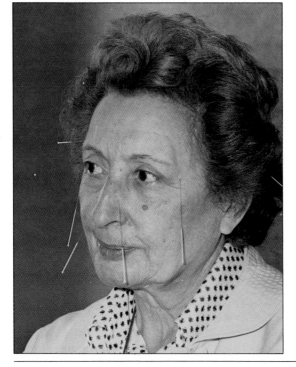

An acupuncture cure for smoking used in a Paris hospital involves the insertion of six needles into the face. With this cure, an 80 per cent success rate has been claimed.

thousand years later, another emperor, Hui Chung, employed an artist to sketch the organs of dissected criminals; and, not long afterward, the Emperor Jen Chung ordered artisans to build him a model of the human body in bronze, showing the nervous system in its entirety.

Despite the widespread and evidently successful use of acupuncture in China, the technique caught on only very gradually in the West.

Nothing much was known about it in Europe until 1712, when Wilhelm den Ryme – a Dutch doctor of the East India Company – published an account of it. In our own century a number of doctors in America and Europe have begun to take a serious interest in the practice – ironically, at the very time that many Chinese doctors are abandoning it in favor of what they believe are more sophisticated Western therapies.

WHY ACUPUNCTURE?

Nobody knows exactly how acupuncture works. All that can be said for certain is that a needle inserted into a particular part of the body will often relieve pain in another, apparently unrelated, part. How and why this happens has never been adequately explained.

The theory is based on a nerve-linked connection between the organs of the body and the body surface. When an organ is painfully diseased, related acupuncture points on the body just below the surface of the skin are stimulated with a needle, thus making the pain disappear. Although certain points are directly related to certain organs, the point and the organ may be in widely separated parts of the body. A headache, for instance, can sometimes be cured by sticking needles into a toe; and biliousness by a needle in the shoulder.

The ancient Chinese divided the nervous system into 12 meridians – imaginary lines connecting the acupuncture points for each of the main organs, including the heart, lungs, liver, kidneys, and bladder. For example, the heart meridian runs down the inside of the arm to the little finger – which, interestingly enough, is almost exactly the course of pain experienced in cardiac arrest. Every acupuncture point on each of the 12 meridians was given its own name and function. Thus the point *yung nen* (cloud gate) on the lung meridian can be stimulated to relieve shortness of breath, asthma, rheumatism, tonsillitis, and acne; while *tian xi* (heavenly ravine) on the spleen meridian relates to such ailments as bronchitis, cough, and – strangely enough – peptic ulcer.

In recent years Chinese techniques of acupuncture, which are still based on the ancient meridian system, have received world-wide publicity because of their well-documented success as an anesthetic in operations. A few years ago an American heart specialist, Dr. E. Gray Dimond, was present at an operation in China for the removal of a man's lung, in which the only anesthetic was an acupuncture needle inserted into the left arm. "The thorax gaped wide open," the American physician later reported. "I could see his heart beating, and all the time the man was chatting cheerfully and quite coherently. When the procedure was about halfway finished the patient declared that he was hungry; the surgeons called a pause and gave him a jar of stewed fruit to eat."

Skeptical Westerners attribute the success of most acupunctural procedures to some form of subtle hypnosis, but this seems unlikely for a number of reasons – not least, that the Mongolians have used acupuncture on animals for centuries. What is true, though, is that acupuncture depends for its success very much on the state of mind of the patient. It does not work for everyone. Even in China, patients are carefully screened for their suitability before having surgery under acupuncture rather than modern anesthetics.

Meridian lines provide a guide for acupuncturists, showing at which points the needles should be inserted to influence the flow of energy to various areas of the body. There are 12 main lines covering the head and body, each line representing an internal organ.

The cult of the dead

The whys and hows of mummification

ALTHOUGH ancient Egypt and mummies are indelibly linked in the minds of most of us, the word "mummy" is not Egyptian. It seems to be derived from the Persian word *mummia*, which means bitumen, or tar. Mummies were given the name because the preserved corpses are often blackened by age, and the people who first found them believed – wrongly as it turned out – that the Egyptians preserved dead bodies by soaking them in tar. The first mummies in Egypt were probably soaked in nothing at all, and were created entirely by accident. Long before the rise of the pharaohs 5,000 years ago, peasants of the Nile valley, reluctant to use scarce fertile land for graveyards, buried the naked dead in sandy soil on the edge of the adjoining desert. In time, the shifting sands must have exposed some of the bodies, which were often laid to rest in graves only two or three feet (about 1 meter) deep. And observers noticed that hot sand had dried the bodies so effectively that the normal process of decomposition had been arrested, leaving centuries-old corpses with skin, hair, and a startlingly lifelike appearance. Some of these bodies, which are not technically mummies, have retained that appearance down to the present day.

As Egyptian society became more closely organized under the pharaohs after 3100 BC, religious belief in an afterlife developed into a virtual cult of the dead. The devout came to believe that preservation of the body was not only possible but essential if the dead were to be able to enjoy paradise. A body that lost any part of itself in the grave, it was thought, would be deprived of that part for all eternity. This is perhaps one reason why the representations of human figures that decorate Egyptian tombs usually include both arms and both legs.

Once physical preservation became the focus of preparation for life after death, it became important, at least for those who could afford it, to be buried in secure stone tombs rather than in the ground. Since this removed bodies from

THE EMBALMER'S RECONDITE ART

During the more than 3,000 years that mummification was practiced in Egypt, techniques changed. But most scholars agree that when the art of embalming was at its height (around the 10th century BC), this is how a top-flight embalmer would go about his task:

He begins by making a cut about four inches (10 centimeters) long in the left side of the abdomen. Through this small incision, made with a flint knife, he pulls out all the internal organs with the exception of the heart (which he and his clients believe to be the seat of the emotions). He cleans each organ piece by piece in wine and spices, including myrrh and cinnamon, and he also flushes out the abdominal cavity with cedar oil in order to dissolve the remaining soft tissue. Now he is ready to remove the brain, which is done by forcing a hooked instrument up through a nostril into the skull and scraping out the cavity, which is then infused with cedar oil and spices to flush out residues of brain matter.

When he has cleaned every part of the body thoroughly, the embalmer packs all the organs and

Anubis, the heavenly embalmer, half-god, half-man, shown at work in this detail from the Papyrus of Anhai, c.1250 BC.

the body itself in powdered natron (a mixture of sodium carbonate and bicarbonate) to dry them. They remain there for about a month, after which he removes them and washes every part in more scents and spices. From beginning to end of the embalming process he has paid scrupulous attention to minor details. At the start, for instance, he attaches covers to each of the corpse's fingers so that no nails are damaged or lost.

He now wraps the dried internal organs individually in linen cloth and puts them in the abdominal cavity (or, instead, he may store them separately in earthenware or alabaster jars), which he further packs with stuffing material such as sawdust, wads of linen, tar, or mud. When this has been done, he sews up the original cut. Because the natron treatment has probably ruined some of the body's hair, he must also weave artificial hair into what remains of the original, and he must insert painted eyes into the skull's sockets. There remains the most technically difficult of his jobs: a restoration of the by-now-shrunken lines of body and face to lifelike fullness.

To perform this ancient type of plastic surgery, the embalmer works his way slowly over the body, making tiny cuts and packing carefully molded wads of linen under the skin, just as a 20th-century cosmetic surgeon might use silicone implants to improve the look of his living clients. Even the lines of the face and neck are restored in this way, with packing laid in the mouth to hold the cheeks in position. And, finally, the embalmer – now truly an artist – colors the face and sometimes the whole body with the colored earth called ocher (red if the body is male, yellow if female). The corpse is now ready for bandaging. The embalmer wraps each limb separately in tight layers of resin-smeared linen, then the head and torso, finally the entire body. It is a long, slow job. On some mummies that have been unwrapped in modern times total length of the bandages has added up to more than 8,000 feet – about a mile and a half (over 2 kilometers)!

The embalmer's task is at last over, some 70 days after he took it on. He returns the mummy to the family, who will probably have made separate arrangements for a wooden case, shaped like a human figure, in which to place it, and for a tomb. As far as human ingenuity can ensure, the dead Egyptian is now physically immortal, ready for an eternity among the gods.

contact with the sand that had halted their decay, substitute techniques had to be developed, and these were passed on as trade secrets from generation to generation by a new breed of craftsmen – the embalmers. Instead of sand, Egypt's embalmers learned to rely on a naturally occurring rock salt called natron, which is a powdery mixture of sodium carbonate and sodium bicarbonate (what we today would speak of as washing soda and baking soda, respectively). Natron acted like a sponge, drawing out the moisture from a body laid in it. Perfumes and various solvents were used for cleaning out internal organs, and the body was finally wrapped and sealed within hundreds of yards of linen bandages. Valuable and intricately worked amulets were often concealed among the layers of bandages to help guard the dead person from evil spirits on the journey to paradise.

The earliest carefully embalmed and bandaged mummies that we know of date from about 2600 BC. Embalming techniques reached their zenith under the 21st dynasty of pharaohs between 1085 and 945 BC. Then, gradually, commercialism began to replace devotion. Instead of attempting to preserve a body completely, embalmers took to concentrating only on the superficial appearance of the mummy (rather as modern undertakers do when preparing the dead for a final viewing). The body was sealed inside and out with a thick coating of resin – or, occasionally, honey – which hid the decay of tissues but did not halt it. Strong perfumes concealed the lingering smell, and lifelike portraits on the wooden cases within which the mummies were put began to replace the painstaking but bandage-hidden art of preserving the flesh itself. Because of this, mummies dating from later periods have often been discovered in an extremely poor state of preservation.

Even as late as the first century BC, though, the embalmer's craft remained highly respected, and his skills commanded an enormous price. According to a contemporary Greek author, Diodorus Siculus, who lived for some time in Egypt, first-century embalmers offered three grades of service. The third and cheapest grade was reasonably priced, he says, though he does not specify the cost; whatever it was, even this sum was probably out of reach of the bulk of Egypt's population, laborers and farmers who buried their dead where and as they could. The second grade cost 20 minas, which has been estimated as the equivalent of around $3,000. The first-class treatment, aimed at preserving all parts of the body, cost a talent (more than $10,000 in modern terms).

Many poor people, denied the luxury of embalmed wholeness in the hereafter, continued to bury their dead in sandy graves – where, as it turned out, their bodies had a rather better chance to resist disintegration than those of the artificially preserved. Over the long centuries of the pharaohs, almost all tombs containing anything of value were broken into and ransacked by grave robbers. Unrestrained by religious fear of the dead, the thieves not only opened the outer cases but even tore apart the mummies themselves to remove any valuables that had been laid in among the bandages. Priests eventually rewrapped most desecrated bodies, but inexpertly. From outside, the rewrapped corpses often seem to be well preserved, but X-ray photographs of many mummies have shown that only wads of cloth and jumbles of unrelated bones now lie beneath the bandages.

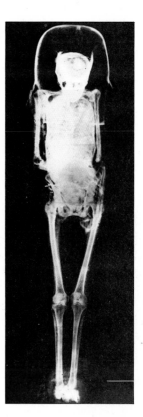

Through X-ray photography, it is now possible to reveal what lies within the bandages that encase a mummy without disturbing the wrappings and allowing air to affect the corpse.

Dentistry – an ancient skill
Turtle brains and golden wires

THERE'S nothing new about toothache. Archeological research into the mouths of mummies has shown that more than 4,000 years ago the ancient Egyptians suffered from just about every dental problem now known – although, since sugar was not a part of their diet, caries (the decay that results in cavities) was not nearly as common as it is today. What seems to have plagued the Egyptians most was dental attrition – surface wear so bad that the teeth were gradually worn down to mere stumps level with the gums. Such attrition, often noted in mummy finds, was probably due to the high content of grit in Egyptian bread. It must have given rise to excruciatingly painful abscesses, either in the roots of teeth or in surrounding soft tissues.

Egyptologists had realized for many years that some form of dentistry was practiced as long ago as the 16th century BC. Egyptian medicine was the most advanced in the ancient world, and physicians often specialized, as do

X-ray photography of mummified heads has proved that dental problems were just as common in ancient Egypt as they are today. This person (at right) suffered from severe abscesses and advanced attrition (wearing down of the teeth) – probably caused by eating coarse and gritty foods.

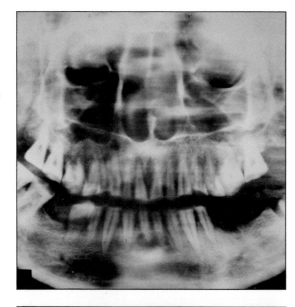

Two teeth recovered from an ancient Egyptian burial site had been joined together by a piece of gold wire, indicating a fairly sophisticated form of dentistry. However, it has also been suggested that the teeth may have served as an ornament worn around the neck and fastened by the wire.

The inscription on the paneling (above) of the third-dynasty tomb of Hesi-Re gives him the title "Chief of the Toothers and Physicians."

modern doctors, in the ailments of a single organ or area of the body. There is a famous medical text, known as the Ebers Papyrus, which dates from around 1550 BC and in it we find many "tooth specialist" prescriptions. A loose tooth, for instance, was treated by the application of a paste composed of a mixture of ocher, crushed seeds, and honey; inflamed gums were eased by chewing and then spitting out a combination of dew-saturated beans and dates mixed with milk – a treatment that was continued for nine days. But until quite recently it was generally believed that Egyptian dentistry was hardly more sophisticated than the Ebers Papyrus prescriptions suggest. Before 1952 the closest approach to dental craftsmanship that had been found in the mouth of a mummy was a gold wire binding a couple of teeth together, probably because they were loose and in danger of falling out unless attached to more secure neighbors.

But was the skill of Egyptian dentists even more sophisticated? Did they in fact use some of the techniques that lie at the heart of modern dentistry – in particular the craft of prosthetics (the artificial replacement of missing teeth)? For many years, a few Egyptologists and dentists in the field have contended that the ancient Egyptians did indeed know how to make the kind of partial dentures we call "bridges," and that, in fact, the practice of reconstructive dentistry

AND EYE SPECIALISTS TOO

In the fifth century BC, when Egyptian civilization was already very old, the Greek writer Herodotus traveled through the country, observing the people and their customs with a keen eye. One thing he noted with admiration was the extent of specialization among physicians. "The practice of medicine is so divided," he wrote, "that each physician is a healer of one disease and no more. The country swarms with medical practitioners, some for the eyes, others for the head, others again for the teeth, or for the intestines, or for some of the obscure diseases." Nor was this a recent development. Doctors (by no means all, but many) had been specializing in Egypt for 2,000 and more years before the time of Herodotus.

For example take Iry, a medical man whose tombstone was discovered near the pyramids at Giza in 1926. Iry lived sometime between 2270 and 2100 BC, and he is commemorated on a huge limestone slab (known as a *stele*) resplendent with hieroglyphs that identify him as Royal Ophthalmologist (eye-doctor to the court). Interestingly enough, the description also credits him with having been a magician.

The Ebers Papyrus, a medical treatise compiled about 700 years after Iry's death, is our chief source of information about eye diseases in ancient Egypt.

They were much the same as those we suffer from today: poor sight, crossed eyes, cataracts, and conjunctivitis. Prescriptions for healing, though, were somewhat different. One recommended cure for weak eyes was a mixture of honey, red lead, and water from the eyes of a hog, to be injected in the patient's ear. Another, for strabismus (crossed eyes) was a salve composed chiefly of turtle brains. Such cures, we are told, work best when the patient completes the cure by twice repeating a magic formula: "I have carried out the instructions and applied the medicine: the crocodile is weak and powerless" (the crocodile being one of the animals, according to ancient myths, that caused eclipses by stealing the eye of the sun).

There are no extant records of the practice of eye surgery, such as the removal of cataracts, in ancient Egypt. But it would be wrong to assume that the eye-doctors' medicine was entirely a matter of turtle brains and mumbo-jumbo. Much that they prescribed makes better sense than it seems to at first glance. What, for example, about their recommendation of liver in one form or another as a treatment for night blindness? Until quite recently, all that modern medicine could offer for combating certain kinds of night blindness was cod-liver oil and liver extracts.

originated in Egypt. But whenever somebody claimed to have found an apparent example of restorative work such as artificial teeth or bridgework in the mouth of a mummy, the finding was hotly disputed. No incontrovertible evidence turned up until 1952, when, in a burial ground about 30 miles (48 kilometers) northwest of Cairo, a professor in the Department of Antiquities at Cairo's American University found an artificial bridge made of real teeth in the crushed bones of a 4,500-year-old skull.

The bridgework consists of three teeth (there was probably also a fourth) held together by gold wire. This is clearly not a case of loose teeth being made more secure. The roots of two of these had been scraped to shape them for wearing, and the third was a "live" tooth serving as an attachment for one side of the bridge. Moreover, one end of the gold wire that was bound around two of the teeth passed through a hole drilled in the third, suggesting that a similar hole was drilled in a now-missing live tooth on the other end. Tartar deposits on the teeth indicate that the bridge served its owner for a considerable time before death.

At the time of its discovery, the significance of the bridgework seems to have been overlooked. In 1974, however, Professor Shafik Farid, who made the original find, called it to the attention of a colleague, Professor Zaki Iskander, and an American orthodontist, Dr. James E. Harris of the University of Michigan dental school, and, after a careful study of the evidence, the three men published their findings in the December, 1975, issue of the *Journal of the Michigan Dental Association.* Their conclusion is as follows: "the preparation of this bridge ... proves beyond any doubt that the Egyptians practiced dentistry in its true sense as far back as the Old Kingdom (2700–2200 BC)."

Rats, rice, peanuts, and jade

A common bond

ALL THE best-known theories about early "discoverers" of America share a common feature: Whether Irish, Welsh, Scandinavian, Phoenician, or Italian, the first explorers sailed westward from Europe. Scholars accept that the American Indians migrated to the New World from Asia at least 12,000 years ago, near the end of the last Ice Age, when the Bering Strait was still a land bridge. But no one till recently had seriously considered the possibility of further traffic between ancient Asia and the Americas after the land masses were separated by rising sea levels.

Modern scholars however, have found tantalizing shreds of evidence that Chinese seafarers may have crossed the broad Pacific Ocean many centuries before the first transatlantic voyagers set foot on American soil. To be sure, no incontrovertibly ancient Chinese artifact has been unearthed in the New World, and no suggestion of such an extraordinary voyage exists in China's official archives. Yet baffling links have recently been found, which seem inexplicable without some sort of early contact between the two shores of the Pacific – and contact in both directions at that. The earliest and most puzzling link is, of all things, the humble peanut.

Botanists agree that the peanut plant originated in South America and that its seeds can survive neither digestion by birds nor long immersion in salt water. Although China is now a leader in world production of peanuts, it is known that the plant was not grown there in modern times until this century. How is it, then, that shriveled peanuts dating from about 3000 BC (as verified by radiocarbon analysis) have been found in the Chinese coastal provinces of Kiangsu and Chekiang? Does it not seem likely that the plant was somehow transferred from one hemisphere to the other by human hands?

There are other puzzles, too – a whole catalogue of similarities between Chinese and South or Central American cultures that stretch coincidence to the breaking point. Take, for instance, the custom of placing jade beads as magic charms in the mouths of corpses. The Aztecs and Maya of Mexico did this – as did the Chinese. Stranger still, on both sides of the Pacific the green jade was sometimes painted with red ocher. Similar customs can exist, of course, in widely separated cultures, but it is unusual to find repetition of such precise details. In the same way, it may not be surprising that both the ancient Shang dynasty of China (1525–1027 BC) and one of Mexico's oldest civilizations, the Olmecs (about 1300–900 BC), worshiped big cats (tigers in China, jaguars in Mexico) as earth gods. But it seems extremely

The peanut plant, which originated in South America, has provided tantalizing clues to the possibility of early links between China and the American continent.

odd that in representations of the cats that they worshiped both cultures frequently depict them as lacking a lower jaw.

Among other possibly significant correspondences: Wheeled clay models of animals from around the time of Christ have been found in Mexico; such models were being made by the Han Chinese in the third century BC, but it is particularly startling to find these models in America, since no American culture put the wheel to practical use before the arrival of Europeans in the 15th century. Thin copper axes were used as currency in Aztec Mexico and Ecuador, and the Chinese also had ax-shaped coins. Conical-lidded cylindrical pots on clay tripods are known to have been made in Han China; and pots with the same features dating from the fifth and sixth centuries AD have been found at sites in both Teotihuacán in Mexico and Kaminaljuyú in Guatemala.

Chinese legends tell of a land called Fu-sang, a paradise said to lie beyond the "eastern ocean" (the Pacific). A fifth-century-AD Buddhist monk named Hui Shen recorded an account of a visit he claimed to have made to Fu-sang. And because there are odd similarities of detail between his account and American realities, some commentators have interpreted his story as further confirmation of Chinese contact with the New World.

Most modern authorities remain skeptical, though. For one thing, Hui Shen claimed to have seen carts, horses, and cattle in the far-away "paradise," and all of these are known *not* to have existed in the Americas during this period. Moreover, the skeptical experts adduce three striking pieces of negative evidence that appear to refute arguments in favor of early Chinese exploration of the Western hemisphere: No rice, no millet, no rats. Biologists and botanists agree that none of these forms of life existed in the Americas before 1492; yet they should have done so if the Chinese had really been there. Rice and millet have been staple crops in China since the dawn of history, and long-distance voyagers in ancient times invariably carried a supply of grain so as to replenish food supplies by pausing to grow crops wherever possible. As for rats, since the two types that prey on man were able to spread throughout the scattered islands of

The Olmecs of Mexico and the Chinese both worshiped big cats – the Olmecs jaguars, the Chinese tigers. Interestingly both peoples showed their feline gods minus a lower jaw, as is the case with the bronze tiger, above, and the stone jaguar, shown at right in front of the Castillo Pyramid at Chichen Itza in Mexico. Such similarities suggest possible contacts across the Pacific Ocean between these two ancient cultures.

Polynesia by stowing away on tiny open-decked canoes, they would surely have done the same on anything even remotely resembling a Chinese junk. Yet neither species reached America until Columbus came along.

In 1974, in an effort to test the attractive belief that the skeptics were wrong, a writer and scholar named Kuno Knöbl built a replica of a Chinese junk dating from the second century AD. The 60-foot-long (19 meters) boat, copied from a clay model found in Canton in 1954, was built without metal; it was held together by 1,000 wooden bolts and 3,000 wooden nails. Knöbl's aim was to follow the Kuroshio Current across the North Pacific from Japan to California in order to show how an ancient junk could have reached America. The voyage was not a success. The boat took four months to reach the middle of the Pacific, where, riddled with holes made by the wood-boring teredo worm, it sank.

Knöbl's failure did not end the debate, of course, since one unsuccessful voyage does not prove that all such voyages would have failed. And the puzzles still remain. If the Chinese did cross the Pacific, how did they leave the rats behind? But if they did not, who took the wheeled models to Mexico – and brought back with them some peanuts to China?

Translating the past
The first foreign-language dictionary

FOR 15 PAINSTAKING YEARS, in the dust and heat of northwest Syria, an archeologist had doggedly probed the secrets of the mound of Tell Mardikh, one of the many mounds, or *tells*, that are dotted across the arid plains south of Aleppo. For Dr. Paolo Matthiae of the University of Rome, these had been years of mounting excitement, for this was clearly no ordinary site. Digging methodically into the mound, his team had unearthed a splendid gate, an enormous city wall, and the outlines of a royal palace, temples, and many houses. In 1968, the fifth year of the excavations, an inscription was found on a broken statue which revealed the name of this city. It was Ebla, hitherto known to archeologists only from a few inscriptions found in Egypt and Mesopotamia dating back to 3000 BC.

Then came the big discovery. In 1974, in one of the palace rooms, a workman on Matthiae's team found 42 small clay tablets each of which was covered in signs and inscriptions. In the following year, as the dig neared completion, the archeologists discovered another two rooms, full of tablets, more than 15,000 in all. They were piled on the floor where they had fallen when fire consumed the shelves on which they had been stored.

At first, no one could decipher the cuneiform (wedge-shaped) signs on the tablets. They were written neither in Akkadian nor Sumerian, two cuneiform scripts known to modern archeologists, but in an unknown language. The signs resembled the cuneiform script of Sumer, and some but not all of the symbols were identified as Sumerian. The breakthrough came with the discovery of more than 100 bilingual tablets, containing lists of Sumerian words and their Eblaite equivalents – the world's earliest known foreign-language dictionaries.

Syllable by syllable, word by word, the scholars were able slowly to come to grips with the ancient language of Ebla using their knowledge of Sumerian. And as they did so, they realized that the history of the region would now have to be rewritten, for it had always been believed that 4,500 years ago Syria and Palestine had been little more than a buffer-zone between the empires of Mesopotamia in the east and Egypt in the south. But the discovery of the Ebla archive changed this view completely. Here was proof, in a wealth of detail, of the mighty Syrian kingdom that Ebla had once been.

The sheer size of the Ebla archive is astounding: It is over four times greater than all other surviving records from the same period put together. The thousands of stacked tablets – it will be years before all of them have been fully read and analyzed – tell of Ebla's rich and far-ranging trade with famous cities hitherto thought to have been founded much later, notably Gaza and Beirut. The archive also contains invaluable historical chronicles, and records of treaties with neighboring states, showing that Ebla's power extended at least as far east as the River Tigris, 300 miles (nearly 500 kilometers) away. Closer to Ebla, many lesser city-states, towns, and villages are recorded as having been payers of tribute to what was obviously, in effect, an important imperial capital.

One of the most interesting finds was a group of tablets written in the shaky handwriting of students trying to master the Eblaite language. Some of them have an X mark, in the steady hand of a teacher, indicating that the student had made a mistake in the exercise, and had been corrected by his instructor. One pupil has been identified as Azi, and his career has been traced through a sequence of tablets bearing his name. Starting as a student, he passed his examination to become a scribe. Later, he is identified as a *dub-zu-zu*, Sumerian for "one who knows the tablets," a high accolade. Finally, he appears as the top administrator of Ebla.

When more tablets are deciphered, perhaps scholars will be able to compile a complete biography of Azi, more than 4,500 years after his death, as they will also be able to fill out the story of Ebla's rise and fall for which archeologists have so far only been able to provide an outline. Not much is known yet of Ebla's history other than that it was a thriving city and commercial center until it was attacked and sacked by Akkad warriors around 2300 BC. It managed to shake off this alien rule, but finally succumbed to Amorite nomads who overran Syria around 1800 BC, and burnt the city to the ground.

With the passing of the centuries, Ebla's ruins receded ever deeper within the rising mound of Tell Mardikh. But the massed records compiled by the scribes of Ebla have survived, to unfold their city's glorious past to the world.

More than 15,000 tablets written in cuneiform script have been found in the archive at Ebla. Documents such as this tablet accounting wages for palace workers have provided archeologists with a mass of detail about life in the city of Ebla at the height of its power, 4,500 years ago.

Tomb or temple?

The riddle of Malta's Hypogeum

BENEATH A food store in the busy Maltese town of Paola lies one of the most extraordinary monuments of the Mediterranean world. It was discovered by workmen on a building site in 1902. Cutting into the rock to make a water tank, they suddenly broke through into a vast underground chamber, carved out of solid limestone. At first, they used the cavity as a dump for building debris, and they filled the cavity with rubble. But one workman realized that this was no natural cave, but a manmade chamber. Accordingly, he reported the find to some local archeologists.

The archeologists removed all the rubble so that they could explore the site. They uncovered a labyrinth of rooms extending three stories into the ground to a depth of over 30 feet (10 meters). This Hypogeum, a Greek word meaning "beneath the earth," excited all who saw it. Here was an excavation on a grand scale. The architectural features, including pillars and roofs, followed the same designs as those used in many ancient Maltese tombs and temples. However, while every other temple was built on the surface, the Hypogeum is unique because it was constructed entirely below ground level. The more that the archeologists uncovered of the Hypogeum, the less certain they became that it was a temple, particularly when they found the bones of up to 7,000 people beneath the debris. What then was the purpose of the Hypogeum and when was it built? The second question was easier to answer than the first. Other temples on Malta, similar in style to the Hypogeum, were constructed in about 2400 BC, a period in which the Stone Age inhabitants of the island indulged in an orgy of temple building. They used picks and wedges of horn or antler, driven into the rock by stone mallets, two of which have been found, together with flint and obsidian tools for the finer work.

Little is known about these people, but their architectural prowess is evident in all their buildings. One room in the Hypogeum above all bears witness to their talents. In this room, which is known as the "Oracle Chamber," there is an opening behind which there is a cavity just large enough to contain one person. If a man sits in this cavity and talks in a normal voice, the sound is carried without distortion around the chamber – female voices are too high-pitched to achieve the same effect. The sound is carried along a ridge carved in the wall around the entire room just below the ceiling. The designer of this room clearly understood the acoustic effects resulting from such a device.

Discovery of this echo chamber led the archeologists to think that the Hypogeum was a religious building and that this room was perhaps a sanctuary for an oracle. But while the oracle must have been a man, the object of worship was probably female, because the archeologists unearthed two statuettes of sleeping women, reclining on their sides, together with other statuettes of grossly fat, perhaps pregnant, women. This evidence suggested that a cult of Earth-Mother worship was practiced at the Hypogeum. Whatever the form of worship, the physical character of the Hypogeum must have been daunting, not to say terrifying to those who came to pray and consult the oracle. Such features as a temple without light, deep underground, and capable of transmitting the voice of an unseen person in an eerie and supernatural way around a large room would inspire and surely demand devotion.

What then is the significance of the 7,000 sets of human bones found in a small chamber measuring less than 40 feet (12 meters) across? The bones were not intact skeletons, because the bulk of 7,000 corpses could not have fitted into such a confined space. The disconnected bones in the chamber provide evidence of a dual form of burial, a common practice among primitive people. The second burial consisted of eventual reinterment of the bones after the bodies had decomposed in an initial burial ground. Was the Hypogeum the final resting place for worshipers in the temple? And if the whole temple complex celebrated life, did it also accommodate death? Did the religion of these early inhabitants of Malta embrace worship of the dead?

No one knows when the bones were placed in the chamber or why. Nor do they know if the Hypogeum changed its nature at some stage from a temple to a necropolis, or whether the Hypogeum was originally built to serve both purposes. Many temples on the surface were imitations of earlier rock tombs. Perhaps the Hypogeum represents a reversal of this pattern – a tomb built in the style of an above-ground temple. Such questions remain unanswered and the riddle of the purpose of Malta's unique Hypogeum will probably stay unsolved.

Carved out of the solid rock 4,500 years ago, the Hypogeum is similar in design to the above-ground temples built elsewhere in Malta. The rooms (one of which is shown at left) contain such architectural features as pillars, window niches, and elaborate door lintels. The whole building probably served as a temple dedicated to a female deity, such as the sleeping woman (above).

The puzzling labyrinth

Was the vast Cretan maze a royal palace or a mausoleum?

FOUR THOUSAND years ago, the Mediterranean island of Crete was the center of a glittering civilization. Its people, the Minoans, were traders and seafarers whose material wealth and culture antedated the rise of mainland Greece by many centuries. The legend of Atlantis – an advanced society lost to the world when the gods, angered by its arrogance, ordered the sea to engulf it – may have stemmed from the fate of the Minoans, for the abrupt end of their civilization has been seen as the result of tidal waves caused by a volcanic eruption, which devastated the island of Thira (now Santorini) 70 miles (110 kilometers) away.

Memory of Minoan civilization and its achievements faded. For over 3,000 years nothing survived but a popular legend about King Minos of Crete and his ravenous Minotaur, half man, half bull, lurking in a dark underground labyrinth. Then in the early 20th century a British archeologist, Sir Arthur Evans, unearthed the remains of the Minoans' capital city, Knossos. It was a sensational find. The city itself was big; with its nearby port, Knossos must have had a population of about 100,000. But Evans's most impressive discovery was a vast building that he and most other archeologists took to be a royal palace. Built on several levels, some of them

INSIDE THE MINOTAUR'S LAIR

The baffling layout of the Minoan palace of Knossos suggests that it was probably the historical source of the legend of the Labyrinth. Bewildering arrays of staircases – sometimes as many as three in the space of 30 feet (8 meters) – link rooms with others on different levels. Corridors leading from one courtyard to another twist and turn, so that the visitor without a guide loses all sense of direction.

According to ancient Greek tradition, Pasiphae, Queen of Crete and wife of King Minos, had an affair with a white bull sent to Crete by Poseidon,

The minotaur – half-man, half-bull – has been portrayed in many works of art. This 19th-century painting by G.F. Watts is one of the few to attribute the mythical beast with human characteristics and emotions.

god of the sea; and the fruit of this affair was the Minotaur, an enormous monster with a bull's head attached to a human body. Minos imprisoned the creature in a labyrinth designed for him by Daedalus (the mythical inventor whose son, Icarus, died when he flew too close to the sun). Later, after Minos defeated Athens in war he exacted a terrible tribute: Seven Athenian youths and seven maidens had to be delivered to Crete every year to feed the Minotaur. The young people were sent into the Labyrinth to wander helplessly until the great beast found and devoured them. This cycle of sacrifice ended only when the Athenian hero Theseus joined the band of victims and won the love of Ariadne, one of Minos's daughters. Ariadne gave him a ball of thread so that he could retrace his path out of the Labyrinth after killing the Minotaur.

To modern ears the legend may sound like no more than a grim fairy tale. But the ruins of the palace at Knossos provide hints, other than the maze-like complexity of the structure, that the tale grew out of historical fact.

Bull-worship, for example, seems to have been a central feature of Minoan religion, probably because, as in other ancient cultures, the bull was regarded as a symbol of virility. And several frescoes at Knossos show young acrobats apparently doing somersaults directly over the horns of a charging bull.

If such feats were attempted during Cretan religious ceremonies or athletic contests, the central participants probably had as little chance of survival as the Athenians in the Minotaur's maze. When Sir Arthur Evans, the 20th-century archeologist who discovered Knossos, asked experienced Spanish bull-fighters about the feasibility of doing a somersault over a bull's horns, the unanimous verdict was that it would be a once-in-a-lifetime performance. Nobody would live to try it twice.

underground, the palace was rich in marvels. Brightly colored frescoes of marine life and dancing girls, of bulls and acrobats, blazed on the walls. There were stone silos, remains of musical instruments, bronze axes and arrow-heads, and a checkerboard nearly three feet (1 meter) square made of gold-plated ivory inlaid with crystal and pieces of glazed pottery. Polished alabaster gleamed on flagstones in the reception rooms, on what seemed to be a king's throne, around doorways, and on the down-ward-tapering columns that were an evident hallmark of Minoan architecture.

Was this complex, luxurious edifice really a royal palace? That conclusion, generally accepted by archeologists and historians, has been seriously challenged by a German scholar, Hans Georg Wunderlich, who, in a book published in 1972, argued that the great building in Knossos, far from being the home of living kings, was a house of the dead, a giant mausoleum. According to Wunderlich, huge earthenware jars that most archeologists thought were for storing grain, oil, and wine were actually used as burial vessels in which bodies could be preserved by being soaked in honey; the stone "silos" were tombs; and wall paintings symbolized the passage of the soul to the afterlife and depicted possessions that the dead would need there. Even the elaborate plumbing, Wunderlich insists, was not for the living but was probably necessary for the process of embalming.

As evidence for his surprising conclusions, Wunderlich points to several interesting facts. The site of the Knossos structure, for instance, is an unlikely one for a palace since it is highly exposed and not easily defensible against attack by land. Then, too, there is a shortage of springs at the spot, and it would have been difficult to channel water through pipes in sufficient quantities to support a large living population. Moreover, there are no rooms that are obviously kitchens or stables in the palace area; would residents have had no need for food or transport? And rooms that have been identified as royal apartments are damp, windowless, below-ground chambers – an improbable arrangement when siting living quarters in the balmy climate of the Mediterranean.

Probably the strongest single argument against Wunderlich's theory is that no traces of mummified corpses or burial have been found at the site (apart from children's bones that date from the Stone Age, thousands of years before the rise of Bronze Age Minoan Crete). Even if grave robbers later emptied the palace, it seems incredible that they would not have overlooked or discarded a few tell-tale articles. And in 80 years of patient excavation and study, nothing to indicate that people were buried in the palace has been discovered. The Wunderlich book raises some provocative questions to which the answers may yet be found beneath the rubble and dust of ages.

Planning a family
Population control among the ancients

A CONCOCTION MADE of crocodile dung may sound like a brew from a witch's caldron, but this odd ingredient was seriously recommended for use as a vaginal suppository in the earliest known document on contraception, an Egyptian papyrus dating from about 1850 BC. And, strangely enough, it sometimes had the desired effect. The ancient Egyptians knew nothing about the existence or the function of sperm (a scientific discovery that would not be made until the late 17th century of our own era), but they somehow learned that conception could – occasionally, at least – be prevented by the insertion of certain compounds into the vagina.

Prescriptions for suppositories using sticky substances must have proved a fairly effective birth-control measure. They can be found not only in pre-Christian documents but in records from the Islamic world until the 11th century AD and in those of some parts of Africa and India – where elephants replaced the Egyptian crocodile as a source of dung – up to the 13th century. The ancient Egyptians, though, seem to have been more concerned than most other early peoples with contraceptive ways and means. Detailed prescriptions and gynecological instructions have been preserved in their papyri. Among Egyptian recommendations are potions to be drunk, irrigations of the vagina with certain drugs, post-coital douching (often with a liquid containing wine and garlic), and instructions on how to bring about abortion – one of the less-favored methods of controlling the birth rate.

Many women in ancient Egypt believed that charms (such as that illustrated on a medical papyrus, above, dating from 1700 BC) could protect them against women's disorders and problems in childbirth.

ODD BELIEFS AND OUTLANDISH THEORIES

Until the first century AD, many people believed that the complete animal, with all its organs already in place, existed in miniature in the "germ" (an accepted term for "seed" or "semen"). And it was thought that each germ contained the germs of all its descendants, one within the next, like a nest of boxes. Thus the notion that a mother was not a parent of her child but merely a provider of nourishment – the field upon which the father had sown his seed – was quite common, even among great Greek writers. For instance, Aristotle supported the general idea that females did not contribute seed to the embryo. On the other hand, Hippocrates, followed by Pythagoras and Plutarch, believed that both men and women formed semen and that fertilization involved a kind of representative extract from each parent.

Among the fascinating theories of the ancients: A group of doctors in Sicily believed that boys develop in the womb more quickly than girls because male fetuses occupy the right, and warmer, side. And many peoples attributed conception not to sexual intercourse but to the impregnation of women by wind, water, plants, or animals. The Hindus blamed – or extolled – the ibis; the Japanese, the butterfly and the crane; some American Indians, the red spoonbill; and ancient Teutons believed (as many of us once did) in the stork. Thus the best way to avoid conception was to stay out of the paths of such creatures.

Trobriand Islanders apparently did not believe that sexual intercourse had anything to do with pregnancy, but thought that children originated in the spirit world. And in nearby Papua, New Guinea, two ideas predominated: That eels in a stream could impregnate a woman, or, more commonly, that the semen formed the children, making repeated intercourse necessary.

One prescription (in the 16th-century-BC Ebers Papyrus) is remarkable in that the ingredients of acacia extract and honey, with which lint was to be moistened before insertion, can form a jelly containing lactic acid, and lactic acid is today universally recognized as a conception-inhibiting agency. In some modern countries women who have recently borne children are advised to prolong the period of lactation abnormally in order to stave off further conception. And this sometimes effective, but unreliable, method of birth control may well have been common among the Egyptians.

Why were they so eager to limit births at a time when infant mortality and short life expectancy already kept the population down? The cost to a family of extra mouths to feed must have been a major consideration, but it has been suggested that a primary reason for the concern with birth control was cosmetic. In other words, Egyptian ladies dreaded the physical results of multiple pregnancies. Significantly, many of the papyri containing contraception recipes also discuss lotions and ointments for beautifying the skin and hair. In many such concoctions olive oil is a major ingredient; yet, strangely, it was the ancient Greeks, not the Egyptians, who used olive oil as a contraceptive. (Like similar substances inserted into the vagina, it could have a contraceptive effect by gumming up and reducing the mobility of sperm.)

The Greeks of the Classical Age were strongly in favor of population control and seem to have had few qualms about methods of achieving it. Both Plato and Aristotle, for instance, advocated limiting the size of families not only by means of contraception and abortion but by the exposure of unwanted infants. And followers of Hippocrates, the fifth-century-BC "father" of Greek medicine, invented an intra-uterine contraceptive device consisting of a lead tube filled with mutton fat, which could be partially inserted through the cervix into the uterus. It is now well known that a foreign body introduced into the uterus can prevent conception – and so it could fairly be said that the IUD dates from the time of Hippocrates.

Most contraceptive techniques among pre-Christian peoples, other than coitus interruptus, were practiced by women. There is some evidence, though, that sheaths made of animal membranes were used by males in both Greek and Roman times. And in the second century AD a gynecologist named Actios (of Amida, in modern Turkey) made the surprisingly reasonable suggestion that the penis should be washed in brine or vinegar – both highly spermicidal – before intercourse if sexual partners wanted to avoid pregnancy.

The ancient Hebrews, of course, believed it to be their religious duty to propagate the race. Birth-control methods do not appear among official prescriptions for the good life in either their writings or those of the early Christians, whose faith was rooted in the Old Testament as well as the New.

It was not until 1843 that the cellular union of the sperm and ovum was observed, with the result that at last contraception could, for the first time, be based on scientific fact rather than mere speculation. Nevertheless it is interesting to note that, in the days when conception was scarcely understood, contraceptive devices and techniques were remarkably similar to those used in our more enlightened day – obviously the ancients learned from experience.

An early lawbook
Still good sense after 4,000 years

OUTSIDE THE whitewashed walls of the courtroom, the sun blazed down relentlessly on the Euphrates valley, crossed by irrigation canals lined with date palms, and dotted with green fields of wheat and barley. Within, the judge and his clerk listened attentively to the plaintiff as he put his case against a local contractor who, the plaintiff claimed, had built him a house so incompetently that its walls bulged dangerously. Witnesses were called; the contractor was forced to admit the justice of the case; and, after consulting appropriate statutes, the judge ruled that the house be rebuilt at the contractor's expense.

That sounds like a reasonable judgment to modern ears. Yet the incident occurred nearly 4,000 years ago in ancient Babylon. The scene as described is not a fanciful reconstruction; just such a case – or something like it – must have happened, since it became the precedent for law number 233 in the Code of Hammurabi: "If a builder has built a house . . . and does not make his work perfect . . . , that builder shall put (it) into sound condition at his own cost." The 282 laws that comprised the code were not ethical commandments like those of Moses – divinely inspired for a pastoral people – but a series of precedents suitable for the Babylonian empire, whose great capital city, Babylon, was a trade center that was constantly humming with disputes and conflicting claims.

Several copies of the code on clay tablets still exist, but the best and most famous version, which was discovered by French archeologists in 1901, is a monumental tablet of black stone seven feet six inches (2.5 meters) high on which the laws are inscribed in 49 cuneiform-packed columns. This now-renowned stone slab (or *stele*) was undoubtedly set up in some sort of civic center as a permanent reminder to the public of an outstanding achievement of Hammurabi, the man who ruled Babylonia during its golden age (the first half of the 18th century BC). Though not the first written code of laws – those of neighboring Ur-Nammu, for example, are three centuries older – the Code of Hammurabi is the earliest complete code to have survived.

Although several of Hammurabi's judgments seem harsh to us today, they do compare rather favorably with some laws still current in the Middle East. Others, indeed, are humane by any standard. Hammurabi's law on adoption, for example, states: "If a man has taken an infant for adoption and brings him up, that child shall not

The Code of Hammurabi – dating from 1800 BC – is one of the earliest written codes of law to have survived. Inscribed on a huge stone tablet, it not only deals with matters of law but also provides an accurate picture of the life style and attitudes during Hammurabi's reign. The upper part of the tablet shows Hammurabi standing before the god of justice.

"BY THE RIVERS OF BABYLON"

Hammurabi, sixth king of the Amorite or Old Babylonian dynasty, put his city on the map as the greatest metropolis of western Asia. During his reign in the 18th century BC, the power of Babylon was pushed northwestward to the Mediterranean and southward to the Persian Gulf. So extensive an empire over the densely populated and turbulent "Land of Two Rivers" (ancient Mesopotamia) could not last forever; but for a very long time after Hammurabi's death Babylon remained the commercial and cultural capital of the vast area that came to be known as Babylonia.

Mesopotamia, like Egypt, was a land so enriched by the silt of its rivers that two magnificent harvests of wheat, barley, and dates were produced annually. Unlike Egypt, the land lacked unification and was fiercely divided among many city-states until the rise of Babylon as a central power under Hammurabi's immediate predecessors. Nothing before his time, however, could compare with what was achieved in the days of Hammurabi and the following centuries of Babylon's supremacy. Apart from their military prowess and legal accomplishments, the Babylonians excelled in the splendor of their architecture and in science. Mathematics and astronomy were developed to a point where scholar-priests could predict eclipses with astonishing accuracy (though they never suspected the rotation of the Earth around the Sun). It was to the same area, given the name Neo-Babylonia by modern archeologists to distinguish it from the old city of Hammurabi's days, that captive Jews were brought in the sixth century BC, where, says the psalmist, "By the rivers of Babylon, there we sat down, yea, we wept, when we remembered Zion." There, two centuries later, Alexander the Great, having conquered half Asia, breathed his last. It was only then that the city began its decline as the main center of East-West trade, being replaced by the much newer city of Seleucia, to which Babylon's inhabitants were removed in 275 BC, leaving the once-great city's walls to crumble into sand.

All Babylon's glory was made possible by the wealth brought in by trade. The Babylonians were primarily merchants, and trade had depended critically on the existence of written laws, Hammurabi's greatest and most abiding legacy to his native city.

be reclaimed." Here, again, given the attitudes prevalent at the time, is a remarkably compassionate law on divorce: "If a nobleman wishes to divorce his wife because she has not borne him children, he shall pay her the full amount of her marriage price and also make good to her the dowry she brought from her father's house. Only then may he divorce her." Or this law, dealing with desertion: "If the husband has gone away and there is not enough maintenance for the household, his wife may enter another man's house without blame."

Other laws, though, are more cruel. In keeping with the ancient (and sometimes modern) notion of tit for tat, "If a man has put out the eye of a free man, they shall put out his eye," says one clause of the code. But only a fine is required as punishment for putting out the eye of a slave. Equal protection for all classes of society is an entirely modern concept.

How India acquired the caste system
The legacy of the Aryans

"THEY ARE SO degraded that a twice-born Hindu considers it necessary to bathe if he is touched by one of them ... They are not allowed to draw water from the village tank, the village barber will not shave them, the village washer-woman will not wash their clothes." In spite of recent laws that have attempted to root out the age-old disabilities of the Untouchables, those comments made in a census report of 1911 still define the position of many of the lowest of the low on India's long ladder of castes. The enduring stigma of such pariahs – the "children of God," as their champion Mohandas Gandhi called them – is a tragic legacy of the Aryans, warlike people who began to invade India from the northwest more than 3,000 years ago.

Before the Sanskrit-speaking Aryans arrived, India was already the home of several cultures, including one advanced civilization, that of the Harappan people of the Indus valley. The light-skinned Aryans, who conquered and colonized the northern portion of the sub-continent before 1000 BC, had little respect, however, for the dark-skinned natives whom they defeated in battle. Though illiterate and initially nomadic, the Aryans felt superior because of their military might. The Harappan people, with their planned cities and irrigated fields, their script, arts, and crafts, were far more sophisticated – but they were no match for the hard-riding, fort-destroying invaders, so the Aryans enslaved them; and it was out of this new multi-racial India that there gradually emerged a complex caste structure which still exists.

When they took over in India, Aryan communities were already divided into three castes: the Brahman (priests and scholars); the Kshatriya (kings, warriors, and nobles); and the Vaisya (merchants and workers). The pre-Aryan Indians, who became servile or semi-servile cultivators of the soil and ordinary laborers, now comprised a fourth major caste, the Sudra. Members of the original Aryan castes were the only people entitled to be "twice born" – the highest of all states, in which physical birth is followed by symbolic birth – the initiation into an upper caste. As the system evolved and grew increasingly complex, a great number of human beings whose primitive way of life was considered "unclean" found themselves at the bottom of the heap, and these were literally "outcasts" – that is Untouchables. It is evident that there was a racial background to this hierarchy and that its origins must have lain in skin color: the Sanskrit word for caste, *varna*, means "color."

Our knowledge of early Aryan society in India comes from the *Rig-Veda*, a collection of sacred hymns compiled around 1000 BC. The *Rig-Veda*, which reflects Aryan culture during the centuries when it was merging with those of the Harappan and other conquered peoples, was handed down orally through many generations of Brahmans until the 14th century AD, when it became written literature. Modern Hindus refer to it as the fountainhead from which later Indian philosophy and religion flowed. The Vedic hymns tell us in detail about the life of Aryan tribesmen who enjoyed gambling and drinking and gloried in their swift horses, light chariots, and prowess in battle. With the help of the subservient Sudras, many of whose gods they adopted, the Aryans took to settled farming, but their nomadic tradition of cattle-rearing gradually acquired a special aura (perhaps romanticizing a long-past "golden age"). The sacred status of the cow in modern Hinduism dates back to ancient Vedic times.

Menial tasks such as temple-sweeping (above) were reserved for the Untouchables – the lowest of the low in the Indian caste system.

As custodians of the *Rig-Veda*, the Brahmans imparted sanctity to the hereditary caste system of Aryan-dominated India. But religious pressure could not counteract the forces of climate and human nature. By the beginning of the West's Christian era, 1,000 years after the original compilation of the *Rig-Veda*, members of the three upper castes could no longer be distinguished simply by their complexions; interbreeding with dark-skinned locals had blurred such distinctions. Racially mixed castes emerged, the system became more and more firmly based upon vocations, and people who did the most menial kind of work – refuse-collecting or disposing of dead animals – became the Untouchables. A vast network of sub-castes (*jati*), which were immediately concerned with type of employment, developed; and a person's *jati* became more important for purposes of identification and status than his or her main caste (*varna*).

It now became an accepted fact of Indian life that the members of a caste did the same sort of work, and that they alone did it. Ideally, they might marry only one another. And, if strict, they would eat only food prepared by others belonging to their caste. Yet, far from producing a static, closed society, this vertical division of the population made it easier in later centuries for India to assimilate new ethnic peoples. Every new group took on the characteristics of a separate sub-caste and was thereby fitted into the larger caste structure.

Even when certain groups broke away in repudiation of the caste system, they simply ended up as new castes. When Islam reached India early in the 13th century, it appealed to many of the underprivileged as a casteless religion. In practice, though, many Muslims observed caste restrictions, and there are Muslim castes in India today. Similarly, Jewish and Christian populations in the subcontinent have often formed bodies akin to castes. When industrialization produced new occupations and new social and political roles, the system adapted once again to accommodate them as castes. Most remarkably, parliamentary democracy in India actually reinforced the ancient systems because caste organizations were set up to influence politics in their own particular members' interests. Thus far, the system has not been destroyed, and the Brahmans have maintained their position at the top of the ladder, with the lowest rung just as firmly – alas – in the possession of the Untouchables.

Indra, the Aryan god of war and thunder, was one of the most powerful of the Vedic gods. Here he is shown brandishing the daggers of war and conflict, and riding the elephant Airavata, symbolizing a rain-cloud.

WHO WERE THE ARYANS?

Strictly speaking, "Aryan" is not the proper name of a people or group of peoples; it comes from a Sanskrit word meaning "kinsmen" and it correctly applies to all individuals who speak one of the Indo-European family of languages. But the term "Aryan" is generally, though incorrectly, used in a more restricted sense to identify a single group whose restless movements were responsible for much of the development of ancient history throughout Eurasia after 2000 BC. As land-hungry migrants, certain Sanskrit-speaking tribes were indomitable; they had domesticated a wild species of horse that lived in their homeland in southern Russia, and they could use its power and mobility in and out of battle. Their mother-tongue moved with them; as they encountered new environments and mingled with other races, it eventually evolved into many languages, including Latin and ancient Greek.

Genuine knowledge about the Aryan invaders of India was long confused by a racist myth that gained currency in the 19th century and was enthusiastically promoted by Adolf Hitler and the Nazis in the 20th. This myth suggested that a white "master race" was responsible for all the progress of humanity, both early and recent. But it was horse mastery and the subsequent use of war chariots, rather than innate superiority of physique or mind, that ensured Aryan triumphs.

One way to belittle a foe

The Jivaro head-shrinkers

DO YOU RIDICULE the notion that you can keep trouble at bay by knocking on wood or putting a hex on someone you fear? You're probably right. Still, primitive rituals for warding off enemies do occasionally seem to work, or have worked in the past – perhaps because of the deterrent effect of the general knowledge that such rituals are being practiced. Consider the case of the Jivaro Indians, one of the very few tribes that survived the Spanish conquest of South America without losing their identity as a distinctive culture.

Around AD 1450, when the Incan army of Tupac Yupanqui invaded a south-Ecuadorian province of the kingdom of Quito, word spread through the Incan ranks that this was to be no ordinary war of conquest. They were hardened soldiers for whom the horrors of war meant little; but that particular group of enemy fighters – the Jivaro – gave the Incas pause. The Jivaro were head-shrinkers. Not content with decapitating their enemies and keeping the heads as trophies, they were famous for shrinking heads to crush the immortal spirit of the fallen dead.

The Incas could hardly be appalled at the idea of cutting off heads and carrying them proudly homeward; they often did it themselves. (In fact the practice had been common in South America as much as 3,000 years ago.) But since they believed that a person's soul resided in his head, they dreaded the possibility of the soul losing its potency. And destruction of the enemy's spirit is just what the Jivaro were known to achieve. They shrank heads in a ritualistic manner that made the resident souls incapable of exacting revenge upon those who had captured them.

Tupac Yupanqui won his war of conquest, but without overcoming the Jivaro, who melted back into the jungle from which they came.

Others took heads and prized them as spoils of war. Once, however, a Jivaro had ceremonially shrunken a severed head and imprisoned the enemy's soul, the *tsantsa* (to give the end-product its native name) was no longer valued. The avenging soul of a dead warrior – its *muisak* – would seek out its owner's killer and pursue him unless effectively neutralized in this fashion, the Jivaro believed. If they feared anything, it was the wrath of an escaped *muisak*.

Most of the captured heads were taken from the neighboring Achuara tribe, for there was a long tradition of hostility between the two peoples. (If no Achuara were in reach, Jivaro communities sometimes made war on each other, but they were careful to observe among themselves a strict code of conduct that prohibited decapitation.) The shrinking of captured heads, a process which took several days, would occur either at home-based ceremonies after the warriors' return from battle or, quite often, during the homeward journey. Each step in the communal process would be marked by ritual dances and feasting. The completed *tsantsas*, with eyelids sewn together so that the *muisak* could not see the outside world, and mouths sewn too so as to permit no escape, were ceremonially wrapped in cloth and placed in earthenware jars, which were frequently buried beneath the victorious warriors' huts.

Toward the middle of the 19th century the Indians discovered that *tsantsas* were a valuable asset – as trophies not for themselves but for European and North American collectors. So they began to sell modern shrunken heads to local traders in return for cheap manufactured goods, usually rifles. At one point demand for *tsantsas* became so great that new sources of supply had to be found. Many shrunken heads subsequently sold to museums around the world

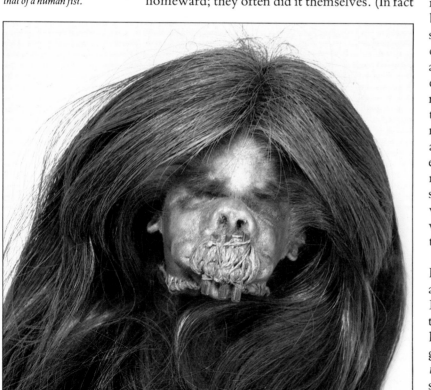

Using tried and tested methods, generations of Jivaro Indians have been shrinking human heads to a size no bigger than that of a human fist.

are in effect counterfeit – the work of unscrupulous forgers who applied Jivaro techniques to the heads of anonymous paupers unclaimed from the hospital morgues of Ecuador and Panama. You can usually recognize an authentic Jivaro *tsantsa* when you see one in that it is no bigger than your fist, and the contours and facial features of the full-size head (assuming you know what its long-dead owner looked like) have been in no way altered by the shrinking process.

The Incas and other Indian tribes of the pre-Colombian era have long since disappeared, destroyed almost at once by the Spanish, but the Jivaro are still identifiable as a tribe today. Indeed, there are strong grounds to indicate that they were still shrinking heads as recently as the 1960s, and in isolated cases may even be doing so now, despite stiff penalties imposed by the governments of Ecuador and Peru. Documentary evidence is naturally scarce, especially as the Jivaro are intensely wary of outsiders, but a reasonably accurate picture of their head-shrinking activities has nevertheless been built up by 20th-century anthropologists.

HOW TO SHRINK A HUMAN HEAD

The process of shrinking a head Jivaro-style usually took about six days – partly, of course, because of the ceremonial aspects, but also because the flesh needed to dry out between stages. The first and most important step was to remove the skull. This was done by making a vertical slit in the nape of the neck and peeling off the outside as if skinning a rabbit. The skull itself, along with eyes and teeth, was thrown into the river as a present for the anacondas. With sentries standing guard, the head-skin was boiled in water – perhaps containing some sort of astringent to prevent the hair from falling out – until it had contracted to just under half its original size. While still too hot to handle, it was lifted out with a stick and hung up to cool off and dry. Then the inner surface of the head-skin was scraped completely clean of flesh and the eyelids were sewn up.

By now the skin would be pale yellow and thick and rubbery to the touch. To reduce the head still further, the Jivaro Indians used a number of rounded stones that had been heated in the flames of a fire. One by one the stones were dropped through the neck aperture and rolled around evenly in the head to keep its shape from becoming distorted. As the sizzling flesh continued to shrink gradually, the stones were replaced with progressively smaller ones until, at last, even the smallest would no longer go through the aperture. Facial hair had to be singed off and what remained of the neck tightened with the thin, strong stem of a vine sewn around it to keep it in proportion to all other features. To complete the shrinking process, hot sand was poured into the head. Once the sand had cooled, the original head was little bigger than a man's fist. As a next step, the lips were skewered with three splinters of chonta-palm wood (an especially hard local wood) before they were sewn tightly together.

Much remained to be done, however, before the head became a finished *tsantsa*, the shrunken head within which the conquered enemy's vengeful soul was imprisoned. The skin was blackened with balsa-wood charcoal to keep the avenging spirit in darkness, and a red-and-black seed was sometimes placed under each firmly closed eyelid to make it bulge realistically. Finally, a hole was drilled in the top of the head and a bark string inserted to allow the head-taker to wear the *tsantsa* around his neck at the celebratory feasts.

The Thira eruption

The big bang that shook the Mediterranean world

THIRA (known today as Santorini), a crescent-shaped island in the Mediterranean 70 miles (110 kilometers) north of Crete, is actually part of the rim of a sunken volcano. Sometime around 1500 BC that volcano was the scene of one of the most devastating eruptions in history. Modern scientists agree that it was at least four times more violent than the greatest such catastrophe of our era, the 1883 eruption on the island of Krakatoa off the coast of Java, which hurled an estimated five cubic miles (18 cubic kilometers) of rock into the air, was heard by people 3,000 miles (4,800 kilometers) away, created tidal waves that killed nearly 40,000 people, and affected weather conditions around the world. And historians are now trying to link the eruption of Thira with some of the most famous dramas and mysteries of the ancient world in the belief that an understanding of the effects of the eruption may help to explain hitherto puzzling events.

For example, might it not have been responsible for the beginning of the end of Cretan civilization, which faded away with strange rapidity, toward the end of the 15th century BC? The great Minoan society on the island of Crete had reached a cultural peak during the 16th century BC. Its seafaring people had extended their influence over the whole of the Mediterranean – and perhaps well beyond it, to such outposts as Brittany in France – and they had developed some of the earliest known written scripts, had made beautiful pottery, jewelry, and gold- and silver-ware, and had built magnificent palaces such as those at Knossos and Phaistos. Yet all this was laid to waste within a few decades – a remarkably short time for the collapse of a civilization that had clearly not been brought about by invading armies. What else could possibly have brought about such a swift and irreversible decline?

Invasions and earthquakes are the two explanations most commonly put forward. But neither one nor the other, nor both combined, have ever convinced some historians. Instead, they suggest that the eruption of Thira, more than anything else, dealt Minoan Crete a mortal blow. The tremendous convulsion only a relatively short distance away would, it is argued, have showered the Cretans with blinding hot ash and noxious sulfur fumes. Then, at its height, the Thiran volcano could have fallen in upon itself, causing millions of gallons of seawater to pour into the roaring white-hot chasm beneath the surface, only to emerge again as a huge explosion of steam. When the resultant tidal wave, which was estimated to be well over 300 feet (100 meters) high and laden with scalding pumice, hurtled down upon the island of Crete, it must have engulfed and smashed everything for miles inland.

True, the disaster did not entirely destroy the island race – at least, not immediately. We know that homes and palaces were repaired. But life was never the same again, and Cretan civilization soon sank into oblivion.

The catastrophe at Thira also suggests the most probable source of the legend of Atlantis – that mystifying and wonderful island civilization that is said to have disappeared suddenly and without trace. Legends about glorious lost civilizations were already old and encrusted with myth according to Plato when he wrote about Atlantis in the fourth century BC, more than 1,000 years after the Thiran cataclysm, yet Plato is in fact the first author to mention this story. What some authorities now contend is that, because of the tendency of legends to exaggerate the incident that gives them birth, Plato described the island of Atlantis as 10 times bigger, and the time of its lost civilization as 10 times

earlier, than the facts warranted. If this error is corrected, the facts about Atlantis as set forth in Plato's story – its geography, its time scale, the nature of its culture – correspond in some striking details to the island of Crete and all that we now know of Cretan culture. So is it not likely that the story of Atlantis is simply a mythical and much embellished version of what happened to Minoan civilization, created in the wake of that awesome tidal wave?

That same wave would have swept onto the shores of Egypt – and could it not have caused the extraordinary series of events recounted in the Book of Exodus? An Egyptian inscription recording certain occurrences during the reign of Queen Hatshepsut (1490–68 BC) refers both to the departure from Egypt of a group of subject people and to a natural phenomenon that sounds very much like the action of a tidal wave. This presents a problem to scholars since the exodus of the Hebrews from Egypt is generally believed to have taken place during the reign of Ramses II (1290–24 BC). But the Bible itself gives no precise indication of the dates of the events recorded in the Book of Exodus; they *could* just as easily have occurred during Queen Hatshepsut's reign, although in that case it seems strange that the Bible refers to a pharaoh, not a queen, of Egypt.

In the light of this historical possibility the Old Testament account takes on a remarkable new significance. To start with, the plagues of Egypt – of flies and cattle, hail, locusts, darkness, and the rest – are exactly the kind of natural upsets associated with intense volcanic activity. And, proceeding to the exodus itself, Biblical scholars have long accepted that the term "Red Sea" (over which the Hebrews are said to have crossed) may well be a scribal misinterpretation of "Sea of Reeds," which is the name of a lake that lies close to the Mediterranean coast. Thus the Hebrews pausing on high ground after having passed the Sea of Reeds, could have seen the pursuing Egyptian army suddenly drowned in the waters of a mighty tidal wave.

The eruption at Thira would certainly have been visible from the shores of Egypt – all the more so if, as scientists believe, the prevailing wind at the time was from northwest to southeast – and so there could have been a "pillar of cloud" by day and a "pillar of fire" by night, accompanied by "darkness and early nightfall." For Moses and the Hebrews fleeing from the pursuing Egyptians such wondrous happenings, and the deliverance they brought, were nothing less than the latest in a succession of miracles wrought by the hand of God.

THE EXODUS

The Hebrews living in Egypt were treated as little better than slave labor, forced to perform menial, exhausting tasks in building grandiose monuments to glorify the reigns of the pharaohs. Their lot was unbearably harsh but at the same time, probably during the reign of Ramses II, they were allowed to leave after a succession of plagues had driven the Egyptians to believe that the Hebrews' God would punish their captors if they were kept indefinitely. Led by the visionary Moses, the Hebrews began the long migration known to us from the Bible as the Exodus.

Scholars have suggested four possible routes that they may have taken to the Promised Land. All would have entailed appalling privations, for the great horde of people, with their beasts and possessions, had to traverse the mountains and deserts of Sinai. The most celebrated incident in this long march is the crossing of the Red Sea, or, as most scholars now agree, the Sea of Reeds, close to the Mediterranean shore. The Hebrews were being pursued by an army sent by the pharaoh. According to the Old Testament, the waters miraculously parted, allowing the Hebrews to cross to the other shore. God then instructed Moses: "Stretch out your hand over the sea, that the water may come back upon the Egyptians . . ." This Moses did and the Egyptians were engulfed.

Whether the Hebrews were saved by the miracle described in Exodus or by some trick of nature we do not know. Certainly the Sea of Reeds could easily have brought disaster to Egyptian chariots. Then again, might there not have been a violent tidal disturbance caused by the Thira eruption? What is beyond dispute is that the Hebrews escaped and continued their long march.

The Egyptians engulfed by the Red Sea, as vividly depicted in this early-14th-century manuscript.

The mystery of the Basques

Will it ever be unravelled?

IN 1981, the Spanish destroyer *Marqués de Ensada* was sabotaged while at anchor at Santander, in northeastern Spain. An explosion ripped a large hole in the boiler area of the vessel, but fortunately no one was injured. The attack, which was just one of the most recent incidents in the continuing struggle for Basque self-determination, was the work of ETA, the Basque nationalist movement called *Euzkadi ta Azkatasuna*, or *Euzkadi* (the Basque name for their country) *and Liberty*.

The Basques are a proud people who live in northeastern Spain and southwestern France. Distinctive in appearance, they are of medium height, with narrow faces and thin, prominent noses. Their complexions are dark, though not as dark as those of French people and Spaniards in the same areas. Even more unique is their language. It is Western Europe's only living language that does not belong to the Indo-European group. Its origins still baffle linguists

and of various claims perhaps the most fantastic is that it was spoken by the Creator.

A close study of Basque vocabulary shows that most words bear no resemblance to any known language. It is extremely hard to learn and few outsiders have ever mastered its complexities. With some justification, Manuel de Larramendi, who wrote the first Basque grammar in the 18th century, called his book *El Imposible Vencido* (*The Impossible Conquered*). The difficulty of the language is compounded by the fact that there are eight officially recognized dialects and 25 subdialects. The vocabulary and dialect can vary from village to village and even from house to house, a complexity that perhaps gave rise to a favorite Basque legend about the Devil who apparently once visited the Basque country. Forced to leave after seven years, he had learned only the words for "yes" and "no."

Since the 19th century, scientists, linguists, and archeologists have suggested a bewildering

Basque dancers entertaining the crowds at festival time are carrying on a centuries-old tradition, whose origins are shrouded in obscurity.

array of solutions to the mystery of the Basques. About 20 peoples have been proposed as their ancestors, including ancient Egyptians, Hittites, Phoenicians, Ligurians, North and South American Indians, and Eskimos. Some people have even suggested that the Basques are survivors of the lost continent of Atlantis. The most popular of the theories link the Basques with the ancient Iberian or Celtiberian races, with the Berbers of North Africa, or with peoples of the Caucasus region between the Black and Caspian seas in the USSR.

The latter theory was based on some similarities between the Basque language and languages of the Caucasus. The theory seemed to be proved in the early 19th century when archeologists found Caucasian-type skulls in the French Basque country. The triumph proved to be short-lived when the French archeologist Dr. Paul Broca also discovered skulls, but of an ancient European type in the Spanish Basque region in the 1860s.

The shapes of the skulls found by Broca differed sufficiently from the modern Basque skull that no definite links could be established, although his finds seemed to support the theory that the Basques were descended from a traditional European people, probably the original inhabitants of the Iberian peninsula.

The first detailed archeological exploration of Basque territory was carried out by two Basques – Telesforo de Aranzadi and Jose Miguel Barandiaran – who in 1918 discovered weapons and paintings in the caves of Santimamiñe in the region of Cortezubi, northeastern Spain. These finds bore witness to the existence of a primitive hunting people in the region during the Upper Paleolithic period. In 1936, two types of Upper Paleolithic skull were found in the Urtiaga cave. One was of the kind previously found by Dr. Broca, while the other closely resembled a modern Basque skull. This provided the strongest evidence to date that the Basques are descended from Upper Paleolithic stock. For the first time, it could be shown that the Basques might be indigenous to the region they now inhabit.

Even so speculation about the Basques and their language will doubtless continue. As the Basque historian Arnauld Oihénat has said: "It is difficult to write the internal and external history of this race, for there exists no single ancient document concerning them."

Egypt's bearded queen
The monumental ambitions of Hatshepsut

THE TEMPLE OF Deir el Bahri near Thebes, capital city of ancient Egypt, is perhaps the finest achievement of Egyptian architecture, rivaling the Sphinx and the Pyramids in majesty and magnificence. Set in a bay of cliffs on the west bank of the Nile, a complex of pale limestone colonnades rises from a series of three terraces, exquisitely proportioned against the massive backdrop of raw rock. Myrrh trees imported from the exotic land of Punt once lined the long avenues of approach to this splendid structure – dedicated by its royal patron to the god Amon, for whom it had been conceived as a corner of paradise. And – remarkably – that royal patron was a woman pharaoh in a land where male supremacy was sacred.

Deir el Bahri was just one among the many architectural wonders commissioned by Queen Hatshepsut. Throughout her lands she erected statues, restored temples, and built new shrines. Typical of her ambitious projects were two giant obelisks at Karnak, each hewn from a single block of red granite and pointed with gold so that "their rays might inundate the Two Lands whenever the sun rose between them . . . on the horizons of heaven."

The Egyptians of Hatshepsut's time – some 1,500 years before the birth of Christ – had no word for "queen"; there was only "the wife of the king" since it was taken for granted that a man must sit upon the throne of the pharaohs. Although several royal wives, such as the beautiful Nefertiti, gained renown and a measure of power, only a very few ruled in their own right. Among these Hatshepsut stands supreme. Some historians single her out as history's first noteworthy woman.

She began her regal career as the wife of her half-brother, Thutmose II. When he died, she became regent for his (but not her) son, Thutmose III. Driven by burning ambition, she quickly pushed the young Thutmose into the background and had herself proclaimed "king," with all power in her hands even though her hapless stepson retained the nominal status of joint ruler. Thereafter she seems to have reveled

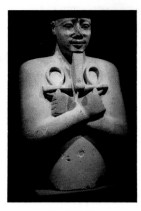

Despite the fact that Hatshepsut's successor, Thutmose III, attempted to have her face and name erased from all monuments, several portraits of the queen still exist. Some even show her wearing her ceremonial beard (above).

HOW TO LIFT AN OBELISK – THE SKYSCRAPER OF THE PAST

One of the most arresting sights amid the ruins of ancient Egyptian temples at Karnak on the east bank of the Nile is a granite obelisk 97 feet (30 meters) tall, which still stands some 3,500 years after it was first erected. The obelisk was one of two raised during the reign of Queen Hatshepsut; the other fell victim centuries ago to an earthquake and has lain ever since at the foot of its partner.

It is calculated that each obelisk weighs more than 320 tons, and archeologists have long pondered the puzzle of how they were put up. The Egyptians of Hatshepsut's day had not invented the capstan or the winch; they knew nothing of jackscrews or even a real block and tackle. Yet they were able to take a heavy, awkwardly shaped block of granite and lift it upright – no mean feat even today. How did they do it?

Evidence left by the Egyptians themselves is sketchy. We know that the obelisks were quarried in Aswan and floated down the Nile on a huge barge towed by at least 27 smaller vessels. And we know that, as well as being difficult, the operation

was extremely hazardous, because a similar task carried out on behalf of Ramses IV, in the 12th century BC, cost the lives of 800 men. But we can only guess at how the obelisks reached their final resting place.

Two theories have been put forward – one by an English archeologist, Reginald Engelbach, the other by a Frenchman, Henri Chevrier. Both depend on a mountain of sand with a funnel-shaped pit at one end, into which the obelisk was gently lowered at an angle of 34 degrees. Chevrier argues that it could then have been pulled upright with ropes; Engelbach, contends that there must have been some sort of levering action. Either theory is plausible, but Chevrier's is perhaps the more likely since he has practical experience of the problem. He once spent two archeological seasons dismantling and re-erecting a 60-foot-high (18 meters) monument dating from the seventh century BC. When the job was completed, he stood on the top surrounded by flags while the workmen below gave him a standing ovation.

One of the two obelisks raised at Karnak by Queen Hatshepsut (above left). The other obelisk (above right) was erected by Thutmose I.

The diagram at right illustrates Chevrier's hypothesis of how Hatshepsut's obelisks were raised. Each obelisk was lowered by ropes down a slope of sand into a pit. Ropes were then used to pull the obelisk upright, while a brick wall restrained the obelisk from toppling over.

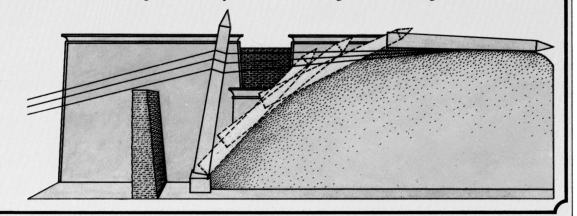

in "kingship." Several portraits show her wearing male garb and the traditional masculine pharaoh's headgear. In some effigies she is even depicted with a ceremonial beard. In addition, she assumed almost all the honorary titles normally reserved for male pharaohs. (One notable exception: She was never known as "Mighty Bull" – an epithet that must have been considered inappropriate even for this commanding figure of a woman.)

Inscriptions make extravagant claims for Hatshepsut's beauty, but we do not know what she really looked like. Her images sometimes portray her as a slender girl, sometimes as a man of athletic build. No matter which, she must always have looked regal, especially to government officials through whom she ruled. One particularly important official was an architect named Senenmut, who, as Minister of Public Works, was responsible for the building program. But the queen's own vision must surely have lain behind the funeral temple of Deir el Bahri. Its porticoes bear majestic friezes that

celebrate Hatshepsut's lineage and deeds. Designed to perpetuate her claim to greatness, the temple was more than a place of worship; it was a gigantic piece of propaganda.

One famous series of reliefs on the temple walls illustrates an expedition to the fabled land of Punt (identified, though only tentatively, by modern scholars as Somalia, in the southern coastlands of the Red Sea). Punt was celebrated in Egypt for its myrrh trees and for exotic products such as ebony, ivory, and gold. The voyage is depicted as such an achievement that Hatshepsut was popularly credited with having "discovered" Punt. But this was not so. Egyptian expeditions to the mysterious land had been going on for at least 1,000 years before Hatshepsut's day. She herself, we now believe, created and nurtured her image as the queen who sponsored epic adventures.

This was one way to compensate for a lack of notable military successes during a long reign. Although the queen is characterized in one inscription as a "born conqueror" and as the anointed "serpent of the royal god, Horus, spitting fire against the enemy," there is no evidence to support these bold words. No great conquests by Hatshepsut's armies are named or illustrated anywhere among the artifacts of her reign – which, in fact, appears to have been both peaceful and prosperous. Her vague claims to martial glory were probably designed only to satisfy the masculine warrior-pharaoh tradition.

She undoubtedly had to project a conquering-hero image because her position was precarious despite her successes in the fields of commerce and architecture. The woman's face behind the false beard must have troubled many an orthodox mind during the 21 years of her "joint"

reign with her stepson; and he himself clearly harbored savage resentment against the woman who wielded power that was rightfully his. As soon as Hatshepsut died and Thutmose III became sole ruler of Egypt, he set about having most of her effigies destroyed or defaced and her name deleted from monuments throughout the land. And after waiting in the wings for 21 years, he went on to establish a reputation as one of ancient Egypt's greatest war leaders.

Only in one way did Thutmose honor the memory of his remarkable stepmother: He permitted her to be buried in Egypt's royal cemetery, the Valley of the Kings – the rarest of privileges for a woman.

The message of the "dragon bones"
News of ancient China

LESS THAN a century ago, most historians assumed that organized society in China began sometime around 1100 BC. There was, indeed, a tradition that a shadowy government known as the Shang dynasty had flourished before the dawn of recorded history, but stories about the Shang were generally rated as little more than legends (much as Western scholars once believed that Troy and the Trojan War were almost wholly fictitious). Such doubts no longer exist, however. They were eventually dispelled as the result of a fortuitous chain of circumstances.

In 1899 a doctor in Peking prescribed some medicine for a family who were suffering from malaria. The head of the family, a man named Wang I-yung, happened to be a paleographer (an expert in ancient scripts); the prescription was a traditional concoction containing something called "dragon bones"; and before crushing the "bones" after procuring them, Wang noticed that they were not bones at all but pieces of yellowed turtle shell with scratch marks on them. His curiosity aroused, he examined the scratches and discovered to his vast surprise that they were some kind of writing. The characters were either primitive pictograms – symbolic picture writings with, for example, a crescent representing "moon" and a circle "sun" – or ideograms, as in modern Chinese. This was obviously a very old inscription of a type that Wang had never seen before, and so he bought up his pharmacist's stock of "dragon bones" and subjected them to intense scrutiny.

The "bones," which included pieces of animal bone as well as turtle shell, contained enough of the meaningful scratch marks to convince Wang that they were relics of the Shang dynasty and were about 3,400 years old. With the publication of his findings, accepted notions of the date when the Chinese had begun to use ideograms were demolished. Not only that. It became clear that the Shang dynasty was not a mere legend. The people of the Shang were now recognized as the first literate civilization in China, with the world's earliest-known extant writing system, which, once paleographers could decipher it, revealed at least a partial picture of its society.

Wang's discovery inspired other scholars, as well as curio collectors, to search feverishly for inscribed "dragon bones." Their search proved remarkably successful throughout northern China, though not in the south; and the many fragments unearthed in the early years of the 20th century soon provided answers to two out of three obvious questions. First, why had the Shang scribes written on bones and shells rather than on a more likely – if less durable – medium such as the bark of trees? And, secondly, why was the writing always arranged around cracks or cuts in the fragments, suggesting that cracks and cuts were not accidental damage but were somehow related to the accompanying inscriptions? The answer to both questions turned out to be that these were all pieces of what came to be known as *oracle bones*. Far from being accidental, the cracks resulted from the bones' being deliberately subjected to extreme heat; the

Shang believed that the appearance and position of the cracks foretold the future. Thus the writing around a given crack records both a question and the oracle bone's answer. Shang citizens from the king down apparently relied on oracle bones not only for predictions but for guidance in making decisions about anything from the conduct of war to building a house or going on a trip. For a long time after Wang's original feat of detective work, however, one important question remained unanswered: Where did the Shang people live; where exactly was the urban center of their dynasty situated? We now have the answer to that one, too.

For many years, the inhabitants of an area around An-yang, an archeological site in the northern province of Honan, had been haphazardly digging up and selling long-buried white-pottery objects and fine bronze vessels. After the significance of oracle bones became a matter of common knowledge among collectors, An-yang's diggers also found it profitable to sell "dragon bones" that were constantly being unearthed in their territory. In 1928, though, dismayed by the careless dispersion of so many archeological treasures, the Chinese government stopped the plunder by authorizing controlled digs in the area. Those excavations are still going on today. They have resulted in the finding not only of huge quantities of oracle bones – up to 17,000 in one pit – but of the remains of what was undoubtedly the Shang capital city, including a palace 92 feet (30 meters) long flanked by royal workshops in which Shang artisans once manufactured stone tools, bone arrowheads, and superbly ornamented bronze vessels. Also unearthed have been other impressive dwellings and temples built of brick set on stone bases, with roofs held up by large wooden pillars; thatched-roofed houses that probably belonged to commoners; a great many beautiful pieces of porcelain and bronze; remains of wheeled vehicles; royal tombs decorated with vast stone sculptures; and underground corridors filled with human skeletons (the victims, perhaps, of mass sacrifice).

This, archeologists agree, was the site of Great Shang, the last capital city of the dynasty. And other sites across northern China have revealed even more evidence of the Shang people – a people now at last rescued from what was once thought of as their "mythical" past.

An oracle or dragon bone (at right) was commonly ground into powder for use as an ingredient of some Chinese medicines, until it was realized that the scratch marks on the surface of most of these bones were examples of the earliest Chinese writing.

HOW TO CRACK THE FUTURE

The notion that the position and shape of cracks in heated bones can foretell the future was already old 3,500 years ago, when the Shang Chinese were basing every decision, vital as well as trivial, upon it. Archeological evidence suggests that the priest-diviners who worked with "oracle bones" did their job in this way:

Having chosen a suitable material – either the undershell of a turtle or a bone from the shoulder blades of domestic cattle or water buffaloes – the diviner polished the shell or bone, then scratched a question on its surface with a stylus. The question on one still-extant bone, for instance, reads: "The king asks whether he should go hunting on the tenth day of the month." Next, the diviner cut a groove in a part of the bone adjacent to the query and touched it with a red-hot bronze point, causing a maze of cracks to appear on the surface. Having studied the results and obtained the required information from whatever gods or spirits of the dead governed such matters, he scratched down the answer, which might be a simple "yes" or "no" or a comment such as "It is a satisfactory day for hunting."

The priest-diviners seem to have given some fairly poor advice from time to time, and their predictions must have missed the mark more often than not. Yet the oracle-bones system persisted for centuries; no Shang ruler dared to make war or build a palace without consulting the bones. So perhaps they worked sometimes.

THE SHANG DYNASTY

Tradition has it that the Shang was the second of three dynasties that governed northern China between, roughly, the 18th and 11th centuries BC. It is not known whether the three ruled successively or simultaneously, each gaining the upper hand at different times, for no detailed records of the period exist. Because of the oracle bones and the An-yang excavations, however, we do know that the Shang power base lay in the Yellow River valley and that Shang kings ruled over a largely agricultural village-based people with a remarkably high level of civilization. Shang bronzesmiths cast vessels still unsurpassed for artistry; astronomers devised a calendar of 365 days; a decimal system of counting was in use; and traders used an elementary form of coinage for financial transactions. Great Shang, the last and most splendid of the dynasty's three capital cities, covered an area of about 24 square miles (62 square kilometers) stretching along both banks of the Huan, a Yellow River tributary.

Shang rulers inhabited palaces consecrated with human sacrifices; the victims, often in a kneeling position and fully armed, were built into the foundations for luck. Poorer subjects lived far less grandly, in thatched-roofed pits.

The strength of Shang society lay largely in the way it was organized in clans. Each clan shared the same surname, worshiped the same ancestors, and obeyed the royal will as guided by priest-diviners. This tight organization enabled the rulers to mobilize powerful armies and use forced labor for digging ditches for flood control and irrigation. Shang troops wielding the bronze-bladed kō – a dagger-ax with a tongue-shaped blade – stamped Shang authority across the breadth of northern China from Inner Mongolia in the west to the China Sea in the east. The last king of the dynasty was overthrown in about 1100 BC, when a tribe from the northwest, called the Chou, captured Great Shang (now known to have been sited at modern An-yang) and set up a new dynasty.

This ornately decorated wine vessel is an example of the bronzework for which the Shang dynasty was especially famed.

The strange disappearance of Queen Nefertiti

And an even stranger explanation

THE REIGN of the Pharaoh Amenhotep IV (about 1372–1354 BC) shook Egyptian civilization to its foundations. Soon after coming to the throne, the pharaoh swept aside ancient Egypt's time-honored gods in favor of a single supreme deity – the Aton, or Disc of the Sun. Abandoning the great temple at Thebes, the capital city on the banks of the Nile, with its presiding deity Amon, he and his beautiful wife, Nefertiti, set up a new capital at Amarna, on an uninhabited tract of land 200 miles (300 kilometers) to the north. By royal decree the shadowy sanctuaries of the past were abolished and the new religion made the law of the land. In Amarna the pharaoh and his wife worshiped their Sun god in courtyards open to the sky so that every corner was penetrated by life-giving solar rays. So intoxicated was the pharaoh with his new faith that he changed his name to Akhenaton ("It Goes Well with Aton") and renamed the city Amarna, Akhetaton, in tribute to the celestial power.

Historians still quarrel about the character of Akhenaton and the extent of Nefertiti's influence over him. Some have exalted him as the pioneer of monotheism, history's first great advocate of peace, love, and artistic creativity. On the other hand, he has been condemned as an unstable fanatic whose mystic obsessions were

Queen Nefertiti of Egypt's remarkable beauty has been re-created in this famous bust, renowned for its realistic quality and probably sculpted during the queen's lifetime.

catastrophic for Egypt, which declined because of his neglect of the skills of warfare and diplomacy. And some have suggested that he was actually unfit to rule and that major decisions were mostly made by his wife. If this last theory is true, it raises some fascinating questions.

Undeniably, Akhenaton was odd. He even looked peculiar, with an elongated skull, drooping jaw, slack, protruding lips, broad hips, and a distended belly; it seems likely that he suffered from a disorder of the endocrine glands. Many representations of both him and Nefertiti survive, and some of them exaggerate the pharaoh's ugliness, as if to exalt his unique nature. Nefertiti, by contrast, was truly beautiful, as evidenced by the miraculously lifelike bust found in the workshop of an ancient Egyptian sculptor. Her face was slender and refined, a mask of timeless elegance with more than a hint of intelligence in the taut features.

The queen's origins – like much else in her life – are shrouded in mystery, but her loveliness is well known. The name Nefertiti meant "The beautiful one has come," and the pharaoh, who seems to have felt something close to reverence for her beauty, called her his Mistress of Happiness and Lady of Grace. She was no mere adornment to Akhenaton's household, however. She appears to have been constantly at his side, and the couple are often portrayed in scenes of domestic intimacy – playing with their daughters, eating meals together, riding side by side in a chariot. Wherever and however they are depicted, the disc of the sun is always shown above them, its rays descending on pharaoh and queen alike. So Nefertiti seems to have shared her husband's near-divine status. Was she really the power behind an unstable monarch's throne?

A sickly and unworldly dreamer, the pharaoh could well have required someone to keep him in touch with reality – a role which Nefertiti could easily have fulfilled. Yet, in the 12th year of Akhenaton's reign something happened to the Lady of Grace. The name Nefertiti disappears from inscriptions on plaques and monuments dating from that year on, and she is not mentioned again. Did she die or fall into disgrace for some reason?

There is another possibility, though. In the final stages of Akhenaton's 17-year reign, an elusive male figure named Smenkhkara governed Egypt as Akhenaton's co-regent. The identity of this newcomer remains speculative; he may have been the pharaoh's son by a minor wife (Nefertiti seems to have borne only daughters). But a new and intriguing theory has recently been proposed: Might not Smenkhkara have been none other than Nefertiti herself?

Startling as the idea appears, it is not entirely implausible. One of Smenkhkara's names, for example, was very nearly the same as a name by which Nefertiti was also known – Neternefruaton. The theory, which explains both the mysterious disappearance of the queen and the equally mysterious rise of the new co-regent, is based on the assumption that an increasingly enfeebled Akhenaton was losing his grip on the reins of power, and that Egypt's strong-willed Lady of Grace posed as a man in order to keep her husband on the throne. We have no evidence to support this bizarre suggestion – but then there is only shadowy evidence in support of much of what we think we know about this perplexing period of ancient Egyptian history.

Both Akhenaton and the mysterious Smenkhkara died in about 1354 BC. The successor, a boy named Tutankhaton, had been brought up as a worshiper of the Aton. But the cult of the Sun god did not long outlive its royal patron. Three years after becoming pharaoh, Tutankhaton abandoned Amarna and reopened the royal court at Thebes. New statues of the old gods were erected, and Tutankh*aton* changed his name to Tutankh*amon* in tribute to the Amon of Thebes. In time the city of Amarna was razed, and the whole Amarna episode (sometimes called the Amarna Revolution) came to be reviled. The names of the heretic pharaoh and his wife were savagely chiseled away from monuments in order to propitiate the traditional gods, and Akhenaton's glittering vision was forgotten. But, fortunately, despite these deliberate attempts to erase her memory, the world will always remember Nefertiti as long as her exquisite sculptured head remains.

Pharaoh Akhenaton and his wife Nefertiti discarded Egypt's traditional deities such as Amon in favor of the Sun god Aton. The couple were usually portrayed symbolically basking in the sun's rays. This family scene shows them playing with their three daughters.

Bearers of the purple

Bringing riches to the rich

THEY HAVE BEEN called the bedouins of the sea. From their homeland in the Levant they shipped fabulous cargoes the length and breadth of the Mediterranean. Roman emperors were to buy and wear their luxurious purple cloth; Egyptian pharaohs were embalmed in fabrics treated with their cedar oil; Solomon called upon the talents of their craftsmen to adorn the Temple at Jerusalem and to build and furnish his palace.

Who were these enterprising and inventive people? They were the Phoenicians, who inhabited a coastal strip of land in the eastern Mediterranean, corresponding to modern Lebanon plus small areas of Israel and Syria. Semitic in origin, they are referred to in the Bible as Canaanites; and the Hebrew patriarchs fulminated against their heathen practices. But even the Old Testament authors recognized their genius for trade. In Hebrew, *kena' ani* means "merchant" as well as Canaanite.

It was the ancient Greeks who gave the Canaanites the name by which they are best known. "Phoenicia" means roughly "the land of purple," and the Phoenicians' most renowned export was a rare purple dye whose exquisite beauty was sung by poets throughout antiquity. The dye was only one of their much-sought-after products. Sidon, one of the two leading Phoenician cities, was famous for the manufacture of fine glassware such as highly colored beads, bottles, vases, and goblets. Both Sidon and the other big city, Tyre, produced richly embroidered fabrics, delicate carvings of wood and ivory, and incomparably well-wrought metal objects. Homer describes Sidonian silverware as "the most beautiful in the world," and it was 10th-century-BC Tyrian craftsmen who built Solomon's Temple and palace and filled them with ornaments of gold and silver.

In about 1200 BC, the Canaanites were forced by invaders to look seaward for their livelihood,

PHOENICIAN EXPLORATIONS

The Phoenicians were amazingly accomplished navigators, always searching for new markets and new sources of raw materials. We know that they founded trading posts on the coasts of Spain and Morocco beyond the Strait of Gibraltar, and that they often sailed to the region around Cadiz to pick up loads of copper and lead ore. If the Greek historian Herodotus is to be believed, a Phoenician fleet circumnavigated Africa in about 600 BC on an expedition organized by the Egyptian Pharaoh Necho. According to Herodotus, the expedition set out via the Red Sea and returned three years later via the Strait of Gibraltar.

Since it was another 2,000 years before European seafarers managed to round the Cape of Good Hope, the account seems hardly credible. Yet in an intriguing footnote to his narrative, Herodotus says that the Phoenicians claimed to have had the sun "on their right hand" as they traveled westward; in other words, the sun was to the north. Ironically, Herodotus disbelieved this part of the story, while to modern geographers, aware that a ship must cross the Equator in order to circumnavigate Africa, it is the most credible part of the story.

Did the Phoenicians also get to Britain? The suggestion has often been made, but with no direct evidence to support it. A much more startling claim for their seamanship is that it might have brought them to America. As evidence, enthusiasts have cited Mexican pottery figurines that appear to have Semitic faces, and have pointed out that a number of American Indian peoples

worshiped bearded gods though the continent's native inhabitants were all beardless. Could the gods have been modeled perhaps on bearded Phoenician visitors?

Most scholars dismiss this theory. Phoenician galleys, powered mainly by oarsmen although sometimes equipped with mast and sail, were chiefly used for island-hopping or for skirting long coastlines within sight of land. The routes to the mineral riches of Spain, for example, were dotted with staging posts and warehousing centers that allowed the seamen to drop anchor overnight. It might have been possible for the Phoenicians to circumnavigate Africa or reach Britain in stages. A venture across the Atlantic, however? Most unlikely, even for these remarkable navigators.

- ┄┄ Possible voyage around Africa
- ▓ Area settled by Phoenicians c.500 BC
- ▭ Sea trade routes

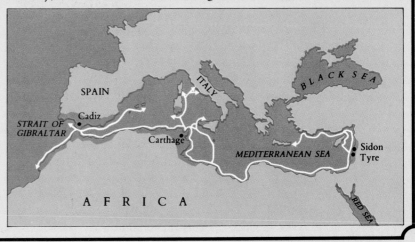

Phoenician traders, shown here in a painting by the 19th-century artist, Lord Frederick Leighton, dealt in a variety of luxury goods, in particular the purple cloth for which they were renowned.

and so built the greatest maritime empire the world had yet seen. Phoenicia was at its most prosperous between the 12th and eighth centuries BC, a long period during which her people monopolized maritime trade. They were the Mediterranean's middlemen, with commercial routes linking all parts of the then-known Western world. It may possibly have been largely in order to maintain communication within this vast trading area that the Phoenicians devised an alphabet – an innovation that was to form the basis of all written language in the West. After the eighth century, though, their power began to decline, partly because the Greeks gradually developed Mediterranean colonies and broke Phoenicia's monopoly of trade, and partly because of increasing domination of the coastal homeland by successive powers – Assyria, Babylon, Persia, and eventually Rome.

Yet Phoenicia's native civilization did not die, nor did the ingenuity of her people. The technique of glassblowing, for example, was a Phoenician invention of the first century BC. And meanwhile, more than ever, there remained her purple dye. Imperial Roman priests and officials prized their robes adorned with Tyrian purple above all other garments, for the exquisite color became associated with, and symbolic of, the most exalted rank. Emperors wore purple tunics; senators wore tunics with a double purple stripe down the front; the garments of other aristocrats often had a narrow purple stripe extending from each shoulder downward. The manufacture of Phoenician purple, in fact, outlasted the Roman empire. The dye was still being imported from the Levant to Europe as a rare commodity in the early Middle Ages, though by then Phoenicia itself had long since fallen to the Saracens.

CASTING THE DYE

The coastal waters of ancient Phoenicia abounded in two kinds of dye-bearing shellfish: the murex and the buccinum. In both there is a long sac or vein filled with a yellowish fluid that turns purplish when exposed to light. Purple-dyeing became a major industry in Tyre and Sidon, the Phoenicians' main cities, but Tyre was especially celebrated for the quality of its dye. Although the Phoenicians were secretive about their manufacturing arts, much has been learned about the way they produced dyes.

The mollusks were gathered in deep water by dropping down narrow-mouthed baskets baited with mussels and frog meat. Once harvested, the shellfish were hauled off to dye pits, where their sacs were removed, pulped, and heated in vessels of lead so that extraneous matter could be skimmed off. A mordant (fixative) was added to make the dye color-fast. The pits were located downwind of habitation since, though purple delighted the eye, its manufacture offended the nose. The Phoenicians were able to produce a range of colors that varied from pale pink to deep violet by mixing the murex and buccinum fluids in differing quantities.

Archeologists have found immense heaps of empty shells at the remains of dye pits excavated near both Tyre and Sidon. In fact, until other methods of producing the color were introduced, the two types of mollusk were so intensively exploited that they have become almost extinct off the shores of present-day Lebanon.

A dive into the past

Submarine archeologists explore the world's oldest known shipwreck

Some of the copper ingots which were part of the cargo of a Phoenician merchant ship that was wrecked around 1200 BC.

STANDING IN THE stern of the boat, the olive-skinned trader was feeling pleased. The voyage had been profitable. He had taken aboard a ton of bronze and copper ingots at his last port of call on the island of Cyprus and he was making good time on his voyage to the Aegean, where he hoped to sell the cargo to Greek metal-workers. A strong, westward current was carrying the 35-foot (over 10 meters) planked boat along the southern coast of Turkey and he would soon be dropping anchor at the harbor of Finike to take on fresh water for the final leg of the journey.

But the trader never reached Finike. In the island-studded waters off Cape Gelidonya, the vessel suddenly struck a reef of jagged rocks just under the surface. Its bottom was ripped open, and weighed down by the metal ingots, it sank like a stone in 90 feet (27 meters) of water. Whether members of the crew managed to swim ashore or were swept away by the current, they never returned; and so the boat and its cargo lay virtually undisturbed on the sea floor.

For 3,000 years the wreck remained hidden there until the 1950s when sponge divers from the Turkish fishing village of Bodrum, 180 miles (290 kilometers) west of Cape Gelidonya, came across it. The divers were not particularly excited by their find, because the Turkish coast is littered with such debris. But in 1958, Peter Throckmorton, an American diver and writer, visited Bodrum to hunt for ancient wrecks. In a chance conversation, he heard that the captain of a sponge boat was planning to dynamite a wreck to obtain its cargo of bronze for scrap. The captain's enthusiasm was muted, however, because, he said, the metal was "rotten." Throckmorton quickly realized that such a description could be applied only to bronze that had been corroded by the sea over an extremely long period. Realizing the implications, he dissuaded the captain from dynamiting the ship.

By adapting the equipment and techniques normally used on land, archeologists have found that they can investigate underwater discoveries much more thoroughly.

Among the many items recovered from the 3,000-year-old wreck of a Phoenician trading vessel was a stone cylinder-seal, believed to have belonged to the merchant.

In June 1959, Throckmorton returned to Turkey with friends aboard an American yacht. The team pinpointed the site of the wreck and collected enough evidence to persuade the University of Pennsylvania to sponsor a full-scale archeological expedition. Up to that time, most undersea excavations had been undertaken by professional divers, while the scholars waited impotently on the surface. In 1960, however, the expedition's leader, a 27-year-old American archeologist named George Bass, adopted a new approach: Instead of trying to turn divers into scholars, he trained archeologists to dive and in doing so pioneered an exciting new branch of practical scholarship.

The results were astounding. Using the same painstaking techniques that archeologists use on land, measuring and recording the precise positions of everything they found, Bass's team pieced together a picture of life aboard an ancient eastern Mediterranean trading ship.

Most perishable goods and much of the boat itself had disintegrated. But the boat had sunk so fast that much of the cargo, though concreted together by limestone deposits and marine organisms, was still stacked in neat piles. And fragments of matting, in which the rough-edged ingots had been wrapped, had also survived.

Over several months, the team found the remains of tin and copper ingots (the earliest evidence of industrial tin), stone anvils, hammers and "rubbers" (used for beating the cast metal into polished sheets), the merchant's seal, an elegantly carved stone cylinder that may have been a family heirloom, and several sets of weights that were used by traders. The divers also brought up scrap metal consisting of broken pieces of bronze tools and weapons, including axes, adzes, knives, and spearheads, which were obviously intended to be melted down for re-use. The ingots and scrap metal would be exchanged for Greek wine, olives, and oil.

Of all the finds, perhaps the most poignant were everyday items, including good luck charms, a bronze mirror, and olive pits and fish bones, possibly the remnants of the crew's last meal. There was even a bronze skewer of the kind still used in Turkish cooking.

Once all the artifacts were salvaged, they were studied. Each item had to be matched against similar artifacts from around the Mediterranean. They were dated by laborious comparisons of styles, particularly of pottery, and the results were cross-checked against other dating techniques, such as carbon-14 analysis of fragments of wood. Piecing the jigsaw together took seven years. Such painstaking work was ultimately rewarded as Bass's team established that the shipwreck had occurred during the late Bronze Age in about 1200 BC and that the trader was a Phoenician, who bought and sold metal and cast his own ingots from fragments smelted in temporary kilns he built ashore: the team had found the world's oldest known shipwreck.

In doing so the archeologists also overturned some long-cherished beliefs about the ancient world. Most significantly, classical historians had long believed that Homer's *Odyssey* – set in the 13th century BC but written several hundred years later – was completely inaccurate when it stated that Phoenician traders were operating at the time. Evidence from the shipwreck, however, proved these historians wrong. Not only did the finds from the shipwreck confirm that as early as 1200 BC there was Phoenician activity in the Mediterranean but also it confirmed certain technical aspects of Homer's writings as they relate to shipcraft of that time.

The mysteries of Eleusis
Intimations of immortality

RELIGION WAS all-pervasive in ancient Greece. There was the familiar Greek pantheon of anthropomorphic gods and goddesses, including Zeus, Hera, Athena, and Apollo, who controlled all natural forces. These deities were worshiped with prayers and sacrifices both in the home and in public ceremonies at shrines and temples. Alongside this public religion, however, were mystic cults, often linked with female powers, that began before the classical period. Possibly the most highly venerated of these cults was the Mysteries of Eleusis. The word mystery comes from a Greek word meaning "to close the eyes" and the Mysteries of Eleusis were closely guarded secrets. They were protected by such sanctions as death for any impure person who spied on the sacred rites, or the confiscation of the estate of any initiate who disclosed the secrets of the cult. Above all, the initiates respected their oaths, believing that, in keeping the secret of the mysteries, they held the key to immortality.

Many of the mysteries remain a secret. However, scholars have pieced together a fragmented picture of the Eleusinian Mysteries from references, often oblique, in ancient texts, and from the excavation of the great temple complex at Eleusis, once the prosperous center of a rich farming region and now a dusty industrial suburb of Athens. Here, particularly in the great Temple of Demeter (the Telesterion), archeologists uncovered sculptures and vase paintings that depicted some of the rites.

The ritual of the Eleusinian Mysteries was expressed in the legend of the goddess Demeter (or Ceres, goddess of corn and agriculture) and her daughter Persephone, who was abducted by Hades (Pluto), king of the underworld. After an intervention by Zeus, Persephone was allowed to return to the world for eight months of the year, but for the other four months, she had to languish in the underworld. The myth symbolizes the burying of seed and the emergence of new crops, a form of death and resurrection.

The Eleusinia festival consisted of three stages. The first, or Lesser Eleusinia, was held every February; its ceremonies were concerned with the purification of initiates, and rams and hogs were often sacrificed. The second, or Great Mystery, was celebrated in September/October. Some people who had been initiated into the Lesser Eleusinia, called *mystae*, set out for Athens to Eleusis to fetch relics and sacred objects required in the ceremonies, returning the next day along the Sacred Way which linked Eleusis to the Athenian suburb of Ceramicus. The *mystae*, who could be men or women or even slaves, gathered in a huge, noisy crowd on the third day. They were then told to be silent by the *Hierophant*, the high priest.

The *Hierophant* demanded: "Is there anyone present whose hands are not clean? Is there anyone with a voice that cannot be understood? Is there anyone who is guilty of murder or sacrilege, or who has surrendered to black magic? Let him withdraw." The lesser priests and priestesses then checked the credentials of the *mystae*, administered oaths of secrecy and collected their fees – the treasury of Eleusis became extremely prosperous in consequence. From this point, the *mystae* began to fast.

On the fifth day, ceremonies were held to honor Dionysus and Asclepios (the god of healing). On the sixth day, the *mystae* probably rested, while the *kykeon*, a sacred drink, was prepared probably from a mixture of malted

The mythical abduction of Persephone (Proserpine) by Hades, king of the underworld, has inspired generations of artists. This scene, entitled The Rape of Proserpine, *was painted by Charles de Lafosse.*

barley and the mint known as pennyroyal. The main part of the ceremonies began on the seventh day, when the *mystae* set out in procession for Eleusis, watched by the citizens of Athens. At the head of the procession, a statue of Dionysus as a young boy was hailed by shouts of "Iacchus! O Iacchus!" (Iacchus being another name for Dionysus). At the bridge over the Kephisos River, old women mocked the *mystae*, re-enacting part of the legend that recounts how an old woman cheered the grieving Demeter as she searched for Persephone. At this point, the *mystae* started drinking the sacred *kykeon*, which had by now begun to ferment.

At Eleusis, the secret rites were held during the Mystical Nights. They included a torchlight walk, symbolizing a journey through the Underworld, and perhaps a performance by the priests and priestesses of a mystical drama. The last night of the Mysteries represented the third and final stage of the ceremonies. It was known as *Epopteia*, a "seeing."

The darkness was dispelled by a brilliant fire, and the *Hierophant* chanted: "The Mistress has given birth to a holy boy, Brimo has given birth to Brimos, that is, the Strong One to the Strong One." This meant that the Goddess of the Dead, Persephone who was wife of Hades, had given birth to a son, a symbol of resurrection and rebirth. The climax may have been the display of a symbolic ear of corn, whose meaning was exalted in the minds of the initiates as a symbol of renewal and, hence, immortality. The ceremony had a profoundly ecstatic effect on the *mystae*. Perhaps it was a form of mass hypnotism aided by fasting, an intoxicating drink, and the bright light of the fire appearing out of the darkness. The Eleusinian Mysteries persisted until they were suppressed, along with other pagan rites, by the Roman Emperor Theodosius I in AD 395. By that time, many Greeks had already embraced the new religion, Christianity, which offered all believers, not just initiates at a particular place, the hope of eternal life.

Desert strikers

Doormen to the afterworld

FOR SOME 500 years the pharaohs of ancient Egypt were buried in the Valley of the Kings, interred in huge tombs carved out of the rock by gangs of workmen under their employ. Succeeding generations have frequently portrayed these workmen as slave labor, eking out a miserable existence under brutal exploitative conditions. But were the Egyptian workers really as down-trodden, and were the pharaohs always as cruel and harsh as they are so often made out to be?

In fact, according to written records found in the tombs, a group of these tomb workers (who were laborers rather than slaves) organized the first recorded strike and sit-in in history; using now commonplace methods, they actually obtained all they demanded.

But were they discontented because of truly unbearable conditions? Traditionally the Egyptian pharaohs were buried in the pyramids. But despite the ingenuity of the builders, tombs were frequently plundered. As a result the Pharaoh Thutmose I decided, some 3,500 years ago, to create an underground tomb for himself in what came to be known as the Valley of the Kings on the west bank of the Nile, accessible to the capital city of Thebes and yet concealed from

possible robbers. From that time on, throughout the period of the New Kingdom (1567–1085 BC) all the pharaohs were buried in that same Valley of the Kings.

The arduous work of burrowing into the softish rock, constructing tortuous passages, hidden doors, and false chambers, was carried out by a permanent company of skilled craftsmen who also decorated the interiors of the tombs. They were housed in a specially constructed village called Deir el-Medineh, on a barren site in the desert. (This village, known to the Egyptians as the "Place of Truth," still exists and the 20th-century visitor can walk about its streets and see what remains of its 70-odd mud-brick houses.) The houses were in lines facing directly onto the street, each single-story house consisting of four rooms, one behind the other. Although none had its own water supply, there was a public tank outside the main gate of the enclosure wall.

More detailed knowledge of the living conditions of the workmen stems from thousands of *ostraca* – fragments of limestone and pieces of broken pottery covered with hieratic writing (a shorthand form of hieroglyphs) and, in some cases, with drawings. They were discovered by

French archeologists excavating the site between 1922 and 1947. Among the information on these "pages" are detailed records of the workmen's names and duties, and the progress of work on various tombs. (On one *ostracon*, it was even noted that a workman was absent because he had had an argument with his wife.) Organized into two gangs, each under a foreman, his deputy, and the inevitable scribe, the men worked an eight-hour day for eight days at a stretch, during which period they slept in simple huts close to the tomb they were working on. Every ninth and 10th day was a holiday, when they went home to their wives and children in the village. There were also holidays on the great festivals of the principal gods.

Wages were paid in kind – wheat for bread and barley for beer – and were issued monthly from the royal treasury, and a few female slaves were allocated to each gang to grind the wheat into flour. Washermen were employed to do the laundry and potters to replace the vessels the workmen seem to have broken with such abandon. The men were also supplied with rations of fish, vegetables, wood for fuel, and body oil, which was in great demand by men working in hot dusty conditions. From time to time, the pharaoh himself would reward his skilled tomb workers with luxuries, such as meat, wine, salt, and Asiatic beer.

Isolated in the desert and unable to grow their own food, the villagers relied on the prompt delivery of supplies, normally on the 28th day of each month, but, occasionally, the laden donkeys failed to arrive on time. In the 29th year of the reign of Ramses III, no supplies had reached the village for several weeks, and eventually the workmen threw down their tools and made their way to the great mortuary temple of Ramses II. There they sat down in orderly fashion, refusing to go back to work until the pharaoh had been informed of their desperate plight. A temple scribe was consulted who, after hearing the men's case, ordered that the workers should be given a month's supply of grain from the supplies allotted to the official scribes. The men staged further strikes over the next few months, until the backlog of monthly payments had all been delivered.

As far as we know, no one was punished for daring to dictate terms to the pharaoh in this way. It seems from the evidence of these records that, far from being the ruthless despots portrayed in many Hollywood films, the rulers of ancient Egypt were less tyrannical – and the workers less docile – than we have sometimes been led to believe. These men did not work as "slave labor," but, of course, they were in a special position; they knew full well that their work was absolutely vital to the pharaoh, whose journey to the next world could not be made unless his tomb, his "house of eternity," was decorated, furnished, and completed in time to receive his earthly remains.

The Valley of the Kings, royal burial ground of the ancient Egyptian pharaohs, was situated within easy access of the country's capital, Thebes. Some of the excavated ruins of Thebes can be seen in the foreground of the photograph, with part of a modern village behind them.

The mysterious mound builders

A vanished people

One group of North American mound builders, known as the temple-mound Indians, etched intricate designs onto shells. The engraving on the conch shell (at top) would look like the drawing (above) if unrolled and laid flat.

WHEN EUROPEAN explorers ventured into North America in the 16th and 17th centuries, they found a magnificent wilderness totally untamed. Almost all of them commented that though they had seen signs of civilized life – groups of buildings, monuments, and artifacts in Mexico and other lands to the south – no civilization, ancient or modern, seemed to have left its mark on North America. The vast and fertile continent was peopled, and apparently always had been, by semi-nomadic Indians who lived off the land and created nothing durable.

In the 18th century, however, colonists reaching the Ohio and Mississippi river valleys in their drive to the West came upon strange mounds of earth overgrown with trees and shrubs. It was clear from the distinctive shapes of the mounds that they were man-made. And as more and more were found in a huge area of central midwestern and southern America, the early settlers began to look upon these mounds as evidence of some long-vanished and forgotten culture. Some of the mounds were low and fashioned into gigantic effigies of animals. Others were conical piles as much as 100 feet (30 meters) high, or flat-topped pyramids with their bases covering many acres. The settlers also discovered great areas enclosed by earthen walls, especially in the region of the Ohio River and its tributaries. For example, at what was to become Newark, Ohio, there were earthworks forming two large circles, a square, and an octagon, all interconnected by long avenues covering an area of four square miles (10 square kilometers). Could this perhaps have been the capital city of an ancient people? Certainly, the 18th-century European Americans were convinced that such elegant work could not have been done by either contemporary Indians or the ancestors of the Indians they knew.

This conviction was strengthened when, digging into many of the mounds, the settlers found a wealth of extraordinary artifacts: exquisite pottery; beautiful engraved stone pipes; intricate stone carvings; and effigies of birds and serpents in copper and mica. Since the mounds that contained such objects also contained human bones,

---

RICHLY STORED GRAVES AND TEMPLE PLATFORMS

The mound builders of North America were probably three separate groups of Indians who lived at different times and constructed earthworks of varying styles for different reasons. Archeologists speak of the pioneers of mound building as the Adena people (named after a site near Chillicothe, Ohio). The Adena people began to construct low mounds in the shape of animals and high burial mounds in about 1000 BC. By about 300 BC another group, the Hopewell people (again named for an Ohio mound site), were building huge enclosures of earthen walls surrounding burial mounds. The goods that the Hopewell people buried with their dead were far more elaborate and finely wrought than the Adena artifacts. They included copper breastplates, ornate headdresses, writhing serpents carved of stone and glittering mica, sculptured images made of polished stone, and highly decorated pottery. One Hopewell skeleton has been found bedecked with thousands of fresh-water pearls.

The Hopewell people were traders, who brought exotic materials for fashioning their goods from great distances. Obsidian, for example, came from the Rockies, mica from the Appalachians, conch shells from the Gulf Coast, copper from the Great Lakes region. There were also trading links with Florida, which may have brought in Mexican influences as well. But the Hopewell people seem to have made no attempt to establish physical domination over the peoples with whom they traded. They remained centered in the Midwest, exporting their fine goods in return for raw materials and peacefully living in small river-valley farmsteads. They continued to thrive and to build thousands of burial mounds until some time in the sixth century AD, when, with unrest spreading throughout North America, their trading network fell apart. Within two centuries the once great Hopewell people either became absorbed into simpler peoples or were vanquished by more aggressive tribes. And no more burial mounds were built.

The third and last group of mound builders, the Mississippian people seem to have begun their work soon after the end of the Hopewell period. Centered largely in the South, they specialized in what archeologists call temple mounds – truncated earthen pyramids on whose flat tops wooden temples were built. The temple-mound Indians, whose craft spread widely over America from about AD 900 onward, were even more gifted than the Hopewell people at making beautiful artifacts. They were still building their mounds when European explorers came to North America early in the 16th century, but by the time of the first settlers the custom had ended, and the religious rites that had engendered it were forgotten.

it was obvious that these were burial mounds, the focus of a society that, like the ancient Egyptians, sent its dead into the other world accompanied by rich hoards of ornaments. By contrast the animal-shaped mounds were evidently just what they seemed to be – animal effigies, probably created for religious reasons; while the large flat-topped mounds appeared to have been platforms for temples. The earthen walls, too, it was generally agreed, were more likely to have enclosed sacred spaces than to have been built around cities. As the archeologist Ephraim Squier remarked of the Newark site in 1848: "In entering the ancient avenue for the first time, the visitor does not fail to experience a sensation of awe, such as he might feel in passing the portals of an Egyptian temple." What seemed surprising was that this supposedly advanced society of the far-distant past had left no traces of its cities and highways.

Such finds seemed to indicate that the mound builders were a profoundly religious people of great skills but little appetite for the conquest that creates empires. But who were these people? When did their civilization flourish?

The mystery soon began to grip the public imagination and a number of intriguing theories sprang up: perhaps the builders were Vikings; or Asian Indians who had come to America by way of the Bering Strait (and had presumably gone back by the same route); or the 10 lost tribes of Israel; or Phoenicians from the ancient city of Tyre; or they were Welshmen. In other words, it was assumed that they were almost anything but American Indians.

In 1839 this assumption was contradicted by an eminent ethnologist, Samuel G. Morton, who produced evidence that the skulls taken from the mounds were identical in shape to the skulls of Indians who had recently died. The mound builders, he contended, were the forebears of present-day Indians. Few people, however, accepted this startling conclusion. Even archeologists like Squier found it hard to believe that the Indians could ever have possessed the skills of the mound builders. Finally, in 1881, Congress ordered the Smithsonian Institution's Bureau of Ethnology to mount a special investigation. A team led by Cyrus Thomas, an Illinois naturalist and archeologist who was himself a staunch supporter of the lost race theory, labored for seven years on the problem, unearthing and examining thousands of artifacts. Some of these, the team discovered, were undoubtedly of comparatively recent European origin, and Thomas was eventually forced to change his mind. A few of the mounds,

he reported, were "constructed and used subsequent to the occupation of the continent by Europeans, and some, at least, of the mound builders were therefore none other than known Indian tribes."

Ironically, the debate need never have happened. Back in the early 16th century, one European explorer, the Spaniard Hernando de Soto (1499–1542) saw some Indians building mounds in the southeastern part of what is now the United States and recorded the fact. When his observations came to light in our own century, they confirmed the theory that until about a century before Europeans actually settled in North America, certain Indian tribes were still constructing mounds for religious purposes, and that no lost civilization had ever existed. In demolishing the myth of the mound builders, America lost a glorious past, but dignity and respect were restored to the Indian people.

During the 19th century, teams of workmen led by archeologists excavated a number of man-made mounds in North America. One such excavation (shown at top) has been remembered in a vast panoramic painting of significant events in the history of the Mississippi valley area. Entitled Monumental Grandeur of the Mississippi Valley, *it was completed around 1850.*

Coiled over 1,254 feet (380 meters), the sinuous bends of the Great Serpent Mound in Ohio (above) show up clearly in an aerial photograph.

The Assyrian came down like a wolf on the fold

Stability with cruelty

"BLOODTHIRSTY GHOULS who showed no mercy to their victims"; "The Romans of the East – they brought stability to the ancient world"; "The rod of God's anger against the Hebrews." Opinions about the Assyrians certainly differ. Their reputation for cruelty to their subject peoples is unrivaled in history, a reputation founded on Biblical texts – the Hebrew prophets viewed the awesome Assyrians as God's punishment – and on their own war records and inscriptions. In the states that they conquered, the Assyrian kings erected victory *stele*, upright monuments carved with reliefs and inscriptions, celebrating their bloody victories. Such stele also served to remind the vanquished people of what would befall those tempted to rebel, and enhanced their self-propagated images of cruelty. It was a cruelty of which Assyrian kings were proud:

"I built a pillar against his city gate," boasted King Ashurnasirpal (who ruled from 883 to 859 BC) of his exploits against his enemies, "and I flayed all the chiefs who had revolted, and I covered the pillar with their skin. Some I walled up within the pillar, some I impaled upon the pillar on stakes, and others I bound to stakes round about the pillar. I made one pillar of the living and another of heads, and I bound their heads to tree trunks round about the city. Their young men and maidens I burned in the fire." Shalmaneser III (859 to 824 BC), who waged war for 31 years of his 35-year reign, crowed " I destroyed, I devastated, I burned with fire . . . 250 cities I destroyed . . . Awe-inspiring terror I poured out." Even allowing for slight exaggeration for propaganda purposes these accounts provide a horrifying insight into Assyrian terror tactics. In a cruel age the Assyrians surpassed their enemies and glorified their bestial acts. But who were the ferocious people who founded this empire of terror, and is their reputation justified?

The Assyrians were essentially a Semitic tribe of hardy, ruthless fighters centered on the town of Ashur on the west bank of the River Tigris. This commanding position over Mesopotamia brought them into conflict with neighboring tribes over trade routes and scarce resources, as they all squabbled over the remains of the once-powerful and now declining Babylonian empire. The Assyrian empire reached its greatest territorial extent in 671 BC when its powerful armies annexed Egypt and Syria. Its kings were bred to be tough, wrestling lions to prove their manhood, educated as both

---

THE ASSYRIAN ARMY

It was the Assyrian army that won the empire for Assyria. Hundreds of years before the Roman legions conquered the ancient world, the Assyrian army triumphed over its enemies through a combination of highly skilled troops, superior weapons, and strict discipline.

The original Assyrian soldiers were tough peasant farmers recruited from the rugged highlands of northern Iraq. An army of conscripts, they served Assyrian objectives well for over 300 years, but as the empire grew and its enemies became stronger, a permanent army was needed. King Tiglathpileser III (745–727 BC) enlisted fighters from the outlying provinces of the empire – horsemen from Iran, camel drivers from Arabia and infantrymen from Anatolia and Syria – to form a fulltime standing army. Citizens of Assyria were still liable to be conscripted, but they could send slaves to fight in their place. Later the army relied on mercenaries from hostile tribes who were attracted by the promise of rich booty. These elements weakened the army and contributed to its eventual defeat.

We have few exact figures for the number of soldiers engaged in battle – King Ashurnasirpal mentioned 50,000 at one battle, and Shalmaneser III claimed to have 120,000 men in the field in the battle of Qarqar in 853 BC. What is obvious from the carved reliefs in the royal palaces depicting the army is the importance of the engineer corps, invaluable for besieging hostile fortified towns. These men filled in moats, constructed earthworks, dug tunnels, and used enormous battering rams to breach gates or walls. The vital infantry section consisted of archers and slingers, who had no defensive weapons, and lancers who were protected by a coat of mail and a tall shield. Cavalrymen, armed with a small bow or a long spear, initially rode bareback, but later their horses were protected by armor. Fast, light, two-wheeled chariots were used, enabling the Assyrians to outmaneuver their opponents. The army was followed on its long treks by male and female servants and many supply wagons.

Such records as we have are vague as to the organization of the army, although we do know the names and ranks of the officers. Assyrian war records are more concerned with recording victories than with detailing the mundane life of the common soldier.

able warriors and administrators. They treated the petty states surrounding their homeland as their private hunting ground, and grew rich on the booty pillaged. Local chieftains would tremble at the approach of the mighty army, descending on them like a whirlwind from the desert, and hastened to pay the king tribute and swear eternal allegiance. Once they had done this, they had nothing to fear, but woe betide the unfortunate prince who did not keep his promises. A holocaust of revenge was launched against the offender.

But were the Assyrians merely blood-seeking barbarians anxious only to pillage and kill in the name of Ashur, their god? An examination of their empire reveals them to be skilled in many fields. An efficient system of tribute in money and men kept the empire rich and safe. Administration was in the hands of extremely competent local governors handpicked by the king. The Assyrians constructed magnificent cities–Nineveh, which housed a library stocked with over 20,000 cuneiform tablets, Khorsabad, and Kalah, all providing us with numerous examples of their fine art. Assyrian reliefs are noteworthy for their realism–their artists could exquisitely capture the pathos of a wounded beast, for example. And their skills in constructing aqueducts and devising new methods of metal-casting were unsurpassed at the time.

But life was by no means pleasant for the citizens of Assyria, especially if they fell foul of the law. "If a man has caught a man with his wife and has then brought a charge against him and proved it against him, both of them shall be put to death; there is no guilt in this." If a woman gave shelter to a wife running away from her husband, both of them were liable to have their ears cut off. However, "leaving aside the penalties relating to a married woman which are inscribed on the tablet, a man may flog his wife, pull out her hair, split and injure her ears. There is no legal guilt in it." A felon in Assyria was either executed, flayed, blinded, fettered, enslaved or thrown into prison. We do not know whether these laws were carried out to the letter, although there are mentions in Assyrian records of the court receiving a payment of silver and then waiving further punishment, much in the same way that today some offenses are punished by either a stay in prison or the payment of a fine. Assyrian citizens were not often put into prison: they were put to work as slaves.

Such was the nature of Assyrian society–one built on force and sustained by fear. But it is too easy to be blinded to the significance of the Assyrian empire by the violent propaganda of its kings. Out of their fractious, quarreling world they built and maintained an empire which lasted for over 300 years until it was brought down by the rival power of the Medes and the Persians to the east. The Assyrians brought stability to the ancient world, and it says much for their art and technology that such achievements have outlived their formidable reputation as the most cruel people in history.

This reconstruction of the royal palace at the Assyrian capital of Kalah (modern Nimrud) gives some idea of the magnificence of Assyrian architecture at the height of the empire.

800 BC–AD 500

THE CLASSICAL WORLD

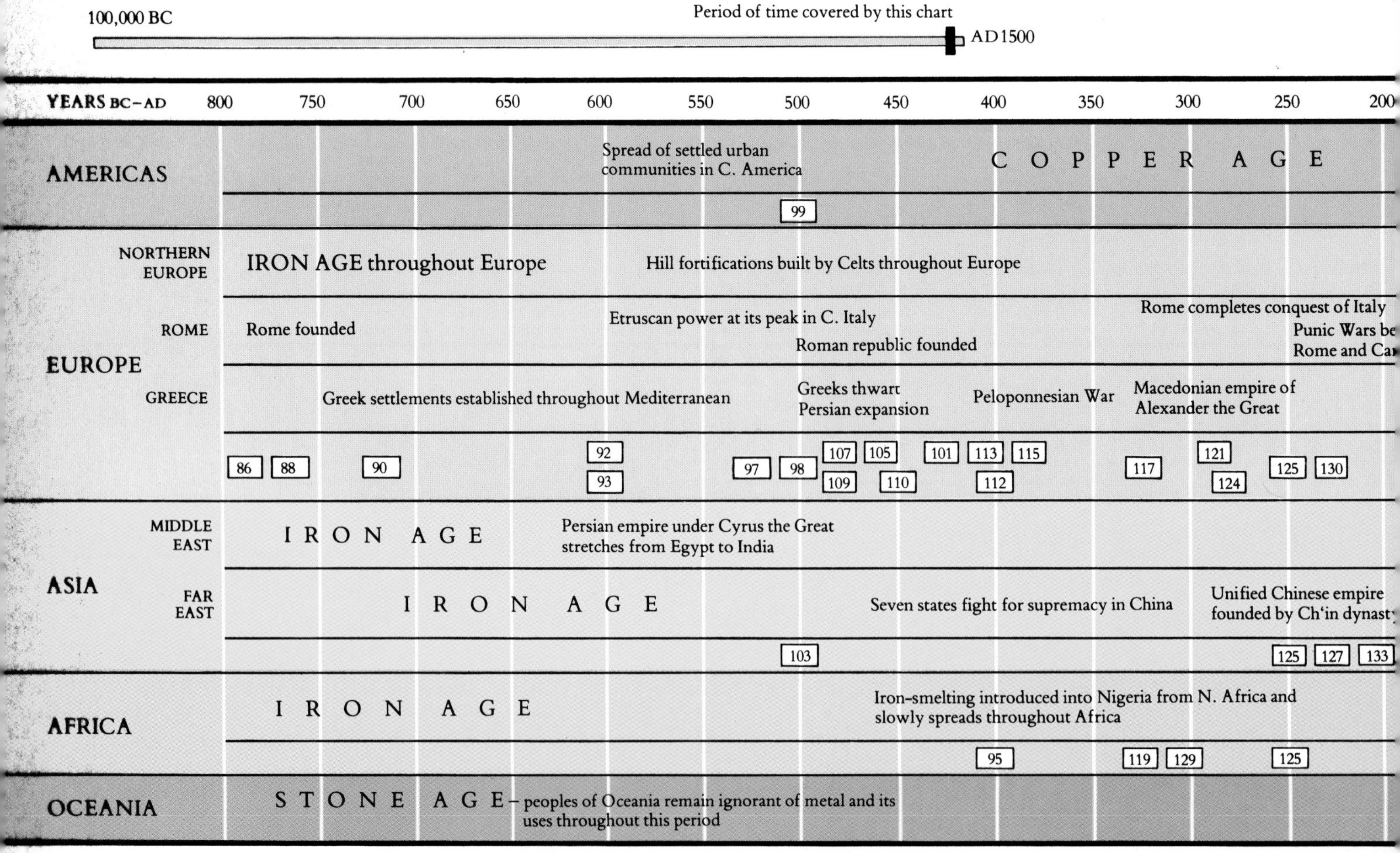

Period of time covered by this chart

100,000 BC

AD 1500

YEARS BC–AD	800	750	700	650	600	550	500	450	400	350	300	250	200

AMERICAS — Spread of settled urban communities in C. America   C O P P E R   A G E

99

EUROPE

NORTHERN EUROPE — IRON AGE throughout Europe   Hill fortifications built by Celts throughout Europe

ROME — Rome founded   Etruscan power at its peak in C. Italy   Roman republic founded   Rome completes conquest of Italy   Punic Wars be Rome and Ca

GREECE — Greek settlements established throughout Mediterranean   Greeks thwart Persian expansion   Peloponnesian War   Macedonian empire of Alexander the Great

86 88 90 92 93 97 98 107 105 109 110 101 113 112 115 121 117 124 125 130

ASIA

MIDDLE EAST — I R O N   A G E   Persian empire under Cyrus the Great stretches from Egypt to India

FAR EAST — I R O N   A G E   Seven states fight for supremacy in China   Unified Chinese empire founded by Ch'in dynast

103 125 127 133

AFRICA — I R O N   A G E   Iron-smelting introduced into Nigeria from N. Africa and slowly spreads throughout Africa

95 119 129 125

OCEANIA — S T O N E   A G E — peoples of Oceania remain ignorant of metal and its uses throughout this period

---

Shown in the chart above are page references to each article appearing in this section of the book. The subject of each article is listed here.

86 Homer writes *Iliad* and *Odyssey*?
88 First Olympic Games run in Greece
90 Vestal Virgins cult organized in Rome
92 Delphic oracle housed in temple to Apollo

93 The mysterious Etruscans living in Italy
95 Egyptians worshiping cats
97 Samos tunnel constructed
98 Greek city-state of Sparta flourishing
99 S. American goldsmiths at work
101 Women in Greece profit from Peloponnesian War
103 Tattooed man buried in Siberian grave
105 Silver from Laurium helps Greeks to defeat Persian fleet

107 Herodotus, the "father of history," born in Halicarnassus, Asia Minor
109 Greek theatre playing to packed houses
110 Empedocles names the four elements
112 Alcibiades accused of mutilating statues in Athens
113 "Symposium" held at Athens house of Agarthon
115 Aristotle born in Greece

117 Philip II of Macedon dies in Vergina
119 Foundation of library in Alexandria
121 Iron Age farming in Britain
124 Archimedes born in Syracuse, Sicily
125 List of "Seven Wonders of the World" first compiled
127 Terracotta army guards the tomb of Chinese emperor Ch'in Shin-huang-ti
129 Carthaginians sacrifice their children
130 Hannibal crosses the Alps

Because the modern world, Oriental as well as Occidental, has been profoundly influenced by the cultural and political achievements of classical Greece and Rome, we sometimes tend to over-stress their importance and to neglect the history of other societies that flourished during the centuries from, roughly, 800 BC to AD 500. In fact, as the variety of subject matter dealt with in this section indicates, the classical world extended over a far wider area than just that of the Mediterranean basin. The Americas, the islands of the Pacific, and much of Africa south of Egypt did indeed remain untouched by the forward thrust of Eurasian civilization. By the beginning of the Christian era, however, with the Roman empire at its height, there were thriving societies in contact with one another from Japan and China in the Far East, across Asia through Persia in the south, and onward through all Europe to the British Isles.

No period of history, not even our own, has been more fruitful than the classical period. In the dozen or so centuries that elapsed between the rise of the Greek city-states and the break-up of Rome's European empire, literary, artistic, philosophical, and scientific ideas of enormous consequence sprang from the lively minds of Eastern and Western peoples alike. And these were the centuries, too, that saw the swift spread of the great religions – Buddhism, Judaism, Christianity – that have shaped the thinking of much of mankind.

150	100	50	0	50	100	150	200	250	300	350	400	450	500

Mayan civilization in C. America

N. America reverts to STONE AGE
S. America in BRONZE AGE

Moche Indian civilization in Peru

176

First urban centers built by Romans

Nomadic tribes from Asia threaten Roman empire

Angles and Saxons occupy Britain after Romans withdraw

Roman empire founded

Empire at its greatest extent
Barbarian invasions threaten security of empire

Christianity spreads throughout empire
Empire split into two
Destruction of empire in the West

Greece conquered by Rome

140 135   146 142   186   156 160 165 169   158   138   183   189   191
      150   152   148 162 166 172   184

Roman empire expands in Middle East

Sassanid empire rules Persia and Mesopotamia

Han dynasty rules China

Unification of Japan under first emperor

152 154   165 174   178   187

Romans occupy Egypt

Expansion of kingdom of Axum in Ethiopia

143 145   180   182

Gradual settlement of eastern Polynesia

133 Chess first played in China?
135 Farming manual written by Cato
138 "Peutinger" map aids Roman tourists
140 Suppression of Bacchanalian orgies by Roman senate
142 Antikythera "computer" made
143 Cleopatra commits suicide
145 Colossus of Thebes starts to talk
146 Tollund Man buried in Denmark
148 Romans fight Druids on Mona, Wales

150 Danebury hillfort built
152 Roman trading contracts with India flourishing
154 Josephus born in Jerusalem
156 Pliny loses count of number of baths in Rome
158 Leisure center thriving in Bath
160 Boudica defeated by Romans
162 Emperor Nero blamed for fire of Rome

165 Treasure of Temple of Jerusalem moved to Rome
166 Eruption of Vesuvius buries Pompeii
169 Colosseum officially opened in Rome
172 Mithraic religion spreading throughout Roman empire
174 Paper invented in China
176 Moche Indians making pots
178 Death of Sujin, first Japanese emperor?

180 Ptolemy studies the stars
182 Roman brothers take Christianity to Ethiopia
183 Emperor Diocletian outlaws inflation
184 Constantine sees vision in the sky
186 Tiberius cares for his troops
187 Simeon Stylites takes up residence on a pillar in Syria
189 Rome sacked by Alaric the Goth
191 Attila the Hun dies in Italy

Who was – or were – Homer?

We do not even know his real name

THE *ILIAD* AND *ODYSSEY*, regarded as incomparably great literature ever since they were first written down (probably in the eighth century BC), are universally attributed to a Greek poet called Homer. We today call him Homer because the ancient Greeks did, but we are not sure that the epics are the work of a single poet, or that he was, or they were, named Homer. A seventh- or sixth-century-BC poem refers to a "blind man living in Chios" (an Aegean island). This unverified notion of blind genius has held the literary imagination for nearly 3,000 years.

Our only reliable source of information about the poet is the poems, where clues are scanty. We can be fairly certain, though, that Homer was what the ancient Greeks called a "singer" – a public performer of *oral* poetry. The reason we are so sure of this is that the Greeks as a people were actually illiterate until just before Homer's time; they did not have an alphabet – and consequently could not write things down – until they acquired one from the Phoenicians, an eastern

Mediterranean people with whom they traded, toward the middle of the eighth century BC. Before Homer's day, stories could be passed along only orally, and their poetic form helped "singers" to memorize them. But singers did not merely recite poems by rote. When asked to perform at feasts or public ceremonies, they would pluck a story out of their repertory and *re-create* it on the spot.

The subject matter of the song-story gave each performer his framework and guidelines. There would also be a regular metrical pattern, along with repetition of certain word-combinations. But beyond these fixed, standardized elements, more talented singers could improvise, making changes from one performance to another. With each singer modifying a given poem in his own way, the poem would grow and evolve through the years. As finally written down, the *Iliad* and *Odyssey* must surely have been end-products of this snowballing process. Scholars agree that both poems contain all the ingredients of orally transmitted poetry:

The 10-year war between the Greeks and the Trojans, vividly described in Homer's Iliad, *ended with the infiltration of Troy by Greek soldiers, hidden in a wooden horse. The Greeks emerged from the horse under cover of darkness, opened the city gates, and set fire to Troy. This painting by Giovanni Tiepolo shows the Trojans dragging the horse through the city streets.*

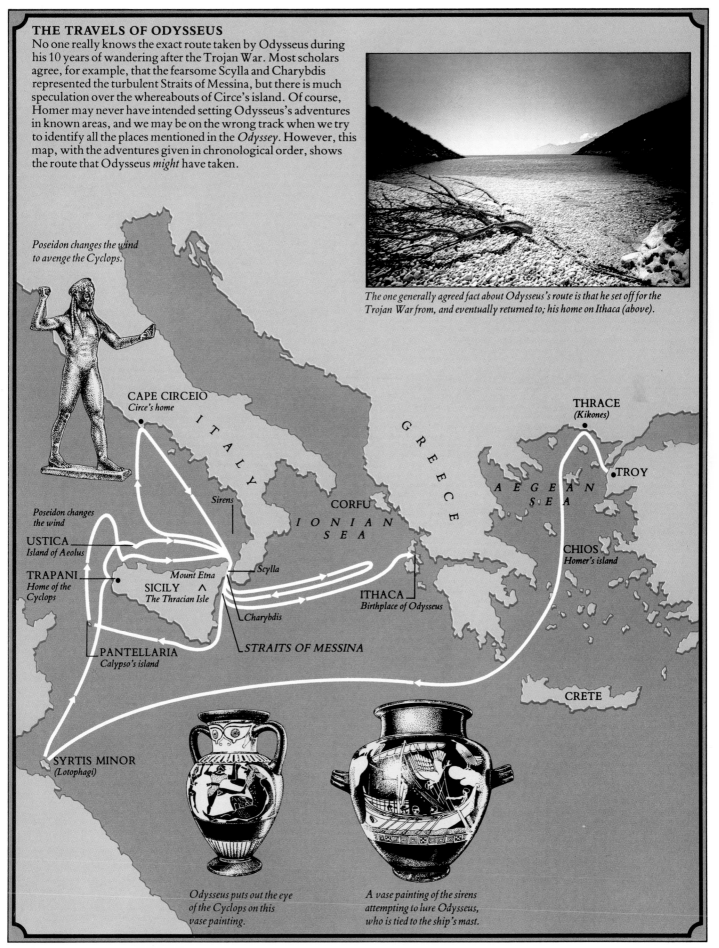

THE TRAVELS OF ODYSSEUS

No one really knows the exact route taken by Odysseus during his 10 years of wandering after the Trojan War. Most scholars agree, for example, that the fearsome Scylla and Charybdis represented the turbulent Straits of Messina, but there is much speculation over the whereabouts of Circe's island. Of course, Homer may never have intended setting Odysseus's adventures in known areas, and we may be on the wrong track when we try to identify all the places mentioned in the *Odyssey*. However, this map, with the adventures given in chronological order, shows the route that Odysseus *might* have taken.

The one generally agreed fact about Odysseus's route is that he set off for the Trojan War from, and eventually returned to; his home on Ithaca (above).

Poseidon changes the wind to avenge the Cyclops.

CAPE CIRCEIO
Circe's home

THRACE
(Kikones)

TROY

ITALY

G R E E C E

CORFU

Sirens

*I O N I A N
S E A*

*A E G E A N
S E A*

CHIOS
Homer's island

*Poseidon changes
the wind*

USTICA
Island of Aeolus

Scylla

TRAPANI
*Home of the
Cyclops*

Mount Etna

SICILY ∧
The Thracian Isle

ITHACA
Birthplace of Odysseus

Charybdis

PANTELLARIA
Calypso's island

STRAITS OF MESSINA

CRETE

SYRTIS MINOR
(Lotophagi)

Odysseus puts out the eye of the Cyclops on this vase painting.

A vase painting of the sirens attempting to lure Odysseus, who is tied to the ship's mast.

the constant repetition of formalized descriptive phrases and speech patterns, the use of traditional myths and legends, plenty of brisk action, and so on. Heroic tales about the Trojan War and the wanderings of Odysseus undoubtedly appealed to early Greek singers and their audiences. And some episodes in the Homeric epics read as though they might once have been short poems in their own right. Moreover, some incidents include details that seem to date from earlier times than others – a fact which suggests that there were several "contributors" over a long period of time.

What probably happened, then, is that a hugely gifted singer appeared on the scene just when the acquisition of an alphabet made writing possible. Gathering up a mass of accumulated oral material, he used it as bricks and mortar for building two enormously rich epics; he then either wrote them down himself or, perhaps, dictated them to a scribe.

This is a pretty safe assumption about the genesis and composition of the poems. It remains possible, though, that there were two "Homers." Apart from the fact that some of the language of the *Odyssey* appears to belong to a later period than that of the *Iliad*, the epics differ widely in theme and tone. The *Iliad*, for example, focuses on the events of a few days and emphasizes martial deeds, whereas the *Odyssey* covers a 10-year period and specializes in magic and fantasy. Partly because the *Odyssey* is so much less concerned with brutal warfare, one famous commentator on the work – the 19th-century English novelist Samuel Butler – went so far as to argue that the author of the *Odyssey* was, in fact, not a man but a woman!

At any rate, the cumulative evolutionary process might well have continued after the initial writing down of the poems, with later singers adding new elements to the written epics (of which no manuscript earlier than the third century BC survives). But stylistic similarities between the poems strongly suggest that, at some point in the construction, a single unifying force played a major creative part. Since we are unlikely to discover any more than that, we may as well continue to call that force Homer.

Professionalism in ancient Greece

All in the games

Javelin throwing is one of the 10 parts of the traditional decathlon event, which has been a highlight of the Olympic Games for over 2,000 years.

HIS CHEST still heaving from his exertions, the victorious young athlete stood waiting, his naked body gleaming with oil and sweat under the hot sun. He was about to receive a wreath of olive leaves for having won an Olympic Games race against the finest athletes of the day. But his smile of triumph was not just for the coveted wreath. Still to come were a procession and feast in his home town, verses in his honor by a great poet, and – the *real* prize – security for life in the form of a pension (which would be discreetly recorded in the municipal accounts as "rations") which could be as much as 100 times the annual rate of pay for a Roman soldier at the time. In other words, a well-paying professionalism in sports is not a 20th-century invention. The athletes who competed in the Olympics in ancient Greece were professionals; they were on the "games circuit," much as modern tennis stars are on the tennis circuit.

It had not begun that way. The Olympic Games, traditionally believed to have started in 776 BC, were the oldest of four major competitions in the Greek world – the Pythian, held at Delphi every four years, and the Nemean at Nemea and Isthmian near Corinth, both of which were biennial. All four sets of games originated as part of religious festivals, and the only prizes awarded were wreaths of leaves. The Olympic games were of supreme importance; so much so that years were reckoned in Olympiads (the four-year periods between games), and to win a wreath there was an unparalleled honor. Indirect material gains became substantial, though, especially since there was a good deal of cash on offer at less exalted competitions that grew up and were sponsored by more than 300 Greek towns and villages, and athletes renowned for their victories at major games could profit by doing the rounds.

When the Olympics began, the contestants were all amateurs, mostly wealthy aristocrats with enough time and money to train properly. The Greeks were keen on athletic prowess, partly because it fitted men for war but also because they believed it developed *arete*, a word that means "excellence, valor, virtue," and gymnastic exercises formed part of the basic education of every Greek boy. In time, however, people let

Olympia, a peaceful valley in the Peloponnesus, was a sacred place dedicated to the worship of Zeus, father of the gods, and it was in his honor that the Olympic Games were founded, according to tradition, in 776 BC. In fact, Olympia may have been the site of some sort of ritualistic sports event for as much as 500 years before the traditional founding date; but the Greeks always reckoned the Olympiads (four-year-long periods between games) as beginning in 776, when the first recorded winner, a man named Coroebus, won the 200-meter (218 yards) sprint.

At first the sprint was the only race, but other events were added over the next two centuries, including at one time a musical contest for trumpeters. By the middle of the sixth century BC, the games usually included chariot and horse races (traditional opening events); the pentathlon (five related contests: discus, standing long jump, javelin, 200-meter sprint, wrestling); three events for teenage boys (200-meter race, wrestling, boxing); three races for men (200, 400, and 4,800 meters); men's wrestling and boxing; and the pankration (a-no-holds-barred event combining elements of judo, boxing, and wrestling, in which only biting and strangling were forbidden).

Gradually through the centuries, pure sportsmanship gave way to professionalism, and honest professionalism to corruption. In about AD 50, nearly two centuries after Greece had become a province of Rome, the first athletes' union, or professional association, was formed. In AD 67 the vainglorious Roman Emperor Nero took part in the Olympics and surprised nobody by winning several special events. By the end of the fourth century AD the games had fallen into such disrepute that the Emperor Theodosius ordered them halted. They were not revived until 1896, when the modern Olympics began.

For most of their long history, the Olympic Games were a male stronghold. All contestants performed entirely naked and barefoot. No women were allowed to take part or even watch. But in 404 BC, one woman beat the ban. She was the mother of Pisidorus, a boy boxer who had been trained by his father. When the father died, his widow took over the training and, dressed like a man, came to the stadium to watch her son compete in a boxing bout.

Unfortunately, when Pisidorus won, she jumped over the barrier to congratulate him, the masculine clothing slipped, and she exposed herself. Because her father, brothers, and son were all Olympic winners, she was not penalized, but to forestall further such incidents it was decreed that thenceforth trainers must also be naked. It was not until late in the Roman period of the games that women were made welcome, first as spectators, then as participants. By that time total nakedness was no longer acceptable.

The Olympic Games are held every four years at a site chosen by the International Olympic Committee. The original site was Olympia in Greece (above left); in 1976 the games were held in Montreal (above).

their enthusiasm for physical achievement run away with them. A large body of professional athletes grew up – men so over-trained in their own particular sport, such as boxing or running, that they became unfitted for any other vigorous activity, such as a military campaign. Because it was considered good for a town's image to have successful athletes, public funds were devoted to their training and upkeep, and it was no longer just the aristocracy who competed in the great games. In fact, true amateurs were dubbed *idiotai*, meaning "laymen" or "amateurs," in the pejorative sense in which we today sometimes use the word.

The only group of competitors who retained their amateur status throughout the long history of the Olympic Games were the owners of horses that took part in equestrian events. As in modern racing, it was the owners (often well-off people) who were awarded the prizes won for them by professional charioteers or jockeys. As the numbers of professional participants increased, various forms of corruption crept in. The first recorded case of bribery happened in the 98th Olympics in 388 BC, when a boxer, Eupolus of Thessaly, paid three opponents to throw their fights. Eupolus was found out and fined, but corruption was there to stay. Money from accumulated fines was used for erecting a row of statues of Zeus, the god of the games, near the entrance of the Olympic stadium.

The greatest of Greek gods could not bring pure sportsmanship back to the games, though. After Greece came under Roman rule in 146 BC, the sacred element gradually diminished, and the Olympic Games became occasions for little more than personal gain and popular entertainment. Only one vestige of their once high principles remained to the end: The formal prize was never more than a wreath of wild olive.

Were the Vestal Virgins pure?

And what if they weren't?

IN 471 BC, Urbinia, one of Rome's highly revered Vestal Virgins, was brought to trial to answer terrible charges made by a slave that she had broken her vows of chastity and had performed holy rites while no longer a virgin. According to the Greek writer Plutarch, one of the two men accused with her committed suicide, while the other was beaten and executed. An even worse fate awaited Urbinia. After being found guilty and whipped with rods, she was bound securely and driven in a covered litter through the silent streets of a sorrowing Rome to a field beside the Colline Gate. There she was buried alive in a subterranean tomb, with only enough food and water to last her for 30 days, and left to die.

To comprehend such a barbarous execution, one must understand the significance and special status of the Vestal Virgins in Roman society. The origin of the Vestal Virgins as an organized cult can be traced back to about 715 BC during the reign of Numa Pompilius, the second King of Rome. It lasted more than 1,000 years and was finally suppressed by the Emperor Theodosius in AD 394, although its influence had been declining since AD 313 when the Roman Emperor Constantine legally recognized Christianity.

At the time of Urbinia, there were six Vestal Virgins who served Vesta, the Roman goddess of the hearth. Living together in what was known as the Vestal College, the Vestal Virgins performed an important religious role because they guarded the perpetual fire that burned in her temple – an evocation of prehistoric times when fire was difficult to procure. Fire was central to the worship of Vesta. Because of its purity and sterility, the Romans believed that it could be tended only by virgins.

The appointment of a Vestal Virgin occurred whenever there was a vacancy in the Vestal College, something that happened on average once every five years. The Pontifex Maximus or the chief priest chose 20 candidates, usually daughters of patrician families, between the ages of six and 10, one of these then being selected by lot. The chosen child entered the Vestal College, passing out of her father's control and under the control of the Pontifex Maximus. With little appreciation of the trials and temptations that lay ahead, the child was committed to 30 years of virginity and holy service. Afterward, she was theoretically free to live a normal life and marry although in practice few Vestal Virgins did so; there was a superstition that such marriages were never happy and so most preferred to remain virgins.

The Vestal Virgins lived in the Atrium Vestae on the southeast of the Roman Forum. They could leave it only if they were sick. For at least eight hours every day, each Virgin had the responsibility of keeping alight the sacred fire in Vesta's temple. The Vestals had other duties too. They offered prayers for the public, carried water from a sacred spring, and prepared food for ritual purposes. They performed many religious functions at such events as agricultural festivals and, paradoxically, took part in fertility rites. Their sanctity was such that they were trusted to guard wills, treaties, and other important documents, and treasure. Wills of emperors were lodged with them – Julius Caesar's was in their custody for six months. This service was probably voluntary and was regarded as a compliment to them.

The Vestal Virgins enjoyed many honors and privileges not accorded to other Roman women.

They traveled in ornate chariots and even such high-ranking men as consuls and praetors (annually elected magistrates) made way for them. If they met a person being led to execution, they had the power to grant a pardon. They were also exempt from taking an oath when giving evidence in court. And they were allocated splendid seats in the front row at gladiatorial games although women were usually given the uppermost – that is, the worst – seats in the stadium. The Vestals were women of property because the government endowed them with a large amount of money when they joined the cult. And because they had direct access to the head of government, they could exert considerable political influence.

At the same time, Vestal Virgins were subject to awesome disciplines. The Pontifex Maximus could punish them severely for carelessness. The punishment for letting the fire go out was a scourging. And the execution by burial for breaking vows of virginity was a reflection of the Roman view that the purity of the Vestal Virgins was a token and guarantee of the welfare of Rome itself.

However, fewer than 20 Vestals were incarcerated in the 1,000-year-long history of the order, partly because the severity of the penalty was a potent deterrent. And some of these gruesome sentences may have been unjust, arising from the Roman superstition that military and other disasters may have been caused by misconduct among the revered Vestal Virgins.

THOSE WHO ESCAPED

Marvelous, if improbable, stories were told about charges against Vestal Virgins that were proved false. One Vestal, named Aemilia, was accused of letting the sacred fire go out. Beseeching Vesta to come to her aid, she threw a strip of her linen robe on the cold embers. The linen burst into flame, a miracle that proved her innocence beyond doubt.

Tuccia, another Vestal Virgin falsely accused of losing her virginity, carried a sieve filled with water through the streets and did not spill a drop. All charges against her were immediately thrown out. A number of writers, including Saint Augustine, refer to Tuccia's miracle and also to that of Claudia, the most spectacular one on record. Claudia was also accused of losing her virginity. Fearing she would be condemned, she tied her girdle to the prow of a ship grounded in the Tiber River. She prayed to Vesta, asking her to command the ship to move, proving that she was a virgin; when she pulled the girdle, the ship followed.

The Vestal Virgins were dedicated to the worship of Vesta, the Roman goddess of the hearth and household. Although this 19th-century painting by the French artist Hector Leroux shows a large number of Vestals gathered together in the temple, we now know that there were never more than six at one time.

The Delphic oracle
Prophecy at the center of the world

IN ANCIENT Greece, people did nothing important without first asking the advice of the gods. Greece had many oracles where the gods could be consulted, but the most famous and influential of them all was the one at Delphi, on the southern slopes of Mount Parnassus, site of Apollo's temple. Delphi was so highly esteemed by the Greeks that they regarded it as the very center of the world, the actual central spot being marked by an *omphalos*, or navel stone, in the Temple of Apollo.

Delphi was never a large place, compared with the great city-states of Athens and Sparta, but its influence and power were enormous. The site of Delphi has been continuously occupied for more than 3,300 years, and it appears to have been a religious center from early times. It was first dedicated to the worship of the Earth goddess Ge, or Gaea. According to legend, Apollo, the Sun god, killed Python, a fierce serpent that guarded Ge's shrine, and took over the shrine for himself. Apollo was the son of Zeus, and was regarded as his mouthpiece.

The Delphic oracle was housed in Apollo's temple, and the oracular messages were spoken

The oracle at Delphi was the most famous of all the Greek oracles. This 19th-century artist's impression shows a man consulting the Pythia, or priestess, who is seated on the customary gold tripod with a bowl-shaped seat, said to represent the throne of Apollo.

by a priestess known as the Pythia. The Pythia was the only female oracle in Greece, a fact which suggests that she represented a continuation of the ancient worship of the Earth goddess Ge. How each Pythia was chosen is not known, except that she was an ordinary peasant woman with no special qualifications. The Roman historian Diodorus Siculus reported that the original Pythias were young virgins. However, at one time a lecherous questioner of the oracle had carried off and raped one of them, and thereafter women over the age of 50 were selected. Married women were not excluded, but they had to leave their husbands if they were appointed.

People often consulted the Delphic oracle on matters of religion. The answers given usually seemed to suit the religious observances of the particular place from which the questioner came. And because many questioners wanted to know whether a certain course of action was right or wrong, the oracle was able to give a strong lead on moral issues. The Greek writer Herodotus recorded that a man named Glaucus once asked the oracle whether he could appropriate some money and swear that he never had it. The oracle replied that he would die eventually whether he broke his word or not, but that terrible things would happen to the family of a man who did such a thing. The prophecy was fulfilled. Glaucus's family died out.

Unbelievers also met with problems. A skeptical Greek, Daphnitas, asked whether he would find his horse, although in reality he did not own one. The oracle's reply was: "You will find your horse, but will be thrown from it." Daphnitas boasted of how he had exposed the oracle. But one day, after insulting the king, he was executed by being thrown from a cliff commonly known as "the Horse."

Another story, probably embroidered by the Delphic priests, told how Croesus, the wealthy King of Lydia in Asia Minor, sent envoys to several oracles. The envoys were instructed to ask, on the 100th day after their departure, what the king was doing at that time. In this way, he hoped to assess their quality. Delphi was the only oracle to give the correct answer, namely that Croesus was stewing lamb and turtle in a bronze caldron. Croesus made some extremely valuable gifts to Delphi, and later asked the oracle whether he should attack the Persian empire. The reply was: "If Croesus crosses the

Halys River, he will destroy a great kingdom." Accordingly Croesus confidently went to war. However, the Persians defeated him and overran Lydia and the Greek settlements in Asia Minor. The red-faced Delphic priests pointed out that the prophecy could be taken two ways, and thereafter were careful to make the prophecies even more ambiguous.

The Greek historian Plutarch recorded that in the early days of the shrine, the oracle was available for consultation on one day a year. This was supposedly Apollo's birthday, when the god entered a mortal body. According to tradition, pressure of business eventually brought Apollo to Earth once a month – though he was absent during the three winter months. Prophecy days lasted from dawn to dusk and Plutarch recorded that, at its busiest, there were two Pythias working shifts, with a third, probably a trainee, as back-up. Preparations began at dawn when the Pythia took a ritual bath to purify herself. The chief male priest, the Prophetes, and his assistants were also expected to undergo a similar purification ceremony.

Those wanting to question the oracle took their places in line, the order being decided partly by rank and partly by drawing lots. The questioner had to sprinkle himself or herself with holy water and pay a large fee. He did this by buying a holy cake which he offered on an altar outside the shrine. Private enquirers paid much less than those who represented one of the city-states. The worshiper also had to sacrifice a sheep or goat on another altar. Finally he entered the inner sanctuary of the shrine to put his question to the oracle.

There, the Pythia was seated on an ornate tripod, a three-legged bowl. The Pythia was in a trance, which was probably self-induced. One theory suggested that the trance was caused by chewing roasted laurel leaves, but a modern scholar who tried this experienced nothing. Another theory was that the trance was the result of breathing in volcanic fumes that rose through a crack in the rock under the shrine, but geologists have found no source for such fumes. However her condition was induced, the Pythia chanted and shouted mostly meaningless utterances – to the layman. The Prophetes interpreted the raving and then gave the answer to the questioner in verse or in prose. Some of the verses were such doggerel that educated Greeks wondered how Apollo could stoop to such appalling poetry.

No one knows how much the final answers were based on the sounds made by the Pythia, or whether they were entirely the work of the priests. For the most part, they seem to have been either capable of several meanings or couched in such general terms that they could fit various situations. However, Greek writers record that, although some prophecies were disastrously wide of the mark, many others came true. The success of the oracle was that between the eighth and fifth centuries BC especially, it exerted great moral, political, and economic influence. Its utterances often determined questions of war and peace, trade, and the founding of colonies. The oracle's power declined in later Greek and in Roman times, and the Christian Emperor Theodosius finally closed the shrine at Delphi in AD 390.

The elusive Etruscans

Forerunners of the Romans

THE WORLD'S museums are well stocked with artifacts created by the Etruscans, the people of Etruria (in the northern and western parts of the Italian peninsula) who flourished for several centuries before the third century BC, when their culture was obliterated by the rising power of Rome. Scores of Etruscan burial grounds throughout Italy have yielded up superb examples of the art and craftsmanship of this once-rich nation – and yet the Etruscans remain among the most mysterious of lost civilizations. Why? Why do we know so much more about the structure and functioning of ancient Egyptian society, for instance, than we do about the Etruscans, with whom the Egyptians had trading relations?

One essential element in the complex answer to that question is that nobody has yet found an Etruscan Rosetta Stone. Until the early 19th century the literature of ancient Egypt was also a closed book because scholars were unable to interpret Egyptian hieroglyphics. The Stone, found near the Rosetta mouth of the Nile River, contained a long inscription carved in hieroglyphics along with a translation in Greek; and when, in 1822, the French linguist Jean

A bronze table candelabrum – an example of highly skilled Etruscan metalwork.

The two gold tablets inscribed in Etruscan, found with another inscribed in Punic at the temple site of Pyrgi, are among the few written Etruscan documents ever found. The tablet shown above contains the longer of the Etruscan inscriptions. The holes around the edges are marks for nails probably used to fix the tablet to the temple door.

Etruscan tomb paintings have provided much valuable information about this ancient people. Entertainers at a banquet are shown in this tomb painting from the Etruscan city of Tarquinia.

François Champollion published his discovery of the direct relationship between the easily readable Greek text and hieroglyphics, it became possible for scholars everywhere to unravel the mysteries of ancient Egypt's written language.

No Etruscan literature as such has been discovered, but we have a large number of inscriptions, most of which are funerary – simple identifications, for the most part, of those commemorated – and scholars are now able to read and understand a number of words, which are written in an alphabet that resembles Greek lettering. But nobody understands much about the structure and syntax of the language, which seems unrelated to Greek or Latin. If scholars could only find the key to the Etruscan language, the scarce amount of written material that survives might not tell us much about the everyday life of the Etruscans, but the language itself may have links with languages in other parts of the world, and so provide us with a clue to where the Etruscans originated – a question over which even the ancients disagreed.

And there is at least one document that modern Etruscologists yearn to be able to read, for it promises a tantalizing glimpse into an aspect of Etruscan life that may not be merely funerary. Toward the end of the 19th century, a long Etruscan text turned up in the wrappings of a mummy which had been brought to Europe from Egypt by an official of the Hungarian chancellery, as a souvenir of his travels. He, of course, had no idea he possessed a valuable Etruscan document. After his death, the mummy was eventually passed to the Museum of Zagreb, where it was unwrapped and the Etruscan script, on the underside of the bandages, discovered. The experts, naturally enough, took several years to identify the script, since the source of the mummy suggested that the language was of Egyptian origin. Finally identified by a team of German experts as Etruscan in 1892, it revealed 216 lines of text which appeared to be some kind of religious tract. Known as the Book of the Mummy, the cloth was obviously just a portion of a large piece. Experts who have examined both the mummy and the cloth believe that the body inside, a girl, may not have been an Etruscan but that the bandages in which she was wrapped were simply cut from a linen roll that had been written on and then brought to Egypt either by Etruscan traders or by colonists. The Egyptians were notoriously careless about where they obtained their embalming cloth.

So far, although philologists have been eagerly grappling with the enigmatic document ever since its identification as authentically Etruscan, no one has managed to break the "code" of its language. "The plain fact," as one scholar so accurately puts it, "is that an unknown language can only be deciphered by comparing it with a known language."

As recently as 1964, for instance, the leading Italian expert on the Etruscans, Professor Massimo Pallottino, dug up three gold tablets while excavating the site of an Etruscan temple at Pyrgi (modern Santa Severa) near Rome. Two

of the tablets were inscribed in Etruscan and one in Punic, the language of the Phoenicians and one that linguists already knew. Could this be what they were searching for? Was the Punic a literal rendering of one or both of the Etruscan texts? After months of hopeful suspense, during which scholars worked feverishly to compare the known Punic with the unknown Etruscan, an unhappy truth emerged; the gold tablets were a fascinating discovery, but no comparison of language seemed possible; though very probably dealing with the same subject, the Punic is not an exact rendering of the Etruscan, and there is too little of it to provide a reliable key to the grammar of the lost language.

So we're still hoping for a lucky find – something like the Rosetta Stone – to unfurl the mysteries of the Book of the Mummy. Is it not possible that such a key still exists somewhere underground in Italy?

WHAT DO WE KNOW ABOUT THEM?

For the most part, we can only speculate about Etruscan civilization. We know that the Etruscans ruled much of the Italian peninsula for at least 300 years before they were ousted by the growing power of Rome and that they were a deeply religious people who produced a wealth of beautiful art treasures and traveled and traded widely at a time when their neighbors in Italy could apparently achieve little beyond living off the land. Most of the rest of our knowledge comes from Roman accounts of their predecessors; the Romans were probably biased commentators, often contemptuous of those people they had conquered. According to some Roman observers, the Etruscans were cruel, immoral, and sensual; yet after crushing their might and virtually annihilating them as a separate entity, the Romans employed individuals from Etruria as prophets and seers because the Etruscans were believed to have a special ability to divine the will of the gods.

Like the Greeks before them, even the Romans speculated about the origin of the Etruscans, partly because of a strangely oriental quality in their art and partly because the language was unlike any other in the western Mediterranean area. Since they were effective seamen who traded extensively with Greece, North Africa, and the Near East, they could have emigrated from almost anywhere.

Interest in Etruscan civilization was revived in 1828, when a plowman at Vulci, some 50 miles (80 kilometers) northwest of Rome was startled by the sudden disappearance of one of his oxen, which seemed to have fallen though a hole in the field. The "hole" turned out to be an Etruscan tomb, and further searches revealed a network of tombs, all richly stocked with a fascinating variety of painted and carved objects – ceramics, bronzes, sculptures, and jewelry – which, when they reached the market, set off a great wave of Etruscomania among collectors. As it happened, there were vast numbers of Etruscan tombs and other repositories of artifacts to be found by anyone who searched with sufficient diligence. Peasants and landowners alike, scenting the heavy odor of money, were soon engaged in plundering the wealth beneath the soil. Unhappily for today's archeologists and historians, much important information about the Etruscans has undoubtedly been lost or destroyed in the continuing race for profit since the searchers and plunderers of the tombs tended to throw away any objects which seemed to them to have no immediately evident value.

Etruscan artifacts eventually became such a valuable commodity that a brisk trade in fakes came into being. No less a body than New York's Metropolitan Museum of Art was swindled by clever forgers when, around 1920, it paid $40,000 for a pair of "Etruscan" warriors (now labeled more accurately as "20th century AD in style of fifth-century-BC Etruscan work").

Life and death

A crate of cats

IN 1952, a long-forgotten crate of objects excavated in ancient Egypt was found in the dusty vaults of the Natural History Museum, London. It was to reveal fascinating clues about a long-outstanding mystery, namely the ancestry of the domestic cat, one of the most popular of all domestic animals. The crate contained 192 mummified cats dating from the fourth to the second century BC. There were also mummies of seven mongooses, three dogs, and a fox. The mummies had been excavated at Giza, near Cairo, and donated to the museum in 1907 by the distinguished 19th-century Egyptologist, Sir W.M. Flinders Petrie. But, as with much of the biological material collected by Sir Flinders Petrie, it was not accompanied by any information on where it came from.

The discovery of the mummified cats was especially important because unlike the only other evidence we have of the domestication of

The startling discovery in 1952 in a London museum of a crate containing the bodies of Egyptian mummified cats gave rise to renewed speculation about the origins of this popular domestic animal. The mummified cat shown above dates from the first century BC – approximately 200 years later than those found in 1952.

cats, which also came from ancient Egypt, this find throws light on their ancestry as well as on their role in society. In the fourth century BC cats were revered – probably because they killed the rodents that attacked grain stores – and they were featured in religious cults. Bubastis in the Nile delta was the chief cult center of the goddess Bast, who was portrayed either as a cat or with a cat's head, and catacombs at Bubastis yielded hundreds of thousands of mummified cats in the second half of the 19th century. At the time, however, archeologists had no interest at all in these finds – perhaps because most people considered the cat to be too common to be worthy of serious attention – and the finds were sold as cheap fertilizer.

With the rediscovery of the crate, interest in the origins of the domestic cat was revived. Zoological research revealed that of the 192 cat mummies in the crate, three were larger than the rest and were the remains of Jungle Cats (*Felis chaus*): the other 189 closely resembled the common African Wild Cat or Egyptian Sand Cat (*Felis libyca*). In fact these 189 mummies were thought to be a half-stage between the African

Wild Cat and the modern domestic cat, a conclusion that solved the identity of the chief ancestor of modern pet cats. But some controversy will forever surround the cat's origins, a consequence of the fact that domestic and wild cats can interbreed. Hence, in certain areas, *Felis chaus* and others, including the European Wild Cat (*Felis silvestris*) and the Chinese Desert Cat (*Felis bieti*), have without doubt also made invaluable contributions to the development of this popular domestic animal.

The study of the mummies also overturned some long-held theories about the role of the cat in Egyptian society. Herodotus, the Greek historian, wrote in about 450 BC that Egyptians never killed cats, such was their reverence for the animals. But most of the mummified cats were under 12 months in age, only two had passed their second birthday. These cats were, therefore, not family pets that had died naturally and been mummified as offerings to Bast. Instead, they were probably reared by priests and killed before they were fully grown. Their mummies may well have been sold by the priests as votive offerings to the goddess.

THE CHANGING ROLE OF CATS

Cats have experienced changing fortunes at the hands of people. The Egyptians, who first domesticated them, revered felines and founded a religious cult centered on the cat goddess Bast. For the Egyptians, the pupil of the eye symbolized the sun's orb, and cats, whose eyes contract and dilate in a most pronounced fashion also became linked in their mythology with the sun. Bast eventually merged with the goddess of pleasure. Bast's annual festival at Bubastis every spring was a time of boisterous and drunken revelry and, according to the Greek traveler Herodotus, as many as 700,000 people participated. Bast's great temple at Bubastis was 500 feet (152 meters) long and built in part of superb red granite. Around the feet of Bast's statue roamed the sacred cats of the temple.

So great was the Egyptians' regard for cats, wrote Herodotus, that an entire household would mourn and shave their eyebrows as a sign of grief when a pet died. Dead cats were embalmed, their bodies preserved with oil of cedar, and interred in sacred vaults. When a cat was killed in anger, or even accidentally, the rage of the Egyptians was dreadful: In 80 BC, after a Roman soldier in Egypt accidentally killed a cat, a mob rushed to his quarters and put him to death.

The Egyptians were not alone in loving cats. The Romans, Chinese, South American Indians, and others featured cats in their religions. The prophet Muhammad (AD 570–632) is said to have adored his cat. One day, when it was lying against his arm and he had to move, he severed the sleeve of his robe rather than awaken his pet.

Unhappily, cats have not always enjoyed this esteem; the gods of one religion often become the devils of another. For example, the Romans identified Bast with Artemis, or Diana, goddess of the moon. In turn, Artemis was identified with Hecate, Queen of the Underworld and chief of the witches. This image haunted cats in the Middle Ages and later, when they were thought to be the familiars of witches. Many also thought that the Devil took the form of a cat. In 1344, a black cat, identified as the Devil, was said to have caused an outbreak of the disease St. Vitus's Dance in France. And near the end of the 15th century, the pope ordered the Inquisition to hunt down all cat worshipers. Superstitions led to the drowning, beating, and burning of many thousands of cats. In other words, cats were ill-treated largely because of misguided Christian zeal. For example, there was an English superstition that absolution at Shrovetide could be achieved by beating a cat to death. In Ypres, Belgium, cats were hurled from a tower during Lent for the same reason.

Other than its association with Hecate, the cat was singled out as the Devil's servant in part because of its nocturnal habits. And its sensitive response to atmospheric changes led people to believe that the cat could both foretell storms and actually cause them. But perhaps the main cause behind our forebears' mindless hatred of cats was the disconcerting characteristic that cats share with snakes, an unblinking gaze. Napoleon was one of many who found their stare unnerving. Some even find it terrifying.

World-class engineering

The ancient Greeks gouged through a mountain

IN THE OPINION of the Greek historian Herodotus, who lived in the fifth century BC, three of the greatest works of his countrymen were to be seen on the island of Samos. Two of these constructions – a magnificent temple and superb artificial harbor – have been destroyed, but the third still exists and remains one of the most striking monuments of antiquity, in many respects rivaling the Egyptian pyramids. After making a detailed study of it in the early 1960s, science historians Stephen Toulmin and June Goodfield rate it as the best preserved of all ancient Greek works. Why, then, is such a marvel virtually unknown? Simply because it is not an artifact of great beauty but a brilliantly engineered structure that lay unobserved for many centuries. First rediscovered in the late 19th century, it still lies underground where it was meant to be, for this nearly forgotten wonder is a tunnel.

Measuring six feet high and six feet across (2 meters by 2 meters), the Samos tunnel, which was built in about 525 BC, travels 3,400 feet (1,000 meters) through an entire mountain. But the fact that gangs of workmen managed to gouge a way through limestone rock 2,500 years ago is not the most amazing feature of the tunnel. What the Greeks did that had not been done before, and that would not be done again for a long time, was to dig from each end simultaneously to meet eventually inside the mountain far below the summit.

Samos lies in a commanding position in the Aegean Sea near the coast of Turkey. Anyone who controls Samos controls the trade routes of the southeastern Aegean. With this in mind, the tyrant Polycrates transformed his capital into a rich and elegant city at the foot of Mount Castro – an ideal site for a stronghold – and ringed it with high walls extending from its harbor up to the summit of the mountain. However, there was a major flaw in the defenses. The city had no fresh water within the walls, and so its defenders would be forced to capitulate quickly if Samos were besieged. There was a spring at a short distance beyond the far side of Mount Castro; the problem was how to bring its water safely to the city in time of war?

In his search for a solution, Polycrates called in an engineer named Eupalinus, and it was decided that a tunnel must be bored through the mountain to bring the water from its source to the city; and he ordered Eupalinus to complete it with the utmost speed. This meant that, to save time, one gang of workmen had to begin digging within the city while another gang set to work on the other side of the mountain. Their almost impossible goal: to tunnel toward each other and meet in the middle.

From an exhaustive survey of the mountain and the tunnel, Stephen Toulmin and June Goodfield have deduced that Eupalinus determined where the digging should begin at each end by placing a number of poles in a straight line up and over the mountain, using the sea level to measure the height of one pole above the next. They estimated their position by always keeping the light from the ventilation shafts in sight. The digging itself was done by means of chisels and pickaxes, and it appears to have gone well until the two gangs neared each other, when Eupalinus may have had second thoughts about his calculations. At any rate, deep inside the mountain one of the two sections of the tunnel starts to curve as if blindly seeking the other. Interestingly enough, the calculations had been correct to begin with; if the tunnelers had maintained their original course, they would have met head-on. Instead they failed to meet by a distance of about three feet (1 meter). At this point in the digging process it must have been clear to each gang where the other was, for they could surely hear one another through the rock as they hacked away at the limestone. One gang appears to have stopped work while the other made an abrupt turn and burst through.

This slight deviation apart, Eupalinus had been precise in his measurements – too precise, as it happened. The completed tunnel is nearly level, sloping only six feet (2 meters) over a total length of 3,400 feet. Because such a slope is not steep enough for water to flow through, it became necessary to dig a channel in one side of the tunnel floor. The channel, through which the spring water flowed to the city, sloped more steeply than the tunnel and fed a reservoir 25 feet (8 meters) below the tunnel exit.

As a defense measure, the Samos tunnel was a double-edged sword. It could sustain the city in a siege, but only if the far entrance was concealed and its location kept secret. Once an enemy knew about it, they could both cut off the water supply and use the tunnel as an invasion route. Fortunately for Polycrates and his successors,

Samos, a tiny island near the coast of Turkey, is the site of one of the greatest engineering achievements of the classical world – the Samos tunnel, gouged through a mountain of limestone over 2,000 years ago.

the mouth of the tunnel remained undisturbed for nearly a century. When the Athenians attacked the city in 439 BC, it was still invulnerable. Legend has it that, unable to breach the fortress, the wily Athenians offered to lift their siege if given a hostage. At last, then, wisdom deserted the Samians. They gave the besiegers a cantankerous old man who, angered by this insult, revealed the location of the tunnel to his captors.

The city's water supply was cut, and the Samians had no option but to surrender, wounded in their Achilles' heel.

Only traces remain today of Samos's former glory, but the tunnel can still be visited and explored. Unlike most of the great structures of the ancient world, it is in almost perfect condition, a living testimony to the ingenuity of an extraordinary people.

How the Spartans learned to be spartan

Faced with conformity or death, they had no choice but to conform

The warrior ideal was all-important in the Spartan state, where every adult male was expected to present himself in full Spartan armor (above) at a moment's notice. Only after undergoing rigorous military training from an early age could a citizen be considered a true Spartan or "Spartiate."

THE WORD "spartan" – from Sparta, the ancient Greek city-state – means "austere," with overtones of brave and admirable indifference to pain. Most of us have heard about the Spartan boy who hid a fox inside his shirt and permitted the animal to gnaw away at his flesh rather than reveal its presence by so much as a grimace. Or we have thrilled to the heroic (if somewhat exaggerated) account of how, in 480 BC, a few hundred Spartans at Thermopylae held a narrow pass to the last man against the Persian hordes of Xerxes, thus permitting the main Greek army to retreat to safety. So we tend to associate the Spartans with praiseworthy qualities such as courage, discipline, and self-denial. History, however, can be distorted when transformed into legend and so we are entitled to ask whether the Spartans *were* in fact so admirable.

Sparta, in the Peloponnesian peninsula, became the dominant power of the Greek city-states as the result of a series of wars that culminated in the defeat of Athens at the end of the fifth century BC. She achieved dominance at the cost of art, culture, and philosophy (the features of civilization that we today speak of as the "glory that was Greece") and focused exclusively on the maintenance of an incomparable military machine. To do this meant a stern way of life that affected everybody in the state. Not that every individual became a warrior. But the families who held political power and had full citizenship were all headed by land-owning military men with a background of rigorous training and discipline. These were the true Spartans – the "Spartiates." Inferior groups of non-citizens – the poor and landless and vast numbers of state-owned "serfs" – had almost no rights at all, and certainly no influence on social attitudes or behavior.

The ruling classes ran the city-state like an army camp on a permanent war footing. Highly suspicious of outsiders, the Spartiates maintained a high degree of self-denying equality among themselves, rejecting all show of wealth; even their money was not gold or silver but plain, unadorned iron bars. The most important element in their life was duty to the state. Family ties and individual needs were overshadowed by the citizen's duty to transform himself into an efficient cog in the military machine. And this duty began at birth. Newborn babies of both sexes were inspected by a council of magistrates empowered to condemn to death by exposure any who were sickly, weak, or deformed. Boy children who passed this inspection were required to leave home at about eight years of age and to undergo state education and military training, with an emphasis on physical fitness. They were given a minimum amount of food, wore only one garment whatever the weather, slept on thin beds of rushes on bare ground, and faced constant tests of endurance and obedience, sometimes including floggings, from which many boys died stoically, without showing any sign of weakness. At the same time, they were encouraged to steal food, not just to supplement the meager diet but to test their initiative. Any boy caught in the act was flogged – not for stealing, but for being caught.

Adult Spartiates had to be permanently ready for war. When not fighting, they spent much of their time in competitive athletics, hunting, or living rough in the countryside, armed with daggers. They were also expected to keep an eye on their lands, of course, and to produce further generations of warriors. Girls did not leave home for this youthful training, but were otherwise raised much like boys, with similar emphasis on fitness in the hope that healthy women would bear healthy children. Marriages were arranged by families, with state approval. And Spartan women, excluded from politics and warfare, were generally counted as citizens and were not supervised so strictly once they proved capable of bearing children. Adultery was said to be unknown in Sparta, as sex with a socially acceptable lover was condoned; for example, it was considered a blessing, not a shame, if a married woman bore strong children by more than one man.

Eventually, Sparta went into decline, but spartan behavior persisted. By the first century BC, when all Greece was under Roman rule, legendary spartan endurance had degenerated into sadistic sideshows, tortures withstood without a whimper for the edification of Roman tourists. Despite this debasement of spartan qualities, the concept of spartan behavior retained its glamour. Today, too, endurance, courage, and social responsibility remain desirable human qualities. But we may perhaps be excused if our admiration for spartan behavior does not extend to Sparta's reality, especially when we take into account the resemblances between some of the darker episodes of 20th-century history and Sparta's callous cruelties, such as the disappearance (liquidation?) of 2,000 Helots during the Peloponnesian War.

THE GREEKS HAD A WORD FOR IT

Like Sparta, several place-names of ancient Greece have found their way into the English language as descriptive words. An inhabitant of the isle of Lesbos, for instance, was and is a Lesbian – but so, today (without the capital L), is a female homosexual, thanks to the alleged inclinations of the seventh-century-BC poetess Sappho, who lived in Lesbos. People of the Peloponnesian region of Arcadia prided themselves on the untroubled beauty of their simple rural lives, and so a serene life of rustic bliss and pastoral pleasures may now be termed "arcadian." Classical Greek architecture in its most splendidly refined form existed in Attica (Athens and its surroundings), and today's modest top-of-the-house attic takes its name from the small upper story that often rose above the main columns of Attic buildings.

As for that useful word "laconic," characterizing statements that are brief and crisp, we must go back to Sparta and the region that surrounded it, Laconia, where the people were known for their brusqueness of speech. An immortal instance occured in the fourth century BC, when Philip of Macedon was leading his armies out to conquer the world. Philip wrote to the Spartans, "if I enter Laconia, I shall level it to the ground." The Spartans replied, laconically, with only a single word: "if."

America's first gold rush

The conquistadors found that "all that glisters is not gold"

IN 1492 Christopher Columbus and his followers saw gold jewelry on Arawak chiefs in the West Indies – a sight that triggered the most ruthless gold rush in history. The lure of precious metal brought Spanish conquistadors across the Atlantic, through inhospitable jungles, and up and down mountain ranges until, within 40 years the majority of the known gold-producing regions of the New World were theirs. And, unlike their 19th-century successors, they did not have to soil their hands by digging; American gold was highly accessible – as accessible, the Indians reckoned when they saw the swords of their conquerors, as iron must be in Spain. All that was needed was a bit of bloodshed (Indian blood, of course).

The natives of pre-Columbian America prized the gold for its beauty, presuming that the shiny yellow metal had a divine origin. In Mexico, the Aztecs called it the excrement of the gods, while the Incas of Peru thought it to be the sweat of the sun. All the Indians fashioned ceremonial objects and regalia from it and adorned their temples and palaces with it. The Peruvians reserved both gold and silver for the exclusive use of the ruler (the Inca himself), other noble personages, whether living or dead, and the gods. Gold was not valued as a major item of currency, and the Indians would have been puzzled by the familiar European image of a miser fingering his hoard in lonely greed. The glittering metal existed to be displayed, admired, and even utilized, since, because it resists corrosion, it could be turned into functional things such as fishhooks and needles.

So the Spaniards did not have to go prospecting for gold. They seized vast quantities of it to bring back to Europe. Unfortunately for posterity, however, it was primarily the bullion they wanted, not the beauty of the workmanship

A copper-gold alloy known as tumbaga was used by pre-Columbian South American Indians to cast this staff head in the shape of a bird. It may have served as a ceremonial spear-thrower hook.

ATAHUALPA'S RANSOM

In exchange for his freedom, Atahualpa offered his Spanish captors enough gold to fill his prison rooms. In this near-contemporary engraving, an Inca presents a small part of the ransom required to the haughty conquistadors.

While looting Mexico, the conquistadors were fascinated by rumors of a fabulous "kingdom of gold" farther south. The rumors probably stemmed from exaggerated accounts of a ritual observed in Colombia among the Muisca Indians, who allegedly inaugurated the reign of a new king with a ceremony in which the naked monarch, his body powdered with gold dust, dropped offerings of gold and emeralds into a sacred lake. No legend could have been more calculated to whet a conquistador's appetite, and Francisco Pizarro was determined to find the golden kingdom of "El Dorado" (literally, "the gilded man").

Making their way down to Peru, Pizarro and his men captured Atahualpa, emperor of the Incas. Deprived of the support of his retinue, most of whom the Spaniards had killed, Atahualpa offered to fill his prison apartments with gold in exchange for freedom, and Pizarro accepted the offer – a genuine one since Atahualpa was *the* Inca (supreme ruler of the Incas), and gold was a royal monopoly. It was the Inca's prerogative to award the use of gold to his courtiers, priests, administrators, and warriors. Their golden ornaments, even golden gloves and sandals, were all symbols of royal favor. At Cuzco, the Inca capital, the royal palace was adorned with a precious-metal garden with life-size stalks of golden corn and golden animals and birds. If this was not itself El Dorado, the Spaniards must have thought it a reasonable substitute for the real thing.

Atahualpa's prison chamber – 22 feet long, 17 feet wide, and 8 feet high (7 by 5 by 2.5 meters) – was heaped high with gold; and two other, smaller rooms were filled with silver. So the emperor kept his side of the bargain; but the conquistadors did not release him. Instead, Pizarro had him first baptized, then garroted. Needless to say, none of the priceless gold and silver, which included treasures from the Temple of the Sun at Cuzco, survived the Europeans' melting pot. It took nine smiths a whole month to melt down the gold objects and turn them into gold bars.

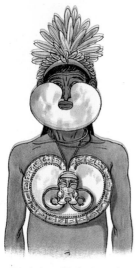

Greedy for gold, the Spanish melted down the work of perhaps the world's finest goldsmiths. A few items did survive, however, including this nose ornament of an Aztec warrior, now in the Gold Museum in Bogotá.

that had been lavished upon it by the Indians. The techniques of pre-Columbian American goldsmiths, dating back to at least 500 BC, were as advanced as those of the finest metal-workers of the Old World. Colombia and Ecuador were the main centers of innovation and design, but each culture had a distinctive style. Peruvian goldsmiths, for instance, liked the dramatic impact of large expanses of shimmering gold, whereas the Colombians delighted in adorning the heads of long cloak pins with delicate figures of spiders and mythological beasts, and the craftsmen of Ecuador often combined platinum with gold by means of powder metallurgy (a sophisticated technique not perfected in Europe until the 19th century).

A few Spaniards were not insensitive to such splendors. One Franciscan missionary, having observed the work of Mexico's Mixtec goldsmiths, remarked upon their superiority over similar craftsmen in Spain: "They could cast a bird with a movable head, tongue, feet, and hands ... they cast a fish with all its scales, one scale of silver, one of gold, at which Spanish goldsmiths would much marvel."

Because of their preoccupation with the artistic potential of gold, as opposed to its monetary value, the Indian goldsmiths liked using a copper-gold alloy known as *tumbaga*. Not only was tumbaga harder than pure gold, but it was also easier to cast and it reproduced fine decorative detail more accurately. But the alloy looked like pure gold because of an ingenious finishing process; after *tumbaga* items were consigned to the melting pots for bullion, many a conquistador must have discovered the truth of the maxim: all that glisters is not gold.

It says something for the beauty of Indian goldwork that a hard soldier like Cortés, the conqueror of Mexico, could not bring himself to melt down all the treasures of Montezuma, the Aztec leader. Instead, he sent some outstanding pieces intact to Charles V, the Holy Roman Emperor. When, in 1520, the great Renaissance artist Albrecht Dürer viewed these "wondrous things," he was astounded by what he termed the "subtle genius" of the anonymous goldsmiths of far-off America.

Very little pre-Columbian gold escaped the melting pot, however; the bulk was consigned to the melting pots to make bullion, and most of the beautiful objects that survived did so because the Indians hid them or they remained buried in tombs. Grave-robbing has been carried out, in fact, ever since the days of the conquistadors, and many a priceless treasure has been melted down into currency. As recently as a decade ago, it was common practice among grave-robbers in Panama to sell ancient gold objects to dentists to be melted down for use as dental fillings. Fortunately, an increasing interest in pre-Columbian art in the United States, Europe, and Latin America has pushed the price of ancient goldwork high enough to ensure that it no longer ends up in people's mouths. Instead, future finds will no doubt go to museums, where we can all share Dürer's delight in the subtle genius of Indian goldsmiths.

Women's lib in ancient Greece

What the Spartans taught the Athenians

THE ATHENIANS of the Classical Age worshiped a number of goddesses. They believed that the Graces and Muses were feminine, and so were the guardians of justice, wisdom, and peace. Their city-state itself was named for Athena, daughter of Zeus, and her image overlooked the city from a supreme vantage point on the Acropolis. And yet, at the height of their civilization, in the fifth century BC, and despite their veneration of immortal women, many of the male citizens of Athens seem to have behaved toward *mortal* women as if they existed only in order to breed further generations of male Athenians.

It is a curious fact that the brutal Peloponnesian War – between Athens and culturally inferior Sparta that was to last intermittently for three decades and ended with the total defeat of Athens – actually benefited the women. For although the war was disastrous for their fathers, husbands, and sons, the resulting social upheaval gave them more rights and freedom than they had ever enjoyed before. Just as the great wars of the first half of our own century began to emancipate women throughout the Western world, so the Peloponnesian conflict enabled their ancient Athenian counterparts at least in some measure to loosen if not throw off entirely their shackles.

The records and literature of Athens tell us almost nothing about what life was like among the hard-working lower classes. But the women

The leisured ladies shown in this frieze painted around 420 BC are in their gynaikon, *the women's quarters in a wealthy Athenian household. Usually situated on an upper story, and always remote from the street, the* gynaikon *accommodated the women of the household in strict seclusion.*

of the middle and upper classes, with time on their hands and a social position to maintain, had to behave impeccably if they wanted to keep their place in society. Prior to the early years of the Peloponnesian War, which began in 431 BC, this meant in effect that a respectable woman was expected to live in almost total seclusion. It was scandalous for a well-bred woman to appear in public; she was not even permitted to leave the house except on certain religious or family occasions. Even shopping was taboo; her husband or her slaves took care of it.

Nor was life much better indoors. Greek marriages were usually arranged as a matter of convenience, with love matches the exception rather than the rule. Women were subject to severe and degrading penalties if they were found to have committed adultery, but their husbands took sex as it came; promiscuity whether with courtesans or boys, was accepted as "normal" behavior. A wife's main function was to run the house and bring up her children – and to keep out of sight while doing it. She was allotted a special part of the house known as the

gynaikon – the women's apartments – generally at the back of the house or upstairs, and had a great deal of explaining to do if caught elsewhere. If her husband was entertaining male guests, she did not eat with them. She saw to it that food was properly prepared, and then left him to enjoy it in the company of his friends while she ate in her own apartments.

Much of this changed gradually as the Peloponnesian War dragged on. By 404 BC, after 27 years of warfare, Athens was on its knees, many of its accepted attitudes gone forever. People from all walks of society now turned their backs on outmoded conventions in favor of enjoying the best things in life while they still could. After one siege of the city, it is believed that more than a quarter of the population, including the great statesman Pericles, died of plague. A survivor, the soldier-historian Thucydides, has recorded the effect of the disaster on public morality: "These sudden changes of fortune which people witnessed – the wealthy struck dead overnight, paupers taking possession of their riches – made them more willing to

SAPPHO – THE LESBIAN WHO WASN'T

Although the status of women in ancient Athens left much to be desired, women in other parts of Greece often enjoyed a relatively free and pleasant existence. Hints of a charming picture of life on the island of Lesbos, for instance, have been left by the poetess Sappho, whose work dates from the sixth century BC. Only a few fragments of her verse survive, but the bits we have are exquisite, combining verbal melody with great power of expression and evocations of physical beauty.

The Greek poetess, Sappho, is shown here making her suicidal leap from a cliff by the 19th-century French painter Antoine Jean Gros. The legend of Sappho's unrequited love for a man was probably invented long after her death.

There is some evidence that Sappho was a schoolmistress who ran a boarding school for aristrocratic young girls, preparing them ultimately for marriage and motherhood; and it is against this background that what remains of her poetry should be read, for it reflects the deep and often passionate affection she felt for some of these girls and the sense of loss she suffered when they left her to get married. The word "lesbian" has since been coined to explain the profound love between women, but there is very little contemporary evidence to indicate that her fondness for girls expressed itself physically. Later comedies, performed in Athens, caricatured her as a lustful woman-chaser, but they were not meant to be taken literally, any more than should the traditional story that she committed suicide for her unhappy love of the handsome ferryman Phaon by jumping off a cliff.

We actually know almost nothing about Sappho's personal history beyond the facts that she was probably married and had a daughter named Cleis. She would certainly not have been considered particularly good-looking by her contemporaries; she was small and dark at a time when the classical ideal was to be tall and fair. And she spent some time at Syracuse in Sicily (probably because of civil disturbances at home) but soon returned to Lesbos, where she apparently lived to old age. It is not the facts of her life – or, indeed, her sexual proclivities – that matter, but her poetry. Scholars agree that even the little that has survived justifies Plato's later opinion of her as the classical world's Tenth Muse.

indulge openly in pleasures that they would before have taken care to conceal. They sought quick returns for their money, and saw immediate self-gratification as the one reasonable pursuit in a world where they, and their wealth, were liable to perish at any moment."

Live now, pay later was the message, and the women of Athens were probably as quick as the men to take advantage of the newly liberal atmosphere to do more or less what they felt like doing. In this they were following the example of the enemy, for although Spartan military discipline was much more stringent than that of Athens, it paradoxically encouraged women to enjoy a more outgoing and vigorous existence. "Spartan maidens," explains a character in a play by the Athenian playwright Euripides, "are allowed out of doors with young men, running and wrestling in their company, with naked thighs and girt-up tunics." Toward the end of the fifth century, however, it was not only Spartan maidens. The girls of Athens too began to hitch up their skirts and enjoy the open air. Not surprisingly, this eventually led to so much trouble that by the next century, a special magistrate – a *gynaikonomos* – had to be appointed with the sole task of keeping the city's women under control. In particular, he was supposed to keep them from becoming spendthrifts – a job that (no doubt in the men's opinion) gave him more than enough to do. For the first time in Athenian history women were asserting their rights as people, and they became increasingly aware that they had some strong weapons with which to fight the battle for liberation. In 411 the playwright Aristophanes presented his comedy *Lysistrata*, in which the women of all the Greek states are shown as striking a blow for peace with their mightiest weapon: They go on a sex strike, denying their bodies to their husbands until the men give up fighting. A few years earlier such a theme for a play would have been much less likely.

Emancipation still had a long way to go. After their brief respite from oppression in the fifth century BC Athenian women found that their lot once again sank to the level at which it had been during the so-called "Golden" Age.

Frozen tombs

The tattooed man of Pazyryk

IN 1948, the Russian archeologist Sergei Rudenko opened a burial chamber dating from about 500 BC. Inside was the body of a tattooed man and his wife or concubine. The burial chamber was one of five large and nine smaller chambers at Pazyryk on the Altai steppes near the Mongolian border of western Siberia. By a strange quirk of nature, the couple with their normally perishable belongings, including everything from shoes and socks to carpets, bottles, and a wooden table, were largely intact – they had remained frozen for around 2,500 years. For Rudenko, who had first investigated the site more than 20 years earlier, this was the find of a lifetime.

The most important discovery in the tomb was the body of the man. Although damaged by robbers, who had entered the tomb some time after the burial, enough remained to give Rudenko a unique insight into the lifestyle and physical appearance of a tribal chieftain at the start of the Iron Age. For that period, the man was remarkably tall at five feet nine inches (1.76 meters) and physically powerful. The front of his head had been shaved and the head had been scalped. From a slight bone deformation in the legs, Rudenko deduced that the man had spent many years on horseback, as befitted the leader of a nomadic people.

Undoubtedly, however, the tattoos were the corpse's most fascinating feature. They covered his arms, legs and much of his trunk. Most of the designs depicted mythical monsters: creatures with wings and cats' tails; lion-griffins with snakelike bodies; and deer with long antlers and eagles' beaks. The tattoos were a remarkable display of imagination and a work of art in their own right. They also indicated that this man's customs were very similar to those of the Scythian people. The Scyths, who were famed for their tattooing, were a warlike people who lived in Central Asia between the seventh and third centuries BC. The Greek physician Hippocrates, who lived between about 460 and 370 BC, wrote that "the whole mass of the Scyths, as many as are nomads, cauterize their shoulders, arms, and hands, chests, thighs, and loins, for no other purpose than to avoid weakness and flabbiness and to become energetic." In addition, Hippocrates tells us, the Scyths

Tattooing was a painfully acquired status symbol among the Scyths. The elaborate body designs were effected by skilled tattooists who pricked deeply into their clients' flesh and then filled the holes with a black liquid. This piece of skin, decorated with animals, both real and imaginary, is from the right upper arm of the chieftain buried in the tomb at Pazyryk. The tomb froze soon after the burial, thus preserving the body until the present day.

WHY DID THE TOMBS FREEZE?

The ancient Siberians built graves to last, but they had no idea that freak conditions on the Altai steppes would preserve their handiwork long after they had passed out of history.

The Altai steppes have long and severe winters and short, cool summers, but the average annual temperature is not usually low enough for permafrost: that is, for the subsoil to remain permanently frozen. The climate certainly contributed to the condition of the graves, but it was their particular construction that caused them to be preserved.

All the large burial chambers uncovered by Rudenko were built on the same pattern. The main chamber at the bottom of the burial shaft, about 16 feet (5 meters) deep, was walled with stout larch logs and roofed with more logs and a covering of rocks. Above the rocks was a mound of earth about six feet (1.8 meters) thick. Above the earth was a cairn of loose stones, 14 to 18 feet (4 to 5 meters) high, perhaps 150 feet (50 meters) in diameter. More than anything else, these stones caused the graves to freeze. They kept out summer warmth, but allowed frost to enter in winter.

Stones are poor conductors of heat, and the earth beneath the cairns became permanently frozen almost as soon as the burial mounds had been completed. Even so, they did not freeze in time to prevent the partial decomposition of food in the form of goat flesh and the horses buried with their masters. The human bodies escaped destruction only because they had been embalmed, and the cavities filled with grass.

Rudenko was surprised, however, that the robbery of the tomb of the tattooed man appeared to have had no significant effect on the freezing process. At first, he wondered if the refrigeration was perhaps caused by the sudden exposure of the burial chambers to cold air let in by the robbers' tunnel. Subsequently, he concluded that the bodies had frozen very soon after burial, and that the later robbery was not the cause of the refrigeration. But there was no doubt that the break-in must have occurred within a few years of the burial, not long after the followers of the dead had left the area, because the marks left by the intruders showed that they were still using the same bronze tools rather than the iron tools of a later period.

The body of a tattooed man was found in what came to be known as Barrow Two of the 14 burial chambers excavated at Pazyryk. Barrow Five is shown, with its grave goods, in cross-section (below). Like the other chambers, Barrow Five was constructed of wooden logs covered in layers of soil and stones (inset).

lived in four-wheeled wagons, two or three to a family. Rudenko found the remains of such a wagon in another burial mound on the Altai steppes, together with draft horses that had been slaughtered so that they could accompany their master into the next world.

The tomb of the tattooed man also contained the remains of several riding horses. Each horse faced east and beside it were its bridle, saddle, and head decorations. The tomb enclosed a collection of domestic articles, including a piece of carpet, some felt stockings, a bronze mirror in a fur case and a silver mirror in a leather bag, as well. There were fur and beads in abundance, together with gold pendants from earrings that had been overlooked by the robbers. Rudenko also found a near-perfect wooden table, with four legs carved in the shape of tigers standing on their hind legs. Earthenware bottles containing some dregs of *koumiss* (fermented mare's milk) and a pouchful of cheese were there to sustain the dead couple on their journey. Sources of consolation included the remains of a harp and a bag of hemp seed for growing cannabis. Mature hemp had been used for weaving a man's fine shirt, which had intricate stitching and red woolen braid along the main seam.

One bizarre object was a false beard lying beside the man's head. It was made of human hair, dyed the color of dark chestnut and sewn onto a leather strip. Although no male corpses in the excavations had beards or moustaches, representations on pendants suggested that Scythian men often wore beards. Perhaps these beards were all artificial, worn for reasons we shall never know.

Most curious of all, however, was the wide variety of skull types found in the tombs. Although he had only a few specimens, Rudenko identified not only the Europeoid type, but also two distinct forms of Mongoloid skulls, long-headed and broad-headed. He attributed this racial variety to the practice of chieftains marrying princesses from distant tribes for political reasons. Rudenko pointed out that similar facial differences occur among modern Kazakh and Kirgiz people.

The Mongoloid skulls may also have belonged to Hunnish aristocrats, because a tribe of migrant Huns probably drove the Altai chieftains out of this area toward the end of the third century BC. At first, the Huns may have intermarried with them. By the end of the century, however, they probably resorted to more violent methods, because all evidence of the ancient Altai people as a distinct cultural group in the region ends abruptly at that date. No trace of their existence after this has ever been found.

A lucky find

A silver strike that changed the course of history

AT THE START of the fifth century BC, a crisis occurred in the eastern Mediterranean that was to have profound effects on the development of Western culture. In 499 the Ionian Greek cities on the west coast of Asia Minor, under the leadership of Miletus, rebelled against their Persian overlords who had controlled Asia Minor since about 547 BC. Aided by Athens, the Ionians continued their struggle until the armies of the Persian King Darius crushed the revolt in 494. This was the opening phase of the Greco-Persian wars. In 490 Darius launched an expedition against the Greek mainland, but his army was badly defeated by the Athenians at the Battle of Marathon, the first major military setback in the history of the Persian empire.

Many Athenians thought that the threat of a Persian invasion had been lifted. However, a group led by the general, Themistocles, thought otherwise. Themistocles feared that the situation in Athens would make resistance difficult.

Some years before, a group of slave-miners working in the government-owned silver mines at Laurium, 25 miles (40 kilometers) southwest of Athens, had discovered an immensely valuable vein of high-quality silver. Within a very short time, the new seam had yielded several tons of pure silver. Public opinion in Athens was divided on how the proceeds of this silver strike should be used. One group demanded that every adult male citizen receive an equal share of the profits. Another group, no less influential, was led by Themistocles, a shrewd, tough, ambitious leader. He advocated that the funds from Laurium should be used to finance the building of triremes. As their name implies, these warships had banks of oars at three levels. In battle, when speed and maneuverability were essential, all three banks, involving about 170 men, were employed. Otherwise, only one bank at a time would be used. Triremes could maintain rowing speeds of up to five knots, and the record stood at about eight knots. To provide extra power, these highly effective warships were equipped with a square sail.

Enough money was voted to build 100 triremes, half the number that Themistocles thought would be needed in the event of another Persian invasion. Worse still, the funds, it seems, were allocated for only one year. However, news that the Persians had begun to plan an invasion led to the instigation of a swift shipbuilding program. Before long, Athens could boast a fleet of more than 200 vessels. In addition, thousands of crew members and marines, or hoplites—infantry equipped with swords and javelins, up to 40 of whom were carried on the deck of each trireme—had to be enlisted, trained, and paid. Without silver from Laurium, none of

Greek fleet consisted of about 300 triremes, approximately 160 coming from Athens and over 100 from Sparta and her allies. In the battle, the Persian fleet, because of its numerical superiority, lacked the room to maneuver in the narrow strait. Confusion reigned and the Persian ships were easy prey to the Greek triremes, heavy and clumsy though they were. The Persian ships were rammed and either holed or crippled as their oars were sheared away. The vessels were then boarded by the ferocious hoplites. The action lasted most of the daylight hours. By sunset the Persians had lost about 200 ships, including those severely disabled, while the Greek losses were much lighter, perhaps as few as 40 ships. There were also more Persian casualties than Greek, for the simple reason that most of the Greeks could swim and the Persians couldn't. But as the victors were in a position to recover many of their damaged vessels and

The trireme was the standard fighting ship used in the Battle of Salamis in 480 BC. Shown here in cross-section, with the three banks of oars that gave the boat its name in elevation above, a typical Greek trireme was approximately 120 feet (40 meters) in length and 18 feet (6 meters) in width. It was steered by a helmsman, the most skilled man on board, who directed the ship from the stern. The majority of the sailors were poor citizens of Athens, who derived pride and some power from their key role in naval warfare.

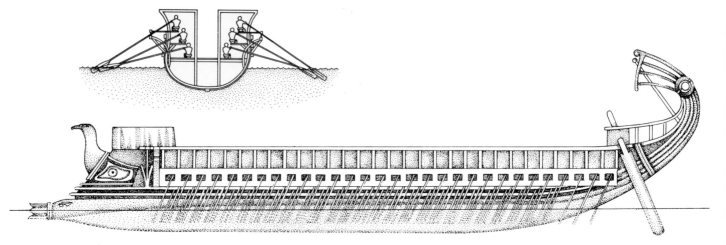

this could have happened. The importation of materials needed for shipbuilding also stimulated foreign trade and brought many financial benefits. Athenian drachmas, known as "owls" from the figure stamped on them, became an international currency.

In 480 the Persian armies, under King Xerxes, son of Darius, swept into Europe from Asia Minor. They destroyed a small Spartan force at Thermopylae and occupied most of Greece, including Athens, which was burned.

The Greeks stationed their fleet in the confined waters off the island of Salamis, about 10 miles (16 kilometers) west of Athens. They then lured the Persian fleet by making Xerxes think that they were about to retreat without a fight. On September 20, from a nearby hill, Xerxes watched his fleet advance against the Greeks. The Persians had more than twice the number of vessels, acquired from subject peoples, including 300 Phoenician and 200 Egyptian craft. The

crews, the Persians, in headlong retreat, were forced to abandon many ships and men.

The victory at Salamis was crucial. Without ships, the Persians were unable to safeguard their supply routes and had to withdraw most of their troops from the Greek mainland. A year later, Greek victories at the Battle of Plataea, about 50 miles (80 kilometers) northwest of Athens, and another naval engagement at Mycale in the eastern Aegean Sea, marked the final defeat of the Persian invasion. Because of that "fountain of silver, treasure hoard of earth," as the Greek poet Aeschylus called the lucky strike at Laurium, Athens emerged as the dominant naval power in the eastern Mediterranean and the leader of the Greek world. Shortly afterward, it became the center of the dazzling intellectual and artistic achievements of the classical period. Had the Persians won, they might have occupied Western Europe and changed the character of subsequent Western civilization.

The history of Herodotus

Serious historian or great storyteller?

"IN THIS BOOK, the result of my enquiries into history, I hope to do two things: to preserve the memory of the past by putting on record the astonishing achievements both of our own and of the Asiatic (barbarian) peoples; secondly, and more particularly, to show how the two races came into conflict."

These words were written by Herodotus in the introduction to his *History*, an account of the Greco-Persian wars at the end of the sixth, and during the fifth, century BC. In the first century BC, the Roman orator Cicero dubbed Herodotus "the Father of History" for this achievement, although some detractors preferred to call him "the Father of Lies."

Little is known of Herodotus's life. He was born in Halicarnassus, a Greek town on the coast of Asia Minor, in the 480s BC. He was therefore too young to have any firsthand knowledge of the Greek victories in 480 and 479 that finally ended the Persian threat. As a young man, Herodotus and his family moved, for political reasons, to the island of Samos, off the coast of Asia Minor. From Samos, Herodotus wandered through the Mediterranean region, gathering information, asking questions and recording the answers. He later claimed that in preparing his *History*, he had sought the opinions of people from "40 Greek cities" and the views of "the inhabitants of 30 nations."

He traveled as far north as southern Scythia, north of the Black Sea, as far east as Babylon, and as far south as Upper Egypt. He also sailed west and visited Libya. But he did not reach the Atlantic. He had heard of "a sea beyond Europe," although he could not confirm its existence, "having never found anyone who could give me firsthand information."

Herodotus spent some time in Athens, whose civilization he greatly admired. There and in other Greek cities, he was acclaimed for his readings from his *History*. Almost certainly, because of his foreign origins, he never achieved Athenian citizenship. Perhaps disappointed, he settled in the Greek outpost of Thurii, which had been founded in 443 on the Gulf of Taranto in southern Italy. His tomb has been found at Thurii, although the exact date of his death is unknown. He probably died in about 429 BC, after the start of the Peloponnesian War between his beloved Athens and Sparta, which began in 431. The *History* of Herodotus is contained in nine books. These books include much information not directly connected with the Greco-Persian conflict. For example, Book II is concerned with the geography, history, and ethnography of Egypt. The other books contain many digressions about the people and territories he had visited. He describes "beasts in Libya that go without water." He writes of the Babylonians who wore "linen tunics right down to their feet," and who had "long hair and cover themselves with perfume."

Anecdotes, clearly intended to amuse, also abound. He tells of how the rich King Croesus of Lydia offered an Athenian, Alcmaeon, "as much gold as he could carry away." The ingenious Alcmaeon arrived "wearing a tunic with deep folds, hanging in front, the widest boots he could find, then sprinkling them and his hair full of gold dust – he even filled his mouth with it." Croesus burst out laughing and doubled the gift. Such tales must have been well received at public readings, although they invite criticism from those who think that history is a serious matter.

The *History* is, therefore, less a chronology of events than a fascinating blend of information of many kinds. It also has an epic quality and shows the influence of Homer's *Iliad* and the *Odyssey*. It is undoubtedly one of the great European prose works and is probably read today as much for its literary merit as for its historical content. But Herodotus was no credulous peddler of myth and magic. In collecting information, which was often based on hearsay and probably suffered in translation–Herodotus spoke only Greek – he often found several versions of the same incident. He reacted disarmingly by saying: "My business is to record what people say. But I am by no means bound to believe it – and that may be taken to apply to this book as a whole." Although a committed supporter of Athens – the people who named him "the Father of Lies" were implacable opponents of the Athenians – he was not the man to be ungenerous to the enemies of that city.

The accounts of the battles of Marathon, Thermopylae, and Salamis were central to his theme and they are beautifully written, with personal touches that illuminate the tragedy and nobility of war. His statistics are often absurdly exaggerated. He writes of millions of soldiers, when he means hundreds of thousands. But hyperbole is a minor fault. It is the religious element in the *History* that gives the modern reader most difficulty, because Herodotus clearly believes in the intervention of the Greek pantheon to influence the course of events. Even so, he is probably the first writer to seek to explain historical events primarily through human behavior. To reveal the autocratic nature of the Persian Emperor Xerxes, Herodotus tells how he boasted of the discipline of his army, saying that, "left to their own free will, they will do nothing." An exiled Spartan general replied that the Greek democrats feared the law "more than your subjects fear you." One of the law's consistent commands, he added, was "not to retreat before any number of men – but to remain in their ranks and conquer or perish."

Is Herodotus "the Father of History?" He has only two rivals. Hecateus, the only prose writer mentioned by Herodotus, was a fellow Ionian, who sought to reconcile Greek mythology with the genealogy of Athenian families. He also wrote a travel book. But his work totally lacks the stature of the *History*. The other contender is Thucydides, who as a boy attended a reading by Herodotus and was moved to tears. Thucydides, a rich Athenian, adopted a far more serious and intellectual approach to history. He expressed his distaste for the methods used by Herodotus to popularize and dramatize his accounts. But while Thucydides might take the mantle of the historians' historian, Herodotus is certainly the historian for the ordinary person. And with his forceful yet compassionate, humorous, and vivid style, Herodotus gives us a far greater feel of what it must have been like to live in the ancient world.

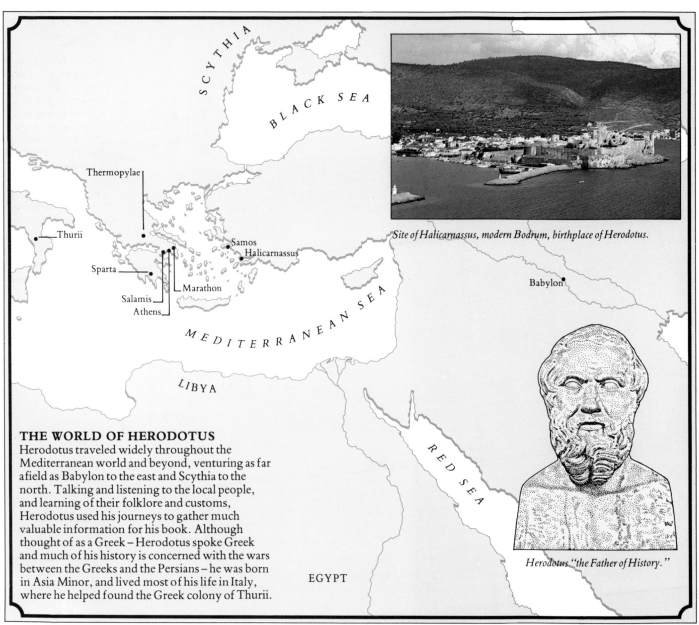

Site of Halicarnassus, modern Bodrum, birthplace of Herodotus.

Herodotus "the Father of History."

THE WORLD OF HERODOTUS
Herodotus traveled widely throughout the Mediterranean world and beyond, venturing as far afield as Babylon to the east and Scythia to the north. Talking and listening to the local people, and learning of their folklore and customs, Herodotus used his journeys to gather much valuable information for his book. Although thought of as a Greek – Herodotus spoke Greek and much of his history is concerned with the wars between the Greeks and the Persians – he was born in Asia Minor, and lived most of his life in Italy, where he helped found the Greek colony of Thurii.

Theatre-going in ancient Greece

Something for everyone

NEARLY 2,500 YEARS have passed since the great *theatron* of Dionysus was built on a hillside in Athens, and in all that time the vocabulary of the theatre has retained much of its ancient flavor. For instance, audiences in Greek theatres, which were outdoor semicircular structures, faced a stage placed behind a circular dancing place (in Greek, literally, the *orchestra*) where members of the *chorus* could dance and sing. The actors changed costumes in a tent called the *skene*, and in between scenes they perhaps peered nervously into the rising tiers of the theatre to see how the *kritai* (the judges, whence our word critics) were reacting to their efforts. Tradition has it that the first man ever to play a role on the Greek stage was named Thespis, and we still speak of actors as thespians.

The experience of going to the theatre, however, is very different today than it was in the fifth century BC when the greatest Greek dramatists lived and Greek theatre was at its zenith. A time-traveler to the 20th century from ancient Greece might well feel more at home at the Edinburgh or Salzburg Festivals than watching a play on Broadway. Athenian drama took the form of a yearly competition that had much in common with the almost orgiastic festival spirit that sometimes enlivens such musical gatherings as rock festivals. Works were performed once rather than regularly, as they are in modern theatrical centers such as New York, Berlin, Paris, and London; instead, they were the main feature of an annual festival – the festival of Dionysus, which the Athenians looked upon as the most exciting event of the year. This was held every spring in honor of the god of wine (called Bacchus in later centuries in Rome) and for sheer spectacle it would certainly be difficult to beat.

The festival began with a public holiday and an opening ceremony consisting of a procession of men wearing brightly colored robes and carrying enormous phallic symbols to herald the coming of spring, the season of fertility, and continued with the sacrifice of a bull at the theatre on the southern slopes of the Acropolis. The festival was religious in origin, and did not completely break away from its religious roots until long after the fifth century BC. Most of the 14,000 or more spectators who crowded in to the first day of the festival took care to arrive early so as not to miss the opening ceremonies.

We know very little about those ceremonies or about the composition of the audience in the golden age of the Athenian theatre, although we do know that there were no female performers. We are not even sure of the size of the theatre in fifth-century Athens. Theatres were gradually built in cities and towns throughout Greece, and the one that has best survived into modern times – in the Peloponnesian town of Epidaurus – dates from the fourth century BC, by which time the great days of Athenian tragedy were already a thing of the past.

By the end of that century the annual festival had become a largely social occasion, with people of both sexes vying with one another for the offstage limelight. Everybody wore festive clothes, and garlands of ivy leaves were an almost obligatory headdress. Seats closest to the stage were reserved for city dignitaries and foreign ambassadors, the ones farthest away and apart from the others are thought to have been for prostitutes. Tickets were made of lead, and people who were dissatisfied with their seats could buy others from one of the many scalpers (or ticket touts) doing business outside the gates. Almost certainly, the scalpers' best customers were the snobs and social climbers, who, according to the late fourth-century writer Theophrastus, would do anything to be seen sitting near important officials.

Festival events included musical entertainments, choral singing, and usually five plays a day, acted by splendidly costumed men wearing elaborate masks. Five plays at one sitting may sound like the makings of a long, hard day, especially since three of the plays were usually tragedies. But Greek dramas tended to be short, each play probably lasting no longer than an hour and a half. And there was a great deal of audience participation. People shouted down bad actors, cheered good speeches, and sometimes there was even physical violence. Noisy partisanship was rife, since the Athenians offered a prize for the play judged by the official *kritai* at the end of the festival to be the best. The reward was an ivy crown – a sort of classical Tony award – and Greeks of all classes seem to have cared very much who won it. There is a story that when, in the fifth century BC, Sophocles won the crown with his first attempt at a tragedy (now lost), the old master Aeschylus, who had also entered the competition for that

In classical Greek drama, the actors (always men even if they were playing female characters) wore stock masks to portray particular emotions or roles. Two typical examples are the "comic" mask (top) and the "slave" mask (bottom). This device was accepted unquestioningly by the audiences of the time for whom individual characterization was less important than it is to present-day theatre-goers.

year, left the country in a fit of rage. And Euripides, too, left Athens toward the end of his life, perhaps because his plays and his ideas were uncongenial to Athenian audiences.

As time went on, audiences at the festivals became more and more sophisticated, and more and more difficult to please. They were increasingly ready to boo and hiss and even throw stones, fruit, or nuts if something failed to measure up to their expectations. A third-rate actor is said to have admitted that, during a performance in a provincial town, he was showered with enough figs and other such things to stock a fruit store. A crane-like device called a *mechane* was

sometimes used for accomplishing the descent of the god toward the end of a tragedy, and this *deus ex machina* (literally "god from a machine"), in the form of an unfortunate actor swinging into view dangling from the end of a rope, invariably struck some members of the audience as extremely funny. Eventually, comic writers learned that they could raise an easy laugh by getting an actor to pretend to be stuck in mid-air and frantically signal a stagehand to lower him to the ground.

Until a quarter of a century ago, the only Greek plays known to be still extant were a few by each of the three great tragic dramatists of the fifth century, Aeschylus, Sophocles, and Euripides, and several by their contemporary Aristophanes, a superb writer of extremely bawdy comedies. Of the many other playwrights nothing had survived except some fragments from the pen of Menander, a popular writer who reached the height of his fame around 300 BC. Menander wrote more than 100 comedies, many of which were either translated into Latin, or closely imitated by two Roman playwrights of the following century, Plautus and Terence. So scholars knew a great deal about Menander's work, but only at second hand, as no one had read or seen any of his comedies in the original Greek. In 1959, however, a complete papyrus manuscript of Menander's comedy *Dyskolos* ("The bad-tempered man") that had been discovered in Egypt was published. The find was interesting in itself, of course, but perhaps the most exciting thing about it is its proof that even after 20-odd centuries we need not assume that our quest for the Greek past has ended. Some day, to our surprise and delight, we may find other things to add to our knowledge of the Athenian theatre in its golden age.

Familiar scenes from popular drama were often featured on Greek vase paintings. In this painting, Alcemene is being sacrificed on the pyre by her jealous husband Amphitryon – a scene from a Euripidean tragedy, which was painted in about 350 BC.

The four elements

What can the matter be?

IN ABOUT 625 BC, Thales, who is rated the world's first great scientist, was born in the Greek city of Miletus. And it was he who asked what is arguably the most important and profound question in history: "Of what is the Universe made?" His answer was simple – water. His reasoning: water can be solid and gaseous as well as liquid. It is also essential to life and so Thales concluded that everything must be made of water. Of course, Thales was wrong

and his theory was soon disputed. But the basic idea that all matter can consist of a simple element was vitally important because it set in motion a long train of discoveries which culminated in the achievements of modern chemistry.

Many philosophers thought they had "improved" on Thales's conclusions during the next 200 years, but it was the persuasive – and eccentric – thoughts of the great philosopher, Aristotle, that were to endure for centuries.

THE MYSTERIOUS QUARKS

All matter – from the humblest micro-organism to the grandest of galaxies – is made up of combinations of elements. These basic substances, of which 107 have been discovered, consist of particles called atoms, so small that they can be discerned only in the most powerful microscopes. Each element has its own particular kind of atom, which explains why one element differs from another. Knowledge of how atoms interact when elements combine to build substances has enabled scientists to produce some marvelous new materials.

Inside the atom, scientists have found even smaller particles that can be juggled to provide nuclear power. The latest theory holds that the atom is composed of six even tinier particles called quarks. These are classified in accordance with the attributes "up" (u); "down" (d); "sideways" or "strange" (s); "charmed" (c); "top" or "truth" (t); "bottom" or "beauty" (b). These oddly named particles cluster together to form the nuclear particles – electrons, protons, and neutrons – which make up atoms. Although they have never been detected there is strong theoretical evidence pointing to the existence of u, d, c, s, and b. However, it is in doubt, and there are a number of so-called "topless" theories against it. The odd word "quark" comes from James Joyce's novel *Finnegans Wake*.

Earth

Fire

Water

Air

The ancient Greeks believed that all material things were made up of four basic elements: Earth, fire, water, and air, depicted in these illustrations based on medieval German paintings (above).

Aristotle built upon the ideas of another great philosopher, Empedocles, who had suggested that all matter is composed of four elements: earth, fire, air and water. Aristotle added a fifth element to the list – ether, which he claimed was the sole constituent of the heavens (a concept that survives in the word "ethereal"). In this world, Aristotle believed, the four elements of Empedocles made up all matter. But each element itself consisted of a single primary material that was affected by pairs of four qualities – hot, cold, dry, and wet. Thus, Aristotle claimed, earth was cold and dry, fire was hot and dry, water was cold and wet, and air was hot and wet. Further, the four elements each had a natural position in the order of things. Earth had the lowest position; then came water; air lay over water, while fire had the highest position. And he argued that this was why rocks fell through water, raindrops fell through the air, bubbles rose in water, and smoke ascended to the sky. These theories were, of course, utterly wrong but Aristotle and his predecessors had developed the idea of elements joining together like "building blocks" to make matter – a concept that even today lies at the very heart of modern science.

About 100 years previously, during the fifth century BC, another idea of fundamental importance had also originated from Miletus; the concept of the atom. The idea of the atom was first put forward by the Greek philosopher Leucippus who proposed that matter was made of atoms. His ideas are known to us through his brilliant pupil Democritus. He said that all matter could be cut into smaller and smaller pieces. However, he said there would come a point at which the pieces could not be cut into anything smaller; he called these pieces *atoms* from a Greek word meaning "uncuttable." According to Democritus, these tiny individual particles were eternal, unchangeable and indestructible.

They were grouped in different patterns and between the atoms was empty space. Further, atoms obeyed fixed laws of nature, not the whims of gods.

These ideas were uncannily prophetic but at the time they had to compete with the overwhelmingly convincing ideas of Aristotle and were swamped. It is interesting to speculate on what might have happened if the Greek ideas of elements and of atoms had been developed then, instead of two millennia later.

SCIENTISTS OR DREAMERS?

What kind of men were the philosophers of ancient Greece? Some idea can be obtained from contemporary writings. Plato describes Thales as a dreamer who one night fell into a well while stargazing. A servant girl mocked him for trying to find out what was in the heavens, when he could not make out what was at his feet. But Aristotle challenges this view of Thales. He recounts the legend that Thales, tired of being taunted for his failure to become rich, used his knowledge of the weather to predict a bumper olive crop. He quietly bought up all the olive presses in Miletus and, when the glut occurred, charged highly for the use of them. Having made a fortune and proved his point, he immediately abandoned business and returned to philosophy.

Empedocles, on the other hand, was a mystic. He was convinced that he was immortal and would be taken up into heaven and made a god. Either in exultant expectation of his deification or in deep despair that the heavenly chariot had not arrived, he jumped into the crater of Mount Etna and was killed.

Democritus seems to have been a more worldly soul, because he was known as the "laughing philosopher." Some ascribe this title to a code of conduct that led him to be cheerful all the time, believing that laughter was an asset in personal relations. However, others contend that he was laughing at the follies of humanity.

Sacrilege in Athens

Was it a frame-up?

Hermes, the god who presided over travelers and commerce, was so greatly revered in Athens that there were statues of him at every street corner of the city. The mutilation of these statues the night before the Athenians embarked on an important naval mission in 415 BC outraged the citizens and led to general panic.

THE GREEK CITY-STATE of Athens was in the grip of war fever. All through the spring and early summer of 415 BC its shipwrights had been busy fitting out a fleet, arms had been prepared and supplies gathered. Volunteers flocked to join the expedition, which was to go to Sicily in aid of Athens' ally, the tiny city-state of Segesta. Segesta had asked Athens for help against its rival, Selinus, backed by the even stronger Sicilian city of Syracuse.

Volunteers were eager to come forward, for one of the three commanders of the expedition was Alcibiades, perhaps the most flamboyant Athenian of his day. He was young, about 35, and wealthy, a brilliant general with several successful campaigns to his credit, and a skillful and eloquent politician. True, he was also inclined to be wild and dissolute, and had the reputation of being an inveterate womanizer. But he also had the knack of making himself agreeable to people, and was known to be a friend of the sober philosopher Socrates. As the Greek poet Aristophanes put it, the Athenians both hated and loved Alcibiades.

Then, just as the preparations were almost complete, panic broke out. On the morning of June 7 the Athenians awoke to discover that during the night a terrible sacrilege had been committed on the Herms, the square pillars each adorned with a bust and phallus of the god Hermes which stood at street corners all over the city. Almost all these statues had been mutilated, their features hacked and defaced. The superstitious citizens felt that this was an evil omen for the success of the expedition, for Hermes was the god invoked by travelers before setting out on a dangerous journey. But who was guilty of this terrible deed? Rumor was rife. So began one of the most baffling, and mysterious, of events in Athenian history.

At first the sacrilege was thought to be a drunken frolic by high-spirited youths. But the damage was too widespread for that, and had obviously been well organized. Then suspicion fell on the rival city-state of Corinth, which had founded the colony-city of Syracuse, with which Athens might soon be at war, and which therefore had a vested interest in frightening the Athenian expedition off. Furthermore, staunch republicans suggested that the mutilations foreshadowed a coup by the aristocrats, who hated Athens' democratic form of government.

Nowhere was the blasphemy more fervently discussed than in the Assembly, the governing body of Athens. The Assembly met regularly, and its initial discussion of the affair came to no new conclusion. Then, in mid-June, came a new sensation. A citizen named Pythonicus rose in the Assembly and solemnly accused Alcibiades of blasphemy, not in the act of mutilating the Herms, which he carefully avoided mentioning, but in parodying, at a drunken party, the sacred rites or Mysteries celebrated at the nearby sanctuary of Eleusis. In the eyes of the Athenians, this was an even greater blasphemy than the mutilation of the Herms, for the Eleusinian Mysteries were supposed to be secret.

Alcibiades denied the serious charge, for if found guilty he faced a possible penalty of death, and he demanded an immediate trial, confident of acquittal. But he was outwitted by Androcles, a proletarian leader who hated the aristocratic Alcibiades, who wanted time to drum up more evidence. He protested that the naval expedition could not be held up while one of its generals was tried, and must sail at once. Alcibiades could face trial after the war was over. This agreement swayed the Assembly, which ordered Alcibiades to take up his command.

So off went the fleet to Sicily, in search of glory, commanded by Alcibiades and two fellow-generals, one of whom was Lamachus, a bluff, blustering general who though experienced was inclined to be rash in battle. The other was Nicias, an avowed enemy of Alcibiades.

The Assembly was by now thoroughly alarmed, and began a witch-hunt for the perpetrators of the mutilation of the Herms. Informers came forward to denounce a whole host of people; those of the accused who could do so fled, others were arrested, and many were summarily tried and executed.

Then an aristocratic lady named Agariste, a distant relative of Alcibiades, came forward in the Assembly to give evidence, and renewed the charge against Alcibiades of profaning the Eleusinian Mysteries. Outraged, the Assembly promptly sent a ship to bring Alcibiades back from Sicily to face trial. Alcibiades surrendered, but on the way home he escaped. He was wise to do so, for the Assembly condemned him to death in his absence.

Was Alcibiades guilty, or was he framed? The contemporary historian Thucydides confessed himself baffled, as indeed were many other Athenians at the time. The evidence suggests that Alcibiades was innocent of mutilating the Herms, because he had nothing to gain and much to lose if the Sicilian expedition had been cancelled as a result, but he may very well have been guilty of profaning the Eleusinian Mysteries since such parodies were fashionable among the young bloods of the time. It was unlikely that the Athenian populace would have tried to frame Alcibiades, because they stood to gain from a successful war, and Alcibiades was the general most likely to gain victory. As for Agariste, her personal reason for denouncing her relative is still unknown. Of all the suspects, the person most likely to gain was Nicias, who had opposed the expedition all along and would have been delighted to see it called off.

If Nicias was the arch-plotter, his plan misfired, for the Sicilian expedition was a disaster after Alcibiades' departure, and the Athenian force was wiped out. Lamachus was killed, and Nicias, left in sole command, bungled things. Eventually he surrendered to the enemy, who put him to death.

And Alcibiades? After an exile of eight years he returned in triumph to Athens, and was again appointed to command that city's forces.

Symposiums

Don't let the name fool you

IT IS EASY to picture the scene: Night has fallen, lamps are lighted, supper is finished, the guests have turned to the real business of the evening, drinking and talking. An honored guest has just been discussing – very soberly, in the circumstances – love, about which all of them have been expressing opinions. Suddenly there is a disturbance and in stumbles a gatecrasher – a charming but tipsy young man, extravagantly dressed and with outrageous manners – who tries to persuade everyone else to have a few more drinks. For a moment it seems as if the quiet good fellowship of the evening is about to decline into a boisterous frolic. But the other guests manage to calm the intruder down, and the evening returns to a lofty level.

A common enough occurrence, perhaps, but this is no common party. The time is 416 BC, the place is Athens at its zenith, and the guest who has been talking is none other than Socrates, one of the greatest of Greek philosophers. The drunken intruder is Alcibiades, brilliant but unscrupulous politician and military leader, most glamorous and dissolute of the young rich. The party is being held at the house of Agathon, a poet, and among the other guests is Aristophanes, the famous comic playwright. After Alcibiades calms down, Socrates and Aristophanes carry on the discussion about the nature of love; they talk till dawn, long after the other guests have fallen asleep on their couches (guests reclined rather than sat).

With dancers, girl flutists, and naked boys serving wine to the men-only guests, Greek "symposiums," such as the one illustrated below, were far from serious affairs. Although there was much philosophical discussion and argument, such talk often took second place to the entertainment and debauchery that accompanied the drinking.

The events of that night were described – or perhaps largely invented – some 30 years later by Socrates's great disciple Plato in a lengthy dialogue known as the *Symposium*. The word "symposium," which has come to mean "a conference or discussion of a serious subject," meant simply "a drinking session" in ancient Athens, and Plato's symposium seems to have been far more decorous than most.

Even so, there was always a serious – or, at least, a ritualistic – element in Greek drinking parties. Wine played an almost sacramental role in all aspects of life, social as well as political and religious. A child's first taste of wine marked his or her acceptance in the community. At every stage of official ceremonies (there were usually three stages in a formal symposium) there were libations – the pouring of a few drops of wine in honor of either a god or, at a symposium, the good spirit (*agathos daimon*) invoked to bless the party. This "good spirit" was felt to be essential. The Greeks were half-fearful of the potent effects of wine. As hot-blooded as they were quick-witted, they felt the need to control and civilize their drinking – though they did not always succeed, as the Alcibiades incident shows only too clearly.

A "symposiarch" (master of drinking) was chosen at the start of every party. He would ordain the mixture of wine and water (the Athenians thought it not only dangerous but barbaric to drink unwatered wine), the rate at which the wine circulated, and even the number of cups each guest was allowed. In Plato's account, the drinking is moderate, partly because some of those present already have hangovers. And Socrates and his companions decide to dispense with such frivolities as the girl-flutists and dancers (whether girls or boys) that generally enlivened such get-togethers. Instead, after the amusing incident of the arrival of Alcibiades, they concentrate on philosophizing about love – heterosexual, homosexual, and non-sexual (Platonic) love.

Apart from the entertainers, who were often, it must be admitted, practitioners of less seemly arts than flute-playing and dancing, women were not normally present. There may have been female equivalents of the all-male banquets, but no written evidence of women's parties survives. Our knowledge of the procedures, both decorous and highly indecorous, at symposiums comes almost entirely from paintings on Greek vases and drinking cups, and from two detailed accounts: Plato's *Symposium* and another party – again with Socrates among the guests – described by Xenophon, who was a soldier and landowner rather than a full-time philosopher. Xenophon's *Symposium* is set five years earlier (421 BC) than Plato's and tells of a

---

THE TWO PORTRAITS OF SOCRATES

The Greek philosopher Socrates (whose marble bust is shown above) founded a school of philosophy in the fifth century BC which was to flourish for many years. Although he never recorded anything in writing, his teachings were elaborated upon and immortalized by his pupil, Plato.

Socrates is the most famous of all philosophers because of his pupil Plato's extensive accounts of his life and words. But what about the reality behind the figure? He wrote nothing himself; everything we know about him comes from other sources, chiefly Plato and the landowner-historian Xenophon. They agree about the basic facts of his life and death, but they present very different images of the kind of man he was – and how are we to choose between those images?

Socrates was born around 469 BC and lived for 70 years, through the greatest days of Athens and on to its crushing defeat by Sparta. He held minor public office and fought bravely as a foot-soldier. He was married to a woman named Xanthippe, who was reputedly ill-tempered and ugly, and they had a son. He also more or less laid the foundations of Western moral philosophy, and he died for his beliefs, accused by his city of neglecting the traditional gods and of corrupting young people by encouraging them to query traditional ideas and assumptions. Given the choice of death or exile, he chose death and was forced to kill himself by drinking hemlock. His memory was revered by a large circle of pupils of varying ages and abilities; they had paid no fees for the privilege of sitting at his feet and exploring pathways toward truth by the Socratic method of asking questions and listening to answers that invariably raised further questions.

But what was Socrates himself really like? In Plato's dialogues – so named because Plato, long after the event, gives us vivid re-creations of a number of question-and-answer sessions – the great philosopher is portrayed as a high-minded seeker after absolute truth, prepared to use quiet humor to this end but basically a serious and rather austere character. He is also depicted as inclined toward homosexuality (like Plato himself) with a comparatively dismissive attitude toward women.

On the other hand, Xenophon's *Symposium* – which may have been written to counter Plato's – shows us a jovial Socrates, who not only enjoys wine and girl-entertainers but prefers not to discuss serious subjects until the festivities have ended. He comes across as unquestionably (like Xenophon himself) interested in women, and charmingly insists that they are in no way inferior to men, except in terms of physical strength, provided they're properly taught. That, according to Xenophon, is why Socrates married a woman as surly as Xanthippe; if he could teach *her*, reasoned Xenophon, he could teach anyone.

Each of the two vivid characterizations seems to reflect the preferences and temperament of its writer. Which, then, is closer to the truth?

drinking party in honor of a lad, Autolycus, who has just won a contest in the Panathenaic Games. Here jollity *does* reign. A dancing girl and boy remain throughout the evening, and Socrates cheerfully joins in the fun, even doing a dance of his own that raises a general laugh.

The many depictions of drinking parties on Greek vases and cups indicate that informality of this sort was much more common than dignified behavior. These show naked or topless girls dancing, playing musical instruments, or cavorting in a variety of ways before the reclining guests, each with a three-legged table beside him for his food and drink. Naked boys are rarely far off with decanters of wine. At gatherings like these, conversation must have been light and inconsequential. Nor was sex taboo if the graphic illustrations on some of the ancient vases are to be believed.

And when the party was over? Well, all we know for certain is that at the end of Xenophon's *Symposium*, after seeing a short erotic play about the love of Dionysus and Ariadne, most of the married men hastily call for their horses and ride off to make love to their wives. That, at least, is how Xenophon tells it.

The other side of Aristotle
Classification was the name of the game

ARISTOTLE, who lived from 384 to 322 BC, was the most influential of the Greek philosophers, both in his own day and for well over 1,000 years after his death. His restless mind encompassed virtually all fields of knowledge, including metaphysics, politics, astronomy, literature, ethics, logic, meteorology, physics, economics, and psychology, and what he wrote about all these subjects had a profound effect upon Western culture. Yet one of the most valuable of his achievements was that he founded virtually single-handed the science of biology – and his work in this field was almost ignored until comparatively recent times.

Animals – as, to a lesser extent, plants – seem to have been a special passion of Aristotle's. He studied them assiduously in an effort to reveal the order and beauty in Nature. But whereas other philosophers were content to reach conclusions on the basis of reason alone, he never ceased to observe the workings of the natural world and to base *his* generalizations on solid evidence. For instance, he describes about 540 kinds of animal – an enormous undertaking for a man who lacked microscopes, reference books, or other aids, and who nonetheless tried to classify and study the life style of every creature whose existence he had heard of. To broaden his horizons, he solicited, and got, the help of many students and colleagues, one of whom was Alexander the Great, who brought his former tutor accounts and specimens of many exotic forms of life that he encountered in his campaigns through distant lands.

Examples of Aristotle's meticulous observations of animal life, particularly in the area of reproduction and prenatal existence, abound. He noted, for instance, that the heart of an embryo chick inside an egg takes shape four days after laying as "a tiny speck of blood on the white of the egg that beats and moves as though alive." Several such discoveries were subsequently disbelieved because nobody else was painstaking enough to repeat his observations. Thus his finding that certain dogfish embryos are attached to a structure like a placenta in the womb was largely ignored until finally confirmed in AD 1842. And his description of the unusual breeding behavior of a certain kind of catfish was considered ridiculous until it was first observed in American catfish, then – as late as 1856 – found in a hitherto unsuspected Greek species that was the very one he had based his observations upon. Similarly, it was not until 1842 that zoologists fully confirmed his account of the extraordinary mating procedure of the octopus, in which the male employs a specially developed tentacle.

On the basis of his observations, Aristotle classified animals into groups, trying to discern some order in the sheer diversity of living creatures. Other thinkers had endeavored to do this, too, classifying animals according to their appearance as "winged," "footless," and so on; but he realized that this was the wrong approach and argued – rightly – that, for example, dolphins are related to human beings in spite of their fish-like appearance because both dolphins and human beings bear their young in the same way. His scheme of classification separates animals and plants into two kingdoms, divides animals into the two main groups that we today call vertebrates and invertebrates, and recognizes that plant-like creatures such as sea anemones and sponges are in fact animals – all reflecting a system of Nature that is in many respects the one biologists accept today.

He was not omniscient, of course, and his observations led to many wrong conclusions. For example, he considered the heart to be the seat of intelligence and the brain to be merely an organ for cooling the blood supply to the heart. Because he had such remarkable intelligence, though, his ideas were very persuasive – so much so that they dominated thinking in medieval Europe. In fields other than biology an uncritical worship of Aristotle eventually hindered progress. Even as late as the early 1600s, an observant priest who claimed to have seen spots on the Sun was told by his superior to change his spectacles because "Aristotle nowhere mentions spots." And his pronouncements on motion, which included the theory that heavier objects fall faster than light ones,

prevented any real advance in physics and astronomy until they were overthrown by Galileo in the late 1500s. Ironically, then, some of his less valid dicta swamped his most valuable ideas, those in the field of biology.

It was not till 1735 that a comprehensive system of classification based on Aristotle's scheme of Nature was established by the Swedish botanist Linnaeus. Because, as in Aristotle, the Linnaean system suggested a pyramid of life with the various animals gradually ascending in complexity from simple to more intricate, this type of thought led directly to Darwin's theory of evolution. Darwin himself realized how much he owed to Aristotle. When presented with a translation of Aristotle's *Parts of Animals*, he remarked: "I had a high notion of Aristotle's merits, but I had not the most remote notion what a wonderful man he was. Linnaeus and [the French anatomist] Cuvier have been my two gods, though in very different ways, but they were mere schoolboys to old Aristotle."

PHILOSOPHY AND CONQUEST

The first meeting between Aristotle and Alexander the Great, which took place in 342 BC, is shown in this detail from a French medieval manuscript illustrating scenes from Alexander's life.

In 342 BC, at the age of 42, Aristotle was summoned to the kingdom of Macedon to serve as tutor to the son of Philip II. The meeting was one of the most fruitful in history, for the prince, then 14, was to succeed to the throne six years later and to become known as Alexander the Great. The young warrior acquired a great respect for the philosopher and his persuasive ideas. In his meteoric career of conquest, Alexander not only

established a Greek-speaking empire extending from Spain to India, but directly sought to bring about the development and refinement of Greek knowledge, which was to be preserved in Alexandria, the city named after him. It was from there that Greek thought, spearheaded by Aristotle's philosophy, eventually found its way to Europe, providing the seeds from which Western science and culture could grow.

Ancient secrets

Archeologists may have discovered the tomb of Alexander the Great's father

I**N 1977** a season of archeological digging at the village of Vergina in northern Greece seemed destined to end in frustration and disappointment. But in early October the luck of the Greek archeologist Professor Manolis Andronikos of the University of Thessaloniki suddenly changed.

While excavating at the bottom of a pit dug into a large earth mound on the site, he uncovered a curved stone that looked as if it might be a roof. Excavations continued, and a fresco above what was later found to be the front entrance was revealed. It depicted a hunt for wild boar and lions, and was held aloft by two pillars that were as yet only partially visible. The quality of this painting suggested that it might lead to a major tomb. Perhaps it would confirm the professor's conviction that this site, about 30 miles (48 kilometers) west-southwest of Thessaloniki, lay over the ancient city of Aegae, capital of the empire of Macedon. The front entrance was impenetrable, so, in an atmosphere of mounting anticipation, the archeologists removed a keystone from the roof, in the manner of tomb robbers through the ages, and on November 8 Professor Andronikos clambered through into the chamber. His hand shook with excitement as the thin beam from his flashlight probed the inner sanctum of the burial chamber. Could the professor be the first person to enter the inner tomb since it had been sealed? Or had grave robbers vandalized it, looted its treasures, and destroyed its testimony to the past?

The professor was elated to see immediately that the contents of the tomb were undisturbed. The only ravager had been the passage of time: Some of the articles had crumbled into heaps of dust on the floor. At the far end of the chamber stood a great marble sarcophagus, the chest in which the remains of the dead were laid.

In front of the sarcophagus lay scattered remnants of wooden furniture. From one of these pieces, perhaps a bed, a decorative row of gold and ivory figures, about six inches (15 centimeters) high, had fallen to the floor. Among the many other treasures were a man's personal belongings. They included body armor, sandals, leg guards, a scepter, and, most exciting, a royal diadem or headband. The same opulence was evident in a beautiful sword in a sheath of ivory and wood, the remains of a shield, and the first iron Macedonian helmet

ever found. These arms and armor, with their delicate and sumptuous decorations, bore witness that this was no commoner's tomb, where offerings might consist of little more than a few vases; instead, all the pieces were of immense value, made with supreme skill and care.

As the professor and his assistants opened the marble lid of the sarcophagus, they gazed with astonishment at the sight of a fabulous casket of solid gold, later found to weigh more than 24 pounds (10 kilos). The sunburst, a radiating star, embossed on its lid was a royal Macedonian symbol. Here, indeed, was a royal tomb, but who was the king that lay there?

The lid of the casket lifted easily to reveal a fragmented skull and other bones that had been partially burned. Bones and armor had been retrieved from a funeral pyre. The bones would have then been washed and laid in the casket. A delicate wreath of leaves and acorns from the Greek god Zeus's sacred tree, the oak, had been placed over the bones. Among the bones were two teeth, which were later judged to have belonged to a man of more than 32 years of age.

Close inspection of the tiny ivory and gold figures on the floor revealed six portraits. One

---

PHILIP AND ALEXANDER

Philip II (382–336 BC), father of Alexander the Great (356–323 BC), was a brilliant statesman and soldier. He came to the throne of Macedon in northern Greece in 359 BC and formed his scattered tribesmen into a powerful army. Having conquered much of Greece with the aid of his son, he was determined to invade the vast Persian empire, an act of vengeance for the Persian attack on Greece a century and a half earlier. But Philip was assassinated and it was left to Alexander to fulfill his father's dream.

With an army of almost 40,000, an aggressive fighting force, Alexander conquered Asia Minor (roughly present-day Turkey). In a series of brilliant battles, he defeated the Persian King Darius III, taking all his lands and titles.

Driven on by his visions of one empire built up from the territory he had won, combined with his own thirst for fame, he fought on for another seven years, leading his army into Russia and eventually to India. As a result of his conquests, he had mapped unknown territory, founded cities, and opened new trade routes that brought vast areas under the control of the Greeks.

Busts of Philip II (above) and his son Alexander (below).

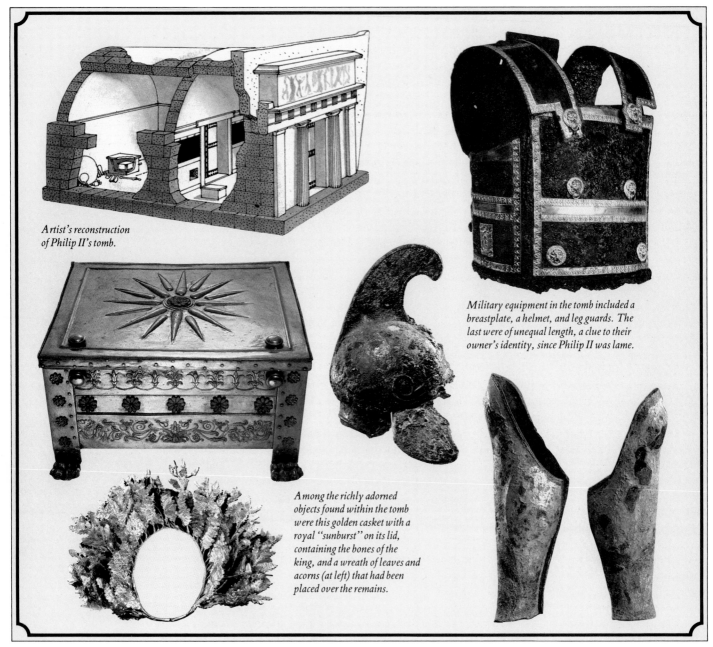

Artist's reconstruction of Philip II's tomb.

Military equipment in the tomb included a breastplate, a helmet, and leg guards. The last were of unequal length, a clue to their owner's identity, since Philip II was lame.

Among the richly adorned objects found within the tomb were this golden casket with a royal "sunburst" on its lid, containing the bones of the king, and a wreath of leaves and acorns (at left) that had been placed over the remains.

most probably portrayed King Philip II of Macedon, father of Alexander the Great. Another was the most beautiful sculpture of the young Alexander that Professor Andronikos had ever seen. A third head, resembling Alexander, was probably a portrait of Olympias, Alexander's mother. The identities of the other portraits remain a mystery.

Further discoveries awaited the archeologists in a second, smaller room. Linked to the main chamber by marble doors hung from bronze bolts, it contained another wonderful fresco. A marble sarcophagus stood next to the wall. An exquisite golden wreath, patterned in the leaves and flowers of myrtle, lay on the floor, while in the corner stood a gold quiver. Leaning against the door was another pair of bronze leg guards,

one of which was slightly shorter than the other. And inside the marble sarcophagus lay a smaller golden casket with a royal sunburst on the lid. Inside, the burned bones were wrapped in a rich purple fabric interlaced with gold thread. It also contained a superb diadem of intertwined golden branches, which must have been the possession of a woman.

The objects retrieved in these excavations, including fragments of pottery, have helped archeologists to date the building of the tomb at between 350 and 325 BC. In this period only one king was buried in Macedon: Philip II.

Philip was a military genius. In the fourth century BC he forged a powerful army which enabled him and his son to conquer the entire Greek peninsula, thus greatly extending the

Macedonian empire. Texts written at the time tell us that Philip had an injured eye and that he had been lamed in battle. The ivory portrait found on the floor of the larger burial chamber showed a mature man of great character, with an injured eye. And the bronze leg guards in the smaller room are those of a lame man.

Philip loved rich banquets, good wine, and women – he had seven wives, not to mention countless mistresses. Olympias, Alexander's mother, was one of his earlier wives. Philip also had a much younger, beautiful wife called Cleopatra, who bore him another son. Olympias regarded this child as a threat to Alexander,

and it was rumored that she plotted Philip's death out of jealousy. It was also alleged that after Philip had been murdered, she also killed Cleopatra and her son. It seems reasonable to suppose, therefore, that the bones of the woman in the smaller tomb might be those of Cleopatra.

The weight of the evidence, including the rich treasure, the trappings of royalty, the sunburst emblem on the caskets, the teeth of a man over 32 (Philip was 46 when he died), the portraits, and the unusual leg guards, has convinced archeologists that the tomb at Vergina is, indeed, that of Philip II, who bequeathed to his subjects his brilliant son, Alexander the Great.

The work of years gone in hours
The destruction of the Alexandrian Library

SOMETIME OVER 1,300 years ago a group of religious fanatics set about the destruction of what were, to them, heretical writings. The flames which the fanatics ignited set the course of learning back for centuries, and threw difficulties in the way of any quest for the past. For these writings were the volumes that made up the Alexandrian Library, the greatest collection of scholarship of the ancient world.

Alexandria, founded in Egypt by the Greek King Alexander the Great in 332 BC, came under the rule of the Ptolemies, descendants of one of the king's generals. This general, Ptolemy I, founded the library, and wrote for it a history of Alexander's campaigns. It was his son, Ptolemy II Philadelphus, who established the library in its glory, not merely as the greatest collection of books in its day, but also as a center of research and study. Its first librarian was a scholar named Zenodotus of Ephesus, remembered for his editing of the Homeric poems the *Iliad* and the *Odyssey*, which he painstakingly assembled from various manuscript sources.

Under Ptolemy II and his heirs, and Zenodotus and his successors, the library at Alexandria was expanded enormously. It was planned to contain a copy, or in some cases the original manuscript, of every Greek work, as well as material from all other parts of the civilized Western world. By the middle of the first century BC, when Alexandrian scholarship probably reached a peak, the number of separate *volumina* (scrolls, and hence our word "volume") ran into hundreds of thousands. Estimates of the numbers vary widely, depending

on which commentator you read, but may have been as high as 700,000. The most likely estimate is half a million. But it must be remembered that each *volumen* held fewer words than does a modern book, so the actual number of complete works may have been rather less.

An army of copyists and scholars prepared the manuscript scrolls. Manuscripts were bought or borrowed for copying and returned (or in some cases borrowed and not returned) from all over the place. Ptolemy II is said to have demanded authenticated copies of the plays of Aeschylus, Euripides, and Sophocles as a condition of supplying Athens with corn during a famine. All books found aboard trading ships docking at Alexandria's busy port were seized and copied. The library and its copyists standardized scroll production, and "Alexandrian editions" were

THE SEPTUAGINT
The translation of the Hebrew books of the Old Testament into Greek was a product of the Alexandrian Library. According to a letter supposedly written by an Alexandrian official to his brother, Ptolemy II wrote to the High Priest Eleazar at Jerusalem asking him to send 72 scholars, six from each of the 12 tribes of Israel, to translate the Sacred Writings for him. This translation, completed appropriately enough in 72 days, became known as the Septuagint, the Seventy. Modern scholars think the translation actually took about 200 years, and was probably made for the use of the big Greek-speaking colony of Jews living in Alexandria at that time.

considered to be the authentic versions. Most of our present-day editions of the Greek classics owe their accuracy to this library. The poet Callimachus, who worked at the library for many years in the third century BC (though not as librarian), devised the first system of classification, in a catalogue that ran to 120 *volumina*.

The library was divided into two parts, the Royal Library with the bulk of the collection, and an Outer Library with about 43,000 rolls in it. We do not know how the collection was divided, or why; nor do we know exactly where it was housed, for the destruction of Ptolemaic Alexandria was so complete that our knowledge of its buildings is minimal.

Unfortunately we know very little about the actual contents of the library. We do know that the intention of the Ptolemies was to make a complete collection of Greek literature, and that though they did not succeed, the collection was certainly very comprehensive. The library also contained many scientific works, such as those of Ctesibius, the second-century-BC barber's son who invented, among other things, a water-clock and a catapult driven by compressed air, and of the astronomer Aristarchus, who in the third century BC knew that the Sun did not revolve around the Earth. Ctesibius's work is lost, and known to us today only by references in other writings, and most of Aristarchus's works have also vanished.

Though the disappearance of such writings undoubtedly held back scientific progress, the lost ground has now been regained and passed; but we can never recapture those miracles of creative art, the literature that was lost in the destruction of the library. Records show, for example, that in the fifth century BC the pioneering playwright Aeschylus wrote at least 70 plays, and that his near-contemporaries Sophocles, Euripides, and Aristophanes wrote, respectively, 113, 92, and 43 plays. All these works were almost certainly in Alexandria's library, yet only seven plays of Aeschylus, seven of Sophocles, 18 of Euripides, and 11 of Aristophanes are extant. In the wry words of a modern scholar, Carl Sagan, "It is a little as if the only surviving works of a man named William Shakespeare were *Coriolanus* and *A Winter's Tale*, but we had heard that he had written certain other plays, unknown to us but apparently prized in his time, works entitled *Hamlet, Macbeth, Julius Caesar, King Lear, A Midsummer Night's Dream, Romeo and Juliet . . .*"

The end of the Alexandrian Library is shrouded in as much mystery as its contents. Part of the library, at least, was accidentally set on fire and destroyed during Julius Caesar's brief campaign in Egypt in 48 BC. The contemporary sources differ in their account of what was destroyed; some suggest that it was a book storehouse, which may have been the building where new acquisitions were held pending cataloguing and incorporation in the main collection; others suggest that it was the contents of the Royal Library itself. However, shortly afterward Cleopatra, the fabled ruler of Egypt made secure on her throne by Caesar, was given the

Alexandria (shown in the manuscript illustration at right) was founded by Alexander the Great in 332 BC, and rapidly became a great intellectual and commercial center. Here the cultures of many races and civilizations found a home, most notably in the city's famous library.

TORN TO PIECES BY THE MOB

One of the last of the many great scholars who worked at the Alexandrian Library was a woman named Hypatia. She was born about AD 370, the daughter of the mathematician Theon of Alexandria. She appears to have lectured on the philosophy of Plato, Aristotle, Pythagoras, and other Greek thinkers, and was therefore regarded by the Christians of the day as a major protagonist of pagan Neoplatonism. Yet one of her pupils was Synesius of Cyrene, who later became Bishop of Ptolemaïs. She was also a close friend of Orestes, who was the pagan prefect of Alexandria.

Hypatia's teachings and her friendship with Orestes provoked the enmity of Cyril, Bishop of Alexandria, a bigot dedicated to the suppression of paganism in all its forms. In 415 there was a riot – one of many in Alexandria – and a Christian mob, led by monks who were possibly carrying out the wishes of Cyril, dragged Hypatia from her chariot as she rode through the streets, stripped her, and flayed her alive with clam shells.

Although little is really known about the structure and decoration of the Alexandrian Library, one of its Great Halls may well have resembled this reconstruction (at left). The two paintings in the hall show, at left, Alexander the Great (founder of the city) and, at right, the god Serapis. Worshiped by both the Greeks and the Egyptians, Serapis symbolized the influence of Greek learning in Egypt.

contents of another library by her lover Mark Antony to replace the burned books. This was the 200,000-volume collection from Pergamum (modern Bergama in Turkey). The Alexandrian Library was again a center for learning.

In the third century AD, Alexandria became a center of Christian worship, and there is some evidence that in AD 391 a mob destroyed the pagan temple of the Egyptian god Serapis, the Serapeum, and with it the part of the Alexandrian Library which was contained within the building. However, the list of scholars who worked in Alexandria after this date shows that some part at least of the library survived this disaster. The final destruction seems to have been at the hands of Arab invaders in 646. The Arabs, in the fanaticism of their new religion of Islam, destroyed all books that did not conform to its teachings. Tradition has it that the scrolls from the Alexandrian Library were taken to the public baths, where for three months they served as fuel to heat the water. In this sadly ignoble manner the collected wisdom of centuries went up in smoke.

Butser Farm

An Iron Age settlement in England

DISCOVERIES of the remains of prehistoric peoples raise as many questions as they answer. How did ordinary individuals and families go about their daily business? How did they cook their food, build houses, make tools, travel about, and so on? To put such questions to the test, to find out what may or may not have been possible at a particular time and place, given the fragmentary evidence we have, a new craft has recently been developed; it is called experimental archeology. The experimental archeologist tries to build a practical way of life upon clues provided by the piecemeal findings of his colleagues.

One of the most fascinating of such experiments has been concerned with one type of culture in the Iron Age – the name generally given to the five or six centuries immediately preceding the Christian era, during which the great civilizations of Egypt, Greece, and Rome flourished while northern and western Europe remained "barbaric." What would life have been like on a British farm in those days? To shed some light upon that question, archeologist Peter Reynolds has re-created – as nearly as possible – an Iron Age farm of about the year 300 BC. He chose for his experiment a site on Butser Hill, a high point on the chalky Hampshire Downs of southern England, where archeological findings indicate the actual existence of just such a farm.

Reynolds started with a fair idea of the materials, livestock, and basic crops available to his prehistoric predecessors. He knew, too, what must be ruled out: all forms of pesticide, weed killer, and fertilizer; even, if possible, rabbits, since there probably were no rabbits in the British Isles before the time of the Norman Conquest in the late 11th century AD.

One of the first items on the program was the building of a farmhouse based on the ground plan and remains of a Celtic dwelling at a site known as Maiden Castle in southwest England. Using Iron Age tools such as a socketed ax and heavy iron hammer, Reynolds and a team of assistants constructed a circular wooden house with a diameter of about 18 feet (6 meters), a thatched roof, and low walls made of daub (a mixture of clay, chalk, straw, and animal hair). It is hard to tell how precisely this resembles an "average" Iron Age British farmhouse; but, simple as it is, the structure has withstood hurricane-force winds and torrential rain, and is therefore sturdy as well as functional. The team

Peter Reynolds's Butser Experiment, begun in 1972, set out to reconstruct life on an Iron Age farm of about 300 BC. The first practical experiment of its kind, the project received worldwide attention and became the subject of a British television documentary in 1977. For the purposes of filming and the convenience of its many visitors, it was decided in 1976 to extend the original farm and to build a demonstration area (at right), the focal point of which was a reconstruction of a large Iron Age round house (above) furnished in the style of the time, and believed to be the largest reconstruction of a prehistoric round house that has ever been undertaken.

erected a second dwelling that had a portion of thatched roof at a more shallow pitch than the rest, but this one proved unsound. From an experimental point of view, failures are as instructive as successes.

Turning to livestock, Reynolds tried to "back breed" by crossing a wild boar with one of the oldest surviving breeds of English pig. This too was a failure; the result of the cross was a litter of striped piglets that could outrun any dog and were almost impossible to catch. So no further attempts to re-create long-gone breeds of domestic animals were made. Instead, the farm has been stocked with modern breeds that Reynolds believes correspond closely to Iron Age breeds – for instance, small shorthorn Dexter cattle imported from Ireland. The cattle have been trained to pull ards, which are the forerunners of ploughs. Basically a wooden spike tipped with an iron point and inserted into a pole, an ard stirs up the soil rather than turning it over.

One of the farm's principal crops is Emmer wheat (seeds of which have been found in the pyramids of Egypt). This ancient cereal does not grow to a uniform height as its modern counterparts do, and so the best way to harvest it is by hand rather than with a sickle. Its grain has a higher protein value than today's more refined varieties of wheat. Among other crops appropriate for an Iron Age farm is the oddly named "Fat Hen" (or Melde), a leafy green vegetable that also has a higher food value than leafy vegetables eaten today such as cabbage or spinach. It can be cooked and eaten, or its seeds can be made into flour.

But having grown their food, how did the Britons store it for future use? At Butser Hill the experimental archeologists are using storage pits dug in the ground – the method probably used by Iron Age farmers. The amount of food produced per acre and the proportion of it that can be stored in pits without rotting has already led to a reappraisal of the total amount of land under cultivation in ancient times and of the population it could support. Reynolds now believes that far more land was farmed by the prehistoric Britons than was previously thought.

The Butser Ancient Farm project, begun in 1972, has been filmed and televised, and people from many countries have studied the results of the experiment. In response to growing worldwide interest, a special demonstration area has been added to the original working farm. This includes a larger round house, based on the plan of a structure excavated at Pimperne (in a nearby part of southwest England), and furnished in Iron Age style, complete with stout metal andirons and clay oven.

Meanwhile, Reynolds and his team, by continuing to test in practical ways all sorts of theories about Iron Age rural life, are helping other archeologists to identify and interpret the evidence found on actual Iron Age excavations. For instance, charcoal – vital to an Iron Age economy – has been manufactured at Butser Hill in pits covered in turf to record the effects on the surrounding soil. Structures and haystacks have been allowed to collapse, and storage pits have been deliberately soiled and abandoned in order to observe what evidence they leave behind. The team have even noted the way the lowly earthworm can, in time, redistribute in the ground such items as pottery fragments.

In all such ways, the Butser Hill project is bringing us closer, in fact and spirit, to an understanding of the sturdy, industrious Britons who were able to repulse the invasions of Julius Caesar and his legions in 55 and 54 BC.

The greatest scientist in the ancient world

The pursuit of pure reason

OF ALL THE great scientists in ancient Greece, the most brilliant was undoubtedly Archimedes. His understanding that principles can be proved to be true simply by testing them to show that they work was probably his most important contribution to scientific thought, because it is the basis of modern science. Like other Greeks, however, Archimedes to a great extent disdained the practical consequences of his work and was proudest of his abstract discoveries. The belief that the application of scientific principles to everyday life was somehow ungentlemanly is borne out by the historian Plutarch. He reported that the philosopher Plato inveighed against inventors and engineers as "corrupters and destroyers of the pure excellence of geometry."

Archimedes was born in Syracuse in Sicily, which was then a Greek kingdom, in about 287 BC and lived there for most of his life. He was a magnificent mathematician – as well as making discoveries, he was the first to calculate accurately the value for pi (π), the number representing the ratio of the circumference of a circle to its diameter, which is used for calculating the surface areas and volumes of spheres, cones, and cylinders. Archimedes considered this his crowning achievement, so much so that he even ordered his gravestone to be inscribed with a sphere and a cylinder.

But today Archimedes is best remembered for his mechanical inventions and practical discoveries. He had the rare ability to look at something and then deduce the principles by which it works. He grasped how and why levers and pulleys work and constructed machines that could raise weights with relatively little physical effort from their human operators. It is said that using a pulley of his own design, he once heaved a fully laden ship from the harbor at Syracuse up onto the shore. Whether or not he did perform this feat, it would certainly have been possible for him to do so, given his knowledge.

The discovery for which Archimedes is best known demonstrates how the need for a solution of a practical problem could spur his genius. Hiero, the King of Syracuse, asked Archimedes to find out whether his crown was made of pure gold or whether it contained some silver. The scientist decided to ponder on the question while relaxing in a bath. He filled the tub to the top and got in. Inevitably, some water overflowed onto the floor. Immediately, Archimedes realized how to solve his problem. If he immersed a crown of pure gold in water, it would displace less water than a crown of the same weight of gold and silver. This is because gold is heavier, or denser, than silver and so an adulterated crown would be bulkier than a crown made of pure gold. Elated at his discovery, the scientist is supposed to have rushed out naked into the street, shouting "Eureka," meaning "I've got it!" He performed the experiment. The gold turned out to be adulterated and Hiero executed the goldsmith. The craftsman's misfortune is our gain. Archimedes had discovered the important principle of specific gravity – the ratio of the density of a substance to the density of water. Pure gold has a specific gravity of 19.3, which means that it is 19.3 times as dense, or as heavy, as an equal volume of water. Silver is much less dense, having a specific gravity of 10.5.

Archimedes went further. He realized that if a substance has a specific gravity of less than 1, it will float in water. This principle is still known today as Archimedes's principle. Apart from

Although best known as a classical inventor, Archimedes' specialty was mathematics. Here, the Renaissance artist Raphael has shown him teaching the principles of geometry, a tribute to the feeling of the Renaissance world that the Greeks had laid the foundations of scientific and mathematical knowledge.

solving problems for the King of Syracuse, Archimedes made little use of his discoveries. He was satisfied simply to demonstrate that they worked by heaving ships or testing crowns. And yet the theories he propounded could have been used, for example, at the time to improve the waterwheel to make it produce much more power, or to build better ships. But the Greeks had little call for mechanical sources of power – slaves, working animals, and some waterwheels were generally sufficient. Instead of utilizing their science to gain a commanding position in the ancient world, the Greeks were conquered by the Romans, who throttled the extraordinary creative energy that seems uniquely Greek. Archimedes, himself, died at the hands of a Roman soldier when Syracuse fell to Rome in 212 BC. The Romans, however, had such respect for Archimedes that after his death they complied with his request and had a sphere, surrounded by a cylinder, engraved in commemoration of the discovery of which Archimedes was most proud – the calculation of the volume and surface areas of a sphere. Even so, Greek science and its practical consequences were lost for nearly 2,000 years.

Although Archimedes' screw (above) bears the scientist's name, there is no evidence that Archimedes invented it.

FROM TOYS TO TURBINES

Two Greek inventors of genius made discoveries of far-reaching consequences. They were Ctesibius, who worked in Alexandria in about 270 BC, and Hero, who lived there about 300 years later. Both built elaborate machines powered by falling weights of moving air or water, and involving complex trains of cogs and levers. Some, such as Ctesibius's water-powered clock and Hero's screw press, had a serious purpose and were used for centuries before being surpassed. But much of their work was of little practical value. For example, Ctesibius constructed the first organ, a water-powered instrument with stentorian tones that reputedly carried for 40 miles (over 60 kilometers).

Hero was renowned for his automatic puppet shows and temples with doors that opened, as though by magic, when a fire was lit on the altar.

Hero also invented sources of power that are now used in the production of electricity. In all of antiquity, Hero was the only person to refer to a windmill. But he described it as being used to power a machine that puffed air into an organ so that, whenever the wind blew, the organ would sound. Hero's most ingenious invention was the aeolipile, a hollow sphere with two spouts mounted above a boiler. Steam was piped up from the boiler into the sphere and, as it issued from the spouts, the sphere spun around. The same principle is applied today in lawn sprinklers and jet and rocket engines. In fact, Hero's aeolipile is a direct ancestor of the steam turbine, but like his windmill, it was regarded only as a plaything and never used to provide useful power. Hero little realized how much his efforts could have improved everyday life.

Fifteen centuries after its invention as a toy, Hero's aeolipile provided the basis for the steam engine, and hence, in the long term, the industrial revolution.

The Seven Wonders of the World

A "must" for ancient Greek travelers

SOME OF THE world's greatest sculptors and architects lived in ancient Greece. It was perhaps natural, therefore, that the Greeks would compile a list of the masterpieces of their day, a list of the Seven Wonders of the World. This list was not merely a catalogue of marvels, but it was also a guide for travelers to the unmissable sights within range of the eastern Mediterranean Sea.

Why were there seven wonders? The number seven has had mystical and sacred connotations from ancient times, partly because it is composed of two lucky numbers, four and three. The many instances of the use of the number in folklore, religion, and literature include the Seven Days of Creation, the Seven Deadly Sins, the seven planets (including the Sun and the Moon) recognized by Greek astronomers, the Seven Wise Men of the sixth century BC, such sayings as the "Seven Seas," and, among later examples, Shakespeare's Seven Ages of Man. Seven must have seemed the ideal number.

The first list was drawn up in the third century BC, during the short-lived existence of one of the wonders, the Colossus of Rhodes. The first recorded mention of the list comes in a poem written about 100 years later by Antipater of Sidon, who lived in Alexandria, that gracious Greek city founded by Alexander the Great in 332 BC. A second list drawn up in the second century BC by a Greek rhetorician, Philo of Byzantium, was the same as Antipater's, except for his inclusion of the Walls of Babylon instead of the Pharos (a lighthouse) at Alexandria.

A WONDROUS LIST

The Pyramids of Giza in Egypt were built between 2700 and 2300 BC as tombs for three pharaohs, Khufu, Khafre, and Menkaure. The largest, the Great Pyramid of Khufu, contains more than two million limestone blocks. It originally stood 480.9 feet (146.6 meters) high.

The Hanging Gardens of Babylon, on the River Euphrates in what is now Iraq, were built by King Nebuchadrezzar (Nebuchadnezzar of the Bible), who reigned from 605 to 562 BC, in an attempt to create an artificial, tree-capped "mountain" in the middle of the flat Euphrates plain.

The Mausoleum at Halicarnassus, on the coast of Asia Minor, was the tomb of Mausolus, Persian regional governor of Caria and almost king in his own right. It was designed by the Greek architect Pythius of Priene and decorated by the Greek sculptors Bryaxis, Leochares, Skipas, and Timotheos. It was about 160 feet (49 meters) high and was topped by a statue of Mausolus and his wife Artemisia, who was also his sister, in a chariot. An earthquake damaged it in about AD 1400. Later, the Knights of St. John removed the stones to build a fortress.

The Temple of Artemis at Ephesus, a Greek city about 35 miles (56 kilometers) south of modern Izmir, Turkey, was built by King Croesus in about 560 BC. It was burned down then rebuilt 200 years later. The Goths destroyed it in AD 262.

The Statue of Zeus, the centerpiece of the Temple of Zeus at Olympia, site of the original Olympic Games in the northwestern Peloponnese peninsula, was a masterpiece of the sculptor Pheidias of Athens in about 430 BC. Made of wood and covered with gold and ivory, it stood about 40 feet (12 meters) high. An earthquake destroyed the temple in the sixth century AD.

The Pharos at Alexandria, Egypt, was the world's first lighthouse. It stood about 440 feet (134 meters) high, and was built by the Greek architect Sostratos of Cnidus in about 280 BC. It fell into ruin after an earthquake in AD 796.

The Colossus of Rhodes, on the Greek island of Rhodes, was more than 100 feet (30 meters) high. It was a statue of the Sun god Helios, designed and built by the sculptor Chares in about 290 BC. It stood by the harbor entrance and did not straddle it, as is popularly believed. An earthquake brought the statue crashing down only 66 years after it was erected. The shell of beaten bronze sheet, which covered the stone and iron framework, was salvaged 900 years later by Arab raiders.

The Walls of Babylon, the alternative to the Pharos cited in the list of Philo of Byzantium, were about 11 miles (18 kilometers) long and 23 feet (7 meters) thick. Magnificent gateways pierced the walls. The finest, the Ishtar Gate, is now in the Pergamon Museum in East Berlin.

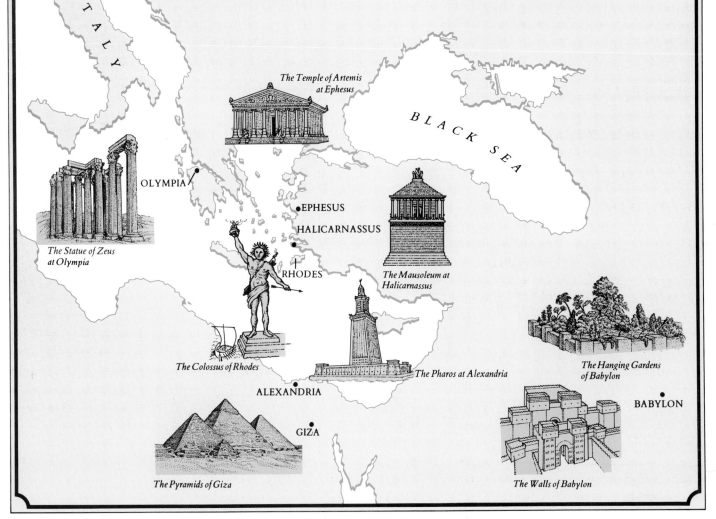

ITALY

BLACK SEA

The Temple of Artemis at Ephesus

OLYMPIA

•EPHESUS

HALICARNASSUS

The Statue of Zeus at Olympia

RHODES

The Mausoleum at Halicarnassus

The Colossus of Rhodes

The Pharos at Alexandria

The Hanging Gardens of Babylon

ALEXANDRIA

BABYLON

GIZA

The Pyramids of Giza

The Walls of Babylon

The lists reflect the Greeks' esthetic values and their admiration for engineering skills, although significantly only one of the wonders, the Pharos, had a practical purpose. Religious considerations affected the choice of the Temple of Artemis at Ephesus and the Statue of Zeus at Olympia, but above all it was the sheer size of the wonders that aroused the awe of the Greeks.

The Greek lists inspired later generations, and many other comparable lists were compiled. One in the Middle Ages included the Colosseum of Rome, the Catacombs of Alexandria, Stonehenge, the Great Wall of China, the Porcelain Tower of Nanking, the Hagia Sophia (the Church of St. Sophia) of Istanbul, and the Leaning Tower of Pisa. Modern lists, as befit our technological age, tend to lay greater emphasis on utility as well as size, and so they include canals, skyscraper office blocks, bridges, and even scientific discoveries and inventions. There are also lists of natural wonders, reflecting the recognition that such spectacles as the Grand Canyon and Mount Everest dwarf human achievements and are much more durable. Of the Seven Wonders of the World listed by the Greeks, only the Pyramids remain.

The terracotta army
Guardians of a dead emperor

IN THE EARLY 1970s, as a number of Chinese laborers were at work digging a well near Mount Li in northern China, they uncovered some pieces of terracotta statuary. These chance discoveries aroused the interest of archeologists, who began excavations in the area. Although they had long been aware that archeological investigations around Mount Li would be rewarding, they were totally unprepared for the vast scale of the treasures they were uncovering. By 1974 a major excavation was underway which has shed much light on early Chinese sculpture and military organization.

The first find was a huge pit which measured 689 feet (210 meters) from east to west, and 197 feet (60 meters) from north to south. Within the pit, the archeologists found 11 parallel corridors, containing about 6,000 life-size figures of soldiers and horses. These figures were symbolically guarding the tomb of Ch'in Shih-huang-ti (c.258–210 BC), the first Emperor of China and builder of China's Great Wall.

An armored archer, one of the army of life-size terracotta soldiers recently unearthed in northern China.

THE FIRST CHINESE EMPIRE

Ch'in, one of the provinces of ancient China, was located in the northwest of the country and corresponded roughly to the modern provinces of Shensi and Kansu. When the 13-year-old Cheng came to the throne in 246 BC, Ch'in was one of the strongest provinces. And, soon after Cheng began to rule personally in 237 BC, he moved against his rivals. With an army of more than a million men, he subdued the other seven major kingdoms of China in a series of campaigns that one chronicler likened to "a silkworm eating its way through a mulberry leaf." By 221 BC, he ruled virtually all of mainland China and so he assumed the title of Ch'in Shih-huang-ti, meaning First Ch'in Sovereign Emperor.

The emperor surrounded himself with men of great ability, including Li Ssu, his grand counselor. Together, the two leaders imposed their stamp on every aspect of Chinese life. They ordered the surrender of all personal weapons, which were melted down and recast as bells and statues. They uprooted and resettled in their capital of Hsienyang thousands of the old landowning class and divided the land into new administrative units. They standardized weights and measures, the currency, the characters of Chinese script, and even the gauges of cart wheels. They built roads connecting the capital with the farthest corners of their empire.

Their most enduring achievement was the completion of the Great Wall of China, built to keep the barbarian peoples to the north out of China. It runs from the north coast to a point near the border with Tibet – a distance of about 1,700 miles (2,700 kilometers). Some stretches of the Wall had been built before the First Emperor's time, but the task of linking them was largely completed between about 220 and 200 BC. Much of the work was entrusted to General Meng T'ien, who had earlier beaten off a Mongol invasion. At least a million workers slaved at the task. Most of those who died were buried where they fell, deep in the foundations or within the Wall itself. The Chinese hoped that the spirits of the dead would appease the gods and demons of the frozen north who were offended by the building of the Wall.

The authoritarian rule of the First Emperor was strong and efficient. But soon after his death, a bitter struggle for power ensued, in which Li Ssu was arrested and tortured, before being cut in two at the waist. Revolts flared up and China once more became divided.

Some historians have suggested that the reason for the construction of the Great Wall of China was not merely to keep out invaders, but to find employment for thousands of disbanded soldiers.

The army of terracotta warriors excavated around Mount Li in northern China date back to the third century BC. The first and largest find, Pit No. 1, contained 11 corridors, in which were found figures of more than 3,000 bareheaded foot soldiers (some of which are shown above), all painted in brilliant colors. Remarkably, no two faces are the same.

while the third appeared to be a military head-quarters, with an elite command unit of 68 figures. In this third pit, a vanguard commander stood six feet four inches (1.93 meters) high, while the guards averaged six feet two inches (1.88 meters). Their exceptional height probably symbolized their importance. A fourth, empty pit was also discovered, suggesting that work on the terracotta army was probably abandoned before it was completed. Work continues at Mount Li, but, by the early 1980s, no attempts had yet been made to excavate the mound and the emperor's tomb.

Historical records show that Emperor Ch'in Shih-huang-ti had a morbid fear of death. He moved around his imperial place of 10,000 rooms, never sleeping in the same room twice for fear of being killed by evil spirits during the night. This fear inspired the construction of the mausoleum to house his tomb and the protective army of terracotta soldiers.

The preparation of the mausoleum obviously took an enormous amount of time and effort. According to an historian who lived between about 145 and 90 BC, a labor force of 700,000 was employed. The work entailed the diverting of underground rivers, the excavation of the burial chamber, halls, and corridors, the construction of surrounding walls, and the building of the central mound, about 4,600 feet (1,400 meters) in circumference. To make it resemble a hill, the tumulus was planted with trees and shrubs. The emperor's tomb was filled with model temples and palaces. Channels of quick-silver (mercury) were mechanically circulated to represent the flow of the Yellow and Yang-tse Rivers. A huge copper dome representing the night sky covered this model of the emperor's domains, and lamps replenished by reservoirs of seal oil illuminated the scene. And, as a truly lethal protection against marauders, crossbows were installed that could fire automatically.

While the work was proceeding, the emperor set off on a tour of the provinces in 210 BC, in search of an elixir of immortality. Ironically enough, it was during this trip that he died – probably from natural causes, despite his constant fear of assassination. His tomb was not yet finished and his top officials, fearful of his successors, decided to keep the news secret for as long as possible. But it was high summer and the body soon began to smell. In desperation, the officials placed a load of rotting fish, which smelled even worse, ahead of the carriage containing the decomposing corpse, which could then be carried, slowly and unappetizingly, to its magnificent resting place.

There were more than 3,200 bareheaded foot soldiers, standing four abreast in nine of the corridors and in two files in the narrower ones. There were also sculptures of bowmen, cross-bowmen, officers (distinguishable because they wore headgear), spearmen, and charioteers. Pottery horses were attached to real chariots. The soldiers' swords, spears, and bows were missing, having been plundered soon after the downfall of the Ch'in dynasty in 206 BC, although many fragments of bronze weapons, including arrowheads, crossbow triggers, spearheads, and swords, have been excavated. The uniformed and mostly armored terracotta soldiers averaged five feet nine inches (175 centimeters) in height. The lower parts of the statues were solid, but the heads, forearms, and hands were hollow. They had been painted in brilliant colors, but only tiny traces of the pigments had survived. And, remarkably, no two faces were the same.

More pits were uncovered in 1976. The second pit contained war chariots and cavalry,

Burnt offerings to Baal

Honor for Carthage's noble families

THOUGH THE PEOPLES of the ancient world were no strangers to cruelty, the ritualistic brutality of one nation in particular never lost its power to shock. Throughout the Mediterranean region the name of Carthage was synonymous with what was surely the most savage of religious observances: child sacrifice. Even the Romans, hardly noted for their softheartedness, were never guilty of such a systematic disregard for human life. As for the Greeks, they were outraged by reports of Carthaginian barbarism. We owe our most striking account of a sacrificial ceremony to the Greek historian Diodorus Siculus (who lived during the first century BC). It took place in the great North African city nearly two centuries before the Romans destroyed it.

Sometime in the dim past, Carthage (literally, "New Town") was founded by merchants from the Phoenician city of Tyre; and by the fifth century BC it had become the focal point of a flourishing trade network, with some imperial pretensions that Rome eventually thwarted, but only after a series of devastating wars (the three Punic Wars). In 310 BC, during an earlier conflict with the Sicilian city-state of Syracuse, Agathocles, tyrant of Syracuse, entered Carthage as a temporary fugitive from his own land and saw one of the atrocities carried out by its inhabitants in the name of religion. Diodorus's retelling of the eye-witness report of Agathocles makes horrifying reading, although we must bear in mind that Diodorus was writing over two centuries after the event.

With Agathocles among the spectators, 500 youngsters were burned to death as offerings to the stern deity Baal Hammon, before whose monstrous bronze statue a pyre had been set alight. The children's bodies, possibly with their throats already cut, were placed in the open hands of the statue, then dropped into the flames. Like most such ceremonies, this one took place at dead of night, to the accompaniment of pipes and tambourines. Masked dancers

Reports of religious rites involving child sacrifice in ancient Carthage seem to have been confirmed by the discovery of earthenware pots, containing the remains of babies and children, in Carthaginian religious sites, such as this temple of the goddess Tanit in Salammbo, Carthage (at left).

joined members of Carthage's powerful priesthood in performing a rite that bereaved parents were required to watch dry-eyed; tears were forbidden since the sacrificial death of a son or daughter was considered a privilege – an honor, in fact, which could only be bestowed on the noblest of families.

Aristocratic Carthaginians apparently needed to be reminded of this privilege from time to time. Prior to the holocaust witnessed by Agathocles they had fallen into the habit of substituting children of slaves for their own in routine ceremonials. This deception had brought down the wrath of Baal in the form of some defeats in battle. And so, Diodorus tells us, Agathocles was present on an occasion when they were paying for their sins and propitiating the god with the charred bodies of their own nobly born children.

Though child immolation of the Carthaginian kind was not common among the ancients, human sacrifice – of captive enemy soldiers, for example – was far from rare. The Phoenician ancestors of the Carthaginians had brought with them a number of fertility cults designed to guarantee plentiful harvests and healthy offspring. Such cults often saw sacrificial slaughter as a supernatural way to regenerate body and spirit and ensure the continuation of the race. Freshly spilled blood, they believed, bought the certainty of more abundant life through a sort of grisly pact with the dark forces in which they placed their trust. Despite the protests of her Mediterranean neighbors with more humane attitudes and less demanding gods, Carthage resisted change. Some of her people paid lip service to relatively tolerant gods such as Zeus and Hera, but most kept faith with the old magical traditions throughout the Classical Age of Greece and the rise of Rome.

We do not know the exact degree of importance that sacrifice bore to religious worship in Carthaginian society. There may have been other forms of communication with the gods, but no information about them is available. Archeological evidence, however, indicates that ritual killings were a widespread activity. Quantities of human remains (including baby teeth), have been unearthed on sites of what were clearly temples or *topheths* (large furnaces combined with altars). And there remain well-preserved gravestones bearing scenes of what are undoubtedly ritual sacrifices. Finds of small-mammal bones also suggest that animal flesh was offered to such gods as Baal and an Earth Mother called Tanit, who was related to the Phoenician Moon goddess, Astarte.

During the centuries of intermittent warfare against Rome, the Carthaginians must have resorted regularly and often to their cult of sacrifice, but Baal, Tanit, and the rest proved to be implacable. The Second Punic War ended in 201 BC with the utter destruction and humiliation of the city's armed forces. Then in 146 BC, after a two-year-long siege during which her last desperate defenders are said to have shut themselves up in a sacred temple and set it alight, the Romans burned the whole of Carthage to the ground – a brutal fate strangely in keeping with the city's fiery past.

Death in the Alps
Echoing passes and hostile gods

TO THE desert-bred North Africans of the Carthaginian army the mountains looked formidable. Austere and aloof, they rose up so sharply that their summits vanished into the clouds. Confronted with a swirling gray world of echoing mountain passes (and probably hostile gods), the shivering soldiers longed for a return to the warm plains they had left behind them. For Hannibal, their commander, the decision to lead an army of 40,000 men, several thousand horses, and 40 elephants across the Alps was the most momentous of his military career. Still only 29, he had been commander-in-chief of Carthaginian forces for three years and had a reputation for audacity second to none. He knew that the Roman enemy, expecting him to invade Italy from the north along the coastal route, had placed an army there to stop him. That was why, in the fall of 218 BC, he decided to go over the Alps even though the feat of taking a large force up and over this rocky and in some places ice-covered terrain had never before been attempted.

Soon after the army began its climb, tribesmen of the hostile Allobroges, who were poised on the heights above Hannibal's men, suddenly attacked. The wounded Carthaginian animals went berserk in the narrow pass along which the

WHY ELEPHANTS?

Although the use of elephants in war is generally associated with Hannibal, they had been used for years before his invasion of Italy, particularly in the Indian sub-continent but also in the Mediterranean world. As early as 326 BC a squadron of 200 elephants fought at the battle of the Hydaspes, when Alexander the Great defeated the Indian King Porus, and they were in use in Italy in 280 BC against the Romans. In many battles the elephant was the tank of its day – a weapon to terrify an enemy that had never before set eyes on such a creature. Horses and human beings alike fled at its approach. This could be a drawback, since horses on the same side would also panic unless trained. And in battle, an elephant that ran amok could cause untold damage to its own army.

Nonetheless, the battlefield elephant was a formidable opponent, especially when large enough to carry on its back a wooden castle full of soldiers. The elephants in Hannibal's army could not do this. They were mainly from North Africa where they were found in the vicinity of Carthage – in present-day Morocco and south of Tunisia – and were smaller than other breeds, measuring only about seven feet nine inches (2.5 meters) from shoulder to ground. Thus they were not much bigger than horses. As a weapon of war, in fact, they probably proved to be more trouble than they were worth. Hannibal went to great lengths to keep them alive during the crossing of the Alps and the severe, north Italian winter that followed, even providing woollen coverings for them. However, of the few that had survived the journey, one by one these now succumbed to the cold. By the time spring came, only one of the original 40 was still alive.

The greatest general of his age, Hannibal was as respected by his enemies as by his own men. He had the gifts necessary for a successful general – personal bravery, concern for his troops, meticulous attention to every detail, and a streak of ruthlessness – yet he was not a flamboyant character, keeping his emotions very much under control.

THE WARS BETWEEN CARTHAGE AND ROME

The wars fought between Rome and Carthage for control of the western Mediterranean are called Punic Wars after the Latin word for Phoenician, because Carthage (near modern-day Tunis) was founded as a Phoenician trading post. The struggle, which began in 264 BC when the Roman army invaded Sicily in an effort to take control of the island from the occupying Carthaginians, was carried on in three separate wars over the course of more than a century.

At the outbreak of the Second Punic War in 218 BC Hannibal was in command of the Carthaginian army in Spain – which was then part of the Carthaginian empire. Since he knew that the strength of the Romans depended on control of Italy, he decided to mount an invasion of the Italian peninsula through the least likely route. And so he led his men through Gaul (modern-day France) and across the Alps – a brilliant move that caught the Romans by surprise. For the next 15 years Hannibal held them at bay in their own territory, harassing their troops and keeping them fully occupied on the home front. A successful tactic of his was to allow the center of his line to be pushed in by the advancing enemy, who would then be surrounded and if possible, destroyed by the Carthaginian flanks.

He did not win the war outright because of Rome's overwhelming military presence and because Roman sea power kept him short of reinforcements from home. Roman generals, moreover, evolved the sensible policy of never fighting him face to face if they could avoid it. When Hannibal finally abandoned the campaign, it was only because a Roman counter-invasion of North Africa forced him to hurry home to the defense of Carthage itself. He got there too late to fight anything but a rearguard action, and peace was declared on the enemy's terms. Some time after the Roman victory in the Second Punic War he went into exile, joining forces with a series of enemies of Rome in Africa and Asia Minor. Eventually, though, the Romans caught up with him, causing him to call for a cup of poison and kill himself, probably in 183 BC.

The Third Punic War lasted from 149 to 146 BC and ended with the destruction of Carthage, whose surviving inhabitants were enslaved.

---

army was strung out; horses and men slipped to their death down the mountainside and chaos reigned. The Carthaginians were near defeat. Luckily Hannibal himself and several thousands of his troops were overseeing the progress of the rest of the Carthaginians from a higher vantage point. They threw themselves into the fray, and the Allobroges fled.

The victorious general and his forces spent a night and day recuperating in an abandoned town at the head of the pass. That first successful battle in the Alps won them a short breathing space, thus enabling the army to make considerable progress. Some days later, local tribesmen, eager for loot, offered to provide guides to help Hannibal find a way through the mountains. The guides took the army through a deep gorge that had a cliff rising above one side of the track, a precipice on the other, and a number of their fellow-tribesmen, armed with rocks, at the top of the cliffs. There was no way the Carthaginians could avoid the onslaught. Boulders crashed down all along the column, causing appalling loss of life; and this time the panic was not confined to the animals. The Carthaginian column was cut in two, and Hannibal and some of the men were forced to spend the night on a large rock formation warding off continual attacks, while the remainder of the army struggled through the darkness.

Hannibal rejoined the rest of his troops the next morning. For a few days the tribesmen continued to harass the Carthaginians, but they were apparently too frightened of the elephants to attack the army directly, and so they withdrew. But now the terrain was changing, becoming more menacing than the worst of human enemies. At the highest point of the crossing, Carthaginian morale nearly evaporated. The slopes all around were covered with ice; there was no grazing for livestock, no shelter, no respite. Without reliable guides, the army often took wrong turnings, forcing the cumbersome baggage train to retrace its steps again and again. The soldiers felt increasingly trapped and defeated. Of the 40,000 men who went into the

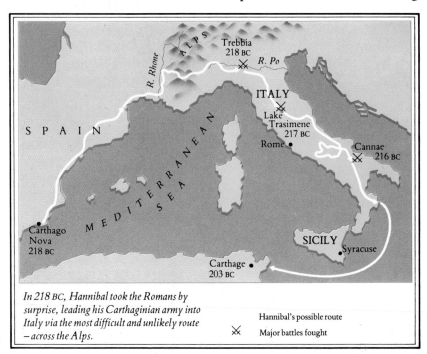

In 218 BC, Hannibal took the Romans by surprise, leading his Carthaginian army into Italy via the most difficult and unlikely route – across the Alps.

⤬⤬ Hannibal's possible route

⤬ Major battles fought

Alps with Hannibal, it is estimated that fewer than 14,000 survived to reach the other side.

On the 10th day of the crossing, with the army at its last gasp, the outlook suddenly changed. For 10 days the soldiers had seen nothing but immense, seemingly impassable mountains in front of them. Now, all of a sudden, they caught a glimpse of their goal: Italy. There, stretched out far below, were the plains of the River Po, warm and inviting in the sunshine. For two days the men camped overlooking the Po, to recover their strength and allow stragglers to catch up. They then began a descent

that took three days and cost more lives. It is a measure of Hannibal's stature as a general that, by the time they reached the bottom of the treacherous slopes, they were once again a disciplined body of men as they poured onto the Italian plain. It was the Romans who had confidently declared war against far-away Carthage. Now Hannibal had done the unthinkable and carried the battle into Roman territory.

Historians still argue about which of several different passes over the Alps the Carthaginians chose to follow; there is no argument about the extent of their achievement.

War by proxy
Moves across the board

CHESS IS A WAR GAME. The board is the battlefield. The pieces are soldiers, engines of war, with a king in their midst. They advance, outflank, fall back in defense, capture or are captured in their turn. Chess is clearly a game that grew out of the clash and tumult of real battle.

Many myths surround the origins of chess. From medieval Persia comes the tale of a legendary battle between two royal brothers, Talkhand and Gav, for the crown. When Talkhand was killed, Gav commanded wise men to invent a game which would explain the tragic events to his grief-stricken mother, the queen. According to another, Arab, story, chess was the brainchild of the mythical philosopher, Sassa. As his reward for inventing the game, the wily Sassa asked his king for a single grain of corn to be doubled in quantity for each square on the chessboard, so emptying every granary in the land and becoming a wealthy man in the process. Yet another legend claims that the game was invented during the Siege of Troy in the 12th century BC.

Despite these claims, the origins of the game are fairly well established: When Alexander the Great marched into northwest India in 326 BC, he was opposed by a mass of cavalry, chariots, and elephants. This traditional type of Indian army, involving four separate divisions, was perfectly reflected by the pieces used in the ancient Indian board game of chaturanga, which means "four parts, or arms." Chaturanga was superseded by a game that was recognizably chess around the year AD 500 (from when we have the first written mention of it), and from

India soon spread to neighboring Persia (modern Iran), where it quickly became popular.

It is from the Persians that we have inherited many familiar chess names and terms. Persian foot soldiers were the *piyadah*, or pawns. The chariot was the *rukh*, or rook (or the castle). Their king was the *shah*, from which the word "chess" itself is derived. *Shahmat* meant "the king is helpless." This is the "checkmate," the critical moment of play when one player's king cannot escape capture, and the game is lost and won. Like the pieces themselves, "checkmate" is a comment upon the state of real warfare in ages past, when a captured king, held for ransom, was of more value than a dead one.

Persia was a vital stepping stone in the history of chess. During the seventh century AD, the old Persian empire fell to Islam; and chess was carried far and wide on the high tide of Islamic conquest: from Spain, and then on into Western Europe, to the gates of Constantinople, from whence the Viking longboats were to carry it to the distant north.

The legend and lore of chess is as rich and varied as the game itself. There is the famous story of Alfonso VI, King of Leon and Castile, who laid siege to the Moorish city of Seville in 1087. The governor of the city, Al-Mutamid, anxious to save his city, offered the king a magnificent chess set and board, of ebony and sandalwood, and challenged him to a game, the winner to keep the set and board, the loser to grant the winner one wish. Alfonso was roundly beaten, and though he did actually keep the set, as the loser he had to grant the governor's wish which was that he raise the siege.

The game of chess is thought to have been inspired by military maneuvers. This Viking chessman, carved from walrus ivory, dates from the 12th century and belongs to what is believed to be the oldest complete chess set in existence.

CHESS AROUND THE WORLD

François Philidor astounds his audience in an English gaming club by playing chess against two opponents simultaneously and while wearing a blindfold.

There is a theory that chess originated in China. While little evidence exists to support this, the Chinese did develop their own distinctive version of the game. Chinese chess, or the river game as it is also known, has several familiar pieces, plus some interesting extras, including cannon – which may testify to their early invention of gunpowder. The biggest difference is the board, which has lines instead of squares, the pieces moving from line to line, and intersection to intersection.

Astronomical chess was another remarkable version of the game, played on a circular board, based on the second-century-AD astronomer Ptolemy's notion of a concentric universe, and with the pieces modeled on the astrological signs for the planets. A special Byzantine form of the game, called in Greek *zatrikion*, was also played on a circular board, but with standard pieces.

"Great chess," once very popular in Russia, especially with Catherine the Great, has provided other interesting variants. The board had many more squares and extra pieces and was marked out in the shape of a large cross, to accommodate four players. The pieces were sometimes named after real or mythical beasts, such as the lion, phoenix, and unicorn. In the 19th century, in Germany, there was an attempt to make chess a card game.

So-called "blindfold" chess is probably the most intriguing version of the game. The player is simply told of his opponent's moves and does not look at the board, retaining all the moves in his or her head. The 18th-century grand master, François Philidor of France, several times played two simultaneous games of "blindfold" chess while carrying on a conversation. On one occasion in the 19th century, the American champion Paul Morphy played eight "blindfold" games simultaneously, winning them all, while some modern chessmasters blindfoldedly play up to 50 or more games, simultaneously.

By the end of the Middle Ages, many changes were made in the game of chess to make it more dynamic. One of the most popular variants, the "courier" game, as shown in this 16th-century painting by von Leyden, involved a board 12 squares deep instead of eight.

Somewhat grimmer is the tale told in the 13th-century Norse saga, the *Heimskringla*, of a match between the Danish King Knut (Canute) and his kinsman Ulf the Jarl (or "Chief," an uncle of Harold of England). Knut made a bad move and lost a knight, whereupon he wanted to take the move again. Ulf scornfully abandoned the game, and, according to the story, for this indiscretion he was later found stabbed to death in a church, on the orders of the king.

In chess, some medieval writers saw images, not of war, but of magic and mysticism. For them the board was a microcosm of the universe, the pieces moving according to the symbols for earth, air, fire, and water. Others couldn't resist sermonizing upon the game. "The rook," asserted one Latin treatise, "stands for the itinerant justices who travel over the whole realm, and their move is always straight, because they must deal justly." The queen, it continued, "moves aslant only, because women are so greedy that they will take nothing except by rapine and injustice" – an interesting comment on the still-limited role of the queen chesspiece at that period, as well as being a forthright opinion on the character of women. The translation of a work in a similar vein, by a Dominican friar named Jacobus Cessolis, was published by William Caxton in 1474, to become one of the first books printed in the English language.

For centuries, chess was also deemed an excellent test of character. Legends and stories abound of kings or lords giving or withholding a daughter's hand in marriage depending upon the play and behavior of a suitor at the chessboard.

Kings and emperors delighted in the "royal game," no doubt partly because it allowed them to live out their military fantasies through its stratagems. Tamerlane, the 14th-century Mongol warlord, was known to be an enthusiastic chess-player and Ivan the Terrible of Russia is said to have died at the chessboard, his own king clutched convulsively in his hand. Louis XIII of France had a traveling chess set and his contemporary, Charles I of England, had inscribed on

his personal chessboard the motto: "With these subjects and this ruler, the battle is waged without bloodshed" – a sadly ironic comment for a monarch destined to lose a bloody civil war and with it his own head.

During the 15th century, the queen – known originally as the minister, counselor, or vizier – became the most powerful piece on the board, and chess assumed its modern form. Interest in it today is stronger than at any time in its long and colorful history, the game being played by young and old alike across the world. Such is the international importance of the game that in 1972, when Bobby Fischer of the United States faced Boris Spassky of the Soviet Union for the world chess championship, which Fischer won, commentators called this historic encounter "war by proxy" – just one more way of describing the world's most fascinating game.

Two outstanding contemporary chess players, the Russians Viktor Korchnoi (at right) and Anatoly Karpov, confront each other in the nail-biting semi-final of the 1974 world chess championship in Moscow.

Farming in republican Rome
Slaves and absentee landlords

O tillers of the soil, most happy men
If they but knew their bliss; on them the earth
Showers her goodness, far from the clash of arms

EVER SINCE the greatest of Latin poets, Virgil, wrote those lines some 30 years before the birth of Christ, people have had a romantic notion of the pastoral joys of Roman agriculture. But most of the "happy" tillers of the soil in the last two centuries of the Roman republic, which came to an end in 27 BC with the accession to power of the Emperor Augustus, had little reason to feel blissful. They were slaves, working in conditions not unlike those prevailing in the plantations of the West Indies in the 18th century.

Virgil's father was a peasant who through thrift and hard work saved enough to buy a small farm, and the Virgilian picture was true of such farms and their owners; but it did not reflect the big-business side of Roman agriculture. This agribusiness came about as a result of the Second Punic War against the Carthaginians. When it ended in 201 BC, Rome had gained, or regained, control over the whole of Italy, but many landowners had been killed, many farms were mortgaged or neglected, and a good deal of unused farmland was for sale. A shortage of ordinary farmers with enough money to buy land was matched by an abundance of patrician (noble) families with money to spare. Consequently patricians bought up large tracts of land – which, of course, being patricians, they could not cultivate with their own hands. Fortunately for them, the war had left Rome with a large number of slaves, since slavery was the normal fate of prisoners of war and there was also a flourishing organized slave trade not related to military conquest.

As a result, during the second century BC the Italian landscape became dotted with *latifundia* – literally, broad estates, which were generally owned by absentee landlords and run by slaves under a slave overseer. Some of the slaves, especially those who were sturdy war captives from Africa, Spain, Gaul, and other lands, could be kept under control only in chains. Otherwise, shackling of slaves was not a common practice.

An insight into Roman farming methods is given in the first Latin farming treatise, *De Agri Cultura*, written about 160 BC by Marcus Porcius Cato, a man who gained fame as a soldier and politician but who also had close personal knowledge of agriculture. Cato suggested that the most profitable methods of farming were, firstly, growing vines for wine-making and olives for oil, followed by raising sheep and cattle, and finally growing cereal crops. The staff of a money-making *latifundium* should be mostly slaves, he wrote, though it might be advisable to hire casual laborers at harvest-time. In fact, the life of a slave was in many ways better than that of a free laborer; a slave-owner had a financial interest in keeping his slaves well fed, properly clothed for cold or wet weather, and healthy, whereas casual workers were entirely on their own.

Like many plantation-owners of pre-Civil War America, some Roman patricians took good care of their slaves when they were too old to work. The first-century-AD biographer Plutarch criticizes Cato himself for "disposing of" his slaves when they were no longer of use to him. And Cato's book describes the harsh treatment that was only too often meted out to slaves who were regarded as simply part of the farm stock, along with the animals and implements. Severe punishment for misbehavior seems to have been taken for granted, and most enslaved farmhands were kept working at all times, regardless of weather or nominal holidays. The working day began at dawn and ended at sundown – only about nine hours in winter, but up to 15 in summer. Although some slaves eventually attained freedom, either by buying it with savings or as a gift from their owners, the harsh Cato does not mention this in his book; presumably his slaves never were given their liberty.

The best-off among rural slaves were the herdsmen, wandering on open pastures with their rich owners' flocks, and thus much freer than those working on crops. It was this partial freedom that gave opportunity for revolt. A slave gang in the fields worked under constant supervision, whereas the herdsmen could not be kept under surveillance. They were never chained, and they had to be armed to defend their animals against brigands and wolves. In 198 BC the herdsmen on a plantation at Setia, south of Rome, revolted; but they were betrayed by two of their number (who were set free as a reward), and the rebellion was quickly and ruthlessly crushed. Two years later, though, it took a Roman legion to put down a rebellion in the region of Etruria. The ringleaders were whipped, then crucified.

The *latifundia* most at risk from uprisings of this sort were in Sicily, then as now a law unto itself. Slave-owners there were, by repute,

A profitable Roman latifundium, or estate, was usually devoted to growing vines and olives (for the wine and oil so dear to Roman palates), with some sheep and cattle rearing, and a little cereal production. Its efficiency was based on the toil of slaves, working long hours under constant supervision, backed up by droves of donkeys.

greedy, cruel, and insensitive. One of them, Damophilus of Enna, not only branded all his slaves but refused to provide herdsmen with clothes. When they protested, he suggested they should help themselves to the garments of travelers. It was an unwise move. The slaves became bandits, robbing and murdering where ever they could. Finally, led by a slave named Eunûs, they were joined by slaves of neighboring farms, and a full-scale revolt began. After capturing the city of Enna and slaughtering many of its inhabitants (including their former owners), they set up their own kingdom, with Eunûs as elected king, and soon had an army more than 20,000 strong. It took the Romans three years, from 134 to 132 BC, to defeat this army and restore Roman rule in Sicily. And it took them another three to crush a second Sicilian revolt (104–101 BC).

The most notorious rebellion of Roman slaves, of course, was not initiated by farm workers. Spartacus, a captured Thracian soldier, was forced to become a gladiator, and it was he and some comrades who started the great first-century-BC revolt. But much of their success (they ravaged southern Italy and defeated five Roman armies during the course of two years) was due to vast numbers of farm-worker followers. By the time the revolt led by Spartacus had been crushed (71 BC), the heyday of huge landed estates was passing, at least partly because Rome's dominion over the Mediterranean world was by now virtually unchallenged, affording few opportunities for slaves to be acquired through war.

Cultivation by slave labor gradually gave place to a system of tenant farming by freemen. Where slaves were still used, their treatment improved. Slave-breeding, once deemed unnecessary, now became essential, and female slaves who produced many children were given their freedom. A century or so after the revolt of Spartacus, Pliny the Younger, writing about his problems with tenant farmers, says: "A number of them have to be supplied with industrious slaves, for I myself have none in chains anywhere, nor does anyone in these parts." By the time the Roman empire in the West fell in the fifth century AD, the position of most slaves on the land was similar to that of freemen.

Imperial travel

The enthusiastic ancient roamers

Below, part of the Peutinger Map, a copy made in 1265 of a Roman map of the AD 200s or 300s. It is named for one of its owners, Konrad Peutinger (1465–1547), who was town-clerk of Augsberg in Germany and acquired it in 1508.

The map is thought to be a reasonably good copy of the original. It is on a series of strips of parchment, and is about 22 feet (6.75 meters) long and about one foot (34 centimeters) wide. Much like the route maps issued by present-day automobile associations, it shows towns, the distances between them, and how they relate to main roads.

The Romans had already hit on one idea made famous by Michelin Guides: the use of symbols to show the relative comfort of the inns and other stopping places along the route. Distances are marked in Roman miles except in Gaul and Persia, where local measures are used.

"YOU'D BETTER not drink the water." This warning, important for modern travelers, was even more so for people of the Roman empire – the water at wayside inns was often toxic. On a journey from Rome to Brindisi in the southeastern corner of the Italian peninsula, the poet Horace (65–8 BC) suffered an upset stomach from drinking bad water, and recorded the experience in one of his poems.

Horace was accompanying a statesman, Gaius Maecenas, on a diplomatic mission. Romans normally journeyed for a purpose, not just to see the sights – but once embarked on a trip, they tended to be as eager not to miss anything as modern rubber-neckers are. Even soldiers took time off in foreign lands for sightseeing. In 167 BC, for example after a campaign in Macedonia, General Aemilus Paulus toured historic spots in Greece: Delphi, the Acropolis at Athens, the statue of Jupiter at Olympia, and many others. The Roman historian Livy cynically suggests that such places were disappointing when visited: but just as modern tourists cannot resist seeing Gettysburg or Flanders or Shakespeare's birthplace, so the Romans took pride in saying that they "knew" the historic sites of their time.

As well as traveling for pleasure, many Romans could find other good reasons for taking to the road. Far corners of the empire required the attention of civil servants, militarymen, and merchants. Young men of good families were sent to famous educational centers such as Athens or Alexandria. Sea voyages were often prescribed by physicians for the health. It was also fashionable to make pilgrimages to places of religious significance. And underdeveloped western parts of the empire offered possibilities for a better life, just as Rome itself attracted provincial youngsters. Women rarely traveled on their own, but they often accompanied men who were going to be away for a long time.

Rich Romans had country estates to which they repaired for vacations. The seaside around Naples was fashionable in spring and cool places in hilly country were popular in hot weather. For less well-to-do citizens there were boarding houses in resorts such as Baiae or Puteoli in the Bay of Naples, where visitors could rent boats and amuse themselves in various ways.

Travel was made easier by a network of roads that were so well planned that many modern highways still follow them. Travelers on government business were entitled to stop off at

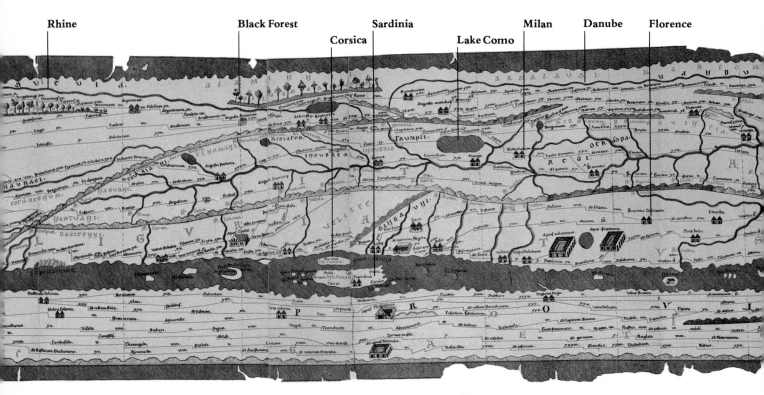

Rhine • Black Forest • Sardinia • Corsica • Lake Como • Milan • Danube • Florence

official rest-houses where necessary comforts and fresh horses were provided. Other travelers could find wayside rest-places of varying quality. Many sold wine, which often cost less than drinking water. They also had a good stock of fleas. But food, except at a few hotels (mostly in Italy, rarely in the provinces) was the traveler's own responsibility. Rich people who made the same journey often were likely to own several conveniently placed houses.

The poor traveled on foot, perhaps with a mule to carry their baggage, whereas people with money had horse-drawn carriages and a very necessary bodyguard. Because of the inadequacy of the rest-places, more or less everyone, rich or poor, had to take along a great deal of luggage – bedding, towels, cooking equipment, tents, and, of course, food and drink.

There was no dearth of maps, guidebooks, or eager native guides at popular spots. And just as today, souvenirs galore were on sale, some the work of craftsmen, others those gimcrack items "for the tourist trade." If you took a trinket back to Rome or across a frontier between provinces, you were likely to have to pay duty on it. The empire's customs officers were as vigilant as their 20th-century counterparts.

In spite of the discomfort, travelers went on traveling. Pliny the Younger, writing to a friend in the first century AD, grumbled about people's preference for distant wonders over those at home. "There are many objects of interest in and near our city that we have not even heard of, much less seen," he wrote. "If they were in Greece, Egypt, or Asia, or any other land that advertises its marvels, we'd have heard of them . . . and examined them long ago."

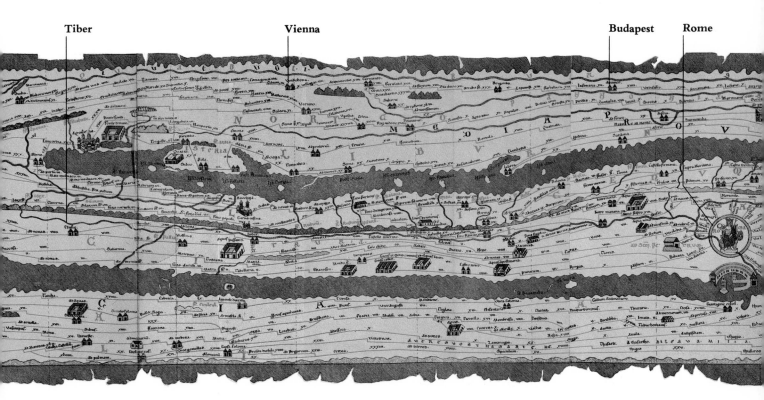

Tiber   Vienna   Budapest   Rome

Bacchus defeated

When prohibition hit Rome

The rites of the secret Bacchanalian cult, introduced into Rome from Greece in the second century BC, are shown in this detail from a wall painting in the Villa of the Mysteries at Pompeii. The term "Bacchanalian" simply denotes drunken revelry today, but in the second century BC it carried decadent and, for some, even sinister overtones.

A YOUNG ROMAN NOBLEMAN, Publius Aebutius, was the heir to great wealth but still under the guardianship of his stepfather when the stepfather tried to persuade him to join a group known as the Bacchanalians. Why, Aebutius wondered, was the older man – who was not normally eager to amuse his stepson – so determined to introduce him to the joys of this Greek cult that had recently sprung up in Rome? A friend gave him the answer: The Bacchanalians were noted for debauchery; once initiated into their wine-soaked and perverted "religious" rites, he faced almost certain degradation and ruin – no doubt what his stepfather intended, so as to get his hands on the young man's fortune. Incensed, Publius Aebutius went to the Roman senate and told that august body about the allegedly immoral activities of the Bacchanalians, whose membership was burgeoning, particularly among the affluent young. Thus began a series of scandals, accompanied by harsh repressive measures, that shocked citizens of the Roman republic in 186 BC.

Alarmed at what they heard from Aebutius, and intent on stamping out the growing passion in Rome for exotic luxuries and a hedonistic way of life, the senate acted swiftly. That same night, the city's gates were closed, potential escape routes blocked, and a trap sprung on known and suspected adherents of the growing cult. A decree forbidding gatherings of Bacchanalians was drawn up and an inquiry launched into their activities. The inquiry discovered that not only were the votaries of Bacchus indulging in every imaginable form of dissipation, but they were also committing all sorts of crimes, from the forging of wills to murder. Publius Aebutius had not been guilty of exaggeration. The only question that troubles modern historians is whether or not the city fathers were themselves guilty of exaggeration in their reaction to Aebutius's story, but since, by its very nature, the cult of Bacchus was secretive, we now have no way of assessing their action.

But why did the Roman state come down so hard on the Bacchanalians? It is understandable that the authorities felt that suppression was necessary. The victorious end in 201 BC of a crucial war with Carthage left Rome practically undisputed mistress of the Mediterranean, but

AWASH WITH WINE

The Romans may have disapproved of the worship of Bacchus, but it can truthfully be said that they lived in a world almost awash with wine. Lacking tea or coffee, and unable to drink the frequently impure water, they drank wine routinely, added it to water to purify it, and used it both as an antiseptic and a preservative for food. Since they were also without sugar, although they did have honey, sweet wine formed a vital part of their diet. Indeed, the great vineyards of France were first planted by the Romans.

Most Roman wine was fairly rough stuff, however – drunk within a year of its pressing and almost always mixed with water. The richer Romans preferred mellower, older vintages, but storage of wine presented a problem; since the cork was not in regular use until the later stages of the empire, bottles or flasks had to be sealed with lead or wax, materials that too often leaked air into the fluid, causing it to turn to vinegar. (Vinegar that became insipid through prolonged exposure to air was called *vappa*, which became slang for "blockhead." This term of abuse survived, interestingly, in modern Neapolitan dialect as "wappo." Carried across the Atlantic by Italian immigrants, it was somehow abbreviated into "Wop," an ethnic insult for all Italians.)

In the beginning, wines from the Greek islands held first place among Roman connoisseurs, but the establishment of an Italian wine industry was well under way by the first century BC, when the poet Horace could agree to share with a friend a bottle of "the finest Falernian" – a heavy red wine from grapes grown on Mt. Falernus southeast of Rome. But the ancient Romans treated their fine wines with less reverence than do modern devotees of Bacchus. Horace, for instance, asks his friend to bring a small flask of spikenard, a powerful spice, to add flavor to the Falernian. This was not an abnormal suggestion. Salt or salt water or various spices might be added, and often the brew was heated (heat, it was thought, increased the alcoholic effect).

Tampering with wine in the cask was also common practice, frequently for fairly disreputable reasons. The wine merchants of Massilia (Marseilles, France) were notorious for trying to make young wines look older by keeping them in smoke-filled cellars so that the casks would darken and the wines would mature faster – presumably because of the heat rather than the smoke. In short, many of the elements of wine-forgery as well as wine-snobbery were evident in the Roman world of 2,000 years ago.

victory brought wealth as well as power; and the traditional virtues of patriotism, toughness, and austerity were giving way to a love of luxury and voluptuous ease hitherto associated in the Roman mind with the effete Greeks. It was also apparent that the uninhibited abandon of the cult appealed mainly to the young.

There was also the deep-rooted fear of a breakdown of law and order. Outbursts of unbridled enthusiasm like the rites of Dionysus (the Greek name for Bacchus, god of wine) were celebrated every spring in Greece. But they were unknown in Rome before the early second century BC, when a young Greek priest imported the strange, wild ceremonies into central Italy, although the cult was well-established in the more Greek-influenced south of Italy as early as the fifth century BC. The Bacchanalians began holding secret meetings, usually in caves or cellars, at night. Sworn to secrecy and encouraged to get drunk, it was alleged that initiates engaged in sexual immorality. Too much wine and too little discipline inevitably led to infringements of Roman criminal law as well as to indulgence in forbidden physical delights.

During the weeks that followed Aebutius's revelations, more than 7,000 people of both sexes were imprisoned. Of these, any found guilty of nothing worse than joining the cult were left to rot in jail; those who had committed unlawful acts (often of a sexual nature) were executed. Guilty women were handed over to their relatives, who were instructed to carry out the prescribed capital punishment in private, but girls who had no family were publicly executed along with men. It is possible that more people were killed in this campaign against an unwanted new "religion" than in any of the later attacks on Christianity. Christians, at least, would be given a chance to recant. The Bacchanalians, on the other hand, were not often offered such an opening for escape.

Persecution of the Bacchanalians was followed a few years later by an even more puritanical attempt to put the clock back to a simpler, more frugal past. In 181 BC an old-fashioned patrician named Cato induced the senate to pass laws imposing high taxes on such foreign luxuries as fine carriages, perfumes, silk clothes, and highly educated slaves – one of the most popular imports from the East. In the long run he and others like him proved powerless to defeat the trend toward self-indulgence. The worship of Bacchus in secret rites, however, was successfully prevented from becoming firmly established. Although we do not know the end of the story of Publius Aebutius and his stepfather, we know that, in public affairs at least, the moral youngster triumphed decisively over the scheming old man.

The orgiastic cult of Bacchus attracted the enthusiastic support of many of Rome's "bright young things." Meeting at night, their festivals were riotous occasions where they would consume great quantities of wine and dance by torchlight to the music of flutes. Inevitably, drunkenness and debauchery resulted, to the horror of those citizens who believed in the traditional virtues of Roman society.

The Antikythera mechanism
A mechanical puzzle

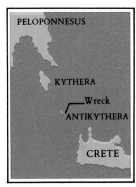

The island of Antikythera is situated in the eastern Mediterranean between the island of Crete and the Greek mainland. It was off the coast of this small island that a group of divers found the 2,000-year-old mechanism that has revolutionized our understanding of ancient Greek technology.

AS SO OFTEN happens, one of history's most spectacular scientific discoveries came to light by pure chance. Shortly before Easter in 1900, a party of Greek sponge divers ran into fierce gales and their boat was driven off course. Captain Demetrios Condos realized that his survival depended upon escaping the lethal straits off Crete, and so he turned northeastward to the calm waters at the northernmost tip of Antikythera Island.

For a week the storm continued to rage and, to maintain discipline and keep his crew occupied, the captain sent divers to hunt for sponges. One of his most experienced men, Elias Stadiatis, plunged to a depth of 140 feet (42 meters), pulled down by the heavy lead weights attached to his diving suit and the soles of his boots. Suddenly, he yanked the rope linking him to the ship, a sign that he wanted to ascend immediately. Stadiatis emerged in a state of shock. He muttered something about "naked women and horses," but would give no further explanation. Captain Condos was very curious and determined to solve the mystery. He descended to the sea bed and there found an ancient ship which had sunk in about 80 BC, its treasure of statues and other objects plainly visible.

At the end of November 1900, salvage work on the wreck began; it continued for nine months. The Greek government provided a ship to assist in the work but weather conditions were so hazardous and underwater techniques so primitive that one diver died and two were seriously injured. Eight months later, when all the treasure had been housed in the National Archeological Museum in Athens, a most important object was discovered by Valerios Stais, a hawk-eyed museum archeologist. What he found were the remains of a bronze clock-like mechanism, later to be known as the Antikythera mechanism, that had up to this point been disregarded among a pile of unexamined bronze and marble pieces. A fragment of the mechanism bore an ancient inscription. The letters later proved to have been inscribed in the first century BC, and the most complete part of the inscription was similar to an astronomical calendar written in about 77 BC.

In 1902 Stais's announcement of his discovery of what he claimed was an ancient Greek astronomical device provoked a controversy that was not to be resolved for nearly 70 years. For historians had earlier believed that the existence of such a complex mechanism was impossible, that the ancient Greeks, despite their mathematical brilliance, had virtually no mechanical technology – a phenomenon partly attributed to their dependence on slaves and partly to the low status ascribed to mechanical occupations. Now, however, the discovery of the Antikythera mechanism – the first great find of underwater archeology – seemed to put an end to this long-cherished belief. Even so its purpose and function were still to be established and the following years saw the emergence of a variety of theories: Initially the mechanism, which was about half the size of a portable typewriter, was thought to be an astrolabe, an instrument used by navigators to measure the angular distances of heavenly bodies above the horizon. Some believed that it might be a small planetarium, of the kind that the mathematician Archimedes was said to have made, while others maintained that it was too complex to be either. The most conservative academics even argued that it must have been thrown overboard from some other vessel passing over the wreck centuries later.

Finally, in 1975, the strange mystery of the Antikythera was solved when Professor Derek de Dolla Price of Yale University announced the conclusions of his long research into the mechanism. His work had included cooperation with the Greek Atomic Energy Commission which used gamma rays on the fragments to enable him to see the mechanism's internal network, comprising more than 30 bronze gears. Here, stated the professor, was a computer, made in about 87 BC for calculating the motions of the Sun, Moon, and planets. The four pieces of broken mechanism, with their sophisticated gear wheels, dials, and inscribed plates, were such that the professor compared its discovery in an ancient wreck to "finding a jet plane in King Tutankhamun's tomb!" Indeed, so revolutionary were the findings that there were some who insisted that the creators of the mechanism could not have been ancient Greeks, but rather aliens from outer space.

The recovery of the Antikythera mechanism shattered popular beliefs about ancient Greek technology. Today, experts acknowledge that mechanical technology was an important element in Greek science and that this mechanism is a forerunner of modern scientific hardware.

A FORERUNNER OF THE COMPUTER AGE

The Antikythera mechanism, also called the Rhodes calculator, has been described as a Greek wheeled computer of the heavens. It was probably made by a pupil of Posidonius, a philosopher who had settled on the island of Rhodes around 87 BC. Or it might have been the work of a Greek astronomer, mathematician, and philosopher, Geminus, a contemporary of Posidonius.

The mechanism mathematically mimicked the movements of heavenly bodies, at a time when many Greeks still believed that the Earth was a circular disc supported by a great ocean, above which was the hemispherical bowl of the sky. The planets and the Moon were thought to move along certain geometrical paths. The object of the mechanism was to reveal their motions and so dispense with the need for further calculations.

The mechanism must have resembled a modern mechanical clock, but the evidence points to the fact that it was an astronomical device that happened to use mechanisms that were later to be adapted to tell the time. Some experts suspect that its main users were not astronomers, but astrologers who wanted to know the aspect of the heavens at any given time, past or future. The mechanism had three dials: one in front and two at the back. The dial at the front contained two concentric bands. One band was inscribed with the names of the signs of the zodiac. The other, movable band had the names of each month in Greek on it. A pointer indicated the position of the Sun in the zodiac for each day of the year. The dials at the back seemed to indicate lunar and planetary movements. A handle turned once every day set the mechanism in motion.

The sophistication of the Antikythera mechanism is most extraordinary when the device is placed alongside the sundials, water clocks, and horoscopic instruments of its time.

Archeologists have made a replica of the original Antikythera mechanism using more than 30 gears from the original device. Its workings suggest that it had been designed to plot the movements of the Sun, Moon, and planets.

What sort of woman was Cleopatra?

Beauty was not her main weapon

GREAT LITERATURE (mainly Shakespeare's play *Antony and Cleopatra*) and somewhat trashy movies have portrayed Cleopatra as a sexy seductress, a beautiful *femme fatale*. But was this most memorable Queen of Egypt merely a promiscuous, frivolous beauty? If, as is suggested in Shakespeare's play, one of her lovers called her his "serpent of old Nile," was he referring to her sinuous, uncapturable loveliness or to her ruthless bite? Will the real Cleopatra please stand up?

The *real* Cleopatra, as modern scholars have discovered from studying records as well as legends, was indeed an alluring woman. She was not a great beauty, though; she seems, in fact, to have been rather plain. Her portrait, as it appears on Egyptian coins of the time, shows a vivacious countenance, with a sensitive mouth, large eyes, and a surprisingly big, hooked nose. Writing more than a century after her death, the Greek biographer Plutarch says: "Her beauty, we are told, was not of the incomparable kind that instantly captivates the beholder. But she had irresistible charm . . . along with a peculiar force of character that pervaded her every word and action and put all who associated with her under her spell." So her personality seems to have been more powerful than her looks. Far from specializing in empty-headed frivolity, she was intelligent, able to speak six languages, and well versed in history and philosophy. Above all, though, she appears to have been a skillful, ambitious ruler and negotiator. In fact, Cleopatra can best be characterized as a brilliant political operator, who used her charm as a weapon for gaining power. This is the key to her relations with the two great Romans – Julius Caesar and Mark Antony – who became her lovers.

Egypt was nominally independent but was in fact a protectorate of Rome when 18-year-old Cleopatra and her husband, Ptolemy XIII, inherited the throne jointly in 51 BC. As was the custom in ancient Egypt, the king and queen were brother and sister as well as husband and wife, and they soon became rivals rather than loyal helpmates. By 48 BC, When Caesar led a military expedition into Egypt, Cleopatra had been deprived of power, and it seems probable that she set out to seduce Caesar less for love than in order to recapture her throne. At any rate, her efforts to captivate the Roman hero were crowned with success: Caesar crushed her opponents and restored the joint rule – under

Roman authority – of brother and sister. Not long after that, Ptolemy was killed in battle; Cleopatra bore a son nicknamed Caesarion ("little Caesar") by the people of Alexandria; and she was sole ruler of Egypt, although she shared the throne for a while with her 13-year-old brother (and husband number two), Ptolemy XIV.

In 44 BC, Cleopatra – still only 25 years old – was in Rome, when her hopes of securing Egypt's position as a protectorate of Rome and thus enhancing her own power, were dashed by Caesar's assassination. She now returned to Alexandria, the capital city of Egypt, and awaited the outcome of the power struggle that followed Caesar's death. By 42 BC she was probably convinced that Rome's – and thus Egypt's – future was in the hands of Mark Antony, whose only remaining rival was Caesar's young but apparently sickly nephew, Octavian. So when Antony asked her to come for a meeting at Tarsus in Asia Minor (Turkey), Cleopatra once again set forth on a mission to conquer a conqueror.

She approached Tarsus by sailing up the Cydnus River in a lavishly decorated barge. Cunningly, however, she did not enter the city but moored nearby, so that Antony was obliged to come to *her*. Then, according to Plutarch, she revealed the bounteous gifts she had brought, symbols of Egypt's wealth and importance – gold, precious stones, horses, even slaves. Her chief aim, probably, was to impress Antony, but she succeeded in seducing him as well. So once again she made use of a Roman hero and his power. They returned to Alexandria as lovers, and she soon bore Antony's twins.

Meanwhile, however, Octavian had been growing in power and authority. In 40 BC, as an act of self-protection, Antony returned to Rome and married Octavian's sister. Cleopatra, alone on the Egyptian throne (her second brother-husband having been "liquidated"), spent her time strengthening Egypt's economy and building up its defenses.

Then, in 37 BC, Antony returned to the Middle East, intent on forming a power base there – and Cleopatra, who knew he needed her, was ready for him. She financed his military campaigns in and around Persia, and in return he made over great tracts of land to her and their children. Effectively, he fulfilled this shrewd woman's yearning to restore Egyptian greatness. It has also been claimed that he married her, although his Roman wife, Octavian's sister, still lived.

But at this point Cleopatra's star began to wane. Octavian convinced the Roman people

HOW DID CLEOPATRA DIE?

In Shakespeare's *Antony and Cleopatra*, the Egyptian queen, determined to escape public humiliation after the defeat of her fleet and the suicide of her lover, kills herself by baring her breast to the fangs of an asp (a small poisonous snake). This was not entirely a poetic invention. The Greek biographer Plutarch suggests that she died of a snake bite on her arm; the breast is a romantic addition to the story. Plutarch points out, however, that there are various accounts of the manner of her death, any one of which may be true. She may, for example, have taken poison, which she reportedly kept in a hollow comb, ready for use when necessary.

If she did die from a self-induced snake-bite, it would probably have been that of a cobra rather than of an asp, which is a kind of viper. The evidence we have about her indicates that Cleopatra was too clever and knowledgeable to force a slow, painful death upon herself. If she had indeed considered different poisoning methods she would have known that the effects of viper venom are agonizingly slow, whereas a cobra bite induces nervous paralysis and a quick, relatively easy end.

Whatever the method, it is certain that Cleopatra committed suicide. Her children would perhaps have been better off had she taken them with her. Caesarion, reputed to be the son of Julius Caesar, was executed. Of the children born of the liaison with Mark Antony little is known for sure, although the daughter may have escaped execution by being conveniently married off to the king of far-away Mauretania.

Royal emblem of the Egyptian pharaohs and possibly used by Cleopatra as a means of suicide, the cobra was one of Egypt's earliest deities. Here the cobra decorates the headdress of Tutankhamon (ruled c. 1348–1340 BC).

that they were threatened by a rival empire with its capital in Alexandria. And in 31 BC the Roman senate stripped Antony of his political offices and declared war on Cleopatra. Soon afterward the combined fleets of Antony and Cleopatra were routed by Octavian's ships in the Battle of Actium, near the western coast of Greece. The lovers escaped to Alexandria, but it was all over for them. Antony killed himself by falling on his sword. Cleopatra was left to the mercy of Octavian, the man who would soon be known as Augustus, the first of a long line of Roman emperors.

There is reason to believe that she would willingly have made peace with Octavian on much the same terms as she had offered Caesar and Antony. But she was nearly 40 years old by 30 BC, when Octavian followed her to Alexandria. Perhaps she was tired; perhaps she looked her age. In any event, Octavian did not succumb to her charms. Rather than be carted back to Rome as a prisoner of war, she committed suicide.

Did she, then, choose to die because her lover had killed himself? Was she a lovelorn lady? An over-sexed voluptuary? The answer to all such questions appears to be no. The real Cleopatra was an ambitious women, with politics in her bones and a bright eye for the big chance. Her only failing was that, in the end, she had backed the wrong man.

Impersonations for the screen have tended to glamorize the Egyptian queen, Cleopatra, although the sculpture (above) dating from c. 30 BC shows her with a firm chin and unattractively large nose. Theda Bara (left) in the 1917 Hollywood film Cleopatra *is remembered for her stunning role but a true likeness was not attempted; the film makers sought to show a beautiful woman according to the taste of the period but with little regard for historical accuracy.*

The talking Colossus

A miracle or a confidence trick?

WHEN THE Greek geographer, Strabo, visited Egypt's top tourist attraction nearly 2,000 years ago, his reaction was, to say the least, cynical. He recorded that he had heard "a noise like a blow of no great force." He was not sure whether the sound had come from the base of the statue, or had been made by a bystander. But he felt sure that the statue itself had not made the sound. Yet for the next 200 years the statue that had become known as the "vocal Memnon" continued to draw crowds of wondering visitors, many of whom believed that they were indeed witnessing a miracle. Every day, at sunrise, the statue before them would "talk."

The vocal Memnon was one of two giant statues (known as the Colossi of Memnon) in the city of Thebes, the ancient capital of Egypt some 300 miles (500 kilometers) south of Cairo. In 27 BC an earthquake struck the city with great severity, damaging one of the statues; the giant split across its body and the upper part of the magnificent structure was hurled to the ground.

It was soon after the earthquake that reports began to circulate that the damaged statue had begun to "talk" around sunrise, and visitors would make dawn trips to the statue to hear it.

Another Greek geographer, Pausanias, visited Thebes around the middle of the second century AD. In his *Guidebook of Greece*, the only guidebook to have survived from the ancient world, he expressed his surprise at hearing the "talking" statue. He wrote: "Every day at sunrise it cries out, and one would compare the sound most nearly to the breaking of the string of a harp or a lute."

However, the sightseers who thronged the streets of Thebes believed that they had heard the voice of Memnon, the legendary King of Ethiopia who was said to have been slain by the Greek hero Achilles in the Trojan War.

For 200 years visitors marveled at the talking statue. Then, early in the third century, a Roman emperor, Septimius Severus, who ruled from AD 193 to 211, also went to Thebes. A man of wide administrative and military experience, he was concerned about the dilapidated state of the "talking" Colossus. He ordered his engineers to replace the part of the statue that had fallen down. But from the day the statue was repaired Memnon's voice was never heard again.

How then did the statue "speak"? A possible explanation is that the sudden, fierce heat of the sun expanded the cold, damp stone unevenly along the cracked surface. This might in turn have set up vibrations that were interpreted as a melodious voice. Or the sound might have been caused by a current of expanding air making its way through a damaged section of the stone.

Skeptics attribute the phenomenon to human intervention – an ingenious subterfuge to guarantee that gifts and offerings would continue to pour into the shrine. Perhaps the Theban priests were expert ventriloquists. Or perhaps they concealed someone at the base of the statue before dawn. If so, they must have been incredibly skillful or lucky to have kept up the deception for so long.

The twin Colossi of Memnon have stood guard in Thebes, ancient capital of Egypt, for over 3,000 years. But their present serenity is deceptive for one of them, damaged in an earthquake in 27 BC, was regularly heard to speak, giving rise to a mystery that has yet to be completely explained.

TOURIST INSCRIPTIONS

The Colossi of Memnon are really twin statues of the Pharaoh Amenophis III, as attested by inscriptions of the pharaoh's name and royal title on the backs of the statues. Amenophis, called "the Magnificent," reigned from about 1417 to 1379 BC. By the time of the earthquake, he had been forgotten and the Greeks and Romans were convinced that the statues were likenesses of the Ethiopian King Memnon.

The statues formerly guarded the entrance to an enormous temple complex, which was totally destroyed within about 100 years of its construction. The statues, however, still exist. Carved from red sandstone, they tower 64 feet (19.5 meters) above the ground. Their massive shoulders are 20 feet (6 meters) broad, while the fingers are more than 4 feet (1.2 meters) long.

On the legs and base of the "talking" statue are many inscriptions of the names of distinguished visitors, often with lengthy messages. These early graffiti are so beautifully engraved that they were probably the work of professional stone-cutters. Archeologists have logged more than 100 inscriptions, including 61 in Greek and 35 in Latin. About one-third of them are dated, ranging between about AD 14 and 205. The inscriptions reveal the firm belief of the visitors in the miraculous sound. One inscription from about AD 89 to 91 reads:

Thou still hast thy voice, O great Memnon,
e'en though
By destroyers thy body was smitten,
For Mettius heard it, and can say it is so.
This poem by Paeon was written.

The mystery of the Bog people
Murder victims or winter sacrifices?

IN MAY 1950 Danish peat-cutters uncovered the body of a man in a Danish bog called Tollund Fen. They thought they had stumbled on a murder victim and immediately sent for the police. But the police were accustomed to such reports. With the help of a representative of the local museum it was very soon established that this was no recent murder victim but a character from some ritual drama played out perhaps as much as 2,000 years previously. As a result, it became a case not for the police, but for Professor Peter V. Glob, a leading Danish authority on the Bog people, Iron Age men and women whose bodies somehow ended up in the sour peat-bogs of northwest Europe.

Tollund Man, as the 1950 find became known, is one of the finest specimens of the Bog people. The most remarkable feature of the body was the wonderfully intact face. As Professor Glob later wrote: "His face wore a gentle expression – the eyes slightly closed, the lips softly pursed, as if in silent prayer. It was as though the dead man's soul had for a moment returned from another world, through the gate in the western sky."

Lying on the right side, as if asleep, the body was tanned a dark, leathery brown, while the peat had turned the short-cropped hair reddish-brown. The contours of the body had been somewhat distorted and flattened by the weight of the overlying peat. But the air of serenity pervading the grave was soon shattered. Further excavation revealed a noose around the dead man's neck. He had met his death by hanging.

Cutters in northern Europe have been extracting peat from the bogs to use as fuel for hundreds of years. During this time the bogs have yielded occasional grim finds, much to the consternation of the superstitious cutters who could recall tales of the Devil, or of sinister, unexplained disappearances in the locality. Several hundred Bog people came to light in this way. Their bodies, slightly shrunken and sometimes incomplete, had assumed the color and texture of hide due to the tanning action of the acid peat. In some cases the bones were decalcified. Only the skin and organs survived.

Such bodies were usually hastily reburied in the peat or laid to rest in consecrated ground. In more recent times and especially since World War II, the bog finds have been recognized as dating from antiquity. As a result archeologists have scrutinized them closely for the light they shed on the past. Modern methods of dating, such as pollen analysis and carbon-14 techniques, place most of the Bog people whose bodies have so far been discovered in the Iron Age, between about 100 BC and AD 500.

Most numerous and best documented are the Danish finds, particularly those in north and central Jutland. These finds include Tollund Man and his Iron Age neighbor, Grauballe Man, unearthed in a bog 11 miles (17 kilometers) farther east in 1952 and again closely examined by Glob. Like Tollund Man, Grauballe Man was buried naked. Though misshapen by the pressure of the peat, the body was extremely well-preserved. Grauballe Man had also met a violent end. His throat had been cut, almost from ear to ear, and the skull was fractured. The body had also sustained other injuries, some of which may have occurred after death.

Violence is a recurrent theme in the many peat-bog finds. Hanging, strangulation, throat-cutting, bludgeoning, or decapitation are the commonest causes of death. Exceptions include a girl of about 14 found in Schleswig in northern Germany. Archeologists think that she was drowned in the shallow water of the bog after having been blindfolded. The body of this girl, who lived in the first century AD, had been weighted down with branches and a large stone, as had the body of a man, also found in 1952, who had been hanged and buried just 16 feet (5 meters) away.

An important 19th-century find was the body of a woman, aged about 50, who may have been buried alive in a Jutland bog. Wooden crooks driven in tightly over each knee and elbow joint had fastened her body securely to the underlying peat. Strong branches, laid horizontally across

A face from the time of Christ, undisturbed for 20 centuries in the peat-bogs of the Tollund Fen, Denmark. This amazingly well-preserved head seems to be that of a man tranquil in death – yet a noose was about his neck. Was he executed for some crime? Or perhaps sacrificed to a demanding Iron Age god?

the body, were also clamped into place with crooks embedded in the peat. An observer of the find described the look on the dead woman's face as "one of despair."

What is the meaning of these often gruesome finds? Tollund and Grauballe Man have been subjected to closer scrutiny than any earlier bog finds. Full post-mortems, laboratory analyses of body tissue, and radiographic examinations have been constructed, showing among other things that Grauballe Man had rheumatoid arthritis in the spine. Incredulous assistants in the police laboratory at Aarhus even took Grauballe Man's fingerprints. The condition of the hands showed that he, like many Bog people, had not been accustomed to rough manual work. In both cases the stomach contents, analyzed by paleobotanists, gave valuable clues to the events surrounding the deaths of these men. The last meal of both men had consisted of a sort of gruel made from various grains and wild-flower seeds. The complete absence of summer or autumn foods suggested that both men had died in winter or early spring.

This discovery supports a theory of Professor Glob's. He has argued that the Bog people were not executed criminals, but victims sacrificed to a northern fertility goddess at winter celebrations held to hasten the arrival of spring. "It was on just such occasions that bloody human sacrifices reached a peak in the Iron Age," wrote

Glob, who has also made the point that the peat-bog burials seem to have nothing in common with normal Iron Age burial customs, whereas they do bear the stamp of ritual killing enacted at a time when this practice was known to be widespread. Even so, no absolute or conclusive explanation has yet been established.

After a year's preservative treatment to perfect the tanning process begun in the peat-bogs, Tollund Man's serene head was sent to the Silkeborg Museum in central Jutland, barely six miles (9 kilometers) from the dank peat-bog in which it was found. Displayed alongside Iron Age artifacts, it remains the world's best-preserved human head from antiquity. Meanwhile, in the Museum of Prehistory at Aarhus, Grauballe Man is preserved complete – a tallish, dark-haired man in his late 30s who lived around AD 310. Both men now bear silent testimony to the dark practices of a dark age.

Celtic "barbarism"

Defeated through religion

The great Gundestrup caldron, a Celtic votive vessel made of silver, was found in Denmark in 1891. This detail, which shows a human victim being offered to the War god, corroborates Roman accounts of lurid Celtic practices. But the barbarians' religion also had a strong mystical dimension – a quality lacking in the more arid official cults of the urban Romans – and the caldron testifies to the sophistication of Celtic craftsmanship.

WHEN, IN AD 60, Roman troops launched a devastating attack on the island fortress of Mona (present-day Anglesey) off the northern coast of Wales, they were determined to crush not only a military base but a religious center. Mona was a holy island, the heartland of Celtic Druidism, and the aristocratic Druid priesthood constituted the backbone of Celtic resistance to the expanding power of Rome in Britain. As the invading troops waited to cross the water in their landing craft, they could see white-robed Druids moving among the warriors opposite, "raising their hands to heaven and screaming dreadful curses," in the words of the Roman historian Tacitus. As if to make the scene doubly spectral, black-robed women with disheveled hair were urging on the Celtic men, howling and brandishing torches.

For a time the Romans hesitated; then, recovering, they crossed to defeat the ill-equipped defenders of Mona. Military victory was not enough, though. The Romans then proceeded to do something uncharacteristic: They destroyed the Celts' sacred grove of oak trees, putting an end to centuries of mysterious rites connected with the worship of strange gods.

Normally, the Romans were tolerant of the religions of the peoples they conquered. Why did they so ruthlessly try to destroy that of the Celts? The answer, according to imperial apologists, was that civilized Rome despised the "barbarous impiety" of human sacrifice and head-hunting that the Druids countenanced in the name of religion. Yet human sacrifice had been practiced in Rome until 97 BC, when the senate finally banned it; and bloodthirsty gladiatorial contests were all the rage in the imperial capital at the very moment the troops were destroying the sacred groves of Mona. The real reason why Rome wanted to deprive the Celts of their faith was that the priesthood – the noble Druids – had an incomparable power to spur their people on to great feats of bravery. It was fear, not distaste for a "barbarous impiety," that lay behind Rome's intolerance.

The Greeks as well as the Romans had long known and respected the formidable fighting qualities of Celtic tribes, whose peoples and culture had swept across Europe from their beginnings somewhere northeast of the Alps. These tall, muscular, fair-haired warriors had swooped down upon the urban south, sacking the holy city of Delphi and even raiding Rome itself in the fourth century BC. By the time Julius Caesar began his conquest of Gaul in 58 BC, the Celts had spread throughout Western Europe and into the British Isles. It was mainly for military glory that Caesar set out to subjugate the "barbarians" to the north and west of Italy. His accounts of Gallic life, which constitute one of our chief literary sources, were probably written partly to justify his attacks on the Celts and so should be viewed with caution. The success of Rome's legions was such that Celtic identity and culture were eventually destroyed or absorbed by other peoples – except in the areas that were difficult to subdue because of their remoteness: Far-away Britain, Ireland, and northwestern France (the area now known as Brittany), for example.

Until the decisive battle at Mona these northerners, who were to retain their Celtic language and identity, were still living in a "heroic age" of endless intertribal fighting, punctuated and encouraged by heavy drinking bouts and oral poems glorifying war. Their society was divided rigidly into three strata – warrior nobles,

Druids (who also belonged to the nobility), and peasants, among whom were craftsmen as well as tillers of the soil. The warriors lived only to fight, and on occasion they fought from chariots made of wickerwork and driven at speed along the enemy lines. Often yelling at the top of their voices, the warriors would hurl javelins before leaping down to fight. With their faces painted blue, with great horned helmets on their heads, and drunk with strong beer and battle lust, they must have made an imposing sight.

And always in their midst were the priests, goading them on to even greater glory. The Druids themselves abstained from fighting, but in no other respect were they men of peace. It is hardly surprising that the Emperor Claudius, after his conquest of southern Britain in AD 43, banned all forms of Druidism in the Roman empire, or that, a few years later, Suetonius Paulinus, then governor of Roman Britain, commanded his troops at Mona to kill the Celts' priests as well as their fighters.

THE DRUIDS

In doing away with Druidism, the Romans suppressed a priesthood of great culture and complexity. Though in Rome itself almost anyone of the right social status could assume the office of priest for a god such as Apollo or Mars, Druids in the Celtic world were trained for up to 20 years to prepare for their positions as guardians of the secret lore of their religion (whose tenets were as mysterious to the Romans as they are to us). Once a Druid had passed initiation tests, he belonged to a caste apart from and even above the warrior class.

Druids served their tribes not only as priests but as judges and historians. They carried out their religious rites, which involved human sacrifice, in dense woodland areas (the "sacred grove"); and it is possible that the Romans were influenced by their observation of heavy, threatening forests in the cold and misty north – so different from the sunlit lands of the Mediterranean – to exaggerate reports of occult and demonic practices. Both Julius Caesar and his near-contemporary Strabo, a Greek geographer and historian, agree that ritual sacrifice among the Celts was not indiscriminate. For example, although the victims were usually burned alive in wickerwork cages shaped like enormous heads, this fate was normally reserved

for prisoners of war, kept alive for the purpose, and was seldom visited upon innocent Celts.

Another Roman writer of the first century AD, Pliny the Elder, paints a fascinating word-picture of white-robed priests celebrating the sixth night of the new moon by cutting a growth of holy mistletoe from its parasitical position on a sacred oak tree (the word "Druid" means "Knowing the oak tree" in Gaelic, the language of Britain's Celts). The mistletoe, cut with a gold sickle, was dropped onto a white cloak spread out below, and was then used in magic potions, says Pliny. So the Druids seem to have been herbalist healers too.

Most Celts were illiterate, but Druids could read and write, and many knew Latin as well as their own language. They were students of the stars, too, and not only practiced a form of astrological "crystal-gazing" but also had an understanding of astronomy equal to that of the Romans. Their calendar, for instance, was based on a year comprising 12 30-day months with interspersed extra days. After the destruction of the sylvan religious center at Mona, however, Druidism lost its authority and prestige. Within a few generations the Druids had dwindled into little more than sorcerers.

Betrayed only by their footwear and spectacles, present-day British Druids act out the summer solstice ceremony of their Celtic ancestors at Stonehenge – the most spectacular ancient religious complex in northern Europe.

Danebury: A Celtic hillfort

Fortified hilltop settlements first appeared in Europe around 2000 BC, when Bronze Age peoples used the more easily defensible hills as natural refuges for the tribe and its flocks. These earliest defenses were encircled by a row of stakes mounted on a raised bank and further protected by a surrounding ditch, but later hillforts were constructed with vertically walled ramparts of timber and stone. From 1000 BC substantial hilltop defenses were built by Iron Age Celts throughout Western Europe, and by the second century BC were a common feature of the Celtic world, protecting their inhabitants from raids by other tribes out to seize valuable livestock.

British hillforts varied in size from small, defended farmsteads and single fortified dwellings to huge enclosures surrounded by miles of ramparts. In southern England, certain forts, of which Danebury in Hampshire is a good example, seem to have acquired a dominant status by the second and first centuries BC, controlling up to 40 square miles (100 square kilometers) of surrounding countryside.

Roughly 330 yards (300 meters) wide, Danebury has been excavated in a broad strip across its center, giving us at least a partial knowledge of life within the fort. The earliest buildings, probably grain stores, date from the sixth century BC, but there is no sign that the site was lived in then, though it may have had a protective palisade. By the early fourth century BC, a timber-faced rampart surrounded the fort, and from that date there are signs of continuous occupation according to an organized plan. Houses and grain-storage pits were built to the north, and rows of rectangular structures, probably storage barns, to the south. Later the scheme was modified, and houses may have been more evenly distributed. Four rectangular buildings toward the center of the fort may have had a religious function, for later Roman temples have been found in several hillforts, and it seems likely that they were the successors of earlier buildings. The presence of ritual burial pits at Danebury confirms that it was a sacred site.

In the third century BC, the west entrance was blocked and the ramparts heightened with chalk and earth to rise steeply from a deep ditch. This gave the defending inhabitants the advantage of a safe height from which to discharge sling shot. The fort's weakest defense point was the gate, which was eventually strengthened in about 100 BC with the construction of two projecting bastions and a command post. An outer earthwork enclosed a tract of pasture where beasts could be driven in to safety.

The remains of domestic activities at Danebury show that in effect it was a walled town, with a large and flourishing population and an administration strong enough to organize major building works. The presence of unworked shale and iron ingots, and of conical pits probably used as clay settling tanks, suggest that metal items, shale ornaments, and pottery, were made for distribution elsewhere.

Danebury's prosperity declined after the coming of the Romans, when the forts were forcibly cleared and people were attracted to the new towns. When central authority collapsed after the Romans withdrew in the fifth century BC, some hillforts once again served as refuges and were refortified, but the arrival of the Normans in 1066 finally ended their role.

Raised granary

Houses in Danebury hillfort were circular in shape, with a conical overhanging roof of thatch or turf supported by walls of stakes or wattle, weatherproofed with daub and possibly faced with turf. The only substantial timbers used were for the doorframes. Some houses had small enclosures flanking the path to the door where food was grown and livestock kept.

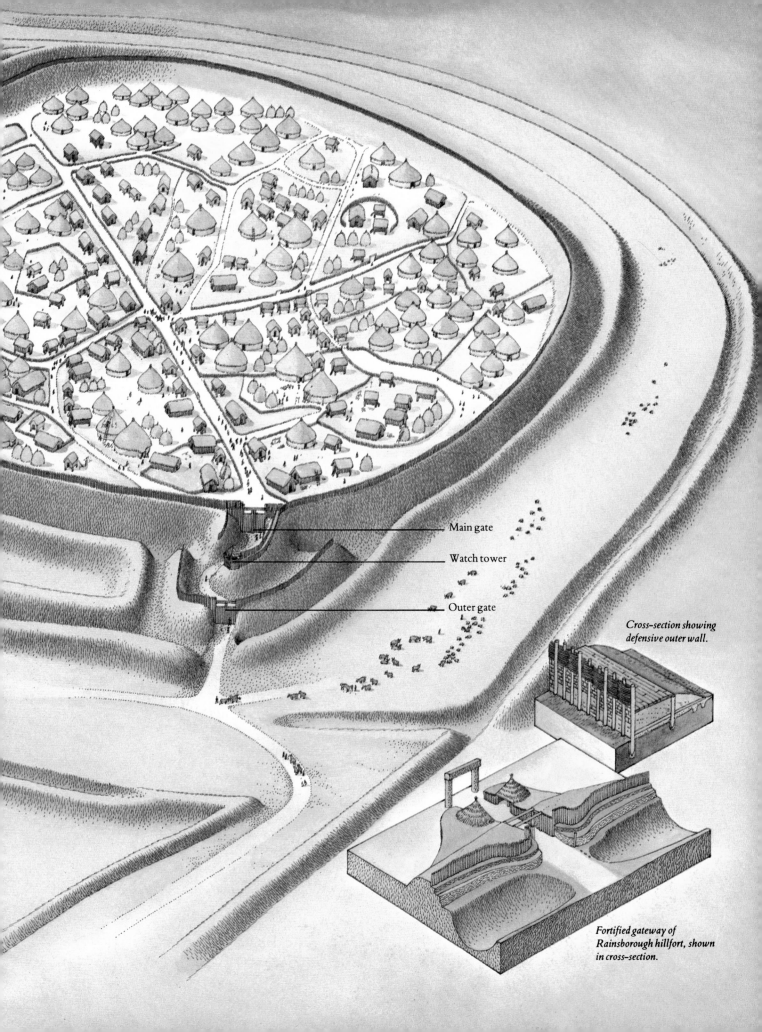

Main gate

Watch tower

Outer gate

*Cross-section showing
defensive outer wall.*

*Fortified gateway of
Rainsborough hillfort, shown
in cross-section.*

Buried treasure

Money that couldn't be spent

IT HAS LONG been known that the Romans followed in the steps of Alexander the Great and reached India – no mean feat in a time when communications were neither easy nor quick. That the Romans were willing to make this arduous journey thousands of miles to the East is understandable, given that Eastern luxury goods have traditionally brought great profits to any Europeans trading in them. But did the Romans have anything to offer the Indians, whose culture was so different that there would seem to be little they needed from the Roman traders? Roman coins have been unearthed in southern India, some found, as one would expect, individually. However, most had been buried together in large quantities.

Did a few enterprising Indians hold a monopoly on trade with the West, raking in money they were unable to spend in their own country? Or did these hoards of money have some special significance for the Indians who collected them? Only by carefully piecing together the evidence of this East–West trade have historians been able to provide an unusual answer to the riddle of India's buried treasure.

In the peace and stability of the Roman empire, trade and commerce flourished, supplying a demand from wealthy Roman citizens for the luxuries of other cultures and continents. Furs and amber were imported from the barbarian north, Africa yielded up ivory, gold, spices, and wild animals for the amphitheatres, and from the sub-continent of India came the fabulous products of the exotic Orient.

During the reign of Augustus (27 BC to AD 14), commerce with India flourished. Entrepreneurial interest in the riches of the East, famed since the time of Alexander the Great, was stimulated by the many trade missions that arrived in the Roman world from India. One mission brought such wonders as a man born without arms, a large river turtle, snakes, and a partridge "as big as a vulture." But other missions arrived with pearls and precious stones – offerings that were to prove more representative of the imports that flooded into Rome as 120 monsoon-borne ships sailed each year from Roman-controlled Egypt to India, to pick up their precious cargoes.

The active agents in this trade – the wholesale merchants of Roman civilization – were Alexandrian Greeks. Alexandria in Egypt was the main Western port through which Eastern goods, and raw materials, passed. In India, the traders first established themselves in trading stations along the Malabar coast. There they had access to spices – especially pepper – muslin cloth, perfumes, and ivory. By the end of the first century AD, traders were dealing in pearls and gemstones from what is now Sri Lanka, and they also acquired products that reached India from farther east, notably Chinese silks.

All these commodities had to be paid for in one way or another, but in a country largely without a coin currency, and requiring little that the Roman traders had to offer, problems of payment inevitably arose. This difficulty was overcome in an ingenious way.

By the first century BC, Roman trade with the East had reached its peak, with spices, ivory, and jewels being important trading commodities. This detail from a wall painting in Ostia, dating from between the second and third centuries AD, shows a typical Roman trading ship being loaded up.

When the first Roman coins were unearthed in India in 1775, it was assumed by archeologists and historians that the hoards in which they had been discovered represented the collected savings of Indian traders which had been abandoned or lost due to some unfortunate or unforeseen incident. But historians have now come to realize that the Indians were interested in the coins not as currency – a meaningless concept to them – but as bullion.

Each hoard therefore represents a whole unit of stamped silver and gold, which was weighed out and then bartered for a specific wholesale purchase, just as silver ornaments are sometimes weighed out in exchange for purchases in Indian bazaars today. The fact that Roman gold and silver was already subdivided into reliable units, coins, was a matter of great convenience to the Indians and fostered much goodwill. The scholar Pliny reported that it was the unvarying quality of Roman coins – which were all the same weight and of the same gold or silver content despite the heads of successive emperors imprinted upon them – which impressed the King of Sri Lanka and inclined him favorably toward the honest traders of Rome.

To emphasize that they were no longer to be used as currency, many of the coins found in India had been defaced by an incision across the imperial head. But despite their lack of interest in the exchange value of the coins, the Indians were by no means oblivious to the charms of the designs of the coins, designs they admired so much that pierced or looped imitations of Roman coins, made of terracotta and probably once gilded, were made in India to be worn as jewelry. Imitation in this case was indeed the highest form of flattery.

But this continuous flow of coins to the East was not, from the Roman point of view, a sound basis for commerce. Soon export restrictions were imposed and when Roman silver coins were debased under Nero, Indian confidence in the bullion value of Roman money was undermined and they refused to accept any more Roman coins. The traders had to find substitute bartering material and so began to offer goods instead: high-quality tableware, glass, linen, coral, lamps, worked gems, and wine. And the great amount of Mediterranean pottery fragments found in India at Arikamedu near Pondicherry, where a major Roman trading station was excavated in the 1940s, indicate that the traders were successful with this new strategy. In the warehouses of Arikamedu, Italian pots and dishes, fine wines, and tableware were stored, and in its workshops jewels were worked and muslin cloth was made and dyed.

But this trade with India was not one upon which the health of the Roman legions, or the security of the people of Rome, depended. The crisis-ridden third century AD was a period of commercial decline in the Roman world, and as business confidence faltered, direct trade with India came to a halt. Intermediaries, such as Arabs and Persians, took over the trade. The merchants of Alexandria stopped sailing with the monsoon. To the peoples of the West, India once again became a mysterious, inaccessible land of legend.

Many articles of Arretine ware – so-called because of its manufacture in Arezzo, Italy – have been found in old trading stations in India, evidence of Roman trade with the sub-continent. This bowl, with its molded decoration, is a typical example of a popular Roman export commodity.

MASTERING THE MONSOON

The conquests of Alexander the Great (who ruled from 336–323 BC) first brought the Mediterranean world into contact with India. But the growth in particular of the mighty Parthian empire in Persia meant that the ancient trans-Asian land routes became effectively barred to regular traffic from the Mediterranean to the sub-continent. For a safe and less laborious route, merchants turned their attention to the sea.

In the first century BC a Greek merchant named Hippalus discovered how to use the southwest monsoon to sail to, and from, the Indian sub-continent. He also provided a relatively accurate geography of the area, and soon Hippalus's wind was being utilized by other merchants for regular trade on an unprecedented scale with the East. In July and August, for 40 days, merchants well-versed in the ways of the monsoon voyaged from Arabian ports directly to the Malabar ports on India's southwestern coast. In December and January, having transacted their business, they returned via the Red Sea, or the Persian Gulf, to the Mediterranean. By the first century AD the trading depots on the east coast of India – previously reached overland – were now linked by circumpeninsular sea traffic. Direct trade links with Sri Lanka were established and some ships were sailing as far east as Burma, Malaya, Vietnam, and even China.

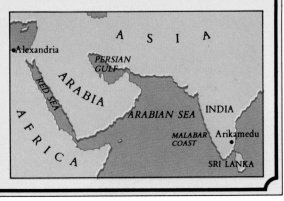

Traitor or patriot?

The riddle of a Jewish historian

Josephus unashamedly adopted the name Flavius, family name of his emperor-patron Vespasian, thus betraying his eagerness for acceptance by the Roman establishment. Back home in Judaea, however, such traits confirmed his unsavory reputation as a "quisling."

HISTORY IS FULL of prophets who have not been honored by their own people. And the history of Josephus – the chronicler of the Jews – teaches us that this truism can also apply to historians. Accused by his fellow-Jews of treachery to his compatriots while benefiting from his friendship with the Romans who had conquered them, Josephus has gone down in history as a man who, for personal gain, turned his back on his heritage. But does Josephus deserve such a reputation, or was he – as he himself believed – a patriot and a friend to his people in their time of need?

As a Jew, Josephus started life with impeccable credentials. He was born in AD 38 of a noble, priestly family in Jerusalem, a clever and studious boy, so precocious that by the age of 14 he claimed he was being consulted by priests and other learned men of the city on matters of Jewish law. He continued his education until he was 19, becoming a member of the Pharisee religious sect. His choice of sect is significant for an understanding of his later career, because the Pharisees were distinguished from other Jewish groups by their down-to-earth attitude toward Roman rule. Unlike groups such as the Zealots, who were militantly anti-Roman, the Pharisees believed that religious integrity could co-exist with the Roman political order.

In AD 64 Josephus, by then an ambitious young priest and scholar, was sent to Rome to plead for the release of certain Jewish priests who were being detained there. He was successful in this mission, thanks to the favorable intervention of the Emperor Nero's wife, Poppaea. Josephus enjoyed his stay in the cosmopolitan imperial city and while there he was impressed by Roman military might. This reinforced his Pharisee belief in the futility of a Jewish armed revolt against the all-powerful Roman military presence in Judaea, a conviction that was later to lead him into compromise.

When he returned home, however, the storm clouds of revolt had already gathered over his country. Josephus was quickly drawn into the bitter and bloody rebellion, which was to culminate in the destruction of Jerusalem by the Romans in AD 70. To remain neutral in such a

---

JUDAEA: THE RELUCTANT PROVINCE

Judaea was conquered by Pompey in 63 BC and from then until AD 44 the area was ruled as a Roman protectorate by a series of puppet rulers. The tranquility of Judaea, which provided a strategic land-link between the imperial provinces of Egypt and Syria, and formed a barrier against the hostile Parthian empire in the east, was of vital importance to the Romans. Accordingly, they were anxious to ensure the passive cooperation of their Jewish subjects.

The Jews were granted complete religious freedom, being asked to make a daily sacrifice for, rather than to, the emperor, who was the focus of loyalty to Rome. This was an unusual dispensation for a subject people, as was their exemption from military service and the considerable leeway allowed to them in the running of their own affairs. Even so, the Romans occasionally displayed great insensitivity to Jewish traditions. In AD 39 and 40, for example, the mad Emperor Caligula tried to have a statue of himself set up in the Temple in Jerusalem. War would have ensued from this attempted desecration, if Caligula had not been murdered in AD 41.

Although dependent on Roman support for their power, not all the puppet rulers of Judaea were disliked. King Agrippa I was very popular both with his Jewish subjects for whom he was a devout Jew, and with his Gentile subjects, for whom he was a cultivated Hellenistic monarch. But he was too independent in his ways for Roman comfort and when he died in AD 44, his kingdom was brought under direct Roman rule as the procuratorial province of Judaea. Under a series of greedy and incompetent procurators, political tensions mounted in the province and the militantly anti-Roman Zealots gained influence.

The Zealot movement began in the year AD 6 after a Roman census (the necessary preliminary for an assessment of tribute) made the Jews conscious of their subjection to a foreign, heathen emperor. The revolt of 66 was started when a daring youth named Eleazar interrupted a sacrifice to the imperial cult. Led by Menahem, who was the son of the Zealot founder and acclaimed as the long awaited Messiah-king, the Zealots gained control of Jerusalem after this incident.

The Roman reaction was swift and brutal. The last flames of revolt were put out in 73 when the defenders of the rock fortress of Masada by the Dead Sea chose to commit mass suicide rather than surrender. Jewish nationalist aspirations were not yet crushed, however. In 132–35, the Jews rose again and this time the Romans left nothing to chance. The rebels were forcibly deported and their lands were laid waste.

struggle was almost impossible, and Josephus felt that he could have some influence as a counselor of moderation among the Zealot-inspired rebels. He became military commander of Galilee, and it was during this period that an event took place which was to provide ample fuel for Josephus's detractors. The rebellion was going badly for the Jews, and Josephus and 40 of his men were forced to take refuge in a cave hide-out. When the besieged men decided to kill themselves rather than give in, Josephus suggested that, instead of suicide, each man, in turn, should kill his neighbor. They were to cast lots, the first man killing the second, and so on. Through "jugglery," Josephus contrived to draw the last lot and as one of the two survivors in the cave, he persuaded his intended victim to surrender with him to the Roman army, which was led by Vespasian. If it had not been for his quick wits, Josephus might have been sent to Nero in Rome as a prestigious Jewish prisoner. But he "prophesied" that Vespasian would become an emperor. This prediction, which was probably nothing more than a shrewd guess inspired by Vespasian's obvious popularity with the army, came true in AD 69 after Nero had been dethroned and his three short-lived successors had met with equally inglorious ends. The new emperor – Vespasian – rewarded Josephus with his freedom, and more.

Granted Roman citizenship and a pension, Josephus began his new life as Flavius Josephus, the darling of the Roman establishment. He accompanied the imperial army, now led by Vespasian's son Titus, to the besieged city of Jerusalem, where he implored his fellow-countrymen to surrender. Needless to say, the people of Jerusalem did not appreciate these attempts at persuasion from a man whom they regarded as a careerist defector. But it is to Josephus's credit that he used his influence to obtain the release of many of his friends after the city had been sacked, and he refused to accept the loot he was offered.

Settled in Rome with his fourth wife – an aristocratic heiress – in the palace that had been occupied by Vespasian as a private citizen, Josephus devoted the rest of his life to literary labors. Through his writings Josephus appears as a conceited and often smug person, but one who was constantly aware of his Jewish background and identity. However, he claimed to be a realist, who had come to terms, as had many other of his compatriots, with the political and military strength of a Rome that had proved remarkably tolerant of frequent Jewish disturbances until finally provoked by the Jewish

revolt in AD 66. He had tried – and failed – in Judaea to present the situation to his people in the same light, and so in Rome he used his gifts as a historian to celebrate and explain the history and heritage of his people to the Gentile world. This loyalty to his culture is best demonstrated by his last book, *Against Apion*, a vigorous defense of Judaism, its customs and philosophy, against the anti-Semitic slanders of the day.

If his activities in the war earned him an ambiguous reputation, his writing finally branded him as a traitor in the eyes of some of his fellow-countrymen. In *The Jewish War*, which was written after the end of the war, between AD 75 and 79, Josephus described the conflict in which he himself had played a prominent role, first as a rebel leader and then as a privileged observer with the victorious Roman army. But this was history with a propagandist purpose. Josephus wanted to dissuade other peoples in the Middle East from rebelling – futilely, in his opinion – against the massively superior Roman war machine. He was also concerned about the image of his people in the Roman world, asserting that the Jews had rebelled only because they had been led astray by fanatical visionaries. *The Jewish War* was of course music to Roman ears and the work was quickly given official support and encouragement.

Ironically, it was Josephus, a Jew despised by his own people, who attempted to educate the Gentile world about the history and traditions of Jewish culture. This 14th-century illustration shows the 10 Tribes of Israel being taken into captivity, an episode that was described in Josephus's book The Antiquities of the Jews.

Naturally enough, it was not so popular with those Jews who had fought in the war – men who remembered the heroic last stand at Masada and the sacking of Jerusalem. For them, it was especially galling to read the author's account of his own, not wholly commendable, behavior during the revolt. Josephus was obviously embarrassed by his past. He was ambiguous about his motives as a rebel leader and remarkably callous about the unhappy fate of the men he had fought with. And the incident of his "capture" by the Romans in particular indicates that Josephus was at best certainly no hero.

He never regained the affection of his people. When he died, aged about 70, no memorial was raised in his native city of Jerusalem. But in Rome a statue was erected in his honor. A rare tribute to a representative of a conquered race.

So was Josephus a realist who tried to reconcile the grandeur and power of Rome with the proud and independent heritage of the Jews, or a cunning opportunist, always ready to turn events to his advantage, no matter who suffered in the process? Josephus himself believed the former, but it is unlikely that the Jewish people will ever agree with this view of him.

Roman comforts
Ungodly cleanliness

IS CLEANLINESS next to godliness? Not according to many citizens of the Roman empire, most of whom believed that cleanliness was next to decadence. They were speaking of the almost universal custom of public bathing, and of all that went with it.

From the early days of the republic (about 400 BC), the homes of the rich often had a private bath (*balneum*), which was more like a small indoor swimming pool than a modern bathroom. As the republic grew into a mighty empire, and towns and cities also grew in size and wealth, the practice of bathing spread to all sections of the community. Public baths became so popular that the historian Pliny the Elder, living in the first century AD, could not keep count of the number of public *balneai* in Rome

The Roman spa and baths at Aquae Sulis, now Bath, in England, became an internationally popular leisure complex, where the naturally warm spring water was renowned for what were believed to be its curative properties.

alone, but reckoned them in hundreds. Best of these were the *thermae* – baths that included a hot room (*laconicum*), hot bath (*caldarium*), cool room (*tepidarium*), and cold bath (*frigidarium*). If you went for a bath, you would normally begin by limbering up with a ball game or other exercises in a special recreation room, then strip, sweat it out in the *laconicum*, cleanse your skin with oil, have a hot bath, cool off, and take a final invigorating plunge into the *frigidarium*. In this respect the *thermae* were like a modern gymnasium, Turkish bath or sauna, and public swimming pool combined.

This, however, was only half the picture. The great *thermae* of Rome and other cities were built like palaces, with marble columns, vaulted ceilings, beautiful mosaic floors, fountains, and statues. The baths of Caracalla in Rome covered nearly 28 acres (11 hectares) and could accommodate over 1,500 bathers at a time. The *thermae* of the Emperor Diocletian in the center of Rome were even larger. And most *thermae* offered a great deal more than the games rooms, hot rooms, and baths; they had shops, bars, and cafes, even libraries and theatres.

Thanks to state and/or private financial aid, admission was usually cheap or free. Rich and poor alike went to the *thermae* to see or be seen. They became such popular centers for rest and recreation – and merrymaking – throughout the empire that even people who could afford private bathrooms frequented them. The philosopher and statesman Lucius Seneca describes in a letter to a friend written about AD 40, what it was like to live near such an establishment. He complains of the noise, incessant

THE FOUNTAINS OF ROME

Over 220 million gallons (about a billion liters) of water a day once flowed into the imperial city of Rome to serve its baths and hundreds of other public pools and fountains. This vast, continuous flow was carried by 10 main aqueducts – stone conduits covered with slabs and raised above the ground on arches of stone and brick. The ruins of one, the Aqua Claudia, still bestride the country in the neighborhood of modern Rome.

Aqueducts elsewhere in the Old World are among the finest monuments to Roman civilization. For example, the Pont du Gard in southern France, which still spans a broad ravine, attaining a height of 160 feet (47 meters) on three tiers of arches, was planned 20 centuries ago by the soldier and engineer Marcus Agrippa; it formed part of a large system of conduits, some of them running through hillsides, that brought water to the city of Nîmes. Rising high above the Spanish town of Segovia, a two-tier Roman aqueduct built of sections of cut stone without the use of mortar or cement remains virtually intact. Greatest of all in its day was the Zaghouan aqueduct in North Africa, which zig-zagged its way for more than 130 miles (over 200 kilometers) across desert and mountain, bringing the waters of a large spring to the city of Carthage. Considerable sections of it still remain today.

Once arrived in the cities, water was distributed through a system of reservoirs, cisterns, and pipes, and this public supply was often tapped illegally by private individuals. Roman plumbing included lead tanks and piping – though as early as the first century BC, another great engineer, Marcus Vitruvius, was already warning that lead in water was a health hazard. The main alternative was ceramic pipes, built in sections and fitted together by joints sealed with a mixture of quicklime and oil. There were also excellent sewage systems. In Rome itself the main sewers (*cloacae*) were stone tunnels, large enough in places for an oxcart to drive through. The oldest and biggest of them was the Cloaca Maxima. Its mouth, an arch with a diameter of 16 feet (5 meters), can still be seen where it empties into the River Tiber.

There were, however, limitations to Roman ingenuity. While cities were well endowed with public baths and fountains, few private dwellings had running water, and armies of slaves were employed as water carriers. Similarly, drains and sewers served only the streets and other public places, and domestic plumbing in general was quite primitive. Large houses and villas had their own cesspits, but people in the crowded cities were as likely as not to empty their slops straight into the streets. Drenchings were a hazard of big-city life.

---

grunts and shouts of those at play and exercise, the cries of food and drink vendors, the splashing and shouting of the bathers. In particular, he singles out the professional hair-plucker "with his penetrating, shrill voice, for the purpose of advertisement, never holding his tongue except when he is plucking armpits and making his victim yell instead."

So they were large, crowded, noisy places. But what about the decadence? The famous Roman orgies – known to us through old movies and the popular imagination – were generally conducted in private. But there was much else at the baths to titillate and tempt anyone in the right mood. For a long time, many *balneai* permitted mixed bathing, which often led to prostitution. Some baths, in fact, were little better than brothels. In others, the proximity of so many naked men and women in the hot rooms and pools led to a good deal of what we today would call wife swapping. The situation became so scandalous that, in the second century AD, the Emperor Hadrian finally banned mixed bathing. Thereafter, the sexes used the baths at different hours.

Drunkenness was also a problem. It was easy to work up a thirst either in the hot room, or through exercise, and easier still to slake it with a few large cups of wine. This, in turn, led to quarrels and fights, and attracted pickpockets,

tricksters, and other petty criminals on the lookout for befuddled victims. (The frequent chase and arrest of thieves in the baths was something else that Seneca complained about.)

In other ways, too, many Romans saw evidence of decadence in their bathing customs. They remarked upon the way the rich loved to flaunt their wealth, arriving at the public baths in their finest robes, with a bevy of slaves to undress them, massage their bodies with oil, clean them again with a strigil (a special kind of metal or ivory scraper), and soak them in rare and expensive perfumes. Some disapproving ancients even frowned on the preliminary games and exercises, as well as on the ritual of oiling and scraping. Keeping clean was one thing, argued the moralizers, but to make a cult of athleticism was, they claimed, bound to sap the moral fiber of the empire.

Today, you can stand amid the ruins of one of these great baths and, if *you* want to moralize, consider how the pleasure-loving Romans brought about their own downfall. At the same time, you may want to remember that such places were masterpieces of Roman art and architecture, triumphs of engineering. Most of the Romans loved their *balneai* and were honest in their perception of them. One Roman commented: "Baths, wine, and women corrupt our bodies – but these things make life itself."

Bath: A Roman leisure center

The development of a Roman town at Aquae Sulis, now the English town of Bath, was almost entirely due to the existence there of the hot-water springs that emerged from the ground at a temperature of 120°F (49°C) and at the rate of over a quarter of a million gallons (over a million litres) a day. It was the ideal place for the Romans to construct, soon after their conquest of Britain, thermal baths in a massive leisure complex that would rival any they had built before outside of Italy. In keeping with the style of similar structures in Italy, particularly with that of the Colosseum in Rome, the outside of the complex was extremely plain, with its heavy vaults and walls devoid of decoration. In contrast, the interior was designed to provide a harmonious and beautiful setting that would please the eye of the bathers as they enjoyed the facilities of the spa. Baths, halls, and hot rooms, were decorated with fine columns, pillars, arches, windows, and well-dressed masonry. The baths at Aquae Sulis continued in use until the fifth century AD when the town was abandoned and the baths buried. Excavated and partially restored in the 18th century, the baths are still supplied today by the hot-water springs.

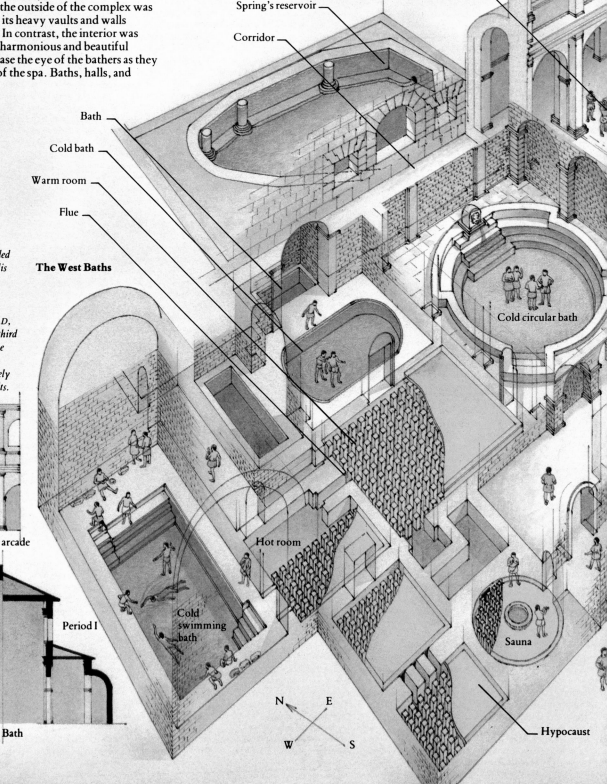

The Great Bath
Archeologists have concluded that the baths at Aquae Sulis underwent five major consecutive periods of alteration. It was probably during the second century AD, in what was known as the third period of alteration, that the Great Bath and the rooms adjacent to it were completely re-roofed with cement vaults.

Elevation of Great Bath arcade

Period III   Period I

Section across the Great Bath

The West Baths

Spring's reservoir

Corridor

Water supply from spring

Bath

Cold bath

Warm room

Flue

Cold circular bath

Hot room

Cold swimming bath

Sauna

Hypocaust

N E S W

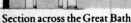

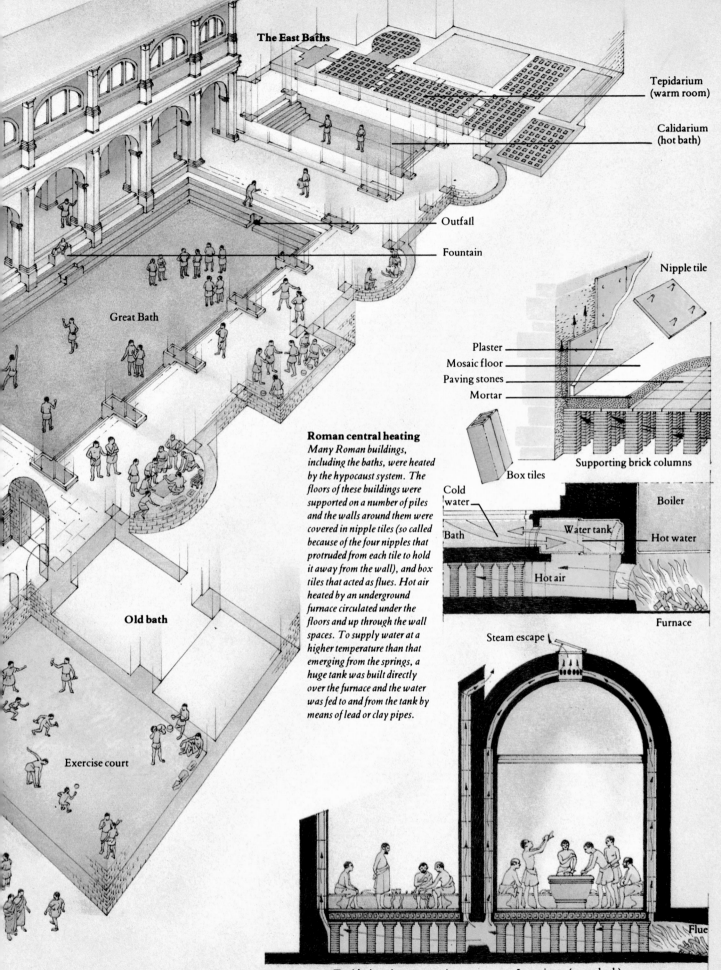

The East Baths

Tepidarium (warm room)

Calidarium (hot bath)

Outfall

Fountain

Great Bath

Nipple tile

Plaster

Mosaic floor

Paving stones

Mortar

Box tiles

Supporting brick columns

Roman central heating
Many Roman buildings, including the baths, were heated by the hypocaust system. The floors of these buildings were supported on a number of piles and the walls around them were covered in nipple tiles (so called because of the four nipples that protruded from each tile to hold it away from the wall), and box tiles that acted as flues. Hot air heated by an underground furnace circulated under the floors and up through the wall spaces. To supply water at a higher temperature than that emerging from the springs, a huge tank was built directly over the furnace and the water was fed to and from the tank by means of lead or clay pipes.

Cold water

Bath

Boiler

Water tank

Hot water

Hot air

Furnace

Steam escape

Old bath

Exercise court

Tepidarium (warm room)

Laconicum (sauna bath)

Flue

Boudica

A rebel queen versus the Roman empire

IN ABOUT AD 60, the King of the Iceni – a Celtic tribe in eastern Britain – died, leaving no male heirs, only a widow and two teen-age daughters. As loyal supporters of the Romans, who had invaded Britain 15 years earlier, the Iceni had enjoyed rights and privileges, such as limited autonomy, that Rome generally accorded cooperative subject nations. Now, though, it seemed that the King of the Iceni had bequeathed part of his kingdom to the Roman Emperor Nero, and the procurator (imperial representative) of Britain, a greedy man named Decianus Catus, was quick to take up this "bequest" by wringing extra protection-money out of the apparently leaderless Iceni and confiscating much of their territory.

But they were not leaderless; the king's widow, Boudica, had taken the throne for herself, and she immediately asserted her right not to be mistreated. As the new ruler of a nominally independent tribe, she refused to pay up or to permit her land to be plundered. Decianus was furious. He gave orders that the defiant woman should be stripped and flogged, and the orders were obeyed. The Roman soldiers even added some extra punishment of their own: In Boudica's presence, they - several of them, according to one account – raped her young daughters.

That is the end of the girls' story; we do not know what became of them. Their mother, however, became an avenging fury. From that day, she devoted her life to leading her people in a terrible crusade of vengeance against the foreign oppressors. She must have had an exceedingly forceful personality. The Iceni followed her into active revolt unquestioningly, and several neighboring tribes soon joined the fray. By the winter, Boudica had gathered together an army many thousand strong (up to 100,000, according to one estimate), and the rebels were on the march, directing their resentment against three eastern population centers known to be full of Roman settlers and British "collaborators": Camulodunum, Verulamium,

This statue of Boudica captures her fiery spirit. Cast in bronze, it stands in London near to the Houses of Parliament, and was erected in 1902.

and Londinium (modern Colchester, St. Albans, and London). Inflamed by their majestic leader, the Iceni and their allies vowed to sweep all before them as bloodily as possible, to burn, to ravage, and to take no prisoners.

Boudica chose her moment well, for the military commander of Britain, Suetonius Paulinus, and half his troops were fully occupied at the time in a campaign far off to the west. In an orgy of fire and slaughter the three towns were invaded and virtually destroyed by the rebellious hordes. Roman garrisons were not the only targets. Boudica in her wrath declared that no one who had been willing to live peacefully with the conqueror was to be spared. The horror of her vengeance upon women friends of the Romans – if Roman accounts are to be believed – is graphically depicted in the words of the second-century historian Cassius Dio: Boudica's followers "hung up naked the noblest and most distinguished women, and then cut off their breasts and sewed them to their mouths, to make the victims appear to be eating them; afterward they impaled the women on sharp skewers . . . All this they did to the accompaniment of sacrifices, feasting, and wanton behavior . . ." The toll of dead in the three towns has been estimated as around 70,000. And Decianus Catus, the civil servant whose avarice and cruelty had sparked the flames of rebellion, was forced to flee to the continent.

Meanwhile, Suetonius Paulinus and his men hurried back toward London, determined to stop the uprising. At that point Boudica made her great mistake. Flushed with victory and strong in the knowledge that her forces outnumbered those of Paulinus by at least five to one, she thought she could wipe out the Romans and complete the liberation of Britain by meeting the enemy in open battle. Her courage was a match for anyone's but Paulinus was an experienced general in command of crack troops; she knew nothing of advanced military techniques, and her "army" was just an ill-equipped, ill-organized throng.

At some time in AD 61, not long after the death of Boudica's husband, Paulinus stationed his men at a spot in a narrow gorge (which has never been identified) not far from London, where their rear was secured by dense woodland. There, in orderly ranks, they awaited the approach of the over-confident Britons. Before long an enormous crowd rushed forward in grand disarray. Behind the half-naked men, who were armed with slings, a variety of makeshift missiles, heavy spears, and long swords, came wagons loaded with women and children – an eager audience for what they must have imagined would be a gloriously gruesome spectacle. Some of the shouting men rode in light chariots, and at their head stood the queen herself. "She was huge of frame, terrifying of aspect, and with a harsh voice," says Cassius Dio. "A great mass of bright red hair fell to her knees. She wore a great twisted golden necklace and a tunic of many colors, over which was a

BRITAIN UNDER THE ROMANS

When the Emperor Claudius invaded Britain in AD 43, the natives were a Celtic people who, although fairly uncivilized by Roman standards, had left their earlier savagery far behind them. In the past they *had* painted their naked bodies blue and *had* lacked social organization, and many barbaric attitudes and customs still survived. But they had been much influenced by earlier temporary Roman incursions, especially those of Julius Caesar in 55 and 54 BC. Some rulers of tribal kingdoms welcomed the conquerors and accepted a subservient status in return for imperial protection. Rome's legions were forced to go on fighting in order to subdue many tribes in northern and western parts of what is now England, but by AD 60, six years into the reign of the Emperor Nero, the civil administration had established a good measure of peace and security with the help of client kingdoms in the northeast and southeast.

Roman greed, corruption, and brutality were beginning to turn friends into enemies, however, when, following the death of her husband and her own shameful mistreatment, Boudica led the Iceni, joined by the forces of other sympathetic tribes, into armed rebellion. Roman casualties were high at first, and so, after eventually crushing the revolt, Rome seems to have learned a lesson from the experience. The military governor, Suetonius Paulinus, advocated a series of harsh reprisals on the shattered natives; but instead of accepting his advice, Nero called him and some of his advisers back to Rome and appointed milder men as both civil and military governors of the island. Under their more benign rule peace was restored. The surviving Iceni, though treasuring the memory of their courageous warrior-queen, soon adjusted themselves to the restraints and comforts of the Pax Romana, and there were no further major outbreaks of war against the empire.

Britain remained Roman until the middle of the fifth century, when Roman garrisons were withdrawn and rushed to the defense of Rome itself, leaving the island virtually unprotected against new hordes of invaders such as the Germanic Angles, Saxons, and Jutes. Hundreds of years of direct Roman rule, however, had a profound effect upon the British people, and on their towns, cities, language, and culture.

thick mantle fastened by a brooch. Now she grasped a spear, to strike fear into all who watched her ..." But the Romans were not afraid. As the Britons jumped down from their chariots and began to hurl missiles at the disciplined ranks in front of them, Paulinus's men sent an ordered volley of javelins into the air. Then another. And then the well-armed and shielded Romans drew their short swords and charged. Before long the rebel forces began to stampede, and the battle turned into a rout; but there was little chance to retreat since behind the rebels lay a nearly solid barrier of wagons bearing the women and children who had come expecting to gloat over a massacre.

Though the Romans slew men, women, and children indiscriminately, the valiant queen seems to have survived. Cassius Dio attributes her death simply to sickness, but a more reliable historian, Tacitus, says she poisoned herself – perhaps a more appropriate end for this firebrand who would not succumb to outrage.

WHAT'S IN A NAME?

The Roman historian Tacitus (about AD 55–120), who first wrote down the story of the ferocious British queen who defied Rome's legions, called her Boudicca. Somehow, though, in copying down his original manuscript the name was misread – and universally accepted for many centuries – as Boadicea. It was not until our own century that scholars ferreted out the truth: The familiar name Boadicea was wrong! And, for that matter, so was Tacitus. For a number of philological reasons the queen's name must actually have been Boudica, with only one *c*. So Boudica it is, and Boudica it must remain – at least until another generation of scholars determine otherwise

However you spell it, the name derives from the ancient British word *bouda*, meaning "victory." So you may prefer the happy, if unsanctioned, alternative of calling the warrior-queen not Boadicea nor Boudicca nor Boudica, but Victoria the First.

The truth about Nero

Does he deserve his reputation?

As a young man, Nero had naturally thick copper-colored hair that was arranged by his barber in rings of curls, one above the other. He wore a beard until his early twenties. A handsome youth, he became fat in later years, with a fleshy face and a thick neck.

IS IT TRUE that the Roman Emperor Nero set fire to his city, "fiddled" while it burned, and then, blaming the Christians for the fire, ordered them to be "thrown to the lions"? The answer may well be no. Nero did many foolish things and committed a number of crimes, but most modern historians agree that, whatever else he may have been guilty of, he was probably innocent of the two appalling misdeeds for which he is most notorious.

Nero was only 16 when, in AD 54, he succeeded his stepfather, Claudius, on the imperial throne. At that time the use of violence was standard practice among those who wanted to get and keep power. The reigns of Claudius and his predecessor, Caligula, had been blood-soaked, and young Nero soon contributed to the tradition by ridding himself of various important people whom he considered dangerous or, for some reason, burdensome. Nonetheless, he was in many ways a good ruler, and the first years of his reign were widely hailed as the dawn of a golden age. He reduced taxes, improved the economy, and was kind-hearted toward people in general. The Roman historian Suetonius speaks of his pleasant manners. Once, for instance, when the senate passed a vote of thanks

to him, the emperor responded by saying simply, "Wait till I deserve it." Far from being extravagant, young Nero prudently avoided costly military campaigns to extend the already overstretched empire. Nor did he encourage public indulgence in cruelty. Although he delighted in lavish public spectacles – which the people also liked – he had actually forbidden gladiatorial fights to the death. The Roman empire prospered, and, for a while at least, the young emperor's popularity seemed assured.

Gradually, though, he became increasingly vain about his skills as an artist and administrator and more and more convinced that, so deeply was he loved, he could indulge his every whim. His native generosity turned to reckless extravagance, draining the treasury, and his growing belief in his omnipotence led to a series of coarse and cruel acts that alienated powerful elements in Roman society such as the senate and the army. By AD 64, when he had been on the throne for 10 years, the populace in general had become restive. And so it seems only natural that he should have been held in some measure responsible for the misery that resulted from the great fire that ravaged Rome in that year. Moreover, opposition hardened when it became

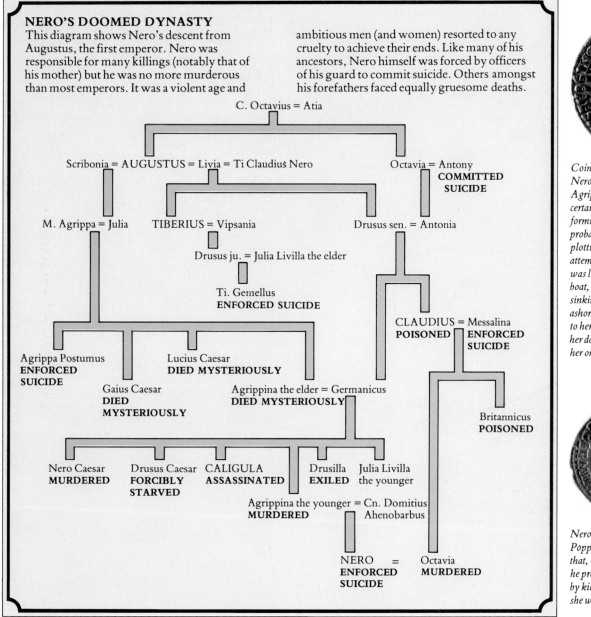

NERO'S DOOMED DYNASTY

This diagram shows Nero's descent from Augustus, the first emperor. Nero was responsible for many killings (notably that of his mother) but he was no more murderous than most emperors. It was a violent age and ambitious men (and women) resorted to any cruelty to achieve their ends. Like many of his ancestors, Nero himself was forced by officers of his guard to commit suicide. Others amongst his forefathers faced equally gruesome deaths.

C. Octavius = Atia

Scribonia = AUGUSTUS = Livia = Ti Claudius Nero   Octavia = Antony
COMMITTED SUICIDE

M. Agrippa = Julia   TIBERIUS = Vipsania   Drusus sen. = Antonia

Drusus ju. = Julia Livilla the elder

Ti. Gemellus
ENFORCED SUICIDE

CLAUDIUS = Messalina
POISONED   **ENFORCED SUICIDE**

Agrippa Postumus
ENFORCED SUICIDE

Lucius Caesar
DIED MYSTERIOUSLY

Gaius Caesar
DIED MYSTERIOUSLY

Agrippina the elder = Germanicus
DIED MYSTERIOUSLY

Britannicus
POISONED

Nero Caesar
MURDERED

Drusus Caesar
FORCIBLY STARVED

CALIGULA
ASSASSINATED

Drusilla
EXILED

Julia Livilla
the younger

Agrippina the younger = Cn. Domitius Ahenobarbus
MURDERED

NERO = Octavia
ENFORCED SUICIDE   **MURDERED**

Coin bearing the images of Nero and his mother, Agrippina. We cannot be certain why Nero ordered this formidable lady's death, but he probably feared that she was plotting against him. His first attempt miscarried: Agrippina was lured on to a collapsible boat, but in the confusion of its sinking, she managed to swim ashore. Nero then sent officers to her house, where they struck her down and then cremated her on her couch.

Nero and his second wife, Poppaea. Historians agree that, although Nero loved her, he probably caused her death by kicking her in a rage when she was pregnant.

generally known that Nero wanted the main feature of rebuilt Rome to be a gigantic imperial palace – a fabulous building designed to cover a full third of the city. It is not surprising that people were soon whispering that the emperor had destroyed the city purposely to make room for his "golden" palace (which, incidentally, was partly built, but entirely demolished after his death in AD 68).

Most of what we know about Nero comes from the writings of Tacitus and Suetonius, two historians who wrote about 50 years after his death, when his reputation had sunk very low. Of the two, only Suetonius says that Nero started the great fire and sang while enjoying the spectacle. (He would have accompanied himself on a lyre had he done so; violins were not invented till the 16th century.) We now know from contemporary records that the emperor was not even in Rome when the fire started, but was staying at his villa in Antium, 35 miles (56 kilometers) away. We also know that when he heard that Rome was burning, he hurried back, not to sing but to make frantic efforts to stop the blaze and to organize aid for its victims. The conflagration apparently started by accident and spread so devastatingly because the city, apart from its monumental public buildings that were mostly built of stone, consisted of a jumble of close-packed wooden houses.

Interestingly enough, Suetonius says nothing about Nero's blaming Christians for the fire. That story comes from Tacitus; and modern historians believe that in this case, as in many others, Tacitus is repeating unauthenticated gossip. In fact, there were few Christians in Rome in

Nero's day. They were persecuted, of course, but so was everyone else who denied the divinity of Rome's emperors. There is no evidence that Nero favored brutal treatment of Christians or than *anyone* was murdered by being thrown to lions during his reign, although neither is there any real evidence that Nero did not have Christians and members of other sects killed in equally gruesome ways. There *is* evidence that he was quite tolerant of new beliefs. He is even portrayed in a fresco in Rome's Palatine Chapel deep in conversation with St. Paul.

In later centuries, however, the Christian Church took the word of Tacitus and named Nero as an Antichrist. This was too harsh a judgment. Though certainly no hero, he was neither an arsonist nor an arch enemy of Christ and His followers.

A 19th-century – and misleading – view of Nero enjoying the martyrdom of Christians. In fact, Nero never persecuted Christians but rather showed a tolerant curiosity to these people who worshiped an invisible god.

HOW THE EMPEROR LOST HIS POPULARITY

Although Nero's reign began well and he seems to have been at first both public-spirited and self-controlled, he soon developed a taste for wild night-life – a taste that he indulged with more and more abandon during his 14 years as Roman emperor (AD 54–68). According to the nearly contemporary historian Suetonius (born about AD 67), the emperor made a habit of prowling the streets in disguise, looting shops, attacking passers-by – even killing some who resisted – and drinking. On one occasion he was beaten up by a senator whose wife he had molested during one such drunken revel. Thereafter he never went out after dark without a discreet escort of soldiers.

Vanity about his skills not only as ruler of a vast empire but also as an artist swelled gradually into megalomania. In about AD 60 he began to participate in public performances, playing his own musical compositions on a lyre, declaiming his own poetry, starring in stage plays, and competing in chariot races. Nero invariably expected a full house to witness his performances, and spectators were encouraged enthusiastically to applaud his every word and deed. In competition he is known to have regularly bribed and bullied his way to victory. Suetonius tells about a chariot race, at Olympia in Greece, when Nero fell off his chariot, had to be helped back in, failed to finish the course – and was nevertheless awarded the prize by the Greek judges, who were themselves rewarded by being given large amounts of cash along with the privileged status of Roman citizenship.

Nero's popularity, even among the most tolerant Romans, waned as his private life became not merely a scandal but an outrage. He spent most of his time, and much of the empire's money, feasting at vast orgies. No woman, married or single, noblewoman or commoner, was safe from his attentions. Nor, even, were young boys. It is said that he once had a boy called Sporus castrated in order to preserve his looks, and that the emperor actually assumed the role of bridegroom in a mock marriage in which Sporus was forced to wear women's clothes and a bridal veil.

To pay for his extravagances, Nero eventually confiscated property from the wealthiest families of Rome, exiling or executing their leading members whenever necessary. He had come to think of himself as a god, with the absolute powers of godhead. The magistrates with whom he packed the courts of Rome are said to have been given a simple brief: "You and I," Nero told them, "must see that nobody is left with anything." It is not surprising, then, that the resentment generally felt by Rome's citizens led many to believe that he would have gloated over the flames that destroyed his detractors' city in AD 64.

By AD 66 the emperor was surrounded by enemies. Senators hated him for his arrogance and the insults he heaped upon them. Influential aristocrats detested him because they never knew who might be next on his black list. The soldiers of his legions were increasingly dismayed by his lack of imperial dignity. But Nero ignored the warning signs. Instead, he left Rome for 15 months to tour Greece, whose leaders were always prudent enough to flatter him. During his absence, opposition to his rule grew, and open rebellion flared throughout the empire. He simply laughed off the news. When informed of armed insurrection in the area known today as France, he remarked, "All I need to do to have peace once more in Gaul is to turn up and sing."

He held on to power for only four months after his return to Rome in February, AD 68. In June his palace guard abandoned him and his courtiers fled. The senate issued a humiliating death warrant. The 30-year-old emperor, it ruled, should be executed like a slave: by being tied to a stake and whipped to death. Nero fled to a hut on the edge of a marsh near the city. There, as soldiers closed in, he had no choice but to commit suicide, probably by slitting his throat.

The lost treasure of Jerusalem

A priest's private joke?

IN 1885 a young priest named Bérenger Saunière took charge of the church at Rennes-le-Château, a tiny village near Toulouse in the Languedoc region of southern France. Saunière was poor, with no private resources and such a small income from the parish that it had to be supplemented by gifts from parishioners and by the fruits of his own hunting and fishing. Yet by 1896 he was spending money like a multimillionaire, buying land, building villas and gardens, and – above all – providing some costly improvements for the village and its ancient church. When asked where the money came from, he told his bishop it was a gift from exceedingly rich people, whose identity and motivation for generosity must remain secret because imparted within the privacy of the confessional. And Saunière took the secret with him when, in 1917, he died.

Most people who knew about the mystery (which became a *cause célèbre* in France) had a firm idea about what had happened, however. They believed that the young priest had stumbled upon buried treasure and had managed to sell whatever he found to buyers who agreed to keep his secret. It was even suggested that what Saunière had found was the fabled "lost treasure of Jerusalem" – speculation supported by certain historical facts. To begin with, the enormous wealth of ancient Judaea (sometimes called the "treasure of Solomon"), which was originally housed in the great Temple of Jerusalem, was seized by the Romans in AD 70. It was then put on display in Rome, only to become plunder or booty once more, it has been suggested, when, in AD 410, the Visigoths sacked the city. The Visigoths had conquered much of Western Europe by the end of the fifth century and had built several impressive cities and citadels, among them a hilltop city that became one of the last Visigoth strongholds as their power declined. With the passage of time that fortress-city dwindled into an isolated hamlet called Rennes-le-Château.

So it is possible that Visigoth treasure, including the treasure of Jerusalem, was hidden in one or more of the natural caves and subterranean passages that abound in the mountainous region where Bérenger Saunière came to live in 1885. It is even possible that the Visigoths were not the only medieval people who made use of those hiding places. The Franks, a major power in Gaul by the fifth century AD, were ruled by a succession of kings whom history calls the Merovingians (because legend says that they sprang from a semi-magical monarch named *Merovech*). There is reason to believe that when the last of the active Merovingians, Dagobert II, was assassinated in the late seventh century, his son fled to Languedoc, carrying with him many of the dead king's treasures. And there is a local tradition that the young heir to Dagobert died and was buried in Rennes-le-Château.

Saunière, of course, was aware of the eventful history of the village and the area, and he knew that his crumbling little church, dating from 1059, was built on top of a much older Visigoth structure. In 1891, having persuaded his parishioners to scrape up money for urgent repairs to the church, he had the altar stone removed – and discovered that one of the hollow pillars on which it rested contained aged parchments. Although, at first glance, these appeared to be simply copies of parts of the Gospels, Saunière looked more closely and found signs of a complex code within the copied lines.

This part of the Saunière story is devoid of mystery. With the expert assistance of other

Many strange and even unholy images are to be found in the church of Rennes-le-Château, including this money bag featured in a fresco at the west end of the church. Is it mere decoration – or a clue left by the village priest as to the nature and whereabouts of the treasure he is thought to have found?

A view of the church and village of Rennes-le-Château, the origins of which date back to Visigothic times. The church was extensively renovated and redecorated in the 1890s when its impoverished priest suddenly and unaccountably became immensely rich.

A detail from the Arch of Titus, Rome, showing the triumphant Emperor Vespasian with booty seized from the Temple of Jerusalem, which he sacked in AD 70. Many believe that this treasure ultimately found its way to the village of Rennes-le-Château in southern France.

clergymen in Paris, the code was apparently broken. Saunière recognized allusions to specific landmarks in the area around Rennes-le-Château and noted, too, tempting references to Dagobert (the Merovingian king) and Zion (Judaea) linked with the magic word "treasure." As a first result of his researches he found some long-buried Merovingian relics and made no secret of it. But now the mystery begins; we can only guess at what happened afterward to put him in possession of a fortune – though our guesswork is based on a solid foundation of fact.

Saunière himself left a number of clues. He took personal charge of the elaborate repairs and restoration of his church, and some of the decorations seem puzzling, incongruous, perhaps even blasphemous. For instance, many a clergyman who visits Rennes-le-Château must wonder why they are greeted by a phrase carved in stone above the church door, "*Terribilis est locus iste*" – "This place is terrible" – or why a grotesque statue of the demon Asmodeus stands at the church door, nearly the first thing you see as you enter. The most likely explanation for this and other strange and far from holy images within the church is that they provide clues to the source of the priest's wealth – hints that are like little private jokes. It takes special knowledge, for example, to be able to recognize Asmodeus as the legendary demonic guardian of the treasure of Jerusalem. . . .

Along with what has long been suspected about Rennes-le-Château as a hidden treasure-trove, the history of Saunière and the medieval church has encouraged many treasure-seekers to try to follow in his footsteps. So many, in fact, that exasperated villagers have erected signs that translate roughly as "No Digging." Nobody since Saunière, though, has found a thing. Nor has anyone located the eventual whereabouts of ornaments or jewelry that Saunière may have found and sold. Whatever the treasure was, and into whatever secretive hands it was transferred, the young priest probably got it all, leaving the rest of us with only tantalizing mysteries.

The day disaster struck

An eyewitness account

A stone relief of wine carriers, the sign of a wine shop, which was found intact during excavations at Pompeii.

ON A HOT summer day in AD 79 an 18-year-old student named Gaius Plinius (Pliny the Younger) was staying with his mother and uncle (Pliny the Elder) at a villa in the town of Misenum on the Bay of Naples, about 20 miles from Mount Vesuvius. The day started like any other but within hours had become one of the most momentous days of ancient history as Vesuvius erupted, and engulfed for many centuries the two towns of Pompeii and Herculaneum. Pliny the Elder died that day but Gaius his nephew survived and wrote a remarkable account of the events in two long letters to the Roman historian, Tacitus. These were preserved and excerpts from the letters are translated here:

"On August 24, about one in the afternoon, my mother drew my uncle's attention to a cloud of unusual size and appearance. It was not clear at that distance from which mountain the cloud was rising, though it was afterward known to be Vesuvius. The cloud's general appearance can best be described as being like an umbrella pine, for it rose to a great height on a sort of trunk and then split off into branches. In places it looked white, elsewhere blotched and dirty."

Pliny the Elder was commander of the naval fleet at Misenum. According to his nephew's account, he apparently realized that Vesuvius was erupting and decided to take a few ships across the bay on a rescue mission. They were unable to land anywhere close to the mountain

COUNTDOWN TO CATASTROPHE

Inhabitants of Pompeii and Herculaneum had been subjected to a major earthquake in AD 62, 17 years before the great eruption of Vesuvius. But although the quake flattened many buildings, the victims simply rebuilt their homes and moved back. When, in AD 79, the earth began to rumble again, they were evidently unperturbed at first, carrying on their daily routines as if nothing out of the ordinary were happening. This is the timetable of events in the final days:

Early August Minor tremors shake the region. Cracks appear in walls. Statues shiver on their pedestals. People go on as before.

August 20 The tremors become more severe. Wells and springs dry up as the pressure of molten rock beneath the volcano's lava cap shifts the water table and diverts underground streams. In the normally placid Bay of Naples, giant waves rear up and pound the coast. But, undisturbed, people go about their business as before.

August 24, 10 a.m. The plug of lava in the crater of Vesuvius is blasted into the sky. Molten rock is hurled a mile into the air; it cools into pumice stones as it rains down. Blasts of poisonous gas from the vent kill birds in mid-air.

1 p.m. At Misenum, Pliny the Elder sees the giant pillar of smoke and sets out on the rescue mission that will cost him his life.

Within hours, almost everyone who has been unable to leave the two towns is dead – overcome by fumes, buried by a deep layer of pumice and ashes, or entombed within a buried structure. (Many centuries later, archeologists uncover pathetic scenes such as these in Pompeii: a family group that obviously broke through the wall of a room in which they were trapped, only to choke to death in an ash-filled garden; a group of guests at a funeral feast, apparently gassed to death before they could leave the banqueting hall; a gassed man with his pet dog, which must have survived its master since it seems to have become hungry enough to try to eat his flesh.) Criminals die forgotten in their cells. Gladiators die in their barracks. In Pompeii alone, about 2,000 people – more than one in 10 of the entire population – are killed. In late afternoon a torrent of steam explodes from the crater and mingles with sea spray to generate scorching cloudbursts around Vesuvius. The storm triggers an avalanche of boiling mud and lava, which pours down the mountain's flanks onto Herculaneum, burying the town to a depth of more than 50 feet (16 meters).

August 25, 10 a.m. A second convulsion throws up a vast new cloud of smoke and ashes, which drifts out to sea when the wind changes. Some of the ash falls on Rome, more than 100 miles (160 kilometers) away. Traces are scattered as far away as Egypt and northern Europe.

August 26–28 The rain of ashes and lava continues, less and less ferociously, until the eruption dies down.

This 19th-century tinted engraving of Vesuvius erupting is merely a figment of the artist's imagination, for the eruption so darkened the sky that the details such as those shown here would not have been visible at the time.

August 29 As the smoke clears, the mountain's single conical summit is seen to have vanished, splitting Vesuvius into two smaller peaks. For miles around, the countryside is unnaturally white and level. Thousands lie dead beneath the ashes; thousands more are homeless. At Pompeii the roofs of some of the highest buildings and the tops of a few towers jut from the wind-swirled dust. At Herculaneum nothing at all is visible.

because of hot, thickly falling ashes and pumice (chunks of solidified lava), and so the boats headed for the town of Stabiae, three miles (5 kilometers) south of Pompeii, where Pliny the Elder took shelter at the home of a friend. From there they could see Vesuvius, from which "broad sheets of fire and leaping flames blazed at several points, their bright glare emphasized by the darkness of night."

Any hope of carrying on the naval rescue mission was abandoned by now; Pliny and his party were themselves in great danger. According to Gaius's account: "They debated whether to stay indoors or take their chance in the open, for buildings were shaking with violent shocks and seemed to be swaying to and fro as if torn from their foundations. Outside, on the other hand, there was the danger of falling pumice stones, even though these were light and porous." At daybreak they left the house for the seashore, but as flames approached and sulfur fumes grew insupportable, the courageous 56-year-old naval commander, who suffered from asthma, collapsed and died. His companions then fled for their lives, some reaching Misenum to pass on the news to Gaius.

At Misenum, meanwhile, Pliny the Younger and his mother made for an open field, as far as possible from tottering buildings. Even the sea "seemed to roll back on itself, pushed back by earth tremors. Many fish were beached on the sand. In the other direction gaped a horrible black cloud torn by zigzag flashes and revealing masses of flame, like lightning but much larger." With ashes raining upon them, Gaius and his mother "were enveloped in night – not a moonless night or one dimmed by cloud, but the darkness of a sealed room without lights. Only the shrill cries of women, the wailing of children, the shouting of men could be heard. Some were calling to their parents, others to their children, others to their wives . . . Many lifted up their hands to the gods, but most were convinced that there were now no gods at all, and that this night was the end of the world.

"Finally, the darkness lightened and then, like smoke or cloud, dissolved away. Daylight returned, and the sun shone out, though luridly, as it does when an eclipse is coming on."

On the afternoon of August 25 – not much more than 24 hours after they had first seen the awesome cloud over Vesuvius – Gaius Pliny and his mother staggered, exhausted, back to the villa. They had escaped but thousands of others had perished and lay permanently at rest under a thick blanket of lava and ashes.

The bodies of those killed by the poisonous gases, ash, and pumice emitted by Vesuvius in AD 79 were quickly covered by many further layers of ash and pumice. Rainwater later washed more ash over them, filling any cracks and sealing the corpses inside a hard casing. Only their bones remain today but, by pumping plaster into the cavities left by the original buried bodies, perfect casts of the dead have been formed (below).

A typical street in Pompeii (below right) with its raised pavements and stepping stones to enable pedestrians to cross the muddy road. The stepping stones are carefully spaced to allow cart wheels to pass through. Excavations of streets and houses in Pompeii have given us a unique record of everyday life in a Roman town.

Animals for the Colosseum

From Africa to ancient Rome by oxcart and sailing vessel

SERIES OF "games" in which 9,000 animals were killed marked the official opening of the Roman Colosseum in AD 80. A quarter of a century later, in AD 107, 10,000 animals were among the luckless participants in games staged in honor of the Emperor Trajan's conquest of Eastern European armies. These were exceptional occasions – but even in an ordinary year thousands of animals were killed throughout the Roman empire to satisfy public craving for bloodshed.

Events themselves varied. In some the beasts fought one another; a bear and a bull, for example, would be tethered to the ground to keep them from wandering off, and then egged on by attendants to claw and gore each other. In other games one or more men, known as *bestiarii* (a special type of gladiator armed with net and spear), fought lions, panthers, and other animals to the death. If a man rather than a beast was killed, it hardly mattered, of course, since most gladiators were only slaves. (A notable exception was the second-century Roman Emperor

Commodus, who liked posing in the arena and who once distinguished himself by killing 100 ostriches with bow and arrow, shooting from the Colosseum's imperial box.) Sometimes the wild beasts were treated quite well, when, for instance, criminals and other undesirables were thrown to them unarmed, or when they were used in non-violent circus acts similar in concept at least to those we see today performed by lions and lion-tamers.

The empire needed a constant supply of animals to meet the enormous demand. For provincial stadiums, local species (wolves and wild boars in northern Europe, for instance) were easily procured and served as standard fare, with an occasional tiger or leopard thrown in as a treat. But in Rome itself, where the emperor sponsored the games, exotic species were essential as dramatic evidence of Rome's mastery of most of the known world. Developing the huge network of supply lines to provide the expected ration of lions, tigers, and elephants was not an easy matter. Even today, with modern methods

A tiger is captured for the games in Rome's Colosseum in this detail from the mosaic floor of a fourth-century imperial villa. Thousands of wild beasts were captured and transported to Rome from all over the known world, a vast and complex operation involving much planning and organization. The more dangerous and exotic the beast, the more thrilled were the crowds of spectators.

The games at the Colosseum in ancient Rome were so popular that by the fourth century AD, nearly half the year was set aside for them. Most of the spectators sat on stone benches which were arranged in tiers around the arena. High-ranking citizens and members of the nobility would sit in boxes, where they could watch their favorite entertainment at leisure, as shown in this 20th-century painting by Sir Lawrence Alma-Tadema.

of transportation, moving animals is a difficult and expensive business. To transport wild beasts – in the thousands every year – over hundreds of miles by means of ox-drawn carts and sailing vessels must have been an even more staggering operation in the ancient world.

Africa was the favorite hunting ground because of the diversity of its fauna. For tigers, which are not native to Africa, the Romans had to travel to India and Persia. Roman soldiers stationed in a given area generally had the initial job of capturing animals, and they were sometimes assisted by native hunters. None of our modern rules of sportsmanship applied; the object was to trap or trick beasts into captivity by any method that worked. One trick was to pour wine into a shallow pool, then wait until a creature had drunk enough to become intoxicated and docile, when it could easily be roped. Another was to dig a pit and throw in a small animal, whose cries would attract a predator,

such as a lion or tiger, which, once in the pit itself, could be lured into a baited cage. Pits were also used for trapping elephants.

Large-scale hunts demanded expert coordination and cooperation among the hunters. They might surround an animal and drive it into an enclosure of nets and branches, using flaming torches to keep it under control. Or a number of animals could be forced into a single enclosure and then separated according to species. The capture of lion cubs for taming required similar coordination. A ship would be anchored as near as possible to a previously located lion's den. Several hunters would enter the den armed with lances and shields and force the lioness to retreat, while others seized the cubs and threw them to horsemen, who would then gallop off to the ship, with the enraged lioness in pursuit.

Once captured, the beasts were subjected to long journeys over land and water. To keep as many as possible alive, overland journeys

WHO WERE THE GLADIATORS?

The Romans enjoyed watching fights between men and animals, but their favorite form of entertainment was hand-to-hand combat between armed men. Most gladiators (so named for the *gladius*, or sword, they carried) were prisoners of war, of whom there was always a good supply. As with lions and tigers, new batches of men were constantly needed, for there were numerous games throughout the empire. Fights often ended in the death of an antagonist, and many events would be presented in the course of an afternoon.

Inevitably, many gladiators were unskilled, and some were simply criminals thrust into the arena to "execute" each other for public amusement. But the Romans were connoisseurs; they liked to see men fight *well*. There were a number of gladiatorial training centers in and around Rome, most of which could accommodate well over 1,000 men. The schools had their own arenas, where trainees practiced their skills with wooden swords, and a typical school staff included armorers, masseurs, and doctors in addition to trainers. Considerable attention was given to the men's diet, which included a lot of barley, a muscle-building food. The gladiators were never allowed to forget that they were merely slaves, however, and any who infringed the rules were punished by imprisonment or worse.

The main objective was to turn out men who could both fight well and die well. The gladiator had to show absolute courage, never flinching when a sword was brandished in his face, and always aiming to kill, not merely to maim, the opponent. Normally, some kind of protective armor was worn on parts of the body, such as the arms and legs, where a wound would not be mortal, but the breast was bare and open, protected only by the shield that the fighter usually carried. If, as sometimes happened, a long struggle ended with both combatants still on their feet, they would be allowed to leave the arena alive. More often, one would be dealt an incapacitating blow, whereupon the victor was obliged to pause to allow public opinion to decide the fate of the loser. If he had fought bravely, influential spectators might signal clemency by waving white handkerchiefs; if not, it was, literally, thumbs down to the defeated gladiator.

Some gladiators managed to survive a number of combats, and a few became immensely popular, so popular that in time they might be released from the perilous profession and become freedmen. Ironically, some ordinary members of the Roman public chose to be gladiators and to submit to several years' slavery in a training school and the prospect of violent death. Adventurers, social misfits, even a few noblemen were attracted to the arena. For a while there were also female gladiators, but from about AD 200, combat between women was forbidden.

Gladiatorial combats in ancient Rome were usually fought to the death, when an official dressed as Charun of the underworld (above) would symbolically strike the corpse of the defeated gladiator with a long mallet. Kirk Douglas (below left) realistically portrayed a gladiator in the epic film, Spartacus.

would be interrupted at several places for a week at a time so they could recover from the effects of being jolted along in wooden cages pulled by oxen. An imperial decree required all towns within the empire to provide food for these caravans. Even so, many animals either died en route or reached Rome in severely weakened condition. Those that did arrive were taken to imperial menageries, where some were given plenty of raw meat to keep them in fighting form (a certain third-century emperor, Elagabalus, even fed his carnivorous animals on pheasants). Eventually, they were herded into subterranean parts of the Colosseum, an area honeycombed with cages, ramps, and large elevators for lifting animals into the arena (from which few came back alive).

In the last years of the empire, chariot racing eclipsed the more violent games in popularity. The Emperor Constantine had abolished the lively sport of tossing human victims to wild animals in AD 325, but combats between *bestiarii* and beasts were still taking place in Rome as late as 523. By then, however, the supply of wild animals had thinned out considerably, for indiscriminate hunting had produced a severe shortage of lions in North Africa, and a species of elephant from there was already extinct.

ROMAN HOLIDAYS

The games held in the Colosseum and other arenas in ancient times were not just a diversion, as sports events are for us today; they were central to Roman life. During the reign of Claudius (AD 41–54), 93 days a year were entirely set aside for the games; and the number had increased to 175 days – nearly half the year – by the middle of the fourth century. There was no charge for viewing the games, which were considered one of the basic rights of citizenship. Roman citizens who worked for a living put in a short day. From the richest patrician to the poorest plebeian, the freemen of Rome generally led a relatively leisurely existence, with work concentrated largely in the hands of a multitude of slaves.

The endless spectacle of bloodshed in the arenas probably had its origins in the ritual sacrifices of earlier religions, and it retained a superficial religious significance since official games were presented in honor of the gods. The first gladiatorial combats are believed to have occurred in 264 BC when the sons of a Roman nobleman organized fights involving three pairs of slaves as part of their father's funerary rites. The idea caught on fast, and gladiatorial combats in honor of the dead were soon attracting large crowds in the forum. Gradually the sport lost its ritual character and became an effective means of securing public support for politicians who sponsored it.

The "public relations" value of blood sports involving both men and animals was well understood by rich landowners and victorious generals alike. For example, long before AD 80, when the Colosseum was built, the great Julius Caesar (100–44 BC) treated the citizens to an imaginative spectacle in the enormous Circus Maximus – a spectacle built around a full-scale battle including infantry, cavalry, and 40 elephants. Caesar's flair for showmanship was not the least of the reasons for his popularity.

The tradition of what has become known as "bread and circuses" endured for 400 years after Caesar's death. The Romans demanded entertainment above all else.

Early Christianity's biggest battle
The forces of Mithraism

T HE INCIDENT was neither unique nor even rare in late-fourth-century Rome: An angry crowd had burst into a building that many other Romans venerated as a sacred place of worship; wielding axes, the invaders had hacked gaping holes in wall paintings, smashed sculptured images, and covered the floors with piles of garbage. Now, having desecrated the building, they proceeded to wreck it, leaving the rubble behind them.

Such violence in such places was becoming common. What might surprise many people today was that the angry mob consisted of followers of the Prince of Peace. They were early Christians, and savagery of the kind they had displayed seemed to them necessary because this temple on Rome's Aventine Hill posed a real threat to their young faith. The building had been a Mithraeum – the Latin name for a place where devotees worshiped the god Mithras. Mithraism was only one of several religions that rivaled early Christianity in the centuries when Rome's old gods were losing ground, but it was the most powerful of the rivals, and the early

Mithras sacrifices a bull in this statue by Kritios of Athens. Mithraists held the belief that the bull symbolized potency and fertility.

Christians felt that they had good cause to loathe it. Dating from around the 15th century BC, Mithraism emerged in ancient Persia (present-day Iran). "Mihr" (the Persian form of Mithras) was the word not only for the Sun but also for a friend; and that seems to be how this pagan god was originally worshiped – as both supreme Sun god and god of love. There was, however, a slow shift in emphasis from a belief in the spiritual power of the god to a reliance on his physical power. By the beginning of the third century BC, the militaristic rulers in western outposts of what had been the Persian empire were venerating Mithras as a divine warrior, no longer a loving Sun god but the unconquerable god of soldiers and friend of power. The kings of Pontus in Asia Minor even assumed the name Mithridates (the god's "chosen ones"), claiming that Mithras had cast his divine light upon them.

It was possibly troops of one such "chosen" Mithridates who brought this form of Mithraism into Europe sometime early in the first century before Christ. By the start of the second century AD the faith was spreading all through the Roman empire; it had a special appeal for a number of social groups and peoples. Soldiers, sailors, merchants, slaves – men uprooted from their homes and kin – found comfort in a belief that offered them the protection of a god of power, whose sanctuaries were often located in caves, to symbolize his closeness to the earth, yet whose mysterious rites identified him with fire and water. The Sun-worshiping Celts of Gaul and Britain latched on readily to worship of this new Sun god. Warlike barbarians and proud Romans alike flocked to a god who promised, above all else, victory in battle. Accordingly, caves and temples were dedicated to his worship everywhere along the guarded outposts of the Roman empire. Near the end of the second century, several Roman emperors actively encouraged the worship of Mithras. This was not merely a matter of religious conviction for Rome's emperors, since they quickly realized that the cult was in their interests: Mithraism preached discipline, loyalty, bravery, and self-sacrifice – the very qualities that made and kept the imperial Roman army so effective a military force for so long.

Backed by imperial approval, the faith became so widespread that some historians believe that, without the rise of Christianity, it would have become *the* Western world's religion. So it is hardly surprising that the early Christians felt they had no choice but to fight it with every weapon at their command.

Yet there were some striking similarities between the beliefs and rituals of the rival faiths.

An artist's impression of the Mithraeum on Rome's Aventine Hill, immediately prior to its destruction late in the fourth century. Just as many Mithraic beliefs complemented, or were incorporated into, Christianity, so Mithraeums resembled churches. Inside, altars headed a central nave, which was flanked by benches for worshipers.

Like Christians, the Mithraists believed that their savior had descended from heaven to earth; had shared a last supper with 12 followers; had redeemed mankind from sin by shedding blood; and had risen from the dead. They even baptized their converts to wash away past sins. So there was a strong conviction among believers in Christianity that Mithras was the Antichrist, a devil who had visited the earth earlier than Christ in order to discredit Him at His Coming.

Refusing to venerate the emperor as a god (a respect willingly accorded him by the Mithraists), Christians were treated as second-rate citizens within the Roman empire, persecuted at the whim of hostile mobs and emperors. Even so, their numbers grew throughout the first three centuries AD. Then, quite suddenly, the tables were turned when, in AD 313, Constantine the Great accepted Christianity and it became the official religion of the empire later in the fourth century. Thereafter (despite a brief attempt by the Emperor Julian some 50 years later to revive polytheism) the altars of the pagan god were destroyed, and all traces of the despised religion obliterated. The little that we know about Mithraism and its secret rites comes from casual references in ancient writings, such as those of the Persians who worshiped Mithras in one form or another until Islam snuffed out the faith 12 centuries ago, or from finds of Mithraic ruins. We know about the sacking of the temple on Rome's Aventine Hill around the year 400 because of archeological excavations in the 1930s and 1950s. Archeologists have also discovered that after the Aventine Hill Mithraeum was wrecked, the Christians built a basilica upon the site. Christianity had at last triumphed in Europe.

MITHRAIC INITIATION RITES

Soldiers made the best recruits to Western Mithraism – partly because only men were permitted to become active participants in Mithraic rites, but also because only the hardiest of men could cope with the initiation rites. Initiation into the mysteries of Mithraism was as rigorous as a commando training course. According to some students of the subject – and there is little certainty about the facts of this dead religion – converts could be accepted into the "church" only by undergoing 12 trials, including ordeals by fire, water, hunger, cold, flagellation, bloodletting, and branding. The whole exhausting program lasted from two to seven weeks. Successful candidates swore to keep the rites secret. Then they were baptized.

All new recruits became "brothers" in a group led by a "father." Ambitious brothers who studied Mithraic theology and other lore could go on to reach successive grades of authority; the climb up the ladder symbolized the soul's ascent to heaven, which it would reach after death. From lowest to highest, the seven grades entitled the active Mithraist to call himself in turn Raven, Bride, Soldier, Lion, Persian, Courier of the Sun, and Father, and each grade had a distinctive mask or dress to be worn at rites celebrated secretly in caves.

The battle that made this book possible

An end to the bamboo strip tease

IN AD 751 Muslim forces defeated a Chinese army in a battle fought at Talas in the wilds of Turkestan, midway between the Muslim caliphate of Baghdad and the heartland of the Chinese empire. This – the latest in a growing number of Muslim conquests that followed the death of the Prophet Muhammad in AD 632 – resulted merely in the transfer of desolate Turkestan from Chinese to Muslim rule; and it is one of the least remembered battles in history. Yet it had far-reaching effects on the spread of knowledge across the face of the world. For among the Chinese prisoners hustled in triumph to Muslim Samarkand were experts in a craft that had remained isolated in China for over six centuries: The art of paper-making.

The very presence of paper-makers in a frontier war zone shows the importance of paper in the Chinese administrative system. Before the invention of paper at the beginning of the second century AD, the Chinese had lacked any substance suitable for receiving and storing writings in bulk, whether government archives or works of literature. Far to the west, the papyrus reed of the Nile valley yielded a pith that could be aligned in strips and made up into flat pages, but the papyrus reed did not grow in China. Nor, oddly enough, had the inventive Chinese hit upon the Mediterranean practice of using parchment made from dried animal skin. Instead, before the second century the Chinese had been forced to write on narrow strips of bamboo.

Each strip could hold only a single line of script, and, as a result, books and records consisted of weighty bundles of bamboo strips threaded together; they were difficult to store and handle, and there was inevitable confusion whenever the connecting thread broke and the correct sequence of the book was lost.

Histories of ancient China contain several references to the shortcomings of this cumbersome system. It was said that a whole bamboo grove had to be cut down when somebody wrote a book. In a routine day's deskwork for a state official, document-reading involved the handling of a weight of up to 120 pounds (55 kilograms). The only lightweight alternative to bamboo was silk, and although fragments of "proto-paper" made from silk floss from the second century AD have been found, its use was not continued because it was far too expensive. A pound of silk, China's most costly export, was valued at a pound of pure gold in the markets of the distant Roman empire.

Silk may have had something to do with the invention of paper, though. The process of weaving silk fabric out of filaments spun from dissolved silkworm cocoons was so costly that it no doubt encouraged the search for cheaper fibers. The fibrous inner bark of the white mulberry tree would have been familiar to men of the silk industry since silkworms feed on mulberry leaves; and mulberry bark was the basic substance from which fiber for the earliest manufacture of paper was made.

The facts about how paper was "born" are fairly obscure. According to the ancient official history of the late Han dynasty (AD 25–220), the technique for paper-making was disseminated by a eunuch named Ts'ai Lun, who was the Emperor Ho Ti's minister of public works. The official history is vague about whether or not Ts'ai Lun invented the process, but it certainly credits him with having instructed the court in its mysteries. The fibers used for Ts'ai Lun's paper were a mixture of mulberry bark, hemp, rag, and (oddly, until one remembers the shaggy texture of ageing cordage) old fishing nets. And the new substance was so highly valued by later generations that the mortar in which pulp for the first piece of paper had been beaten was long preserved as a holy relic in China's imperial museum.

Tradition had it that Ts'ai Lun himself, though revered as the patron saint of paper manufacture, came to a bad end. Involved in some sort of court intrigue (the details remain obscure), he killed himself rather than face trial. We know little more about the man, but his invention – if it *was* his – caught on rapidly. Letters on paper that has been dated to within 50 years after AD 105, the year when, it is generally accepted, paper-making began, have been found in a watchtower on the Great Wall of China. The Chinese were also quick to use the stuff not only for writing paper but for wrapping paper, napkins, even toilet paper.

Yet it was not until the capture of those Chinese paper-makers 600 years later that this marvelously lightweight and practical substance found its way westward. Once there, its superiority over papyrus was soon recognized by the Muslims of the Baghdad caliphate, then (more gradually) throughout the Mediterranean world. Although papyrus continued to be used (and even gave the new material its name, "paper"), the Chinese invention was already more fashionable by the late ninth century. "Excuse the papyrus," ends a polite thank-you letter dating from sometime around 890.

As they were unable to use the Chinese mainstay of white mulberry bark, Muslim craftsmen made their paper entirely from rags; to procure the necessary rags, the Egyptians even tore wrappings from mummies. Step by step the craft moved westward – from Samarkand to Baghdad, from Baghdad to Damascus, from Damascus along the North African coast to Muslim Spain. The earliest-known Christian paper-mill was founded in Italy toward the end of the 13th century, and there was one in southern Germany by 1392, only half a century before the momentous invention of the movable-type printing press, which was to have an even greater impact on world civilization.

For many centuries the Chinese alone knew how to make paper. Workers collected bamboo, then soaked and cleaned it (below left); later the bamboo was reduced to pulp and placed in a screen (below) of the same size as the paper required. Once dry, the sheets of paper were ready for use.

Indians who loved deformity

Startling obsessions, bizarre images

TO THE CASUAL observer, the Virú valley on the northern coast of Peru seems an arid, dusty place, a desert wilderness as dull as it is inhospitable. This lifeless valley, however, hides some amazing facts about the people who inhabited it 2,000 years ago and who were apparently preoccupied by some of the more unusual aspects of human behavior such as human sacrifice, sexual perversion, and every kind of physical deformity.

The valley's inhabitants have come to be known as the Moche or Mochica, an Indian tribe who predated the more famous Incas by over 1,000 years. Their sphere of influence extended nearly as far north as the Ecuadorian border, and as far south as the Nepeña valley, some 250 miles (400 kilometers) north of Lima; and from the remains so far discovered – in particular, their unique grave pottery – it is clear that they were a sophisticated people with very unusual ideas about sex and religion.

Although Moche artifacts have been discovered in various Peruvian spots throughout the past hundred or so years, it was not until 1946, when two Columbia University archeologists, Duncan Strong and Clifford Evans, excavated the Virú site, that the significance of Moche pottery really struck home. Strong and Evans found a mass grave containing five people – two women, a boy, an adult male, and an old man of some importance, probably a warrior-priest – which revealed much about Moche attitudes to death and the afterlife. From the contorted positions of the female bodies, for example, it seems likely that they were the old man's wives or concubines who were buried alive at the time of their master's death to share his hereafter. The

boy may have suffered a similar fate, and the younger man undoubtedly did: His knees and ankles were lashed together before burial. Alongside the bodies, Strong and Evans unearthed a number of artifacts, including beads, fragments of cloth, 28 clay pots, and a gold-plated copper mouth mask – confirmation of the Moche's strong interest in the afterlife, for they evidently believed in taking earthly possessions with them; some even arranged to be buried with hollow canes leading from their mouths to the surface of the earth, so that relatives could continue to feed their dead bodies.

It is from the pottery, though – not only the pots unearthed at the Virú site but also the many found elsewhere – that we are really coming to know the Moche Indians. They used pottery to depict a situation or tell a story as other peoples have used paintings, sculpture, and books. The Moche never invented a system of writing. Instead they applied their skills to the production of clay pots either in particular shapes, such as a stirrup-spouted bottle in the form of a drunken figure supported by two friends, or with elaborate scenes painted on the surface. The scenes may portray anything from religious ceremonies and battles to fox hunting and decapitation. It is from this evidence that archeologists are piecing together an absorbing idea of everyday life among the Moche from the first century BC until their eclipse around AD 700.

Religion and its ritual, or something like it, obviously played a large part in their society. A remarkable number of pots depict a particular ceremony – as significant to the Moche, it seems, as the Crucifixion is to Christians – involving the presentation of a goblet to a figure

With no system of writing, Moche Indians used pottery to tell stories and to depict events from their lives. As well as such everyday scenes as a woman straining to lift a heavy pot on to her back (pot A), common themes for decoration were facial deformity (pot B), drunkenness (pot C), and affliction (the figure on pot D suffers from the disease which causes jug ears).

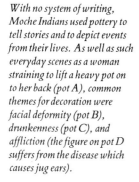

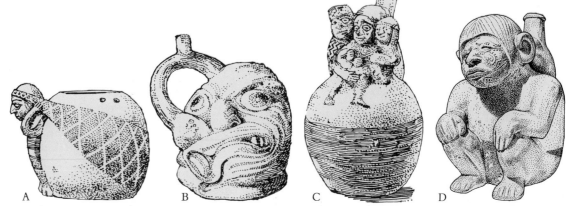

A   B   C   D

THE IMPORTANCE OF SEX IN MOCHE POTTERY

A startling characteristic of the Moche Indians, one that has puzzled archeologists for many years, is their excessive preoccupation with various forms of sexual activity. Much of their pottery is heavily phallic in character, depicting in graphic detail many forms of sexual activity. In fact Moche art depicts all aspects of sexual activity except those that might result in pregnancy; this has led some archeologists to argue that, far from simply having dirty minds, the Moche used pictures as a kind of propaganda for promoting various forms of contraception. Others are not so sure, believing instead that abnormal sex may have had some sort of religious significance for the Indians which has not yet been sufficiently studied.

What is certain, though, is that when the Incas conquered the decendants of the Moche, they discovered that homosexuality, for example, was rife among both sexes. To the Incas any kind of abnormal sexuality was repellent, not least because they thought that sexual activity that did not result in childbirth was a great waste of seed. They attempted to stamp out aberrant practices by ruthlessly destroying the family and property of everyone caught in the act. At best they were only partially successful; records show that sexual deviation was still prevalent when the Spanish first came to Peru.

Exquisitely worked, often in minute detail, Moche pots depict a wide range of pursuits and occupations, such as fishing, farming, and hunting. A hunter closing in on his prey is shown at left.

which has rays of light emanating from his head and shoulders. What the goblet contains is a mystery, but there is a strong suspicion that it might be human blood since most illustrations of the scene also show blood being extracted from captives. Other characters in the drama tend to be part human and part bird, or are anthropomorphized feline creatures, and they are always engaged in activities that reflect a strong taste for the bizarre. A recurring image shows skeletons playing the pipes or engaged in sexual activity, and the incidence of twisted bodies and deformed heads amounts to an obsession. Many Moche pots are deathlike effigies of the blind and physically malformed who suffered from diseases such as leprosy, and dwarfed or mutilated bodies are also commonplace. A Peruvian archeologist, Rafael Larco Hoyle, has suggested that the Moche probably practiced ceremonial punishment by mutilation, but this would not account for many of the grotesqueries in the pottery; the Moche apparently venerated deformity – a reflection, no doubt, of its traditional association with magical powers.

Apart from the preoccupation with the weird, a wide range of day-to-day activities is depicted in the pottery. The range is, in fact, far wider than is usual among other ancient cultures. All sorts of occupations and pursuits were recorded in clay, from women in childbirth or washing their hair to fishermen at work, warriors hunting in the mountains, and various creatures indulging in frankly lewd acts. Cooks, medicine men, weavers, porters, soldiers, priests, and musicians can all be seen at their daily tasks. Whatever the subject matter, however, it always has a storylike quality, whether we are shown a sea lion eating a fish, a bird being shot with a blow pipe, or people engaged in sexual acts. Everything that was important to the Moche – their food, their housing, their hierarchical social structure – found its way sooner or later into their earthenware.

From the fragments discovered at numerous burial sites it has been possible to build up, slowly and painstakingly, a still incomplete picture of this fascinating people. Much work remains to be done, and many sites have yet to be explored, but a definite impression of a strange set of standards has begun to emerge. Although the Moche are long dead, overshadowed by the Inca civilization that superseded them, the pottery they left behind still speaks to us – and the pictures are worth thousands of words.

Japan's imperial family

Prisoners of a myth

ON NEW YEAR'S DAY, 1946, a few months after the end of World War II, the Japanese people heard their emperor's voice for the first time. It is impossible for a Westerner to imagine the impact of the moment when, in a speech broadcast to the nation, Emperor Hirohito repudiated his family's claim to divinity as descendants of the Sun goddess – a notion that had never before been publicly challenged. Until then, all but a few highly informed Japanese had accepted the tradition that the first monarch of a united Japan was the Sun goddess's descendant Jimmu, warrior king of Kyushu (southernmost of the four biggest islands); that Jimmu had conquered and subjugated the rest of the archipelago in 660 BC; and that the imperial line had thenceforth stretched on to our own time, with Hirohito as the 124th of an unbroken line of emperors.

The facts of history in no way support this myth. For one thing, Kyushu and the other Japanese islands were in reality sparsely populated and had at best a Stone Age culture back in the seventh century BC. For another, the earliest written references to Japan date from AD 57, when Chinese chronicles record a visit to the mainland by representatives of one of the "more than 100" states of Wa (the ancient Chinese name for Japan). Obviously, the islands were at that time far from united under a single ruler.

So when *was* the empire established, and who was the first true emperor of all the Japanese? Historians who try to find answers are thwarted at every turn, chiefly because the Chinese chronicles were written largely from hearsay about relatively remote and – to the Chinese way of thinking – under-civilized people. No Japanese chronicles exist prior to AD 712, when a book called the *Kojiki* (*Record of Ancient Events*) was written; the *Kojiki* tells the traditional story of the founding of Japan by the Sun goddess and its unification under her descendant, "Emperor" Jimmu, in 660 BC. There is no doubt that by the seventh century AD, when the *Kojiki* appeared, the islands had become a united empire – and an ambitious one. The empire needed to create for itself a recorded history as old as that of the venerable Chinese; it was a matter of pride. And so the *Kojiki* must be read not as history but as propaganda, replete with "facts" and "dates" that cannot be taken literally.

According to the more reliable Chinese chronicles, the first ruler of a number of Japanese states welded together was a woman. The chroniclers call her Empress Pimiko (a name meaning "daughter of the sun"), but she was certainly not Empress of all Japan since it is known that the islands were racked by internal wars throughout the period of her reign (around AD 183–248) and for long after her death. Her

Supposedly the 124th of an unbroken line of divine Japanese emperors, Hirohito publicly renounced the divinity of his family shortly after the end of World War II, and since then has played only a ceremonial role in public life. A renowned marine biologist, the emperor is seen here at work in his laboratory.

authority seems to have stemmed primarily from the fact that she was probably a shaman, or priest, of the tribal religion, Shinto – a form of extreme patriotism based on the worship of natural and ancestral spirits – which was to become the official religion of imperial Japan.

Pimiko is said to have had magic powers, to have isolated herself behind armed guards in a fortress, and to have had 1,001 servants, only one of whom was male. (Such unlikely details are typical of those that make it difficult to separate fact from fiction in all early accounts of ancient Japan.) We do not know the locale of her home island. Some scholars believe that she held court in Kyushu, but there is no solid evidence on which to base this belief. At any rate, she appears to have bequeathed her lands and authority to another woman – perhaps her niece – named Iyo. And the likeliest candidate for the claim to have been first in the long line of Japanese emperors is a tribal chief from Kyushu who easily subdued Iyo and accorded her the title of imperial princess.

This man's name was Sujin. In official imperial lists he is confusingly named as the 10th emperor but is also cited, along with the legendary Jimmu, as "first emperor to rule the state." Theirs are the only names distinguished in this fashion; and some scholars have suggested that Sujin is the real person whose career gave birth to the myth of the similar-sounding Jimmu. The validity of this theory is enhanced by the fact that both Jimmu and Sujin are said to have set out from their native Kyushu to conquer the much larger neighboring island of Honshu, where the

center of the Japanese empire has been located since the misty beginnings of its history.

We know little else about Sujin other than that he lived at the end of the third century AD and the beginning of the fourth, and by the time of his death in 318 his territory covered most, if not all, of modern-day Japan. Needless to say, the imperial descent from Sujin to Hirohito is by no means clear or direct, but authorities agree that the throne has been occupied by a single family since at least the sixth century – a dynastic record that makes the imperial house of Japan the world's oldest royal family. That is no mean heritage, even without the supernatural intervention of the Sun goddess.

WHY "JAPAN?" WHY "NIPPON?"

The ancient Chinese gave the derogatory name of Wa – meaning "small" or "dwarfed" – to the group of islands that lay some distance off the northeastern coast of their immense country. When the inhabitants of those islands had united to form an empire, they understandably wanted to discard the image of themselves or their land as stunted or backward; and so from the early seventh century AD they adopted a new name meaning "place where the sun rises" in the hope that this would give them greater prestige in the eyes of their Chinese neighbors. The Chinese characters in which this is written are pronounced "jih-pen" in Chinese, "nih-pen" in Japanese.

Thus the modern name "Japan" is an English rendering of the Chinese pronunciation (brought to the West in the early 14th century by Marco Polo), while "Nippon" is our rendering of the Japanese way of saying "Land of the Rising Sun."

Kyushu, from which the first emperor is thought to have come, is today the most densely populated of the Japanese islands. In an effort to support the expanding population of Japan, as much land as possible is made available for growing rice by terracing the hillsides.

Claudius Ptolemy: Genius or fraud?

An astronomical giant with feet of clay

A medieval representation of Claudius Ptolemy, wearing a crown and with the tools of his trade in his hands. During the Middle Ages the revered scientist was sometimes flatteringly confused with the Ptolemaic rulers of Egypt.

Ptolemy's map of the known world, taken from a Dutch copy of the map made in 1486. Its representation of Europe is fairly accurate, but Asia is shown stretching farther to the east than it does. It was Ptolemy's view of the world that encouraged Christopher Columbus to sail westward in the hope of soon reaching the east coast of Asia. Instead he encountered the then-unknown continent of the Americas.

IN SCIENCE'S hall of fame, Claudius Ptolemy has always been honored as a very great scientist. Ptolemy, who was born in Greece in about AD 90 and died in about 168, lived most of his life in Roman Egypt, where he wrote the two books on which his reputation rests: a compendium of geographical knowledge and an encyclopedia of astronomy. Both were extremely influential, helping to shape Western thought for more than 1,000 years. The *Guide to Geography* was revered for 1,400 years as the first world atlas, and maps based on it were still being published in the 1500s. Indeed, it was Ptolemy's maps (which showed Asia stretching much farther eastward than it does) that encouraged many people to believe they could actually reach "the Indies" by sailing west. And Ptolemy's *Almagest* – a 13-volume treatise on astronomy – was accepted as the final authority on the subject until it was superseded by the observations of the Polish astronomer Nicolaus Copernicus in the 16th century.

Even after Ptolemy's belief in Earth as the stationary center of the universe was overturned, he was still regarded as a scientist and astronomer of undisputed genius, and it is as an astronomer rather than a geographer that he is best remembered today. Now, though, an American astronomer, Robert Russell Newton of Baltimore's Johns Hopkins University has challenged that opinion. Newton's verdict, based on an exhaustive analysis of Ptolemy's methods and mathematics, is blunt and uncompromising: Far from being a genius, Ptolemy the astronomer was a fraud.

In a book entitled *The Crime of Claudius Ptolemy* Newton concludes that, in order to support his theories, Ptolemy invented bogus observations and even went so far as to falsify the findings of earlier astronomers. And he declares that by supplanting earlier astronomical textbooks, the *Almagest* "has caused us to lose much of the genuine work in Greek astronomy . . . . There is only one final assessment: It has done more damage to astronomy than any other work ever written, and astronomy would be better off if it had never existed."

As evidence for his crushing assessment, Newton begins by comparing Ptolemy's figures for the position of the Moon at specific times with what we now know it must have been. Many of the claimed observations turn out to be so wildly inaccurate that they cannot be explained by imperfections in ancient measuring instruments; often the observations are far less accurate than similar sightings made centuries earlier. Ptolemy's figures are out by more than a quarter of a degree. That might not seem much, but it is the equivalent of Ptolemy lining up his instruments on the edge of the moon rather than on its center – a gross mistake even for a raw novice and unthinkable in a skilled astronomer. But, significantly, these wrong measurements match almost exactly the figures predicted by Ptolemy's own astronomical equations. Similarly, there are huge inaccuracies in his figures for the position of the Sun at different times of the year – and, again, suspiciously close agreement between the figures and the theories that the observations were supposed to be testing. Does it not seem possible then that Ptolemy juggled his results or even invented them so as to fit his theories instead of rethinking his theories in the light of the results, as a true scientist must always do for accuracy?

On one occasion, Newton asserts, Ptolemy even convicts himself of fraud by reporting an observation that nobody could possibly have made! Attributing the observation to an earlier astronomer named Hipparchus, Ptolemy writes of a lunar eclipse that took place on September 22, 200 BC, at 6:30 p.m. Yet we know that the Moon did not even rise until half an hour later on

that date. So either the original observation was a fake – and Ptolemy should have realized it – or Ptolemy himself either altered Hipparchus's observation or invented one, attributing it to Hipparchus, a widely respected scholar, to give it credibility. Hipparchus's own records have vanished; and since the time fits neatly with Ptolemy's theories, Newton has no doubt about who did the faking.

Further indication that Ptolemy was a charlatan comes, curiously, not from inaccuracies but from an implausibly high level of *accuracy*. Newton points out that reputable scientists recognize that a measurement of any quantity, whether in or out of a laboratory, is subject to error, which can arise because of the angle at which the person making the measurement stands in relation to the measuring device or because the method of measuring or the device itself may be slightly inaccurate. The scientific way around such difficulties is to go on making the same measurement several times and to average the results. If all measurements are done as accurately as possible, the errors should cancel each other out. Thus the raw figures are bound to be spread out on either side of the right figure, and the pattern and size of this spread can be predicted statistically. Yet so often, Newton claims, this pattern is absent from Ptolemy's calculations.

For example, the time Ptolemy gives for the start of the lunar eclipses are accurate only to about the nearest quarter of an hour, partly because there were no precise clocks in his time, and also because the Earth casts a fuzzy-edged shadow, making it difficult to ascertain exactly when the shadow first touches the Moon. If he recorded his times honestly, this imprecision should have meant a variation of at least a quarter of a degree in the pattern of the Moon's movements that Ptolemy calculates. In fact, however, his calculated results agree to within one-sixth of a degree. The odds that such accuracy might occur by chance are 64,000 to 1 against – a probability that looks even more suspicious when added to all the other improbably neat results in the *Almagest*.

The conclusion, says Newton, is inescapable. Ptolemy started with his theories, worked out from them the data he needed to make the theories stand up, then claimed he had actually observed the necessary data. And his detailed descriptions of the measuring devices and the observational methods he used, add an air of credibility to the great hoax.

Newton's work is complex and still controversial, and not everyone is convinced by what he says. But if he is right, Ptolemy's dishonesty did as much of a disservice to him as to astronomy. For the *genuine* information available to a scientist as well equipped as he was, might have been sufficient to enable him to spot the truth about the solar system: that Earth revolves around the Sun. Fourteen centuries later, Copernicus worked this out – despite the extra difficulties imposed on him by trying to make sense of Ptolemy's bogus figures – with mathematical techniques and measuring devices no more sophisticated than those that Ptolemy had. So, ironically, if Ptolemy had spent more time making observations and less time forging them, he might have deserved an even greater reputation than the one he has. Or used to have.

THE PTOLEMAIC UNIVERSE

According to Ptolemy, Earth is a perfect, static sphere, around which all the other bodies in the universe orbit, carried on concentric spherical shells of invisible crystal. There are eight such shells. Closest to Earth is the shell holding the Moon. Then, in order, come Mercury, Venus, the Sun, Mars, Jupiter, and Saturn. (The existence of the outer planets – Uranus, Neptune, and Pluto – was not suspected until much later.) The eighth shell bears all the other stars.

Unfortunately, the major heavenly bodies do not move in the regular patterns demanded by this elegant model. Sometimes they appear to move backward in the sky, and their apparent size varies, suggesting that they move closer to and then farther away from Earth. To explain these irregularities, Ptolemy, like other early astronomers, devised a system of epicycles – smaller revolving spheres set in the larger shells. He believed that the Sun, Moon, and planets are held on these smaller crystalline spheres, and that they move in much the same way as a blob of paint on a ball rolling around the inside of a drum.

Even this modification did not explain all observed movements. So Ptolemy added a further refinement: eccentricity (literally, off-centeredness). In other words, Earth does not lie at the exact center of all the major shells, but is slightly offset. This was enough of an explanation to satisfy the sky-watchers of antiquity. Later, more accurate observations, however, forced even further modifications until in the end the Ptolemaic system became a cumbersome collection of varying eccentricities and epicycles involving, in all, some 80 shells and spheres.

Despite its complexity, the system survived essentially unchallenged until modern astronomers, beginning with Copernicus (1473–1543), swept it all away as they developed the correct theory of the planets orbiting the Sun.

Christianity in Africa

The Romans who came to convert, not conquer

THE STORY of the explorer and missionary, David Livingstone, bringing Christianity to Black Africa in the 19th century is well-known. What is not so well-known is that 1,500 years before Livingstone stepped on African soil, one small pocket of this vast continent was already being Christianized. This extraordinary event was brought about, not by intrepid explorers who were ahead of their time, nor by priests, nor even by a conquering race, but – so the story goes – by a strange quirk of fate that led two young Christian brothers to the court of an Ethiopian king. That it happened at all is remarkable enough; what is even more remarkable is that it took place in the fourth century AD, when a large part of Western Europe was still pagan.

The boys were both Roman citizens traveling with an elderly relative, Meropius, a philosopher from Tyre (modern Sur in Lebanon), a Christian city. Meropius was anxious to visit and explore a land he knew as "India," but which was, in fact, Ethiopia.

The ship on which they were traveling put in to land at a port on the Ethiopian coast, to take in food and water. The boys, Frumentius and Aedesius, who were students, went ashore, taking their books. It was as well they did. For the Ethiopians had just heard that a treaty between Rome and their country had been broken. As an act of vengeance, a party of warriors boarded the ship, and killed Meropius and all his crew.

The bloodstained tribesmen then found the two boys sitting under a tree, deep in their studies. Out of compassion for their youth, they were spared and taken to the king of that part of Ethiopia, Ella-'Amida. He was pleasantly impressed with them and gave them posts at his court. Frumentius and Aedesius soon became such trusted servants of Ella-'Amida's family that on the king's death Frumentius was asked to help with the education of the new king (then only an infant) and to act as an adviser. Frumentius agreed to take on this heavy burden if supported by his brother.

Imbued with the Christian tradition of his native city, Tyre, Frumentius encouraged Christian merchants from Rome to trade in Ethiopia, and in due course even had a number of churches built there. When the young king was old enough to assume control of the country, Frumentius and his brother sought permission to return to their native land. Aedesius hurried back to Tyre where he eventually became a priest, but Frumentius traveled to Alexandria where he took orders as a bishop, before returning to Ethiopia to convert the young king to Christianity. For this act, Frumentius has since been canonized.

We owe this account of the foundation of the Ethiopian Christian Church to two early Church historians: the fourth-century monk and theologian Tyrannius Rufinius, who heard the story from the younger brother, Aedesius, and a fifth-century Greek, Socrates Scolasticus. There seems to be no reason to doubt the basic accuracy of the story, though there are other traditions about Ethiopia's religious history that are obviously romanticized versions.

Christianity in Ethiopia suffered a setback in the seventh century when the country was invaded by Arabs. Although the rulers remained Christian, the population was largely Muslim until the Arabs were finally defeated late in the 13th century. Despite further sporadic Muslim attacks, however, the Christian Church survived in Ethiopia up to the present day.

Haile Selassie, the "Lion of Judah," was the last emperor of his country. Though he was respected for his unfaltering resistance to fascist Italy's invasion of Ethiopia in 1935, impatience at his lack of domestic reform led to his overthrow in a military coup in 1974. He died in the same year.

ETHIOPIA AND THE QUEEN OF SHEBA

Not only was Ethiopia for many centuries the only Christian country in Black Africa, but it also had a strong tradition of Judaism, going back to a legend that is thought to have originated in the 10th century. Ethiopia's rulers claimed to have been descended from King Solomon of Israel and the Queen of Sheba. Modern historians generally agree that the Sheba of the Bible was in the Yemen, but according to the Ethiopian legend, Sheba was in Ethiopia, and the queen seduced by Solomon was an Ethiopian queen called Makeda.

From her union with Solomon, Makeda bore a son, named Menelik, whom Solomon wanted to make his heir. When Menelik refused, Solomon anointed him, gave him the name of David, and decreed that only David and his heirs should reign in Ethiopia, under the title of "Lion of Judah" (a title borne by all Ethiopian rulers until the last, Haile Selassie, who reigned from 1930 to 1974).

By a subterfuge Menelik and his entourage managed to take back with them to Ethiopia the holy Ark of the Covenant, the most sacred object in the sanctuary of the Temple at Jerusalem.

Scholars believe that the legend was originated by the Kings of Ethiopia themselves in a deliberate attempt to assert their right to the throne through their descent from Solomon.

Inflation: An ancient woe

Even in ancient Rome a prices-and-incomes policy was a dismal flop

A coin of Diocletian's reign, bearing the emperor's likeness. The chaos and disasters of the third century forced him to impose major changes on the administration of his empire.

B Y THE STANDARDS of his day, the Roman Emperor Diocletian was not a bloodthirsty man. He did not believe in unnecessary killing. But when, in AD 301, he drew up a set of regulations to curb inflation, he decreed that there could be only one punishment for anyone who broke the law: Death.

Diocletian's edict fixed maximum prices for about 1,000 articles, including food, raw materials, textiles, and transport, and also for wages. The edict, though not the first anti-inflation policy ever attempted, was the first on a very large scale, and the emperor was determined to make it work. He passed the word to every corner of the empire: Anyone who exceeded the maximum price, or who tried to get around the rules by keeping goods off the market, would face summary execution. To a large extent, this was a desperate measure reflecting a desperate situation. Diocletian had come to power after half a century of political upheaval, a time of instability and almost non-stop warfare. The capture of a previous emperor, Valerian, by barbarians in AD 259, for instance, had led to a financial crash in which people had rushed to

turn their money into goods, creating a rate of inflation estimated at 1,000 per cent over 17 years. With prices still soaring in the years that followed, the government was forced to respond by debasing the coinage, so that what looked like precious metal was mostly just copper underneath.

Sounds familiar? The preamble to Diocletian's edict, which carefully diverts attention from the government's shortcomings to put the blame on speculators who gambled on grain futures sounds even more familiar: Responsible for the empire's fiscal problems were "men who have nothing better to do than carve up for their own advantage the benefits sent by the gods . . . men who are themselves swimming in a wealth that would satisfy a whole people, who think only of their gain and their percentage."

Equally familiar to us today is the fact that Diocletian's policy did not work. He discovered, as governments have been discovering ever since, that inflation cannot be beaten simply by legislation. Rather than see their money devalued still further, people once again rushed to stockpile all the goods they could lay their hands on. The black market flourished at the expense of the rest of the economy and, to the best of our knowledge, no heads ever rolled as a result of Diocletian's harsh edict.

The world's first prices-and-incomes policy (even when backed up with the threat of capital punishment) had come to nothing.

The most impressive Roman building still standing in present-day Yugoslavia is Diocletian's vast imperial palace at Split, a combination of fortress and residential villa. Within its walls stands Diocletian's elaborate mausoleum, illustrated below with its adjoining market.

THE EMPEROR WHO GAVE UP POWER TO RAISE CABBAGES

Unusually for a Roman emperor, Diocletian seems to have died peacefully in bed. Of his 26 immediate predecessors only one had been so lucky. Of low birth and a native of what is now Yugoslavia, Diocletian rose rapidly through the ranks of the Roman army to be proclaimed emperor by his troops in AD 284, at the age of 39. For the next two decades he held the empire together during a difficult time, chiefly by dividing the command in two and sharing the burden with a fellow-countryman, Maximian. The partnership was so successful in defeating Rome's enemies, if not in solving her economic problems, that by 305, at the end of a long career, both men were able to abdicate in favor of carefully chosen successors.

Diocletian retired at once to his villa at Salona, near the modern Yugoslav town of Split, where he spent the rest of his life pottering around the garden. Maximian was less contented in retirement. Before long he got in touch with Diocletian and suggested a return to the cut and thrust of life at the top. "Ah," replied Diocletian, happily refusing to leave home, "if you could only see my cabbages, which I planted with my own hands. . . ."

"In this sign conquer!"

The sight that converted an emperor

The insignia that the Roman Emperor Constantine ordered to be emblazoned on his standard before going into battle was the monogram composed of χ and ρ, the first two letters of the Greek word "Christos," or "Christ," and shown above on a Roman silver plaque.

IN THE OPENING years of the fourth century AD Rome's gods were being increasingly challenged by the rising popularity of a different religion – Christianity – and the rulers of the Western empire were determined to stem the tide. Persecution of professing Christians and their sympathizers reached a height – "depth" might be a better word – of cruelty as Christians were strung up on gibbets, beaten, tortured, mutilated, decapitated, or imprisoned for years in filthy dungeons. In the names of Jupiter, Apollo, Minerva, and the other "immortals" who had held sway in the empire's capital for countless centuries, the followers of Christ were being accused of every possible crime, and punished accordingly.

Then, all at once, it stopped. In AD 313 the Roman Emperor Constantine legalized Christianity and declared it the official religion of his empire. Constantine had reigned over western portions of the empire since 306, and for seven years had not lifted a finger in defense of the suffering Christians; in fact, he had been a staunch upholder of traditional paganism. What changed his mind – and, in so doing, changed the face of European history?

Whether fact or legend, the story of Constantine's conversion has inspired Christians ever since it was first told by Eusebius, Bishop of Caesaria (the Roman capital city of Palestine), in

his *Life of Constantine*, which he wrote immediately after Constantine died in 337. On an October day in 312, Constantine and his army were marching on the city of Rome in order to wrest it from the grasp of a rival emperor, Maxentius, when, in the rays of the setting sun, Constantine saw a cross in the sky and, along with it, the words "In this sign conquer." That very night Christ appeared to him in a dream and told him to go into battle behind a standard emblazoned with Christian insignia; only thus would he emerge victorious. So the emperor ordered workmen to fashion a standard made of gold, studded with precious jewels, and bearing a monogram symbolizing his fealty to Christ. Behind that ensign – and, according to some accounts, with a special sign of the cross painted on every shield – Constantine's soldiers defeated the enemy in a battle at the Milvian Bridge on the River Tiber. Maxentius drowned, and Constantine entered Rome, victorious and, from that day onward, a committed Christian.

Did Constantine really have the experience that Eusebius describes? Eusebius says that he heard the story from the emperor himself, who swore in the name of God that it was true and that not only he but the soldiers who were with him saw the radiant cross in the sky. However, a number of questions about the facts behind the story have been raised. To begin with, why was

CONSTANTINE'S ROME

At the beginning of the fourth century AD, the city of Rome was at the center of an empire that stretched across the Middle East, throughout the Mediterranean world, and took in all western Europe including present-day France, Spain, and most of Britain. Toward the end of the preceding century the Emperor Diocletian had decided to divide the empire into eastern and western portions; he ruled the east from a capital city in Asia Minor while his trusted son-in-law, Maximian, remained in Italy to administer the west. But because even this division was insufficient for the control of the vast and restless territories that comprised the Roman empire, there had to be further delegation of power. And so the empire was ruled in fact by a tetrarchy – two emperors out in the field along with the two at "home" bases.

Constantine's father was the imperial ruler of Gaul and Britain at his death in 306, and the troops under his command soon acknowledged young Constantine – then not yet 20 years old – as their

emperor. Meanwhile, Diocletian and Maximian had retired (in 305), and there were rival claimants for both the central thrones as well as the two in the field. As so often in such a situation, a series of bloody battles for power ensued; and one such battle – a decisive one – was the battle between Maximian's ambitious son, Maxentius, and Constantine at the Milvian Bridge in 312. As a result of his victory Constantine became sole acknowledged ruler of the Western Roman empire, with his capital at Rome.

Gradually consolidating his position by force of arms, he was able to declare himself head of the whole empire in 324. Six years later, in 330, he decided to move the capital from Rome, which was an increasingly difficult city to defend, to Byzantium in the east. From Byzantium, renamed Constantinople, Constantine the Great ruled over the entire Roman empire. There were no rivals strong enough to challenge his supremacy during the last years of his reign, which ended with his death in AD 337.

Constantine and his army are shown pointing in amazement at a cross of light in the evening sky in this 15th-century mural (at left). Scholars who doubt that what Constantine saw was truly a vision suggest that he observed what meteorologists call the "halo phenomenon" (above), which is caused by sunlight illuminating ice crystals in the upper atmosphere, giving the appearance of ghostly circles around the sun.

such a startling revelation kept secret until after the death of the emperor? How, too, would it have been possible to create an elaborate bejeweled standard in a single morning, almost on the very day of battle (though Eusebius, if not Constantine himself, is vague about precisely where and when the epiphany occurred)? And why, after being converted to Christianity in such a speedy and miraculous way did the emperor postpone being baptized as a Christian till the last year of his life?

Historians today tend to believe that in an age of superstition, when the Christian Church needed to win support by every possible means, stories about divine visions were bound to gain currency. Everybody at the time, whether pagan or Christian, believed in miracles; and the wonder of Constantine's conversion as narrated by Eusebius had a tremendous impact not only on the bishop's contemporaries but also on many generations to come.

The story as told by Eusebius, then, may not be literally true in every respect. But there can be little doubt that *something* happened to the emperor on the eve of his entrance into Rome. Some scholars have suggested that his "vision" may have been caused by what meteorologists speak of as the "halo phenomenon," which can occur when ice crystals in the upper atmosphere form light rings around the sun. Very occasionally, such rings interlock in a pattern that can suggest a cross to some viewers. Perhaps this explains the vision, if not the dream that followed. In any event, it remains true that Constantine was certainly not a Christian before his victory at the Milvian Bridge and that he thereafter became a militant defender of the faith. For the rest of his life his imperial armies marched behind the sacred *labarum*, the name given to the banner on which Constantine's monogram of Christ was inscribed. And they never failed to emerge victorious *in hoc signo* (in this sign).

Keeping fit in the imperial army
The Romans took good care of their far-ranging legionnaires

ON THE SWORDS and spears of her armies Rome rose to world dominion. But this superb military machine was none the less composed of human beings; and armies seldom remain victorious if they leave their wounded or sick soldiers uncared for. In the early days of the Roman republic there seems to have been little organized medical care within the military forces – no medical corps as such, no equivalent of our modern Red Cross. But when, after gaining control of the Italian peninsula, the armies marched abroad and came into contact with the more cultured Greeks, they learned much from the conquered people and soon adopted Greek medical customs as well as other modes of behavior.

The Greeks had a medical tradition going back to Hippocrates in 400 BC and the establishment of sanatoriums dedicated to the god of healing, Aesculapius. Following Rome's defeat of Macedonia in the second century BC, Greek physicians began to accompany the Romans on their campaigns. Though their skills were simple by modern standards, they had well-made surgical tools and some drugs, and they recognized the importance of rest and recuperation for the recovery of wounded, exhausted, or fever-racked bodies. Gradually, as their frontiers expanded, the Romans under Greek tutelage set up a number of hospitals to serve military camps throughout the empire. An officer who fought under the future Emperor Tiberius in the northern frontier wars during the reign of Augustus (27 BC – AD 14) has left posterity a hint of how well this system worked for him:

"There was not one of us, nor of those above or below our rank, who fell ill without having his health and welfare taken care of by Tiberius with as much care as if this was his chief preoccupation despite his other weighty responsibilities. There was a horse-drawn vehicle for all who needed it, his own litter was at the disposal of us all, and I among others have enjoyed its use. Now his physician, now his kitchen, now his bathing equipment brought for his personal use ministered to the comfort of all who were sick. All the wounded lacked was their home and slaves – nothing else that friends at home could provide or desire for them."

So much for the words of a grateful officer. What about the rest of the army? From the accounts of Cicero and Caesar, both writing in the first century BC, it is clear that ordinary soldiers were by no means neglected. At the very least, they could depend on having somebody come to bind up their wounds on the battlefield. Although the men who did this were called *medici*, they were not trained doctors but ordinary soldiers who had acquired limited but valuable knowledge of first-aid procedures. Their ministrations must have saved many lives even though surgery of any complexity was probably beyond them. On the monument known as Trajan's Column in Rome, there are

The importance of preventive medicine is appreciated today, but Roman soldiers were well fed and regularly drilled 2,000 years ago with the same principle in mind. If injured or ill, they were cared for, as shown in this detail from Trajan's Column in Rome, which features activities at a dressing station for wounded Roman soldiers.

carved battle scenes from the Dacian wars (early second century AD) showing a *medicus* who wears the uniform of an ordinary soldier. We know he is a *medicus* only because he is depicted as binding the wound of a comrade.

Though the skills and knowledge of the *medici* were pretty rough and ready, their work did much to forward the study of medicine. The most famous scholar-physicians of the Roman empire, Celsus (first century AD) and Galen (second century), both commented on the value of warfare in providing practical experience for medical and surgical procedures. The battlefield also provided a steady stream of corpses for dissection and anatomical exploration. Gradually, the army adopted a more professional attitude toward health care for its soldiers. By AD 210 each of the two 1,000-strong cohorts of military personnel in the city of Rome had four doctors attached to it, and the medical men ranked as subordinate officers. If the same system held in the field, every 6,000-man legion must have included about 24 medical officers. In addition, sick soldiers as well as the long-term wounded could be nursed back to health in permanent military hospitals behind the lines.

Nor was preventive medicine neglected. The Romans knew that an army in good health is more likely to win its battles than an ailing one. So, in an age when more deaths occurred as a result of diseases such as malaria or dysentery than from sword wounds, they took good care to place their *castra* (camps) in healthy environments, as distant as possible from malarial marshes yet with a good supply of water. They did not know about bacteria, but they sensed the need for cleanliness and clean air; as early as the first century BC, a learned and thoughtful writer named Varro speculated about the existence of "minute creatures which cannot be seen by the eyes, float through the air, and enter the body through the mouth and nose, causing diseases." And Vegetius, a fourth-century-AD writer, emphasized the importance of siting camps carefully and suggested that "most informed people believe that daily exercise contributes more to soldiers' health than do doctors."

Probably the best health measure of all was an indirect one. By means of their excellent engineering the Romans doubtless prevented many a lethal epidemic, for they were able to pipe clean water to, and remove sewage from, military camps as well as cities.

THE WORLD'S FIRST HOSPITALS

At Inchtuthil in central Scotland archeologists have discovered the remains of one of the world's first hospitals. Constructed during the Roman occupation, the building was almost 300 feet (100 meters) long and 200 feet (68 meters) wide. It had a superb drainage and sewage system, and its division into separate wards connected by a corridor suggests that the architects were aware of the value of isolation in dealing with infectious diseases. From Scotland in the north to Libya in the south, such *valetudinaria* were built throughout the empire and equipped with plumbing and designed with a regard for hygiene that the West would not see again for centuries. Surprisingly, civilian Rome itself had no early *valetudinaria*; sickness was treated in the home. Home care for personnel in the provinces was obviously impossible. Hence the military hospitals.

Typically, these were built around courtyards, with latrines and baths of a high standard attached. By the fourth century AD, this military example was beginning to be followed in civil life, especially among Christians, who regarded visiting the sick as one of their duties. The Emperor Julian (361–63) noted the spread of Christian hospitals – a fusion of old Roman techniques and new religious sentiments. After the collapse of the empire in the fifth century, the techniques were gradually forgotten while the religion endured and throve.

As an indication of the relative sophistication of Roman medicine, these ancient physician's tools are still recognizable as such today. Here, from left to right, are a scalpel, surgical scissors, and forceps for manipulating bones.

Simeon Stylites

Thirty years on a pillar

THE CHRISTIAN CHURCH has conferred sainthood on many people – few as bizarre as Simeon Stylites the Elder, who lived alone on the top of a tall stone pillar in the desert for more than 36 years.

St. Simeon believed that, because the Lord had suffered, His followers should follow His example. As a young monk in his native Syria, Simeon acquired a reputation by chaining his right leg to a rock and performing miracles, mostly by healing people who flocked to visit him. Although later writers may have invented the miracles, it is a matter of record that Simeon had himself walled in during Lent, and that he allowed vermin to crawl over his body rather than harming them. His behavior bordered on the fanatical, and people traveled hundreds of miles to catch a glimpse of him. At first he welcomed the attention, but soon began to find it a nuisance. He was a man who craved solitude, and in desperation he decided that the only way to escape the crowds while getting closer to God was to live on top of a pillar. This supreme act of self-mortification, in which Simeon was far from unique, was designed to elevate the devotee above the worldly pressures and disturbances of day-to-day life.

In AD 423, at roughly the same age as Christ when He was crucified, Simeon settled on one of a number of stone columns in the village of Telnishe, in north Syria, the remains of which can still be seen, having first experimented with living in a confined space by taking up residence on a rock ledge. Simeon's first residential column was 6 feet (1.8 meters) high; during the following six or seven years, he moved on to higher columns, finally settling on the tallest which was about 72 feet (22 meters) high. For 30 years, Simeon never once came down from the top. Food was delivered by ladder, but no one was encouraged to stay with Simeon at the summit. The top of the column was about 2 feet (50 to 60 centimeters) square, probably surrounded by a railing to stop Simeon rolling off

St. Simeon's spectacular career of self-denying isolation from the world inspired a host of imitators and an enduring tradition in Christian monasticism. This medieval picture shows Simeon atop his pillar, while St. Ephrem, who converted much of Syria to Christianity, is being buried (below). In the hills, hermit-monks can be seen in their caves, which were popular niches of isolation.

when he was asleep. It was open to the heat of the sun in summer and the rain in winter.

Simeon lived a life of fasting and prayer. A follower counted the number of prostrations Simeon made in rapid succession during prayer from his kneeling position. He stopped counting at 1,244. His disciples, who gathered around the base of the column, listened intently to every word he shouted down. Simeon was highly regarded as a preacher, a visionary, and a settler of disputes. For example, the text of a letter still exists in which certain priests pledged, at Simeon's insistence, never to charge more than six per cent interest on money loaned, instead of the more usual 12. He also corresponded with important people, sending petitions to the Roman emperor Theodosius II on behalf of the Syrian bishops, or arguing theology with the Patriarch Basil of Antioch. He dictated his letters by shouting down from the pillar.

In his own day, Simeon was venerated, but his popularity owed as much to the common people's love of eccentricity as to his stature in the Church. A few people argued that his self-imposed punishment served no useful purpose, and, with the possible exception of several Lebanese, he made few lasting converts. Nevertheless, when he died in 459, his death was initially kept secret to prevent his followers from carrying off the blessed body. Even so, a few of his teeth were stolen at some point and have since become holy relics. He was buried with much ceremony in the great church of Constantine in the Syrian city of Antioch. Antioch had recently suffered two earthquakes and its citizens hoped that St. Simeon would guard them against future disasters.

Although Simeon was its most famous exponent, the cult of stylitism (living on a pillar) was popular among Eastern Christians as far afield as Egypt, Greece, and Mesopotamia, and was originally pagan in origin, although enthusiastically taken up by the early Christian Church in the East. It never caught on in the West, except briefly in 19th-century Russia, but it remained popular in the East until well into the 12th century. Some stylites with less fortitude lived in small huts on their pillars, while others lived in hollows inside them. One eccentric spent 10 years hanging in a tub suspended between two poles. Stylites were fanatics, motivated by a form of religious masochism that has rarely been equaled. The most fanatical was not St. Simeon, but rather St. Alipius, who was said to have lost the use of his feet after standing on a pillar near Adrianopolis (now Edirne in Turkey) for 53 years, and so spent the next 14 years on the pillar lying on his side.

The end of an empire

The work of barbarians or a case of poisoning?

ON A HOT August night in AD 410, the gates of a starving Rome were opened, probably by a slave, to the Gothic armies camped outside. For three days, hordes of Germanic barbarians under Alaric the Goth pillaged and ransacked the "Eternal City," which had stood unconquered for 800 years. The news stunned the world. In far-away Bethlehem, St. Jerome, a native of Rome, lamented: "When the brightest light on the whole Earth was extinguished, when the Roman empire was deprived of its head, when, to speak more correctly, the whole world perished in one city, I was dumb with silence." For many people, Christians and pagans alike, the fall of the world's greatest city spelled the end not only of an empire, but the end of the world.

But, needless to say, the end of the world was not nigh, nor for that matter was the end of the Roman empire. The city of Rome had collapsed, but the Western Roman empire, of which Rome was the capital, recovered from the blow dealt by the Goths and lingered on until 476 when Romulus Augustus, its last emperor, was deposed by his German commanders. On the other hand the Eastern Roman empire (which had come into being in AD 395, with its capital at Constantinople, now Istanbul) continued until its capture by the Turks in 1453. Although this Eastern empire had become increasingly Greek in life and language, it still considered itself Roman. And within its mighty walls, Constantinople fostered Roman learning and law.

Many factors combined to lead to the eventual fall of the Western Roman empire, and the sack of its capital in 410 was more a symbol of its decline than a cause. In fact, Alaric's Goths were more interested in sharing the benefits of the Roman way of life than in destroying the Eternal City. For many years, Alaric had been asking the

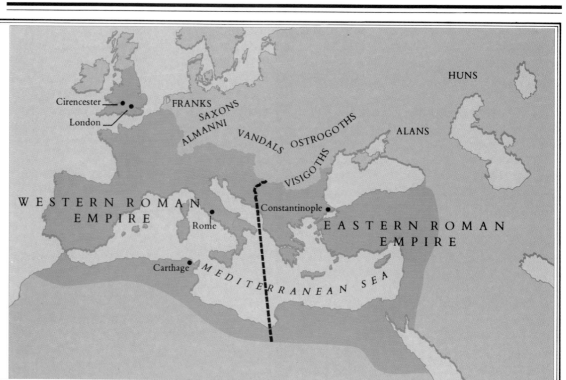

The Romans did not know about the poisonous hazards of lead pipes, but they were well aware of the menace posed by the land- and plunder-hungry barbarian tribes pressing on the borders of their empire – an empire which, as can been seen from this map, had extensive land frontiers that had become too vulnerable to be adequately or easily defended.

When sacked by Alaric and his armies in AD 410, Rome was the most splendid city in the world, a metropolis of over one million people. Buildings such as the Forum, built by the first Roman Emperor Augustus (who reigned from 27 BC to AD 14) dominated the city and expressed in physical terms the might and power of the Roman empire – a power increasingly threatened by the barbarian tribes at her borders.

Romans to give him the title of allied commander and to provide lands for his men. It was despair at Roman double-dealing and delays that finally drove him to attack Rome. The court that the Goths established a few years later at Toulouse under Alaric's successor, Athaulf, was praised by one Roman visitor as having "the refinement of Greece, the elegance of Italy, and the vigor of Gaul combined." Even before they sacked Rome in 410, the Goths had been slowly adopting Roman customs, while generations of Romans living in distant parts of the empire were being increasingly influenced by barbarians, and more and more of Rome's soldiers were being recruited from Germanic peoples who felt little loyalty for Rome.

Alaric's sack of Rome in 410 was not, therefore, a decisive blow to Roman power. But – as the first such defeat in 800 years – it certainly did immense psychological damage, which was perhaps more difficult to repair than pillaged buildings. This factor makes it more understandable why Alaric's capture of the Eternal City rather than a much more devastating destruction perpetrated in 454 by a Vandal, King Gaiseric, has remained in the records as the symbol of the end of a great empire.

Recently evidence has emerged which may also have an important bearing on why the city of Rome fell to the Goths so quickly in the fifth century. Between 1969 and 1976, excavations at Cirencester, in southern England, uncovered 450 skeletons in a Roman cemetery dating from the late fourth and early fifth centuries – that is, on the eve of the fall of the Western Roman empire. Most of the bones were found to contain up to 10 times the normal concentration of lead, the skeletons of children being particularly affected. Some of these people had probably died from lead poisoning, although this could not be proved. What is known from contemporary accounts is that throughout the empire, hundreds of people suffered from paralyzed limbs and headaches, symptoms of chronic lead poisoning. Cirencester was the second-largest city in Roman Britain and so it may be representative of most Roman cities.

The Romans were proud of their excellent water supplies. But water was normally carried through lead pipes. The Romans drank from lead cups, cooked in lead pots, and even used lead oxide to sweeten wine in the absence of sugar. The average Roman must therefore have consumed a large amount of lead during a lifetime – lead that must have caused listlessness and lack of energy. Another consequence of this consumption of lead may well have been sterility. Later emperors were constantly encouraging parents to produce more children, possibly in order to halt a decline in the population, although no detailed or accurate figures exist for population changes in the Roman empire which can confirm this decline. Lead can affect fertility, even at low concentrations, and so it is possible that the Romans were literally drinking themselves to death and extinction.

Lead poisoning, of course, was not the only cause of Rome's fifth-century collapse. And why should the Eastern Roman empire have survived for another 1,000 years after the West went under? As usual, there were a combination of reasons: it had shorter, more defensible frontiers and so was less exposed to invasions. It was also better able to keep the peace at home. However, it is surely also significant that the Eastern Roman empire possessed far fewer lead mines than the West, and so its inhabitants had to make do with – as they thought, inferior – pottery cups and cooking pots.

"The Scourge of God"

Was Attila as bad as they say?

ATTILA THE HUN! His name conjures up a terrifying image of a demonic barbarian, a savage horseman bringing death and destruction to all who stood in his way. It was more than 1,500 years ago that Attila led his galloping forces against the might of the Roman empire to prove himself the greatest warrior of his time; but his reputation as a bogeyman has outlived the centuries. Why? Was he truly so frightening? How does the real Attila compare with the myth?

The man himself made a strong, and not very pleasant, impression on his contemporaries. One Roman historian who visited Attila's stronghold in Wallachia (a region in the south-eastern part of what is now Romania) in AD 449, and whose chronicles tell us much about Attila's court, describes the king as a hideous dwarf with broad shoulders, large head, flat nose, and scanty beard. Another historian who saw Attila in person says: "The haughty step of the king of the Huns expressed the consciousness of his superiority to the rest of mankind, and he had a habit of rolling his eyes fiercely as if he wanted to enjoy the terror he inspired." Attila was superstitious and illiterate, but so were most people of the various tribes that the Romans lumped together as "barbarians." He was obviously intelligent, though, and knew how to make men follow and obey him.

Although Attila's name is often paired with that of another "world" conqueror, Genghis Khan, the mighty Mongol overlord of the 13th century, the comparison is unfair to the great Hun. Whereas Genghis encouraged his soldiers to ravage conquered territory and torture prisoners, Attila was not merciless in battle, and he realized the futility of destroying the spoils of war and murdering prisoners who could be put to useful work. He was as ruthless as Genghis Khan in his pursuit of absolute power – there is no doubt that he murdered his brother, Bleda, in 445 after they had ruled jointly for 11 years – but he was quicker than Genghis and other barbarians to learn respect for the more sophisticated peoples whom his armies overran; while conquering great sectors of the Roman empire, he even employed Rome-trained officials in his court. And though eventually in command of treasure beyond the wildest dreams of the once-poor Huns, Attila remained uncorrupted by this wealth. The Roman commentator who

This stone plaque, bearing a supposed likeness of Attila, was not in fact made until after he had gained the sobriquet Flagellum Dei, "Scourge of God," in the 10th century.

describes the conqueror as a "hideous dwarf" nonetheless writes admiringly about his preference for eating ordinary meat from a wooden plate while his fellow-soldiers gorged themselves on "dainties" served in silver dishes.

No single military force of his day – certainly not the demoralized army of the crumbling Roman empire – could halt Attila's march across northern Europe. Not until Rome joined forces with the Visigoths, another mighty barbarian people, were the swift cavalry and deadly accurate bowmen under Attila's command finally defeated, in 451, at a bloody and decisive battle at Maurica near what is now Châlon-sur-Marne in northeastern France. According to legend, Attila then prepared to immolate himself on a pyre of burning saddles rather than face capture. Retiring southward, the Huns invaded Italy, where for a time they threatened the city of Rome itself. But much of their momentum was spent by then, and in 453 the death of the military genius who had made them what they were spelled the beginning of a quick end to their whirlwind European adventure.

Attila's end at the age of about 47 was as dramatic and strange as any of the events of his lifetime. While still in Italy, he decided to take a new bride (he already had a number of wives), a beautiful young girl named Ildico. After a wine-sodden wedding feast, the happy couple retired to their bedchamber, and nothing was heard of them until late the following day, when, at last suspecting that something might be wrong, attendants made their way into the room. They found Ildico in a state of shock; Attila was lying on his back in a pool of blood, dead, apparently, from an unstoppable nosebleed. Had the pretty young wife murdered him? She was accused of it in some reports, but the Huns themselves seem not to have thought her guilty. Attila was buried in a traditional ceremony by a selected group of horsemen, who were then put to death. (According to legend, they were strapped to their saddles, their throats were cut, and their horses impaled in a ring around the grave, forming a rather gruesome guard of honor for the departed king.)

About five centuries after his death, Attila gained the sobriquet by which he is best – or perhaps the word should be "worst" – known: "The Scourge of God" (*Flagellum Dei*), an epithet used for the first time by the Bishop of Modena in a 10th-century Latin account of the Huns' advance through Europe. No doubt the Christians of Europe *were* terrified by the approach of the Asian hordes, and no doubt the Huns *did* sack churches during the 19 years (434–53) of Attila's leadership. We should not forget, however, that everything we know about the Huns comes from Roman and Church historians; and patriotic Romans and fervent Christians all had their motives for picturing Attila as a monstrous enemy of God. The Romans needed someone almost supernaturally evil to blame for the decline of their "eternal" empire. And Attila's story, including its bloody end, provided the Church with a good cautionary lesson for sinners.

WHO WERE THE HUNS?

The Huns were a nomadic people who came originally from north-central Asia. Their name probably derives from *Hsiung-nu*, the name of a tribe mentioned by Chinese chroniclers over 2,500 years ago. In the centuries before they began to migrate westward, they scratched a poor living from the steppes, hunting and gathering their food rather than relying on agriculture. Having no time to waste on weaving, they wore untreated skins as clothes – and continued to wear them until they disintegrated. Excellent stock-breeders and horsemen, they practically lived in the saddle; it has been alleged that they tenderized meat beneath their saddles before devouring it raw. Hun warriors associated their destiny so closely with their steeds that when Attila was threatened with capture after the battle of 451 that ended his westward surge, he prepared to immolate himself on a pyre of burning saddles – a splendidly symbolic gesture for a great horseman.

Early Hun society was composed of numerous tribes, each headed by a chieftain who held his position because of military skill, not simply inheritance. The westward migration of these tribes in search of richer land in the fourth century AD brought them into contact – and conflict – with other tribes and, eventually, the Roman empire. The separate tribes of the Huns were largely united by the beginning of the fifth century, and full unity along with unprecedented prosperity was achieved under the leadership of Attila from 434 to 453; it was he who realized the immense military potential of his people despite their former poverty and extremely primitive technology. During his dictatorial rule they became not only a military power but a nation of traders.

After Attila's death, however, they were unable to retain their swiftly acquired empire, which, at its height, stretched across Europe from northern Gaul to the Caucasus. Unable to police all their subject peoples and supply their vast army, they were forced to retreat eastward, gradually reverted to old tribal groupings, and eventually lost their identity as a distinct people.

The tyrannical Attila owed his success to his military genius and absolute control of his forces. In this painting by the 19th-century French painter J.E. Delaunay, Attila leads his ferocious but disciplined army against Paris.

AD 450-AD 1500

THE MEDIEVAL WORLD

100,000 BC — Period of time covered by this chart — AD 1500

YEARS AD		450	500	550	600	650	700	750	800	850	900	950
AMERICAS				Mayan civilization in C. America at its peak								
			Throughout this period, Americas remain ignorant of iron and its uses									
					228							
EUROPE			Break-up of Roman empire in the West fragments Europe				Arab invasion of Europe halted by Franks			Charlemagne builds new empire centered on France		
		196	208	198 217					203 / 209	220	224	
ASIA	MIDDLE EAST	Byzantine empire dominates E. Mediterranean			Muslim conquest of Middle East and N. Africa				Abbasid caliphate in Baghdad dominates Muslim world			
	FAR EAST			China reunified by T'ang dynasty						Fujiwara family in control of Japan		
										China ruled by Sung dynasty		
		208		200			212		214			
AFRICA						Kingdom of Ghana prospers on trans-Sahara trade				Muslim trading contacts established with east coast of Africa		
OCEANIA			Throughout this period, Oceania remains in Stone Age, with no knowledge of iron-working or use							New Zealand, the last major uninhabited islands in the Pacific, colonized by Maoris		

Shown in the chart above are page references to each article appearing in this section of the book. The subject of each article is listed here.

196 King Arthur born?
198 Theodora quells a revolt in Constantinople
200 Hsuan-Tsang travels to India from China
203 Viking raiders terrorize much of N. Europe
208 Horses first collared in China
209 Charlemagne crowned emperor in Rome
212 Harun ar-Rashid presides over glittering court of Baghdad

214 Stories of Sindbad's voyages first appear in print
217 St. Benedict lays down rules for monastic life
220 Blueprint for St. Gall monastery drawn up
222 Caves of the Thousand Buddhas in China sealed up
224 Alfred the Great, King of Wessex, takes on Vikings
226 Alhazen tries to dam the Nile
228 Nazca Indians draw lines in the Peruvian desert

230 *Tale of Genji* written
232 Bayeux Tapestry finished
234 Domesday Book compiled for William the Conqueror
236 Cannibalism on the First Crusade
238 Search for legendary Prester John begins
239 Nicolas Flamel claims to have made gold
240 Samurai take control in Japan
243 Birth of Eleanor of Aquitaine, "First Lady of the Courtly Lovers"

The human world of AD 1500 had become a vastly different place from the world at the beginning of the medieval period, for the intervening 1,000 years witnessed rapid changes almost everywhere. Western Europe was transformed from a collection of barely organized states, which had evolved after the collapse of the Roman empire in the West, into a group of complex, powerful, and aggressive Christian kingdoms. Meanwhile, the empires of the East had developed flourishing, forceful civilizations; this was the period of the expansive rise of Islam, after the death of Muhammad early in the seventh century, and the later dominance of the Mongol empires. The period came to an end and the modern age began with the discovery of the Western hemisphere – an unknown quantity to the rest of the world before Columbus returned from his first epic voyage in 1493.

In their isolation, the Americas had developed differently from the Eastern hemisphere, where knowledge of important inventions like paper and gunpowder could spread gradually throughout Asia and Europe. Nevertheless, although the inhabitants of America did without such advantages until the coming of the Europeans, great Mayan, Inca, and Aztec nations formed and prospered. Largely isolated too in this period was sub-Saharan Africa, whose wealth of culture is only now being appreciated, and the islands of Oceania, which remained in the Stone Age until well after the end of medieval times.

| 000 | 1050 | 1100 | 1150 | 1200 | 1250 | 1300 | 1350 | 1400 | 1450 | 1500 |

Chimu empire at its peak — Rise of Aztec empire in Mexico — Inca empire in Peru — Columbus establishes first European contact with New World

264 — 278 — 261 293 312

Spain starts to expel Muslims — Norman invasion of England — Angevin empire of England and France created by Henry II — 100 Years War between England and France — Renaissance flourishes in Italy — Civil war in England

247 — 234 232 236 248 243 — 252 255 268 — 259 — 276 271 — 273 282 287 284 250 289 239 — 297 291 — 299 308 310 305 301 303 312

First Crusade launched to recapture Jerusalem from Muslims — Crusader kingdoms conquered by Saladin — Fall of Acre marks end of Crusades — Mamluks found empire in Egypt — Ottoman Turks slowly expand empire

Mongols under Genghis Khan carve out vast Asian empire — Kublai Khan emperor of China — Mongol empire under Tamerlane

226 230 — 222 247 — 240 236 — 238 — 266 — 276 — 295

Brass and copper portrait heads and regalia cast in W. Africa — Rise of Mali empire — First Iron Age settlement in Zimbabwe — Portuguese explore coastline of Africa

226 — 238 — 245 257 — 270 — 280

245 King Lalibela of Ethiopia carves churches out of rock
247 Recipe for gunpowder published
248 William Rufus, King of England, killed – accidentally?
250 Turin Shroud first shown publicly in France
252 Tournament takes place at Lagny-sur-Marne
255 "Stupor Mundi" born in Sicily
257 Growth of Great Zimbabwe in C. Africa

259 Inquisition set up on papal orders
261 Incas expand empire in Andes
264 Chan-Chan built in N. Peru
266 Genghis Khan assumes control of Mongol tribes
268 Chartres cathedral being rebuilt after disastrous fire
270 Mamluks take control of Egypt
271 War of the Sicilian Vespers
273 English longbowmen overwhelm French at Crécy
276 Marco Polo sets out for China

278 Aztecs start to build capital city of Tenochtitlan
280 Ibn Batuta crosses the Sahara to Mali
282 Order of the Garter founded by Edward III
284 Black Death decimates Europe
287 Hanseatic League wins concessions from King of Denmark
289 Peasants' Revolt quelled by boy king Richard II
291 Nicholas of Cusa exposes Donation of Constantine as a fraud

293 Ozette buried by mudslide
295 Tamerlane the Terrible dies
297 Joan of Arc burned at the stake by the English
299 Vlad the Impaler dies
301 Medicis attacked in Florence
303 Perkin Warbeck lays claim to English throne
305 Leonardo paints *The Last Supper*
308 Lucrezia Borgia born
310 Spain conquers the Moors in Granada
312 Columbus first sails for the New World

King Arthur and the Round Table

An enduring source of inspiration

In this illustration from a 14th-century manuscript, King Arthur lies mortally wounded after his last battle, having ordered the loyal Sir Bedivere to throw the king's sword, Excalibur, into the lake.

The unique and massive Round Table, which still hangs in the Great Hall of Winchester Castle. It was damaged during the Civil War in the 17th century when Cromwell's troops used it as a kind of dart board for target practice.

THE LEGENDS of King Arthur and his gallant knights of the Round Table have enthralled and inspired the Christian world for more than 1,000 years. To some, Arthur and his knights represented champions of civilization against banditry and barbarism, while to others they were defenders of the weak and helpless. In a sinful world, they were shining symbols of courage, faith, and endurance. The legends told in Sir Thomas Malory's *Morte d'Arthur* (written in 1485, about 1,000 years after Arthur is supposed to have lived) even contain the belief that Arthur is not dead, but will return with his knights to resume the struggle to heal the hurts of the world as *Rex Quondam Rexque Futurus,* the "Once and Future King."

A Round Table had been the centerpiece of Arthur's court. Like the round orb held by monarchs at their coronations, the Round Table symbolized power and glory spreading to the confines of the world. But it was much more than that. In real terms, it was a force for harmony and brotherhood. Around it, no knight could feel humiliated by being seated in a lowlier place than another. It was an antidote for jealousy, ambition, greed for higher precedence

and power – those human faults which underlay the turmoil and wars of the Middle Ages. But Arthur decreed that the knights of the Round Table must be the best: "knights which be of most prowess and worship."

For 600 years the top of a Round Table, believed to be major proof of the existence of Arthur and his knights, has hung as a decoration on the wall of the Great Hall of the royal castle of Winchester, once capital of England. In the late 1970s this table was at the center of a fascinating piece of detective work.

A Round Table is not mentioned in the earliest stories about Arthur, and many scholars have maintained that the painted decorations on the table were later additions, since its central image is a rose – symbol of the Tudor dynasty – and a portrait of what appears to be a young King Henry VIII. Analysis of the paintings in the 1970s has shown that they *were* done in the early 16th century. However, the wood from which the table was made dated from before this period, so perhaps Henry VIII had merely added decorations to this royal heirloom?

The table was also examined by an expert in woodworking techniques through the ages. His opinion that the table was probably made in the 14th century was corroborated by carbon-dating, which has established that the wood was probably felled in the 1330s. So who built the table, if not Arthur? The most likely candidate seems to be England's King Edward III who reigned from 1327 to 1377.

The Arthurian legends were well-suited to the emerging ideals of crusading and chivalry in the 11th, 12th, and 13th centuries. Arthur's knights could be emulated by all fighting men as triumphant crusaders in the quest for the Holy Grail, the cup with which Jesus Christ celebrated the first Mass. By the 14th century, chivalry was at its zenith. At that time, Edward III was seeking to invade and conquer France, like the legendary Arthur in his war with the "Dictator Lucius" of Rome. The blend of love of chivalry with respect for the unifying inspiration of the Arthurian legends gave Edward the idea of founding a new, elite order of knighthood. The seat of the new order was the royal castle of Windsor, west of London, where, according to the French chronicler Jean Froissart, Edward announced his plan at a great tournament on April 23, 1344, St. George's Day.

KING ARTHUR: FACT OR FICTION?

If King Arthur existed, he probably lived in the late fifth or early sixth century, a period of British history which is virtually undocumented. The last broken accounts of the fall of Roman Britain date from the early fifth century, while authentic records of Anglo-Saxon history do not begin until the sixth century.

A tough war leader, champion of the Romano-British way of life and an expert in the tactics of the late Roman empire, could have achieved temporary success in rallying people against Anglo-Saxon barbarians. He would have earned, or enforced, the submission of the petty kings of the Celtic west and north – Cornwall, Wales, Northumbria and, possibly, the Scottish lowlands. He would have succeeded best by using mobile but heavily armored cavalry on the late Roman model. This would have included a picked guards force – the origin of Arthur's knightly elite.

In Anglo-Saxon records, no English victories are recorded between AD 530, when the West Saxons took the Isle of Wight, and 552, when they beat the English at Salisbury. This 22-year gap might represent the respite won for the interior by Arthur's victories. Hence we can speculate that he might have lived between 470 and 550, but this is no more than an informed guess.

And what of Arthur's capital, Camelot? Malory's identification of Camelot as Winchester is possible, because Winchester was close to the West Saxon enclave at the head of Southampton Water, facing the Isle of Wight. But we can assume that Jean Froissart's 14th-century assertion that Camelot was Windsor was an attempt to please his patron Edward III, because Windsor was badly placed to defend the west. Similarly, the 12th-century ruins at Tintagel in Cornwall would have been too far west, as would Dozmary Pool. There remains Somerset, in southwest England, particularly around Glastonbury. Somerset was strategically located to block West Saxon forays north from the English Channel coast. And swift moves north and east would also have been possible along the old Roman roads. Recent excavations at the ancient hill-fort of Cadbury, southeast of Glastonbury, have uncovered traces of a Romano-British occupation. And at Castle Cary, five miles (eight kilometers) north of this lonely outpost, is an even more intriguing complex of artificial fortress-mounds, which are, sadly, half obscured by the modern town. Somerset is the most likely site of Camelot, although people from Cornwall, Northumbria, Scotland, or Wales would never agree.

Cadbury

Glastonbury Abbey (above)
Glastonbury Tor (below)
Tintagel (bottom right)

Dozmary Pool

A warrior from Arthurian times, ready for battle.

Monuments to Edward's dream have survived. One is the Order of the Garter, the official name of Edward's new brotherhood of knights. Created in 1348, it remains the senior British order of knighthood today. Another is the great Round Tower at Windsor, which was begun by Edward and was intended, or so it seems, specifically to house a round table. The massive 1¼-ton (1,270 kilograms) table at Winchester is the right size for the tower and was built during Edward's reign.

So, although sadly not the table at which Arthur and his knights sat, the Winchester Round Table demonstrates the enduring aura of Arthurian legends. It is said that Arthur and his knights will return if ever England is in dire need, and in a deliberate evocation of this legend, Henry VII named his eldest son Arthur – a tribute repeated in 1982 when Prince Charles, the Prince of Wales, had his son and heir christened Prince William Arthur.

THE "NINE WORTHIES"

The English printer William Caxton wrote a preface to the first edition of *Morte d'Arthur* in 1485. In explaining his reasons for publishing the epic, he stressed that medieval tradition included Arthur among those paragons of virtue, the "Nine Worthies."

The Nine consisted of three pagans, three Jews, and three Christians. The pagans were Hector of Troy, Alexander the Great, and Julius Caesar. The Jews were Joshua (conqueror of Canaan), David, and Judas Maccabeus. The Christians were Charlemagne and Godfrey de Bouillon, the first Crusader King of Jerusalem, but both were preceded in honor by the "noble Arthur."

The Nine Worthies were "the best that ever were" – the same excellence demanded by Arthur for knightly admission to the Round Table. This confident interlacing of legend with historical fact is and always has been the essence of the Arthurian epic.

Empress with a purple past
The incredible story of Theodora

IN AD 532 Justinian I, ruler of the Eastern Roman empire, was on the point of fleeing from a murderous mob chanting *"Nika! Nika!"* ("Conquer! Conquer!") outside his palace when his wife, Theodora, made an impassioned appeal to him and the frightened officials surrounding them: "... for an emperor to become a fugitive" she cried "is a thing not to be endured ... If you wish to flee to safety, emperor, it can be easily done.... However ... as for me, I hold with the old saying that the purple makes a *fine* winding sheet." Inspired by her words, the emperor and his followers – including a brilliant general, Belisarius – swung into action. Belisarius gathered his forces together and swooped down upon the angry crowd that had gathered in the Hippodrome, a great amphitheatre adjacent to the palace. Retribution was terrible and swift. Justinian's men are believed to have killed more than 30,000 people during the next few hours, throwing many of the bodies into the sea. The so-called Nika Revolt had ended almost before it had begun.

Thanks to Theodora's character and resolve, Justinian emerged from the ordeal more secure and powerful than before. He gave his wife due credit for her heroic stand; immediately following the Nika Revolt, he decreed that she was to have full equality with him as joint ruler of the empire. For the rest of her life she did indeed rule, and with ruthless efficiency. Surprisingly, this regal personage, this great lady dressed in the purple of an empress, was not "born to the purple" at all, was not in fact a "lady," but was of exceedingly humble birth and had begun her adult life as a prostitute.

Theodora's father was a bear-keeper at Constantinople's Hippodrome, a center for the popular sports of bear-baiting and chariot racing. Her earliest associates must have been an assortment of stable-boys, animal-keepers, hawkers, pimps, prostitutes, and petty criminals. Women who valued their reputation shunned the corridors of the Hippodrome, but it was there, when she was 12 years old, that Theodora joined her elder sister on the stage – which was the equivalent in the Eastern Roman empire of entering a brothel.

According to the contemporary historian Procopius, Theodora was not a talented actress, but she was clever, graceful, beautiful, and adept at exhibiting herself in salacious attitudes and situations. Since Procopius is notoriously hostile toward the empress, he doubtless over-emphasizes the more lurid aspects of her background and behavior, but there seems little

doubt about the fact, if not the extent, of her debauchery. Perhaps she did not actually display herself on stage in a coarsely suggestive pose involving a tame goose, as Procopius claims. And perhaps she did not often dine with as many as 40 young men to whom, in the words of the British historian Edward Gibbon, "her charity was universal." But her charms, however and wherever displayed, certainly brought her to the attention of gentlemen in high places. For a time, we know, she was the mistress of the governor of Cyrenaica (in what is now Libya), and she eventually found her way into the arms of the heir to the Byzantine throne, Justinian, first as his mistress and later as his wife. In 527, when Justinian became emperor, Theodora was crowned at his side. She was not yet 30.

By the time of her marriage she had become impeccably respectable, and she apparently remained faithful to Justinian. Few people, in any event, dared question her virtue, for Theodora's displeasure was something to be avoided. She employed an army of spies to listen to gossip; and people who gossiped about her past or spoke harshly about her present conduct were thrown into prison, where they were tortured or left to die. There is a story that she bore – and abandoned – a son during her "professional"

THE RAH-RAH BOYS OF BYZANTIUM

Sports fans of the sixth century AD were as emotional as – and very much more dangerous than – their 20th-century counterparts. The spark that ignited the Nika Revolt, which nearly toppled the throne of Emperor Justinian I in AD 532, was a rowdy free-for-all of rival groups of chariot-racing enthusiasts. Chariot racing – the baseball or football of its day – divided the young men of Constantinople (Byzantium), the capital of the Eastern Roman empire, into two furiously antagonistic camps. After an afternoon spent watching their favorite sport in the city's Hippodrome, heavily bearded fans wearing outlandish "uniforms" and flaunting team colors – blue for one team, green for the other – would wander about in packs, mugging terrorized passers-by, looting, vandalizing, and picking fights with opposition groups.

Rioting of this sort was punishable by death; and it was after one such post-game disturbance, when the authorities were escorting some of the rioters to prison and certain death, that the insurrection began. For once agreeing on a truce, the gangs of blues and greens joined forces to free the condemned men, kill their captors, and break into the city's prison to release its inmates. Sports fans' ranks were later increased by vast numbers of disgruntled citizens, ripe for rebellion because of resentment at heavy taxation and other economic burdens caused by the cost of the constant military adventures and luxurious living of the ruling classes. Within a few days Constantinople was in flames, with furious gangs chanting "*Nika! Nika!*" ("Conquer! Conquer!") as they rampaged their way through the streets. Eventually Justinian and his empress were prisoners in their palace. Resistance to the mob seemed impossible, the emperor's only chance of survival apparently being escape aboard ships that lay in the harbor adjacent to the palace. This was the path the emperor had chosen to follow when the Empress Theodora changed his mind and urged him on to victory.

199

career and that when, as a young man, he discovered he was the illegitimate child of the empress and made himself known to her, he disappeared, never to be seen again. As a firm believer in the Eastern (Orthodox) brand of Christianity, she also sought out and persecuted adherents to the Church of Rome

For her husband and his empire, however, Theodora was probably the best thing that ever happened. In addition to her courage, her political judgment and willpower stood Byzantium in good stead. She built monasteries, orphanages, and hospitals for ordinary people. Significantly, too, she curbed traffic in prostitution by buying many girls from brothels and paying for their

rehabilitation. Under her orders, procuring for prostitution was declared an offense punishable by law. And she constantly urged and inspired Justinian to act in ways that caused some historians to dub him a great ruler.

After Theodora died – in 548, when not quite 50 years old – Justinian the Great ruled for a further 17 years. It is a tribute to the capabilities of the reformed harlot whom he had loved and married that the outstanding achievements of his reign – the Code of Laws, the conquest of North Africa and reconquest of most of Italy, and the construction of Constantinople's magnificent Church of St. Sophia – belong to the days when Theodora shared his throne.

The pilgrimage of Hsuan-Tsang
A medieval folk hero

ALTHOUGH THE splendid civilizations of ancient India and imperial China evolved in relative isolation, with the snow-clad Himalayas as a gigantic natural barrier between them, the two peoples were by no means unaware of each other. There was commercial contact, for example, through arduous overland trails plied by Central Asian nomads, and goods were also exchanged via sea routes. The strongest cultural links, though, were

forged in medieval times not by trade but by religion: Buddhism, which developed from the teachings of the pre-Christian-era Indian seer Siddhartha Gautama, known to his followers as the Buddha (enlightened one).

Knowledge of Buddhism first entered China at the time of Christ. The religion won favor in the imperial court as early as the second century AD; Indian monks then began to filter into China as missionaries, while Chinese pilgrims

A mountainous region in present-day Afghanistan, where intense daytime heat alternates with nights of freezing cold. It was through terrain such as this that Hsuan-Tsang struggled, often alone, in his indomitable resolve to reach the great Buddhist monastery at Nalanda, near Benares, in India. Founded in the fifth century, Nalanda was a magnet for those seeking learning and enlightenment.

made the perilous trek to India to visit holy places and collect sacred texts. Among later Chinese travelers bent on journeying to the fountainhead of their faith and returning to China with renewed spiritual zest, one pilgrim towers above the others as a revered teacher in his own time, and also as an explorer and geographer of importance to future scholars. His name was Hsuan-Tsang, and he was a man of outstanding fortitude, stamina, and charisma – the sort of person whose exploits gave rise to a web of legends from which it is not easy to extricate historical fact.

Born in 602, Hsuan-Tsang was educated in the ancient Chinese tradition of Confucianism, which was more concerned with behavior in the material world than with spiritual matters. Before the age of 20 he was converted to Buddhism, became a monk, and gained swift renown as a learned, virtuous, and indomitable priest. As he grew increasingly aware of the paucity of sacred Buddhist texts in the Chinese language and of apparent contradictions within those that were available, he decided to make his way to India, where he could visit Buddhist centers in order – as he later wrote, in an extensive account of his travels – "to question wise men on points that were troubling my mind."

And so in 629, when he was about 26, he applied for official permission to leave his native land. But because a long delay before such requests could be granted was inevitable in those days when relations between the two countries were strained, he did not wait for an answer. Instead, impatient to be off (an impatience for which he was to apologize to China's emperor long afterward when he had become his country's most eminent priest), he set forth on a solitary journey across desert sands and icy mountain passes that had already spelled death for many well-equipped parties of pilgrims.

It is hard to conceive of a more daunting route than the one that this intrepid traveler chose to follow. He was a tall, handsome man, with a delicate complexion, refined manner, and taste for good living in general and colorful garments in particular. Contemporaries speak of his brilliant eyes and the hypnotic resonance of his voice. Yet this evidently urbane scholar did not flinch at the prospect of leaving his home in northeastern China to walk some 5,000 miles (8,000 kilometers) westward through northern China, across the Gobi Desert, farther westward to Samarkand (now in southern Siberia) via the glacial passes of the Tien Shan range of the Himalayas, then south toward Kabul (now in Afghanistan), and on down to the northwestern

A painting on silk, made in about AD 800, of Hsuan-Tsang equipped as a traveler, with his backpack full of scrolls. On his return to China, he brought with him 75 Buddhist scriptures and a great many sacred images.

part of the Indian sub-continent, still many hundreds of miles away from his goal, the eastern Buddhist center of Nalanda, near Benares.

During the next 16 years, the adventures of the "Master of the Law," as Hsuan-Tsang came to be called, were exciting and varied enough to have made a thrilling series of stories without the need for mythical additions. As he crossed the Gobi Desert (the haunted "moving sands" that sprawl almost endlessly across Central Asia), he nearly succumbed to terrifying mirages of menacing phantom horsemen, and to thirst when forced to do without water for four days and five nights. He came close to losing his life in an avalanche, had to push forward through blistering heat here and constant blizzards there, was attacked by robbers, and was nearly killed by Ganges River pirates. Some of the time, especially at the beginning, he traveled alone, but the strength of his character was such that he attracted followers throughout the pilgrimage.

Though deeply religious and always in quest of religious knowledge, Hsuan-Tsang was also an inquisitive and high-spirited tourist, alert to local color and customs, eager to enjoy but never afraid to criticize whatever he saw. The disregard for cleanliness of some Indian ascetics, for instance, appalled him. Faced with a group of bedraggled self-styled holy men – one smeared with ashes, another naked and covered with sores, a third wearing a wreath of skulls, and a fourth plastered with dung, the fastidious Chinese monk sharply told them that they resembled (respectively) "a cat who had slept in a stove; a withered tree; a vampire in a graveyard; and a pig in a stye."

Eventually, after an extensive period of study at the great Buddhist monastery of Nalanda, Hsuan-Tsang returned to China. In 645, after 16 years' absence, he once more set foot in the imperial capital – but accompanied now by 20 horse-loads of Sanskrit texts and religious relics given to him by Indian Buddhists who were reluctant to let him leave their own shores. His homecoming was triumphant, for his reputation as an intellectual celebrity in a foreign land had preceded him, and the emperor himself wanted to hear about the pilgrim's adventures and observations from his own lips. In fact, Hsuan-Tsang so impressed the emperor that he was offered a government post. But he lacked worldly ambition and preferred to spend the rest of his life writing his memoirs and translating from Sanskrit into Chinese the precious books that he had brought home.

The story of Hsuan-Tsang does not end with his death, which happened in 664. Indeed it is the aftermath that makes the story almost unique in the annals of history: How many other scholar-priests have been posthumously honored by acquiring the legendary status of heroes of folklore to compare with such non-scholarly warrior figures as Alexander the Great or Charlemagne or King Arthur? So many popular tales and fables attached themselves to the memory of Hsuan-Tsang and his travels that they were gathered together in the 16th century and turned into an epic novel, the magically picaresque *Hsi-yu chi* (*Journey to the West*), which is one of the masterpieces of Chinese literature, combining biting satire of human foibles with an authentic sense of spiritual quest – a kind of rambunctious *Pilgrim's Progress*. It is a lasting tribute to the worldly impact of a man whose only ambition was the pursuit of knowledge.

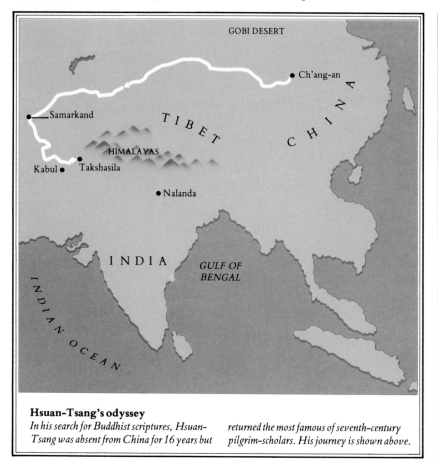

Hsuan-Tsang's odyssey
In his search for Buddhist scriptures, Hsuan-Tsang was absent from China for 16 years but *returned the most famous of seventh-century pilgrim-scholars. His journey is shown above.*

STORM OVER THE GANGES
Hsuan-Tsang's good looks were not always an advantage as he made his way around India. On one occasion the Chinese scholar was captured by river pirates while traveling down the Ganges with a party of companions.

The pirates worshiped the goddess Durga and customarily appeased her with the sacrifice of an especially handsome young man when they could find one. Hsuan-Tsang was obviously a fit dish for the voracious goddess. No amount of pleading by his companions could sway the robbers from their course. They dragged the scholar to a rough earthen altar on a bank of the river and forced him to lie down at the point of a sword. Concentrating his mind on thoughts of the Buddha's paradise, Hsuan-Tsang went into deep meditation.

Suddenly a storm blew up, and waves capsized some of the pirates' boats moored along the shore. The robbers were seized with superstitious awe. "Where does this man come from?" they asked. Hsuan-Tsang's companions explained that he was a famous monk who had come from China to search for Buddha's Law. To kill him, they added, would be an unmitigated crime – as the heavens themselves had indicated by sending down this sudden storm. The frightened robbers released the scholar with profuse apologies and promised to mend their ways in the future.

The Vikings: Destroyers or creators?

Paradox and bloodshed

A Viking warrior's helmet, discovered in Sweden and probably made sometime during the seventh century.

"FROM THE wrath of the Northmen, O Lord deliver us!" From over 1,000 churches, abbeys, and monasteries the cry went up as Viking raids spread over Europe in a great arc from Hamburg in Germany to Bordeaux in France. The terrifying Viking bands appeared at the end of the eighth century, and the savage northerners' long, low ships, with their red dragon prows, were seen sliding swiftly up rivers and estuaries, sailing around headlands, bringing fire, rape, and pillage far inland. In 793 the monastery of Lindisfarne, off the northeastern coast of England, was sacked, its monks slaughtered, its holy treasures stolen. Two years later the Vikings had reached the coast of Ireland near Dublin, by 799 the west coast of France. And the raids worsened in the next century. The annals of St. Bertin Abbey near Rouen in northern France describe the "Danish pirates" in 841 as "carrying everywhere a fury of rapine, fire, and sword"; and a French monk's account of the Danes' siege of Paris in 885 calls the Vikings "wild beasts going by horse

and foot through hill and field . . . killing babies, children, young men, old men, fathers, sons, and mothers. . . They ravage, they despoil, they destroy, they burn. . ." In other words, they were not the sort of people you'd want to meet.

But consider the fact that all the above reports come from *victims* of the attacks – in fact, from churchmen, the only Europeans who could read or write in those days. Even when describing victories over the Vikings, they tend to exaggerate their opponents' numbers and ferocity; when dealing with the sack of churches, no words could be too black. To get a fairer picture, should we not also read some Viking documents? Unfortunately there are none, since the Vikings were not at that time literate. Instead, we must rely for our fairer picture on archeology and on such third-party – mainly Arab – accounts as there are. Then a rather different picture emerges.

True enough, the Vikings did pillage and destroy, especially churches and monasteries. From their pagan point of view, the Christians

---

LIFE AT HOME WITH THE VIKINGS

"Never have I seen people of more perfect physique; they are tall as date palms and reddish in color," wrote Ibn Faldan, the Arab ambassador from the Caliphate of Baghdad on a mission to the "Rus" – that is, the Vikings in the East – in AD 922. His is a rare first-hand report of what the Vikings were like from a civilized but impartial observer. He found them physically impressive but dirty. The report continues:

"They are the filthiest of God's creatures. They do not wash after discharging their natural functions, neither do they wash their hands after meals. They are as stray donkeys. . . . Ten or 20 of them may live together in one house, and each man has a couch of his own where he sits and diverts himself with the pretty slave girls whom he has brought along to offer for sale. He will make love with one of them in the presence of his comrades. Sometimes this develops into a communal orgy. Every day they wash their face and hands in the same water. . . . A girl brings her master a huge bowl of water in which he washes his face, hands, and hair, combing it out also over the bowl. Then he blows his nose and spits into the water. When he has finished, the girl takes the same bowl to his neighbor, who repeats the performance – until the bowl has gone around the entire household."

They were a pretty rough lot, those Vikings in Russia. But they had their sensitive side. Ibn Faldan goes on to describe the cremation of a

Viking chief: how the dead leader's body was placed in a special ship covered with silk brocades, how an older woman called the Angel of Death supervised the ceremonies, how one of the chief's slave-women who volunteered to die with her master was taken into a special tent and stabbed by the old woman – while, outside, the men banged on their shields to drown the slave's cries – and so to the final firing of the ship, with the girl's body burning besides her master's on its brief journey to Valhalla, the Viking heaven.

Twenty or thirty years later, another Arab traveler, the geographer Ibn Rusteh, painted a somewhat more positive word-picture of the Vikings. "They wear exquisite clothes," he writes. "They respect their guests and are hospitable and friendly to strangers. But if one of them is challenged to battle, they stick together as one man until victory has been achieved." Ibn Rusteh had his criticisms too, however: "There is little security among them and much deceit; even a man's brother or comrade is not above killing and plundering him if he can." Both writers agree on the quarrelsome nature of the Nordics and comment on their extortion of tribute from nearby Slav villages.

So, it seems, the Vikings were not a lovable people. Vigorous, enterprising, aggressive? They were certainly all of these things. Only not much fun to live with.

must have appeared unbelievably stupid, cramming their churches with gold and silver ornaments, and leaving them undefended except by the monks and priests. Such rich pickings were obvious targets, as were unfortified towns or villages. But the Vikings did not just leave smoking ruins wherever they went before passing on to fresh pastures for plunder. They were builders as well as destroyers. However, Viking raiders had burst upon an astonished and terrified Europe with such rapacity that the image of the Norse warrior pirate has become a popular stereotype. The Vikings are less well known as a great trading people whose cargo boats exploited the waterways of Europe from Greenland to the Caspian Sea, and they used their new, if illegal, wealth to buy ships in which to carry on trade with far-off countries, or to move their families to settle in lands more fertile than thin-soiled Scandinavia.

Take the case of a Dane named Rorik, who, after repeatedly sacking the port of Dorestad at the mouth of the Rhine, eventually settled down there and became a prosperous merchant. Others were more adventurous, venturing much farther, and founding trading posts that grew into great cities such as Dublin in Ireland and Kiev in Russia. Though the Vikings usually came to raid, they often stayed to trade, for the same river and sea routes that opened up a land to pirates also opened it to merchants. Scandinavian trade was already flourishing in Roman times. Furs, cattle, dairy produce, and Baltic amber were exchanged for luxury goods from the south. There are few historical sources for the succeeding centuries, but evidence of costly ship-burials and treasure hoards tells us that while much of Europe was in turmoil, the Scandinavian peoples continued to trade and grow rich, outside the mainstream of events.

By the 10th century the raids were more or less over and the Vikings had become colonists. In 911, for instance, they were granted the area of France since known as Normandy, where they soon adopted not only the language but the religion of their French neighbors. The Duke of Normandy became one of the most powerful rulers in Europe, and his Christian soldiers conquered the whole of England in 1066 and, a few years later, all of southern Italy and Sicily. Farther north, the Norwegians sailed out beyond the paths of earlier voyagers, who had hugged the

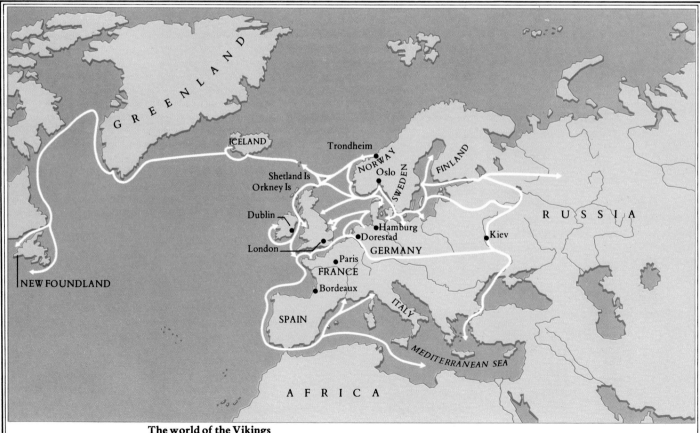

The world of the Vikings
The Vikings were able to travel great distances in their long ships, which were designed and built to be strong enough to cope with the roughest of seas yet light enough to be both fast and maneuverable. The Vikings reached Newfoundland via Iceland and Greenland, and may even have discovered the North American coast, many years before Columbus.

coasts in terror of the deep oceans. With neither compasses nor maps and with single-sailed boats no more than 50 to 70 feet (16 to 23 meters) long, the Vikings daringly explored over vast stretches of unknown water.

On hitherto deserted Iceland they founded a republic of fishermen and farmers, with a unique assembly in which all free men could vote and speak. This, the first democracy the world had seen since ancient Greece, still survives, a living tribute to the productive rather than destructive genius of the Vikings. Farther west loomed a larger, even colder island than Iceland. It was discovered in 982 by a Norwegian called Erik the Red, who – optimistically – named it Greenland. When, a few years later, Erik's son Leif reached a land he called Vinland, which was probably Newfoundland, he too tried to colonize it. His efforts foundered; but, had they succeeded, the discovery of America might have been attributed to a Viking not an Italian.

There is a grave near Fittja in eastern Sweden that once held the remains of a Viking trader (or raider; like many Vikings, he was probably both). When archeologists opened it up, they found dramatic evidence of the full reach of Viking trade: silver pieces from Córdoba in southern Spain, from Egypt and Syria, from Baghdad, and even from as far east as the city of Tashkent in Central Asia.

Viking warriors usually wore full armor to protect the head and torso. Less vulnerable parts were guarded to some extent by thick leather, and each man carried a shield, as well as an ax or a heavy sword.

A knorr: Cargo vessel of the Vikings

The Vikings of the ninth and 10th centuries skillfully navigated both inland waterways and the open sea in search of trade, bartering their native products for such luxury goods as Arab silver and Chinese silk. They also established settlements, and many, such as those on Greenland, depended on regular supplies for their survival. For these voyages, the Vikings developed a hardy sea-going trading vessel known as the "knorr," as well as a smaller, lighter version for use on inland waterways.

We know about these knorrs from the remains of five such boats raised from the bottom of the Roskilde Fjord in Denmark, where they had been deliberately sunk in the early 11th century to form a barrier to protect the town of Roskilde from a sea attack. Knorrs were built for capacity rather than speed, and were deeper and broader than the faster, fighting longships, but they shared their distinctive construction. At either end rose a deep, slightly curved keel to form symmetrical prow and stern posts. The hull was clinker built, (the lower edge of each plank overlapping the one below), and inner ribs were attached to the planking, but not to the keel, producing a flexible structure which rode the sea rather than butting against it. Cross beams for reinforcement supported the decking, or served as rowing benches, and gave the knorr its distinctive strength and resilience despite its light weight and shallow draft. The use of oars supplemented the wind power of the sail, and the boat was steered by an oar-shaped rudder lashed to the starboard (righthand) quarter through the planking, and pivoted on a shaft. In some cases, to improve the steerage and lessen drift, the keel was extended fore and aft.

Despite their sea-going capacity, knorrs were basically open boats, with decking in the prow and stern only, so cargo, crew, passengers, and rations for the journey, were exposed to the elements. Few crew were needed: just enough to manage the sail, steer the boat, keep a lookout, and bail out the water.

The long distances traveled by the Vikings show that they must have been skilled navigators. Though they possessed neither compass nor accurate timepiece, nor any knowledge of longitude, they could follow a course for several days without sight of land. Using their knowledge of latitude judged by the sun and stars they would sail to the nearest parallel and then follow this course until landfall.

For 300 years these resilient traders dominated the seas until succeeded by the bulkier, slower-moving "cog." But the Viking methods of shipbuilding lived on in many of the countries visited by these fearless seafarers, and still survive in parts of Norway.

Viking shipbuilders were skilled at building knorrs, using a range of tools, of which the ax was their favorite even for fine work. Oak was the preferred timber, the logs being split radially to produce strong wedge-shaped planks of uniform breadth. Naturally curved timbers were used, and those not needed were stored under water to keep them supple.

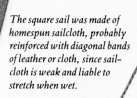

The square sail was made of homespun sailcloth, probably reinforced with diagonal bands of leather or cloth, since sail-cloth is weak and liable to stretch when wet.

Viking "Solskuggafjol," or floating sundial.

Bearing dial, used for determining the ship's position against the sun or stars.

Anchor

Oar

Rigging block (at left) and tackle (at far left) used for sail setting.

Wooden flaps were used to cover the oar-holes when the oars were withdrawn, to prevent an inrush of water as the ship heeled, but spray and leaking at the seams must always have been a problem.

Making the most of horsepower
Hauling Europe out of the Dark Ages

A modern harness has a padded collar supporting rigid wooden or metal hames, to which traces are attached. This arrangement does not interfere with a horse's breathing or circulation, and allows it to put its full weight into pulling, unlike earlier harnesses, which throttled both windpipe and jugular vein.

SOMETIME AROUND the year AD 500, a camel driver in China, whose name we shall never know, came up with an invention that transformed the lives of millions of people, from the steppes of Siberia all the way across Europe and beyond. The invention led to a revolution in agriculture and methods of warfare. It opened up new patterns of trade, travel, and domestic organization. Yet it could hardly have been more simple. It was a horse collar.

Of course horses – like the camels for which the collar was originally designed – had already been in harness for thousands of years, but it was not until the introduction of a rigid, padded collar, properly fitted to the shoulders, so as to protect the neck, that their capacity as beasts of burden could be fully exploited. Always before they had been harnessed with a soft collar around the neck which pulled tight when they began to move and pressed down on the windpipe and jugular vein. To avoid being throttled, they had to throw back their heads in a way that looked supremely attractive, as shown in classical art, but was so inefficient that horses in ancient times were never able to draw a plow, and thus could not make a significant contribution to agriculture.

With the coming of the hard horse collar things began to change. It has been calculated that a team of horses wearing the horse collar can pull a load four or five times heavier than their ancient counterparts could. In the long run, the

A HORSEMAN IN SEARCH OF THE PAST

Historians might never have realized the importance of the invention of rigid horse collars without the work of a retired French soldier, Richard Lefebvre des Noëttes, who loved horses. As a cavalry officer, Lefebvre des Noëttes had worked with horses every day, sleeping alongside them on maneuvers and always concerned with their welfare. This lifelong fascination led him to research a book on the history of harnessing, a task that occupied him on and off for over 20 years until the book's eventual publication in 1931.

In particular, Lefebvre des Noëttes was puzzled by a Roman law that laid down severe punishment for anyone harnessing a pair of horses to a load in excess of 500 kilograms, scarcely more than half a ton. By modern standards, 500 kilos was no load at all for a pair of horses. Moreover, Lefebvre des Noëttes had noticed that the horses in Greek and Roman sculptures always had unnaturally arched necks. Determined to find out why, he conducted a series of experiments with a pair of horses harnessed as shown in classical monuments, with a noose around the windpipe, and he quickly discovered that 500 kilos was indeed as much as they could pull without choking. The conclusion was obvious. With all their achievements, the ancient Greeks and Romans had never learned how to utilize ordinary horsepower!

These stirring steeds, depicted in a frieze from the Parthenon, prance along, heads thrown back, just as heroic horses should – or did when the savage curb bits of the time forced them to.

effect of horsepower on agricultural economics was enormous. Horses did not immediately replace oxen at the plows largely because the upkeep of horses was more costly than that of oxen. But horses did play an increasingly important role after the eighth century, when the hard collar made its first appearance in Europe. And by the 11th century, many European farms must have had horses at work in their fields. Our earliest pictured representation of such activity appears in the border of the famous Bayeux Tapestry, which was woven sometime around 1080; and there is a slightly later tapestry in the cathedral at Gerona, Spain, which shows a team pulling a heavy-wheeled plow. Horse-drawn plows had become the tractors of their day.

The 12th century and the first half of the 13th witnessed what was essentially a revolution in European agriculture, as food yields were raised to levels not surpassed for another 500 years. The revolution was based on improvements in husbandry, together with better-designed plows and a method of rotating crops over three fields instead of two. But none of this could have happened – the agricultural revolution could not have begun – without the invention of the humble horse collar.

In war, too, medieval commanders were able to revise their strategy in favor of heavier loads pulled by pack animals. Trade flourished with larger wagons and, later, canal boats, and long-distance travel by carriage became a realistic possibility. The most profound effect, though, was on the domestic life of the peasant farmer. In the old days peasants had lived next to their fields in hamlets of no more than four or five houses. Now they were free to live in larger villages, traveling to work each day by cart and returning at night to the safety of a larger bustling and fortified community. They had never heard of that anonymous camel driver, but they were enormously indebted to him.

Charlemagne: Emperor of the Romans
The man and the myth

ON CHRISTMAS DAY in AD 800, the great Basilica of old Saint Peter's in Rome, the holiest church of Christendom which traditionally was said to have been built by the Emperor Constantine some 500 years earlier, was thronged with Romans, Lombards, Bavarians, and above all, Franks whose empire then included the Eternal City of Rome itself. By the high altar knelt the lord of all these people, King Charlemagne, who was dressed in a long tunic with a gold belt and jeweled sandals. As he rose from prayer, Pope Leo III lifted a golden crown from the altar and placed it on the king's head. The entire assembly roared out: "Long life and victory to Charles Augustus, crowned by God, the great and peace-giving emperor of the Romans." Charlemagne rose an emperor, the first in Western Europe since the deposition of the last Roman emperor in 476, and the founder of a great empire that was to last for the next 1,000 years.

Like the legendary King Arthur, Charlemagne attracted around himself an aura of myth and legend as a hero, poet, soldier, and statesman. The epic poem *The Song of Roland*, an anonymous work that celebrated his deeds, depicts him as the doughty defender of Christendom against infidels. However, for many years it was widely believed that he was an illiterate man who, even in old age, continued to struggle without success to teach himself to read and write, a landowner interested in farming his estates and preoccupied with war who scarcely deserved the title of Roman emperor. What then was the truth about Charlemagne?

The charge of illiteracy arose from a misunderstanding of a passage in a biography of Charlemagne written by the Frankish historian Einhard, or Eginhard (770–840). This Latin work, entitled *Vita Caroli Magni*, recorded how Charlemagne kept a slate and copybook under his pillow to practice writing. But, Einhard wrote, "he did not get very far because he had begun so late in life." In fact Charlemagne could certainly read a little, and could write well enough for everyday purposes, although he often dictated letters to his clerks. What he could not master was the Carolingian minuscule script, a clear, manageable form of calligraphy fostered by the English scholar Alcuin of York (735–804) in order to promote Charlemagne's program of educational reform. The script was eventually superseded by the Gothic script, but its revival in the Italian Renaissance had such an influence on the new printing trade that it became the basis of modern typography.

This anonymous portrait of Charlemagne in the Uffizi Museum, Florence, shows how the first Holy Roman Emperor must have looked at the stage of his life when he tried to learn to write in the new Carolingian script that was named after him.

Charlemagne is crowned as emperor by the pope in St. Peter's, Rome, on Christmas Day, 800. The impressive ceremony, as depicted in this 15th-century illustration, was calculated to evoke memories of the great Western Empire of the long-dead Caesars, but many tribes – notably the warlike Saxons – were not impressed.

The elegant Carolingian script was only one of the accomplishments of Alcuin, the most brilliant of the international circle of scholars, poets, and artists gathered around the imperial court at Aachen, where Charlemagne's new palace was itself considered a wonder of the age, with its octagonal chapel inspired by Roman models, its great reception hall 160 feet (49 meters) long, its library, and its swimming pool filled with warm water from thermal springs. Here Charlemagne presided over what has been called a "Carolingian Renaissance." He encouraged the copying of precious manuscripts without which much later scholarship would have been impossible, and he also sought to restore literary standards which had been declining since the collapse of the Roman empire. One of his first acts as king was to order the establishment of cathedral schools to improve the generally poor standards of education among the clergy.

What then of his achievements as a soldier and diplomat? Charlemagne was 26 years old when

he became joint King of the Franks in 768. At first he ruled with his younger brother Carloman, but after Carloman's death in 771, Charles, soon to be known as Charles the Great (or Charlemagne as his Latin name was later pronounced by the French), began to enlarge his kingdom. At the start of his reign, his kingdom embraced modern France, Belgium, Switzerland, and parts of western Germany and Holland. By 814 he handed over to his son an empire that also included Austria, Saxony, Bavaria, modern Hungary, northern and central Italy, and northern Spain.

An excellent diplomat as well as general, Charlemagne knew when the threat of force was as effective as its use. For example, when he decided in 788 to crush the unruly Duke Tassilo of Bavaria, he first asked the pope to denounce the duke, which was excellent propaganda. He then mustered such overwhelmingly large armies on all sides that the Bavarians surrendered without a fight. Similarly, when he attacked the

THE FIRST REICH

The coronation of Charlemagne in AD 800 marked the birth of an empire that lasted, in name at least, for more than 1,000 years.

In Charlemagne's day the position of the emperor carried with it the concept of a universal rule over all Latin Christendom because Charlemagne had ruled most of Western Europe. Later emperors were not so powerful; indeed the empire nearly collapsed 100 years after Charlemagne. But it was restored in 962 when Otto I, was crowned emperor in Rome. From this time the empire's crown nearly always adorned the heads of German rulers, and its lands were centered on what is now Germany and the Low Countries and northern Italy. It never again included France, the country that had been the heartland of Charlemagne's empire.

By the 13th century, the emperor was known as the "Holy Roman Emperor," "Roman" because he claimed to be reviving the classical Roman empire, and "Holy" in order to emphasize the sacredness of his majesty. Some emperors claimed to be universal rulers like the ancient Romans, and this led to many disagreements with the popes in Rome. The popes welcomed a distant protector who could be summoned in times of need. But, on the other hand, they did not want a strong king who would interfere with their administration of the Church.

Through the centuries, the Holy Roman Empire became little more than a name. Even in Germany, the emperor found it difficult to make his powers effective outside his own family lands. By the 18th century, the French satirist Voltaire mocked it for being "neither Holy nor Roman nor an Empire." Hence, when Napoleon, who had crowned himself Emperor of the French and did not want rivals, forced the Holy Roman Emperor Francis II to abandon his title in 1806, the end of the empire had little practical effect or impact in Europe.

The thousand-year "Reich" (a German word meaning "empire") was at an end, but the dream of a European empire the size of Charlemagne's lived on. The Second Reich, the Prussian-led German empire founded in 1871, collapsed with Germany's defeat at the end of World War I in 1918. The so-called Third Reich inspired by Hitler lasted for only 12 years, despite his boast that this Nazi Reich would last for 1,000 years – a 20th-century echo of Charlemagne's empire.

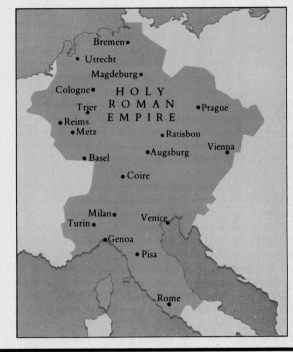

Otto I, the first of many German emperors, inherited Charlemagne's title of Holy Roman Emperor in 962. There was less justification for Otto's pomp and circumstance, however, because although his "empire" (shown at left) extended farther east, it was far smaller than that of his illustrious predecessor. France no longer belonged to the Holy Roman Empire, and the domain that remained would never again enjoy the stability of Charlemagne's reign.

Avars, a nomadic tribe in Hungary who had grown rich by robbing their neighbors, he made an alliance with the surrounding Slav tribes and attracted many to join the fight by promise of booty. As a result, he was able to call on what were, for the time, enormous fighting resources of up to 60,000 men.

Plunder, in fact, was the cause of the defeat Charlemagne suffered at Roncesvalles, which was recorded in *The Song of Roland*. When he had invaded Spain in 778, he did so believing that its Arab rulers were divided and that their Christian subjects would rise to welcome him. He was misled on both scores. The Muslims were united and stopped him from capturing the city of Saragossa, while the Christians were uninterested in Frankish liberation. On their return through a pass at Roncesvalles in the Pyrenees, the Franks' baggage train, laden with booty, was ambushed by Christian Basques, not Muslims. All the Franks guarding it were killed, including Charlemagne's nephew, the Roland of the poem's title. According to legend, Charlemagne, after weeping on the battlefield, led an avenging expedition in person. In fact he never entered Spain again, although his counts captured a strip of land around Barcelona by 801.

Despite the defeat at Roncesvalles, in reality only a minor skirmish, there is no doubt that Charlemagne towered above his contemporaries. His achievements are all the more impressive because they were based on insecure finances, attempts to improve his empire's revenues being a major factor behind the interest that he took in farming.

Charlemagne's successors divided the empire between them in bitter civil wars, and allowed Vikings to raid far into the heartlands of the empire. Charlemagne's fame survived the breakup of his empire although the reality described by Einhard – of a good general, skillful politician, and patron of the arts and scholarship – was later obscured by the romantic image fostered by succeeding generations.

The Arabian Nights

High life in Baghdad

ONCE UPON A TIME, as all best-loved stories start, there lived a king who had become disillusioned with marriage. He was so afraid of his wife's possible infidelity that he decided to marry a new wife each night, and have her killed in the morning before she could betray his love. Shahrazada was the unlucky girl selected one night, but, anxious to save her life, she told the king a story that was not finished when morning came. The king wanted to hear

An illustration by Edmund Dulac (1882–1953) for "The Story of the Magic Horse" in an edition of The Arabian Nights Entertainments *retold by Laurence Housman.*

the end of Shahrazada's tale, and so spared her life for another night. On the next night she finished the first story and was halfway through another when morning came, so the king spared her life yet again.

And so it went on night after night for 1001 nights. The tales that Shahrazada is said to have told the king – a collection of fairy tales and love stories – have been passed down from generation to generation, told and retold a million times by people who have thrilled to the adventures related in the tales of *The Thousand and One Nights* (or *The Arabian Nights Entertainments*), the world's best-known work of Arab literature.

But the tales of the *Arabian Nights* are not purely works of invention, figments of a fertile imagination. They are based on a real place, with recognizable people appearing in the stories. For once, fact is stranger than fiction: The world of the *Arabian Nights* is the world of medieval Baghdad, founded in 762 by the Muslim Abbasid dynasty as the capital of an Islamic kingdom that stretched from Egypt to India. Its ruler, Harun ar-Rashid, was the fifth Abbasid caliph, and the most powerful man of his day, a romantic hero whose glittering reign (786–809) is the subject of so many of the *Arabian Nights* tales. Harun was a connoisseur of music and poetry, a generous patron of the arts. The tales in which he appears portray him as the ideal ruler: just, honorable, and generous: disguised and accompanied by a few close friends, he rambled around Baghdad at night, championing the oppressed and punishing rogues and cheats. Some of the more scurrilous tales, it is true, represent Baghdad's ruler as a drunkard. Since the Koran expressly forbids alcohol, this would have been scandalous, and therefore unlikely, behavior for a devout caliph.

The city he ruled over provides the setting for many of the tales. Baghdad was a rich city, soaking up the mercantile wealth of the East. It was said to be so rich that you would be as unlikely to find a poor man in Baghdad as a Koran in the house of an atheist. Baghdad's leading men, still more their many wives, enjoyed the high life. They competed among themselves in conspicuous consumption, building luxurious houses, and sponsoring lavish entertainments. In his vast Golden Palace, the caliph presided over a court life that was polished, opulent, and fabulously rich. Theologians, scholars, and philosophers catered for the intellect, while bards, jesters, and singing girls catered for the emotions.

The slave trade in Baghdad was a thriving industry, and gifted slave girls went through a rigorous physical and intellectual training before being put on the luxury slave market. Vocal music was encouraged, and royal concubines whose skill of voice and verse charmed the heart of the caliph might hope to emerge from the seclusion of the harem into prominence. Harun's redoubtable mother, Khayzuran, who dominated affairs of state until her death in 789, started her career as a slave girl. His most important wife, an Arab princess by the name of Zubaydah, was also a forceful personality, dazzling the court with her style and grace, and eating only from gold and silver dishes that were studded with gems.

But life in Harun's Baghdad was not all pleasure, and Harun not always the munificent benefactor of entertainment and enjoyment. Despite his impressive gifts and winning personality, he was also capricious, at times cruel, small-minded, and vindictive.

This darker side of his character is illustrated by the tragic fate of the celebrated Barmakid family. Muslim, but Persian rather than Arab, the Barmakids had been the devoted administrators and counselors of the Abbasids for three generations. They ran the caliphate and their personal wealth was at the disposal of Harun's extravagant court. But Arab oil and Persian water would not mix, and in 803 Harun turned against his trusting and trusted servants, and had Jafar Barmakid, for long his companion at private parties and court festivities, murdered. While Jafar's corpse was displayed on a Baghdad bridge, the rest of his family were imprisoned and their goods confiscated. Contemporaries suggested that Harun's wrath had been provoked by a love affair between Jafar and the caliph's own sister Abbasah, and even alleged that in his fury Harun had Abbasah buried alive. Quite what provoked this revenge will never be known, but it probably owes much to Harun's resentment at Barmakid influence over affairs of state, and to feuds between his Persian subjects – who tolerated Jews and Christians – and his more orthodox Arab subjects. The queen mother, Khayzuran, the Persians' most important champion at court, was dead, and the caliph's favorite wife, the haughty Zubaydah, is said to have despised them. Whatever else the court of Harun was, it was obviously a hotbed of jealousy and intrigue.

After the disgrace of the Barmakids, Harun's reign was troubled. Faced with internal revolt and racial conflict, the caliph attempted to solve his problems by dividing his state between two of his sons, one a pure-blooded Arab, the other the son of a Persian slave woman. But this division only institutionalized the rifts, and Harun, for all his many gifts, was no able administrator. Without the Barmakids to help him, his empire crumbled. When he died in 809, the civil war that had been brewing broke out almost immediately, and the authority of the Abbasid caliphs was soon diminished.

But reminders of the brilliant Islamic culture presided over by Harun are to be found in the art and architecture of his reign that still survive in the modern Islamic world. It is therefore appropriate that those he treated best – the poets and storytellers who entertained his court – should have rewarded their generous patron and his glittering city of Baghdad with immortality in the tales of the *Arabian Nights*.

Harun ar-Rashid, the Caliph of Baghdad, appeared in other works of Islamic literature as well as in the Arabian Nights. *In this scene from the poem "Harun ar-Rashid and the Barber" by the 12th-century Persian poet Nizami, Harun notices that, while cutting his master's hair, the barber never moves from one spot. Harun has the floor removed and discovers treasure lying beneath it.*

Sindbad the sailor

Tall tales rooted in fact

THE RIGGING snapped in the wind, the sails filled, and the boat heeled over and surged out to sea. This was no ordinary boat; it was an exact replica of an eighth-century Arab *boom*, built from 140 tons of hardwood dragged by elephants from the forests behind India's Malabar coast. The boat was 87 feet (28 meters) long and its 60-foot (18 meters) mainmast and 75-foot (22 meters) main spar had each been cut by hand from a single tree trunk. And, because medieval Arab shipwrights used no iron in the construction of their ships, since iron was a scarce commodity, and nails tended to crack the timbers, not a single nail had been used in the construction of this 20th-century vessel. Instead, 20,000 holes had been drilled by hand in its planks and ribs, which were meticulously stitched together with around 400 miles (650 kilometers) of rope made from coconut fibers.

On just such a boat Sindbad the Sailor – the legendary merchant whose seven voyages are recorded among the 1,001 tales of *The Arabian Nights*–would have set sail from Baghdad and Basrah (in present-day Iraq) on his search for adventure and profit. On just such a boat he would have traveled to the valley of the rocs, giant birds big enough to swallow elephants whole, or to the home of the terrifying Old Man of the Sea, and to all the other strange, wonderful – and, of course, fictitious – places described in the great storybook.

But this time the crew were not characters in a tale. The boat, which was built on the shores of the Persian Gulf, crewed by Arabs from the Sultanate of Oman, and named *Sohar* (after

Sindbad's supposed birthplace), set sail on a November day in 1980. It was under the command of Tim Severin, an Englishman who has made a specialty of testing theories about the factual background of ancient legends.

Three years earlier, Severin had sailed a 36-foot (11 meters) boat made of wood and leather from Ireland to Newfoundland, thereby proving that St. Brendan, a sixth-century Irish monk, *could* have used a similar boat to visit North America nearly 1,000 years before Columbus. Now, in the belief that the fictional exploits of Sindbad were probably based on actual experiences of Arab seafarers between the eighth and 11th centuries, he had re-created another vessel from the past, intending to penetrate to the far side of Asia. Along the way, he was determined to look at that part of the world with the eyes of a medieval sailor who might have brought back accounts of adventures that could conceivably have been exaggerated into Sindbad's magic marvels.

Despite pests that infest sailing vessels, corrosive salt, heat, and tropical storms, the handstitched *Sohar* survived over seven months at sea, covering 6,000 miles (over 9,000 kilometers) from Oman to the fabled Chinese port of Guangzhou (Canton). The ancient shipbuilding techniques that Severin had followed for constructing his boat seemed to work better than some more modern methods. The hull, for instance, was protected on the outside with a waterproof mixture of simple tree gum and lime, and on the inside the coconut ropes were preserved simply by being swabbed with vegetable oil. The result: Even the voracious teredo worms, which, by chewing their way through the toughest planks, have been the bane of later tropical explorers, did no significant damage to *Sohar*'s hull. And the voyage served its main purpose very well, for Severin managed to track down some titillating links between the Sindbad tales and the real world.

In the seventh voyage, for instance, Sindbad – sold into slavery by pirates – is sent by an ivory dealer into a forest where he discovers an elephants' graveyard. Even today, no one knows exactly what happens to dead and dying elephants, as very few carcasses are ever found – despite one unconfirmed report of an elephant having been seen carrying the bones of another to an undiscovered destination. So it does seem

In this scene from The Arabian Nights Entertainments, *the intrepid Sindbad is being carried off to a valley of diamonds by a ferocious roc – a mythical bird capable of swallowing elephants whole.*

possible that the animals have a special communal graveyard and that knowledge of its existence, if not of its exact location, was the foundation for this Sindbad tale.

In another tale, Sindbad goes to a far-away land that has been identified as Sri Lanka (formerly called Ceylon, but known to the Arabs as Serendib, the place-name from which we get the English word "serendipity," meaning "the knack of chancing upon pleasant things without looking for them"). Here he finds a valley of diamonds; they are guarded by deadly snakes, but he manages to escape with his pockets stuffed full of gems. Although diamonds are no longer mined in modern Sri Lanka, the island is richly supplied with a variety of other valuable stones, such as sapphires and rubies.

Just as in the Sindbad story, these are mined from alluvial beds on valley floors, and miners' pits – cool, damp refuges from tropical heat – often become the lairs of snakes. Moreover, the gem trade, Severin found, is still largely controlled by Muslims, whose faith was brought to Sri Lanka by Arab sailors in the seventh century.

During another voyage, Sindbad is buried alive (only temporarily, of course) with his dead wife on what is called the Island of Women – a reversal of the once-common Indian practice of *suttee*, in which a widow was expected to throw herself onto her husband's funeral pyre. Severin believes that inspiration for this highly unusual situation almost certainly came from Arab sailors' observations of funerary customs on Minicoy, a tiny island near the Laccadives off India's west coast, which was once dominated by a strongly matriarchal culture.

Two of the most famous Sindbad legends – the stories of the Old Man of the Sea and the Island of Cannibals – may well have stemmed from medieval sailors' experiences on Sumatra,

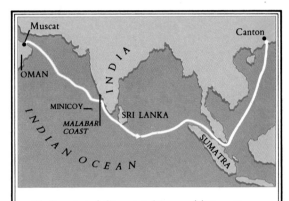

Tim Severin took this route in his successful attempt to prove that sailors of Sindbad's day could have crossed the Indian Ocean to China.

Tim Severin's craft Sohar was constructed using only the materials and skills that would have been available to medieval Arab mariners. The vessel was stitched together with coconut cord made from the husks of coconuts rotted in seawater and then spun by hand, giving it a life expectancy more than five times that of a nailed ship. The mainmast was made from a single tree trunk.

the jagged, blade-shaped island that lies alongside the west coast of the Malay Peninsula. In the Old Man of the Sea episode, Sindbad, who has been shipwrecked, comes across a hairy, leaf-covered creature sitting by a stream. Assuming that the creature is an old man, Sindbad compassionately helps it to cross the stream by carrying it upon his shoulders; but when they reach the far side, the creature – which never speaks, merely gesturing and grunting – refuses to dismount. It tightens its legs around Sindbad's neck until the merchant nearly faints, then rides him like a beast of burden, choking and beating him into submission while it feeds on fruit from the trees. Sindbad eventually notices the rough black skin of its legs and realizes that his tormentor *is* a beast, not an old man. Escape becomes possible only after several weeks, when Sindbad tricks his captor into drinking fermented fruit

juice and kills it when it becomes tipsy. Severin points out that the image of the Old Man of the Sea corresponds closely to a description of the orang-utan, a highly intelligent ape that is native to Sumatra. The orang-utan resembles a wizened old man, has rough black skin on its legs and lives on fruit. In addition, although biologists regard the orang-utan as a timid creature, many Sumatran people in remote forest villages still fear the animal, believing it to be an extremely dangerous form of human being.

The second episode that Severin associates with Sumatra occurs when Sindbad and his crew are cast away on a strange island where they are taken to a village of apparently hospitable natives and lavishly feasted. Only Sindbad himself, suspicious of such generosity, refuses to eat – and so realizes that the food is drugged as he watches his companions sink into stupefaction.

HOW THE ARABS FOUND THEIR WAY

Medieval Arab sailors used a wooden kamal *to ascertain position by holding its bottom edge in line with the horizon and the knotted cord (each knot represents a harbor) in the teeth to secure the rectangle at the correct distance. If the North Star appears in position A, the desired harbor's latitude is to the south; if in position C, to the north; if in position B, ship and harbor are in the same latitude.*

Under the clear skies of the tropical oceans that early Arab sailors crossed, they navigated largely by the stars – so much so that modern Arab seafarers still commonly identify directions by the names of stars rather than compass points. They had no way of measuring longitude, but since the

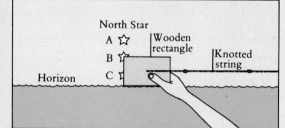

coastlines they traded along – eastern Africa, India, and Southeast Asia – ran roughly north and south, they had no great need to know how far east or west they were at most times. What they did need, and what they had, was a device for measuring latitude in order to know whether to sail north or south along the coast to a given port. It was quite easy for them to identify which coast they were on, since, as master mariners, they were familiar with the general appearance of all the coasts that lay along their trade routes.

The Arabs' latitude-measuring device was a kind of sextant known as a *kamal*. Though so simple that Tim Severin was able to make one easily when, in 1980–81, he duplicated the conditions and route of a lengthy medieval Arab voyage, the *kamal* proved to be sufficiently precise to permit him to judge his boat's position to within 30 miles (48 kilometers) – a tiny margin of error in the vast Indian Ocean, and one that would be unlikely to cause difficulties. A *kamal* consisted of nothing more than a wooden rectangle attached to a knotted string, with each knot representing the latitude of a known port. By holding the appropriate knot between his teeth, the navigator could set the rectangular *kamal* at the right distance from his eyes for judging his position relative to that port. All he had to do was to take a sighting on the North Star (Polaris) with the rectangle's bottom edge in line with the horizon.

The North Star's height above the horizon is a constant factor at every latitude. At the North Pole it is directly overhead, and at the equator it is just barely visible on the horizon. So if the star was higher than the top of his *kamal*, the Arab navigator knew that his boat was too far north for the desired port; if the star was lower than the top of the *kamal*, it meant that the boat was too far south; if the star was in line with the top, the seafarer knew that he was already at the right latitude for the port he wanted to reach.

Day after day, the sailors become fatter and more lethargic. Finally Sindbad, after discovering their hosts' sinister motive when he sees the head man sitting down to a banquet of human flesh, escapes; but it is too late to save the drugged crew. The last he sees of his men, is when they are on all fours in a field, guarded by herdsmen and cropping the grass like cattle.

Cannibalism, Severin learned, was not uncommon on the Indonesian islands during the Middle Ages. But the distinctive feature of the story, which ties it directly to Sumatra, is the use of drugs to tranquilize victims. In northern parts of the island, Severin reports, hashish is still used as an herb in cooking. Arab merchants must certainly have come into contact with cannibals and the drug they used because Sumatra was on the direct route to a nearby spice port where the Arabs regularly traded for camphor, a widely used ingredient in their medicines.

Daily life in a monastery
It wasn't easy, but it had its compensations

FROM THE MEAGER comfort of their straw mattresses and coarse blankets, monks in Benedictine monasteries all over medieval Europe were roused by bell-ringers at 2 a.m. Moments later they would hurry along cold stone corridors to the first of the day's six services in the huge church (there was one at the heart of every monastery), where the altar, gorgeous with gold and silver ornaments, glowed in the light from hundreds of candles. Ahead of the monks lay a day identical to all others, with an unvarying routine of four hours of religious services, another four of meditative private study, and six of manual labor in fields or workshops. Hours of prayer and work were interspersed with periods of meditation, and the monks were usually in bed by 6:30 p.m. In summertime they could look forward to only one meal – without meat – to break the day; in winter there was a second meal to help them sustain the bitter cold.

This was life according to the "Rule of St. Benedict" laid down in the sixth century by Benedict of Nursia, the canonized Italian founder of the Benedictine Order. St. Benedict prescribed a life of poverty, chastity, and obedience for monks, under the monastic guidance of an abbot, whose word was law. Louis the Pious, ruler of the Carolingian empire from 814 to 840, encouraged monks to follow the rules of St. Benedict. And by the year 1000 the routine of virtually all monasteries in Western Europe was modeled on that of the Benedictines, just as many of the buildings themselves were based on the "blueprint" drawn up for the monastery of St. Gall, Switzerland, in 820. St. Benedict's Rule was formulated while he was the abbot of the Abbey of Monte Cassino (in southern Italy), founded in 529 and still one of the world's great monasteries. Benedict himself was its first abbot, and it was he who established the pattern of self-sufficiency advocated by earlier monastic rules – total reliance on its own fields and workshops – that governed Western Christendom's monasteries for centuries, and that continues to do so in many modern establishments.

In every early Benedictine monastery life was lived entirely in common. Central to the daily routine was what St. Benedict called the "work of God" – long and increasingly elaborate services of praising and praying. Everything else was secondary to this. The manual labor that the Rule commanded existed not only to provide the monks with food, clothing, and other necessities, but to keep them from idleness and to nurture the soul by disciplining the body. Later, as the abbeys grew richer, chiefly through gifts from devout men, individual sleeping cells replaced communal dormitories; and laborers were hired to till the fields, releasing many monks for other duties, including the scholarship for which the Benedictine Order was to become so justly renowned.

In their walled gardens the monks grew herbs for medicinal use, and at some time – nobody knows quite when – they hit on the idea of adding certain herbs to brandy, thereby inventing the liqueur, Benedictine. It may seem strange to associate monastic life with a luxurious alcoholic drink, but wine had always been a permissible beverage for Benedictine monks. It went well with their simple meals, which consisted largely of bread, eggs, cheese, and fish. Though meat was forbidden in the early centuries, some abbeys later added poultry and game birds to the menu, since the founder had not specifically named them among forbidden foods. Throughout all meals, though, silence

This 11th-century manuscript from the monastery at Monte Cassino is illustrated by scenes from the life and times of the saintly Benedict. From left to right, and top to bottom, the illustrations show: St. Benedict writing the Rule for monks of his order, and his last moments, dying of a fever; the burial of St. Benedict, and a vision seen by two monks, far distant from each other, of the route by which their founding abbot ascended to Heaven; the mad woman who was miraculously cured after sleeping in the cave that had been occupied by St. Benedict while living as a hermit, and St. Gregory with his completed Life of St. Benedict, of which these illustrations form a part.

reigned. Thus St. Benedict's Rule, though severe in most respects, managed to achieve a balance between asceticism and indulgence.

Benedict himself obviously knew something about human nature. Though monks were required to rise very early, he advised them to "encourage one another gently because of the excuses of the sleepyheads," and he permitted summertime siestas. Further, the first psalm of the day was to be recited slowly in order to give late-comers a chance to catch up. Silence was recommended, but in terms of a "spirit of taciturnity" rather than complete dumbness; and, in fact, a special room, with a fire in winter, was set aside for monks to converse in. In similarly considerate fashion, the monks were provided with plain but clean clothes, including a change of robe and under-tunic. St. Benedict had no desire to imitate the extreme asceticism of monastic societies in Egypt or Syria. Baths, though, were discouraged, except for the sick, as being over-luxurious.

Within their unvarying routine, the Benedictines lived and worked in absolute obedience to their abbot. They elected him, but he then exercised complete authority over them as long as he lived. It was the abbot who determined the tone of his monastery – whether it would excel in austere holiness, in its cooking, or in scholarship. Within their massive walls, which no Christian would dare to attack, the monasteries contained libraries in which was kept intact much of the literary heritage of the ancient world during the centuries when Europe was ravaged by invasion and internal warfare.

In fact, the security, both economic and physical, that a monastery offered its brothers must have been one of its chief attractions. For century after century, the Benedictines and monks of other religious orders lived without fear of hunger, war, or dismissal. And they always had the comfort of knowing that, in the end, they stood a better chance of salvation than the uncloistered, earthbound peasant or knight.

THE FIRST CHRISTIAN MONKS

Ever since the days of the Old Testament prophets, holy men and women of all religions have felt the urge to live austere lives in the wilderness, whether alone or in lonely communion with others of the same mind. The earliest such Christian community was a group of people who chose to retire to the Egyptian desert almost 300 years after Christ's crucifixion. The movement began when St. Anthony of Egypt (known as the "desert father") established a monastery dedicated to a withdrawal from worldly comforts on a mountain close to the Red Sea. Then, a few years later, the monastery of Tabenna was set up in upper Egypt, and the life style it adopted was widely emulated in later Middle Eastern monastic societies.

Tabenna's 1,300 monks each had to serve three years before being accepted into the order. They lived three to a cell and were not allowed to sleep lying down. They ate frugal meals together in the same hall, but had to cover their faces and were forbidden to talk to each other or look around. When not at prayer, they worked as blacksmiths, bakers, carpenters, or at similar trades. Some were scribes, a profession that became increasingly important. Others wrote sermons and religious treatises, some of which contributed much to the fundamental teachings of the early Church.

By the beginning of the sixth century, when St. Benedict founded one of Europe's greatest monasteries at Monte Cassino, communities of monks, as well as solitary anchorites, were scattered throughout Egypt. Legends spread of the hermits' affinity with wild animals, of holy men living in harmony with lions, panthers, and even crocodiles. But the enduring image of the Egyptian monastic communities was of self-denial combined with good works. It was this that caught the imagination of European Christians and inspired them to establish their own monasteries.

The distinctive habits worn by medieval monks and friars (and nuns) proclaimed their order. The seven shown here are, from left to right, Cistercian, Dominican, Premonstratensian, Augustinian or Austin friars, Franciscan, Carmelite, and Benedictine. With only slight modifications, most of these habits are the same today.

The medieval monastery: A masterplan

None of the great Benedictine monasteries built in Western Europe at the time of Charlemagne have survived to the present day, but we know what they must have looked like and how they worked from a remarkable plan which survives in the library of the monastery of St. Gall, near Lake Constance in Switzerland. Drawn up in about 820, this masterplan for a monastery, which was never built, depicted the ideal monastery and what it should include.

The Rule of St. Benedict decreed that monks should lead a self-sufficient life devoted to meditation and worship, and the monastery was planned with this in mind. Specific in every detail, the plan gave a function to every building, describing its layout and furnishings. In the center of the monastery was to be the church, serving both the monks, and the laity of the local parish who had access to the west end of the church only. At both the east and west ends of the church a semi-circular colonnaded area was labeled "paradise," suggesting a pleasant enclosure for contemplation and prayer. The eastern end of the church was to be for monks alone, where they would worship eight times a day. To the south lay the main cloisters around which were the monk's living quarters. Elsewhere accommodation was provided for the abbot and any visitors, the servants, and for a school. To the east of the church were to be two monasteries in miniature, housing novitiates and sick monks, with the doctor's house nearby. The monks' physical needs were looked after in the gardens and workshops, where laborers and craftsmen could provide those services which made the monastery independent of the outside world.

At first Benedictine monks worked their own land, but as the abbeys grew richer, they employed laborers, such as this plowman shown in De Universo, a manuscript dating from 1023 and kept in the abbey of Monte Cassino, Italy.

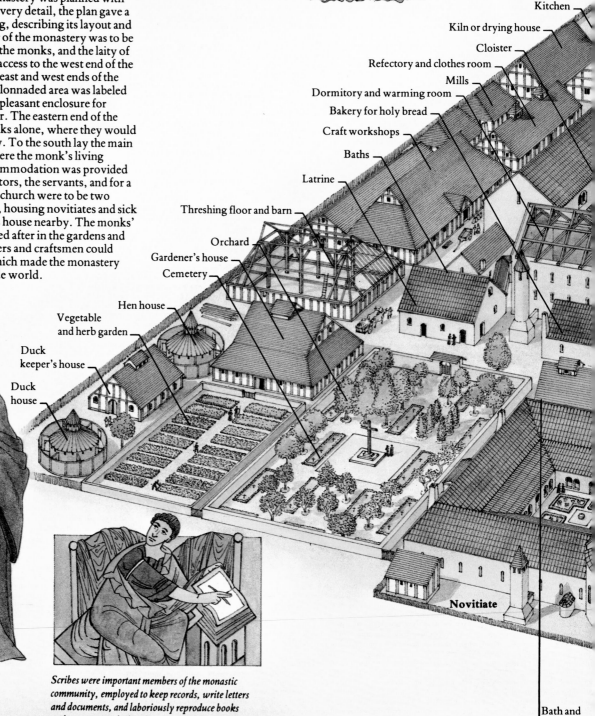

Kitchen
Kiln or drying house
Cloister
Refectory and clothes room
Mills
Dormitory and warming room
Bakery for holy bread
Craft workshops
Baths
Latrine
Threshing floor and barn
Orchard
Gardener's house
Cemetery
Hen house
Vegetable and herb garden
Duck keeper's house
Duck house
Novitiate
Bath and kitchen

Benedictine monk wearing the habit of the order.

Scribes were important members of the monastic community, employed to keep records, write letters and documents, and laboriously reproduce books and manuscripts by hand.

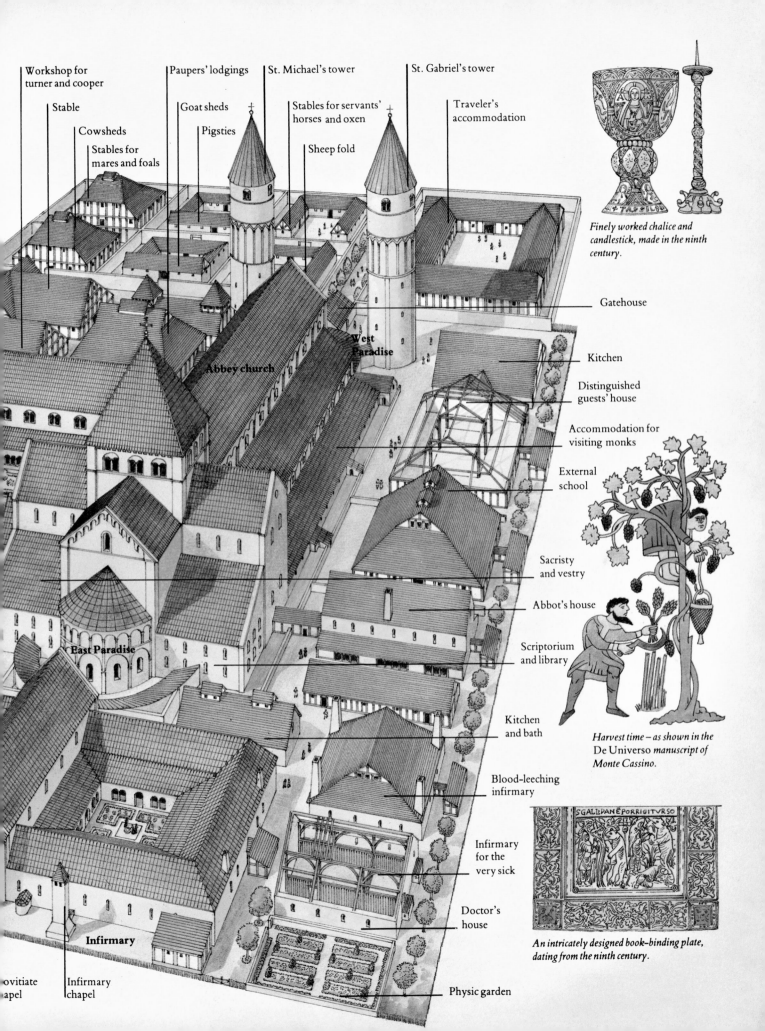

Workshop for turner and cooper

Stable

Cowsheds

Stables for mares and foals

Paupers' lodgings

Goat sheds

Pigsties

St. Michael's tower

Stables for servants' horses and oxen

Sheep fold

St. Gabriel's tower

Traveler's accommodation

Abbey church

West Paradise

East Paradise

Infirmary

Noviciate chapel

Infirmary chapel

Finely worked chalice and candlestick, made in the ninth century.

Gatehouse

Kitchen

Distinguished guests' house

Accommodation for visiting monks

External school

Sacristy and vestry

Abbot's house

Scriptorium and library

Kitchen and bath

Blood-leeching infirmary

Infirmary for the very sick

Doctor's house

Physic garden

Harvest time – as shown in the De Universo manuscript of Monte Cassino.

An intricately designed book-binding plate, dating from the ninth century.

Cave bandits

Scholarly skulduggery

THE TOWN OF TUN-HUANG lies on the edge of the vast Gobi Desert, in a harsh, inhospitable region of western China, where temperatures fall far below freezing and howling winds heap up huge dunes of grayish drift sand. Yet Tun-Huang has been celebrated for centuries, for it was once an important stopping place of the Great Silk Road, along which caravans laden with silken fabrics bore their exotic cargo from China westward. And although this ancient trade route has been long abandoned, visitors still flock to the old town because, in the barren foothills to the southeast, they can see one of the most remarkable sights in the whole of China: A vast honeycomb of rock-cut cave temples known as the Caves of the Thousand Buddhas.

The walls of the caves are decorated with hundreds of vivid frescoes that add up to a magnificent panorama of ancient Chinese life and thought; and also on view are about 1,000 painted Buddhist sculptures, which give the caves their traditional name. In addition, they once housed a unique library of perhaps 300,000 volumes – whose texts, dating from the 11th century and earlier, dealt with farming, medicine, law, Buddhist philosophy, astronomy, history, literature, and geography – along with a collection of beautiful textiles and painted scrolls. But the library and art collection have been much depleted. And thereby hangs a tale – a tale of what some commentators have called "scholarly skulduggery."

By the end of the 19th century the caves had become a desolate place of Buddhist pilgrimage, their mouths choked with drift sand swept in from the desert. Appalled at the deterioration, a monk named Wang Tao-Shih gathered together a team of laborers and made it his business to restore the holy site to something of its former splendor. While clearing out one of the caves, the workmen opened up a crack in the frescoed wall and uncovered a secret chamber that was crammed to the roof with ancient manuscripts and other objects. Since Wang was no scholar, he sent off some specimens to the provincial governor, who responded by simply telling the monk to seal up the no-longer-secret chamber and await further instructions. Thereafter Wang remained sole guardian of the treasure.

News of the discovery traveled, however, and came to the attention of an archeologist named Aurel Stein. Born in Austria but naturalized British, Stein, who worked for the British government in India, had no special knowledge of Chinese culture. What he did have in abundance was the adventurer's instinct for a "find." He lost no time in making his way to the caves in the company of a Chinese assistant named Chiang, and eventually they became acquainted with Wang, who seemed rather unfriendly. Writing about their first meeting, in May 1907, Stein says, "He looked a very curious figure, extremely shy and nervous, with a face bearing an occasional furtive expression of cunning which was far from encouraging." The eager archeologist quickly realized that it would take a great measure of diplomatic skill to get even a glimpse of the treasure.

So he proceeded cautiously, claiming that he wanted merely to photograph the wall paintings. Only after some time did he broach the

Among the many priceless treasures removed by Aurel Stein from the Caves of the Thousand Buddhas was this painting on silk of Vaisravana, the god of wealth, with his masked attendants.

subject of the manuscript cache. Might a single specimen be obtained for examination? The monk was clearly perturbed. For the time being, the subject was dropped.

Then Stein renewed his enquiries, sweetening them with flattery and cajolery, plus an offer of financial help for the work of restoration that was the monk's all-important objective. Bit by bit Wang was won over. First he brought out some manuscripts for scrutiny; at last he was persuaded to permit Stein and Stein's assistant to enter the secret chamber.

Astonished by the sheer volume of documents, they removed a few from their canvas wrappings and were even more astonished at their state of preservation, for the thick scrolls were neither brittle nor decayed. The bone-dry atmosphere of the chamber, sealed off in an arid desert valley, had acted as a preserving agent through the course of nine centuries. And among the unfurled scrolls were superb textiles in silk and brocade and gorgeous banners with painted figures of Buddhist divinities, their rich colors apparently as fresh as when first applied.

Inwardly exulting, Stein kept an outward show of nonchalance, giving Wang the impression that the magnificent relics he was handling were just "miscellaneous rubbish." The deception worked. Soon the monk, no longer wary, gave his British guest a free hand to inspect the contents of the chamber – and so Stein was ready for the next move. A selection of bundles, he

THE SECRET OF THE CHAMBER

When Aurel Stein was first permitted to enter a concealed chamber within the Caves of the Thousand Buddhas, he could scarcely believe what he saw. "The sight of the small room disclosed was one to make my eyes open wide," he wrote. "Heaped up in closely packed layers, but without any order, there appeared in the dim light of the priest's flickering lamp a solid mass of manuscript bundles rising to a height of nearly 10 feet (3 meters). They filled, as subsequent measurement showed, close on 500 cubic feet (14 cubic meters). . . . The area left clear within [was] just sufficient for two people to stand in."

Why was this amazing collection of art and literature hidden in a secret place? Research has shown that none of the manuscripts dates to a period later than the reign of the Emperor Chen Tsung (AD 998–1022). It is known that the nearby town of Tun-Huang was conquered by waves of Tartar (Mongol) horsemen early in the 11th century, and so it now seems likely that the treasured objects were being protected from threatened destruction by the invaders. And the very fact of their existence was no doubt forgotten during the long years of Tartar occupation.

An illustration from The Diamond Sutra, which was composed in about AD 868 and is thought to be the world's oldest printed book. It was one of thousands of manuscripts removed by Aurel Stein from the Caves of the Thousand Buddhas.

said, should be temporarily taken away for scholarly research. Far from being a sacrilege, it would be an act of religious merit to allow Buddhist scholars to study the manuscripts and works of art. Stein, of course, dared not offer to buy objects from the sacred Caves of the Thousand Buddhas. But he delighted Wang with a steady trickle of "donations" for the restoration project. Thus Wang's commitment to guard a sealed chamber was gradually and almost imperceptibly dishonored.

And it was all done in secret. Night after night, Stein's Chinese assistant came to his employer's tent bearing ever heavier loads of treasure. In the end the man who was to be knighted by the British government for his exploits managed to amass 24 cases of manuscripts, containing some 3,000 text rolls, and five further cases containing textiles and over 200 paintings. The whole priceless haul cost him four "horseshoes" of silver (which he estimated at 500

rupees, or less than $50 in modern currency) in "donations" to the honest but misguided monk. Stein's booty went to the British Museum, which still holds it. The art works in particular are of inestimable value since they are paintings dating from the T'ang dynasty period (AD 618–907), which are exceptionally rare. Some of the paintings are so large that they must have been hung from cliffs on ceremonial occasions. It is not surprising that Stein has been characterized as a "robber" and a "bandit." Certainly, his cleverly planned archeological con-trick violated China's cultural heritage. Still, it must be remembered that the China of Stein's day was a crumbling and lawless empire; had he not removed the collection, it might have perished through neglect or been broken up by scavenging dealers and disappeared into the hands of private collectors. Whatever his ethics, Stein's quest for glory helped to preserve a part of the past from the peril of oblivion.

The most restless of royal minds

The monarch who feared only himself

SCHOLAR, WARRIOR, and lawgiver, King Alfred (849–99) was the only English monarch to be granted the title of "Great." Yet he was a religious fanatic who was so obsessed by a sense of sin that sexual activity, even when sanctified by marriage, seems to have frightened him into virtually permanent psychosomatic illness. During the festivities that celebrated his marriage at the age of 20 to a splendid young lady of noble birth, he suddenly collapsed, overcome by a mysterious ailment that no doctor could diagnose. Throughout his

Alfred the Great was a generous patron of art and culture. This, the so-called "Alfred jewel," made of cloisonné *enamel, rock crystal, and gold, demonstrates the high quality of Anglo-Saxon workmanship during his reign. The inscription reads, "Alfred ordered me to be made."*

life – he lived to be 50 – he suffered from what his biographer calls "excruciating pain" or the "nervous dread" of it, "rendering him, in his own opinion, almost useless for both religious and secular duties."

Bishop Asser, the biographer who told the world about the sexual fears and probable hypochondria of Alfred the Great, was not only a friend of the king but a sturdy advocate of his greatness. Some modern historians, however, are unable to believe Asser's account of the harrowing wedding day and Alfred's lifelong emotional and physical weakness; this, they insist, simply does not accord with the bishop's stories of the Anglo-Saxon king's achievements in war and peace. But other scholars argue that Alfred's sexual tensions, far from being out of character with military and intellectual superiority, could have been a major *cause* of his greatness; positive action gave him much-needed relief from the demons that haunted him.

Nobody today argues about one fact: Alfred was indeed great. In the second half of the ninth century England was fragmented into several kingdoms, usually at odds with one another and constantly under Viking (Danish) attack. Alfred became King of Wessex in the southwestern corner of the country in 871, and by the time of his death 28 years later he had dramatically transformed the scene: Anglo-Saxon England was largely unified and freed from the Viking menace. All this, and more, was primarily due to the tortured character and, above all, the tenacity of this remarkable man.

No person or group seemed able to halt the Danish series of invasions during the early years of Alfred's reign. Marauding Viking forces spread westward across the land, assisted by constant forays here and there from the sea, for they were a seafaring people whereas the Anglo-Saxons were mostly farmers. By 878 all of Alfred's kingdom of Wessex was endangered. The will to resist the pagan invaders had nearly evaporated; some of Alfred's people submitted to the Vikings, others fled, all apparently abandoned hope – all, that is, save the king himself, who never lost his intense Christian faith in the rightness of his cause. For a while he seems to have gone into hiding, but he and his forces carried out guerrilla attacks against the invaders while at the same time gathering increasing support from loyal subjects. Finally, at the battle of Edington in Wessex Alfred and his men emerged victorious. Not only was the Danish threat to Wessex lifted, but as the enemy retreated eastward Alfred followed, eventually driving the Vikings out of London and becoming in effect leader of the Anglo-Saxons (as well as the gradually Christianized Viking settlers) throughout the land. Meanwhile, Alfred had the foresight and imagination to realize that the best insurance against further invasion from seafaring enemies was a powerful English navy, and he introduced a new design of ship to provide coastal defense.

But Alfred the Great, driven perhaps by a creative urge strong enough to deflect "sinful" sexual impulses, wanted something more than military renown. Having achieved peace, he resolved to become a scholar king. Literacy was not a regal requirement in his day; in all the years of the ninth, 10th, and 11th centuries, Alfred is the only Anglo-Saxon monarch who, we know, could read and write. Convinced that learning was the key to a better life for all, he gathered scholars around him, and he himself worked with them in translating a number of instructive books from Latin to English. Copies were sent to every bishop in the land, so that knowledge might spread as it had before the collapse of Roman civilization. Free men of all classes were encouraged, for their own good, to learn to read. And, determined that there should be a permanent record of present and former times, Alfred commissioned a work known as *The Anglo-Saxon Chronicle*, a history of the Anglo-Saxon people up to and including his reign, which is still read and studied today. Not without justification Alfred the Great has been called "the father of English prose."

Nor is that all. Toward the end of his life, Alfred supervised the preparation of a code of laws based on the principle that certain crimes – excluding treason – could be atoned for by payment of money to the victims or their families rather than mutilating or executing the criminal – common punishments of the day. Alfred was also an inventor. Significantly, his outstanding achievement was to devise a form of primitive clock, comprising notched candles joined by a fuse, so assembled that six candles spanned a period of 24 hours. His invention reveals his dedication to using his day in the most productive way possible – so much for prayer, so much for work, so much for enjoyment, and so on.

King Alfred was not only a brilliant soldier, scholar, and lawgiver, but he was also the liberator of his country and a statesman who worked tirelessly for the betterment of his subjects. His greatness is magnified, not diminished, by the fact that a bitter sense of sin made him physically ill. Lesser rulers have compensated for self-doubt by cruelty toward others; Alfred the Great, on the other hand, vented his fears and frustrations upon himself alone.

According to Alfred, society was divided into men (a term that included women) who fought, men who worked, and men who prayed. He, however, managed to fulfill each of these roles, and this statue at Wantage, Oxfordshire, shows him holding a scroll, symbol of the scholar and law-giver.

Alfred the Great was renowned for his Christian piety, and in this illustration from the Venerable Bede's Life of St. Cuthbert, *the long-dead, seventh-century saint appears to the king at his court. Such an association between Alfred and a revered saint confirmed the king's status as a man of God.*

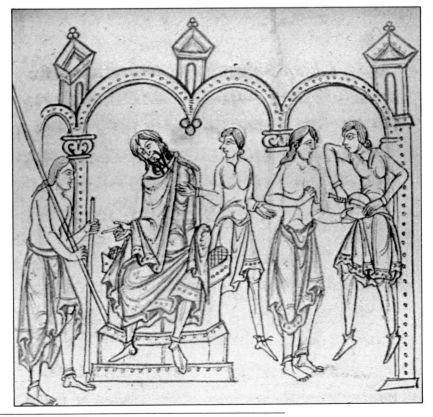

The "mad" scientist of Cairo

Laying the foundations for photography

IN 1971, amid vast celebrations, Egypt's Aswan High Dam – 375 feet (114 meters) tall, 11,811 feet (3,600 meters) long, and creating a lake of 2,000 square miles (5,180 square kilometers) – was completed. At last the age-old problem of the Nile, with its excessive and destructive flooding, was solved, and the precious water could be used for irrigation. Few of those present at the official opening of the dam were aware that a "mad" scientist who lived 1,000 years ago had envisaged just such an engineering feat and that he failed to accomplish it only because the technology of his age could not meet the requirements of the gigantic project he had conceived. Far from being a lunatic (which many of his contemporaries believed him to be), the Arab thinker Ibn al-Haitham, whom Western historians call Alhazen, was a far-sighted genius, the greatest of medieval Islamic scientists; and his name deserves to rank with those of Kepler, Leonardo da Vinci, and Isaac Newton for originality and daring.

Alhazen, born in Iraq in 965, had so thoroughly mastered mathematics, philosophy, physics, and medicine by the age of 30 that the Caliph of Egypt, Al-Hakim, who took a great interest in science, invited him to pursue his studies in Cairo. Not long after joining the scientific establishment that the caliph subsidized, Alhazen advanced the notion that the Nile should and could be dammed, and that the gorge at Aswan was the logical site for it. The enthusiastic caliph immediately ordered Alhazen to do the job and sent him off with a troop of engineers and laborers. After studying the site at first hand and discussing technical problems with his team, however, the scientist decided that the scheme to dam the river was impractical with the tools at his command.

Unfortunately for him, he had raised high hopes in the mind of the caliph, who had a nasty habit of executing men who disappointed his expectations. Knowing this, Alhazen courageously admitted failure but sensibly indicated that he could hardly be held responsible since he was out of his mind. Islamic law frowned on cruelty to madmen, who were considered as in some way "touched" by God, and so the apparently mad scientist was not killed but merely imprisoned. He remained in prison, where he was permitted to continue his studies, until the death of Caliph Al-Hakim in 1021 brought about his eventual release.

From then on he supported himself by copying and selling Arabic versions of Greek masterpieces such as those of Euclid and Ptolemy, but devoted most of his energy to research. Among the discoveries he now made and wrote about in a remarkable treatise entitled "On Optics" was the realization that vision does not depend on the emanation of rays of light *from* the eye *to* an object, but on light rays striking the eye as they travel outward in straight lines from every angle of the object. He was also the first to offer an explanation as to why the farther off an object is, the smaller it appears – an obvious truth to us today, but not fully accepted until the 17th century. For Alhazen was a scientific pioneer, so far ahead of his time that it is easy to understand why he could seem unhinged to his less advanced contemporaries.

If he had had disciples to enlarge upon and expand his ideas, the history of scientific progress might have been different. For instance, he demonstrated that if an object is placed in a dark room and irradiated by light passing through a tiny hole, an inverted image of that object would appear on a white screen – one of the first principles of photography. But nobody thought of putting this principle to use, and so cameras were not a medieval Egyptian invention, as they could have been. Nor were lenses: Alhazen's inquisitive mind wandered into many fields of knowledge, as his vision of a dam at Aswan shows, but he made something of a specialty of

The cycle of summer flooding and springtime drought in Egypt and the Sudan was not controlled until 1971, when a massive dam was completed at Aswan. And yet 1,000 years earlier, a "mad" Arab scientist, Alhazen, had proposed damming the mighty Nile at precisely that point.

THE GOLDEN AGE OF MUSLIM SCIENCE

Alhazen's lifetime coincided with a flowering of philosophical and scientific thought in the Muslim world. Muhammad had died in 632. Within 100 years his followers had carved out an Arab empire that stretched from India to Spain. Though it soon broke up politically, this great area remained unified in terms of religion, economics, and even, to a certain extent, language. Samarkand, Baghdad, Cairo, Toledo, Cordoba, and other great cities of the Muslim world, all became intercommunicating centers of learning.

The Arabs were eclectic, absorbing from their subject peoples – Greeks, Jews, Persians, Christian Syrians – whatever appealed to them in thought as well as in solid matters such as architecture. But they were fascinated above all by the Greek philosophers, especially Aristotle. Translations of ancient philosophical and scientific works were disseminated and studied in hundreds of schools throughout Islam. While the schools of Cordoba in Spain – where Jew, Christian, and Muslim could live together at ease under the tolerant Moorish conquerors – became especially famous for, among other things, a library of 600,000 volumes, the rest of Western Europe was sunk in the bookless depths of the Dark Ages. In fact Muslim Spain reintroduced Aristotle to Christian Europe in the 12th century through the work of Averroes, an Arab scholar and philosopher.

Most Muslims were content to take the ancient Greeks' interpretations of the natural world on trust. But, in addition to Alhazen, there were a few exceptionally original thinkers such as Avicenna (980–1037), who is said to have written some 250 books, chiefly in the fields of experimental physics and medicine. These scholars had an immense influence on later European thought – in particular, on mathematics and chemistry. Our word "algebra" derives from the Arabic word for the system, *al-djabr*; the word "chemistry" from *Khemia*, an old name for Egypt, where chemical studies were particularly advanced in medieval terms. Ammonia, borax, nitric acid, and sulfuric acid are only a few of the chemicals discovered and identified by Muslim scientists. And the medieval Arab mathematicians were instrumental in teaching the rest of us the concepts of zero and the decimal system, without which there could be no modern arithmetic or numerical notation.

By the 13th century, however, the Muslim world had fallen into decline, due in part to internal conflicts, the Mongol invasion and conquest of Persia and Iraq, and the gradual reconquest of Muslim Spain by the Christians – all of which left little enthusiasm or encouragement for the pursuit of science and the creative arts.

Arab scholars were early masters of such diverse subjects as linguistics, mathematics, and architecture; and public libraries, such as this one at Hulwan near Baghdad, catered for their needs. Each housed thousands of volumes, stored flat.

studying the eye itself; he laid the groundwork for the later invention of the lens in his description of the structure of the eye – so accurate that much of it passed straight into standard medical books after 1246, when his Arabic treatise on optics was translated into Latin. The very word "lens" comes from the Latin word for "lentil" because Alhazen wrote that that part of the eye was roughly lentil-shaped.

What was most unusual about him as a medieval scientist was his preference for validating theories by demonstrable evidence rather than by unquestioning reference to ancient authorities such as Archimedes or Aristotle. His methods anticipated those of Galileo (who is said to have dropped weights from the Leaning Tower of Pisa to disprove Aristotle's dictum that heavy objects fall faster than light ones). Of the many practical experiments Alhazen devised to test his theories, perhaps the most fruitful were those designed to examine the refraction of light. For example, he immersed glass cylinders in water to test how light is deflected when entering a medium of different density. He also conducted various experiments to determine the magnifying power of lenses, and even built a lathe on which to turn curved lenses.

In a deeply conservative culture, such experimentation took courage as well as imagination, for both religious and political leaders were likely to frown at "dangerous" new ideas. Alhazen's truly scientific methods continued to strike most people as a form of insanity for fully six centuries after his death in 1039.

Lines in the desert

The mystery of the Nazcas

THE PURPOSES of many extraordinary human achievements remain shrouded in mystery and still provoke lively argument among scholars. Such controversy has surrounded a remarkable discovery made in the Nazca desert, an arid plateau near the town of Nazca in southern Peru. This region was once the home of the Nazca Indians, whose culture was absorbed into the Inca empire in the 15th century, only to be virtually wiped out in the Spanish conquest. The remains of a temple containing six pyramids located on the Nazca River testified to the former existence of a major civilization, but such clues were few.

In 1926 a research team led by Julio Tello, a pioneer of Peruvian archeology, arrived in the area. Without realizing it, they were literally standing on what was possibly the Nazca people's greatest yet most baffling achievement. The discovery came about when, late one afternoon, two of the team, a Peruvian named Mejía Xesspe and an American called Alfred

Kroeber, climbed a hill. From that vantage they could see long faint lines that were invisible at ground level crisscrossing the desert. On examination, the team found that the lines had been made by clearing away stones on the surface to reveal pale-yellow soil. When exposed, the soil gradually darkens to a purplish-brown like the rest of the desert surface, which explained why the lines could be seen only from above.

An early theory that the Nazca lines were ancient roads was soon rejected when aircraft, crossing the desert in the late 1920s and in the 1930s, discovered an enormous patchwork of complex markings. In addition to lines, air travelers could look down on huge rectangles and other geometric shapes, together with exquisite line drawings of animals, including a monkey, a spider, a hummingbird, and even a whale, as well as flowers, hands, and spirals, ranging in size from a few feet to 600 feet (183 meters) across. These lines clearly acted as something more than just roads.

Photographed from an altitude of 5,000 feet (1,500 meters), this view of the Nazca plain shows, among the conventional tracks used by the villagers, almost perfectly straight lines traveling eastward from a church in the village to hill shrines, one some six miles (9 kilometers) away. The lines have been plotted on the diagram (inset).

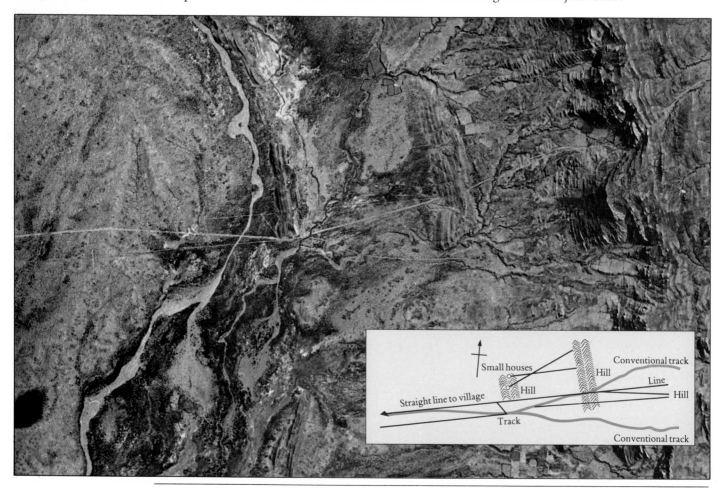

Even though some of the lines were miles long, deviation from the straight was no more than a few yards in a mile, whatever the terrain, and several lines extended onto hilltops. Why should the Nazca Indians have marked the desert in this way? The patchwork of lines was certainly not meant to be an artistic creation, because the Nazca had no way of looking down on them. Further, however impressive the lines may appear on air photographs, they do not represent a major feat of ancient science or engineering. It would have taken 1,000 Indians only three weeks to clear the necessary stones. Perfect straightness was probably achieved by lining up sighting poles and stretching cord between them. This simple method would have required no more than three poles or even two when used in association with a distant reference point.

What intrigued scholars was not the making, but the purpose of the lines. In 1941 the American archeologist Paul Kosok pioneered Nazca investigation, discovering many drawings and plotting the lines and patterns. He concluded that the lines were intended for astronomical observations. His theory inspired a German mathematician, Maria Reiche. From 1946 she has spent her life trying to unravel the mystery of the lines. Like Kosok, she believed that the lines pointed to prominent stars or to the Sun, enabling the Nazca Indians to calculate dates. She thought that the animals and other figures may have represented star constellations, and so the whole extraordinary web of markings was probably a huge calendar.

Maria Reiche found many possible alignments of the marks to the Sun and to stars, but she lacked firm proof to support her theory. In 1968 Gerald Hawkins, an astronomer with the Smithsonian Astrophysical Observatory in Washington, D.C., turned his attention to the Nazca lines after discovering similar astronomical alignments at Stonehenge, southern England's famous Neolithic temple. Hawkins had a powerful tool to probe the secrets of the Nazca people. This tool was a computer, into which he fed data obtained from a thorough survey of the lines. His objective was to find out whether each line had pointed to the Sun, Moon, or to a prominent star in the last 7,000 years. The results showed several striking alignments. For example, a feature called the Great Rectangle had pointed to the Pleiades star cluster in AD 610, plus or minus 30 years. The date almost coincided with the radiocarbon dating of a wooden post found elsewhere in the lines. This demonstrated the antiquity of the features. But the computer failed to solve the mystery of the lines,

View of a Bolivian church, in front of which stood a number of sacred places and shrines, such as that in the foreground. Offerings and sacrifices had to be made by the Indians at each shrine in turn.

because the number of definite alignments was no more than would have occurred by chance.

In 1977, a British movie maker, Tony Morrison, entered the story. Morrison had made several television movies in South America, which included accounts of the work of Maria Reiche and Gerald Hawkins. He had also become fascinated by the enigma and resolved to find the solution. Morrison was convinced that the answer lay in the knowledge of the customs and religion of the Nazca people. Although the Nazcas had vanished long ago, sites with similar lines existed elsewhere in the Andes and so he hoped that the Indians living on such sites might be able to reveal their purpose.

Morrison's quest was inspired by Mejía Xesspe, who had uncovered the lines in 1926. Xesspe told Morrison that he believed that the lines were *ceques*, an Indian word for pathways made for religious purposes. Xesspe had made this suggestion as early as 1939, but he had found no proof. Morrison, however, discovered that a Spanish chronicle dating from 1653 told how Indians at the Inca capital of Cuzco venerated shrines placed along lines radiating from the Temple of the Sun. The lines on the Nazca desert connected piles of stones. Was it possible that these stone mounds were shrines connected by straight sacred pathways?

Morrison visited the Peruvian city and hunted for the pathways. But he was unsuccessful. All traces of them had been obliterated. Undeterred, he carried on his search in neighboring Bolivia. There, in June 1977, in a remote region inhabited by the Aymara people he found a perfect set of lines, cleared not in stony desert but in scrub-covered land. The lines displayed the same precision and an equal disregard for obstacles that characterized the Nazca lines. They also connected shrines made of piles of stones, many of which were on hilltops.

The Aymara Indians worshiped at these mounds, believing them to be inhabited by the spirits of their ancestors or by local gods. The spirits and gods were placated with minor sacrifices or offerings of coca leaves, a mild narcotic. Morrison found that several lines joining shrines converged at a church. The Indians made their way to church along the lines, pausing respectfully at the shrines en route. To deviate from the pathways was, in their eyes, to stray into the domain of evil spirits. The Aymara also believed that the higher a shrine, the more powerful its spirits. This explained why pathways climbed straight over difficult terrain to reach hilltops, as they do at Nazca.

In his book, *Pathways to the Gods*, Morrison vividly describes his adventures and his belief that the lines are sacred pathways. He suggests that the Nazca drawings were probably sacred representations of gods and animal spirits, while large, cleared areas were probably sites for religious gatherings. The age of the Nazca lines is uncertain, because the evidence is sparse. The best that can be said is that they are probably between 1,000 and 2,000 years old.

The enigma of the Nazca lines is not totally resolved. Morrison's conclusions require corroboration and some lines do have astronomical alignments, whether by accident or design. And much remains to be learned about the history and ways of life of the Nazcas themselves. The Nazca lines are now guarded and preserved for future investigators, because every unturned stone may conceal vital clues.

The mystery of Murasaki
And the world's first blockbuster

Hoodo, or Phoenix Hall, Uji, Japan, so named because its plan was thought to resemble a bird in flight. It was possibly to this small palace that Murasaki Shikubu accompanied the Empress Akiko on the death of the emperor, and here she may have written part of The Tale of Genji.

ALMOST 1,000 YEARS ago a quiet, retiring Japanese lady dipped her brush in the blackest of ink and wrote (in Japanese of course), "At the court of an emperor (he lived it matters not when) ..." So begins *Genji Monogatari* (*The Tale of Genji*), one of the earliest, and one of the greatest works of Japanese prose, and a world classic. A blockbuster of a novel, it has been compared with such lengthy works of fiction as Marcel Proust's seven-part *Remembrance of Things Past* and Leo Tolstoy's *War and Peace*; but at over 600,000 words, it is twice as long as *War and Peace*, and the story spans three-quarters of a century, deals with four generations, and contains 430 named characters along with many hundreds who are not given names.

Yet though this book rests at the foundation of Japanese literary art, we know very little about its author, not even her real name. She is known as Murasaki Shikubu, but the first of those names is simply that of a character in her

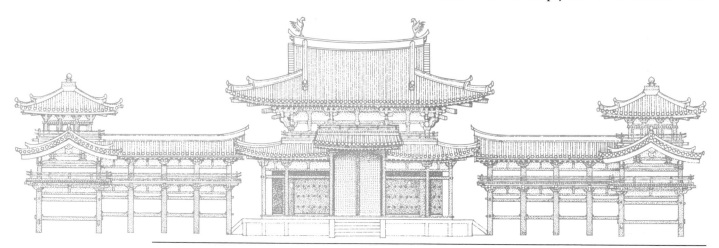

HOW GENJI WAS BORN

It seems probable that Murasaki began to write *The Tale of Genji* for something to do in the years just after her husband's death, and went on with it during her career as lady-in-waiting to the Empress Akiko. Legends accrue to all great literary figures, however; and just as there are many stories about the "real" source of Shakespeare's genius, so, according to one story, *The Tale of Genji* had a more dramatic origin than the pedestrian one of a widow's need to fill the lonely hours. It seems that the bored empress commanded Murasaki to write something new and entertaining in order to help *her* pass the time. At a loss for inspiration, and never having been an author before, Murasaki went to a religious temple to pray for guidance. Her prayers worked so well that, as inspiration struck her, she could not wait but seized the sacred scrolls from the altar and began to write on them. This was, of course, a sacrilegious act. As penance she later made exquisitely beautiful copies of the scrolls to replace the ones on which she had scribbled.

Tourists are still shown the room in the temple where Murasaki is alleged to have begun work on her epic masterpiece.

This 19th-century Japanese silk recalls Murasaki Shikubu at work on her great novel, The Tale of Genji.

book, and the second is the title of the official post held by her father. One important reason for her anonymity is that she was an attendant at the court of the Empress Akiko in the 11th century, at a time when aristocratic ladies' names, apart from those of princesses, were not mentioned in public. Still, although her name and most solid facts about her remain a mystery, scholars have managed over the centuries to form some credible impressions of her life and life style partly from a not especially illuminating diary which she kept for a couple of years, and which still survives.

Murasaki was born into a minor branch of the supremely powerful Fujiwara family, whose members established a firm control over the imperial court and virtually ruled Japan from 866 to 1160 as emperors in all but name. So although her father was only a provincial governor, her connections were of the highest order. While her brother was being given a thorough education in Chinese history and literature – then considered essential for a civil-service career – Murasaki was permitted to study along with him (a rare privilege for Japanese women). Around the year 1000 she was married to an officer in the Imperial Guard, and they had at least one daughter before his death only a brief year or two after their marriage.

As a young widow, Murasaki lived quietly at home, and it is at this time that she is generally supposed to have begun work on *Genji*. In either 1005 or 1006, through her father's influence, she was given a court appointment as lady-in-waiting to the 19-year-old Empress Akiko, wife of the Emperor Ichijo. When Ichijo died in 1011, Akiko and her retinue retired to a minor palace. Nobody knows whether or not Murasaki accompanied the widowed empress. The writer's diary, clearly written while she was at court, covers only the years 1007 to 1010.

To many Westerners, the most puzzling aspect of *The Tale of Genji* must be, not that its author was such a nebulous, unknowable person, but that she was a *woman*. How could a woman write one of the earliest, and finest, of Japanese novels at a time when few women, even of the aristocracy, were considered capable of reading, let alone writing, great literature. But this apparent puzzle is easier to solve than any of the others about Murasaki. In her day, Japanese men read and wrote in Chinese. This was the classical tongue; Japanese was reserved for common, everyday affairs – and for women. Thus writing in the Japanese language was largely in the hands of the ladies. Murasaki's own daughter became a writer, and only a little less famous than Murasaki is her contemporary, Sei Shonagon, the author of a short collection of writings called *Makura no Soshi* (*Pillow Book*).

What distinguishes *Genji* from other novels is its scope and breadth of vision. Largely the story of a young prince – his love affairs, his travels, his efforts to acquire an education – it closely reflects and recreates the court life that Murasaki knew. The court of her day was a hot-house in which frivolity flourished, for the emperor, the nominal ruler of Japan, was involved in little but ceremony and rather boring ceremony at that – while all active affairs were handled by the Fujiwara family. What the court specialized in was gossip and back-biting, and Murasaki was a keen listener and brilliant reporter; in a rare passage of self-revelation, she says in her diary that other people regarded her as shy, unsociable, conceited, and spiteful, whereas she was really gentle. She seems also to have been a lady of virtue, unlike many of her fellow-courtiers. Not surprisingly, a work of the importance of *The Tale of Genji* has attracted a multitude of scholars and critics. More than 10,000 books have been written about it; they range from textual commentaries to dictionaries and concordances, and books by one group of scholars are often entirely devoted to attacking the scholarship of rival groups. Like Shakespeare, Murasaki has her Baconians – scholars dedicated to proving that somebody else, not she, wrote her book. But as no other writers of the period have been found whose work is comparable in excellence, time has largely demolished the work of such doubting Thomases.

The Bayeux Tapestry
Storyboard propaganda

NO CAMERAS were present to record what was probably the most memorable and significant event in English history – the invasion and conquest of that country in 1066 by William, Duke of Normandy. Instead, a few years after the event, a unique visual record was painstakingly stitched together that in its color, detail, and drama is as vivid as any modern documentary film.

The Bayeux Tapestry, some 230 feet (70 meters) long and consisting of 72 embroidered story-panels, presents in picture form the events from 1064 to 1066, and in particular, the story of the relations between Harold of England and William of Normandy, rival claimants to the English throne. In what has been described as a "feudal drama" that includes scenes of oath-taking and betrayal, banquets and ship-building,

According to legend and a scene from the Bayeux Tapestry (above), a star of ill-omen appeared over London during the weeks before the Norman invasion of England. Calculations have since established that such a phenomenon – whether boding good or ill – did indeed occur in the form of Halley's comet.

The Bayeux Tapestry is a prime source of information on the everyday lives of medieval working people, for written evidence from the period is sparse. In this panel from the tapestry, a banquet is being prepared for Duke William of Normandy by men wearing the basic tunic, which was usually gathered at the waist by a belt for ease of movement.

bloody slaughter and violent death, the tapestry portrays Harold's alleged oath of allegiance to William, his subsequent coronation, the Norman invasion, and finally the Battle of Hastings (1066) when Harold was slain and William the Conqueror seized the English crown.

At Bayeux, the ancient market town in northwest France where the 900-year-old tapestry is now kept under glass, tradition has it that the tapestry was the work of Matilda, wife of William the Conqueror. Today, however, most historians believe that the tapestry was produced, probably under the direction of a highly gifted artist, on the express orders of Odo, Bishop of Bayeux and half-brother of William.

Odo was an ambitious and worldly man who played a leading part in the invasion of England. After the Conquest he became Earl of Kent, in southern England, and shared with two other barons the task of ruling England when William was out of the country. The tapestry was commissioned shortly after 1066, and although it was possibly made in France, it was more probably produced in England, then renowned for its needlework. More particularly, it was probably created by English craftswomen in a workshop attached to the ancient monastery of St. Augustine's in Canterbury, capital of Odo's earldom and center of a flourishing school of drawing. The theory that the tapestry was produced in England is further supported by spellings of some of the names, which are in Anglo-Saxon, or Old English, rather than in French. Without doubt Odo would have had a motive in commissioning the tapestry. His motive may have been self-glorification, as he figures prominently in the later part of the story, and until recently it has been thought that the tapestry was intended as a religious decoration for his new cathedral at Bayeux, which was dedicated in 1077. This theory was first challenged in 1966, however, chiefly on the grounds that the earliest mention of the tapestry's presence in the cathedral was not until 1476.

Moreover, nothing in the tapestry suggests an ecclesiastical origin; the whole theme is one of war and conquest, arguing strongly against its suitability for display in the cathedral. Increasingly, it is believed that the tapestry was entirely secular in origin, and meant to decorate Bishop Odo's palace, not his cathedral, as propaganda justifying the Norman invasion of England. Certainly, although the tapestry purports to be a factual narrative, the underlying theme, particularly the suggestion that Harold betrayed William after having promised allegiance to him, is most strongly biased toward the Norman cause.

Propaganda or not, the Bayeux Tapestry remains nevertheless a remarkable document. Its factual accuracy may be suspect, but, with its wealth of dramatic and colorful detail, it remains at the very least an extraordinary work of art – the only surviving representation of the last successful invasion of England.

King Harold, who lost his throne and his life during the Battle of Hastings, is traditionally thought to have been killed by an arrow entering his brain through his eye. Some modern scholars now contend that the soldier whose death from an arrow is shown on the Bayeux Tapestry was not Harold, who may be the man shown on another panel being struck down by a sword.

WHAT IS THE BAYEUX TAPESTRY?

Despite its name, the Bayeux Tapestry is strictly a piece of embroidered needlework rather than a woven tapestry.

It consists of eight strips of linen of varying length, carefully joined together to produce an entire piece 230 feet 10¼ inches (70.34 meters) long and about 20 inches (50 centimeters) wide. The figures are worked in wool of eight colors; red, two shades of blue, three greens, and two yellows. Besides the main story-panels there are narrow borders at the top and bottom containing animals, fables, and scenes of everyday life. In all, the tapestry contains more than 600 human figures and over 700 animals, as well as ships, trees, and buildings. This extraordinary wealth of detail provides a unique source of information about the everyday life of people in this period.

For working purposes the design was probably first drawn onto the linen. Linen strips would have been mounted on frames so that embroiderers had both hands free for easier working. Teams of craftswomen may have been involved, working simultaneously, and despite its size and complexity, it has been estimated that the tapestry could have been completed within two years.

The simple materials used – wool on fabric rather than gold thread on silk – probably contributed to its survival; for the Bayeux Tapestry is one of the few pieces of medieval needlework to have survived until the present day. The earliest mention of the tapestry was in 1476 in an inventory of Bayeux Cathedral.

It was displayed there for only one week a year, during the Festival of Relics, and for the rest of the time was stored among the cathedral's treasures, so reducing the danger of damage or discoloration.

Even so the tapestry has been at risk. In 1792 during the French Revolution, it was almost destroyed when revolutionaries seized it and proposed to use it to cover wagons of a military baggage train. It was rescued by a local administrator, but had to be rescued again two years later when it was decided that the tapestry should be used as a float decoration during a public procession. That year, finally, it was designated a national treasure and stored accordingly. Although subsequently moved on various occasions, most particularly during times of war, the tapestry was finally returned to Bayeux in 1945 where it has remained ever since.

England's total wealth: $100,000

That was a few years ago, of course

IN THE PUBLIC RECORD Office of the City of London lies one of history's most unusual books: A 900-year-old, two-volume survey, hand-written in Latin, of almost the whole kingdom of England – a breakdown of the population and an assessment of property values unparalleled in any country or at any other time until modern census and valuation methods became possible. The book came to be known as the Domesday (Doomsday, or day of judgment) Book because people of the 11th and 12th centuries saw it as the monarch's means of passing judgment on his subjects' right to the use of "his" possessions.

In 1066 William, Duke of Normandy, conquered England by force of arms, slaying the country's Anglo-Saxon King Harold (who had held the throne for only nine months) at the Battle of Hastings. Thereafter, William, known to his contemporaries and posterity as the Conqueror, set about reorganizing his new kingdom, and incidentally rewarding his army of Norman and French barons and knights. By 1085 the reorganization was largely complete in the southern half of the kingdom. With half a dozen exceptions, every native owner of large estates had been dispossessed and replaced by the conqueror's followers. As conqueror, William claimed rights over all the land in the country. He kept a sixth for himself and his family and allocated a quarter to the Church; most of the rest went to 170 Norman noblemen. William's reign is discussed in *The Anglo-Saxon Chronicle*, a narrative history of England written by monks over a period of nearly 300 years. William is criticized for the severity of his rule, but is also praised as a just monarch.

In return for grants of enormous estates, every one of these tenants-in-chief, as they were called, had to provide armed knights in time of war, pay certain dues, and attend any councils the king might call. The 170 great land-holders leased some of their land to "vassals," some of them warrior-knights. Some of these sub-tenants in turn let out parts of their holdings, and so on, creating the pyramid-like social structure characteristic of the feudal system.

In 1085 William felt it was time to take stock. He spent the Christmas season at the city of Gloucester, in western England, where, according to an old account, he had "very deep speech with his Witan [or council of advisers] about this land and how it was peopled and with what sort of men." As a result of this "deep speech," the king decided to have a survey made of the whole country. To carry out this survey, the shires (counties) of England were divided into seven general areas; a group of royal commissioners was authorized to go through each area, shire by shire, requiring local citizens to answer under oath a series of questions in order to determine the ownership and value of all the property in every manor and village, both at the time of the survey and 20 years earlier in 1066, just before the Norman Conquest.

Each group of commissioners held court hearings at every place they visited. They grilled not only the tenant-in-chief (a Norman in most

---

Animals, implements, and people were all recorded in the Domesday Book.

A TYPICAL ENTRY

A typical entry in the Domesday Book is this one, which refers to property around the Abbey of Westminster – now in the heart of London, but in 1086 a sparsely populated rural area – and its Lord of the Manor, who was the abbot himself:

"In the village, where St. Peter's church stands [i.e. Westminster Abbey], the abbot of the same place holds 13½ hides. There is land for 11 plough teams. To the demesne belong nine hides and one virgate, and there are four plough teams. The villagers have six plough teams, and one more might be made. There are nine villagers with a virgate each, one villager with a hide, nine villagers with half a virgate each, one cottager with five acres, and 41 cottagers rendering a shilling each yearly for their gardens. There are 25 houses of the abbot's soldiers and of other men, who render eight shillings a year. Total value £10 in all; when he received it the same; in the time of King Edward £12."

The "demesne" was land under the lord's direct control, not rented out; a "hide" was about 120 acres (48 hectares); a "virgate" about 30 acres (12 hectares); and there were 20 shillings to the pound sterling. The value of the estate had dropped by £2 between the time of Edward the Confessor (early in 1066) and its take-over by the new owner.

cases), but also the sheriff (shire-reeve, or chief magistrate), and for each community its priest, reeve, and six representative *villani* (small land-holders). Questions were set out with great precision: The citizens were asked who held each manor; who held it 20 years ago in 1066; its value at that time, at the time when it was transferred to its new owner, and at present (1086); how many people of each class lived on the manor; and the amount of woodland, meadows for grazing, mills, fisheries, and animals within its borders. A monk of the time wrote: "So narrowly did he [William] cause the survey to be made that there was not one single hide nor rood of land, nor (it is shameful to tell, but he thought it no shame to do) was there an ox, cow, or swine that was not set down in the writ."

The Domesday survey did not cover four counties in the extreme north of England (Northumberland, Cumberland, Durham, and Westmorland) nor a few towns such as Winchester and London. But from it William – who died in 1087, soon after the completion of the survey – and his immediate successors gained a good idea of the material worth of their country, and therefore of what revenue they could raise from taxes. According to the calculations of modern scholars, the value of all the surveyed manors and villages added together totaled around £73,000 (something between $100,000 and $150,000 at modern exchange rates).

The facts and figures in the Domesday Book yield many clues to the state of England almost exactly 900 years ago. For example, the large northern county of Yorkshire was valued at a startlingly small amount. Why? Because people of the northern counties had rebelled against the Normans in 1070 and William suppressed the revolt with great severity, burning houses and whole towns in what historians speak of as "the harrying of the North." The results of this devastation still showed up 16 or 17 years later; the survey describes many places in Yorkshire with the single word "waste." Small wonder that the full value of Yorkshire plus its neighboring county of Lancashire – a vast area – was only £1,200 (around $1,800) out of the country's £73,000 total. By contrast, the total value of three much smaller eastern counties (Essex, Norfolk, and Suffolk) amounted to more than 10 times as much.

We can even trace the route taken by William's army from the battlefield of Hastings on the southern coast to London, by comparing the value of various estates before the Conquest and immediately afterward, as recorded in Domesday, when they passed into Norman hands. Some 217 relatively small estates, at intervals of about 25 miles (40 kilometers), appear to have lost up to 20 per cent of their value. Since 25 miles was about a day's march for an army, it seems likely that it was William's army foraging for supplies and perhaps doing a little vandalism on the side that accounts for the 20 per cent drop.

It is a tribute to the skill of the commissioners and their officials that modern scholars have been able to find remarkably few errors in the Domesday Book. It is undoubtedly one of the most enlightening sources historians have ever had in their quest for the past.

William the Conqueror, founder of the Norman dynasty in England, was as able economically as he was militarily. His introduction of feudalism to England was perhaps the most dramatic effect of his iron rule.

The Domesday Book, displayed on the casket in which it was originally kept. It consists of two volumes. One contains the account of Essex, Suffolk, and Norfolk, the most prosperous counties at the time, and the other the account of the rest of England save the most northerly counties.

The untamable Tafurs

Why the Turks called some Christians "living devils"

THROUGHOUT THE bitter winter of 1097–98 the Turkish garrison of the Middle Eastern city of Antioch could look down from the city walls and watch a besieging army of Crusaders gradually starving to death. While the Turks had a good stock of food, the Crusaders, in a barren land far from help, were in dire straits. It was essential for them to capture Antioch, the gateway to Syria, but it looked as if hunger rather than the Muslim enemy would frustrate their hopes. Some of the knights and barons rode far off to scavenge for food, others ate their horses, which were also famished; lesser men paid high prices for dogs or rats, or were doomed to die unfed.

One day, though, the astounded Turks looked down upon a scene that made them gasp. The most ragged and desolate-seeming of the besiegers were roasting great chunks of meat and ostentatiously gorging themselves. Then Turkish amazement turned to horror. The meat, they discovered, was coming from the dismembered bodies of some of their own comrades, killed a few days before in a skirmish outside the walls. And when this supply had run out, the still-hungry mob began digging up a nearby cemetery in search of recently killed corpses. Shocked beyond measure, the emir (commander) of the Muslim forces sent envoys to the leaders of the Crusade to protest. But the Europeans sent back word that they could do nothing to stop the cannibalism. The noble Crusaders had to admit that "all of them together could not tame the Tafurs."

"Tafur" was not the name of a strange man-eating race. It was simply a word, probably Flemish in its origin, meaning something like "rabble," and it was what upper-class participants in the great First Crusade called the vagabond crowd who accompanied them through Europe on the road to Jerusalem. Tafurs do not fit into our traditional image of Crusaders, who were certainly not cannibals.

The Tafurs were a different breed from the mounted knights in armor. Barefoot, dirty, dressed in ragged sackcloth, covered with sores, unable to afford swords and spears, they carried pointed sticks, clubs, and even shovels into the fray. But what they lacked in weapons they made up for in ferocity. When charging into battle, screaming and gnashing their teeth at the enemy, they were out for blood and had no interest in taking prisoners for ransom. The Turks called Crusaders in general "Franks" because most participants in the First Crusade came from France or Belgium; but Tafurs, they said, were "not Franks but living devils."

Liberation of Jerusalem was not the aim of the Tafurs; they had a far greater yearning for their own liberation. The years before the First Crusade had been a time of drought, plague, and famine. For European peasants life had always been tough; now it had become intolerable. And so, when the First Crusade was proclaimed in 1095, with fiery talk of Jerusalem, the Heavenly City "flowing with milk and honey," thousands of ill-fed, ill-clad, ill-housed peasants took the words literally and decided to make their own way to this fruitful place that the noble Crusaders would soon win back for them. In hordes numbering tens of thousands, including many women and children, the deluded peasants swarmed through Hungary and the Balkans, first spending what little money they had, then stealing and pilfering in order to stay alive. At the city of Constantinople (modern Istanbul) the Greeks, unable to control them, agreed to ferry

In his appeal for a Crusade to "liberate" the Holy Land in 1095, the pope made calculated references to the overcrowding and famine then prevalent in Europe. Inspired by the hope of a better life, many poor peasants set off on Crusade under the leadership of a mystic called Peter the Hermit. Here, some stragglers are seized by Hungarian soldiers and marched into captivity.

them across the Bosphorus into Asia Minor. But when the weary masses got there, they were ambushed and massacred by the Turks, who found them easy prey. Only a scanty remnant of perhaps 3,000 escaped to await the arrival of the main body of Crusaders.

It was this remnant, embittered but hardened by experience, that followed the knights like a ragged shadow, more eager than ever to reach the promised land. By now a dogged determination to win through had welded them into a single-minded, merciless band, and they even had an elected "king" – reputedly a former knight who had thrown in his lot with the poor. At first the shaggy mob embarrassed the official army of Crusaders, who contemptuously called the peasants "Tafurs," but before long their embarrassed contempt changed to fear. They were no longer easy prey for the Turks, either; instead, they struck terror into enemy hearts.

After a nine-month siege, Antioch finally fell to the Crusaders. There was much looting, raping, and killing of Muslims and Jews in the city, and the Tafurs may well have been responsible for a good deal of such cruelty. The following year, too, when Jerusalem was captured, a large number of prisoners were slaughtered instead of being held for ransom, and that crime has also been laid at the door of the savage survivors of the peasant mob. But this type of accusation is based largely on conjecture, not established fact. There can be no dispute about the episode before the walls of Antioch. The Tafurs did, indeed, eat human flesh in order to escape starvation.

THE CRUSADES

In 1095 Pope Urban II appealed for soldiers to march eastward in order to help their fellow-Christians throw off the Muslim yoke. The appeal sparked off a response far greater than expected. Shouting "*Deus le volt*" (God wills it), thousands of noblemen, knights, and commoners vowed to recapture the Holy Land, especially Jerusalem. Few of them had a real idea of where Jerusalem was, but it soon became a symbol that was to lure to the East kings and emperors as well as successive waves of lesser men over the next 175 years. Though the name "crusade" was later applied to proselytizing military campaigns such as that against the pagan Slavs, it primarily refers to the attempts in the 11th, 12th, and 13th centuries to conquer or defend Jerusalem. There were no fewer than nine of these (not including the tragic Children's Crusade), but only the original expedition of 1096–99 was entirely successful. It was called a "crusade" because all participants had a cross (Latin: *crux*) sewn onto their clothes.

After capturing the Holy City in 1099, the Crusaders declared Jerusalem a kingdom and chose one of their leaders, the Duke of Lorraine, as its first king. Lesser states were established to the north, at Tripoli (in modern Lebanon), Antioch (in Syria), and Edessa (now known as Urfa, in Turkey). In 1144 the Muslims captured Edessa, and it was this loss that sparked off the Second Crusade – which, although led by the King of France and the Emperor of Germany, failed to achieve its aim. Edessa remained in Muslim hands; and in 1187 Jerusalem fell to Saladin, Sultan of Egypt, thus bringing on the Third Crusade, with three monarchs – Philip of France, Richard the Lion Heart of England, and the German emperor – all following the Cross. This time again, nothing permanent was achieved: The German emperor drowned in a river on his way; Philip quarreled with Richard and went back to France; and Richard, who captured the port of Acre in Palestine but could not regain Jerusalem, was himself captured and held for ransom by Leopold of Austria on his way home. The Fourth Crusade, of 1202–04, never got near the Holy Land but was diverted to attack and loot the wealthy city of Constantinople (now Istanbul).

Eight years later, thousands of boys and girls, most of them not yet in their teens, also set off for the East, led by a French shepherd boy who was convinced that unarmed innocence would prevail where armed might had failed. Most of these participants in what came to be known as the Children's Crusade either died en route or ended up in the slave-markets of North Africa.

Only one of the five remaining Crusades had even partial success in reaching its goal. That was the Sixth Crusade, a largely peaceful expedition that negotiated a truce with the Muslims and a temporary return of Jerusalem to Christianity in 1228; but the city was once again surrendered to the Muslims in 1244.

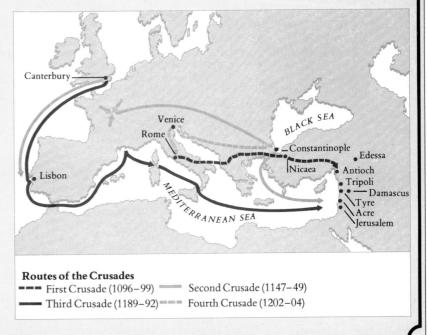

Routes of the Crusades
- ▪▪▪ First Crusade (1096–99)   ▬▬ Second Crusade (1147–49)
- ▬▬ Third Crusade (1189–92)   ▪▪▪ Fourth Crusade (1202–04)

Prester John: A king who never was?

The search for a Christian nation in the Orient

In this portrait, from a map of 1558, the legendary Christian King Prester John is shown presiding over his kingdom situated in the area of present-day Ethiopia.

CHRISTIAN RULERS in 12th-century Europe were preoccupied with the problem of security. Western Europe had emerged from the centuries of chaos known as the Dark Ages only to become a battleground for fractious princes and ambitious churchmen. But worse than the danger of internal warfare was the menace of non-Christian powers. Europe's eastern fringes were under constant threat from the well-organized forces of Islam, and much of Spain was still ruled by Muslim Moors. Meanwhile, the great Crusades to recapture the Holy Land were foundering upon the rocks of Turkish military might. So when a bishop from a Christian colony in present-day Lebanon arrived at the papal court in 1145 with reports of a powerful *Christian* kingdom in the East, the courts of Europe buzzed with the news. Here, it seemed, was an ally who might attack the heathen Muslims from the rear.

The bishop told the pope that the kingdom, lying in the Far East, "beyond Persia and Armenia," was headed by a priest-king called Iohannes Presbyter (John the Elder – rather like the elders of the modern Presbyterian Church) who was a direct descendant of one of the Magi, the three wise men who had visited the infant Jesus. Iohannes Presbyter, said the bishop, had recently defeated the Muslim Kings of Persia

and would have marched on Jerusalem to help the beleaguered Christians there, but had been forced to return home because his army was unable to cross the River Tigris.

Where, exactly, *was* home for Iohannes Presbyter (later anglicized to Prester John)? The only answer appears in a letter, allegedly written in about 1165 by the priest-king himself, addressed to both the Byzantine Emperor of Constantinople and the Holy Roman Emperor. Prester John's realm, it claimed, encompassed "the three Indias." To medieval mapmakers this phrase made impressive sense. They knew the three Indias as Nearer India, Farther India, and Middle India. Nearer and Farther India were, respectively, the northern and southern portions of the Indian sub-continent; Middle India was actually the African region later known as Ethiopia, which lay about halfway along the sea-and-land route from Europe to India via a corner of Egypt and the Red Sea. So the search for Prester John's Christian kingdom could now begin; and during the next three centuries a number of explorers did their best to find it.

They "found" it almost everywhere, and yet nowhere. The Venetian traveler Marco Polo, who spent nearly 25 years in Asia between 1271 and 1295, identified Prester John's people with the Tartars and reported that descendants of Prester John held territory on the plain of Kuku Khotan about 300 miles (500 kilometers) northwest of Beijing (Peking). Until late in the 15th century, Europe's rulers clung to the dream of discovering an oriental Christian ally against the dreaded Muslims. In the 1490s, for instance, they were heartened by a report from the Portuguese explorer Vasco da Gama (the first European to sail around southern Africa) that he had heard about – though not seen – a king called Preste Joham who reigned in the interior of East Africa somewhere north of Mozambique.

Then, in the 16th century, the Muslim threat to Europe receded. And as fear faded, so did the drive to find Prester John's legendary realm. Today, more than 800 years after the first report seized the imagination of a continent, all that survives is a handful of cryptic references in ancient manuscripts – plus a world of speculation. For although the kingdom of Prester John was never found, there is reason to believe that it was not entirely a figment of the imagination of a 12th-century bishop.

WHO WAS THE MAN BEHIND THE TALE?

Like many famous legends, from the Siege of Troy to King Arthur and his knights, the story of Prester John seems to be a mixture of fact and fancy, and scholars still argue about where one begins and the other ends. There is agreement, however, on at least some elements: The Muslim Kings of Persia *were* defeated in battle just before the first news of Prester John burst onto the European scene in 1145; there *were* Christians living in Central Asia and India; and there *was* a Christian empire in Ethiopia.

The battle that overthrew the Persians took place in 1141 near Samarkand, just north of present-day Iran. The victors in that battle were Central Asian Mongols under a commander known as Gur-Khan. Some historians believe that this name might have been pronounced

Yuhanan by Arabs when news of the battle reached the Middle East, and that it could then have become the Latin Iohannes, or John.

Among other candidates for the mantle of Prester John, the most probable, according to modern historians, are the 12th-century Emperors of Ethiopia, all of whom were Christians and known to have been in touch with Rome. It even seems likely that a letter apparently addressed to Prester John by Pope Alexander III in 1177 was really intended for the Ethiopian court. If this theory is correct, the mortal remains of the fabulously wealthy king may still be lying, undiscovered and undisturbed, somewhere in the interior of what is today – ironically – one of the poorest nations in the world.

Home-made gold

An alchemist's dream come true?

THE ALCHEMISTS of the Middle Ages, who included both talented scientists and charlatans among their number, dreamed of finding a miraculous substance called the philosopher's stone or the great elixir, that would transmute a common metal, such as lead, into gold and would confer immortality on its owner. They believed that only those in a state of grace or completely in tune with the harmony of Nature could expect to discover it. To guard their secrets, the alchemists used an obscure language of metaphor and allegory so that no one outside their circle might understand their writings.

No alchemist ever discovered the secret of the philosopher's stone – with one possible exception: A Frenchman, Nicolas Flamel, who by his and other, seemingly authoritative, accounts preserved in the Bibliothèque Nationale in Paris, first fashioned the stone in 1382 and used it to make silver from lead, and gold from mercury.

Nicolas Flamel was born in about 1330, probably at Pontoise, north of Paris. He became a public scribe in Paris, working in a tiny booth near the Church of St. Jacques-la-Boucherie. There he taught noblemen how to write their signatures. He also had a flourishing business producing illuminated manuscripts and devotional books. One night Flamel had a strange dream in which an angel appeared holding out a book and telling him to read it. But as he reached out for the book, the vision disappeared.

The dream was prophetic. In 1357 Flamel was offered a book which he recognized as the book in the dream. This ancient volume was called *The Book of Abraham the Jew* and Flamel quickly realized that it contained formulas for transmuting metals, but he could make no sense of its strange symbols. The book also included a curse on all who read it, excepting only priests and scribes. Flamel, himself a scribe, felt safe and he sought the help of alchemists to penetrate its secrets, but to no avail.

By 1378 Flamel realized that his only hope lay in finding a Jew who could understand the book. This was not easy, because the Jews had been persecuted and most had been driven away from France. However, he eventually met an elderly converted Jew named Maître Canches, who grew increasingly excited as he examined Flamel's copy of the book. He declared it to be the lost book of the *cabala*, a religious philosophy based on ancient scriptures that had been developed by rabbis. He began to explain the mysterious symbols but before the work was finished, he fell sick and died.

Fortunately for his quest, Flamel had learned enough to wrest the secret of the philosopher's stone from the book's pages. Three years later, on January 17, 1382, he was able to make a

In the Middle Ages, when modern distinctions between "science" and "magic" did not apply, the alchemist bent on transmuting a base metal into gold (shown above in this 15th-century painting by "Il Stradano") in the course of his experiments often made progress in the science of chemistry. The work of medieval alchemists flourished side by side with advances in optics, mathematics, and astronomy that were to be of long-term benefit to mankind.

substance he called the white elixir. Adding some of it to molten lead, he transmuted the lead into pure silver. Three months later, Flamel produced a red elixir, which he then added to mercury to produce gold.

Flamel made several more transmutations and apparently amassed enough gold to found 14 hospitals, build three chapels, make gifts to seven churches, and perform many other charitable acts. He acquired considerable fame, not only as an alchemist, but also as a philanthropist and as a most devout man. Flamel died in 1417 and his home and tomb were later ransacked by people searching for the philosopher's stone.

But were these searches doomed from the outset? Did Flamel succeed where others before and after him had failed? If he did discover the philosopher's stone, it certainly did not give him immortality – despite claims that he was spotted enjoying a night at the opera in Paris in 1761. The church in which he was buried has since been demolished but his tombstone can be seen today in the Musée de Cluny in Paris. The records in the Bibliothèque Nationale demonstrate that he did make the charitable gifts that

were attributed to him, although his business could have provided sufficient wealth to account for them. And what happened to *The Book of Abraham the Jew*, which eventually gave up its secrets to Flamel? He bequeathed it to his nephew and, about 200 years later, it came into the possession of the French Cardinal Richelieu who, having no Maître Canches of his own, was unable to interpret its strange symbols. Shortly after Richelieu's death, the book was lost.

As for the transmutation of metals, modern scientists know of no way in which lead can be changed into silver, and mercury into gold, short of employing particle accelerators and nuclear reactors. In other words, they know of no way in which Flamel, given the scientific knowledge of the day, could have succeeded. Yet Flamel himself seems to have believed that he attained his goal. However, perhaps his real greatness lay, not in his power to turn base metals to gold but, as his critics claim, in his ability as a master confidence trickster who succeeded where others failed – in achieving lasting fame as the "sole discoverer" of the legendary and elusive philosopher's stone.

Warriors of feudal Japan
They chose death before disgrace

ON NOVEMBER 25, 1970, as a protest against what he saw as the decadence of Japanese society, the internationally respected Japanese novelist, Yukio Mishima, publicly committed hara-kiri (the honorable form of suicide traditionally reserved for Japan's samurai, or warrior class). This ritual suicide horrified the world and left Japan stunned. Not only had the country lost one of its most gifted writers; the event also struck disquieting chords in the nation's soul. For it showed that, alongside Japan's booming material prosperity, the austere values of the ancient samurai still lived on. Indeed, Mishima's blood seemed to reproach an entire generation of Japanese.

The samurai warriors are well known to modern moviegoers – almost as familiar figures as medieval knights or the gunslingers in Westerns. But who were these proud warriors who shaped the character of a nation?

Local clans, bound by ancestral loyalties, were a feature of Japanese society for many centuries. The nation was united under one emperor possibly as early as AD 300, but imperial authority

Ceremonial swords are made in Japan today in much the same way as they have been for centuries. Here a blade is being polished in the traditional manner on a raised floor.

THE DIVINE WIND

During the 13th century, the Mongol hordes swept across Asia, founding an empire which stretched from Eastern Europe to Korea. In 1260, after imperial China had fallen to the barbarians, the Mongols began to look eastward, toward the islands of Japan.

In 1274, a Mongol army landed on the southern Japanese island of Kyushu, and engaged Japan's samurai armies in fierce fighting. That night, however, a typhoon scattered part of the Mongol fleet, and the invaders were forced to return to the mainland in disarray.

In 1281, the Mongols landed a second invasion force numbering tens of thousands of men. For two months, the proud samurai held a defensive line against the Mongol onslaught; and then a second typhoon came to their aid. Again it destroyed much of the Mongol fleet, and thousands of invaders fell to samurai swords while attempting to withdraw. The Mongols never attacked Japan again.

The second typhoon came to be known as *kamikaze* – "the divine wind" – and became linked in Japanese minds with victory. The term kamikaze was adopted toward the end of World War II by the Japanese pilots who committed suicide by deliberately crashing their aircraft into enemy craft, so guaranteeing a direct hit.

The highly stylized Kabuki drama is still a popular form of Japanese entertainment. This 19th-century print shows actors impersonating samurai warriors in action.

was always precarious, and a number of emperors were in fact puppets of warlike noblemen competing for power. By the 10th century AD, the aristocratic Fujiwara house had come to guide the nation's affairs. The emperor was still the nominal ruler – but clan members monopolized all positions of power.

Under the Fujiwara, Japanese aristocrats gravitated toward the cities and the imperial court at Kyoto. In the provinces, the power vacuum was filled by new and ambitious clan leaders who, like the barons of feudal Europe, maintained armed forces of their own. Their fighting men were known as *bushi* – or (in a later term of Chinese origin) *samurai*, a term meaning "one who serves."

The samurai at first acted, in the famous phrase, as "the teeth and claws of the Fujiwara." Later, however, the military men forced their way closer to the centers of power, until in 1156, one of the leading samurai families exploited disputes within the imperial family and supplanted the Fujiwara – and for some 700 years afterward, Japanese life was completely dominated by the warrior class.

The notion of total loyalty was at the core of the samurai tradition. Every true samurai, whether illustrious knight or mere spear-bearer, was bound by oath to one lord or another. Clan chiefs themselves owed allegiance to the emperor, whose title and divine ancestry was still revered, even though he lived cloistered in his court and was impotent to act. Obedience was an absolute ideal. No samurai was allowed to question – or even pause to consider – an order. Young warriors were made to undergo grueling tests to harden them. Above all, they were trained to believe that their lives belonged to their master to dispose of as he would. When a master died, in battle or in bed, his retainers sometimes felt obliged to commit suicide to honor their bond of service. (A classic of the Japanese theatre, the *Chuchingura*, celebrates an incident in 1703, when 47 samurai committed mass hara-kiri rather than be left without a lawful lord to lead them.)

The term *hara-kiri* means "abdomen-cutting," and this excruciating form of suicide was the exclusive privilege of the warrior class (women might slit their throats, and merchants could take poison). The abdomen was considered the very core of a man's being, and elaborate rules of etiquette were developed around its mutilation. The cut, for example, was to be made horizontally, from left to right; a second upward jerk of the knife was supposed to finish the job off. It was difficult to achieve a quick or certain death with this method, so an assistant was occasionally required to finish the job by cleaving the victim's head from his body.

A samurai might resort to hara-kiri for a number of reasons; out of shame, devotion, or – as Mishima had done – in protest. On the field of battle, suicide was often committed to avoid capture, for to a samurai, death was preferable to the disgrace of surrender. A samurai who was taken prisoner was forever dishonored.

Before the samurai became so powerful, they were regarded by fastidious courtiers as bandits and barbarians. As their influence grew, certain individual samurai were treated as god-like heroes, whose praises were sung throughout Japan. Neither image, of course, is completely true. Certainly, lawless and arrogant samurai were a problem, especially during prolonged periods of peace. They were a class apart which produced nothing, and despised commerce. It was, for example, a mark of good breeding for a warrior not to recognize the different values of coins in circulation. If a tradesman seemed suspicious of the coins he was given by a samurai, it was perfectly legal for the warrior to cut him down on the spot. No one was allowed to interfere. Occasionally, an unsuspecting commoner might have his head severed merely as "killing practice" for the samurai; the blow was delivered with a single warning whoop.

Not all was violence in the samurai code, however, for the warrior's life was seen as a moral progression. Samurai in fact became deeply influenced by Zen Buddhism, a creed which taught respect for all living things. It was these same warriors who popularized the famous Japanese tea ceremony, a calm ritual designed to stimulate feeling for simple things. It was probably the Zen pursuit of the pure and uncluttered which appealed to the warriors; a philosophy that exalted a man's intuition and will above his ability to learn.

But however ascetic or noble in spirit, a samurai was still essentially a war machine. Two swords – one long, one short – were his key weapons, and immense craftsmanship was lavished on producing their razor-sharp blades. High-ranking cavalrymen were also armed with bows and arrows, while the lowliest samurai fought mainly with a spear. They all wore armor, comprising six pieces: helmet, mask, breastplate, sleeve, shin guard, and loin guard.

By 1600, the samurai class made up some six per cent of the population, and much had changed since the early days. No longer, for example, could any soldier of valor rise to the highest command; the military class was more rigid and hierarchical. Luxury and corruption had also tainted the martial tradition. Yet the great samurai houses continued to dominate national life until the reign of the Emperor Meiji (1867–1912). A major reformer, he restored the central authority of the imperial throne and transformed Japan almost overnight into an international power to be reckoned with.

After surviving 29 years on a Philippine island, ready to resist any attack by the Allied forces, Lt. Hiroo Onoda surrenders his sword in 1974 on the instructions of his former military commander.

Even so, the samurai tradition endured in military and cultural life. During World War II, for example, Japanese officers would commit hara-kiri rather than submit to the shame of surrender, while kamikaze pilots willingly went to oblivion to serve their emperor. The Mishima suicide of 1970 was followed by an equally sensational event four years later. In 1974, Hiroo Onoda, an imperial army lieutenant from World War II, emerged, aged 52, from the jungles of a Philippine island and finally surrendered his sword – 29 years after the end of the war. He had been posted to the island in 1944, and having received no direct command to surrender, had continued the struggle, surviving in jungle hideouts. When parties were sent to bring in the mysterious recluse, they were met with gunfire from hidden positions.

Onoda only surrendered when his former commanding officer (by now a retired Kyushu bookseller) was flown out to rescind his order to keep on fighting. It was neither fear nor eccentricity that had inspired the lieutenant's long ordeal – but the spirit of the samurai.

Love in the Middle Ages

The attainable scorned in favor of the unattainable

THE ROMANTIC image of a knight in shining armor, forever ready to serve his lady love, has come down to us through the ages, and shows no signs of losing its glitter despite the efforts of spoil-sport historians to point out that neither armor nor lovely ladies were invariably spotless in medieval times. How did this glamorous idea of heroic, generally unfulfilled courtly love gain currency? If one group of people can be credited with (or blamed for) responsibility, it was the troubadour poets of 12th-century France. And if one person, more than any other, helped to nourish their cult, that person was Eleanor of Aquitaine, who married Henry II of England.

Medieval courtly love, or *amour courtois*, was itself inspired by a variety of beliefs and situations. One of these was a mystical notion of love

THE LANGUAGE OF THE TROUBADOURS

The word "troubadour" comes from the old Provençal language; the verb *trobar* means "to find," in the sense of finding (inventing) verses and melodies. Provençal, a cross between medieval Italian, Spanish, and French, was originally spoken in Provence and other parts of southern France. Thanks to the art and fame of the troubadours, it spread through much of Western Europe and for a time became an international language, second only to Latin.

The troubadours made a ritual of courtship, and, like all rituals, theirs had a special vocabulary to define various phases of ceremonial "worship." The opening stage was the *fegnedor*, when the aspiring lover gazed mutely upon his lady from afar. Next came the *precador*, when he declared his feelings of adoration. With the *entendedor* stage he was accepted as the lady's suitor. The final stage of *drut*, in theory at least, saw the eventual consummation of his love.

There was also the *tenson*, a special type of debate or competition among troubadours on the merits of each other's verses. The famous song contest in Wagner's opera *Tannhäuser* and today's Welsh eisteddfods (music festivals) draw some of their inspiration from the *tensons* of the troubadours.

The formal courtship of the Middle Ages is shown in this 15th-century manuscript illustration.

This discreet lady uses a pulley to raise her lover, undetected, from the street. Such pulleys, which were often a permanent feature on the front of medieval town houses for raising furniture to the upper stories, must have facilitated many romantic intrigues.

as a kind of divine sickness – a notion that probably spread to Europe from Islam by way of the Crusades and Moorish Spain. There was also a growing cult of the Virgin Mary. The magnificent new cathedrals were studded with shrines and statues to the Queen of Heaven. Such worship replaced the earlier Church view of women as sinful descendants of Eve with a new image of woman as exalted.

These radical ideas about the nature of love and of the female herself were in marked contrast with the realities of medieval Europe, whose feudal system empowered kings and barons to barter their womenfolk in marriage and pack them off to grim and loveless existences. Courtly love came into being to redress the balance, to render to women the adoration and devotion they seldom found in marriage. And its apostles were the troubadours of southern France – poets and musicians from many walks of life who, through their verse and song, tended to influence the courtiers and nobles they entertained, much as the media have the power to influence people today.

The troubadours saw courtship as the chief purpose of their art. In their songs they expressed their yearnings, their moments of hope and joy, their willingness to sacrifice life and liberty for a lady's favor and in defense of her honor.

Eleanor's homeland of Aquitaine in southwestern France – the rich and abundant "land of waters" – was perhaps the most civilized part of Europe in the 12th century; and women were generally treated with more respect there than elsewhere. Eleanor, who had grown up in the court of her grandfather, Duke William IX, himself a renowned womanizer and poet, encouraged the art of the troubadours, and many of the finest of these minstrels made her the focal point of their flattering verse. Most celebrated of her literary suitors was Bernard of Ventador, a poet who, obeying the code of chivalry, never dedicated his songs openly to the queen – in view of her marriage to the tempestuous Henry Plantagenet, it would hardly have been wise to do so – but left no doubt that the lady addressed as *mos aziman* ("my magnet") was Eleanor.

Non-physical adoration was partly serious, partly an elaborate game. Sexual appetites in the Middle Ages were no less strong than they have always been. While a troubadour was gracefully idolizing his chosen lady from a discreet distance, affecting to swoon at a glance from her, he was usually quite ready to satisfy his lust elsewhere without ceremony. During the Crusades, indeed, the Muslims were frequently shocked by the licentiousness of the women who followed the Christian armies, which contained

FIRST LADY OF THE COURTLY LOVERS

A scene from the 1977 British television series The Devil's Crown, *featuring Jane Lapotaire as Eleanor of Aquitaine.*

Queen Eleanor of Aquitaine can stand beside Cleopatra of Egypt and Elizabeth I of England as one of history's most remarkable royal women. She was born around the year 1122, and died 82 years later – an astonishing life span for that time. Her first husband was Louis VII of France, whom she accompanied on a Crusade to the Holy Land. They were divorced in 1152 and she went on to marry Henry Plantagenet, Count of Anjou and Duke of Normandy; and after Henry was crowned Henry II of England in 1154, she shared his rule of the Angevin empire that extended from the borders of Scotland to the Pyrenees in southwestern France.

Her sons Richard (Coeur de Lion) and John were both Kings of England in their turn. She supported Richard when, as a young man, he and two other brothers rebelled against their father; and when the revolt failed, she was imprisoned for nearly 15 years, right up to the time of Henry's death. But she never lost either her spirit or her enormous influence over her sons. At Richard's accession to the throne in 1189 she was already in her late sixties but still notably vigorous, personable, and eager to assist in increasing the power of her family.

Like most strong-minded women, Eleanor was extravagantly praised and bitterly vilified by contemporaries and later commentators. She was called bitch, harlot, monster. Shakespeare writes of her as a "canker'd grandam." To others, though, she was an "incomparable woman," immensely charming and sexually attractive. It is a mark of her personality that we remember her not as a queen of England and France, but as someone in her own right – as Eleanor of Aquitaine.

many troubadours flaunting sweet tokens of spiritual fidelity to distant goddesses.

Hypocritical and even cynical though it may have been, the troubadours' elevation of womanhood opened a whole new world of European literature. Eleanor's daughter, Marie de Champagne, encouraged the French poet Chrétien de Troyes to retell the Celtic Arthurian legends in terms of courtly love. Stories we all know about Lancelot, Guinevere, the quest for the Holy Grail, and the rest would be very different had they not been painted in troubadour colors. Dante immortalized his Beatrice, Petrarch his Laura, in the spirit of courtly love. Centuries later, the romanticism of the 12th century was to pulsate again in the poetry of Tennyson and the lyrical prose of Fitzgerald's *The Great Gatsby*.

New Jerusalem in Ethiopia
A miracle in stone

FROM THE TAWNY mountains of Wallo province in northern Ethiopia rises one of the most breathtaking sights in the world – a stupendous assemblage of 11 Christian churches, each hewn from a single block of rock. This is the miracle of Lalibela, the holy city of an ancient Ethiopian king after whom the city is named. None of the churches was "built"; each was carved from the mountainside as a gigantic piece of sculpture, with naves, aisles, altars, and even courtyards all chiseled out of the landscape. Glowing red amid surrounding olive groves, the place is a petrified wonderland.

A 16th-century Portuguese priest, Francisco Alvarez, the first European known to have visited the site, described the monuments as edifices "the like of which cannot be found in the world." More than 400 years later, Lalibela still possesses the power to amaze as, wandering through carved halls, courts, and galleries, the visitor is constantly astonished by new buildings, gateways, and terraces. Though we do not know precisely who created this enchanted labyrinth, there is no doubt that it grew from the visionary impulse of King Lalibela, who ruled over Ethiopia in the early 13th century. Lalibela, who was born in the city – then named Roha, but later renamed in tribute to the king's achievements – was a member of the Zagwe dynasty, a royal house that reigned during a period of about 150 years when the ancient line of kings claiming descent from Solomon and Sheba was temporarily broken. But although he was not of the purest lineage, he remained true to the religion of the traditional dynasty. Ethiopia had embraced Christianity as early as the fourth century.

Legend has it that Lalibela conceived his plan for a holy city of churches after Christ appeared to him in a dream and that angels assisted the stonemasons in their work. Even on the level of prosaic fact, the sculptured rock monuments are so awe-inspiring that it seems incredible that they could have been carved by human hands alone. At any rate, many scholars believe that native craftsmen must have been assisted by masons and sculptors from other lands, possibly even from Alexandria and Jerusalem. Nobody, however, can argue that the style of the churches is other than uniquely Ethiopian.

There are hundreds of other rock-hewn churches scattered throughout central Tigre province, and they testify to a distinctive Ethiopian tradition. All are true monoliths – that is, edifices formed from single blocks of rock – and all are decorated both inside and outside, though none can compare with those of Lalibela in design and finish. Such churches exist nowhere else in the world; even the rock-cut temples of Egypt are simply sculpted facades in the rock face, masking rude caves behind.

The skill and ingenuity of the masons almost defy belief. It has been estimated that around 130,000 cubic feet (100,000 cubic meters) of rock had to be chiseled out of the Lalibela site in order to create the standing architectural wonder of a community of 11 churches, four of which are totally detached from the mountainside, the remainder in different degrees of attachment. All the buildings broadly follow the layout of Byzantine churches, with their basilicas and three ritual entrances. Yet each church is an individual creation, and everything, from the most majestic columns to the most delicate tracery, was carved from the rock as it stood almost exactly 800 years ago. To achieve such master works, the masons probably began by cutting a deep rectangular trench into the mountainside, freeing an immense, rough oblong of rock within. They then worked at the raw stone, both

Most of the churches at Lalibela are unadorned, their stone walls and ceilings devoid of any decoration. A few, however, are colorfully decorated with complex geometric designs or figurative scenes from Bible stories, such as the mural shown above. Such murals are painted either on plaster or directly onto bare rock.

inside and out, starting from the top. After an upper level was shaped, it was sculpted in detail; the craftsmen then proceeded to the level below. The rock itself, because fairly soft, must have been easy to carve, but we can only guess at how the long galleries were lighted and ventilated while work was going on. It is possible that sunlight was reflected into the galleries by means of bronze mirrors, thus dispensing with the need for smoking oil lamps.

Some of the churches remain in their pits; they and their surrounding courtyards only visible from above. The heavy summer rains of the region must have made flooding a hazard for the builders, but they solved the problem by cutting the bottom of each pit at a slope to carry rain-water away from the working area, and they also slanted roofs and gutters ingeniously in order to minimize danger from torrential rain-fall. It is a tribute to the skill of the craftsmen that modern archeologists working at the site have found that the original precautions guarantee safety during even the heaviest cloudbursts.

Until recently the rock-hewn churches of Lalibela were accessible only by mule train. Attempts at restoration were made during the years between World Wars I and II, but serious work did not begin until 1967. Today Lalibela is a prosperous market town with a paved road and nearby airstrip, and the churches are visited by flocks of tourists and pilgrims whenever seasonal conditions – and the political situation – permit. But an aura of mystery still lingers about the site. What was it that inspired the Ethiopian king to sponsor such an ambitious project at such a time in such a place?

One theory to explain the timing, the scale, and the grandeur of the conception has recently

All the churches at Lalibela are carved out of the solid rock, but the church of St. George is the only one in the shape of a cross. The projection above shows the three, west-facing, doors, a typical feature at Lalibela.

gained a number of adherents. During the early years of King Lalibela's reign the Crusades were in full swing, and it was in 1187 that Jerusalem was captured by the Saracens under the great Sultan of Egypt, Saladin. With the Holy City in Muslim hands, Ethiopia's faithful were so stirred in spirit that their zealous sovereign was impelled to reshape his birthplace as an alternative center for pilgrimage and worship, a bastion of Christianity in the hills of East Africa. The church-city of Lalibela, in short, may well have been conceived as a New Jerusalem.

That may be just a theory, but one fact about the churches remains incontrovertible: At Lalibela a burning faith, brilliant artistry, and supreme technological virtuosity combined to create what has been justly called a veritable and lasting wonder of the world.

Of gunpowder and guns
From China to Europe

WHEN KNOWLEDGE of how to make gunpowder came to Europe in the 13th century, the potential effect was as explosive as the substance itself – it changed the face of warfare for centuries to come. Gunpowder was also one of the major factors in ending the feudalism of the Middle Ages. Until the beginning of the 15th century, feudal barons ruled over their lands in secure, well-provisioned castles which could withstand years of siege. Gunpowder changed all this. Cannons and grenades could turn a once-impregnable fortress into a crumbling trap, without any lengthy tunneling (done to undermine the walls) or for the hand-to-hand butchery of an infantry assault. And so power slipped from the hands of many barons into those of a few kings, whose centralized governments were strong enough to control manufacture and use of the shattering new weapons.

Strangely, however, scholars are uncertain about the origins of gunpowder. Until recently they were still arguing about whether it was invented by the Chinese, by Arabs, or by Roger Bacon, a remarkable English scientist and Franciscan monk. Today, most experts concede that credit should go to the Chinese, but doubts persist as to when the "black dust" was first used. Some scholars believe that its ingredients – saltpeter (potassium nitrate), charcoal, and sulfur – may have been determined as early as the ninth century AD. Others date the invention from a recipe published in 1044 by a chemist named Wu Ching Tsao Yao. Nor is it clear what the Chinese used gunpowder for, although many experts now believe that the Chinese had small firearms as early as the 11th century. Others argue that they rammed gunpowder into bamboo tubes only to make signal rockets and fireworks. It has also been suggested that during

ROGER BACON: PROPHET OF SCIENCE

Roger Bacon, born into a wealthy family of English country people in about 1214, spent approximately half of his life as a humble Franciscan friar, but he perhaps deserves to rank alongside the 15th-century genius Leonardo da Vinci as a scientific visionary. Kept in confinement by church leaders for his critical attitude toward authority, he nonetheless continued studying and thinking about the material world until his death in around 1294, and he is recognized as a founder of modern science. Consider this passage from one of his books – a passage of breathtaking foresight (written originally in Latin, of course):

"Machines of navigation can be constructed without rowers so that the largest ships . . . will be moved by a single man at a greater speed than if they were full of men. A chariot that will move with incalculable speed without any draught animal can also be constructed . . . and flying machines in which a man can sit in the middle of the machine revolving an engine by which artificial wings are made to beat the air like a bird."

Bacon is generally credited with having been the first person to suggest ways to improve eyesight by the use of lenses (spectacles), an innovation which came into use during his lifetime. And he urged a reform of the then inaccurate calendar along the lines finally adopted by Pope Gregory XIII in 1582, and still in use today. But modern scientists pay homage to Bacon more for his advocacy of scientific *methods* than for his work on gunpowder or his technological prophecies. He saw more clearly than most of his contemporaries that experimentation must play a central role in advancing our knowledge of the world, and that "pure" logic – so dear to the hearts of most medieval scholars – could tell us little without the aid of precise measurements and observations.

A portrait of Roger Bacon, whose ideas earned him imprisonment before his true stature as a scientist was recognized.

Gunpowder transformed medieval warfare. Shown below in this medieval illustration is an early cannon using stone-shot ammunition.

the 13th century the Sung dynasty of China was using flame-throwers and explosive grenades in its long war against Genghis Khan.

Information about the requisite ingredients of the explosive black dust reached Europe via the

Arabs sometime before 1243, when Roger Bacon (who could read Arabic) wrote what is certainly the first European recipe for gunpowder. By means of a mixture of seven parts of saltpeter to five of charcoal and five of sulfur, he wrote, an enemy "might be either blown up bodily or put to flight by terror caused by the explosion." Bacon's formula was very soon strengthened, under pressure of constant European conflict, by an increase in the proportion of saltpeter (modern blasting powder contains about 75 per cent of this).

Then, sometime after 1300, it was discovered that if the powder was enclosed in a tube, it could propel objects great distances. Nobody knows who made the discovery – and thus invented the first real firearm. Although Roger Bacon foresaw gunpowder bombs, he does not seem to have speculated about this other possibility. The most likely candidate seems to be a German monk known as Berthold Schwarz (Berthold the Black, an epithet possibly acquired because chemical expertise was thought of as a kind of sorcery). According to tradition, he blasted a metal block – the first bullet – into the air by igniting gunpowder in a container.

Whether or not that story is true, both gunpowder and guns were being manufactured in England in the 1340s and probably in Flanders and Italy before then. In the early years, the effects were occasionally as dreadful to those who fired the cannons as to those fired upon, for accuracy of aim could not be guaranteed. Horses of both friend and foe were equally alarmed and frequently the weapon blew up in the face of the gunner. But in the roar of battle against the French at Crécy and Calais in 1346, smoke from the black dust signalled the beginning of the end of chivalry and knighthood and introduced the age of the gun and indiscriminate slaughter.

The death of William Rufus

A medieval murder mystery

LATE ONE AUGUST afternoon in AD 1100, William II of England – generally known as William Rufus ("Red") because of his florid complexion – went on a stag hunt in the New Forest, then a royal game preserve stretching over a large area of southern England, with his younger brother, Henry, and a number of attendants. When the party split up into small groups, the king and his close adviser,

Walter Tirel, rode off together. What then happened remains a fascinating mystery. The facts, as far as we know them, were as follows:

A stag passed near the king and he loosed an arrow, which struck the target but did not kill. For a moment he remained motionless in the saddle, shielding his eyes against the slanting evening light to watch the stag's course. In that instant Tirel shot, and his arrow, missing the stag, struck the king, who fell forward, driving the arrow deep into his chest as he hit the ground; death was instantaneous. Tirel fled the forest and escaped to France. Henry and the rest of the hunting party galloped off to the nearby city of Winchester, where the royal treasure was housed, leaving William's body where it lay. Having seized the treasure, and knowing it to be safe in his possession, Henry hastened to London, where he was crowned Henry I on the third day after his brother's death.

Those are the facts. The question that has never been satisfactorily answered is this: Did William Rufus really die by accident, or was he assassinated at the instigation of his ambitious young brother? Or – a bizarre notion that has recently gained some credence – was he the self-appointed victim of a macabre pagan rite?

The reason some people had for taking this "witchcraft" theory seriously is that throughout his reign (1087–1100) William openly jeered at Christianity, plundered Church property, and most probably believed in pagan gods. After his death it was easy for people to believe stories about portents of impending disaster that were said to have occurred on the eve of the hunt in the New Forest. For example, it was said that William had awakened from a nightmare screaming with terror as a result of a premonition of dying in a welter of blood. And a certain monk also claimed to have had a dream that night – a dream in which a crucifix had kicked the king to the ground, where he lay breathing fire and smoke. Furthermore, there were reports alleging that in a conversation with Walter Tirel the king had urged Tirel to slay him because, according to William's "religion," he had outlived his usefulness as a monarch, and a king with waning powers must be ritually sacrificed.

These and similar stories may well have been popularly accepted because of the general detestation of a cruel and apparently unchristian king who had quite possibly died accidentally. But it also seems possible that they were invented and disseminated as a smoke screen to hide the truth. There are good reasons for arguing that the incident in the New Forest was engineered by William's brother Henry, who had much to gain by William's sudden death.

William Rufus was the second of the three sons of William the Conqueror, who divided his empire among them by leaving Normandy in France to the eldest, Robert; England to William; and a considerable sum of money but no territory to young Henry. Disputes and often open warfare were endemic among the older brothers, but in 1096 they became reconciled when Robert decided to go on a Crusade and needed money to finance the expedition. He borrowed what he needed from William, pledging Normandy as security. In the summer of 1100, though, while Robert was on his way back to France newly married to a rich woman, William decided not to permit his brother to regain Normandy by repaying the debt. Instead, he began making preparations for a campaign to retain the territory, and those preparations were interrupted by the hunt in the New Forest.

Meanwhile, if Henry *wanted* to secure the throne of England, it must have seemed clear to him that he would have to act fast (and the great speed with which he did act immediately after William Rufus's death suggests some earlier planning on his part). If he had waited until Robert returned to Normandy, almost anything could have happened. So it seems quite likely that Henry decided to organize matters so as to have only one brother instead of two to contend with. With William dead, and Robert in a distant land, Henry could seize the English throne to which he had no rightful claim. A further important piece of evidence supporting the belief that Henry was responsible for the hunting "accident" is that Walter Tirel was never prosecuted, nor were his lands seized.

But was it in Henry's nature to organize such an odious crime? No doubt he was despotic and often cruel (on occasion he punished offenses against the state by blinding or castration) and his reign was one of calculated terror, but some historians maintain that he was incapable of fratricide. Moreover, they ask, what had Tirel to gain by collaborating with an enemy of William Rufus, his friend and patron? To the end of Tirel's life, indeed, he denied that he was guilty.

Might there, then, have been a third arrow, fired not by Tirel but by an unidentified member of the hunting party? Some historians think so. And some still insist it was not murder at all but an accident. Hunting in those days was a dangerous sport. Forests were dense, and many a mounted huntsman smashed his legs against trees or was brought down by branches. Arrows loosed in the excitement of the chase were always a source of danger; in fact, Robert's bastard son had been accidentally shot in the same forest some years before his uncle's death.

Still, skeptics like to point out that those who consider Henry incapable of fratricide can hardly praise him as a model of fraternal love. During the 35 years of his reign as Henry I, he wrested Normandy from his only remaining brother and kept him imprisoned in England until Robert's death at the age of 80.

Though the luckless King William II of England is shown in this woodcut mortally wounded by an arrow as he sits on his throne, it was well known that he met his death while hunting in the New Forest. Mystery surrounds the event, but many writers at the time thought it divine vengeance for the savage methods his father William the Conqueror had used when clearing the area of Anglo-Saxons to plant the forest for his personal use.

The greatest Christian relic

Masterpiece or forgery?

IN A CHAPEL of the cathedral at Turin in northern Italy lies a shroud that millions of Christians revere as the burial cloth in which the crucified body of Christ was wrapped. On the cloth, which is about 14 feet (4.5 meters) long and three feet six inches (1 meter) wide, a dead and disfigured body has somehow left its imprint. At the top can be seen the compelling features of a bearded man so like the commonly accepted face of Christ that those who cherish the shroud are convinced that the resemblance must be more than mere coincidence. If genuine, the cloth is the most impressive and moving relic to have come down to us from the time of Christ. But *is* it genuine? For centuries, skeptics have repeatedly proclaimed their doubt of its authenticity.

Controversy still rages – but 20th-century science has, surprisingly, made the voice of the skeptics less strident than it used to be. Tests by impartial scientists are producing increasingly firm evidence that what is revered by so many is in fact the shroud of someone who was crucified in Palestine around the time that Jesus died. Whether the body was that of Christ can probably never be finally ascertained.

The burial cloth under investigation bears the marks on its lefthand portion of the front, on its righthand portion the back, of a man around 35 to 40 years old and about five feet six inches (1.6 meters) tall. There is evidence of a wound in the ribs and of bleeding from the forearms; and something sharp enough to cut the skin – a crown of thorns? – seems to have been bound

THE MANDYLION THEORY

The compelling face on the Mandylion, which was revered by the Byzantines and which some historians believe to be one and the same with the shroud in Turin and now in possession of the pope. The Mandylion has inspired many artists through the centuries, and is featured in this detail from a work by the 15th-century Flemish painter Hans Memling.

Where was the Turin Shroud before 1357, when the impoverished de Charny family began to show it to fee-paying pilgrims in the French provincial town of Lirey? Skeptics who answer that question by insisting it was a relatively recent fabrication have used as a key argument for their case the fact that the image of the face on the shroud conforms closely to the conventional image of Jesus – bearded, commanding, with a V shape at the bridge of the nose. This, they contend, reflects the derivative character of an obvious medieval forgery. The weight of evidence, however, points another way, to the probability that the long line of traditional portrayals of Christ stems from the image on the Turin Shroud itself.

According to a legend of great antiquity, one of the disciples healed the leprosy of King Agbar of Edessa (now Ursa in southern Turkey) by letting him touch Christ's burial cloth, and the cloth remained in the possession of Agbar, who was the first pagan ruler to be converted to Christianity. When his successor, Ma'anu, reverted to paganism, the Christians of Edessa protected the shroud by hiding it in a niche in the city wall, where it was discovered nearly five centuries later. It is not legend but a historical fact that the Byzantines so prized a holy relic that they called the Mandylion (a name derived from a Greek word for an ecclesiastical robe) that they organized an expedition in 944 to wrest it from the Muslims who had gained control of Edessa. From then until the sack of Constantinople in 1204, the Mandylion was carefully guarded; it was on show to the public only twice a year. After 1204 it disappeared and was never seen again.

And what was this precious object? It was some sort of image of Christ's face imprinted on a piece

of cloth, and there can be no doubt about its influence on religious art after its discovery in the city wall of Edessa. Before the early sixth century, Jesus was often pictured as short-haired and clean-shaven. Thereafter he is always shown as long-haired, bearded, and with a pronounced V above the bridge of his nose – all features that correspond to the image on the Turin Shroud. Is it not likely, then, that the Mandylion lost in 1204 resurfaced as the shroud 150 years later?

One drawback to this theory is that the Mandylion is reputed to have borne only the face of Christ, not his entire body. But it has been pointed out that the shroud shows signs of having been folded so that only the head might have been open to view. The Byzantines kept the Mandylion in a frame; they may not have been aware of its full significance. In any event, there is a good possibility that it was rescued from the sack of Constantinople and taken to France by members of the Knights Templar, a wealthy military-religious order renowned for its piety and bravery. It would have been very much in character for this organization to preserve such a relic.

Chiefly because of the order's wealth, the Knights Templar made many enemies within the Christian world. One of these was France's King Philip IV, who, determined to suppress the Templars, had many of their leaders burned at the stake in 1313. One man among Philip's victims was named Geoffrey de Charney – a variant spelling for de Charny. Could Geoffrey's heirs have been the very people who put the Mandylion, now recognized as the burial cloth of Christ, on display in 1357? This is at least a plausible hypothesis to explain the sudden appearance of so awesome a relic after a lapse of many centuries.

around the head. One of the most controversial issues, of course, is the unanswerable question of how the shroud came to bear such clear imprints of the body it covered. Another equally vexing problem arises from the fact that there is no authenticated record of its existence before 1357, when it was publicly exhibited at the small French town of Lirey.

At that time the cloth belonged to a noble French family, the de Charnys, who never explained how it had come into their possession. Among the many people both inside and outside the Church who nevertheless had faith in its authenticity were the powerful Dukes of Savoy, to whom the controversial relic was bequeathed in 1453. At first they kept it in their capital city of Chambéry, where it was slightly damaged by fire in 1532. Then, in 1578, they moved their capital to Turin, where the shroud was enshrined in a cathedral chapel built expressly for it. It has lain there ever since, venerated by many, but the Catholic Church itself has never firmly declared it valid.

The first of the scientific tests that have gone a startlingly long way toward validating the relic took place in 1898. It was not a test at all, in fact, but a photograph taken by an Italian named Secondo Pia, who was as astonished as everyone to discover that the features of the body were etched far more distinctly on the negative than on the positive photograph. Subsequent examination involving increasingly accurate techniques culminated in 1978 with the arrival at Turin of a team of specialists from a number of countries. They were permitted to use every possible modern method for validating ancient objects except one – the carbon-14 process, which is the best-known technique for dating certain objects with a fair degree of accuracy. The reason for this exception is that the process destroys small portions of the object being examined, and the authorities understandably balked at the thought of any such damage.

One theory generally advanced by skeptics is that the figure imprinted on the shroud was simply painted sometime in the 14th century, and this theory has been supported by an American expert on forgeries, Walter McCrone. Contending that the bloodstains are unnaturally red for 2,000-year-old blood and that they were probably composed of a mixture of iron-oxide pigment and rose madder (a pigment much used by medieval artists), McCrone has produced a clever imitation of the shroud. Unlike the original, however, his paint penetrates the linen, showing through on both sides; and over 1,000 analyses by highly respected scientists since 1978

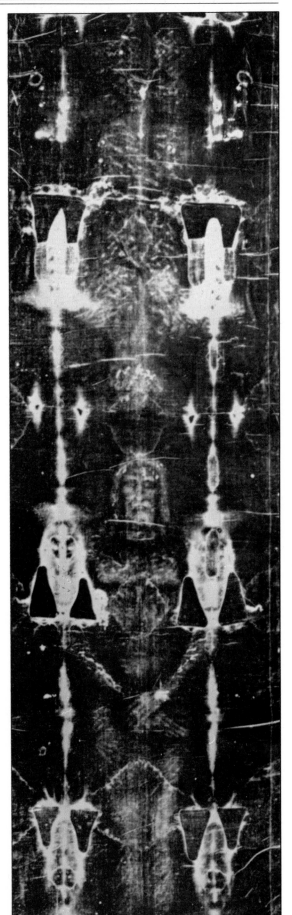

One of the Turin Shroud's mysterious, or miraculous, qualities is the way that the outline of a tortured figure on the cloth is revealed more clearly in a negative photograph, as shown here, than in a positive. For many Christians, this baffling phenomenon confirms the burial cloth's sacred authenticity; but whether or not it was Christ's shroud, the undeniably ancient linen is a very moving testimony to the painful death of an imposing-looking man.

How was the shroud so draped over the corpse that both front and back images appear? Here is one possible explanation, conceived by the 16th-century painter Giorgio Giulio Clovio.

have proved that the image on the Turin cloth could not have been made by paint. On the contrary, what looks like blood has been found to contain the right mixture for blood of calcium, protein, and iron. And analyses of all parts of the cloth not marked by bloodstains find them to be simply linen yellowed with extreme age.

Furthermore, pollen analyses indicate that the linen comes from the Middle East, which is the only area where 33 of the 49 different species of spore in the cloth grow. Textile experts have also concluded that the weave of the linen is of a type common in Palestine 2,000 years ago and that its fibers contain traces of cotton, which does not grow in Europe. If the shroud *was* forged in the Middle Ages, the forgers must have gone to the trouble of procuring cotton as well as certain kinds of plant spore in order to delude 20th-century scientists.

Even more strongly supportive of the authenticity of the relic is the striking 3-D effect that can be obtained by looking at the image through an instrument termed the "3-dimensional scanner." No known painting produces this effect; how it could have been achieved by even the most brilliant of forgers has baffled observers. They agree that the likeliest explanation of the 3-D phenomenon is that it was produced either by a combination of embalming spices and the bitter sweat of a tortured body or by "scorch" of the linen resulting from the chemical effects of an unusually high body temperature.

There remains little conviction among those who have examined the shroud that it was a medieval fake; it was much more probably the burial cloth of a crucified first-century Palestinian. But until the Church grants permission for a carbon-14 test to be performed, the exact age of the shroud can only be guessed at.

Sporting knights played for keeps
Tournaments – spectacular and lethal

AS THE SUN went down one day in 1180, the bodies of dead men littered the field of Lagny-sur-Marne. Blood soaked the ground; the cries and groans of the wounded rent the air. Was this the gory end of a battle between a French army and an invader? No. There had, indeed, been a clash of arms, but men had died and suffered severe wounds not for a patriotic cause, but in the name of sport. For Lagny-sur-Marne had staged a tournament – the

most lavishly spectacular entertainment the Middle Ages had to offer. More than 3,000 armed and mounted knights had lined up and charged at each other that day. Had you been there, according to a contemporary report, "you would have heard such a crash of lances that the earth was strewn with fragments. Great was the tumult upon the field." It was a tournament *à outrance* (literally, "to the utterances," or, as we might say, a fight "with no holds barred").

Pope after pope spoke out against such "execrable and accursed" diversions. Church spokesmen condemned the tournament, because of the carnage involved, and also because the many fine knights who were needlessly maimed or even killed were wanted to fight in the Crusades. They also decried the debauchery surrounding the main event. Eventually the Church threatened participants with excommunication and even refused Christian burial to knights who fell in tournaments.

Such fulminations were of no avail. The allure of tournaments between two "sides" of fighters, each side consisting of a great number of knights often organized and led by the wealthy heirs of the great barons who challenged each other to a tournament, was too strong. Besides, these bloodthirsty games provided vital training for the real business of war. "A knight cannot shine in war if he has not prepared for it in tournaments," declared one chronicler. "He must have seen his own blood flow, have had his teeth crackle under the blow of an adversary." Moreover, engaging in large-scale games was one of the few ways for a youngster to make a name for himself in medieval history. He could begin by becoming the squire to a knight-at-arms, grooming horses, caring for armor and weapons, and accompanying his master to tournaments and wars. Tournaments themselves often included practice bouts between such apprentices. Later, the squire might graduate to knight-errant – the name given to men who traveled from tournament to tournament, offering their skills and valor to one side or the other, in pursuit of fame and fortune.

Tournaments are thought to have originated in France and were an established part of life in that country by the 11th century: The sport soon caught on elsewhere, especially in England, where it became fashionable to celebrate marriages, coronations, and feast days with a grand

Only the elite could afford the costly equipment of the jousting knight. In this illustration from a medieval manuscript, the King of Naples is shown in the attire of an armed knight.

ONE ROAD TO THE TOP

The most celebrated English knight-errant in the medieval world of arms was a 12th-century man named William Marshal, whose surname derived from his father's job as marshal, or court official responsible for organizing the supply and care of horses, on the estates of Matilda of Anjou, daughter of Henry I. At the age of eight William was attached to the household of a Norman baron, William of Tancarville, to serve as the baron's squire. This was the beginning of his rise from relative obscurity as the fourth son of a fairly minor official to the title of Regent of England.

William had earned his spurs as a knight-errant by the time he was 21, and he quickly became famous for his prowess in combat. In 15 years of competition, he reportedly fought on the victorious side in 500 tournaments. During one encounter, his helmet was so badly dented that, to remove it, he put his head on an anvil while a smith hammered him free.

As a reward for his skill and valor in the lists, King Henry II invited William to become a courtier. Soon afterward he went on a pilgrimage to the Holy Land, returning to fight at Henry's side against Henry's rebellious sons, Richard, Geoffrey, and John. And following the king's death in 1189, his son and successor Richard appointed him Earl of Pembroke, guardian of the Welsh border country.

William was rapidly becoming the most important and powerful peer of the realm, and was the natural choice of his fellow barons to become Regent of England in 1216 when Henry III came to the throne as a minor. For three years until his death William ruled England like a king, his life an extraordinary tale of a knight-errant who rose to the top.

Jousting is once more a popular sport, although today strict rules of conduct must be followed to prevent injury.

When jousting was at its most popular, as many as 3,000 knights might be involved in a tournament simultaneously. In this illustration, heralds blow their trumpets as the signal to commence, while lords and ladies watch the glamorous heroes of the field from the safety of a raised enclosure.

tournament. Most events were local affairs with local men, but a few were international events, involving knights from many different countries. The stakes could be very high. Losers might be lucky if they forfeited no more than their horse and armor, but for those taken prisoner, ransom demands could be very heavy.

Once the challenge had been issued, and the time and place for a match were agreed on, preparations went ahead in an atmosphere of mounting excitement. Heralds galloped from castle to castle, and town to town, proclaiming the event. Crowds converged in their thousands upon the appointed place. Stands erected for ladies and other privileged spectators were bedecked with pennants and tapestries (though once the contest was under way, the participants were sometimes lost to view, pursuing one another for miles over open country). The arrival in the field of contestants was the occasion for fanfares and the unfurling of more heraldic flags and banners. Ladies often led their favored knights into the "lists" – the field of contest – by a gold or silver chain, bestowing upon them a personal token, such as a handkerchief or ring, before retiring to the safety of the stands.

With much noise and animation two opposing lines of fighters would, at last, form – each on horseback and armed with the customary lance and sword and shield, which they would have to resort to if unhorsed. At a given signal from the organizer of the event, the fighters charged. There were rules of fair play, of course, as laid down by the Code of Chivalry (blows could not be delivered too high or too low, for example) but once the charge had

developed into what was called a mêlée, with large numbers of knights milling around, some still on horseback, others unseated and struggling on the ground, it was almost impossible to control events. That was when the real damage was done – knights crushed beneath horses' hooves, trapped and suffocated within badly battered helmets, arms half severed by blind swings from broadswords. Sportsmanship could soon turn to blood lust in the mêlée.

The fight would continue until the signal to cease was given or until one party was completely defeated. The wounded were then taken home and cared for, hopefully living to fight in another tournament another day.

By the end of the 14th century the character of tournaments had changed. Knights encased in heavy, shining armor, with shields emblazoned with their coats of arms, plumes atop their helmets, trotted ponderously around engaging in single combat. Jousting or tilting (slightly different but similar forms of combat) between only two men became the favorite sport and rivaled the team tournament in popularity. It could be an exciting spectacle, but it rarely led to anything worse than having the wind knocked out of a knight who was unhorsed. Old warriors were often scornful of the new style; they looked back nostalgically to the days of their fathers, when a mass tournament effectively prepared a man for battle. As one chronicler, commenting on the results of those headlong charges and desperate mêlées, put it: "Then will the knight be able to confront actual war with the hope of being victorious." He might have added, "If he lives that long!"

The Wonder of the World

East meets West

THE CROWDS who turned to stare at the long processions accompanying the emperor on his travels were in no doubt that they were seeing the most remarkable of medieval monarchs. Nothing like this extraordinary traveling court had ever been seen before in Europe. First came the advance guard of Saracen cavalry, whose Arab horses and Eastern garb must have struck the watching Italians or Germans as wildly exotic. Next, bobbing about in palanquins high on their horses, came the veiled beauties of the famous imperial harem guarded by giant black eunuchs. Then followed the cavalcade of the court itself, brilliantly dressed knights and courtiers overshadowed by the emperor himself, a rather small man, with flaming red hair. Behind him came the long lines of pages carrying on their wrists the hooded falcons so dear to their master. And behind them came the imperial menagerie, with its swift-pacing leopards and cheetahs, its camels and its giraffe – the first ever seen in Europe and a present from the Sultan of Egypt. Finally, when the dust had swallowed the last straggling cooks and clerks, mothers would tell their children they had just seen the Emperor Frederick, wonder of the world.

Frederick II, King of Sicily, Holy Roman Emperor, King of Jerusalem and Cyprus, who lived from 1194 to 1250, was to his followers and supporters indeed "Stupor Mundi," the world's wonder, a second King David or even a Messiah, come to restore the golden age of Rome, to purge a corrupt Church, and establish universal

MEDIEVAL BIRD–WATCHING

Many medieval princes were keen hawkers, going out with their falconers to watch the grimly beautiful birds of prey strike their quarry high in the sky, but normally such interest in birds stopped at the doors of their cages. For Frederick II, though, a passionate devotion to the sport extended to all aspects of the birds' lives and led him to write a famous book on the subject, *De Arte Venandi cum Avibus* (*Of the Art of Hunting with Birds*). A truly scientific study, it remained the standard work on the subject right up to the 18th century. Frederick probably wrote it toward the end of his life. Though he acknowledged the *Zoology* of Aristotle, then regarded as completely infallible, he noted that "in many cases the Greek philosopher seems to have departed from the truth." That Frederick was able to put Aristotle right was due to the long hours he spent observing the birds from the hunting boxes scattered throughout his lands. Of the six volumes, the last four are very technical, but the first two are fascinating revelations of Frederick the natural scientist. He noted that birds which get their food by scratching the earth have the inner toe of each foot serrated for the purpose, and discovered the truth about the nesting habits of the cuckoo by taking home a strange chick and watching it grow. He also noticed the migration of birds over southern Italy and attempted artificial incubation of eggs, using the sun's rays.

But it was falcons and falconry which fascinated him most, and on this subject he was the pre-eminent practitioner of his day. His prize falcons came from a country he called Yslandia, a snowy island between Norway and Greenland which he describes in his book in some detail. It says much for his devotion to the sport that he could contemplate capturing and importing wild birds from Iceland to his native Sicily, a transport problem that would be difficult to solve even with today's sophisticated methods.

Frederick II, emperor and expert on falconry, seated on his throne with a falcon perched nearby.

— falcon manuscript text fragment:

oiffiaha e
ivius au
miquam
er fola fi
oebem
pito ipm
inun9 vn
aim ans
pria qad
τ nos no
dea l.in
ontmu
uoebant
alleg ros
imu

peace. But to his many enemies, who included the pope, he was the Antichrist himself, a mocker of true religion and friend of infidels and Jews. Had he not openly doubted the immortality of the soul, and declared that both Moses and Jesus were the greatest frauds in history? Did he not converse with Arab philosophers and keep a harem? When he went on crusade to the Holy Land, instead of massacring the Muslims in the proper manner, had he not made a peaceful treaty with them, leasing back from their Muslim owners the Christian holy places? Little wonder that the pope twice excommunicated him and stirred up rebellions against his rule.

But who was this man who attracted such venom and about whom there were such contradictory opinions? His grandfathers were Frederick Barbarossa, Holy Roman Emperor and King of Germany, who had died on crusade in 1190, and William II, King of Sicily and southern Italy, two of their age's greatest rulers. His father, the Emperor Henry, had married Constance, heiress to Sicily, but had died in 1197 when Frederick was only three, leaving his infant son to grow up unprotected in Palermo. Sicily had variously been occupied by the Greeks, Arabs, and the Normans, and its cities were cosmopolitan melting pots for medieval Europe. The young Frederick was kept in Palermo, while his elders fought out their power struggles. Talking to Jewish merchants or Arab or Greek craftsmen, Frederick certainly had a very different education than that of most young princes of his day.

By the time he was called to the imperial throne in 1212, aged 18, Frederick was already a most unusual man. In an age of faith, when the Church ruled people's minds rigidly, Frederick might be considered a rather lukewarm, perhaps even skeptical, Christian, prepared to admire the good side of Islam and Judaism. He employed Jewish doctors and Arab soldiers, and was eager to soak up the wisdom of infidel cultures from Arab and Hebrew philosophers and scholars.

Though the story of his meeting with St. Francis of Assisi is apocryphal, it epitomizes his inquiring attitude to religion as to most things. St. Francis was returning from a pilgrimage to the Holy Land in the fall of 1221 when he came to Bari, in southern Italy. Frederick was holding court in a castle there and invited the saint to come and spend the night. Into the tower room where his holy guest was sleeping, Frederick introduced a beautiful woman to seduce him, spying through a crack in the wall. St. Francis awoke, scattered hot coals from the fire on the floor, and lay down on them, inviting his temptress to join him. The girl withdrew, the emperor entered the chamber, and spent the rest of the night in conversation with the saint. Ascetic and mystic, Francis was a complete contrast to the doubting, sensualist emperor, yet both had much in common, desiring peaceful relations with Islam and wanting to reform a corrupt Church. What they are supposed to have said has unfortunately not been recorded.

Usually, though, the emperor spent his time on more worldly pursuits. His court was a center for poets and artists, graced by beautiful women, where the troubadours of Provence found a second home. Frederick himself was no mean poet, his verses in Italian influencing the great Florentine poet Dante. In his building projects, Frederick anticipated the later rediscovery of Greece and Rome. The gates at Capua, now destroyed, used Roman models, and his statues and gold coins were classical in design, with their portraits of the laureled emperor.

Frederick's laws were strikingly humane, particularly to women, who were allowed to inherit property and were protected by anti-rapist laws. His administration was fairly advanced, as was the plumbing of his palaces, for the emperor enjoyed frequent baths. In his experiments with the natural world, Frederick was also ahead of his time. Such a reputation did not help him in his long-drawn-out quarrels with the papacy, which disliked his innovations and distrusted his intentions. Inciting the restless north Italian cities to rebel against his rule, the popes wanted to keep their own states in central Italy free from imperial pressures and that, rather than any religious cause, was the real reason for their attacks on Frederick. In such a spirit of temporal rivalry, accusations and lies flourished in place of truth, with both sides accusing each other in a vicious battle of propaganda.

Certainly not the "Antichrist" of his detractors, Frederick ultimately was more of an enigma than a wonder to an age in which many were unable to appreciate such individuality. He was a man who seems to have been born ahead of his times, a precursor of the Renaissance at the height of the Middle Ages, a skeptic in an age of faith. When he died suddenly in 1250, such was the aura that surrounded his life that many refused to believe that he was indeed dead. Impostors appeared who claimed to be him, the Divine Emperor, the Savior of the World. But in death he failed as in life he succeeded. Within 25 years, his heirs were all dead – casualties of the continuing battle with the papacy. And with them also died the dynasty of Stupor Mundi, the Wonder of the World.

Who built Great Zimbabwe?

And why was it abandoned?

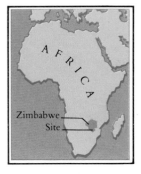

Site of the "Great Ruins" on the southern slope of the high plateau between the Zambezi and Limpopo Rivers in present-day Zimbabwe. The ruins are situated in a fertile, evergreen area between the Matabeleland goldfields to the west and the trading ports on the Indian Ocean to the east, suggesting that they were once the focal point of an important commercial network.

WHEN, TREKKING through bush country in southern Africa, a German geologist named Karl Mauch came across the ruins of huge, stone walls, apparently of an abandoned city, he was certain that this could not have been the work of native Africans. Black Africa was a land of primitive mud huts, was it not? These ruins, which were called Zimbabwe ("stone houses") by people who lived in the area, must, Mauch believed, have been built by visitors from a more northern, more sophisticated society. But Mauch, who made his discovery back in 1871, has been proved wrong. The impressive granite city was certainly the work of a black African people. And it is appropriate that the name of the country where these ruins are located has been changed from Rhodesia to Zimbabwe.

The impressive ruins stand in a magnificent, ever-green setting at the head of the valley of the Mtilikwe River in the southeastern corner of the country. Scattered over 60 acres (24 hectares), the stone structures, now roofless, are dominated by a stone-walled enclosure which has been dubbed the "Acropolis" because of its hilltop site, misleadingly because its purpose was to impress, not to defend. In the valley below stands a temple in a walled enclosure more than 100 yards (92 meters) long and 70 yards (64 meters) wide. Between the two large ruins lie the remains of many smaller buildings.

Puzzled by the fact that none of the Africans in the area knew anything about the history of the massive stone structures, Mauch decided that they must have been a by-product of the gold trade that, according to the Bible story of the Queen of Sheba, flourished in the vicinity 3,000 years ago. And several "experts" later supported his theory that Great Zimbabwe had been planned and built as a trading post by skillful architects and workmen imported from some ancient civilization such as Egypt or Phoenicia. Others disagreed about the whys and whens, but one opinion among 19th-century students of the ruins remained practically unanimous: The ancestors of local Bantu people were simply not capable of designing and building such imposing structures. One intriguing suggestion was that Zimbabwe may have been the site of King Solomon's mines, which, according to legend, provided vast riches for the sumptuous court of Solomon, the son of David.

But could the African Acropolis really have been built 1,000 years before Christ? To many archeologists this seemed doubtful, especially after a Scottish expert, David Randall-MacIver, published his conclusions drawn from a study of the ruins, that the stone structures were only hundreds instead of thousands of years old, and that they were the work not of foreign travelers but of black Africans. These findings, announced early in this century, were upheld by an English archeologist, Gertrude Caton-Thompson, who, in 1929, wrote: ". . . examination of all the existing evidence, gathered from every quarter, still can produce not one single item that is not in accordance with the claim of Bantu origin and medieval date." And this view has been borne out by the researches of later archeologists. What is more, it accords with the likely history of the Bantu-speaking peoples, a group who gradually migrated southeastward from the part of Africa now called Nigeria, until, by sometime in the early Christian era, they came to dominate central and southern portions of the continent.

Evidence found in deposits dated by carbon-14 analysis suggests that work on the Acropolis, the earliest settlement on the hill, began as early as the second or third century AD. By around 1200 the area was controlled by the ancestors of the present Shona people, the Mbire, who were skilled miners, craftsmen, and traders, and who formed a well-organized political entity. It was then that the great walls of granite blocks were probably built. The temple and its walled enclosure were constructed slightly later, and further additions seem to have been made during the next two or three centuries.

When and why was the flourishing trading and religious center of Great Zimbabwe abandoned? Historians are now fairly certain that by the start of the 16th century, the inhabitants of Great Zimbabwe had exhausted the food and timber supplies of the area. Possibly there were a series of droughts or crop failures, or extensive cultivation of the land had exhausted the soil, or possibly even a disastrous epidemic had wiped out the herds of cattle and wild game. We do not know, but whatever occurred, Great Zimbabwe's population of over 3,000 slowly dwindled and moved away to better, more productive lands.

One mystery remains. Why did the Mbire people build monumental structures in stone as

The Temple, or Great Enclosure, with walls more than 30 feet (10 meters) tall, as seen from the Acropolis of Great Zimbabwe.

Giving rise to one of the most fascinating mysteries of Zimbabwe, the Conical Tower stands within the Temple enclosure. A superb example of dry-stone masonry, it is 30 feet (10 meters) tall and has a 50-foot (16 meters) base circumference. It is unlikely to have been a watch-tower, since it is solid throughout and is impossible to climb externally, but it may have been built as a religious symbol.

opposed to wood, or mud? One possible explanation seems to be that Zimbabwe was a center of religion, with buildings and structures designed to reflect its importance. But more likely is that Great Zimbabwe was built as a commercial center controlling the wealthy trade between the Matabeleland goldfields to the west, and the Indian Ocean coast to the east. Wall building probably started in order to link up natural stone outcrops on the hill to make stock pens, but most of the walls were built primarily for prestige, to impress Great Zimbabwe's trading parties with the power and authority of its inhabitants. Whatever their purpose, there is no doubting the ability of Great Zimbabwe to impress, for even today in their abandoned state, the ruined walls still astound all visitors with their solidity and power.

In time the Zimbabwe ruins will perhaps yield more of their secrets. They remain a somber, still mysterious relic of a vanished society.

Repent or burn

The ultimatum of the Inquisitors

ON SUNDAY APRIL 5, 1310, Bernard Gui, Inquisitor for the city of Toulouse in southern France, opened the solemn proceedings of an *auto da fé* (literally, an "act of faith") in the great cathedral. On a stage in its center stood a group of penitent heretics–those who had confessed–in their distinctive yellow robes of penitence, ready to make public declarations of faith. The customary sermon was delivered by the Inquisitor, followed by the solemn decree of excommunication issued against all who might in any way obstruct the proceedings of the Holy Office. The confessions of the penitents were then read out to them, one by one, each being asked if he or she accepted it as true. As only those who had confessed were asked, all agreed: No scandalous protestations of innocence were allowed to disrupt the proceedings. Each penitent was then asked to make a declaration of faith and repentance, before each one was brought forward to hear the sentence read out, starting with the least guilty and progressing to the most serious offenders. Last of all came those who, despite the Inquisitor's efforts, had refused to recant the heresy to which they had confessed. These were "relaxed" from the tender care of the Inquisition – that is, handed over to the civil authorities to be burned alive.

To avoid polluting both a holy place and a holy day, the executions took place the next day, in the main square. There, before jeering crowds, the unrepentant heretics were tied to stakes on the pyre, the Inquisitor still calling on them to repent, so that they might save their souls, if not their bodies. As the devouring flames at last died down, the crowd dispersed and Bernard Gui could close the books on a particularly successful heresy hunt: 65 people condemned to life imprisonment and 18 burned, although he normally sent fewer than 10 heretics to be burned at the stake in a typical year, as his records show.

For southern France was at the time, like most of Italy and Spain, in the grips of terror, as the Inquisition strove ruthlessly, implacably, to stamp out all forms of heresy. It began in the 13th century and quickly spread throughout southern Europe. Unlike the later, more famous Spanish Inquisition (which was simply the last phase of this system of persecution, and which persecuted mainly Jewish and Muslim converts to Christianity, who were suspected of being insincere in their conversion) its targets were people who were baptized Catholics but were suspected of being even slightly sympathetic to sects whose teachings diverged from the orthodox. In 1208, Pope Innocent III had preached a "Crusade" (known as the Albigensian Crusade) to wipe out one such heretical sect in Languedoc, and this proved to be only the first step in a long and bitter battle against the heresy that was sweeping through Europe. This particular battle culminated in 1233 with the papal Inquisition instigated by Gregory IX to investigate charges of heresy.

Before his arrival in a town or village, the Inquisitor would inform the local authorities of his intended visit, and the population was summoned to hear him preach. He would then issue a "period of grace" of 15 to 30 days, during which time people could come forward, to confess their own faults and, what is more important, to accuse others. It is not difficult to imagine the terror this must have caused, as people wondered if a resentful neighbor might reveal some thoughtless remark or question uttered long ago and now horrifyingly taken to express some sympathy with the heretics. Often people must have informed through pure malice or in an attempt to save their own skins by accusing others. When the allotted period was over, the Inquisitor acted.

Once summoned before the Inquisitor, a victim's only hope lay in complete confession, naming others suspected of heresy. He or she was not told who the accuser was, and there was very little chance of an acquittal, for the Inquisitor–judge and protector in one–assumed guilt unless there was overwhelming evidence in the victim's favor. Armed with almost infinite authority, exempted from normal regulations, the Inquisitors, chosen for their fervent ardor, operated in the completest secrecy until they could bring their victims to confess publicly at an *auto da fé*. Only those who had confessed but would not retract their heresy–a mere 10 per cent–were burned, but none who entered the dark prisons of the Inquisition ever came out unpunished. In solitude and often in darkness, kept on a diet of bread and water, the prisoner might spend years in gaol before confessing, for time was one of the Inquisitor's chief weapons. Often victims died in prison.

Torture offered the Inquisitor a shortcut after it was authorized in 1252. Though theoretically a victim could be tortured only once, the Inquisitors got round this by calling each further torture session a "continuation" of the first. Witnesses who were under suspicion were also allowed to be tortured, as long as this did not cause bleeding or death.

Once confessions were obtained, the punishments imposed by the Inquisitor would vary according to the degree of heresy. Minor offenses might simply require certain prayers to be said or a pilgrimage to be undertaken. Any of these were infinitely preferable to the punishment for an impenitent heretic, who lost his property as well as his life. The Inquisition could even pursue a man beyond the grave; its long arm reached across frontiers and its memory was everlasting. Only the pope could override its decisions, and even his protests were often ignored, for in some situations, the Inquisition was a law unto itself.

Pope Gregory IX probably did not realize what a monster he was creating in the name of Christ and Christian love when he authorized the Inquisition. For, once started, it proved very difficult to stop, being checked only by the gradual growth of religious tolerance in the 17th century. The Inquisition's trial system, however, was to be absorbed into many of Europe's

THE CATHARS AND WALDENSES

Of the many lesser sects of so-called heretics two stand out: The Waldenses and the Cathars (or Albigenses). The Waldenses were named after their founder, Peter Waldo – a rich merchant of Lyons who, having in the 1170s undergone a conversion, dedicated his life to Christ-like poverty and preaching. In 1183, he and his followers were condemned as heretics and subjected to fierce persecution that never quite stamped them out.

Very different were the Cathars, who had adopted an Eastern dualistic belief that the entire material world had been created by the devil. In the 12th century they created their own church in Languedoc and other parts of southern France, with its own priests called "perfecti" and its own rites. By 1200 they had virtually ousted the traditional Church in this area – partly because the perfecti actually practiced what they preached. The corruption, laxity, and downright incompetence of the "official" clergy of the time were what had turned so many to "heresies" in the first place.

judicial systems, and torture became accepted as a method of obtaining confessions for any crime. The last heretic to be burned by the Spanish Inquisition in 1787 was just one in tens of thousands guilty, at worst, of preferring a different form of religion.

This scene from a 15th-century manuscript shows the French King Philip Augustus watching the Amalrician heretics burn. They believed that all men and women were potentially divine and that religious ceremonies were therefore superfluous. These and other deviants from strict Catholic orthodoxy were executed in great numbers, either by burning or hanging.

An empire held together with string

How the Incas used colored cords to keep accurate records

WHEN IN 1527 Spanish adventurers were exploring the south coast of present-day Ecuador, they found a vast empire that extended over 2,500 miles (4,000 kilometers), from what is now the border between Ecuador and Colombia in the north down to central Chile in the south. The empire, headed by an autocratic king who was worshiped as a descendant of the Sun god, possessed a network of paved roads and irrigation canals, and the complex activities of the many tribes who made up the large population were regulated by an efficient administrative system, with headquarters at the centrally located capital city of Cuzco. The Spaniards marveled at the engineering and agricultural skills of these civilized "heathens" and at the evident profusion of exquisitely wrought gold and silver objects, equal or superior to anything known in Europe. But what was equally marvelous was that the Incas could neither read nor write. They had no alphabet and no written set of numbers; they did not even have an elementary picture language or system of hieroglyphics.

This seemed incredible. It quickly became apparent that the Inca ruler had access to precise information about the status and age of everyone in the empire, food supplies (what they were and where stored), the location and size of his armies, his holdings of gold and silver, and other matters of imperial interest such as recent history and law. How, the Spaniards wondered, could such complexities be compiled and recorded without the aid of written records? They soon had their answer: It was all done with knotted string – and done so accurately that, as one of the invaders expressed it in a published account of the discovery, "not so much as a pair of sandals would be missing."

The Inca system was entirely based on the *quipu* (the word for "knot" in the Inca language, Quechua). This was a cord of at least one foot (30 centimeters) long from which were hung other lengths of string of different colors, with perhaps even more lengths of string hung from these. Using different lengths and combinations of the different colored cords, the Incas were able to record sophisticated information.

With the quipu, for instance, the Incas maintained an annual census, evaluated each year's harvest and kept records of everything from wool to armaments. They recorded the tributes

The Inca empire developed from little more than a farming tribe in less than a century (1476–1534). By the time Francisco Pizarro, a Spanish conquistador, landed in 1527 the highly organized Incas had come to dominate a vast area, covering much of present-day Peru, Ecuador, Bolivia, northern Argentina, and Chile. But because the Inca government was in the form of a centralized autocracy, Pizarro was able to locate his principal victim, the Inca or emperor, and destroy the structure of this civilization in a few months.

WORKING THE QUIPU

The quipu system essentially consisted of varying lengths of different colored cords onto which were tied knots. The combination of colors, position and number of knots indicated what was recorded on the quipu. It is thought that the quipu itself was read from right to left along the main cord, taking each hanging strip in turn. Colors were used to indicate such matters as the object under consideration (yellow, say, for corn on a quipu referring to stores of grain) and its location (a yellow string attached to a blue cord, for instance, indicating that the corn supply recorded on the quipu belonged to such and such a province). And the position and number of knots on a given length of string "spelled out" whatever quantitative information was required. The system was much more sophisticated than it might have seemed at first glance. For example, a black rope attached to others in a certain way could add a time dimension; and numbers in the high thousands could be recorded merely by placement rather than by the tying of innumerable knots. The quipu was also used as a mnemonic device, most notably by the highly skilled quipucamayocs. These men were able to use their quipus to refresh their memories about incidents far back in time. For instance, the

existence in the quipu of a main cord of black thread denoting the passing of time might suggest that it contained historical information. A red cord tied with a big knot to the main cord might indicate the presence of an emperor in the story, with four knots on that string to show that the events took place in the fourth year of his reign. A subsidiary brown string with 10 knots might relate the conquest of 10 provinces, and further colored strings could be knotted in to represent people conquered, cities captured, and so on.

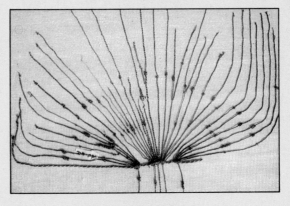

The skill needed to read quipus died out with the Incas, so current understanding of their use is based partly on speculation. In the illustration above, from a book written in Spanish by an Inca, a novice is being instructed in the art. The quipu (at left) like most extant examples, is not intact.

received from conquered tribes and taxes owed to the king by his subjects. And in the absence of a price mechanism using money, the quipus operated as an inventory system for managing supply and demand in such a way as to foresee or prevent shortages.

Obviously, there had to be as many separate quipus as there are books in a modern library, and the system needed trained people to operate it. The keepers of the quipus, known as *quipucamayocs*, were so highly regarded for their skills that they were exempt from taxes and services demanded of the rest of the population. It was an essential part of the education of male Incas of high rank to learn how to use a quipu, and every village had at least three or four highly regarded camayocs, who frequently checked one another's work to make sure that information was properly recorded. Each also had a special area of responsibility – one was in charge of crop records, another census returns, another weaponry, and so on. And for certain types of non-numerical information such as the "reading" of history, legend, and law, it was important to have an excellent memory. The general facts about these matters were passed down from one generation to the next by word of mouth, but the oral records were profoundly supplemented and supported by quipus containing details of dates, numerical quantities and other matters that could be recorded in terms of knots, colors, and placement.

"The empire is governed by the quipu" observed one of the invading Spaniards. Quipus were a key element in the centralizing control system so necessary for such a sprawling domain, and all local quipus were sent to a central registry in Cuzco for the information of the

In their lightning conquest of Peru, the conquistadors enjoyed every military advantage. Horse-borne, armored, and carrying muskets, they easily routed the Incas, who met them with little more than sticks, stones, and arrows.

authorities. It was by quipu that a messenger brought to Atahualpa, the Inca ruler, in the provincial town of Cajamarca the news that an invading Spanish army had landed on the coast in May, 1532. The quipu told the king how many men there were and what arms they carried. The messenger doubtless added startling comments about their horses (animals so strange to the Incas that they thought man and beast were a single monstrous creature).

The Spanish conquest of the Inca empire led to the introduction of a written language and the destruction of most quipus. The new masters of the land never tried to learn much about the secrets of the strings, and so the most complete records ever compiled of an empire and its people were lost. Most of the quipus we see today are in museums but in the mountains of modern Ecuador, Peru and Bolivia a modest form of the Inca quipu is still in use. Even today, descendants of the ancient Incas can be seen keeping track of their sheep by tying and untying knots in long lengths of string.

THE RISE AND FALL OF THE INCAS

The first Incas were a small farming tribe on the east-facing slopes of the Andes in what is now Peru, and they controlled little territory beyond their own village in the Cuzco valley. Constant fighting among rival tribes and the need for more farming land led to the gradual expansion and increasing dominance of the Incas during the 13th and 14th centuries, but it was not until the reigns of two great warriors, Pachacuti Inca and his son Topa Inca, in the 15th century that the Incas became the most dominant group in the Andes. (The name "Inca" was originally that of the tribe's ruling group of families, but it later came to be applied to all members of the empire.) Within about 50 years – from 1438 to 1490 – Inca ownership of a few square miles around Cuzco in central Peru expanded into control of 440,000 square miles (700,000 square kilometers) of mountain, plateau, coastal plain, jungle, and desert containing 10 million people representing over 100 ethnic groups speaking 20 languages.

The glory and power of the Inca empire were short-lived. With only 170 men and some local help from disaffected tribes, Francisco Pizarro conquered the empire in 1532 in the name of the King of Spain. By 1572 the last independent Inca province had been subjugated and the once proud Incas were working almost as slaves for their new masters on big estates and in gold and silver mines. Thousands died in the appalling conditions or as a result of European diseases against which they had no immunity, such as measles and smallpox. The Spanish introduced reading, writing, and their own laws and religion, gradually taking complete control of the land and its people. The Inca empire became merely a province of imperial Spain.

The Inca city of Machu Picchu (opposite), high up in the Andes, was discovered by Europeans only in 1912. Though long abandoned, it was found in a much better condition than other Inca settlements. This mountain-top city was linked to other Inca centers by an impressive network of roads and an elaborate system of messengers running in fast relay. Ironically, it was the very efficiency of this communication system that contributed to the speed of Pizarro's conquest.

Chan-Chan: Desert capital of the Chimu

The city of Chan-Chan, in the desert of northern Peru, was built as the capital of the powerful Chimu empire which extended almost 600 miles (1,000 kilometers) along the Pacific coast of South America. From the 13th to the 15th centuries successive rulers extended the city until it covered 10 square miles (24 square kilometers), but after 1470, when the Incas conquered the Chimu, the city declined, and by the time the Spanish reached the site 65 years later, it was almost deserted.

Archeologists have discovered that the city was dominated by nine great rectangular enclosures, each one believed to be a royal palace. Each enclosure was surrounded by mud-brick walls, possibly up to 35 feet (10 meters) high, and built wider at the base than at the top to withstand earthquakes. Inside, a maze of courtyards, storerooms, U-shaped reception rooms, and kitchen areas housed the royal court, but the existence of very few wells suggests that the total number of people living in each enclosure was small. Some of the rooms were arranged around three or four sides of a courtyard: The remains of textiles found in these rooms suggest that they may have held what was, in effect, the royal treasury (lacking a system of coinage, the Chimu, as accomplished weavers, used textiles as payment for tax and tribute). Each enclosure also contained a burial chamber built of brick surrounded by many rooms containing the riches that were to accompany its royal occupant beyond the grave, as well as the bodies of hundreds of women who were sacrificed to form an entourage for the ruler on his journey. These royal mausoleums were almost certainly built by the ruler to ensure his god-like status in the afterlife, just as the palace would have enhanced his reputation while he lived.

Huddled around the enclosure walls lay a muddle of irregularly positioned buildings whose incomplete outlines suggest that they resembled present-day Peruvian peasant dwellings which have solid walls on the windward side only, the other sides built of poles and matting. Archeologists suggest that the laborers and artisans of the city lived in these houses, 10,000 of which have been found, suggesting a population of up to 50,000 people living in these cramped quarters.

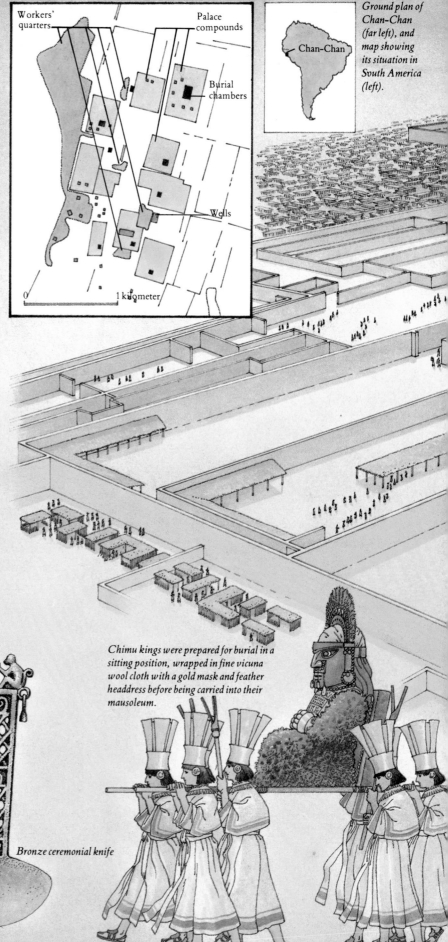

Ground plan of Chan-Chan (far left), and map showing its situation in South America (left).

Chan-Chan

Workers' quarters

Palace compounds

Burial chambers

Wells

0   1 kilometer

Black ceramic pottery vessel representing a Chimu king.

Bronze ceremonial knife

Chimu kings were prepared for burial in a sitting position, wrapped in fine vicuna wool cloth with a gold mask and feather headdress before being carried into their mausoleum.

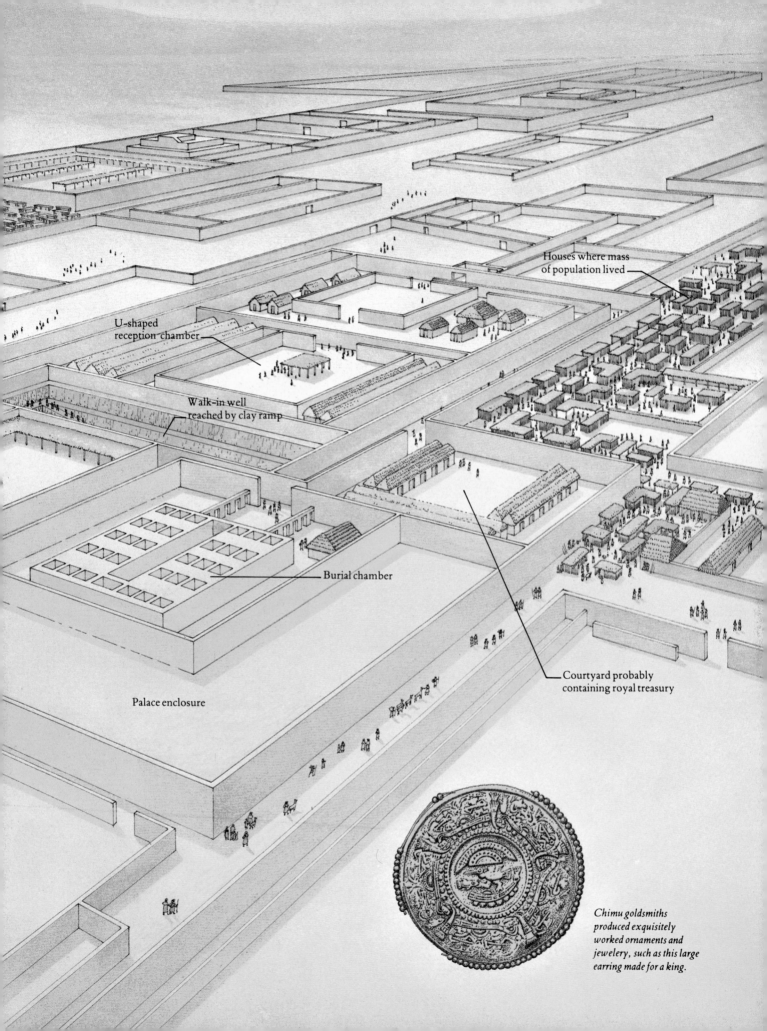

Houses where mass
of population lived

U-shaped
reception chamber

Walk-in well
reached by clay ramp

Burial chamber

Courtyard probably
containing royal treasury

Palace enclosure

Chimu goldsmiths
produced exquisitely
worked ornaments and
jewelery, such as this large
earring made for a king.

The galloping hordes of Genghis Khan
The empire that started on a riverbank

This is the face of Genghis Khan, the first overall ruler of the hitherto unruly and divided Mongol tribes.

ON THE BANKS of the River Onon in Mongolia, at the heart of the immense steppelands that stretch from the Great Wall of China to the Ural Mountains and the plateau of Persia, an immense crowd of nomads assembled in 1206 for a *kuriltai* (general council). They had ridden there on their tiny horses, no bigger than ponies but amazingly hardy, to do homage to Temujin, the once obscure chieftain who had welded a nation out of a chaos of warring tribes. As they listened, gathered in groups under their individual leaders, they cheered the announcement that Temujin was to have a new title. Henceforth he would be known as Genghis Khan, which, roughly translated from the Mongolian, means "universal ruler." In turn, Genghis Khan himself first used the word "Mongol" to define all the people of Central Asia regardless of former tribal identities.

Genghis Khan is a name that has echoed down the centuries, more terrible even than Hitler's or Stalin's, with its associations of empires destroyed and the populations of great cities massacred. For the *kuriltai* of 1206 not only marked the consolidation of the Mongols as a people; it also saw the beginning of seven decades of unremitting conquest. By the time of Genghis Khan's death in 1227 he had carved out an empire reaching from the Caspian Sea to what is now Peking. Within another 50 years his descendants, relying on an invincible combination of horsemanship, discipline, and terror, extended the Mongol frontiers from Hungary and Poland in the west to what is now Vietnam in the southeast. It was the largest empire the world had seen, and it was created with unprecedented speed and slaughter.

The Mongols believed that Temujin, the son of a minor tribal prince, was born (about 1162) clutching a blood clot, as a symbol of his future exploits. During his early years the nomadic Mongol peoples of Central Asia were disunited,

MONGOL RECIPE FOR SUCCESS

Terror, propaganda, deceit, and spying were major factors in Mongol warfare, but at the heart of every triumph rode the Mongol horseman – swift, obedient, fearless, and very, very tough. Bound by iron discipline, with flogging or death the penalty for even minor offenses, he was a formidable fighting machine, capable of a mobility unmatched until modern times.

A Mongol boy was strapped to the saddle of a pony at the age of three, and from then on he spent most of his waking hours on horseback. Mongol ponies could carry their riders up to 80 miles (120 kilometers) a day with only one break for food and water. On the great Eurasian plains their speed and stamina gave the followers of Genghis Khan immense advantages over their enemies. They could concentrate their forces so swiftly as to create an illusion of great numbers.

Mongol armies were tightly yet flexibly organized into *tumans* – groupings of 10,000 warriors made up of 10 1,000-man regiments, each of which was in turn composed of 10 squadrons. *Tumans* were commanded by princes of the blood – relatives of the khan – or by close supporters, and two or more *tumans* formed an army. Though overall unity was maintained by a system of pony-express messengers, individual commanders were given great freedom in the field, a necessity for such far-flung armies. Ahead of each advancing horde rode a screen of scouts, who relayed messages back to the commander. And far ahead of the scouts went swarms of spies,

whose job was to infiltrate cities in order to gather information and spread panic. Within the cities, fifth columnists were often recruited among merchants, a class much favored by the Mongols.

One weapon that served the khans in good stead was the systematic use of terror. Any center of population that did not promptly surrender when challenged could expect no mercy. News of what could happen, as in the total destruction of Samarkand in 1220 and Nishapur in 1221, two of the greatest cities of their time, and the massacre of all their inhabitants, got around fast enough to deter resistance elsewhere. Not that surrender was always effective. The Russian princes of Kiev, who surrendered in 1223 on being assured they would be well treated, were crushed to death beneath the boards on which their Mongol captors were feasting. Two years earlier, when the inhabitants of Herat, a city in the border country around northwestern Afghanistan, had emerged from the city gates after hearing offers of mercy, they were all killed and the city blotted out.

But although the Mongols could be as murderous as our own century's Nazis, they were – unlike Hitler's minions – free of racial or religious prejudice. They might drive peasants before them as a shield, but they did not despise the defeated foe and were, indeed, eager to learn from subjected peoples. In a way, of course, this was their downfall, for as they increasingly fell into the softer ways of the civilizations they conquered, they lost their nomadic vigor.

Few of today's stunt-riders could match the equestrian skills of the Mongols, who were completely at home in the saddle almost as soon as they could walk. Trained to wield both bow and sword while their tough little mounts were in full gallop, the Mongol "cavalry" was the key to the invincibility of Genghis Khan's armies.

and their many scattered tribes were easily manipulated by the inhabitants of settled lands with powerful rulers such as the Chin dynasty of north China. China rather loosely controlled the nomadic peoples to the north and west of the Great Wall, using young Temujin as an ally for attacks on their opponents, chiefly the Tartars, at that time the most powerful of the many Mongol tribes. Another ally of the Chinese – a man whom they valued more highly than Temujin – was a powerful khan (chieftain) named Toghril, whose friendship Temujin had cleverly purchased with a gift of sable fur.

The art of attracting close and helpful associates in such unsubtle ways was an art that Temujin cultivated assiduously in his determination to conquer the world. He was also prepared to mow down former friends when convenient. And so, through a series of wars and shifting alliances, involving at one point the murder of his former ally Toghril and the dispersion of Toghril's tribesmen, Temujin had become lord of the Mongols by 1206.

When he began his campaigns of conquest against the states around him, his people were still inferior to the peoples they subjugated in culture, technology, and governmental skills. Even in numbers the Mongols were often far outmatched by the great armies of China or the old river civilizations of Central Asia. What they lacked in knowledge or numbers, though, they more than made up for in the amazing speed and mobility of their fighting forces. History can show no more awesome example of terror than the surprise and cruel shock of the onrush of

Mongol hordes mounted on their galloping ponies. The terror continued throughout the reign of Genghis Khan and his immediate successors; gradually, though, the Mongols acquired many of the less warlike skills of their subject peoples, and with characteristic efficiency they became expert administrators, metalworkers, hunters, technologists, and so forth.

They also acquired a taste for the good things that are not readily available in a nomadic existence. The Great Khan himself believed he had a divine mission to conquer the world in the name of the Eternal Blue Heaven, but what he offered his followers was the prospect of loot. Military service, though compulsory for all males from age 14 to 60, was not without its rewards. "Future generations of our race," Genghis Khan promised when he was named universal ruler, "will wear gold-embroidered clothes, eat fat and sweet foods, ride fine horses, and hold in their arms beautiful women." By the time he died, he had gone far toward fulfilling his promise.

Under his son and successor, Ugudai Khan, Russia, Persia, Armenia, and Tibet were added to the already vast Asian empire; and Ugudai Khan's nephew Kublai Khan (the monarch whom Marco Polo wrote about) added further lands, including the southernmost portion of China, to his dominions during his reign (1260–94). But Kublai Khan took his grandfather's words rather too literally, turning his back completely on the tough simplicity of traditional Mongol life in favor of the splendors of the Chinese emperors whom the Mongols had superseded. His reign also marked the end not only of Mongol aggression but of the single Mongol state. Kublai Khan ruled his vast empire from the Chinese city now known as Peking, but the subjection and control of China, or Cathay as it was then known, and the constant warfare which that entailed, was more than enough to fully occupy even so talented a man as Kublai Khan. It soon became apparent that the Mongol empire had grown too large to be controlled, even loosely, by one man. After the death of Kublai Khan, separate khanates sprang up in Persia, Russia, and Central Asia, and before long the great empire founded by Genghis Khan had disintegrated. The name of the man who turned a rabble of marauding horsemen into the conquerors of half the known world remained a name to conjure with, however. Even contemporary Chinese chroniclers, who had good reason to hate him, were forced to admit that he "led his armies like a god."

The unknown cathedral builders

Every stone tells a story

THE MIGHTY stone-built columns of Chartres cathedral soar upward and fan out into the vaulting above nave and choir, as though taking wing. Stained glass bathes the interior in a rich and luminous light. The cathedral of Our Lady at Chartres is, for many, the peak of French Gothic architecture.

In the Middle Ages, building a cathedral took so many years that stonemasons, like the craftsmen at work in this Fouquet painting, seldom lived to see the project completed.

In 1194 the existing Romanesque basilica was largely destroyed by fire. Dismay among the local population turned to joy when the fragment of a tunic, said to have been worn by the Blessed Virgin Mary, was recovered from the ashes. Such holy relics were treasured, both for their own sake and for the prestige and trade they brought to the church and town that housed them. The survival of the tunic was taken as a sign of God's grace, and the citizens of Chartres set about the building of a new cathedral in a frenzy of religious ecstasy. The entire town contributed to the building works with labor, gifts of stone, wood, glass, and money.

In 31 years the bulk of the work was done – something little short of a miracle, for the symmetry of design and unity of architectural style found in Chartres cathedral were achieved without reference to any detailed overall plan or guidance from any one overseer or architect. Building work in the Middle Ages was largely in the hands of master craftsmen. With compasses, set square, dividers, and string, they staked out foundations, laid floors, erected walls and columns, added roofs, each master and his team specializing in one particular job. They did not even work to standard measurements, each master using his own preferred rule, be it the ancient Roman foot (of 295 millimeters), the English foot (of 305 millimeters), the Royal foot (of 325 millimeters), or the Teuton foot (of 333 millimeters). The result of this mixture is a masterpiece of *ad hoc* construction.

With no overall plan to guide them, these builders might at least have been expected to follow tried and tested methods of construction. Instead, they strove to raise nave, choir, and transepts to greater heights than had ever been attempted elsewhere, while enlarging windows at the expense of wall space. Hence the need for all those innovative flying buttresses to support their dizzy aspirations. Hence also the disasters that sometimes struck, as at nearby Beauvais later in the century where the choir collapsed twice during its construction. A similar catastrophe was narrowly avoided at Chartres.

Who were these men who raised Chartres from its foundations with the daring of test pilots and vision of artists? Not only do we know little about how they worked, but with a very few exceptions, their names too are lost to us. They have, though, left behind clues to their identity. The observant visitor to the cathedral will notice signs and symbols, such as initials and outlines of fish and faces, chipped into odd corners of the stonework. These were the masons' personal marks, originally made as a tally of work done, now a strangely intimate link with the Middle Ages. Organized as secret brotherhoods to keep the skills of the craft within their control, the masonic guilds engaged in the construction of Chartres cathedral acted much as trade unions do today, protecting the rights and privileges of their members and ensuring proper remuneration for their work.

Some scholars are fascinated by what they see as the link between the cathedral's stonework and medieval ideas about a divine mathematical order, a kind of cosmic geometry, encompassing the universe. A great cathedral, such as Chartres, argue the scholars, was probably built to echo this cosmic order.

They are also intrigued by another question, concerning the cost of the whole enterprise. Who provided the money to finance the building of the cathedral in what was, in the 13th century, a small provincial town of fewer than 2,000 people? It was a colossal building program for such a small community to support, let alone a community without banks or secure sources of credit, yet we have very few details of any financial backing for the work. We know that the diocese of Chartres contained over 900 parishes, each of which would have had to contribute regularly to the cost of the building, and that the town of Chartres had one of the most lucrative annual fairs in France. But could some of the money also have come from the monastic order of the Knights Templar, that elite company of religious knights which had been founded in the Holy Land shortly after the First Crusade in 1099 to wage war against infidels wherever they might be found, and whose growing power was being seen as a threat to the monarchy itself? Many local legends and stories link the Templars to the area of Chartres, and to

VILLARD DE HONNECOURT – MASTER BUILDER

One celebrated name arising from the company of largely anonymous French master builders is that of Villard de Honnecourt. Like many of his colleagues, Villard, who was born around 1200 in the small village of Honnecourt near Cambrai in northeast France, was constantly on the move during the Gothic building boom of the 13th century. Selling his services as an architect and engineer, he joined the workforce on the great Gothic cathedrals of such French towns as Chartres and Rheims and helped in the design and construction of whatever section of the cathedral was currently being built. He once traveled as far afield as Hungary, very much as an American or European technocrat might travel to Third World countries today to advise on building projects.

We would know nothing at all about Villard were it not for the chance survival of his sketchbook, now in the custody of the Bibliothèque Nationale in Paris. Filled with plans, elevations, and sections of buildings; details of stained-glass windows, masonry, and carpentry construction; and sections on roof making and other technical procedures, it affords us a rare insight into medieval building theory and practice.

Beyond such strictly architectural matters, this sketchbook reveals Villard's brilliant inventiveness. He designed a water-powered saw, a crossbow with a new kind of sight, a most ingenious sphere-shaped hand warmer and a decorative mechanical figure designed to follow with pointed finger the daily progress of the Sun across the sky.

Other pages of the book are filled with drawings of people's faces, animals and insects, analyzed in terms of geometric forms. There is also a medical remedy that includes cannabis among its ingredients, and some useful hints about lion taming.

Only 33 pages of Villard's sketchbook are still in existence. They reveal a man of intense curiosity and lively intellect, whose skills were exceptional even in an age peopled with outstanding master builders.

its cathedral especially, but as to any firm evidence in the building itself, the stones are silent.

Whatever the answers to these tantalizing questions, by the time of its dedication in 1260, Chartres cathedral stood as a wonderful example of a work of art, created not by one man of genius, but by the faith and will of a whole community. For centuries it served as all great churches did; not just as a place of worship, but as the focal point of civic life. In times of crisis, or of rejoicing, everybody gathered beneath its roof. Shops and stalls crowded round it, even encroaching within its portals. Miracle plays were performed upon its steps.

Today Chartres cathedral is a Mecca for tourists, historians, and art lovers from all over the world. Those lucky enough to pay a visit on June 21 each year can witness something extra. On that day alone, as the sun reaches its high point of the summer solstice, a single ray of its light shines briefly through a tiny space in one of the stained-glass windows in the south transept. It illuminates a flagstone of a lighter color than the rest, and then is gone again for another year. Someone must have gone to a great deal of trouble to arrange for that to happen. But who, and why? It is just one more of the wonders and mysteries of Chartres cathedral.

Egypt's slave-kings

From lowly mamelukes to lordly Mamluks

FROM SIBERIA to Syria the Mongols had seemed invincible as they crushed one kingdom after another; and so, with their armies sweeping across Syria toward Egypt in the year 1260, they must have been confident that Cairo would soon fall as Baghdad had fallen. They were wrong. When Mongol and Egyptian forces clashed at Ain Jalut, near Lake Tiberias (in modern Israel), the invaders, utterly beaten, were compelled to retreat, never again to threaten Egypt.

The battle of Ain Jalut is notable for a number of reasons, but the most remarkable of these is that the Egyptian army was almost wholly composed of non-Egyptians. Apart from a very small Egyptian force, the soldiers were all either *mamelukes* (an Arabic word meaning "owned men") or the descendants of such mamelukes –

enslaved foreigners who were granted their freedom in return for military services.

The history of the Mamluks – to give them the proper name they are now known by – is an extraordinary one. In the ninth century, the Caliphs of Baghdad began to pack their armies with slaves bought in the Turkish steppes. The practice of procuring adolescent boys from Asian slave markets and training them as soldiers soon became virtually universal among Muslim states. And almost everywhere in the world of Islam the result was the same: The Mamluks stopped fighting wars for their masters; instead, they became the masters.

Egypt's experience is both typical and outstanding. Before the beginning of the 12th century her armies were recruited from unwilling and undertrained peasants, or composed of

MUSLIM BIGWIGS

Titles such as sultan or vizier sound vaguely fictional to modern ears, but they had meanings in the medieval world of Islam as definite as president and prime minister have for us today. Highest of all titles was caliph. A caliph was considered to be the successor to Muhammad, and therefore the spiritual head of all Islam; since he was likely to wield political as well as religious power, rivalry for the caliphate eventually developed. Sultans were more like 19th-century kings and emperors – supreme temporal rulers within their territories but with no spiritual power over the clergy, in

theory at least. During the Mamluk period, the sultans held the real power, relegating the caliph to a position of rather shadowy spiritual authority.

A vizier was the monarch's chief of staff, empowered to execute his orders. Viziers were appointed by the sultans or caliphs concerned. And, finally, the next highest title was that of emir. The word *emir* means "commander," and emirs were commanders in both a military and civil sense. They acted as colonels or generals in Islamic armies, and they could also be governors of large areas of a monarch's territories.

In this painting, attributed to the 15th-century Italian painter Gentile Bellini, the Mamluk governor of Damascus receives a Frankish delegation. Although warriors by training, the Mamluks maintained extensive cultural contacts throughout the then-known world.

Negro slaves and mercenaries, whose loyalty to the sultan was notoriously weak and wavering. To counter resultant military weakness, the Egyptians began to integrate corps of mercenaries from foreign places such as Turkey and Kurdistan into the regular army. In the second half of the 12th century, the great warrior Saladin – scourge of the Christian Crusaders – became, first, Vizier, then Sultan of Egypt; and under his regime a corps of slaves, some bought in the open market, some bought from among Turkish and Circassian prisoners of Genghis Khan, was added to the army. Their performance was first-rate, and so Saladin and his successors gradually increased the proportion of sturdy slaves to unenthusiastic peasants in their fighting forces – until, by the 13th century, the so-called Egyptian army had become almost entirely a Mamluk body.

The attitude toward slavery among the Muslims was very different, of course, from what it was to become in the West in later centuries. Powerful Egyptians who bought young boys to serve as surrogates for themselves and their dependants in Egypt's wars were encouraged to treat them like members of the family, and there was little stigma attached to a servile beginning for either men or women. Mamluk boys were trained in special military schools in Cairo. After reaching manhood they were given freedom, military equipment, and a grant of land to support their families; they were then assigned to the forces of either the sultan himself or one of his colonels. Within the fighting army, though, all commanding officers were, like their troops, recruited from among the Mamluks.

It was therefore inevitable – although Egypt's emirs and sultans, like other importers of military slave labor, failed to realize it – that Mamluk soldiers would loyally obey their field commanders rather than remote Egyptian rulers. And so by the mid-13th century the powerful army that the sultans had built up in order to protect the throne had become strong enough to topple it. When Sultan al-Malik al-Salih died in 1249, the Mamluks murdered his successor and chose one of themselves as monarch. For nearly three centuries thereafter, Egypt and Syria remained firmly in the hands of Mamluk sultans, every one of whom either had begun his adult life as a slave from a foreign land or was the direct descendant of one. Succession to the throne or to any high office was not hereditary among them; it had to be earned (or, rather, fought for). Many of the 50 or more sultans enjoyed extremely brief periods of power, since rival factions constantly jockeyed for supremacy, especially after the first century or so of the Mamluk dynasty. The dynasty finally came to an end in 1517 when the expanding Ottoman (Turkish) empire defeated the Mamluks and occupied Egypt.

Probably the greatest of all Mamluk fighters was Baybars, a general in the army that had trounced the arrogant Mongols at Ain Jalut in 1260. After that victory, nobody could challenge his claim to supremacy. Returning to Cairo in triumph, he began a career as sultan that is still talked about in the city's coffee houses for its peaceful as well as military glories. Yet it was said that this blue-eyed Turk had been sold in a Damascus slave market for 500 silver pieces only a few decades before ascending the throne.

The Sicilian vespers

An evensong massacre

DRUNKEN LECHERS often start fights, but they seldom start wars. Sergeant Drouet of the French occupation army in Sicily was a notable exception. On Easter Monday in the year 1282 he started a war that redrew the map of Europe, reduced the power of the papacy, and humiliated the strongest king in continental Europe. Easter Monday, 1282, was also the day Sergeant Drouet died.

Every year on Easter Monday it was traditional for people of Palermo, the town where Drouet was stationed, to attend a vespers service at the Church of the Holy Spirit, half a mile (just under a kilometer) outside the old city wall. The occasion was always an excuse for a celebration, and as usual there was laughter and singing in the square as the populace waited for the service to begin. Left to themselves, the Sicilians were in great good humor – until the sergeant and a handful of his countrymen tried to join in.

The French had been drinking. Arrogant as occupying troops frequently are, they pushed their way into the middle of the square, ignoring people around them, treating the natives with

CARTING THE STORY AROUND

The incident that led to the War of the Sicilian Vespers has always held a special place in the island's history as one of its most colorful and significant events. The honor of a woman, the pride of the people, the violence, the bloodshed – all of these combine to make a dramatic tale that has been handed down from generation to generation for 700 years, by word of mouth at first and later by other means as well. A Sicilian method of storytelling is the decorated cart, an art form the islanders have perfected over centuries.

Sicilian decorated carts are traditionally painted in red, yellow, blue, and green to symbolize the island's oranges, sun, sea, and grass. Since each cart reflects the status of its owner, the best of them are also elaborately carved all over, from wheels and shafts to front and side panels. The biggest effort is reserved for the back, where the most memorable events of Sicilian history are depicted; and the most frequently portrayed of such events are either episodes from the Crusades or the story of the vespers.

During carnival time in the spring the carts are decked with flowers. Competitions are held, and there is a parade through the streets. The horses wear cocked plumes, the drivers put on their best clothes, and each cart is full of children.

This typical Sicilian decorated cart illustrates scenes from the Norman invasion of Sicily in the 11th century.

obvious contempt. The most insensitive of all was Drouet, who knew what he wanted and intended to get it. Looking around, he spotted a pretty girl in the crowd – a young woman recently married – took hold of her, and began to try his luck. Although her husband was at her side, Drouet was too drunk to care. The girl protested, and her husband lost his temper; before anyone could stop him, he drew his knife and stabbed Drouet to death. At that precise moment, the bells began to ring for vespers.

For a few seconds there was consternation in the crowd. Then the mood changed. Even as Drouet fell to the ground, the Sicilians surged forward and hurled themselves at the French, slashing wildly at their hated oppressors. There could be no turning back now. Long years of repression, injury, and injustice boiled over in the hot sun, and not one of Drouet's fellow-soldiers escaped. On all sides the cry "*Murano li francisi!*" – "Death to the French!" – went up, and it was repeated from house to house and street to street. The massacre that culminated in what historians have named the War of the Sicilian Vespers had begun. It continued for the rest of that day and for most of the night in Palermo, and it quickly spread to every garrison town in the island. Young Sicilians, running wild, dragged Frenchmen from wherever they were hiding and butchered them remorselessly. No one and nothing French – not even Sicilian girls with French husbands or holy men in monasteries – escaped the Sicilian revenge. Within 24 hours of Sergeant Drouet's affront to the young bride, more than 2,000 French men, women, and children lay dead.

With them died the effective rule of the French King of Sicily, Charles of Anjou. Before long the uprising had encouraged Charles's enemies all across Europe to come out in support of the native Sicilians. In return Charles persuaded Pope Martin IV (a fellow Frenchman) to condemn the killings and declare holy war on his behalf. But the move backfired. Holy wars had hitherto been fought in the name of God, but the idea of fighting one for a man as ruthless and unpopular as Charles offended so many Christians that there was little support for this "crusade." As a result, the pope's authority was severely weakened.

Charles himself did not live to see the outcome of the War of the Sicilian Vespers. He died before he had time to crush the revolt, leaving in his wake not the strong empire he had carefully built up, but an empire in deep turmoil, in retreat on all sides, its frontiers crumbling one by one. That single drunken act of Sergeant Drouet's had cost his royal master dear.

The longbow

Deadly weapon of the English people

NAMES LIKE FLETCHER, Bowman, and Archer are common among English-speaking peoples the world over, but few people realize that they derive from an important and revolutionary event in history. This event was the introduction of the longbow by the English army in the 14th century, a major development in the history of warfare. For the first time, peasants and yeomen rather than knights and noblemen decided the fate of battles and of nations. For generation after generation, royal edicts encouraged the planting of yew trees, from whose slow-growing wood the best bows were made, together with regular practice at the archery butts on Sunday afternoons in every town and village throughout the land. Only with such constant training was the strength necessary to pull such a bow acquired. Thus, while the French nobility continued to look down on its foot soldiers as expendable inferiors, and to rely heavily on its knights, the English nurtured and used their bowmen.

The devastating power of the longbow in the hands of well-trained and disciplined soldiers was first revealed to an unsuspecting Europe at the battle of Crécy in 1346, the first vital battle in that long-drawn-out contest between the English and the French which we call the 100 Years War. King Edward III of England had landed in Normandy, northern France, and was advancing on Paris with a smallish army – 2,400 cavalry and 12,000 archers and other infantry – when he came up against King Philip's French army, more than three times as large. The English were forced to retreat hastily toward the coast, but on the hills of Crécy, near Abbeville in northern France, they turned to fight what was then the most powerful army in Europe. It was the morning of August 26, and one important aspect of the warfare of the Middle Ages – the invincibility of the armored knight – was about to be seriously challenged.

The French nobles came charging up on their great horses, confident of victory, and ignored their king's command to wait for the rest of the army, so eager were they to destroy the English. First, though, their Genoese mercenary cross-bowmen were ordered to soften up the enemy by discharging their traditionally deadly weapons. The 5,000 Genoese, who had walked the 18 miles (29 kilometers) of pursuit that day and were hot and tired, were led to the front. But before they could even get within range, a hail of arrows from the 6,000 English archers opposite fell amongst their ranks, cutting them to pieces. Within minutes most of the Genoese were dead or wounded, and the survivors straggled back through the French lines.

A present-day archer in medieval dress shooting over the field of Agincourt. The power and accuracy of the longbow has been demonstrated by reproducing 14th-century models, but the archers had to be fit and skilled, and the monarchs of England made sure that all able-bodied males had plenty of practice.

THE HUNDRED YEARS WAR

Lying full length in his armor at Canterbury Cathedral, the effigy of the Black Prince, Edward III's eldest son and one of his best generals, looks the perfect model of the chivalrous noble warrior. To the inhabitants of much of western France, however, who watched him leading his men on one of the many "chevauchees" – the infamous plunder raids which the English excelled at – the noble Black Prince must have seemed an oppressive brigand and despoiler. As they saw their crops being burned and their houses looted, not only must they have felt fear, but they must also have wondered what all these battles, which we term the 100 Years War, were about.

Calling the conflict the 100 Years War is, in fact, something of a misnomer, for it was not one but a series of wars, which lasted 116 not 100 years. They started in 1337 when Edward III of England announced his claim to the French throne and declared a war that was to last until 1360. Through his French mother, Edward was Duke of Guyeune, and as such had had to swear allegiance to King Philip of France, who felt threatened by the presence of so powerful a duke on French soil. Edward won most of the land and concessions he wanted at the Peace of Brétigny, but by 1373 however, most of the land gained had been won back for the French king.

Henry V of England, Edward's great-grandson, renewed the wars with France and annihilated the French nobility on the field of Agincourt in 1415, aiming, as had Edward before him, for the French throne. Within a few years he too had got what he wanted, forcing the ineffectual Dauphin, the heir to the French throne, into the southern half of his kingdom, where he was to remain until he was inspired by Joan of Arc to restore French fortunes in 1453. By this date, the once-extensive English lands in France were back in French hands, leaving England in control only of the port of Calais on the north coast. With the loss of Calais in 1558, the last English hold on France was gone.

The disparity in power between crossbows and longbows is vividly illustrated in this painting of a scene from the battle of Crécy. In fact crossbows were accurate and their bolts so lethal that successive popes sought to ban their use in warfare. But loading and winding them took valuable seconds – during which time the preoccupied archer was subjected to a continuous rain of arrows from the longbowmen.

The French king had little sympathy for the plight of his mercenaries. "Kill me those scoundrels, they block up our road for no reason," he cried, and the French knights rode forward, to cut down the unfortunate Genoese – and came within the range of the deadly English arrow-storm of 50,000 missiles fired every minute. Squadron after squadron rode forward to founder before reaching the English lines in a chaos of screaming, kicking horses; knights who had dismounted were trapped by their armor. Among them moved the English light infantry with long knives and clubs to finish off the now powerless nobles.

By nightfall the French army was defeated and streaming back; among the dead were the blind King John of Bohemia, a French ally, and the powerful Count of Flanders. King Philip himself had had his horse shot from under him and escaped to Amiens with only five barons as an escort instead of the hundreds who had accompanied him in the morning. The next day was foggy, and new French columns, still advancing, unaware of the battle, were ambushed by English archers. One such encounter alone left 1,562 knights dead on the field.

Crécy was a most unexpected victory and it was followed, 10 years later, by the battle of Poitiers, where once again English longbows triumphed over French cavalry. With this victory England's King Edward was able to force the French to cede the port of Calais in the north and much land in the southwest.

When the French and English met again on the field at the battle of Agincourt in 1415, it seemed that the French had learned nothing from their earlier defeats. Hindered by their heavy armor, the French troops became bogged down in a plowed field, where they presented easy targets for the English archers, who triumphed again.

THE LONGBOW ANATOMIZED

Although bows have been made since time immemorial, the longbow which gave the English their greatest victories in France was a fairly recent development in the history of weapons.

Although in common use for both hunting and sport, the military possibilities of the longbow were not fully realized until Edward I of England came up against the highly effective Welsh archers fighting against English rule of their country at the end of the 13th century.

Once taken up by the English, the longbow was developed into something far more powerful than a mere hunting weapon and, by the mid-14th century, had become the national weapon of the English people. No special skill was required to use it, but it did need steady practice and a great deal of strength.

A typical bow at the time of Crécy was six feet (two meters) long, with the wood straight for a foot above and below the holding space to prevent arrows quivering on release. Yew was ideal for the bows, but oak and maple were also commonly used; for the arrows, three feet (one meter) long and tipped with steel barbs, birch, ash, and oak were all suitable. Though arrows could not penetrate a knight's steel-plate armor directly, they might find vulnerable chinks and could certainly kill his lighter-armored horse. On the ground, the unwieldy knight was easy prey for enemy infantry.

Generally, the English archer came from a non-aristocratic background, but not necessarily a poor one. Equipped with a steel helmet, a steel-reinforced leather jacket, a cloak in which he slept and a good pair of boots, and carrying a water-bottle and a pack for the day's rations, he was self-sufficient. He also carried a sword on a pointed stake which he placed in the ground in front of him to break cavalry charges. Mounted on ponies to increase their mobility, archers were an elite, paid three times as much as the normal infantry. Usually, they were organized in hundreds under their captains who trained them.

After their disasters at Crécy and Poitiers, the French might have been expected to follow the English example and adopt the deadly weapon, but instead they continued to rely on heavy cavalry and crossbowmen. The crossbow, which had been evolving since the 12th century, was more accurate at short range and in the hands of the unskilled, but it suffered from a cripplingly slow rate of fire compared to the longbow – only two shots a minute, compared to the longbow's 10 to 15 a minute – and had considerably shorter range than the 300 yards (270 meters) of the longbow, as the Genoese had discovered to their cost at Crécy. In any case the crossbow was never regarded as more than an auxiliary weapon by the French, who continued to devote their time and money to perfecting their noble cavalry.

This, probably, was initially why they were adverse to importing the longbow into their own country. There were enough peasant revolts in France in the 14th and 15th centuries anyway to make the thought of putting such power into the hands of the commoners very alarming. Nevertheless, the longbow had proved itself to be such a crucial weapon that in 1448 Charles VII of France organized an elite of longbowmen called *francs archiers* whose skills helped tip the balance in favour of France at the end of the 100 Years War. In England, well into the reign of Henry VIII in the 16th century, longbowmen were still a valued part of the army, but the increasing use of firearms in warfare gradually drove them from the battlefield. Although it was suggested even as late as the battle of Waterloo in 1815 that the longbow could be revived, the skills needed had long vanished.

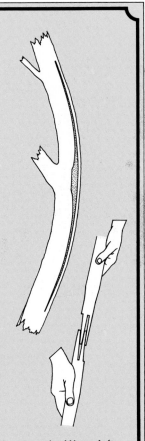

Bows should be made from straight, clean staves; these may need three years or more of seasoning. The best results are achieved by joining two staves at their butt ends by means of a V-shaped joint.

Marco Polo's amanuensis

The story behind one of the world's great story books

Marco Polo sports Tartar costume in this portrait. Explorers of his day, unlike those of the 19th century, usually adopted local attire as being more suitable for the prevailing climate. This adaptability may well have encouraged the friendliness of the peoples encountered by the Polos on their travels.

SEVEN HUNDRED years ago, during a war between the republics of Genoa and Venice, a writer of popular romances named Rustichello of Pisa was imprisoned in Genoa as an enemy alien. Instead of a misfortune this proved a lucky turn of events, for one of Rustichello's fellow-prisoners happened to be a story-teller's dream: He was a Venetian merchant-captain who had been captured by the Genoese in a battle at sea. His name was Marco Polo, and he was brimful of wonderful tales of real-life adventure. From this chance encounter between a writer and a man who had traveled to the ends of the Earth came one of the most important books ever written. The writing was done by Rustichello to Marco's dictation, and the result of their collaboration was the enthralling work known to modern readers as the *Travels of Marco Polo*.

In the year 1260 Marco's father, Niccolo, and uncle, Maffeo, two enterprising Venetian traders on the hunt for new markets, had journeyed overland from the Black Sea coast into the unknown vastness of Central Asia. At this time the whole of Asia, from the Black Sea to the Pacific, lay under the yoke of the dreaded Mongols. But the Polo brothers soon found that they had little to fear from the Mongol khans (rulers), who were more than willing to trade with Europeans. At Bukhara (in what is now southwestern Siberia) the Polos fell in with a messenger of the Great Khan, Kublai, conqueror of China; and in the company of this messenger they traveled overland to Cathay, as China was then called (from the Mongol name *Khitai*).

After being lavishly entertained by Kublai Khan, Marco's father and uncle returned to Italy bearing the Great Khan's greetings to the pope, along with a request for 100 Christian missionaries to be sent to Cathay. The journey back from China had taken them three arduous years, but the Polo brothers, nothing daunted, set off again in the year 1271, little guessing that 24 years would elapse before they once more saw Venice. This time, they took 17-year-old Marco along – on an odyssey that carried them overland to Cathay and home by sea via the East Indies, India, and the Persian Gulf.

Although they failed to bring Kublai all the missionaries he had asked for, the Great Khan welcomed them back with delight and treated Marco with special favor. As Kublai's envoy, Marco traveled the length and breadth of Mongol China; he penetrated as far south as Burma, and was sent by sea on a mission to Ceylon. In addition to remembering everything he saw for

Venetians watch Marco Polo's departure, with his father and uncle, for the East in 1271. Their trek across Asia, 16-year sojourn in China, and journey home by sea took them some 25 years. On their return to Venice, they were thought at first to be impostors.

Marco Polo, his father, and uncle, were among the first Europeans to reach China. There they found a civilization far surpassing any in Europe, a richer and more sophisticated society than any they had encountered elsewhere on their travels. In this scene from a recent film version of the travels of Marco Polo, filmed in Peking, Kublai Khan, escorted by his children, entourage, and guards, receives the three travelers with all honor.

himself, Marco later told Rustichello about all sorts of things he had heard from other people about life in the exotic lands of the Far East. Much of what he claimed to have seen and heard was difficult for his fellow-Europeans to accept. For instance, Venetians fancied themselves as lords of the Mediterranean, inhabitants of one of the richest and proudest city-states in Christendom – and here was this fellow assuring them that they were barbarians compared with the multitudinous dwellers of the "heathen" East. Could the Venetians really credit Marco's statistics (which vary according to which of the many versions of the book is to be believed) about the Chinese city of Kinsai (Hangchow), with its 10 huge marketplaces, 12,000 bridges, 144,000 workshops, and 1,600,000 houses, where costly European luxuries such as pepper were consumed at the unbelievable rate of 10,449 pounds (4,740 kilograms) a day? Or who could seriously believe his stories of springs that gushed oil (the Baku oilfields), rocks that could be ground up and spun into fireproof cloth (asbestos), stones that could be burned like logs (coal), and – instead of honest gold and silver coins – pieces of paper being used as money (Chinese paper currency, complete with inflation caused by printing too much of it)?

Many skeptical Venetians – not to mention some modern scholars – accused Marco of wild exaggeration. His contemporaries nicknamed him, and his book, *Il Milione* ("the millions man"), but they could not reject him as a lunatic or impostor. It might have been a different matter if he had traveled alone, but his father and uncle confirmed the substance of his stories, if not in the same amazing detail. Clearly, Rustichello is telling nothing less than the truth when he says that "from the time when our Lord God formed Adam ... down to this day there has been no man, Christian or Pagan, Tartar or Indian, or of any race whatsoever, who has known or explored so many of the various parts of the world and of its great wonders as this same Messer Marco Polo."

When Marco died (around 1323), his story was already known in much of Europe. Copied and translated into many languages, the *Travels* rapidly became popular and has remained so ever since. The book is not just a compendium of informative facts; it tells a dramatic story, with plenty of action and adventure. Marco had many narrow escapes from death by illness, brigands, shipwreck, pirates, and wild beasts. Some incidents may well have been exaggerated or even, perhaps, invented – though surely not all of them. The major impact of the *Travels* on world history, however, did not derive from the "tall" tales. Marco saw life with a merchant's eye on markets and trade, and it is what he said about probable profits from the procurement and eventual sale of gold, jewels, silk, and spices for anyone willing to meet the cost and dangers of the long road East that caught the 14th-century European imagination.

Within 50 years of his death, the overland route to China that the Polos had traveled was closed to European adventurers by the collapse of the Mongol empire and the rise of the anti-Christian Turks, but Marco's stories of the fabulous wealth of Cathay and the Indies were not forgotten. Nor were his assurances that China and its offshore islands were bounded on the east by an ocean that no doubt stretched unbroken to the coast of Europe. For a certain Genoese merchant-sailor of the 15th century, this belief became a magnificent obsession; Christopher Columbus sailed from Spain in 1492 to cross that "unbroken" sea. A little indirect credit for the discovery of the New World, then, belongs to an obscure writer named Rustichello of Pisa, without whose work Columbus might not have embarked on his search for a western route to the wealth of the East.

Food for the gods
Human sacrifices in the temples of the Aztecs

Within two years of landing in America, the Spaniards made themselves masters of the flourishing Aztec empire.

BERNAL DIAZ, the tough conquistador and chronicler of Hernan Cortés's expedition to Mexico in 1519, was accustomed to the horrors of war and the cruelties of the Spanish Inquisition. But he recoiled at the stench in the temple of Huitzilopochtli in Tenochtitlan, the Aztec Indian capital which stood on the site now occupied by Mexico City, recording that it "was such that we could hardly wait for the moment to get out of it."

The temple was a human slaughterhouse, its walls dark with coagulated blood. Three human victims lay there newly slain, and the priests who had killed them stood by, blood dripping from their stone knives. The Spaniards had uncovered a religion that demanded human sacrifice on a vast scale, so vast that, after the enlargement of this temple in 1487, dedication ceremonies over five days had included mass sacrifices of thousands. No doubt the conquistadors exaggerated Aztec ruthlessness to make their own brutality more acceptable to the leaders of the Christian Church, but records of the time show unmistakably that they were

The Pyramid of the Sun and the Street of the Dead (right), two of the spectacular structures that dominate Teotihuacan, the first major planned city in ancient Mexico. Though it predated the rise of the Aztecs, who had their capital at Tenochtitlan, Teotihuacan remained an important religious center under Aztec rule.

covered most of West Africa. In 1324 the emperor, with a massive entourage and 80 camels laden with gold, arrived in Cairo on his way to Mecca. The emperor and his subjects spent freely, disposing of so much gold that its value fell throughout Egypt, causing inflation. Local merchants swindled the emperor's gullible followers and finally, when Mansa Musa was forced to borrow money, the merchants charged him so much interest that they made a profit of more than 100 per cent. The people of Mali may have been innocent, but their lavish generosity caused a sensation throughout the Muslim world.

Such was the fame of Mali that it eventually led the Majorcan cartographer Abraham Cresques to produce the first map of West Africa ever drawn in Europe. The map depicted the "Lord of the Negroes" seated on a throne in the center of Mali. In his hand he held a gold nugget which he proffered to an Arab trader.

But apart from the stories of Mansa Musa's pilgrimage, little was actually known about the country itself. The Sultan of Morocco, wishing to know more about his neighbors to the south across the desert, decided to remedy this situation by employing Ibn Battuta, whose expeditions of discovery had already earned him a reputation as a fearsome and intrepid explorer, to investigate Morocco's southern neighbors.

Ibn Battuta joined a caravan of merchants to cross the Sahara. After 25 days he arrived at Taghaza, "a village with nothing good about it." Here the buildings were made of rock salt with camel-skin roofs. The village economy was based on its salt mines, the ruins of which still survive. After another five weeks of travel, Ibn Battuta reached Iwalata (modern Oualata in Mauritania). This town at the southern end of the trans-Saharan trade route lay on the northern border of the Mali empire. He found it hot, but the people were hospitable and the women "of surpassing beauty." However, as an orthodox Muslim, he was offended by the fact that the women went unveiled and had friends among the foreign men who thronged the town.

Ibn Battuta's next goal was the capital of the empire. Scholars still argue about the location of this town, but it probably stood about 62 miles (100 kilometers) south of the modern capital, Bamako. There he found Mansa Sulayman, brother and successor of Mansa Musa. Where Mansa Musa had been generous to a fault, Sulayman had a reputation for miserliness. At first the traveler did not see the king, because he fell ill. He recovered after two months and had an audience with Sulayman. Shortly after this he learned that Mansa Sulayman was sending him a present. Ibn Battuta expected some money – the sort of courtesy gift the Arab traveler had come to expect in his unofficial role of ambassador, "but behold, it was three loaves of bread and a piece of beef fried in oil, and a gourd containing yoghourt." Ibn Battuta burst out laughing at this paltry gift, which had been given such a big build-up, and he later said to Sulayman: "I have traveled through the countries of the world and have met their rulers ... yet you have neither shown me real hospitality nor given me anything. What am I to say of you before other

Trading was extensive in medieval West Africa, goods being taken by caravan as far as Europe and the Middle East. Wares included nuts, ivory, skins, and furs as well as weapons and textiles. Trading methods have changed little over the centuries, as may be seen from this photograph of the trading center of Mopti on the Upper Volta.

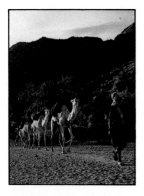

Camels, which can bear heavy burdens over great distances of inhospitable terrain, were indispensable to Arab and African merchants. Camel caravans can still be seen today, but the camel's importance diminished when Portuguese sailors opened up the west coast of Africa in the 15th century.

rulers?" The king then provided a house for Ibn Battuta and five and a half ounces (157 grams) of gold. And when the traveler left Mali, he was given another 16½ ounces (472 grams) of gold.

Despite his meanness, Mansa Sulayman kept an impressive court. Battuta vividly describes how the king, supported by 300 slaves armed with bows or lances, received visitors and petitions. On his arrival at the council, the king was preceded by singers bearing gold and silver stringed instruments and, when in council, he sat under a silken dome. People wishing to appear before the king wore dirty, ragged clothes and sprinkled themselves with dust as a sign of subservience.

Ibn Battuta was particularly impressed with the strong rule and law and order in Mali. No one had any fear of thieves or oppressors. The people were also devout in performing their religious duties. Children had to learn passages from the Koran by heart; those who failed to do so were put in shackles. What did not appeal to the visitor was the fact that female servants, slaves, and small girls went naked. He also disapproved of the practice of eating carrion. Still less did he like the infidels, wild people

from outlying areas, who ate human flesh. He told how a tribal chief came to see the king, accompanied by some of his subjects. As part of his reception gift, Mansa Sulayman gave them a slave girl, whom they promptly killed and ate.

After leaving the capital, Ibn Battuta set off on his return journey to Morocco, traveling along a river which he called the Nile – it was actually the Niger – until he reached Timbuktu, which stands some distance from the river. He did not have much to say about the town, but other Arab writers have described it as a provincial capital and an important trading post. Indeed it took over from Iwalata as a staging post for caravans from North Africa. In time Timbuktu also became a great center for Muslim scholarship and religion.

The empire of Mali finally came to end in the 16th century because disputes over the succession to the throne left the country with no strong government. Further, the Portuguese development of a sea route around the African coast in the 15th century reduced the importance of the trans-Saharan caravan trails, and the great days of Mali, so colorfully captured in his writing by Ibn Battuta, were forgotten.

When knighthood was in flower

And knights wore garters

EVERY YEAR, on St. George's Day (April 23), the traditional date of the mythical martyrdom in the fourth century AD of England's patron saint), there is a ceremony commemorating the founding of the Order of the Garter, Britain's oldest and most exclusive order of knighthood. Today there are those who see this annual event, which takes place in St. George's Chapel, at Windsor Castle, with the queen among those present, as a frivolous anachronism, an occasion for pageantry, nothing more. But the order was no frivolity when it was created by King Edward III in or around the year 1348. For behind the pomp and pageantry was a deadly serious political purpose – an attempt by the king to buy with honors the loyalties of his great and powerful subjects.

During the 14th century big changes were taking place in European society. Based on land and land-holding, it was being transformed by the growth of the market economy and by the increasing importance of towns and merchants. The power of money and wealth had begun to

undermine the class structure, allowing a new merchant class to move up the social scale. Moreover, a class of professional civil servants was being created to administer the realm, depriving many members of the aristocracy of their traditional role in government.

In warfare, too, the situation was fast changing. During the period of the Crusades (the 12th and 13th centuries) knighthood had flourished, with the armored knight on horseback paramount in battle. With the advent of the 14th century, new types of soldiers were coming to the fore, notably the English longbowman, soon to contribute to the destruction of the flower of French knighthood at the battles of Crécy, Poitiers, and Agincourt.

The 14th-century chronicler Jean Froissart cites many examples of how the best of the old and the worst of the new often went hand in hand in the stormy world of his time. He tells, for instance, of the magnanimity shown by England's Black Prince toward the defeated French King John the Good after the battle of

Poitiers in 1356; of how the prince received his royal prisoner, personally served him at table, and honored him as a brave soldier and companion in the fortunes of war. That same prince, however, says Froissart, mercilessly put more than 3,000 men, women, and children to the sword at the siege of Limoges in 1370.

Of the French knight Eustace d'Aubrichecourt, Froissart writes proudly that he "often succeeded in knightly combat with noblemen because he was young, deeply in love, and full of enterprise." But the truthful chronicler is also obliged to record the fact that Eustace "acquired much wealth in ransoms by the sale of towns and castles, through redemptions of the countryside and of houses, and the safe-conduct he provided" – which is a fair description of any gangster operating a protection racket.

This gap between chivalric ideal and harsh reality widened as the 100 Years War – a protracted power struggle between the French and English royal houses that began in 1338 – rolled on. And it was in an effort to tie king and nobility together, to keep chivalry alive and to ensure the loyalty of his powerful vassals, that Edward III established his Order of the Garter, conceived along the lines of King Arthur and his Knights of the Round Table.

The order had no military, social, or economic function of immediate practical value. As originally conceived, it consisted of a fellowship of 26 knights – one of whom was (and still is) the monarch – who pledged to each other "a lasting bond of friendship and honor." Upon the death of any of these, new candidates would be required to submit themselves for election by the remaining company. Today members are chosen by the prime minister and approved by the monarch, and the membership has been increased since the 14th century, but otherwise the original concept remains unaltered.

It is not known why a garter was chosen as the order's chief emblem. Some say it was inspired by Edward's own garter, which he raised aloft as a sign to his troops at the battle of Crécy in 1346. More likely is the story that at a ball in Calais to celebrate the town's capture in 1347, a garter belonging to the Countess of Salisbury (widely rumored to be Edward's mistress) dropped to the floor while she was dancing with the king. Edward retrieved it and was about to hand it to her when he noticed that some bystanders were exchanging meaningful glances; and so, in a spirit of true chivalry, he said, "*Honi soit qui mal y pense*" (loosely translated as "shame on him who thinks ill of this deed") and placed the garter on his own leg. Whatever the reason, a

Edward III confers the Order of the Garter on the Black Prince, his eldest son and one of the ablest military commanders of the time. This is an idealized, Victorian view of the ceremony – the Victorian age saw a great revival of interest in romantic notions of chivalry – painted by C. W. Cope in 1848 and now part of the British House of Lords collection.

JEAN FROISSART

Froissart's *Chronicles of France, England, Scotland and Spain* is one of our most treasured historical records. Jean Froissart was born in Valenciennes in northeast France, probably in 1337, and died about 1410. He was ordained as a priest, but spent much of his time traveling about the courts of Europe. His long life corresponded almost exactly with the first half of the 100 Years War between England and France, and the events of that war form the bulk of his chronicle.

Froissart was entranced by the pomp and splendor of late medieval court life and warfare, which he describes in colorful detail. This high regard for the aristocracy and knightly virtues often led him to gloss over unpleasant realities. His writings, therefore, are of more value as an evocation of time and place than as an accurately detailed record of people and events. Occasionally, however, almost as though acknowledging that the pageantry he loved was little more than a façade for a grimmer reality, Froissart was honest enough to let the account speak for itself.

Her Majesty Queen Elizabeth II, followed by Prince Charles and the Queen Mother, leading the procession of knights at the annual garter ceremony at Windsor in 1982.

blue garter, with its famous French motto, was adopted to represent the illustrious new order that was probably inaugurated on St. George's Day, 1348. At all ceremonies the garter is still worn just below each member's left knee.

Whatever its origins, membership of the order was soon regarded as a high distinction, bolstered by the military reputation of Edward III and his son the Black Prince whose glory reflected on the order. The order had its own herald, and its reputation was spread throughout Europe. With all its pageantry and ritual, its solemn vows and titles, the Order of the Garter has survived up to the present day, long outliving the chivalrous ideals from which it grew. As such, the ceremonial service at Windsor is a reminder of a time when such ideals were first under threat, and a garter came to their rescue.

The Black Death

How it changed the face of Europe

THE WORST HUMAN disaster in history was not a 20th-century world war. It was the 14th-century plague known as the Black Death. In Europe alone a full quarter of the population – some 25 million people – died within the space of four years (1347–51). Today it is thought that this devastation (like that of similar later epidemics) was started by bacteria carried by fleas lodged in the hair of a type of far-ranging rat that flourishes in almost any habitat. Human beings catch the disease either from the bite of the fleas or from the bodily discharges of infected persons. To people of the 14th century, however, the plague looked like nothing less than God's terrible punishment for humanity's sins.

From Central Asia the horror traveled to the Crimea with trade caravans, thence by ship to Mediterranean coasts, and onward, remorselessly, across Europe. Normal life ceased. Fields were left untilled, cattle turned loose to fend for themselves. Corpses were soon being buried,

THE FLAGELLANTS

The horrors of the Black Death provoked a revival of the penitent frenzy of the flagellant, here depicted by Albrecht Dürer.

During the frightening years of the Black Death, there was a revival of the bizarre religious sect known as the Brotherhood of Flagellants. A fanatical cult that had originated in eastern Europe in the 13th century, it soon spread across the continent. The Flagellants believed that an angel had brought down a letter from Heaven stating that the plague was a punishment imposed by God, and that He might be brought to relent only by human acts of self-punishment.

Despite its name, the Brotherhood included women. At intervals each group of Flagellants would set forth on so-called "pilgrimages," marching in somber line, two abreast, eyes fixed on the ground. Each penitent carried a scourge with leather thongs and pointed metal studs. Whenever they reached a place where they could attract an assemblage of onlookers, they would form a circle, strip to the waist, and throw themselves to the ground to be whipped by a man

known as the Master of the Pilgrimage. The "pilgrims" would then rise and, with gathering ferocity, begin to thrash their own bodies until blood ran. Every pilgrimage lasted for $33\frac{1}{2}$ days (the number of years in Christ's life), and during those days the Flagellants were forbidden to wash or to clean their wounds.

There were many such groups, each comprising hundreds, sometimes thousands, of penitents. But the movement was doomed almost from its inception because the penitents' direct appeal to God, without priestly intercession, was offensive to the Church. Church hostility increased when the Flagellants began to proclaim their ability to cast out evil spirits and work miracles, and the pope outlawed the sect in October, 1349. After secular authorities had also taken strong action against the Flagellants (one of the masters was publicly burned to death in the Silesian city of Breslau), support for the cult rapidly waned.

one on top of another, in shallow graves, tipped wholesale into pits, or even left rotting in the streets. City life ground to a halt as contagion spread and people fled from their homes. The air seemed polluted with what one contemporary chronicle describes as "an unbearable stench . . . so fetid as to be overpowering."

Only a few places were spared. In Milan, for instance, the archbishop ordered that, if the infection reached the city, the first three houses where it appeared must immediately be walled up, with the dead, sick, and healthy all entombed within. This was done – and Milan suffered no further. The archbishop, without knowing how the pestilence had spread, had nevertheless hit upon a reliable barrier to it: Isolation. Thus an isolated country house might be a good sanctuary. The writer Giovanni Boccaccio sets his *Decameron* (*c.*1353) in a palace where 10 patrician young people gather to avoid plague-stricken Florence. There, while waiting for the danger to recede, they amuse themselves by telling stories. Segregation could also work on a larger scale. Vast tracts of present-day Poland were spared, perhaps partly because Polish authorities imposed a quarantine.

It was isolation, too, that saved Pope Clement VI, then resident in Avignon, France. On the advice of his doctors he withdrew to a private apartment, where, despite the warmth of summer, he sat in solitude for weeks between two enormous fires kept permanently stoked. Although the doctors could not have known it, their advice made medical sense, for the great heat repelled fleas. Fire also preserved a certain English nobleman who ruthlessly ordered a nearby village to be burned down when it was attacked by the plague. Neither the flames nor the fleas reached his own property.

Apart from such rare instances, the plague took a dreadful toll as it swept through Europe. Yet we see that, during the course of history, such appalling loss of life has often been preceded by economic hardship owing to the pressure of over-population. Catastrophes on a large scale, such as the plague and international wars, have tended to follow on from the problem of overcrowding. Through the centuries, this problem has been solved – not by governments' economic policies – but by "accidental" and enormous loss of life. After the Black Death, the relationship between master and servant

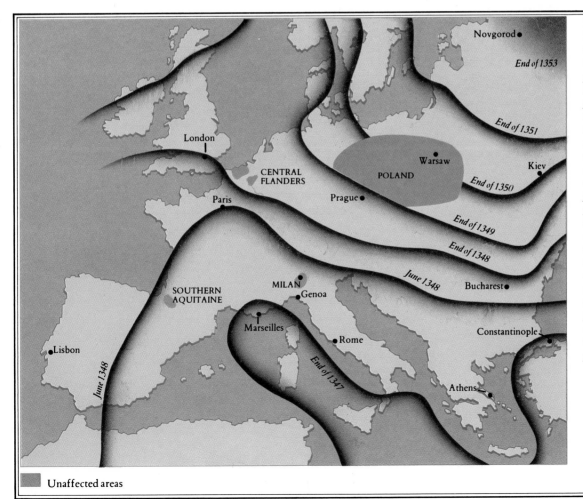

Unaffected areas

The plague years
The Black Death is thought to have erupted in Central Asia, where plague was endemic. Rodents, possibly fleeing from drought or flood, spread it to China and from there it traveled, slowly but relentlessly, with the trading caravans to Asia Minor and the Crimea, where nearly 100,000 people are thought to have perished. The bacillus was then poised to strike at Europe and a convenient means was at hand – trading vessels that plied the Mediterranean Sea. Once the Black Death had reached Sicily, its ruthless passage across most of Europe could not be contained. But small pockets escaped the scourge.

changed significantly. With a quarter of Europe's population destroyed, workers could ask for higher wages, while landowners, faced with less demand for basic commodities such as grain, had to accept lower prices. The resultant economic and social ferment led to sporadic disturbances, particularly among the lower classes, occasionally culminating in uprisings.

Unfortunately, the improvement in the peasants' lot that resulted from the plague was relatively short-lived. By the 16th century, the rapid rise in population meant that the peasantry were even worse off in terms of real wages.

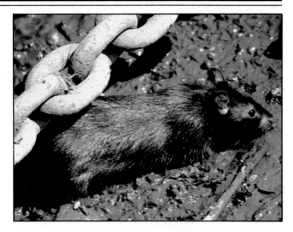

Though the hard-pressed physicians of the time did not know it, plague is caused by the bacillus Pasteurella pestis, *which resides either in the bloodstream or stomach of a flea. The flea, in turn, lodges in the hair of a rodent, its favorite host being* Rattus rattus, *the black rat (at left).*

The scourge of bubonic plague was obsessively interpreted in the art of the 14th and 15th centuries. Many paintings depict a skeleton with either a healthy but doomed young man or, as in the stained-glass representation opposite, a worldly priest.

HOW THEY FOUGHT THE PLAGUE

Physicians in the 14th century were not wholly unskilled. They could remove teeth, set bones, even do skin grafts. In the face of the plague, though, they were powerless. And, unaware of its cause, they could only guess at treatments.

The disease takes one of three forms. It may be bubonic, chiefly characterized by swelling of lymph nodes (buboes, or boils) in the armpits, groin, and site of the flea bite. It may be pneumonic, infecting the lungs and causing the coughing up of blood. Or – most deadly of all types – it may be septicemic, a form in which the bloodstream is rapidly invaded by offending bacteria and death is inevitable within hours.

Confronted with widely differing symptoms, contemporary doctors usually began by trying to draw "poison" from the body by means of bleeding, laxatives, and enemas. Buboes were either lanced or covered with hot plasters. Various haphazard potions ranging from powdered stag's horn to rare spices and compounds of gold were prescribed. Aromatic woods were burned to purify the air, and floors were sprinkled with rosewater and vinegar – measures that succeeded only in masking the stench of decaying flesh.

To forestall attacks, a variety of diets were recommended, and some may actually have been beneficial by making people fitter and therefore more able to fight infection. But the best safeguard was thought to be a mind at peace with God. In fact, the physician took second place to the priest in the sickroom, for the afflicted were always prayed over and given confession before they could have medical treatment. Sick people tended to welcome this, for they knew their plight was hopeless and, despairing, wished for a place in a future world when this world's medicines failed. Not everyone died of the plague. But when stricken people recovered, their survival was normally hailed as a miracle.

Many further outbreaks of the plague have occurred since the Black Death, but only in our own century have we discovered the source of the scourge and its antidote. When the virulent epidemic of 1665 reached London, physicians were not much better equipped to fight it than their earlier counterparts had been. The 17th-century plague, details of which are graphically depicted in the famous diary of Samuel Pepys, took scores of thousands of lives in London alone. Ironically, one 17th-century solution for the problem involved the wholesale murder of dogs and cats – the very creatures that might have helped to slim down the rat population.

The equals of kings and princes
The Hanseatic merchants and their power

IN 1370 the medieval world was shaken to learn that the all-powerful, and till then unbeaten, King of Denmark, Waldemar IV, had been forced to concede vast privileges inside his own kingdom: Not to a rival claimant to his throne, but to a group of mere traders from Germany. These traders were suddenly using military force rather than economic sanctions to become one of the greatest powers in northern Europe. The Peace of Stralsund, signed that year between the group of merchants, known as the Hanseatic League, and the once haughty king – who ruled much of southern Sweden and north Germany in addition to his own kingdom – restored the right of free trade throughout Denmark to the merchants of the Hanse (the word means band or company). This right had been removed in 1363 after two years of war between

Waldemar and the Hanse. However, in 1369 the forces of the Hanse won a resounding victory over Waldemar, which led to the Peace of Stralsund, in which the merchants were also given the right to appoint their own officers to supervise such trade, two-thirds of the revenues from four of Waldemar's Swedish fortresses, and even a right of veto over the heirs to the Danish throne. To a Europe still accustomed to a society dominated by Church and nobility, a merchant league with such powers was rare.

Where had it come from, this league, and how had it developed such strength that it could dictate terms to kings? In fact, its origins date back to at least 1241, when two of the most important north German trading cities, Hamburg and Lubeck, signed a treaty of alliance and mutual protection for trading purposes. Within 50 years there were 19 cities allied together, within a century over 70 – from Reval and Riga in modern Russia to Cologne on the Rhine. Such

a protective organization was essential in the northern Europe of the day, a lawless society tyrannized by pirates, for whom wrecking ships after capturing their cargo was a legitimate, even respectable profession. Unions such as that made by the League needed royal approval, hence the secrecy over the Hanse in its early days before it was formally recognized by the Holy Roman Emperor, Charles IV in 1375. Once it was established, however, no one was powerful enough to crush it.

Lubeck, at the strategic western end of the Baltic, was the League's capital and its wealthiest city, a Venice of the north. But while Venice had grown rich by trading in the East for exotic goods like silks and spices, Lubeck and her allies thrived on the humbler but equally profitable trade in wax, furs, wheat, timber, and above all herring that the Baltic provided in abundance. Medieval Europe was predominantly Catholic, and its frequent fastdays of abstinence from meat created an immense market for fish which the merchants were quick to exploit. Salted and cured, herring was exported with the wheat and rye from Poland and Russia that had come down the long rivers to Hanse ports like Danzig or Riga. In return, the merchants loaded up with wines, textiles, and other products. From London to Novgorod the Hanse controlled and grew rich on an immense network of trade, their convoys offering protection against pirates, their coinage universally accepted.

But heaven help any merchant who tried to contradict or flout the Hanse's regulations. Once a merchant from Bremen continued to trade with Flanders when that region had been embargoed for commercial reasons by the League. For failing to punish him, Bremen was cut off from the Hanse in 1356 so that "for the 30 miserable years which followed she was impoverished; grass grew in the streets and poverty and desolation were everywhere in her borders." On another occasion Brunswick was similarly punished and her trade wiped out until 10 of her leading citizens walked barefoot through the streets of the proud capital of the League in 1374 and begged on their knees before the Council in Lubeck to be readmitted.

London was one of the 120 cities in which the League established "factories" – autonomous trading posts where the merchants lived under Hanse laws. Others included Bruges in Belgium, the greatest of European ports at the time; Novgorod in northern Russia, where the Germans built their own little German town, complete with stores, churches, and Germanic houses; and the Norwegian town of Bergen,

While well-dressed Hanse merchants, the most dynamic capitalists of their day, discuss business, square-rigged vessels bring their goods into Hamburg, an important Hanseatic center. The great wealth and power of the Hanseatic League rested upon its monopoly of maritime trade in northwestern Europe.

where the Germans actually comprised about a quarter of the population, displacing many of the native townspeople. That factory numbered 3,000 artisans and merchants, so lucrative was the trade there.

An almost monastic discipline controlled the lives of the Hanse merchants in Bergen, as in most of their colonies. Vowed to celibacy, they had to sleep within the factory walls (to prevent any of the local women learning commercial secrets in bed). The merchants could only stay for 10 years, had to live in common quarters, and before they were admitted were forced to undergo sadistic initiation rites, such as being beaten until they dropped, or ducked in the freezing fjord waters. These served to entertain the onlookers as well as weed out the fainter hearted, but so strong was the lure of trade that there were always far too many applicants.

For over 100 years after their famous treaty with the Danish king, the Hanse prospered, but early in the 16th century things began to go badly wrong. One major cause for the decline of the League was the migration of the herring from their spawning grounds in the Baltic to the North Sea, where the Hanse's commercial rivals, the Dutch, could catch fish more easily. Another was the growth of Protestantism, which reduced the demand for fish anyway. More serious was the development of new trade routes, after Ivan the Terrible opened the Baltic seaport of Narva to all traders, thus creating competition for the Hanseatic merchants. By 1603, there were only 14 remaining fee-paying members of the League, and by 1648 only Hamburg, Bremen, and Lubeck were still independent cities, the rest having been subjected by the local princes jealous of their wealth.

For Lubeck, left high and dry by the changing trade patterns, there remained nothing but memories of her former greatness, symbolized by her soaring cathedral.

The Peasants' Revolt of 1381

How a boy-king broke the back of rebellion

O N A JUNE DAY in 1381 England teetered on the brink of catastrophe as two unequal forces confronted each other just outside the walls of the city of London. One force was a small company of mounted aristocrats and their followers who were gathered around their 14-year-old king; the other a rebellious crowd of nearly 20,000 peasants and laborers. The rebels had carried out a series of attacks in London. Their targets were the men whom they held responsible for military failure in the war with France, and the high taxes levied to pay for the war. Their demonstration also had structural, political aims. Although they accepted the rule of Richard II, they demanded that all others be made equal regardless of birth, and that Church land be redistributed. These demands showed their strong resentment of the manorial system, which gave them so little chance of a better life. Resentment had grown up because recent improvements in the peasants' standard of living had made them aware of possibilities for the future. Despite their weak position as villeins or serfs, they had been able to demand higher wages after the Black Death (1347–51) had greatly reduced the workforce. But the authorities had responded by passing a Statute of Labourers (1351) intended to control wages and prices. Wages proved easier to control than prices, however, which continued to rise.

The yearning of common people for more liberty and equality had grown swiftly, as reflected in a rhyming slogan that – like a catchy phrase from a modern TV show – gained widespread currency: "When Adam delved and Eve span, who was then a gentleman?" Resentment deepened when, in 1377, '79, and '80, the Council of Regency, which governed the land in the name of young Richard II, levied a series of unprecedented poll taxes in order to meet government expenditure in the French war. When such taxes were payable at the same rate for every individual, whether poor or rich, then they were especially objectionable.

Active rebellion, largely confined to southeastern England, erupted in the late spring of 1381. Refusing to pay their taxes, bands of peasants, armed with swords, axes, and bows and arrows, began to march through town and city centers, burning buildings belonging to the men whom the peasants held responsible for the taxes, destroying legal records that incriminated those who had not paid their taxes, and releasing prisoners from jails. One man released from an ecclesiastical prison was John Ball, a fiery itinerant preacher who had been incarcerated for his

In the Middle Ages, peasants worked remorseless hours at hard, physical labor, often rising at 3 a.m. to tend cattle. They were poorly rewarded and, under the feudal system, most of the land on which they labored belonged not to them but to the lord of the manor.

subversive sermons; he quickly set about urging his liberators on with the revolt. The peasants soon had a secular leader, too, in the passionately committed soldier of fortune, Wat Tyler, whose tempestuous energy, ambition, and force of personality found an appropriate outlet in this revolutionary movement.

The Council of Regency, at first scornful but shortly terrified, were unable to prevent the rebels from converging on London. They were even able to enter the Tower of London, a high-security fortress, and to take away two key members of the Council – Simon Sudbury, Archbishop of Canterbury, and Robert Hales, the Treasurer, whom the rebels held responsible for the poll tax – who were immediately beheaded. Next, they sacked some hated targets such as the Savoy Palace, residence of John of Gaunt, the young king's uncle and chief adviser. On Wat Tyler's orders, nothing was to be stolen, but all was to be destroyed. Gorgeous fabrics were ripped from walls, then slashed and burned or tossed into the Thames; precious jewels were pounded to dust; hundreds of sumptuous garments were burned; furniture was smashed and set fire to. Only one man seems to have been caught disobeying Tyler's order not to steal. Because he had tried to slip a silver coin into his pocket, he was thrown into

the flames that soon enveloped the Savoy Palace. This incident highlights the control with which the rebels maintained their own values while ruthlessly rejecting and destroying the symbols of feudal inequality and injustice.

There was little to hinder the destruction – merely some 500 men-at-arms in the king's entourage. The majority of the poorer classes in London sympathized with the aims of the insurgents. So the king and his frightened councillors were all that stood between the marauding rebels and the destruction of the social order. However, the peasants had agreed to negotiate their demands with the king. But when the two forces met outside the walls of London on that June day in 1381, it looked for a time as if the highly explosive mood of the people could not possibly be defused.

Although the boy-king was mounted on a great war-horse, with a crown on his head and a golden scepter in his hand, he could hardly have appeared a daunting figure to his adversaries. When permitted to speak, he did indeed accede to all their demands. The Peasants' Revolt (to give the rebellion its traditional name) seemed about to culminate non-violently in victory for Wat Tyler and his cheering followers. Then came a sudden shock that might easily have led to disaster. Nobody knows the precise course of events. Somehow, though, Tyler picked a quarrel with one of Richard's knights, made some sort of threatening gesture, and in the next moment lay dead, struck down by the sword of the Lord Mayor of London.

With a roar of outrage the ranks of the rebels fanned out menacingly. Bowmen hastily drew their bows and prepared to loose their arrows. But before confusion could give way to general violence, an extraordinary event occurred: Young Richard, unprompted by his councillors, broke away from the group of noblemen and rode forward alone, crying, "Sirs, what is it you require? I am your captain, I am your king. Quiet yourselves." In that tense moment, with the slender boy's body exposed to the enraged mob, murder and chaos could have followed. Instead, seeing their leader dead and their sovereign raising his hand regally, the rebels cooled down. Richard promised to attend to their grievances, and the crowd dispersed. He had stopped the rebellion in its tracks.

The story has a bleak ending. The lords now had time to reorganize themselves. They assembled troops to quell the remnants of rebellion, and the king's apparent sympathy with the plight of his subjects evaporated; the promises he had made were never honored. The Peasants' Revolt may be said to have been finally suppressed with a symbolic gesture: Wat Tyler's head replaced the head of the Archbishop of Canterbury on a stake on London Bridge.

The fake bequest that devastated Europe
The terrible legacy of this "gift"

THE PERSON who forged the document known to historians as the Donation of Constantine could not have guessed that people would one day be burned at the stake for questioning its validity. In all probability he was simply a loyal servant of the pope, an eighth-century scribe whose only aim was to serve the Church.

The Donation of Constantine was allegedly an edict issued by the Roman Emperor Constantine the Great in AD 315. A legend current in the Middle Ages held that Constantine was suffering from incurable leprosy in 315 and that his baptism by Pope Silvester, the Christian Bishop of Rome, effected a miraculous cure. The eighth-century document was believed to have stemmed from this miracle; it purports to record the grateful emperor's decision to reward the Church by donating part of his empire to it in perpetuity. Thus Constantine is credited with having decreed that "Silvester and his successors" are to rule over the city of Rome "and all the provinces, districts, and cities of Italy and the West . . . forever."

The document adds that Constantine vacated the Lateran Palace in Rome in favor of Silvester, and that he himself carted away the first 12 baskets of earth from the site on the Vatican Hill of what was to become the Basilica of St. Peter. Then, because it would no longer be appropriate for two rulers to live in the same city, he moved eastward to Byzantium, where he set about building himself a new imperial capital.

It was this extraordinary "testament" that provided successive popes with all the excuse they needed to intervene in worldly politics from the eighth century onward. After its first appearance, no fewer than 10 popes and their allies cited the Donation in support of military adventures, using Constantine's alleged bequest to legitimize dubious ambition and persecution of all who seemed to threaten it. The assumption of papal sovereignty over all Europe reached its height in 1300, when Pope Boniface VIII, dressed in imperial armor and accompanied by cardinals wearing the scarlet of Caesar, is said to have declared in public: "I am emperor. I am Augustus." For medieval Italy in particular this idea was to prove disastrous; seesaw battles for power between Rome and various other ambitious states kept the peninsula torn and bloody for hundreds of years. It was not, indeed, until the late 19th century, when the pope's hold on temporal politics was finally shaken off, that the reunification of Italy as a secular state could begin to take shape.

To us today it seems strange that the Donation of Constantine was taken seriously by laymen as well as churchmen, for it is in so many respects palpably spurious. Although the first known manuscript dates from the ninth century, it was almost certainly concocted during the latter half of the eighth in an effort to prove that the pope was not only independent of any earthly emperor but also his superior. Some scholars think the Donation was dreamed up to support Pope

Stephen's struggle against barbarian threats to Rome, in which he was aided by the Frankish King Pepin, Charlemagne's father. Most, however, suspect it was drawn up in the papal chancery under an official named Christophorus.

Yet, despite suspicions raised as early as the 10th century the fraud was not generally accepted as such for almost 700 years. Although the question of Constantine's legal right to give away half an empire was frequently raised by purists disputing the pope's role in temporal affairs, few doubted that the document itself was genuine. The great deception remained undiscovered until the 15th century, when two ecclesiastical scholars finally subjected the text to a thorough examination. The two were a German, Nicholas of Cusa, and an Italian, Lorenzo Valla, who, quite independently of each other, took it upon themselves to go through the Donation document with a fine tooth comb – and swiftly realized that it was riddled with serious errors, including historical facts that could not possibly have been available to Constantine or his contemporaries.

The document has much to say about the city and power of Constantinople, for instance, although Constantine was still in Rome in 315 and had not yet founded his new capital. It describes Roman officials as satraps, a word yet to be invented, and calls the Bishop of Rome a pope almost 200 years before the title came into general usage. Constantine, moreover, is made to refer to himself as the conqueror of the Huns some 50 years before they first set foot in Europe. And if, indeed, he wanted the Church to have half his empire, surely such a momentous wish would have been mentioned again and again in contemporary records. Yet the only pre-ninth-century mention of the bequest occurs in the Donation document itself. No one else – not even Bishop Eusebius of Caesarea, Constantine's contemporary biographer – seemed to have heard of it.

On November 7, 1433, Nicholas of Cusa presented his findings to the Council of Basle, where they were accepted without demur. Seven years later, Lorenzo Valla enlarged on Nicholas's work, producing a ringing condemnation of the Donation and, by implication, of the pope's right to temporal power. Valla was working for King Alfonso of Aragon at the time, and Alfonso was locked in a bitter dispute with Rome over control of Naples. But although it was in Valla's interest to find against the pope, there was no doubting the accuracy of his scholarship. The Donation of Constantine had been, in Voltaire's words, "the boldest and most magnificent" of all forgeries.

NICHOLAS OF CUSA

The breadth of knowledge and inquiring mind of Nicholas of Cusa made him one of the most remarkable men of the 15th century. It was often his fate, however, to pioneer in a field of inquiry without persevering in it – to sow where those who came later would reap. He was ahead of Copernicus and Newton in postulating that the Earth revolves on its axis around the Sun, and he worked out the details of the Gregorian calendar reform long before Pope Gregory XIII put them into practice in 1582. His studies of plant growth were the first to establish that air has weight; and his work as a mathematician – in particular his concept of the infinite – made a significant contribution to 20th-century theories of relativity. He was by turns a lawyer, a geographer, a scientist, philosopher, and priest, an eminent humanist, and a first-class theologian. Indeed, he has been called the model of a Renaissance man.

Nicholas, the son of a fisherman, was born – probably in 1401 – in Cusa, a small town on the Moselle River in western Germany. After studying at Deventer, Heidelberg, Padua, and Rome, he took a doctorate in canon law and, in 1432, became associated with the Council of Basle, which had been convened to deal with ecclesiastical reform. It was here that he denounced the Donation of Constantine as a forgery. Later, he became disillusioned with the council's over-zealous attempts to curb the power of the papacy and threw in his lot with the pope instead. In recognition of his subsequent work for Church unity he was created a cardinal by Pope Nicholas V. He died in 1464.

Although his life was filled with piety and good deeds, Nicholas brought little of his work to fruition. He traveled tirelessly on behalf of Rome, even journeying to Constantinople in an effort to win over the Greek Church to the papacy. But the Church in Europe was destined to be split, and it is ironic that the 16th-century breakaway by Martin Luther and other Protestants was, in small part, made possible by Nicholas's denunciation of the Donation of Constantine. Nor were his attempts at monastic reform any more long-lasting. We remember him today mainly for his scholarship. One of the first maps of Europe is attributable to him; and as a collector of manuscripts he was responsible for discovering texts of the *Natural History* of Pliny the Elder and no less than a dozen lost comedies by the Roman writer Plautus. He left his entire personal library, which was famous in his own time, to an old people's home he had endowed in his native Cusa, where that priceless collection has survived the upheavals of centuries and is still virtually intact.

Pompeii, American style

The mountain that moved

This wooden club found at Ozette has been cleverly carved to represent an owl's head. Its owner probably made it during the slack season before whaling commenced.

TALES ABOUND of lost settlements that the sea has drowned, but this may be the only story you will ever read of a buried settlement that the sea has unearthed.

Ozette is a tiny village, a coastal haven of calm in the northwestern corner of the state of Washington. It lies on a fairly high bank overlooking a broad beach, which is normally cushioned from the full force of the Pacific by a reef three miles (4.5 kilometers) offshore. Until half a century ago the village was the home of a tribe of Indians known as the Makah, who had earned their living at Ozette by hunting whales since long before the coming of settlers from Europe and eastern America. In the 1930s, however, the Makah moved to a town 15 miles (20 kilometers) away because of a government ruling that all Indian children must attend school – and there was no school at Ozette.

Though forced to live at a distance from the stamping ground of their ancestors, the tribal elders kept the past alive by repeating traditional tales of whaling adventures and other lore. There were no written records more than 100 years old, but the memories of the tribe reached back to pre-Columbian times; and one of the tales the elders told concerned a disaster that had occurred so long ago that it sounded to many who heard it like an incredible myth. Once upon a time, they said, a mountain of mud had suddenly descended upon Ozette, burying everything and everybody in its path.

An unlikely story, perhaps, but one who heard it found it fascinating. His name was Richard Daugherty, professor of anthropology at Washington State University. Since an element of fact lurks at the core of almost every legend, Daugherty believed it possible that he might someday find the relics of a buried past somewhere in the area of Ozette. Any such find might be like a time capsule, a key to the daily life of coastal Indian families hundreds of years ago. But how could a modern archeologist trace the path of the muddy mountain that was said to have swept through the village?

Then, in the winter of 1970, Nature gave Daugherty what he was looking for. Freak storms sent water surging up the broad beach to break upon the bank beyond; unable to withstand the battering, part of the bank gave way and collapsed in an avalanche of mud. Soon afterward, on a bitterly cold February morning, a hiker stumbled over the mud-slump and casually picked up something that the sea had washed clean. It looked like a piece of driftwood at first but the finder soon realized that it was a paddle for a boat of some sort, and it was in such good condition that it seemed strange that anyone could willingly have abandoned it.

When news of the mysterious paddle reached Dr. Daugherty, he remembered the recent storms that had brought down part of the ridge of land upon which Ozette stood; and he wondered whether, by chance, this was the area where the Indians had suffered their legendary disaster. Could the paddle have belonged to someone who used it 500 years ago to take his canoe out to the whaling grounds? The hunch was a good one. Upon examination, the site yielded up fish-hooks, a harpoon shaft, part of a

Site of the Ozette diggings. The heavily wooded peninsula is sheltered from the rough seas and strong currents beyond. The Makah Indians who lived here enjoyed reasonable prosperity based on their expert tapping of the natural resources around them, especially those from the sea.

HOW THE INDIANS CAUGHT WHALES

A fully grown gray whale is about 40 feet (12 meters) long and weighs around 20 tons (over 2,000 kilograms). With a flick of its tail it can reduce a small boat to a floating pile of matchwood. Yet for something like 2,000 years, the Makah Indians pitted themselves against these giants of the deep, using frail canoes as their hunting platforms. Only in this century have the Makahs at last abandoned their time-hallowed method of chasing whales, which once furnished them with meat, oil, and bone.

Traditionally, preparations for the hunt started long before the whaling season began. The Makah hunters could rely on one another's courage and skill; but because they believed it was "spirit power" that would make or mar their venture, they observed elaborate rites and rituals during several weeks prior to putting out to sea. An elderly Indian who is still alive remembers having seen his father swimming out into the Pacific and diving and spouting like a whale "to show that his heart was right" for the great undertaking.

On an appointed day the hunt began, with eight men to each canoe. Prepared for a long voyage, if necessary, they took food and water, along with an ingenious device for keeping warm: A box lined with sand, a supply of dry sticks, and some red-hot coals kept alive by being enclosed in large clam shells. Thus they could build a fire and keep it going without setting the canoe alight.

Silently, they would shadow their prey, eventually coming within a few feet – so close that the whale would inevitably capsize the boat if they made the slightest mistake. The moment to strike came when the great target surfaced to breathe. A sturdy member of the crew stood with a harpoon in hand, waiting to drive the weapon home. Inflated sealskin floats attached to the harpoon-rope dragged heavily on the injured whale as it attempted again and again to dive. Then at last, unable to escape and utterly exhausted, it would float passively on the surface, where the hunters would use mussel-shell lances to cut through its fluke tendons and finally reach its heart.

For the weary but jubilant hunters there remained the task of towing 20 tons of whale back to shore. Their first act was to lash the mouth of the dead whale so as to prevent the carcass from becoming waterlogged. Then they attached the sealskin floats to it in order to keep it riding high in the water. Once in sight of land, they would wait for the incoming tide to float their prize ashore.

Makah whalers bring ashore a carcass, which is buoyed up by sealskin bladders. The hunt required great strength – the heavy harpoons were up to 15 feet (5 meters) in length – and good teamwork, as well as, the Indians believed, the favorable intervention of "spirit power."

carved wooden box, and a woven-straw hat, all shallowly buried near where the paddle had been found – and all, as scientific analysis proved, dating from a period before Columbus set foot on American soil. They had survived intact for centuries, protected from decay by a heavy layer of mud that blocked out the air.

Even more exciting was a small section of timber wall, exposed where the bank had slumped. This was undoubtedly part of an ancient Makah house, which might hold an archeological treasure. And so Daugherty set about the delicate job of bringing the house out of the mud. Since digging was impossible because of the fragility of the wooden building and its contents, he and his team of students had to remove tons of wet earth by means of carefully hosed and directed streams of water – a slow process but, in the end, a rewarding one.

The house turned out to be quite big – about 65 feet (21 meters) long and 45 feet (14 meters) wide – and divided into separate units, each with its own cooking hearth and sleeping platforms, so that a number of families probably lived in the one building. Their belongings were strewn about just where they must have lain when the murderous avalanche descended upon Ozette. Among the items literally unearthed by the archeologists were a portion of white blanket with a blue-and-black design clearly visible after five centuries, a wooden bowl carved in the shape of a male figure, fishnets, and some alder leaves, which were green when uncovered but turned brown with exposure as the archeologists watched. One find indicative of the ancient Indians' artistic skill was a handsome representation of a whale's fin carved out of cedar wood and inlaid with more than 700 sea-otter teeth.

Most interesting, of course, were things that revealed the life style of this coastal people. They sometimes cooked, for instance, by dropping fire-heated stones into wooden boxes filled with water; a hole burned through the bottom of one such box suggests that careless cooks occasionally did the Makah equivalent of letting the kettle boil dry. Still intact was a wooden bowl that, when unearthed, reeked of the seal oil it once contained. And while the family meal was being prepared, children could play with toys their fathers had made for them. Daugherty's team found wooden bats shaped like ping-pong paddles, shuttlecocks made of thimbleberry stem, and even a miniature bow-and-arrow set.

And the legend of sudden death proves to be poignantly true. A puppy curled up in sleep died at the same moment as its masters. A half-carved comb that should have decorated the hair of a Makah girl lay where it was dropped, and wood splinters on the floor were never swept up. A few skeletons were found, but not nearly enough to account for the number of sleeping platforms. Perhaps some of the inhabitants had escaped an instant before the catastrophe.

Still, the tragedy of 500 years ago has a bright ending of sorts. For America it has provided what Daugherty terms the "most significant and unique find in northwest coast archeology, truly a national treasure." For the Makah Indians it provides something more. In the words of one modern member of the ancient tribe: "We look in a special way at what is coming from the mud at Ozette, for this is our heritage."

Tamerlane the Terrible
Monstrous pyramids of skulls

OF ALL THE blood-soaked leaders in history, from Genghis Khan and Attila the Hun to Adolf Hitler and Joseph Stalin, none was more steeped in death – if we are to believe the stories of his enemies – than Tamerlane, the 14th-century Tartar warlord who built up a vast empire stretching from China deep into Asia Minor. Born near the fabled city of Samarkand (now part of the Soviet Union) in 1336, Tamerlane lived for nearly 70 years, and probably established an all-time record for prolonged and brutal conquest.

To modern Westerners, he is chiefly known through the fiery play *Tamburlaine the Great*, written by Shakespeare's contemporary, Christopher Marlowe. To the people of his own time, however, his name spelled barbarity on an unparalleled scale. His army of mounted Mongol archers and saber-wielding Tartars ravaged Asia from Syria and Turkey to the edges of China, and from Moscow to Delhi. And wherever it rode, horror rode with it.

When opponents surrendered without a struggle, Tamerlane could be magnanimous,

Tamerlane, seeking glory in death as in his terrible life, was buried in this magnificent domed mausoleum in Samarkand.

FROM DAMASCUS TO THE TAJ MAHAL

Without Tamerlane, one of the world's most beautiful buildings might never have been created. For the most distinctive feature of India's Taj Mahal – its bulging central dome – would perhaps not have been part of an Indian architect's repertory had it not been for another, very different, side to the Tartar ruler: He was a patron of Islamic art and learning.

In Tamerlane's time only one such dome existed – a wooden one atop the great central mosque of Damascus in Syria. Tamerlane, who was a keen student of architecture and often had models of buildings carried back to Samarkand to be copied, could not have overlooked it. He spent at least a month camped outside Damascus when he laid siege to it, in 1400, and the dome dominated the city.

When Damascus fell, in January, 1401, the Tartars sacked it, and the great mosque was burned to the ground. But Tamerlane remembered the dome. He had it copied at Samarkand for his own magnificent tomb, the Gur Amir, parts of which still stand. And from there the dome's style spread northward (where it eventually became the onion shape characteristic of domes on Russia's Christian churches including those on the churches of the Kremlin) and southward across the Himalayas.

The style caught on in India as a result of the exploits of one of Tamerlane's direct descendants, Baber, who overthrew the Sultan of Delhi in 1526 and founded the Mogul empire. It was one of Baber's dynasty, the Emperor Shah Jahan, who put 20,000 men to work for 18 years to create on a riverbank at Agra a mausoleum for his favorite wife, Mumtaz. That mausoleum, the Taj Mahal, completed in 1648, stands today as a unique marble masterpiece, and the shape of the dome at its center derives directly from the mosque that Shah Jahan's cruel ancestor had burned nearly 250 years before.

Was this the face of Tamerlane, the cruel Tartar warlord? Certainly it must bear more than a superficial resemblance to him, for it has been reconstructed scientifically from the despot's skull by the famous Russian anthropologist, Professor Gerasimov.

but he was remorseless with all who resisted – and even with their innocent families. In 1401, in Damascus, Syria, Tamerlane answered a plea for mercy from thousands of terrified townspeople, including women and children, by suggesting that they take sanctuary in the central mosque. According to a contemporary historian (who admittedly may have wanted to blacken Tamerlane's name), his lieutenants ushered some 30,000 women, children, priests and other refugees, into the wooden building, closed all exits, and then put this giant sanctuary to the torch. In another such "merciful" gesture the conqueror promised the city elders of Sivas in Turkey that no blood of the city's defenders would be shed if they surrendered. He kept his promise: The 4,000 Armenian soldiers who had led Turkish resistance were simply buried alive. Christians in the city were either strangled or trussed up and tossed in the moat to drown. And local children were herded into a field to be trampled to death by the Mongol cavalry.

Mass decapitation seems to have been a favorite sport of Tamerlane and his followers. When, for example, the Tartars overran a garrison of Christian Crusaders at Smyrna on the Turkish coast, and ship-loads of reinforcements from Europe appeared over the horizon, Tamerlane's men drove them back by firing a barrage of human heads cut from their captives. After the capture of the Syrian city of Aleppo, the heads of 20,000 of its inhabitants were piled into pyramids about 15 feet (5 meters) high and 10 feet (3 meters) across at the base. These grisly towers, with all heads facing outward, were to serve as monumental warnings.

THE CRIPPLED MAN OF IRON

Tamerlane, the name by which the 14th-century Tartar emperor is known today, is a Westernized corruption of Timur-i-Lenk, meaning "Timur the Lame." He was originally called simply Timur, a word that meant "iron" in his native tongue. As a teenager, however, he was wounded by an arrow in the right knee – probably during a raid on a rival tribe – which left him with a permanent limp; and so he became known as Timur-i-Lenk, particularly among his Persian and Arab enemies, who provide most of our accounts of his life.

When, in 1941, Soviet archeologists opened the jade-covered tomb in Samarkand known to be that of Tamerlane, they found the skeleton of a man about five feet seven inches (1.7 meters) in height – tall for a stocky Tartar nomad. The skeleton's whole frame was twisted because of evident lameness in the right leg, and its right arm and hand seemed also to have been crippled. Despite these disabilities, the archeologists concluded that the body must have been immensely strong and muscular. And historians confirm that although Timur could not walk far because of his lameness, on horseback he was a fearless warrior and a tireless traveler.

Perhaps the largest of several similar towers of death was erected in 1387 after a rebellious mob in Isfahan (in present-day Iran) had massacred 3,000 of Tamerlane's occupying troops. When informed of the revolt, Tamerlane ordered his commanders to collect human heads, giving each commander a quota that must be met. Some of the soldiers, all of whom, like Tamerlane himself, were Muslims, were reluctant to kill fellow Muslims in cold blood, so bought heads from less scrupulous comrades. The result was a sickening market in death. To start with, Iranian heads were selling for 20 dinars apiece. By the end, when most quotas had been amply filled, the price had dropped to half a dinar. When the sated army moved on, no fewer than 70,000 heads had been heaped outside the city walls.

Tamerlane spent his entire adult life at war. The smell of battle was so strong in his nostrils that even when he returned to his capital of Samarkand to celebrate each string of victories, he preferred to live in a campaign tent outside the city rather than take up residence in a glittering palace. At the time of his death, in February, 1405, he was on his way to yet another war, a campaign to conquer the whole of China. Ironically, the brutal conqueror of Asia did not die by the sword. Instead, he died in bed, an old man weakened by illness.

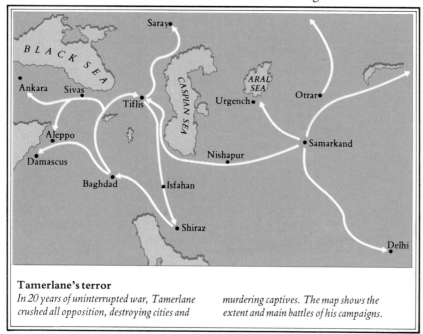

Tamerlane's terror
In 20 years of uninterrupted war, Tamerlane crushed all opposition, destroying cities and murdering captives. The map shows the extent and main battles of his campaigns.

The flames of Rouen

Did they really kill Joan of Arc?

THE HISTORY BOOKS are explicit about the death of Jeanne d'Arc. No question about it, say reputable historians: On a May morning in 1431, she was burned in a public square in Rouen, and there were thousands of witnesses to the tragedy. The route to the stake was lined by an enormous crowd of spectators, who were kept at a discreet distance by 800 English soldiers. Cloaked from head to foot and accompanied by two priests, Joan of Arc (to give her her English name) met her fate after a trial whose result was a foregone conclusion despite her able and spiritied defense. Now the crowd watched the cruel and – from the occupying English force's point of view – conclusive end of a 19-year-old peasant girl who had become the living symbol of French resistance to English occupation.

Ten thousand pairs of eyes saw the flames envelop the slim body of the maiden who had been proclaimed a witch and a heretic; and many of the spectators heard her invoke the name of Jesus and call out to the saints who had inspired her mission to rid France of the English. It took a long time for her to die, but at last, with a final murmured "Jesus," she was gone. People saw the executioner rake back the fire to expose her charred body. Yet there came a time when many French people were convinced of the truth of an insistent rumor that Joan of Arc was not burned at the stake. And some people still believe that it was not really Joan who died on that May morning in 1431.

The devout young shepherdess who donned male attire in order to lead the French army to victory against the English was, of course, the kind of person to inspire a faith in miracles. Under her leadership, the French had raised the siege of Orléans and routed the English at other battles. Joan had endowed the cause of an apparently powerless dauphin with popular fervor and had stood near him when, in 1429, he was crowned Charles VII, lawful King of France. That occasion was the pinnacle of her fortunes, however. Afterward, she failed in an effort to recapture Paris, and during a campaign in the following spring she fell into the hands of the English, who clamored for her public execution because, as a miracle-working morale-raiser capable of electrifying the French soldiers into wild enthusiasm, she was considered a profoundly dangerous enemy resource.

After displaying the charred corpse of the Maid of Orléans (as she had been popularly called), the executioner got a big fire going again, so that there was eventually nothing more to be seen but ashes, which were then dumped into the River Seine. However, there were those who began to talk about miraculous events in connection with the scene they had witnessed. An English soldier was sure that a white dove had risen from the pyre just as the spirit left Joan's body. Others claimed to have seen the word "Jesus" inscribed in the flames. Stories were soon circulating to the effect that Joan's

Death at the stake was quick, for the executioner would usually end the victim's misery. However, Joan's scaffold was so high that he could not reach her. Here Joan is being tied to the stake in a movie version of Shaw's play, St. Joan.

heart and entrails had remained whole and un-scathed by the fire. Soon it was said that the Maid had survived the flames and still lived.

Realizing that this desire of many French people to believe that their heroine had not died might be turned to good account, Joan's two brothers decided to perpetrate a cruel – and, they hoped lucrative – hoax. They had already done well for themselves out of their sister's career, and in 1436, five years after her death, the two brothers gave the rumors that she still lived an impetus that has kept them bubbling through the centuries. Suddenly the two men appeared in the streets of Orléans accompanied by a young woman dressed in armor and mounted on a horse. She was their sister Joan, they asserted, saved from the fire by a last-minute substitution of another woman. In fact, the woman beneath the armor was an adventuress named Claude des Armoises. Before impersonating Joan, she had had a colorful career as a soldier in the pope's army in Italy. Now her martial air and feats of horsemanship delighted people who – as is often the case when a beloved leader is lost – were more than willing to believe the Maid still lived.

So convinced of the truth of the brothers' story were the citizens of Orléans that they discontinued memorial services that had been held ever since their heroine's death. Joan's brothers and their protégée Claude were trusted, wined, dined, and honored – first in Orléans, then in other sections of France – until, after four profitable years, their fraud was exposed. In Paris in the year 1440 Claude made a full confession of her part in the cruel comedy. Her impersonation had had its effect, though; the belief that Joan of Arc had not perished in a public square at Rouen persisted in some quarters despite hard evidence to the contrary.

In 1456, after the real Joan's mission had been completed and Charles VII ruled over an almost totally French France, the scheming brothers forcefully supported their mother's plea for a retrial to clear their dead sister's name of the stigma of heresy and witchcraft. A rehabilitation trial did reverse the condemnation of 1431, but neither brother was called on to give evidence – probably because their earlier effort to exploit Joan's reputation had alienated intelligent churchmen and state authorities. As for the rakish Claude, she managed to retire gracefully, in due course giving birth to children whose descendants still maintain the fiction that she really was the Maid of Orléans.

In 1430 Joan was captured at the siege of Compiègne (above) by Burgundian soldiers, who then sold her to the English.

WAS JOAN ANOREXIC?

Joan of Arc's claim to have communicated directly with God and His saints via "voices" and visions instead of through mediation by the Church enabled the ecclesiastical judges at Rouen to justify their condemnation of her as a heretic. Other aspects of her behavior were also open to censure in the medieval world. Though there was no doubt of her virginity (she willingly submitted to examination by English women), her preference for male dress and her strong, if slim, body could indicate a diabolical lack of femininity to unfriendly minds. Then, too, it was said that Joan did not menstruate, and any such suspension of normal bodily functions aroused suspicions of the workings of evil spirits (rather than, as modern psychologists see it, the effect of mental stress).

There may, however, have been another reason for the failure to menstruate. It was observed that Joan ate very sparingly throughout her spectacular career, and so some historians have suggested that she was a typically intense, ambitious, but emotionally disturbed young woman in the grip of the condition known today as *anorexia nervosa*. One symptom of this disease is amenorrhea.

In captivity Joan shocked her custodians by continuing to wear men's clothes. She argued that her male garments made her better able to defend herself against sexual harassment, to which she was undeniably subjected. Unfortunately for Joan, her male clothing provided her captors with yet more evidence of unnatural influences.

Prototype of Dracula

A pain in the neck

Vlad Tepes, the disarmingly handsome ruler of 15th-century Wallachia, shown in this contemporary woodcut, was the prototype for the blood-sucking Count Dracula.

THOUGH OTHERS before and since 1897 have written stories about vampires, Bram Stoker's famous novel *Dracula*, published in that year, captured the public imagination most and still holds it in thrall. Everybody has heard of *Dracula* or seen the movie (not to mention its various sequels and imitations). But some people do not realize that Stoker's gruesome count is based on a real person, who lived in Eastern Europe over 500 years ago. There are few more terrifying figures in the annals of history.

Both the geographical background of the novel – Transylvania – and the name of its central character are firmly rooted in fact. One of the provinces of medieval Romania was Wallachia, situated between the Transylvanian Alps and the Danube River; and 15th-century Wallachia served as a buffer state between the central European kingdom of Hungary and the Turkish Ottoman empire, which was reaching the height of its power with the capture of Constantinople in 1453. The ruler of Wallachia at that time was known as Vlad Dracul, meaning "Vlad the Dragon," because he had adopted the sign of a dragon as his personal emblem. And when his son, whose name was also Vlad, inherited the throne a few years later, he was given the title of Dracula – "Son of the Dragon."

Born around 1430, Prince Vlad Dracula was well-acquainted with cruelty from an early age. As a boy he was held hostage by the Turks in a fortress called Egrigoz ("Crooked Eyes"). Later, he saw his father murdered and an elder brother buried alive on orders of the Regent of Hungary. During his own frenzied years of rule, Vlad Dracula was destined to put into continuous practice all he had learned – and much more – about violence and savagery.

He became, in fact, better known in his own lifetime as Vlad Tepes, meaning "Vlad the Impaler," because impalement upon an iron or wooden stake was his favored method of disposing of Turkish prisoners or anyone else who

---

THE VAMPIRE MYTH

A belief in vampires is as old as history. Whether shriveled and mummified, cadaverous and gaunt, bloated and slug-like, the image of the blood-sucking vampire leaving its grave at night to enslave its victims, who become vampires themselves, has both sprung from, and preyed upon, the deepest, darkest fears of mankind. People with blue eyes or red hair, babies born with teeth, sufferers from certain brain diseases – all have been linked with the dread image.

The myth of vampirism took an exceptionally strong hold on the imaginations of people in central and eastern Europe, especially in the remote region of Transylvania ("the land beyond the forests"), in the centuries following Prince Vlad Dracula's death in the late 15th century. Horrifying stories of his blood lust were reinforced by frequent outbreaks of the plague with all its attendant terrors, including the fear of being taken for dead and buried alive. Superstitious minds were easily seized by "true" tales about the *nosferatu* – the "undead" – arising from their graves at night to feast upon the blood of the living. There are many recorded cases of corpses being exhumed on suspicion of vampirism, to have stakes driven through the heart, or to be decapitated and burned (a less dramatic form of insurance). And a belief in the efficacy of holy water and a crucifix, or of garlic and herbs, as protection against the curse of the vampire persists today – and not only among avid viewers of old movies.

The gruesome career of Count Dracula acquired a new and even more scary lease on life in 1931 when the first "talkie" version of Bram Stoker's fiction reached the public. So enthrallingly terrifying did the theme prove that it has been estimated that there have been more than 400 screen adaptations. Here, Christopher Lee appears as the fanged archfiend.

incurred his displeasure. As a subtle refinement of this particularly unpleasant form of execution, he would often order the stake to be slightly blunted and greased, so as to prolong the agony of the victim by delaying the ultimate piercing of a vital organ.

His sadism found a number of other inventive outlets. When some Turkish emissaries failed to remove their fezes in his presence, he had the offending headgear nailed to their skulls. To show his detestation of weaklings, he once rounded up a crowd of beggars and cripples, herded them into a large hall furnished for a banquet, ordered all doors and windows barred, and set the place afire. A strong – and in his case deadly – puritan streak also ran through him. Women who were found guilty of adultery during his reign were skinned alive or submitted to other "suitable" punishments that are probably best left to the imagination.

Castle Bran (below), Vlad the Impaler's Romanian residence.

A still extant portrait of Vlad Dracula shows him as a handsome, attractively garbed young prince; and some historians, noting that he doesn't *look* villainous, argue that his image was deliberately blackened by political enemies. They point out, too, that he led a valiant campaign against the invading Turks and so helped save Christian Europe from Islamic conquest; that he supported peasants against the ruthless boyars (the feudal lords of Eastern Europe); and that he restored order to a land torn apart by foreign invasion and civil strife. Apologists also cite certain acts of charity, such as his donation of a gold cup to the fountain in a Wallachian village square. Some have even defended his incineration of the beggars and cripples on the ground that this was really a social-minded effort to stamp out disease in a land that was threatened by plague at the time.

The overwhelming weight of evidence, though, supports most historians' judgment that Vlad Dracula was a monster of cruelty – outstanding even in an age that bred such men as Cesare Borgia, and in the next century, Ivan the Terrible. It is reckoned that Vlad impaled, skinned, strangled, boiled, roasted, or in some other ingenious way put to death at least 50,000 people in his short reign of less than 10 years. He himself, appropriately, met a violent end in 1476, but we do not have an exact account of what happened. He may have been assassinated by political rivals or killed at the hands of the Turks. Whatever the circumstances, rough post-mortem justice prevailed: His severed head was impaled on a stake for public display – a common fate for tyrants in those days.

Vlad Dracula's life coincided with the early spread of the new technique of printing with movable type (invented by a German, Johannes Gutenberg, in 1440); and his atrocities soon reached a wide public. A German publication of 1499 contains a woodcut illustration of the Romanian prince feasting amid a forest of impaled bodies. Some early accounts of his misdeeds hint darkly at cannibalism and blood rites. There is no factual evidence that he liked the taste of blood – though he must have enjoyed the sight of it – but it was only natural that, among the true stories, rumors of his having been an actual demon, a vampire, should have begun to circulate with the passage of time.

Early in our own century, his putative tomb, built on an island in a lake somewhere in Romania, was opened up. It was empty. Had the dead body been removed on a dark night in the remote past and a stake driven through its heart? The idea is not as far-fetched as it might seem.

The magnificent Medici

The bankers who made Florence great

Young Leonardo da Vinci drew this executed conspirator, one of several men who had tried to murder some of the Medicis.

O N AN APRIL Sunday in 1478, Florence cathedral was packed for the celebration of High Mass, ordinary citizens standing shoulder to shoulder in the nave while beneath the vast dome were to be seen the great city's leading families resplendent in velvets and brocades and glittering jewels. Among those nearest to the high altar were members of a wealthy family of bankers, the Medici, who had unofficially ruled Florence for nearly half a century. They included the head of the family, Lorenzo (renowned in history as Lorenzo the Magnificent), who was a swarthy man 29 years old, and with him was his good-looking younger brother, Giuliano.

At the most solemn moment of the ceremony, as the wafer was raised in the ritual of consecration and the great bell of the cathedral sounded its first deep note high overhead, a violent disturbance suddenly broke out among the people standing near the altar.

Two members of the congregation, Bernardo Baroncelli and Francesco de' Pazzi (a jealous rival of the Medici), drew the swords that laymen wore even in church and threw themselves upon young Giuliano de' Medici, hacking and stabbing at him; 19 wounds were later found on his body. At the same time two men dressed as priests pulled daggers from beneath their robes and lunged at Lorenzo. He fell and the four assassins raced out into the street where they had arranged to join other conspirators calling upon the people of Florence to throw off their chains and free themselves from what they referred to as the "tyranny" of the Medici.

The assassins had miscalculated badly. The people did indeed rise – but in anger and grief – and hunted down the murderers and their accomplices, all of whom were eventually found and killed. We have a unique and macabre record of the vengeance of the Florentine people: The young artist Leonardo da Vinci saw the body of one of the assassins dangling from a window of the Palazzo della Signoria (known to modern tourists as the Palazzo Vecchio) and sketched it, meticulously noting the clothes that draped the despised corpse.

Giuliano died of his terrible wounds, but Lorenzo survived to hold sway over the Florentine republic, as his father and grandfather had done before him, for another 16 years. We have good cause to be grateful that Lorenzo survived

the attack on that April day in 1478. Altogether, the Medici family dominated the city-state of Florence for nearly 400 years, from the 14th through the 17th century. They began as merchants, became exceedingly rich bankers with enormous political power, evolved into monarchical Grand Dukes, and finally degenerated, after a long run, into self-indulgent incompetents. It was the Medicis who controlled the city during the 15th century, however, who really made their mark upon history, for they encouraged the flowering of the Renaissance in Italy. And of all the Medicis it was Lorenzo the Magnificent who did most to advance the culture and brilliant vitality of Florence.

The first member of the family to have become deeply involved in the political and cultural life of the city was Lorenzo's grandfather, Cosimo, who was 40 years old in 1429 when he inherited his father's vast banking empire, with branches throughout Europe as well as in most Italian cities. As the richest man in Florence, Cosimo could have led a life of ease, but he continued to manage the family business and even ran a farm as though he were an ordinary peasant, digging and planting with his own hands. Inevitably, too, he was drawn into politics; as his grandson Lorenzo was later to remark: "It goes ill in Florence for those who have

The Medici family used its immense wealth to control the city of Florence. A few of the many city employees can be seen below, receiving their pay from the Medici coffers.

money, but no share in government." The city-state was nominally governed by a nine-man council (the Signoria) selected in an apparently democratic fashion, but this body was, so to speak, "in the pocket" of the wealthy Albizzi family when Cosimo Medici began to purchase political influence. As his power increased, the Albizzi felt threatened. Consequently, in 1433, they trumped up a charge of treason against Cosimo and succeeded in having him banished to the city of Padua.

They should have known better. With Medici funds withdrawn from Florence, the citizens and the government itself suffered. Within a year Cosimo was invited back and the Albizzi were discredited. Thereafter Cosimo – like his descendants – increasingly tightened his grip on the Signoria, which soon became little more than a willingly servile rubber stamp. Cosimo used his power wisely, however. He was a dictator, but not a despot, and in general the people of Florence (apart from rival families such as the Albizzi and the Pazzi) never rebelled against his regime. It was he who began the Medici tradition of patronizing the architects, artists, and literary men who made Florence the fountainhead of the Renaissance.

His son Piero succeeded him in 1464, but Piero suffered badly from gout – a disease that afflicted many of the Medici – and died only five years later, when his son Lorenzo was barely 20. Despite Lorenzo's youth, the Florentines invited him to head their government. He was reluctant to take over the task, but the Signoria was determined to keep the city under what had proved to be beneficial Medici rule. And so Lorenzo took on the job and kept it magnificently for 23 years – until his untimely death, at the early age of 43, in 1492.

Lorenzo the Magnificent was ugly – dark-skinned, heavy-featured, with a big nose and a harsh, squeaky voice. His charming personality, though, made people forget the physical drawbacks. An astonishing mixture of talents and moods, he could be found one day drinking with rowdy cronies in rough taverns, and the next day engaged in philosophical argument with serious scholars. He wrote bawdy songs as well as excellent sonnets. And, like his grandfather, he furthered the arts in every way he could. Michelangelo owed his start in life to Lorenzo's discerning eye and flowing purse. The Medici coffers were at the service of all who were dedicated to the revival (*renaissance*) of classical learning. Under Lorenzo, Florence became the sparkling center of a culture that brought new life to Italy, and ultimately to every corner of Europe.

In addition to his other virtues, Lorenzo de' Medici was a supremely competent statesman, and he skillfully protected Florence from its many enemies not by waging war but by negotiating and building up alliances. He kept the balance of power in Italy so well that, when he died in 1492, the King of Naples ungrudgingly spoke of him as a hero. "This man lived long enough for his own glory," said the king, "but he died too soon for Italy."

THE FLORENTINE STATE

The city-state of Florence, in northern Italy, was dominated by the Medici family for over 300 years.

During the 15th century the city of Florence, with a population of about 60,000, ruled a state composed of surrounding territory within which were half a dozen subject cities – among them, Pisa, Leghorn, and Arezzo – with a total population of some 400,000. The Florentine state was theoretically a democratic republic, but the franchise was, in fact, limited to about 5,000 male members of 21 guilds within the city of Florence; and the guilds themselves were organized in a hierarchical fashion that gave a few prestigious guilds of lawyers, merchants, bankers, and skilled craftsmen most of the actual responsibility for governing the city-state. There was not an elected government in the modern sense of the term. Instead a group of nine citizens was selected, by drawing names of those who were considered to be eligible for office from leather bags, to serve as the governing body (the Signoria) for a term lasting only two months. Of the nine, one was chosen to fulfil the role of *Gonfaloniere* ("standard-bearer," or "leader"), with more power and prestige than the others.

In practice as well as theory, this central organization was normally disbanded after the stipulated period of office of two months and replaced by a new one, with, of course, a different *Gonfaloniere* at its head. Since money ruled the roost in Florence, however, the real governors of the state were its richest citizens. Cosimo de' Medici held the office of *Gonfaloniere* only about three times in his long life (unlike many of his gout-ridden descendants, he lived to be 75); but once having established the fact that his family's financial power was essential for the city's well-being, he remained the real power in control of the Signoria regardless of whose names were fed into and pulled out of the leather selection bags every two months.

There were always challengers, of course. But both Cosimo and Lorenzo de' Medici were remarkable for the force of their personalities as well as their wealth. Under their regimes Florence enjoyed such prosperity and renown that a serious challenge to Medici dictatorship became unthinkable until after Lorenzo's death.

Pretender to the throne

A young Flemish salesman claims the throne of England

THE ENGLISH THRONE has often been in jeopardy. From time to time various "pretenders" have asserted a prior right to the monarchy. Most such claimants have had at least a drop of royal blood in their veins but a few have been little more than swashbuckling soldiers of fortune. One of the most fascinating of these out-and-out impostors was a young man called Perkin Warbeck and it was he who dared to throw down the gauntlet to Henry VII, first of a great line of Tudor rulers.

In 1491 Warbeck laid claim to the English throne. A handsome, regal youth dressed in fine silken garments, Warbeck certainly gave the impression of royal blood. And since he was about 18 years old, many people became convinced that he was the Duke of York, the younger brother of Edward V. Both brothers had mysteriously disappeared (very probably murdered) in the Tower of London in 1483 when they were aged 10 and 12 respectively. A story of his miraculous escape from the Tower spread swiftly and the dashing young "duke" found willing adherents not only in Ireland and England but also in the courts of France and Scotland, Henry's most powerful enemies.

Henry's own claim to the throne was shaky if either Edward V or the Duke of York was indeed still alive and many of his enemies were all too ready to dethrone him if an alternative king could be found.

One of Warbeck's principal champions was Margaret, Duchess of Burgundy, the sister of Richard III and aunt of the lost princes. Detesting Henry, she enthusiastically sponsored her "nephew raised from the dead," installed him

A staircase within the Tower of London, a fortress founded by Julius Caesar and rebuilt over the centuries. It was used not only for defense but also as a royal palace and later a prison. Beneath such a staircase, the bones of two boys, aged approximately 12 and 10 years at death, were found in 1674. The remains may be those of Edward V and his younger brother, the Duke of York.

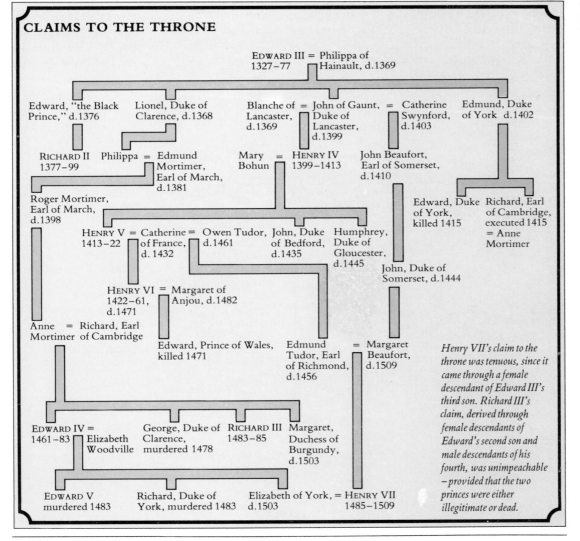

CLAIMS TO THE THRONE

EDWARD III = Philippa of
1327–77   Hainault, d.1369

Edward, "the Black Prince," d.1376
Lionel, Duke of Clarence, d.1368
Blanche of Lancaster, d.1369 = John of Gaunt, Duke of Lancaster, d.1399 = Catherine Swynford, d.1403
Edmund, Duke of York d.1402

RICHARD II 1377–99
Philippa = Edmund Mortimer, Earl of March, d.1381
Mary Bohun = HENRY IV 1399–1413
John Beaufort, Earl of Somerset, d.1410

Roger Mortimer, Earl of March, d.1398
Edward, Duke of York, killed 1415
Richard, Earl of Cambridge, executed 1415 = Anne Mortimer

HENRY V 1413–22 = Catherine of France, d.1432 = Owen Tudor, d.1461
John, Duke of Bedford, d.1435
Humphrey, Duke of Gloucester, d.1445

John, Duke of Somerset, d.1444

HENRY VI 1422–61, d.1471 = Margaret of Anjou, d.1482

Anne Mortimer = Richard, Earl of Cambridge

Edward, Prince of Wales, killed 1471
Edmund Tudor, Earl of Richmond, d.1456
= Margaret Beaufort, d.1509

EDWARD IV 1461–83 = Elizabeth Woodville
George, Duke of Clarence, murdered 1478
RICHARD III 1483–85
Margaret, Duchess of Burgundy, d.1503

EDWARD V murdered 1483
Richard, Duke of York, murdered 1483
Elizabeth of York, d.1503 = HENRY VII 1485–1509

Henry VII's claim to the throne was tenuous, since it came through a female descendant of Edward III's third son. Richard III's claim, derived through female descendants of Edward's second son and male descendants of his fourth, was unimpeachable – provided that the two princes were either illegitimate or dead.

WHAT REALLY HAPPENED TO THE PRINCES?

Did Richard III murder – or order the murder of his two young nephews, one of whom was rightful king? Our impression of Richard as a humpbacked monster whose ugly deeds matched his appearance derives in part from Shakespeare's play *Richard III*, and Shakespeare got his facts from 16th-century historians who were duty-bound to paint the last of England's Plantagenet kings in the blackest of colors. After all, the Tudor dynasty, so magnificently represented by Henry VIII and Elizabeth I, had been established by Henry VII, whose legal right to the throne was questionable, and who had deposed Richard by conquest. It was only natural for the Tudors' loyal spokesmen to vilify the memory of Richard. But were they vilifying his memory, or were they actually telling the truth when they accused King Richard of having cruelly put two innocent young boys to death in the Tower of London?

The Victorians were haunted by childhood innocence and early death, as epitomized in Sir John Everett Millais's painting Princes in the Tower *(1878). The study is idealized (Edward V is thought to have had a disorder of the lower jaw bone) and perpetuates the legend that Richard III was the callous murderer of his two nephews.*

The essential facts are these: When Edward IV died in 1483, he left his sons – 12-year-old Edward V and his 10-year-old brother, the Duke of York – in the care of their uncle Richard. Ostensibly for their own protection, the young princes were taken to the Tower of London and lodged in the royal apartments (a palace, not a prison) while awaiting the coronation day. The marriage of the princes' parents had never been popular with the English people, especially as their mother was a commoner, and soon after Edward IV's death, objections had been raised as to its validity. The marriage was now decreed invalid, making the princes illegitimate and their uncle Richard therefore next in line of sucesssion. He became king, and from that day forward the princes, who had earlier been observed playing in the Tower courtyard, were never seen again.

Did Richard III engineer the decision that Edward IV's marriage was unsanctioned, and thus cause the legal deposition of his nephews? Did he flout the trust with which he had been charged and ruthlessly dispose of the princes? It sounds probable, although, once Richard had become king because of the legal finding against the boys' legitimacy, why should he then risk unpopularity and the possibility of an uprising against him by having them murdered? It has been argued on the other hand that Henry VII had as much to gain as did Richard from the death of the princes. Henry had ended Richard's life and short reign by force of arms in 1485, when Edward V would have been about 14 years old if still alive. Before seizing the throne, Henry had contracted to marry the princes' sister, thus bringing him nearer to the throne. But because he could gain no advantage from the union if his wife was a bastard – and indeed may have believed the evidence against her legitimacy to be false – he ordered the destruction of all recorded testimony to that effect and proclaimed her legitimate, and this automatically re-legitimized her brothers. If the princes had still been alive at this time, Henry would have been faced with a terrible dilemma: As legitimate sons of Edward IV, the princes certainly had a prior claim to the crown Henry now wore.

Interestingly enough, Henry waited until nearly a year after Richard's death before accusing him of the boys' murder. Might the apparent delay have been due to the fact that the princes were still alive when their uncle lost the throne and his life? And was Henry the real villain? Or, if the boys had not been murdered during Richard's reign, why did Richard never produce them as an effective way of silencing the rumors about their death? We still do not know the truth, and probably never shall, although new "evidence" is continually being discovered. We do know, though, that three centuries after these events the bones of two boys were found under a stairway in the Tower. These remains, consistent with the princes' ages, were assumed to be theirs, although it is as yet impossible to date their deaths exactly and so prove a case against one or other of the chief suspects. The bones now lie in London's hallowed repository for England's illustrious dead, Westminster Abbey.

for a time in her home, and coached him in preparation for a confident assumption of his new role. With her assistance and that of James IV of Scotland, who not only recognized the "duke" but provided him with a wife from among his own kinswomen, the personable young man was able to muster enough followers to attempt a series of armed rebellions, none of which was even slightly successful.

Henry did his best to counter these schemes and captured the pretender at the first opportunity, in 1497. Held under loose guard, Warbeck escaped, was quickly recaptured, placed in the stocks, and forced to read out a confessional statement to a London mob. He was then sent to the Tower and was hanged in 1499. The gist of his confession: Far from being an English prince, his name was Perkin Warbeck, and he was born in the Flemish town of Tournai; his own trade was the selling of silks (which was undoubtedly why he could dress so well); and his claim to the throne of England was – to say the least – not valid. Whatever else he was, Perkin Warbeck must have been a good actor.

THE LAW THAT GAVE RICHARD HIS CROWN

In medieval times a contract to marry was considered as binding as an actual marriage, and royal betrothals were usually formalized in the presence of officials of both Church and state. Soon after the death of Edward IV, a churchman – Robert Stillington, Bishop of Bath and Wells – stated that he had officiated at a ceremony many years earlier in which Edward had plighted his troth to a young lady (an earl's daughter, not an insignificant and unpopular commoner) whom he was therefore committed to marry. And so the king's later marriage to a different woman could be considered unlawful and the offspring of that marriage illegitimate. As Protector of the Realm and next of kin among the legitimate members of Edward's family, Richard seems to have been within his rights in assuming the crown – unless, of course, as seems probable, given the intrigues of the time, Bishop Stillington's revelation was a lie.

The battle of Bosworth (1485) witnessed the death of Richard III, the last Plantagenet king, and the accession of Henry VII, founder of the Tudor dynasty. Here Laurence Olivier, in the title role, is seen near the end of the battle in his movie version of Shakespeare's play Richard III.

Leonardo's "Last Supper"

Quest for a masterpiece

AT THE 15TH-CENTURY monastery of Santa Maria della Grazia in Milan, a team of expert technicians has been carrying out a life-or-death operation for the past few years, and the operation will go on for a few more. Equipped with scalpels of surgical precision, tweezers, cotton wool, and microscopic aids, the scientists are trying to revive a patient whose imminent demise has long been predicted. That "patient" is one of the masterpieces of world art, Leonardo da Vinci's mural *The Last Supper*. A masterly creation measuring 28 feet six inches by 15 feet (9 by 4.5 meters), this great painting, located high on a refectory wall, illustrates a moment of intense mystery and drama. Seated at table in the midst of the 12 disciples, Christ has just prophesied: "Verily I say unto you that one of you will betray me."

The instant is brilliantly evoked in the dramatic grouping of the figures. To Christ's left, John and Peter surge forward in anguish, implicitly asking, "Lord, is it I?" Between these two the traitor, Judas, shrinks back. Within other equally energetic groups, each of Christ's followers is

a powerfully drawn portrait. Facial expressions are startled, anxious, doubting, desperate, while attitudes and gestures capture panic and uncertainty. Yet, despite the depiction of shock, a fluid harmony pervades the composition; all the high emotion is resolved into a calm symmetry that focuses on the figure of Christ himself. From the time of its completion in 1498, the painting has been acknowledged as an incomparable achievement, a vision that inevitably comes to mind whenever the Biblical Last Supper is mentioned.

It was probably in 1495 that Ludovico Sforza, Duke of Milan, asked Leonardo to paint the monastery mural, which took the artist more than three years to complete. A contemporary, Mateo Bandello, writes: "Many a time have I seen Leonardo go early in the morning to work on the platform before the *The Last Supper*; and there he would stay from sunrise till darkness, never laying down the brush, but continuing to paint without eating or drinking. Then three or four days would pass without his touching the work. Yet he would spend several hours each day examining it and criticizing the figures to himself." A story – probably spurious – has been told that Leonardo's Judas was based on the monastery's prior, who had complained about the length of time the work was taking. Curiously, Judas has a Christ-like appearance, as

if Leonardo meant the traitor to be a flawed reflection of the Savior. One problem that faced Leonardo was the question of how to make the mural proof against the ravages of dampness and decay. Ever inventive, he devised a sealing compound of gesso, pitch, and mastic, which he applied to the soft stone wall as a background for his painting.

Unfortunately, though, the experimental mixture did not work as he had hoped. With the passage of time, the pigment started to break loose from the base, and deterioration of the painting became noticeable as early as 1517, two years before the artist's death. In 1566, one viewer remarked that nothing was visible but a "muddle of blots." A century later, *The Last Supper* seemed so unsalvageable that a friar cheerfully enlarged a door in the wall below, cutting off the feet of Christ. Yet it was never truly a "muddle of blots." The brilliance shone through, even if dimly. And it survived many perils through the centuries.

During the Napoleonic period, for example, soldiers used the refectory as a storehouse for fodder for their horses. In World War II bombs destroyed the building's roof and righthand wall. Almost worse have been a number of ill-conceived efforts to restore the picture – six such attempts since the early 18th century, most of which have involved "reconstructions" by means of overpainting. By the middle of the 20th century *The Last Supper* had become a faded, crumbling, blemished shadow of itself. Since 1980, however, disintegration has given way to what promises to be a nearly miraculous, if slow, rebirth. The work of scientific restoration – a project headed by the Supervisor of Fine Arts for the Region of Lombardy – began with a meticulous examination of the whole painting. Now, proceeding by fractions of an inch at a time, experts are clearing away the remnants of earlier destructive "restorations" and reconstructing the original as nearly as is humanly possible. The intricacies of working with solvents and scalpels on this crumbling mosaic of paint are mind-boggling. Not long ago, Dr. Giuseppina Brambilla, the leading restorer, said to one observer, "See this flake of blue?" Pointing to a tiny fleck of color on the painting's white tablecloth, she explained: "It has migrated from where Leonardo originally put it, as part of his color for the robe of one of the apostles." And, of course, it was her job to put it back where it belonged.

The mural is a jigsaw of fragments – and an incomplete jigsaw at that. In places where the plaster itself has crumbled there are virtually no clues to original brushstrokes. Even so, remarkable results have been achieved. By 1982 the righthand quarter of the painting was practically complete. Saints Simon, Thaddeus, and Matthew had clearly emerged from the murky accretions of time. In the process, Dr. Brambilla and her associates uncovered some surprising facts about the artist's intentions. St. Simon's beard, for instance, had grown profusely over the centuries as a result of overpainting; Leonardo gave him only a short goatee. Food on the table was originally depicted as half-eaten – a sliced orange and a broken crust of bread – but an unknown hand had unaccountably "corrected" these human details by solidifying the broken roll and putting the orange together again. Elsewhere, vibrancy is gradually replacing darkness. Glinting gold rims have been restored to glasses, and colorful reflections from the apostles' robes to silver tableware.

So far, then, the work of restoration has been a revelation. All lovers of art are impatiently looking forward to what they believe will be a second unveiling of a painting that once again reveals the radiant vision of a superlative genius.

THE UNIVERSAL MAN

Described as "ten men in one," Leonardo da Vinci (1452–1519) was the archetypal Renaissance man: Artist, scientist, architect, anatomist, military engineer, and inventor.

Born in the Tuscan village of Vinci, Leonardo was the illegitimate son of a lawyer and a peasant girl. When he was 14, his father took him to Florence to study art, and he had already become a well-known painter by the age of 20. Ten years later he moved to Milan, where he remained at the court of Ludovico Sforza (later Duke of Milan) for 17 years. Many of the 7,000 pages of his *Notebooks* were compiled during this period. The notebooks contain detailed plans for flying machines, a parachute, a helicopter, a diving suit, a military tank, and a split-level city.

As an inventor, therefore, Leonardo was primarily a prince of visionary possibilities. But as an artist he was responsible for visions that achieved reality, including what are probably the two most famous paintings in the world. They survive in very different stages of preservation. The immaculate *Mona Lisa* is safely housed at the Louvre in Paris, secure behind a screen of bulletproof glass, whereas *The Last Supper* has been, until recently, no more than a noble ruin gradually disintegrating on its refectory wall.

After spending most of his life working – and being appropriately respected and honored – in his native Italy, Leonardo passed his last years in France, at the invitation of the French King Francois I, where he died in 1519.

Leonardo's superlatively inventive mind conceived all manner of mechanical devices centuries before they were developed by others. Illustrated are two pen-and-ink and wash compositions for a tank, a weapon that was not to be employed until 1916.

Lucrezia Borgia

Evil intriguer or innocent victim?

FOR LUCREZIA BORGIA, 20-year-old illegitimate daughter of Pope Alexander VI, August 18, 1500 was a day she would remember as long as she lived. It began in a sickroom at the Vatican, where she was nursing her second husband back to health after a murderous and wholly unprovoked knife attack. Later in the day, she returned after a five-minute absence to find him dead in bed – strangled, she had good reason to believe, at the command of her own brother.

It has never been proved conclusively that Cesare Borgia was responsible for his brother-in-law's murder. But the political climate of the time, together with his own violent nature, make it almost certain that it was he who disposed of his sister's husband to rid the Borgia family of an alliance no longer useful. And although Lucrezia mourned her husband at first – everyone knew that she had adored the young Alfonso of Bisceghe, the nephew of King Frederic of Naples – within a few weeks she had

Pope Alexander VI adorns Lucrezia Borgia with a necklace, a scene from the British television series The Borgias, *showing the close relationship between the notoriously worldly pontiff and his lovely daughter.*

completely recovered her spirits and was seen to be as cheerful and outgoing as ever. To outside observers this was proof – if proof were needed – that Lucrezia was as much a Borgia as the rest of her family, that she entered wholeheartedly into their macabre world of poison, intrigue, lust, and murder. But did she?

The accusations leveled against Lucrezia Borgia over the centuries have been as grave as they are repellent. Historians have regularly argued that she was promiscuous; that she committed incest with her brother Cesare and her father the pope; that the other men in her life were liable to die violently, gruesomely, and without warning; and that her idea of entertainment was to watch 50 Vatican servants and 50 naked prostitutes competing sexually for prizes. She was no angel, certainly – but much of the grosser evidence against her owes more to anti-Borgia propaganda than to the truth.

The gravest charge against Lucrezia – that she went to bed with her own blood relations – is also the easiest to refute. The charge arose from two different sources, neither of which can stand up to close examination. The first to accuse her of incest was Giovanni Sforza, her first husband, to whom she had been married at the age of 13, and he made the accusation purely as a form of self-defense. Their marriage had been a political union, with no love on either side, and when the time came to dissolve it, the Borgia family used Sforza's alleged impotence as the excuse. They claimed that Sforza had never been able to consummate the match. This was blatant nonsense, for Sforza had undoubtedly fathered a child by his previous wife, and himself insisted that he had made love to Lucrezia at least 1,000 times during their marriage – a proud boast, since they never lived together for anything like 1,000 days. But Sforza's pride was hurt, especially when people chose to believe the Borgias' story rather than his own. It was in this frame of mind that he accused the pope of wanting to get rid of him so that he could sleep with Lucrezia himself. The accusation was a wild one, conceived in anger and humiliation, and there was never the slightest evidence to back it up.

It is easy to see, however, why the story so quickly gained currency. During the break-up of her first marriage, Lucrezia seems to have had a love affair with a Spanish page, a handsome young man whose body was discovered in the River Tiber soon after Lucrezia became pregnant. To protect the child with a Borgia name, while preserving Lucrezia from any disgrace, the pope issued a public declaration that the child was Cesare Borgia's by an undisclosed Roman woman. In private, however, for reasons that have never been explained, the pope named himself as the father. When it began to be rumored that the undisclosed woman was Lucrezia, the rumors of incest began to expand and multiply until at length they reached the historians Francesco Guicciardini and Niccolò Machiavelli, who recorded them for all time as well-established fact.

Lucrezia was never as black as she has been painted. She had her failings, admittedly, but she was no worse than many other ladies of her time, and by the standards of the rest of her family she was positively well-behaved. It is significant that when the time came for her third and last marriage, to the future Duke of Ferrara, his ambassador – with no illusions about the Borgias – assessed her character and reported secretly that "She is of incontestable beauty and her manners add to her charm. She seems so gifted that we cannot, and should not, suspect her of unseemly behavior. Apart from her perfect grace in all things, her modest affability and propriety, she is a Catholic and shows she fears God." The ambassador was a diplomat, of course, and knew that one day the future duchess might read what he had written about her -- but his assessment rings true, nevertheless, for it was echoed in many details by several other contemporary accounts.

Lucrezia was just 21 at the time of this marriage, and when she left the Vatican for Ferrara she was never to see either Rome or her father again. She abandoned the vicious world of the Borgias for good, to become in due course Duchess of Ferrara and a lady much loved for her good works, especially the building of convents and hospitals. A list of the 17 books she took with her to Ferrara reveals her strong piety, as well as the scholarship of a woman who could write poetry in three languages – French, Spanish, and Italian. Her past was behind her, with nothing more sinister in it than a few youthful love affairs and a tendency to look the other way when her family was on the rampage. She did not deserve to be tarred with the same brush as the rest of the Borgias. For the remainder of her life, apart from one short-lived indiscretion

THE INFAMOUS BORGIAS

Although Rodrigo Borgia, later Pope Alexander VI, fathered at least eight children by different women, it was the three sons and a daughter by Vannozza dei Cattanei who were closest to him and who have since gone down in history as the most colorful family of a colorful age. Of the four, only Lucrezia and the youngest son – a nonentity named Jofre – survived to a reasonable old age. The pope's favorite son Juan died in early manhood – brutally murdered, if Machiavelli is to be believed, because he and Cesare were rivals for Lucrezia's favors – while Cesare himself outlived his father by only four years before being killed in battle at the age of 32.

The Borgias were a Spanish family of obscure origin. Although the children were all born in Italy, they invariably spoke Spanish among themselves, and to the end of their days they always ate Spanish food and preferred to dress in Spanish clothes. They were outsiders, strangers in Italy, whose first loyalty was to themselves and their clan. Despite their undoubted gifts, they never succeeded in winning the hearts and minds of the population at large, or even the trust of their closest associates. Instead they were hated and feared throughout Italy – usually with reason.

The family's power stemmed from the election of Rodrigo Borgia as pope in 1492. Although he had to bribe his way into the Vatican – being elected on the fourth ballot after a great deal of horse-trading – his political and administrative skills nevertheless made him the ideal man for the job. The independence of the papal states was under threat from the French at the time, in conjunction with their Italian allies, and it took all Rodrigo's ruthlessness and cunning to keep the Church's enemies at bay. In this he was ably supported by his son Cesare, a brilliant student and a skillful captain-general of the Church's armies – although Cesare never fought a major battle, itself the mark of a good tactician. Between them, father and son held the papacy together during a very difficult crisis and kept it intact, earning themselves a terrible reputation in the process.

One of the Florentine ambassadors to Cesare's camp during these years was the political theorist Niccolò Machiavelli. Although no lover of the Borgias, Machiavelli greatly admired the skills he observed in Cesare, and it was to Cesare that he dedicated his classic book on statecraft, *The Prince*. Indeed there is no knowing to what heights Cesare might have risen if events had taken a different turn. As it was, his father died in 1503 – of food poisoning, which revived the legends of the Borgias' involvement with poison plots – and with him the power of the Borgia family. The new pope was a sworn enemy of Cesare and saw to it that his ascendancy came to an abrupt end. Cesare fled to Spain, where he joined the army of his brother-in-law, the King of Navarre, and it was in the king's service that he was killed in a minor military skirmish in 1507.

Pope Alexander VI

Cesare Borgia

with a Venetian poet, she devoted herself to being a good wife and mother, a patroness of the arts, and a strong influence on the court of her adopted state. When she died in childbirth in 1519, worn out after her 11th pregnancy, she was mourned by everyone who knew her. Her husband, whose early indifference to her had given way to a deep love, was so moved by her death that he fainted at the funeral and had to be carried out. The condolences that flooded in to Ferrara from all over Italy were widespread and heartfelt. Lucrezia had been genuinely loved. It was not until later, when historians began to rewrite the Borgia story for their own purposes, that she was misunderstood and the legend of Lucrezia the Infamous was born.

The reconquest of Spain
Christianity drives out Islam

The Great Mosque at Córdoba, the second largest in the world, begun in 785 and enlarged over the following 200 years. After the Christian reconquest of Córdoba in 1236, the Great Mosque was consecrated and in the 16th century a church was built at its center.

IN 1492, after being besieged for a year and a half, Granada, the last Moorish kingdom in Spain, surrendered to the military forces of their most Catholic majesties King Ferdinand of Aragon and his wife, Queen Isabella of Castile. This was the final episode in Christendom's centuries-long battle to reclaim Spain from her Islamic conquerors.

Early in the eighth century, Arab and Berber armies had crossed the Strait of Gibraltar from Africa and had conquered most of the Iberian peninsula apart from the mountainous north. For the next six centuries Spain was largely in the hands of Muslims (Moors); but when the Moorish sphere split up into petty kingdoms after 1002, the northern Christian kingdoms seized the opportunity and began to push gradually southward. The reconquest started as an expansion of frontiers motivated by land-hunger, but it became more popular when it developed into a religious crusade. This came to a triumphant climax when Ferdinand and Isabella, whose marriage had unified Spain's most powerful Christian kingdoms, took possession of the Alhambra, the magnificent palace of Granada's former rulers.

At the time – and for a long time afterward – the reconquest of Granada was seen as the defeat of heathen barbarism by forces of Christian civilization. Today our interpretation of the event is far less one-sided. Under Moorish rule a richly pluralist and extraordinarily cultivated society had flourished in southern Spain. Medicine, astronomy, mathematics, philosophy, and craftsmanship were all so highly valued and made such great strides that the

A triumphant Ferdinand and Isabella receive the surrender of the Moorish kingdom of Granada, the last Islamic kingdom in Spain. The event marked the birth of an aggressive and intolerant Catholic Spain, and is perceived as a watershed in the nation's history. But though this was the final moment of the reconquest, the vestiges of nearly 700 years of Islamic presence in Spain were not so easily erased by the hand-over of Granada to new rulers.

peninsula served as a door through which the learning of the East passed to the rest of Europe. Important Moorish innovations such as irrigation techniques and new crops – for example, oranges, lemons, and sugar – brought enormous benefits to the continent. And under its Arab rulers, Spain's great cities were incomparable centers of culture and learning.

Most brilliant of such centers was Córdoba, the capital of Muslim Andalucía, which fell to Christian forces in 1236. The streets of Córdoba were paved and brightly lighted – unheard-of luxuries in the rude capitals of northern Europe – and the rich among its population enjoyed lavish supplies of pure water. Prosperous citizens lived in grand houses, with marble balconies for summer evenings and hot-air ducts under mosaic floors to provide heating in winter. Nightingales sang in gardens that abounded in flowering shrubs and fruit trees, artificial cascades, and pools full of goldfish. Renowned for her preeminence in art and fashion, Córdoba was a magnet for scholars of all creeds and both sexes (since women were encouraged to do serious study) eager to take advantage of the numerous public libraries the city provided.

Partly because the Muslims in Spain were a minority among their subjects, and partly because such Biblical figures as Moses and Jesus were among the venerated prophets of their own religion, the Moors were remarkably tolerant toward both Christians and Jews. Non-Muslim citizens were subject to a poll tax, but the amount due was related to income and was payable in convenient instalments. It provided such a useful source of revenue that the Moors positively discouraged conversion to Islam. As long as their non-Muslim subjects did not openly insult the Prophet Muhammad or the tenets of Islam, Christians and Jews were free to run their own religious affairs.

In the growing territories of Christian Spain prior to the victory in 1492 over the Moors' last stronghold, Judaism was also tolerated. In fact, the final push of Christian military forces was largely financed by leading members of the large and prosperous Jewish community. But the conquest of Granada, ironically, spelled the end of the peaceful coexistence. Now, egged on by crusading churchmen everywhere, Ferdinand and Isabella set out to rid Spain of all deviant minorities. Offered a choice between expulsion or conversion, some 165,000 Spanish Jews – or, possibly, more – chose exile and dispersion, often after having all their possessions confiscated, or being forced to sell out at a loss. Those who remained as converts were left to the mercy

of the Spanish Inquisition, which had become increasingly cruel since 1478, when Queen Isabella established it in order to make Spain an unwaveringly Catholic country.

As for the defeated Muslims, their lot was at first better than that of the Jews, but even limited tolerance of the religion soon evaporated. The terms of surrender at Granada did, indeed, state that followers of Islam were to be treated with respect and leniency. After a few years, however, this guarantee was openly breached; and in 1501 all Moors still living in the Iberian Peninsula were offered the same bleak choice as the Jews: Expulsion or conversion. They cannot really be blamed for doubting that the reconquest of Granada represented a victory for the forces of "civilization" over "barbarism."

The Generalife gardens in the Alhambra, Granada. Water for fountains and pools was an essential ingredient of Moorish architecture, both for its melodious sound and its cooling of the air. An enduring tribute to Islamic civilization in Spain, the Alhambra was built in the 14th century to accommodate Granada's ruling family.

The discoverer of the New World

Explorer extraordinary or unscrupulous adventurer?

Despite the fame enjoyed by Christopher Columbus after his voyages of discovery, we do not actually know what the explorer looked like, for none of his many portraits were painted during his lifetime. This representation, by an unknown artist, is in the Civico Museo Storico, Como, in Italy.

THE DISCOVERER of the New World, a pioneer who opened up an entire new continent and changed the course of history, a man who did all this in the face of scornful opposition, fired only by his extraordinary belief in himself. Thus has Christopher Columbus been remembered for 500 years, as one of the great heroes of history.

And yet, as so often, there is another side to the story – a side that shows Columbus to have been a liar, a cheat, a blunderer, a tyrant, and, some would say, almost unbalanced in his raging thirst for grandeur.

Columbus's origins are obscure. All that is known for certain is that he was born somewhere in Genoa in Italy around 1451. He first went to sea when he was about 14 and his young manhood was spent in a life of adventurous seafaring. He seems to have had a weakness for tall stories from an early age. According to the rather dubious biography of him written by his son Hernando, Columbus claimed that in February, 1477, he had managed to sail beyond Iceland, yet described the voyage in terms that cast serious doubts on the story.

This woodcut, taken from the published edition of Columbus's first letter describing his discovery of America, shows the arrival of Columbus and his Spanish crew in the New World. Interestingly the ship depicted is not a Spanish caravel, the type of vessel Columbus used on all his voyages, but a Venetian galley, which would have been highly unsuited to the rough waters of the Atlantic Ocean.

But Columbus is best known, and deservedly so, for his four great voyages westward across the Atlantic Ocean, which were to add the Caribbean Islands and the eastern coastline of Central America to the map of the known world. Self-made and self-educated, Columbus had endured seven wretched years of mockery and frustration while trying to find a sponsor for his "Enterprise of the Indies," a voyage to prove that it was possible to reach China and Japan by sailing west from Europe.

Every schoolchild has heard the story of how he eventually persuaded King Ferdinand and Queen Isabella of Spain to finance the journey. No matter that his mathematical calculations were so wrong that the land he discovered could not possibly have been either of those countries. That first voyage was a triumph of one man's faith and willpower to carry on in the face of growing opposition from his crew. Unfortunately, it was these very characteristics that led ultimately to Columbus's downfall. The highstrung and autocratic temperament that could control rebellious sailors in moments of crisis became autocratic despotism when Columbus was struggling ineffectually in his later role as administrator of the lands he discovered.

In the age in which he lived, Columbus was hardly unique in his pursuit of honor, wealth, and power. But his soaring abilities as a seaman of vision were constantly dragged down by his failures ashore. During that long first voyage west in 1492, his men had been spurred on by the promise of a reward from Queen Isabella of a life pension for the first man to sight land. Once back in Spain, however, Columbus claimed that reward for himself and then gave it to his mistress, Beatriz Enriquez, the mother of his son Hernando. It is said that Rodrigo de Triano, the seaman cheated of the reward, left Spain to become a renegade in Morocco.

Honored with the lofty title of "Admiral of the Ocean Sea" for his discoveries, Columbus also insisted on being appointed "Viceroy of the Indies." Once there, however, he found himself saddled with a dead-weight of administrative tasks (colonial governor, town planner, engineer, magistrate) which he was hardly qualified to carry out efficiently. So eager was he for the world to share his belief that this land he had named Hispaniola (modern Haiti and the Dominican Republic) was in fact the Indies (despite the fact that so far the fabled wealth of these lands remained hidden) that he promulgated a law stating that all European settlers should sign a statement to the effect that Hispaniola was India. It was even reported that anyone refusing to sign was punished by having his or her tongue cut out.

So unsuccessful was Columbus's rule as viceroy that in 1500 he was recalled to Spain, Ferdinand and Isabella having decided that however good an admiral he might be, he was certainly no governor. In one of the most famous episodes of the Columbus legend, the admiral was arrested and shipped back in chains. Although treated respectfully on the journey, Columbus refused to have his chains removed, possibly in a bid for sympathy from his royal patrons. If this was his motive, it met with a certain amount of success and Columbus was received back into royal favor, although the king and queen were reluctant to allow him any more say in the government of Hispaniola.

Frustrated in his latest bid for greatness, Columbus, who had already written to Queen Isabella in 1500 claiming that his earlier voyages were divinely inspired, now wrote his *Book of Prophecies*. This was a collection of Biblical texts supposedly showing that he was the God-given agent who would open the wealth of Asia to Spain's rulers and thus supply gold to finance a grand Crusade which would eventually restore Jerusalem to Christian rule.

The king and queen sanctioned this voyage, provided that Columbus did not return to the scene of his failure as viceroy. Stiff-necked as ever, Columbus promptly disobeyed this proviso, but was refused permission to land by the new governor of Hispaniola and was forced to sail on in search of the elusive gold of the Indies.

Recognizing that this voyage, known as the "High Voyage," was also a failure, Columbus returned to Spain, a broken, sick man. Still insisting that he had found the Indies, he wrote to the Spanish Royal Council: "My promises were neither few nor vain. Our Redeemer ordained my path hither: there in the Indies I have brought more lands beneath His dominion than there are in Africa or Europe and more than 1,700 islands apart from Hispaniola, which comprises more than the whole of Spain."

He died in obscurity on May 20, 1506. He had, largely through his own fault, lost the governorship of the lands he had discovered which, though he could not know it, were a year later to be named not after Columbus but after his friend, Amerigo Vespucci. But what can never be taken from the memory of Christopher Columbus is his superb, instinctive skill as a navigator in the unknown – a skill undimmed by his failures as a leader of men and bearer of European civilization to the New World. "To have accomplished the highly improbable," writes the historical biographer, Felipe Fernandez-Armesto, "was insufficient for Columbus – he wanted to conquer the impossible. He died a magnificent failure: He had not reached the Orient. His failure enshrined a greater success: The discovery of America."

Little is known about the Santa Maria, Columbus's *flagship on his first voyage to the New World. It was probably a three-masted vessel weighing about 100 tons, and carried a crew of about 40 in very cramped conditions. This modern reconstruction gives some idea of what the vessel looked like, and how it was rigged.*

INDEX

Page numbers in **bold** type indicate main references

A

Aachen, 210–11
Abbasah, 213
Abbasid dynasty, 212
Abominable Snowman, 11
Aborigines, Australian, 13–14, 23
Abraham, 32, 34, 42
Achilles, 146
Achuara (people), 62
Acropolis, 101, 109, 138–9
Actium, battle of, 145
acupuncture, **46–7**
Adena (people), 80
Adrianopolis (Edirne), 189
Aebutius, Publius, 140–1
Aegae, 117
Aemilia, 91
aeolipile, invention of, 125
Aeschylus, 106, 109, 110, 119–20
Aesculapius, 186
Afghanistan, 200
Africa
    animals, 171
    Christianity in, **182, 238–9,** 245–7
    circumnavigation of, 73
    Mali, **280–2**
    Zimbabwe, **257–8**
afterlife, belief in
    and alchemists, 239–40
    Chimu, 264
    Chinese, 128
    Egyptian, 48
    Greek, 76–8
    Inca and Jivaro, 62
    Moche, 176
    Neolithic, **15–16**
    Sumerian, 42
    see also religious beliefs and practices
Against Apion (Josephus), 155
Agariste, 112–13
Agathocles, 129–30
Agathon, 113
agathos daimon (good spirit), 114
Agincourt, battle of, 273–5, 282
Agra, 295
agriculture
    Copper Age, 30
    Egyptian, 44–5
    European, 209
    Iron Age, 121–3
    Mesopotamian, 59
    Neolithic, 40–1
    Roman, 135–7
    Stone Age, 12
Agrippa I, King of Judaea, 154
Agrippa, Marcus, 157
Agrippina, 163
Ain Jalut, battle of, 270
Airavata, 61
Akhenaton, Pharaoh, 71–2
Akhetaton, Pharaoh, 71
Akiko, Empress of Japan, 230–1
Akkad (people), 54
Akkadian (language), 38–9, 53
Alaric the Goth, 189–90
Alaska, 25
Albigensian heresy, 259–60
Albizzi family, 302

Alcemene, 110
Alchemy, **239–40**
Alcibiades, **112–13**
Alcuin of York, 209–10
Aleppo, 296
Alexander the Great, 59, **117–19,** 133, 152–3, 198
Alexander III, Pope, 238–9
Alexander VI, Pope, 308–9
Alexandria, 116, **119–20,** 138, 144–5, 152–3, 245
Alfonso of Biscegghe, 308
Alfonso V, King of Aragon, 292
Alfonso VI, King of Leon and Castile, 133
Alfred, King, 224–5
"Alfred jewel," 224
Al-Hakim, Caliph, 226
Alhambra, 310–11
Alhazen, **226–7**
Alipius, St., 189
Allobroges (people), 130, 132
Almagest (Ptolemy), 180
Almas (people), 11
Al-Mutamid, 133
alphabet, 74, 86
Alps, 130–3
Altai steppes, 103–4
Altamira, 13
Alvarez, Francisco, 245
Amalrician heresy, 260
Amarna, 71–2
Amazon, 239
Amenhotep IV, Pharaoh, 71–2
Amenophis III, Pharaoh, 146
America, discovery of, 51, 73, 81, 180, 205, 214, **312–13**
American Indians, 14, 51, **80–1,** 293–5
    see also Paleo-Indians and individual tribes
Amon, 67, 71–2
Amorite
    dynasty, 59
    people, 54
amour courtois (courtly love), **243–5**
amphitheatre, 198
Amphitryon, 110
Andalusia, kingdom of, 311
Androcles, 112
Andronikos, Professor Manolis, 117–18
Angel of Death, 203
Angevin empire, 244
Anglesey (Mona), 148–9
Anglo-Saxon Chronicle, 225, 234
Anglo-Saxons, 197, 224–5
Ankara, 296
Anthesterion, 77
Anthony, St., 219
Antichrist, 164, 174, 256
Antikythera mechanism, **142–3**
Antioch, 189, 236–7
Antiochus Epiphanes, King of Syria, 36
Antiquities of the Jews (Josephus), 155
anti-semitism, 155
Antony and Cleopatra (Shakespeare), 143–4
Anubis, 48
An-yang, 70–1
Apollo, 92–3
Aqua Claudia, 157
Aquae Sulis, 156, **158–9**
aqueduct, 83, **157**
Arabian Nights Entertainments, 212–17
Arabs
    Abbasid, 212–13
    in Alexandria, 121
    and gunpowder, 248

Arabs (cont'd)
    Marsh, 33
    navigation, 214–17
    trade, 153
    and Vikings, 203
    see also Islam
Aranzadi, Telesforo de, 67
Arawak (people), 99
Arcadia, 99
archery, 273–5
Archimedes, **124–5,** 142, 227
architecture
    Assyrian, 83
    Carolingian, 210
    Chimu, 264–5
    Copper Age, 30
    Egyptian, 67–8, 78
    Ethiopian, 245–7
    Gothic, 268–9
    Greek, 99
    Iron Age, 122–3, 150
    Islamic, **295,** 311
    Minoan, 56–7
    Neolithic, 40–1
    Roman, 158–9
    Shang, 70
    Stone Age, 54–5
    Sumerian, 39
    Zimbabwe, **257–8**
ard (ancient plow), 123
Arezzo, 302
Arghun, Khan, 277
Ariadne, 56, 115
Arikamedu, 153
Aristarchus, 120
Aristophanes, 103, 110–13, 120
Aristotle, 58, **110–11, 115–16,** 120, 227, 255
Ark of the Covenant, 182
Armoises, Claude des, 298
army
    Assyrian, 82
    Boudica's, 161
    Carthaginian, 130–3
    Chinese, 128
    English, 273–5
    Mamluk, 270–1
    Mongol, **266–7,** 296
    Roman, 174, **186–7**
    samurai, 242
    Spartan, 99
Arretine ware, 145
Artemis (Diana), 96
arthritis, 10, 15
Arthur, King of Britain, **196–8,** 245, 283
Aryans, 60–1
asbestos, 277
Asclepios, 77
Ashur, 82
Ashurnasirpal, King, 82
Asmodeus, 166
Asser, Bishop, 224
Assyria
    empire, 82–3
    inscriptions, 38–9
    and wheel, 36
astronomy
    Arab, 216
    Babylonian, 59
    Celtic, 149
    and chess, 134
    Greek, 142–3
    Nazca, 228–30
    Polynesian, 17–18
    Ptolemy's, 180–1
    Shang, 71
Aswan, 44, **226**
Atahualpa, **100,** 263
Athaulf, 190
Athena, 101
Athens
    city-state, 112–13
    Eleusinian Mysteries, 76–8

Athens (cont'd)
    Minotaur tribute, 56
    and Persians, 105–6
    and Romans, 158
    and Spartans, 98, 101–3
    see also Greece
Atlantis, 56, 64, 67
atom, theory of, 110
Aton, 71–2
Attica, 99
Attila, **191–3**
Aubrichecourt, Eustace de, 283
Augsberg, 138
Augustine, St., 91
Augustinian order, 219
Augustus, Roman Emperor, 135, 144–5, 152, 163, 186, 190
auto da fé (act of faith), 259
Avars (people), 211
Aventine Hill, 172, 174
Averroes, 227
Avicenna, 227
Avignon, 285
Aymara (people), 230
Aztecs, 51–2, **99–100, 278–80**

B

Baal Hammon, 129
Baber, Mogul Emperor, 295
Babylon
    Akkadian inscriptions, 38–9
    decline of, 82
    Hammurabi's Code, **59–60**
    Hanging Gardens, 126
    Herodotus's description of, 107
Bacchus, cult of, 77–8, 109, 115, **140–1**
Bacon, Roger, 247–8
Baghdad, 205, **212–13,** 227, 270, 296
Bahrain, 33
Baiae, 138
Baku oilfields, 277
Ball, John, 289–90
Ban Chiang, 28–9
Bandello, Mateo, 306
Bangkok, National Museum, 28
Bantu (people), 46, 257
Barandiaran, Jose Miguel, 67
Barcelona, 211
Barkmakid family, 213
Basil, Patriarch of Antioch, 189
Basques, **66–7,** 211
Basrah, 214
Bass, George, 76
Bast, 96
Bath, 156, **158–9**
bath
    Carolingian, 210
    Roman, **156–9**
Baybars, Sultan, 271
Bayeux Tapestry, 209, **232–3**
bear, 13, 41, 169, 198
beard
    false, 67, 105
    St. Simon's, 307
bearing dial, 207
Bede, the Venerable, 225
Bedivere, Sir, 196
Behistun Rock, 38
Beirut, 53
Belisarius, 198
Bellini, Gentile, 270
Benedict, St., 217–21
Bergen, 288–9
Bering Strait, 12, 51, 279
Bernard of Ventador, 244
Berthold Schwarz, 248
bestiarii (armed gladiator), 169

Bethlehem, 189
Bibby, Geoffrey, 33
Bible, 64–5
Bibliothèque Nationale, Paris, 239, 269
Big Foot, 11
biology, and Aristotle, 115–16
birth control, *see* contraception *and* population control
bison, 12, 20–2
Black Death, **284–7,** 289
Black Forest, 138
Black Prince, 274, 282–4
Bleda, 191
Blue Nile, *see* Nile, River
boar, 13, 123, 169
boat
    Alfred's, 225
    Arab, 214
    Chinese, 53
    Columbus's, 313
    Hanseatic, 288
    Makah, 294
    papyrus reed, **32–3**
    Phoenician, 73
    Polynesian, 17
    Roman, 152
    Sumerian, 39
    Viking, **205–7**
Boccaccio, Giovanni, 285
Boedromion, 77
Bog people, 146–8
Boniface VIII, Pope, 291
Bolivia, 229–30
Book of Abraham the Jew, 239–40
Book of the Mummy, 94–5
Book of Prophecies (Columbus), 313
boom (Arab boat), 214
boomerang, **23–4**
Bora-bora (island), 17
Borah, Woodrow, 279
Borgia, Cesare, 300, 308–9
Borgia, Lucrezia, 308–10
Bosworth, battle of, 305
Boudica, 160–2
Bouillon, Godfrey de, 198
bow, 12
    see also crossbow and longbow
Boyar, 300
Brahman, 60–1
brain scanner, 25
brain surgery, *see* trepanning
Brambilla, Dr. Guiseppina, 307
Bran, Castle, 300
Brassempouy sculpture, 13
Bremen, 288
Brendan, St., 214
Breslau, 284
Brétigny, peace of, 274
Brindisi, 138
Britain
    Anglo-Saxon, 224–5
    Celtic, 148–51
    and France, 273–5
    Iron Age, 121–3
    Norman, 204, 232–5
    Peasants' Revolt, **289–91**
    and Phoenicians, 73
    Roman, **160–2,** 197
    royal family, 303–5
British Museum, London, 224
Broca, Paul, 24–5, 67
bronze
    as item of trade, 75–6
    see also metal-working
Bronze Age, 19, 24, **28–30,** 70, 76, 150
Bruges, 288
Brunswick, 288
Bryaxis, 126
Bubastis, 96
buccinum, 74

Budapest, 139
Buddha, 200
Buddhism, 200–2, 222–4, 242
building, *see* architecture
bull, 56, 109, 169, 172
bull-fighting, 56
burial customs
  American Indian, 24, **80–1**
  Chimu, 264–5
  Chinese, 128
  Egyptian, **47–9,** 78–9
  Etruscan, 95
  Greek, 117–18
  Hun, 192
  Iron Age, 146–8, 150
  Minoan, 57
  Moche, 176
  Neanderthal, 11, **15–16**
  Scythian, 103–5
  Stone Age, 12, **54–5**
  Sumerian, 42–3
  Viking, 203
Burma, 153
Burton, Robert, 36
Bushmen (Kalahari), 13–14
Butler, Samuel, 88
Butser Farm, **121–3**
butterfly, 58
Byzantium, *see* Constantinople

C

cabala (Jewish mystical lore),
  239
Cadbury, 197
Caesaria, 184
Caesarion, 144
Caesar, Julius, 90, 120, 123, 144,
  148–9, 161, 172, 186, 198, 303
Cajamarca, 265
Calais, 274–5, 283
calendar
  Aztec, 279
  Celtic, 149
  Egyptian, 45
  Greek, 77, 88
  Gregorian, 247, 292
  Shang, 71
Caligula, Roman Emperor, 154,
  162
Caliphate of Baghdad, 174, 203,
  212–13, 270
Callimachus, 120
Caltabellotta, treaty of, 273
camel, 208, 282
Camelot, 197
camera, principles of, 226
camphor, 217
Camulodunum (Colchester),
  160–1
Canaanites, 73
Canches, Maître, 239
cannabis, 105, 217, 269
cannibalism, 215–17, **236–7,**
  239, **279–80,** 282, 300
cannon, 134, 247–8
canoe, *see* boat
Canterbury, 233
  cathedral, 274
Cape Gelidonya, 75
caravel, 312
carbon-14 analysis, 51, 76, 147,
  196, 251–2, 257
Carloman, 210
Carmelite order, 219
cart
  decorated, 272
  development of, 34–5
Carthage, 129–33, 157
  see also Punic Wars
Cary, Castle, 197

Cassius Dio, 161–2
caste system, **60–1**
Castillo Pyramid, 52
Castro, Mt., 97
cat, 51–2, **95–6,** 287
catapult, 120
Cathars, *see* Albigensian heresy
cathedral, builders, **268–9**
Catherine the Great, 134
Cato, 141
Cato, Marcus Porcius, 135–6
Caton-Thompson, Gertrude,
  257
Caucasus
  Basque link, 67
  Hun empire, 192
cave art, 11, **13–14**
Caves of the Thousand
  Buddhas, **222–4**
Caxton, William, 134, 198
Celsus, 187
Celts, 123, **148–51,** 160–2, 173,
  197
cenote (sinkhole), 24
centaur, 239
central heating, 159, 311
ceque (pathway), 229
Ceres, *see* Demeter
Cessolis, Jacobus, 134
Chagar Bazar, 32
Champollion, Jean François, 38,
  93–4
Chan-Chan, 264–5
Chares, 126
chariot
  Aryan, 61
  Assyrian, 82
  Celtic, 149
  Chinese, 128
  Egyptian, 65, 72
  Hittite, 35
  Indian, 133
  race, 89–90, 164, 172, 198–9
  Sumerian, 34, 43
Charlemagne, 198, **209–11,**
  220, 292
Charles IV, Holy Roman
  Emperor, 288
Charles V, Holy Roman
  Emperor, 100
Charles I, King of England,
  134–5
Charles VII, King of France, 275
Charles of Anjou, 272–3
Charles, Prince of Wales, 198,
  284
Charney, Geoffrey de, 250
Charnys, de (family), 250–1
Charoenwongsa, Dr. Pisit, 28
Chartres Cathedral, **268–9**
Charun, 170
Charybdis, 87
chaturanga, 133
Cheng, *see* Ch'in Shih-huang-ti
Chen Tsung, Emperor of
  China, 223
chess, **133–5**
Chevrier, Henri, 68
Chichen Itza, 52
childbirth, 11, 57
Children's Crusade, 237
Chimu empire, 264
China
  acupuncture, 46–7
  Bronze Age, 28–9
  Buddhism in, **200–2**
  chess, 134
  first empire, 127–8
  gunpowder, 247–8
  and Japan, 178–9
  Mongol, 267–8, 276–8
  and New World, 35, **51–3**
  paper-making, **174–5**

China (cont'd)
  plague, 285
  Shang dynasty, 36, 51, **69–71**
  T'ang dynasty, 222–4
  trade, 153
Ch'in Shih-huang-ti, Emperor
  of China, 127–8
Chios, 86
chivalry, 196, 243–5, 248,
  252–4, 282–4
chorus (theatre cast), 109
Chou (people), 71
Chou-k'ou-tien, 16
Christianity
  in Africa, **182, 238–9,** 245–7
  and Anglo-Saxons, 225
  and birth control, 58
  and cats, 96
  Eastern (Orthodox), 200,
    205, 250, 292
  in India, 61
  and Islam, 213, 311
  Huns, 192
  and Mithraism, 172–4
  in Roman empire, 78, 120,
    141, 162–4, **184–5,** 187
  Vikings, 203–5
  see also Crusades, heresy,
    Inquisition, monasticism,
    and papacy
Christie, Agatha, 32
*Chronicles of France, England,
  Scotland, and Spain* (Froissart),
  283
Chuchingura (Japanese play), 242
Chuchunaa (people), 11
Cicero, 186
Circe, 87
Circus Maximus, 172
Cirencester, 190–1
Cistercian order, 219
Civil War (English), 196
Claudia, 91
Claudius, Roman Emperor,
  149, 161–3, 172
Clement VI, Pope, 285
Cleopatra, 120–1, **143–5**
Cleopatra of Macedon, 119
Cleopatra (movie), 145
Cloaca Maxima, 157
clock, 120, 125, 225
Clovis, Giorgio Giulio, 252
coal, 277
cobra, 144
coca, 25, 230
coin, *see* currency
Cologne, 288
Colosseum, 158, **169–72**
Colossi of Memnon, 145–6
Colossus of Rhodes, 125–6
Columbus, Christopher, 53, 99,
  180, 278, **312–13**
Commodus, Roman Emperor,
  169
Como, Lake, 138
Compiègne, siege of, 298
conception, ancient theories of,
  58, 115
Condos, Captain Demetrios,
  142
Confucianism, 201
conquistador, 35, 99–100,
  261–3, 278–9
Constantine, Roman Emperor,
  90, 172, 174, **184–5,** 209,
  291–2
Constantinople, 133, **184,** 189,
  198–200, 205, 236–7, 250,
  291–2, 299
contraception, **57–8**
cooking methods
  Makah, 294
  Neolithic, 41

Cope, C.W., 283
Copernicus, Nicolaus, 180–1
copper
  as alloy with gold, 99–100
  as currency, 52
  as trade item, 32–3, 75–6
  see also metal-working
Copper Age, **30–1**
Córdoba, 205, 227, 310
Corinth, 112
Coroebus, 89
Corsica, 138
Cortés, Hernan, 100, 278–9
cosmetics, 36–7, 79
Council of Basle, 292
"courier game," 134
crane, 58
Crécy, battle of, 273–5, 282–3
Cresques, Abraham, 281
Crete, **56–7,** 63–4, 139
Crime of Claudius Ptolemy
  (Russell Newton), 180
crocodile, 50, 58
Croesus, King of Lydia, 92–3,
  107, 126
Cromwell, Oliver, 196
crossbow, 128, 269, 274–5
Crusades, 196, **236–8,** 244, 247,
  249, 253, 256, 259, 269, 282,
  296, 313
Ctesibius, 120, 125
cuneiform script, **38–9, 53–4,**
  59, 83
currency
  Athenian, 106
  Chimu, 264
  Chinese, 52, 127, 277
  pre-Columbian, 52, 99
  Roman, 152–3
  and samurai, 242
  Shang, 71
  Spartan, 98
customs officer, 139
Cuthbert, St., 225
Cuzco, 100, 229, 261, 263
Cyclops, 87
Cydnus, River, 144
Cyraea vitellus (shell), 32
Cyril, Bishop, 120

D

Daedalus, 56
Dagobert II, King of the Franks,
  165
Damascus, 175, 295–6
Damophilus of Enna, 137
Danebury Hillfort, **150–1**
Dante, 245, 256
Danube
  River, 138
  Valley, 30
Daphne games, 36
Darius, King of Persia, 38, 105,
  117
Darwin, Charles, 116
Daugherty, Richard, 293–5
David, 198
David of Ethiopia, 182
De Agri Cultura (Cato), 135
De Arte Venandi cum Avibus
  (Frederick II), 255
Decameron (Boccaccio), 285
decathlon, 88
Decianus Catus, 160
decimal system, 71, 227
de Dolla Price, Professor Derek,
  142
deer, 20–1, 41
deformity, 176–7

Deir el Bahri, 67–8
Deir el-Medineh, 78
Delhi, 295–6
Delphi, 88, 138, 148
Delphic Oracle, **92–3**
Demeter (Ceres), 77
Democritus, 111
dentistry, **49–51,** 101
"desert father," 210
Diamond Sutra (Buddhist book),
  223
Diana, *see* Artemis
Diaz, Bernal, 278–9
diet
  Aztec, 279–80
  Egyptian, 79
  Neolithic, 41
  Paleo-Indian, 21–2
  and plague, 287
  Roman, 136, 140
  Stone Age, 12
Dimond, Dr. E. Gray, 47
Diocletian, Emperor, 156,
  183–4
Diodorus, 139
Diodorus Siculus, 49, 92,
  129–30
Dionysus, *see* Bacchus
Djibouti, 33
dog, 95, 280, 287
Dolni Věstonice, 20
Domesday Book, **234–5**
Dominican order, 219
Donation of Constantine,
  291–2
Dorestad, 204
Dozmary Pool, 197
drachma, 106
Dracula, **299–300**
"dragon bones," **69–70**
drama
  Greek, 78, **109–10**
  Japanese, 241
Druid, 148–9
Dürer, Albrecht, 100–1, 284
Durga, 202
Dyskolos (Menander), 110

E

earth mother, *see* mother
  goddess
East India Company, 47
Ebers Papyrus, 37, 50, 58
Ebla, **53–4**
Edessa (Urfa), 237, 250
Edward I, King of England, 275
Edward II, King of England,
  196–8, 273–5, **282–4**
Edward IV, King of England,
  303–5
Edward V, King of England,
  303–5
Edward the Confessor, 234
Egrigog, fortress, 299
Egypt
  agriculture, 44–5
  Arab, 226–7
  Assyrian invasion, 82
  birth control, 57–8
  burial customs, 47–9
  cosmetics, 36–7, 49
  dentistry, 49–51
  and Hebrews, 64–5
  Mamluk, **270–1**
  and Mansa Musa, 280–1
  Ptolemaic, **119–21,** 144–5
  religion, **44–5,** 47–9, 71–2,
    95–6
  Roman, 152, 180
  tomb-builders, 78–9
Einhard (Eginhard), 209

eisteddfod, 243
Elagabalus, Roman Emperor, 172
Elamite language, 38
El Dorado, 100
Eleanor of Aquitaine, **243–5**
Eleazar (High Priest), 119
Eleazar (Zealot), 154
electricity, production of, 125
elephant
  and birth control, 58
  in games, 169–72
  graveyard, 214–15
  Hannibal's, 131
  in India, 61, 133
Eleusinian Mysteries, **76–8**, 112
El Imposible Vencido (Larramendi), 66
Elizabeth II, Queen of Britain, 284
Ella-'Amida, King of Ethiopia, 182
embalming, **48**, 58, 73
Emmer wheat, 123
Empedocles, 111
Engelbach, Reginald, 68
engineering
  Alhazen, 226
  Assyrian, 82
  Egyptian, 44, 68
  Greek, **97–8**, 127
  Inca and Mayan, 35
  Roman, **157**, 187
England, *see* Britain
Ephesus, 126
Ephrem, St., 188
Epic of Gilgamesh, 38–9
Epidaurus, 109
Erik the Red, 205
etak islands, 17–18
Ethiopia, **182, 238**, 245–7
Etna, Mt., 111
Etruscans, 93–5
Eunûs, 137
Eupalinus, 97
Eupolus of Thessaly, 90
Euripides, 103, 110, 119–20
Eusebius, Bishop, 184, 292
Euzkadi ta Azkatasuna (ETA), 66
Evans, Sir Arthur, 56
Evans, Clifford, 176
Excalibur, 196
Exodus, **64–5**
experimental archeology, 121
eye disease, *see* health and medicine

F

falconry, 255
Farid, Professor Shafik, 51
"Fat Hen," 123
Ferdinand, King of Spain, 310–13
Fernandez-Armesto, Felipe, 313
Ferrara, 309–10
fertility cults
  Carthaginian, 130
  Greek, 109
  Iron Age, 147–8
  Roman, 90
  Stone Age, 12
  see also religious beliefs and practices
feudalism, 234–5, 244, 247, 289–91
Figgins, J.D., 20–1
Finike, 75
fire
  Neolithic, 41
  and Nero, 162–3

fire (cont'd)
  Stone Age, 11–12, 20–1
  Vestal, 90
fishing, 41, 293–5
Fittja, 205
Flagellants, Brotherhood of, 284
Flamel, Nicolas, **239–40**
flax, 41
flea, 138, 284–7
Flinders Petrie, Sir W. M., 95
Flood (mythology), 39
Florence, 138, 285, **301–2,** 307
Gonfaloniere (Florentine leader), 302
flying machine, 307
Folsom, 20
forceps, 187
forgery, 95, 251–2, 292
Forum, in Rome, 190
Fountain of Youth, 239
France
  and England, 196, 273–5, **297–8,** 303
  and Minoans, 64
  Stone Age, 12–13, 25
  troubadours, 243–5
  Vikings in, 204
  see also Gaul *and* 100 Years War
Francis II, Holy Roman Emperor, 211
Francis, St., 256
Franciscan order, 219
François I, King of France, 307
Franks, 165–6, 209–11
Frederick II, Holy Roman Emperor, **255–6**
French Revolution, 233
Froissart, Jean, 196–7, 282–3
Frumentius, St., 182
Fujiwara family, 231, 141

G

Gaiseric, King, 190
Galen, 187
Galilee, 155
Galileo Galilei, 227
galley, Venetian, 312
Gama, Vasco da, 238
games, 36, **88–90,** 162, 164, **169–72,** 199
gaming board
  Minoan, 58
  Sumerian, 43
gamma ray, 142
Gandhi, Mohandas, 60
Ganges, River, 201–2
Gargas (cave), 13
Garter, Order of, 198, **282–4**
Gaul, 132, 148, 164–5, 190, 192
Gaza, 53
Ge, 92
Geminus, 143
Generalife gardens, 311
Genghis Khan, 191, 248, **266–8,** 271
Genji Monogatari (Murasaki), **230–2**
Genoa, 276, 312
Gerasimov, Professor, 296
Gerona, 209
Ghazan, Khan, 277
Gibbon, Edward, 199
Giza, Pyramids of, 50, 95, 126
gladiator, 162, **169–70**
glass-blowing, 73–4
Glastonbury, 197
Glob, Professor Peter V., 146–8
"halo phenomenon," 185
Gobi Desert, 201, 222
gold
  in acupuncture, 46
  African, 257–8, **280–2**

gold (cont'd)
  in alchemy, 239–40
  Archimedes's experiment, 124
  and King Croesus, 107
  in dentistry, 51
  pre-Columbian, **99–101,** 264–5
  Sumerian, 42–3
  see also currency
goldfield, 257–8
Gold Museum, Bogotá, 100
Gonfaloniere (Florentine leader), 302
Goodfield, June, 97
Gorman, Dr. Chester, 28
Goths, 126, 189–90
graffiti, 146
Granada, kingdom of, 310–11
Gra\Graubelle Man, 146–8
Great Hall, Winchester, 196
Great Mosque, Córdoba, 310
Great Serpent Mound, 81
Great Shang, 70–1
Great Wall, **127,** 175
Great Zimbabwe, **257–8**
Greco-Persian Wars, 105–8
Greece
  birth control, 58
  and Celts, 148
  Delphic oracle, 92–3
  Eleusinian Mysteries, **76–7**
  engineering, 97–8
  games and sport, 88–90
  literature, **86–8,** 102
  use of perfume, 36
  Persian Wars, 105–8
  and Phoenicians, 74
  and Romans, 141, 186
  social life, 113–15
  technology, 142–3
  theatre, 109–10
  women in, **101–3**
Greek Atomic Energy Commission, 142
Greenland, 205–6
Gregory, St., 218
Gregory IX, Pope, 259–60
Gregory XIII, Pope, 247, 292
Gros, Antoine Jean, 102
Guangzhou, 214
Gui, Bernard, 259
Guicciardini, Francisco, 309
Guidebook of Greece (Pausanias), 139, 145
Guide to Geography (Ptolemy), 180
Gundestrup caldron, 148
gunpowder, 134, **247–8**
Gur Amir, 295
Gur-Khan (Yuhanan), 238
Gutenberg, Johannes, 300
gynaikon (Greek women's apartments), 101–3
gynaikonomos (Greek magistrate), 103

H

Hades (Pluto), 77–8
Hadrian, Roman Emperor, 157
Haile Selassie, Ethiopian Emperor, 182
Hales, Robert, 290
Halicarnassus (Bodrum), 108, 126
Halley's comet, 232
Glob, Professor Peter V., 146–8
"halo phenomenon," 185
Hamburg, 203, 288
Hammurabi, Code of, **59–60**
hand-warmer, 269
Han dynasty, 175

Hannibal, 130–3
Hanseatic League, **287–9**
Hapi, 44
hara-kiri, 240–3
Harappa, 33, 60
harem, 213, 255
Harner, Michael, 279–80
harp, 43
harpoon
  Magdalenian, 20
  Makah, 294
Harris, Dr. James E., 51
"Harrying of the North," 235
Härun ar-Rashid, Caliph of Baghdad, 212–13
hashish, 217
  see also cannabis
Hastings, battle of, 233–4
Hatshepsut, Queen of Egypt, 64, **67–9**
Hawkins, Gerald, 229
head-shrinking, 62–3
health and medicine
  Chinese, 46–7
  Egyptian, 37, **49–51**
  Neanderthal, 15–16
  and plague, 284–7
  Roman, 138, **186–7**
  Stone Age, 12, **24–5**
Hebrews, 64–5
  see also Jews
Hecate, 96
Hecateus, 108
Hector of Troy, 198
Heimskringla (Norse saga), 134
helicopter, 307
Helios, 126
helot, 99
Henry I, King of England, 248–9, 253
Henry II, King of England, 243–4, 253
Henry III, King of England, 253
Henry V, King of England, 274
Henry VII, King of England, 198, **303–5**
Henry VIII, King of England, 196, 275
Henry IV, King of France, 273
Herat, 266
Herculaneum, **166–8**
heresy, **259–60,** 297–8
Hermes, 112
hermit, 188, 219
Hero, 125
Herodotus, 44, 50, 73, 92, 96, 97, **107–8**
herring, 288–9
Hesi-Re, tomb of, 50
Heyerdahl, Thor, 33
Hiero, King of Syracuse, 124
Hierophant (high priest), 77
hillfort, **150–1,** 197
Himalayas, 200–1
Hinduism, 60–1
Hippalus, 153
Hipparchus, 180–1
Hippocrates, 58, 103, 186
Hippodrome, 198
Hirohito, Emperor of Japan, 178
Hispaniola, 312–13
Hitler, Adolf, 61, 211
Hittites, 28, 35–6
Holy Grail, 196, 245
Holy Roman Empire, 209–11
Homer, 38, 73, 76, **86–8,** 107
Homo erectus (people), 10
Homo sapiens (people), 10
Homo sapiens sapiens (people), 19
homosexuality, 99, 102, 177
Honnecourt, Villard de, 269

Honshu, 178
Hoodo (Phoenix Hall), 230
Hopewell (people), 80
hoplite, 106
Horace, 138, 140
horse
  absence of, 35
  collar, **208–9**
  and Huns, 192
  and Incas, 263
  as meat, 20
  in medieval warfare, 275
  and Mongols, 266
  race, 89–90
  taming of, 35–6, 61, 105
"Horse," the (cliff), 92
Horus, 69
hospital, first, 187
Ho Ti, Emperor of China, 175
Hsienyang, 127
Hsiung-nu (people), 192
Hsi-yu chi (Journey to the West), 202
Hsuan-Tsang, **200–2**
Huang Ti Nei Ching Su Wen (Yellow Emperor's Classic of Internal Medicine), 46
Hui Chung, Emperor of China, 47
Hui Shen, 52
Huitzilopochtl, 278–9
Hulwan library, 227
human sacrifice
  Aztec, **278–80**
  Celtic, 148–9
  of children, 129–30
  Chimu, 264
  Iron Age, 147–8
  Moche, 176–7
  Shang, 70–1
100 Years War, 248, **273–5,** 282–4, 289, 297–8
Hungary, 211, 278, 299
Huns, 105, **191–3,** 292
hunting
  Hittite, 35
  Magdalenian, 20
  Makah, 293–4
  Neanderthal, 11
  Paleo-Indian, **20–2,** 24
  Roman, 171
  medieval, 248–9
Hyksos (people), 35
Hypatia, 120
hypnotism, 78, 93
Hypogeum, **54–5**

I

Ibn al-Haitham, *see* Alhazen
Ibn Battuta, **280–2**
Ibn Faldan, 203
Ibn Juzayy, 281
Ibn Rusteh, 203
Icarus, 56
Ice Age, **11–13,** 19, 21, 51
Iceland, 205, 255, 312
Iceni (people), 160–2
Ichijo, Emperor of Japan, 231
idiotai (amateurs), 89
Igor, 205
Ildico, 192
Iliad (Homer), **86–8,** 107, 119
"Il Stradano," 239
Incas
  and Chimu, 264
  and Jivaro, 62–3
  and Moche, 177
  and Nazcas, 228
  Spanish conquest of, **99–100, 261–3**
  and wheel, 35

Inchtuthil, 187
India
    Alexandrian conquest, 117
    caste system, **60–1**
    and China, 200–2
    and Columbus, 312–13
    Mogul, 295
    and Romans, **152–3**, 171
Indo-European (language), 61, 66
Indra, 61
Industrial Revolution, 125
inflation, 183, 277, 281
Innocent III, Pope, 259
Inquisition, 96, **259–60,** 311
Ireland, 123, 203, 303
Iron Age, 24, 28, 103–5, 146–8
    hill fort, **150–1**
    settlement, **121–3**
irrigation
    Aztec, 279
    Egyptian, **44–5,** 226
    Harappan, 60
    Moorish, 311
    Shang, 71
    Sumerian, 39
Isabella, Queen of Spain, 310–13
Isfahan, 296
Ishtar Gate, 126
Iskander, Professor Zaki, 51
Islam
    Abbasid empire, 212–13
    and Christendom, 236–7, 238, 244, 256, 300
    in Ethiopia, 182
    in India, 61
    and learning, 121, **226–7**
    in Mali, 280–2
    Mamluk, 207
    and Mithraism, 174
    in Spain, 310–11
    in Sri Lanka, 215
    and warfare, 296
Istanbul, *see* Constantinople
Italy, 204, 256, 291–2, 301–2
    see also Rome
Ithaca, 87
Ivan the Terrible, 134, 289, 300
Iwalata (Oualata), 281–2
Iyo, Japanese Princess, 179

J

jaguar, 51–2
James IV, King of Scotland, 305
Japan
    Fujiwara, 230–2
    imperial family, **178–9**
    samurai, **240–3**
jati (sub-castle), 61
javelin-throwing, 88
Jen Chung, Emperor, 47
Jerome, St., 189
Jerusalem, 73, 154–5, 165–6, 182, 198, 236–8, 245, 247, 313
Jewish War, The (Josephus), 155
Jews
    in Alexandria, 119
    and Assyrians, 82
    Babylonian Captivity of, 59
    birth control, 58
    Exodus, 64–5
    in France, 239
    and Frederick II, 256
    in India, 61
    and Islam, 213, 311
    and Phoenicians (Canaanites), 73
    religious practices, 37
    in Roman Empire, 154–5
    see also Judaea *and* Palestine

Jimmu, Emperor, 178
Jivaro (people), **62–3**
Joan of Arc, 274, **297–8**
John of Gaunt, 290
John the Good, King of France, 282
Josephus, **154–6**
Joshua, 198
Journal of the Michigan Dental School, 51
jousting, 252–4
Judaea, **154–5,** 165–6
    see also Palestine
Judas (Iscariot), 305–6
Judas (Maccabeus), 198
Julian, Roman Emperor, 174, 187
Justinian I, Roman Emperor, 198–200
Jutland, 23

K

Kabul, 201
Kalah, 83
kamal (Arab sextant), 216
kamikaze, 241–3
Kaminaljuyú, 52
Karnak, 67–8
Karpov, Anatoly, 135
Kazakh (people), 105
Keller, Ferdinand, 40–1
Kephisos, River, 78
Khafre, Pharaoh, 126
Khartoum, 45
Khayzuran, Queen, 213
Khorat plateau, 29
Khorsabad, 83
Khufu, Pharaoh, 126
Kiev, **204–5,** 266
Kinsai (Hangchow), 277
Kirgiz (people), 105
Kit Carson (Colorado), 21–2
knight
    and longbow, 273–5
    and tournaments, 252–4
Knights of the Garter, 196, **282–4**
Knights of St. John, 126
Knights Templar, 250, 269
    see also chivalry
Knöbl, Kuno, 53
knorr, **206–7**
Knossos
    palace **56–7**
    possible destruction of city, 64
Knut (Canute), King of England, 133
Kojiki (Record of Ancient Events), 178
Kokachim, Chinese Princess, 277
Kokorevo I, 20
Koran, 212, 282
Korchnoi, Viktor, 135
Kosok, Paul, 229
Kostienki, 19
koumiss (milk), 105
Krakatoa eruption, 63
Kremlin, 295
kritai (a critic), 109
Kritios of Athens, 172
Kroeber, Alfred, 228
Kshatriya, 60
Kublai Khan, 267, 276–8
Kuku Khotan plain, 238
Kuo, Prince of, 46
kykeon (drink), 77–8
Kyoto, 241
Kyushu, 179, 241

L

labarum (banner), 185
labyrinth, legend of, 56
Laccadive Islands, 215
Laconia, 99
Lagny-sur-Marne, 252
lake dwelling, **40–1**
Lalibela, **245–7**
Lamachus, 112–13
Langash, 39
language and literacy
    Aztec, 279
    Basque, 66–7
    Carolingian, 209–10
    Chinese, 69
    cuneiform, **38–9, 53–4**
    development of, 20
    Druidic, 149
    English, 225
    Etruscan, 93–5
    Greek, 86–8
    Indo-European, 61
    Japanese, 231
    monastic, 220–1
    Phoenician, 74
Languedoc, 165, 260
Larco Hoyle, Rafael, 177
Larramendi, Manuel de, 66
Lascaux (cave), 13
Last Supper, The (painting), **305–7**
Lateran Palace, 291
latifundium (Roman farm), **135–6**
Laurium (mine), **105**
law
    Assyrian, 83
    Babylonian, **59–60**
    English, 225
    medieval, 305
    Roman, 208
lead (pipes), 157, 159, **190–1**
Lebanon, 74
Leghorn, 302
Leif Erikson, 205
lens, 226–7, 247
Leo III, Pope, 209
Leochares, 126
Leonardo da Vinci, 301, **305–7**
Leopold of Austria, 237
lesbianism, 99, 102
Lesbos, 99, 102
Leucippus, 111
Leyden, Lucas von, 134
library
    Alexandria, **119–21**
    Arab, 227, 311
    Charlemagne's, 210
    Chinese, 222
    monastic, 219–20
    Nineveh, 39, 83
Life of Constantine (Eusebius), 184
lighthouse, 125–6
Limoges, siege of, 283
Limpopo, River, 257
Li, Mt., 127–8
Lindisfarne, 203
Linnaeus, Carl, 116
lion, 82, 164, 169–72
"Lion of Judah," 182
lion-taming, 269
Lirey, 250
Little Salt Spring, 24–5
Livingstone, David, 182
Livy, 138
loom, 30
London, 161, 287, 289–91
longbow, **273–5,** 282
Louis VII, King of France, 244
Louis XIII, King of France, 134

Louis the Pious, 217
Louvre, 307
Lubeck, 288–9
Luther, Martin, 292
lyre, 43, 163–4
Lysistrata (Aristophanes), 103

M

Macedonian empire, **117–19**
Machiavelli, Niccolò, 309
Machu Picchu, 263
Maecenas, Gaius, 138
Magan, 33
Magdalenian culture, 20
Magi, 238
Maiden Castle, 123
Makah (people), 293–5
Makeda, Queen of Ethiopia, 182
Makura no Soshi (Pillow Book), 231
Malabar Coast, 152–3, 214, 277
Malaya, 153
Maldive Islands, 281
Mali empire, 280–2
Mallowan, Max, 32
Malory, Sir Thomas, 196–7
Malta, 54–5
Mamluks, 270–1
mammoth, 12, 21
Mandylion, 250
Mansa Musa, 280–1
Mansa Sulayman, 281–2
maps, 138, 180, 238, 280–1, 292
Marathon, battle of, 105, 107
Marc Antony, 121, 144–5
Margaret of Burgundy, 303
Maria della Grazia, monastery, 305
Marie de Champagne, 245
Mark Antony, 121, 144–5
Mark, St., 307
Marlowe, Christopher, 295
Marqués de Ensada (naval destroyer), 66
Marshal, William, 253
Martin IV, Pope, 272
masonic guild, 269
Massilia (Marseilles), 140
Matabeleland, 257–8
Matilda of Anjou, 253
Matilda, Queen of England, 233
Matthew, St., 307
Matthiae, Dr. Paolo, 53
Mauch, Karl, 257
mausoleum, 57, 126, 264, 295
Mausolus, 126
Maxentius, Roman Emperor, 184
Maximian, Roman Emperor, 183–4
Mayan empire, 35, 51
Mbire (people), 257
McCrone, Walter, 251
McJunkin, George, 20–1
Mecca, 280–1
Medici family, **301–2**
medicine, *see* health and medicine
medicus (army medic), 186–7
Meiji, Emperor, 242
Melanesia, 16–17
Meluhha, 33
Memling, Hans, 250
Memnon, King of Ethiopia, 146
menagerie, 255
Menahem, 154
Menander, 110
Menelik, 182
Meng T'ien, General, 127
Menkaure, Pharaoh, 126
Meropius, 182
Merovingian dynasty, 165

Mesopotamia
    as cradle of civilization, 28, **34–5**
    trade, 32–3
    see also individual civilizations
Messiah-king, 154
Messina, Straits of, 87
metal-working
    Copper Age, 30
    Phoenician, 75–6
    spread of in Southeast Asia, 28–9
    Sumerian, 39
Metropolitan Museum of Art, New York, 95
Mexico
    Aztec, 99–100, **278–80**
    Mayan, 35
    Olmec, 51–2
    and Phoenicia, 73
Michael, Byzantine Emperor, 273
Michelangelo, 302
Micronesia, 16–17
Milan, 138, 285, 306–7
Miletus, 105, 110–11
millet, 52
Milvian Bridge, battle of, 184
Minoans, 56–7, 63–4
Minos, King of Crete, 56
Minotaur, **56,** 139
Misenum, 166–8
Mishima, Yukio, 240, 242
Mississippian people, 80
Mithraism, **172–4**
Mixtecs, 100
Moche (Mochica) people, **176–7**
Mohenjo-Daro, 33
Mona (Anglesey), 148–9
Mona Lisa (painting), 307
monasticism, 188, **217–21**
Mongols (Tartars)
    use of acupuncture, 47
    in China, 127, 223, 227
    under Genghis Khan, **266–8**
    and Japan, 241
    and Mamluks, 270
    and Marco Polo, 238, 276
    under Tamerlane, **295–6**
Monte Cassino, Abbey of, 217–20
Montreal, 89
Moors, *see* Spain
Mopti, 281
Morphy, Paul, 134
Morrison, Tony, 229–30
Morte D'Arthur (Malory), 196, 198
Morton, Samuel G., 81
Moses, 37, 64–5
mother goddess
    Carthaginian, 130
    Greek, 92
    Stone Age, 12, 55
mound-building, **80–1**
Mtilikwe, River, 257
Muhammad, 96, 174, 227, 270
muisak, 62
Muisca (people), 100
mulberry bark, 175
mummy, **47–9, 95–6,** 175
Mumtaz, Mogul Queen, 295
Murasaki, Shikubu, **230–2**
murex, 74
Musée de Cluny, Paris, 240
Museum of Prehistory, Aarhus, 148
Muslim, *see* Islam
muslin, 153
mutilation, **13–14,** 177
Mycale, battle of, 106
myrrh, 67–8
mystae (initiates), 77–8

N

Nalanda, 202
Naples, 138, 166, 292
Napoleon, 96, 211
Narva, 289
Nasser, Lake, 45
National Archeological
 Museum, Athens, 142
Natural History Museum,
 London, 95
Natural History (Pliny), 292
navigation
 Arab, 214–17
 Chinese, 51–3
 of Columbus, 312–13
 and the monsoon, 153
 Phoenician, 73
 Polynesian, **16–17**
 and Ptolemy, 180
 Viking, 205–7
Nazca (people), 228–30
Neanderthal man, **10–11,
 15–16**
Nebuchadrezzar, King of
 Babylonia, 126
Necho, Pharaoh, 73
ndrua (double canoe), 18
Nefertiti, Queen of Egypt, 67,
 71–2
Nemean games, 88
Neolithic era, 40–1
Nero, Roman Emperor, 36, 89,
 153–5, 160–1, **162–4**
Newark (Ohio), 80–1
New Forest, 248–9
Newfoundland, 205
Newton, Robert Russell, 180–1
Nicholas of Cusa, 292
Nicholas V, Pope, 292
Nicias, 112–13
Niger, River, 282
Nîmes, 157
Nimrud, 83
Nineveh library, 39, 83
"Nine Worthies," 198
"Nippon," 179
Nishapur, 266, 296
Nizami, 213
Noah, 39
Non Nok Tha, 28
Normandy, 204
nosferatu (the "undead"), 299
Novgorod, 288
Numa Pompilius, King of
 Rome, 90
Nun (primordial ocean), 44

O

oak, 41, 117, 148–9, 206
obelisk, 67–8
obesity, 12
Octavian, 144
 see also Augustus
Odo, Bishop, 233
Odysseus, 87
Odyssey (Homer), 76, **86–8,**
 107, 119
Oihénat, Arnauld, 67
"Old Man of the Sea," 214–16
Oleg, 205
Olmecs, 51
Olympias, 118–19
Olympic Games, **88–90**
 Nero and, 164
Oman, 214
omphalos (stone), 92
Onoda, Lt. Hiroo, 242–3
On Optics (Alhazen), 226

oracle
 bones, **69–70**
 chamber, 54–5
 at Delphi, **92–3**
orang-utan, 216
orchestra (in Greek theatre), 109
Orestes, 120
Orléans, siege of, 297–8
Osiris, 44–5
ostracon (pottery fragments), 78
ostrich, 169
Otrar, 296
Otto I, Holy Roman Emperor,
 211
Ottoman empire, 271, 299–300
ox, 20, 35, 209
Ozette, **293–5**

P

Pachacuti Inca, 263
Pacific islanders, **16–18,** 25, 40
palace
 Alhambra, 310–11
 Assyrian, 83
 of Charlemagne, 210
 Chimu, 264–5
 Ebla, 53
 of Harun ar-Rashid, 212
 Inca, 100
 Minoan, **57–8,** 64
 of Nero, 37, 163
 of Sennacherib, 44
Paladru, Lake, 41
Palatine Chapel, 164
Paleo-Indians, **20–2,** 23–4
Palestine, 24, **154–5,** 184,
 236–7, 252
Pallottino, Professor Massimo,
 94
Panama, 101
Panathenaic games, 115
Panuco, 35
Paola (Malta), 54
papacy, 211, 256, **291–2,** 309
paper, **174–5**
Papua-New Guinea, 58
papyrus, 174
Papyrus of Anhai, 48
parachute, 307
parchment, 174
Paris, 193, 203
Parnassus, Mt., 92
Parry, Wilson, 25
Parthenon, 208
Parthian empire, 153–4
Parts of Animals (Aristotle), 116
Pasteurella pestis (bacillus), 287
Pathways to the Gods (Morrison),
 230
Paul, St., 164
Paulinus, Suetonius, 149, 161
Paulus, Aemilus, 138
Pausanias, 139, 145
Pazyryk, 103
Pazzi (family), 302
peanut, 51, 53
Peasants' Revolt, **289–91**
Peloponnesian War, 99, 101–2,
 107
pentathlon, 89
Pepin, King of the Franks, 292
pepper, 152, 277
Pepys, Samuel, 287
perfume, **36–7,** 49, 107, 153,
 157
Pergamon Museum, East
 Berlin, 126
Pergamum (Bergama), 121
Pericles, 102
permafrost, 104
Persephone (Proserpine), 77–8

Persepolis, 38
Persians
 and Arabs, 213
 and chess, 133
 empire, 92–3, 117, 133, 153,
 173
 see also Greco-Persian Wars
Peru, 24–5, 35, 99–100, 176–7,
 228–9, 261–4
Peter, King of Aragon, 273
Peter the Hermit, 236
Petrarch, 245
Peutinger Map, 138–9
Phaistos, 64
Pharisees, 154
Pharos of Alexandria, 125–7
Pheidias of Athens, 126
Philidor, François, 134
Philip IV, King of France, 250,
 273–5
Philip of Macedon, 99, **116–19**
Philo of Byzantium, 125–6
philosopher's stone, 239–40
Phoenicians, **73–6,** 86, 94–5,
 129–30
photography, 226
Pia, Secondo, 251
Pien Chueh, 46
pilgrimage, 138, 281
Pimiko, Empress, 178–9
Pimperne, 123
Pisa, 302
Pizarro, Francisco, 100, 261, 263
"Place of Truth," 78
plague
 Biblical, 64–5
 bubonic, **284–7,** 299
Plataea, battle of, 106
Plato, 58, 64, 102, 111, 114–15,
 120, 124
Plautus, 110, 292
Pliny the Elder, 149, 153, 156,
 166–8, 292
Pliny the Younger, 137, 139,
 166–8
plow, 123, 208–9
Plutarch, 58, 90, 93, 124, 136,
 143–4
Pluto, *see* Hades
Po, River, 133
Poitiers, battle of, 275, 282
Poland, 25, 285
pollen analysis, 16, 147, 252
Polo, Marco, 179, 238, 267,
 276–8
Polycrates, 97
Polynesia, 16–18
Pompeii, 141, **166–8**
Pompey, 154
Pont du Gard, 157
Pontifex Maximus, 90–1
Pontus (kingdom), 173
Poppaea, Roman Empress, 155,
 163
population control
 Aztec, 279
 Egyptian, 57–8
 and lead, 191
 and plague, 285–7
Porchnev, Professor Boris, 11
Portuguese, in Africa, 282
Poseidon, 56, 87
Posidonius, 143
potter's wheel, 34–5, 39
pottery
 development of, 20
 Bronze Age, 28
 Copper Age, 30–1
 Moche, **176–7**
Premonstratensian order, 219
Prester John, **238–9**
Prince, The (Machiavelli), 309
printing, 134, 175, 209, 300
Procopius, 198–9

Prophetes, 93
Proserpine, *see* Persephone
prostitution, 198, 200
Protestantism, 289, 292
Provençal (language), 243
Ptolemy, Claudius, 134, **180–1,**
 226
Ptolemy family, 119, 144, 180
Punic Wars, 129, **132,** 135, 140
Punt, land of, 67–8
Puteoli, 138
pyramid, 50, 95, 126
Pyramid of the Sun, 278
Pyrgi (Santa Severa), 94
Pythagoras, 58, 120
Pythia, 92–3
Pythian games, 88
Pythios of Priene, 126
Python, 92

Q

Qarqar, battle of, 82
quark, 110
Queen Mother, of England, 284
Queir[ó]s, Paolo Fernandes de,
 17
quern, 30
quipu, **261–3**

R

Rainsborough hillfort, 151
Ramses II, Pharaoh, 64–5
Ramses III, Pharaoh, 79
Ramses IV, Pharaoh, 68
Randall-MacIver, David, 257
rat, 52–3, 284–7
Ravenna, 199
Rawlinson, Henry, 38
Reconquest, of Spain, **310–11**
"Red Sea," 64–5
Reiche, Maria, 229
reindeer, 12, 19–20
religious beliefs and practices
 African, 257–8
 American Indian, 80–1
 Aztec, 278–9
 Carthaginian, 129–30
 Celtic, 148–50
 Egyptian, 44, 71–2
 Greek, **76–8, 92–3,** 101–3,
 108, 112–13
 Japanese, 179, 242
 Jewish, 154–5
 Makah, 294
 Minoan, 57
 Mithraic, **172–4**
 Moche, 176–7
 Nazca, 228–30
 Neanderthal, 11
 perfume in, 37
 Roman, **90–1,** 172
 Shang, 70
 Stone Age, 12, **54–5**
 Sumerian, 42–3
 see also individual religions
Renaissance, 124, 209, 301–2,
 307
Rennes-le-Château, 165–6
Reva, 287
Reynolds, Peter, 122–3
Rhine, River, 138
rhinoceros, 12
rice, 52
Richard II, King of England,
 289–91
Richard III, King of England,
 303–5
Richard the Lion Heart, 237, 244

Richelieu, Cardinal, 240
Riga, 287
Rig-Veda (Aryan sacred
 hymns), 60–1
roads
 Chinese, 127
 pre-Columbian, 36, 263
 Roman, 138–9, 197
Romania, 191, 299–300
Romans
 army, 186–7
 baths, 156–7
 birth control, 58
 empire, decline and division
 of, **184, 189–93,** 209, **291–2**
 farming, 135–7
 games, 89, **169–72**
 use of perfume, 36
 religion, 90–91
 tourism and travel, 99, **138–9**
Rome
 and Britain, 148–9, **160–2**
 and Carthage, 130–3
 and Egypt, 144–5
 and Etruscans, 93, 95
 and Greece, 138–9, 187
 and India, 152–3
 and Mithraism, 172–4
 and Palestine, 154–5
 and Pompeii, 166–8
 see also Christianity
Romulus Augustus, Emperor,
 189
Roncesvalles, 211
Rosetta Stone, 38, **93–4**
Roskilde Fjord, 206
Rouen, 297
Round Table, **196–8**
Rudenko, Sergei, 103–5
Rurik, 205
"Rus," 203
Russia
 Alexander the Great in, 117
 Mongol, 266–8
 and stylitism, 189
 Viking, 203, **205**
Rustichello of Pisa, 276–8
Ryme, Wilhelm den, 47

S

Sagan, Carl, 120
Sahagun, Fr. Bernardino de, 279
Sahara Desert, 280–2
St. Bertin Abbey, 203
St. Gall, monastery of, 217, 220
St. George's Chapel, 282
Saint Joan (Shaw), 297
St. Peter's, Basilica of, 209, 291
St. Sophia, Church of (Hagia
 Sophia), 200
St. Vitus's Dance, 96
Saladin, Sultan, 237, 247, 271
Salamis, 106–7
Salammbo, 129
Salisbury, 197
Salona, 183
Samarkand, 174–5, 201, 227,
 266, **295–6**
Samos, 97, 107
samurai, **240–3**
Sanskrit (language), 61, 202
Santa Maria (Columbus's ship),
 313
Santander, 66
Santa Severa, 94
Santimamiñe (caves), 67
Santorini (Thira), 56, **63–5**
Sappho, 99, **102**
Saracens, 74, 247, 255
 see also Crusades
Saragossa, 211

Sardinia, 138
Sasquatch (Big Foot), 11
Saunière, Bérenger, 165–6
Savoy, Dukes of, 251
scalpel, 187
Schleswig, 147
science
 and alchemy, **239–40**
 Arab, **226–7**
 Greek, **110–11, 115–16,
  124–5,** 142–3, 180–1
 medieval, 247–8
 Renaissance, 292, 307
scissors, 187
Scotland, 187, 197, 303
screw press, 125
sculpture, **11–12, 126–8,** 208
Scylla, 87
Scyths, 103–4
Sea of Reeds, 64–5
seal (commercial), 33, 36, 76
Second Reich, 211
Segesta, 112
Segovia, 157
Sei Shonagon, 231
Seleucia, 59
Selinus, 112
Seneca, Lucius, 156–7
Senenmut, 68
Septimus Severus, Roman
 Emperor, 146
Septuagint, 119
Serapeum, 121
Serendib, 215
Severin, Tim, 214–17.
Seville, 133
sextant, 216
sexual practices
 Bacchanalian, 140–1
 and Roman baths, 157
 Greek, 102–3
 Moche, 176–7
 Spartan, 99
 and troubadours, 243–5
Sforza, Giovanni, 308
Sforza, Ludovico, 306–7
shadoof, 44
Shah Jahan, Mogul Emperor,
 295
Shahrazada, 212
Shakespeare, William, 143–4,
 304
Shalmaneser III, King of
 Assyria, 82
shaman, 178
Shamash, 59
Shanidar, 15
Shaw, George Bernard, 297
Sheba, Queen of, 36, 182, 245,
 257
shellfish, 74
Shinto, 179
ship, *see* boat
shipwreck, 75–6
Shiraz, 296
Shona (people), 257
Shoshone (people), 21
Shub-ad (Puabi), Queen of Ur,
 42–3
Siberia, 11, 103
Sicilian Vespers, War of, **271–3**
Sicily, 112–13, 132, 136–7, 204,
 255–6, **271–3,** 285
Siddhartha, Gautama, 200
Sidon, 73–4
silk, 141, 152, 175, 206, 222, 305
Silkeborg Museum, 148
silver
 in acupuncture, 46
 and alchemy, 239–40
 Laurium, 105–6
 Sidonian, 73
 Sumerian, 42–3
 see also currency

Silvester, Pope, 291
Simeon Stylites, St., **187–9**
Simon, St., 307
Sindbad, **214–17**
siren, 87
Sivas, 296
Skavlem, Halvor L., 22
skene (tent), 109
Skipas, 126
skull
 American Indian, 81
 Aztec, 279
 Basque, 67
 Egyptian, 50–1
 Mongol, 105
 Neanderthal, 10–11
 Tamerlane's, 296
 trepanning of, 24–5
slavery
 Arab, 213, **270–1**
 Assyrian, 82–3
 Babylonian, 59
 Roman, **135–7,** 141, 157,
  169–70
Slavs, 203, 205, 211, 237
smallpox, 263
Smenkhkara, 72
Smyrna, 296
Socrates, 112–15
Socrates Scolasticus, 182
Sohar (ship), 214–15
Solecki, Ralph S., 15
Solomon, King of Israel, 36, 73,
 165, 182, 245, 257
Solskuggafjol (sundial), 207
Somalia, 68
Song of Roland (epic poem), 209,
 211
Sophocles, 109–10, 119–20
Sostratos of Cnidus, 126
Soto, Hernando de, 81
Spain
 Basques in, 66–7, 211
 Carthaginian, 132
 and Inquisition, 259, 278–80
 Moorish, 133, 175, 211, 227,
  238, 244, **310–11**
 and New World, 278–80, 313
 Stone Age, 11
Sparta, **98–9,** 101–3, 106
Spartacus, 137
Spartacus (movie), 170
Spassky, Boris, 135
spectacles, 247
spikenard, 140
Split, 183
sponge-diver, 75, 142
sport, *see* games
Squier, Ephraim, 24, 81
Sri Lanka, 152–3, 215, 276–7
Stabiae, 168
Stadiatis, Elias, 142
Stais, Valerios, 142
standard, of Constantine,
 184–5
star "compass", 18
Statute of Labourers, 289
steam turbine, 125
steatopygia, 13
Stein, Aurel, **222–4**
stele (monument), 82
Stephen, Pope, 292
Stillington, Robert, 305
Stoker, Bram, 299
Stone Age, 11–14, 16–20, 23–5
Stone Age "Venuses," **11–12**
Stonehenge, 149, 229
Strabo, 149
Stralsund, peace of, 287–8
Street of the Dead, 278
strike, 78–9
Strong, Duncan, 176
Stupor Mundi, **255–6**
stylitism, 189

Sudbury, Simon, 290–1
Sudra, 60
Suetonius, 162–3
sugar, 140, 311
suicide, 42–3, 144, 164, 240–3
Sujin, Emperor of Japan, 179
Sumatra, 215–17, 277
Sumeria, 34, 38–9, 42–3, 53
Sung Dynasty, 247–8
surgery, *see* health and medicine
suttee (Indian funeral practice),
 215
Switzerland, 40–1
sword, 240, 242
symposium, **113–15**
Symposium (Plato), 115
Synesius of Cyrene, 120
Syracuse, 102, 112, 124, 129
Syria, 53, 82, 187–9

T

Tabenna, monastery of, 219
Tacitus, 148, 162–4, 166
Tafurs, **236–7**
Taghaza, 281
Taj Mahal, 295
Tamburlaine the Great
 (Marlowe), 295
Tamerlane, 134, **295–6**
Tana, Lake, 45
Tangier, 281
Tanit, 129–30
tank, 307
Tannhäuser (Wagner), 243
Tapia, Andres de, 279
tapir, 21
Tarquinia, 94
Tarsus, 144
Tartars, *see* Mongols
Tashkent, 205
Tassilo, Duke, 210
tattoo, 103
taxation
 Assyrian, 83
 Chimu, 264
 Egyptian, 44
 feudal, 289–90
 Inca, 263
 Moorish, 311
 Norman, 234–5
 Roman, 141, 154
tea ceremony, 242
te lapa, te mata (glory of the seas),
 18
Telesterion, 77
Tell Mardik, 53
Tello, Julio, 228
Telnishe, 188
temple-mound, 80
Temujin, 266–7
Tenochtitlan, 278–9
Teotihuacan, 52, 278
teredo worm, 53, 214
Terence, 110
terracotta
 coins, 153
 statues, 127
Thaddeus, St., 307
Thailand, 28–9
Thales, 110–11
theatre, Greek, **109–10**
Thebes, 71–2, **79,** 145
Themistocles, 105
Theodora, Byzantine Empress,
 198–200
Theodosius I, Roman Emperor,
 78, 89–90, 93
Theodosius II, Roman
 Emperor, 189
Theon of Alexandria, 120
Theophrastus, 109

thermae, 156
Thermopylae, 98, 106–7
Theseus, 56, 139
Thespis, 109
Thira, *see* Santorini
Third Reich, 211
Thomas, Cyrus, 81
Throckmorton, Peter, 75–6
Thucydides, 102, 108, 112
Thurii, 107–8
Thutmose I, Pharaoh, 78
Thutmose II, Pharaoh, 67
Thutmose III, Pharaoh, 67, 69
Tiber, River, 139, 157, 184
Tiberius, Roman Emperor, 186
Tiepolo, Giovanni, 86
Tiflis, 296
tiger, 51–2, 169, 171
Tiglathpileser III, Assyrian
 King, 82
Tigris (boat), 33
Timbuktu, 282
Timotheos, 126
tin, *see* metal-working
Tintagel, 197
Tirel, Walter, 248–9
Titus
 Arch of, 166
 Emperor, 155
Toghril, 267
Tollund Man, **146–8**
tool-making, 12, **19–20, 22,** 25,
 30
Topa Inca, 263
topheth (temple), 130
Toulmin, Stephen, 97
Toulouse, 189, 259
Tournai, 305
tournament, 196, **252–4**
Tower of London, 303–5
trade
 African, 258, 280–2
 American Indian, 80
 Arab, 217
 Athenian, 106
 Chinese-Indian, 200
 Etruscan, 93–4
 Hanseatic, 287–9
 and horse-power, 209
 Mesopotamian, **32–3,** 53
 Phoenician, 73–6
 and plague, 284–5
 Roman, 141, **152–3**
 Venetian, 277–8
 Viking, 204–7
Trajan
 Column, 186
 Emperor, 169
transport
 of animals, 169–72
 development of, 34–6
 see also tourism
Transylvania, 299
Treasure of Jerusalem, **165–6**
trepanning, 24–5
Tres Zapotes, 35
Trials of Marco Polo
 (Rustichello), 276
Triano, Rodrigo de, 312
Tripoli, 237
trireme, 105–6
Trobriand islanders, 58
Trojan War, 86, 146
troubadour, **243–5,** 256
Troy, siege of, 133
Troyes, Chrétien de, 245
Ts'ai Lun, 175
tsantsa (shrunken head), 62–3
Tuccia, 91
Tudor
 dynasty, 303–5
 rose, 196
tumbaga (alloy), 99–100

Tun-Huang, 222–3
tunnel, Samos, **97–8**
Tupac Yupanqui, 62
Turin Shroud, **250–2**
Turkestan, 174
Turks, 189, 236–7, 278,
 299–300
turtle
 brains of, 50
 giant, 24
 shell, 69
Tutankhamon, Pharaoh, 72,
 144
Tutankaton, Pharaoh, 72
Tyler, Wat, **290–1**
Tyrannius Rufinius, 182
Tyre (Sur), 73–4, 129, 182

U

Uffizi Museum, Florence, 209
Ugudai Khan, 267
Ukraine, 30
Ulf the Jarl, 134
ulo aetahi (glory of the seas), 18
underwater archeology, 41,
 74–5, 142
Untouchables, **60–1**
Ur, **32–4, 42–3**
Urban II, Pope, 237
Urbinia, 90
Urgench, 296
Ur-Nammu
 laws, 59
 ziggurat, 39
Urtiaga (cave), 67

V

Vaisravana, 222
Vaisya, 60
Valerian, Roman Emperor, 183
valetudinarium (hospital), 187
Valhalla, 203
Valla, Lorenzo, 292
Valley of the Kings, 69, **78–9**
vampire, 25, **299–300**
Vandals, 190
varna (castle), 61
Varro, 187
Vegetius, 187
Venice, 276–8, 288
Venus of Lespugue, 12
Venus of Willendorf, 12
Vergina, 117
Verulamium (St. Albans),
 160–1
Vespasian, Roman Emperor,
 155, 166
Vespucci, Amerigo, 313
Vestal Virgins, **90–1**
Vesuvius, Mt., 166–8
Victoria, Lake, 45
Vienna, 139
Vietnam, 153, 266
Vikings, 133, **203–7,** 211;
 224–5
Villa of the Mysteries, 140
vinegar, 140
vineyard, 136, 140
Vinland, 205
violin, 163
Virgil, 135
Virgin Mary, cult of, 244
Virú Valley, 176
Visigoths, 165–6, 192
Vita Caroli Magni (Einhard),
 209
Vitruvius, Marcus, 157
Vlad Dracul, 299

Vlad Tepes (Vlad the Impaler), **299–300**
Vladimir, Viking Prince, 205
"vocal Memnon," 145–6
volcanic eruption, 56, **63–5,**
166–8
Voltaire, François, 211, 292
volumen (scroll), 119
Vulci, 95

W

Wa, 178–9
Waldemar IV, King of
Denmark, 287–8
Waldensian heresy, 260
Wallachia, 191, 299
Walls of Babylon, 125–6
Wang I-Yung, 69–70
Wang Mang, Chinese Emperor,
46
Wang Tao-Shih, 222–4

Warbeck, Perkin, **303–5**
water, 138, 140, **157,** 187, 191,
311
Waterloo, battle of, 275
Wessex, 224–5
West Indies, 99
Westminster Abbey, 234, 304
We, the Navigators (Lewis), 17
whale, hunting 293–4
wheel
invention of, **34–5,** 52, 70
water, 125
White Nile, *see* Nile, River
Wight, Isle of, 197
"wild men," 11
William Arthur, Prince of
Britain, 198
William IX, Duke of Aquitaine,
244
William Rufus, 248–9
William the Conqueror, 204,
232–5, 249
Winchester, 196–8, 249
windmill, 125

Windsor Castle, 196, 198, 282
wine, 114, **139–40,** 166, 191,
217
witchcraft, 249, 297–8
women, status of
Arab, 213
Assyrian, 83
Egyptian, 67–9
Greek, 89, 92, 98–9, **101–3,**
114
Japanese, 231–2
medieval, 133, 243–5, 256
Moorish, 311
Roman, 90–1, 137, 141, 170
Women, Island of, 215
wooden horse, 86
Woolley, Sir Leonard, 42–3
"wop," 140
World War I, 25
World War II, 241, 243, 306
writing, *see* language and
literacy
Wu Ching Tsao Yao, 247
Wunderlich, Hans Georg, 57

X

Xanthippe, 114
Xenophon, 114–15
Xerxes, 98, 106
Xesspe, Mejía, 228–9
Xocotlan, 279
X-ray, 25, 49–50

Y

Ydonis, 239
Yellow River, 71
Yemen, 182
Yeti, 11
yew, 273, 275
Ypres, 96
Yslandia, 255
Yugoslavia, 183

Z

Zaghouan aqueduct, 157
Zagwe dynasty, 245
Zambezi, River, 257
zatrikion (Byzantine game), 134
Zealot Revolt, 154–5
Zen Buddhism, 242
Zenodotus of Ephesus, 119
Zeus, 89, 92, 101, 117
ziggurat, 39, 42
Zimbabwe, **257–8**
Zion, 166
Zubaydah, Arab Queen, 213

Picture Credits and Acknowledgments

B = Bottom, C = Center, L = Left, R = Right, T = Top

Prof. Leslie Alcock: **197** TR. Aldus Archive: **263**. Russell Ash: **171**. Ashmolean Museum, Oxford: **224**. Australian Information Service, London: **23**.
Michael Baigent: **165** T & B. BBC Television: **244** B; **308**. Bibliothèque Nationale: **120** (Sonia Halliday). **155** (Giraudon); **209** (Edimedia); **227** (Sonia Halliday); **260** (Giraudon); **267** (Weidenfeld & Nicholson); **268** (Giraudon); **274** (Edimedia). Biofotos: **287** (G. Kinns). Bodleian Library, Oxford: **225** B; **234**; **276** B (Robert Harding Associates). Lee Bolton: **240**. Janet & Colin Bord: **197** TC. Bridgeman Art Library: **61**; **74**. British Library: **65**; **83**; **213**; **223** T & B; **231**; **248**; **253**; **280**. British Museum: **34**, **38** B, **44** B, **57**, **96**, **110** (Michael Holford); **133** (Photoresources); **145** B (Michael Holford); **153**; **196** T (Robert Harding Associates); **208** (Michael Holford). Bulloz: **116**.
Camera Press: **135**; **182**. J. Allan Cash: **226**; **300**. Peter Chèze-Brown: **197** BR; **258** T & B. City Art Museum of St. Louis (Eliza K. McMillan Fund): **81** T. Peter Clayton: **50** B. Colorsport: **88**; **89** R. Daily Telegraph Colour Library: **273**; **303** (Tim Mercer). Department of the Environment (Crown Copyright): **283**. Ecole Nationale Supérieure des Beaux Arts, Paris: **77**. Edimedia: **236**; **286**; **298**. Ekdotike Athenon: **117**; **118**. E-T Archive: **243**. Mary Evans Picture Library: **92**; **247**.
Werner Forman Archive: **2–3**; **25** T; **168** B; **281**; **310** T. Fotomas Index: **167**.
Gemäldegalerie/Bildarchiv Preussicher Kulturbesitz: **134**. Georg Gerster/John Hillelson Agency: **81** B; **179**; **246**. Richard Greenhill/(c) Sindbad Voyage: **215**; **216**. Susan Griggs Agency: **6**; **168** T; **254** T.
Sonia Halliday: **44** T; **45**: **68** (Verity Weston); **79**; **169**; **183**; **185** T; **199** (Jane Taylor); **245**. Robert Harding Associates: **100**; **127** T & B; **128**; **197** BL; **222**; **282**; **295**; **311**; **312** T. James Harris & Kent Weeks, X-Ray of Amenhotep I in *X-Raying the Pharaohs*. (c) 1973 Charles Scribner's Sons. Reprinted with the permission of Charles Scribner's Sons: **49**. Hermitage Museum, Leningrad: **103**. Thor Heyerdahl: **32** B. Michael Holford: **48**; **52** R (Ianthe Ruthven); **129**; **156**; **190**; **196** B; **232** T & B; **233**; **278** (Ianthe Ruthven). Horniman Museum, London: **62** (Michael Holford).
Image Bank: **17**. International Photobank: **197** TL.
Kobal Collection: **145** T; **170**; **297**; **299** B; **305**.
Lauros-Giraudon: **193**; **270**. Erich Lessing/John Hillelson Agency: **87**. Louvre, Paris: **38** T (Michael Holford); **59** (Edimedia).
William MacQuitty: **37**; **52** L; **67**; **146**. Manchester Museum Mummy Project: **50** T. Mansell Collection: **91**; **114**; **154**; **164**; **191**; **201**; **290**; **312** B. Meteorological Office, London: **185** B (R.N.Hughes). Roland & Sabrina Michaud/John Hillelson Agency: **47**; **200**. Marion & Tony Morrison: **228**; **229**; **261** L & R; **262**. Musée Baron Gerard, Bayeux: **103**. Musée d'Antiquités National, St. Germain-en-Laye: **13** (Jean Vertut). Musée de l'Homme, Paris: **11**. Musée des Beaux Arts, Tours: **254** B (Lauros-Giraudon). Museo Correr, Venice: **276** T (Giraudon). Museum of Mankind, London: **279**. Museum of the American Indian, Heye Foundation, New York: **21**; **80**. National Archeological Museum, Athens: **101**. National Gallery, London: **86**. National Library of Medicine, Bethesda, Maryland; **50** C. National Maritime Museum, London: **180** B (Michael Holford). National Museum, Copenhagen: **147**; **148** (Werner Forman Archive). National Palace Museum, Taiwan: **266**. George Ortiz Collection, Switzerland: **99**. Ostia Museum: **172** (Michael Holford).
Photoresources: **12**; **55** T & B; **140**; **152**. Picturepoint: **108**. Popperfoto: **242**. Public Record Office, London: **235**. Dr. Peter Reynolds/Butser Ancient Farm Project Trust: **122** T. Rex Features: **46**. Ann Ronan Picture Library: **125**; **180** T. Theodore Rowland-Entwistle: **14**. Royal Holloway College, University of London: **304** (Bridgeman Art Library).
Carl Sagan Productions Inc: **121**. Salmer Archives: **66**; **310** B. Scala: **94** T & B; **188**; **239**; **250**; **252**; **301** T & B; **306**; **309** B. Science Museum, London: **313** (Hamlyn Group). Screenpro Films: **251**. Ronald Sheridan: **32** T; **89** L; **109** T & B; **143** B; **163** T & B; **166**; **177**; **184**; **186**; **225** T; **284** B. Sidney Sussex College, Cambridge: **219**. David Simson: **149**. Smithsonian Institution: **28**, **29** (Ruth Kirk); **143** T (Photri); **293** T & B (Ruth & Louis Kirk). Sotheby, Parke Bernet & Co: **205** (painting by Carl Haag). Staatliche Museen, Berlin: **71**; **72** (Bildarchiv Preussicher Kulturbesitz). Staatsarchiv, Hamburg: **288** (E-T Archive). Statens Historiska Museet: **203** (Werner Forman Archive). David Strickland: **160**. Sygma/John Hillelson Agency: **178**. Syndication International: **284** T.
Tate Gallery, London: **56**. Peter Throckmorton: **75** T & B. Gianni Tortoli: **54**. Turkish National Museums: **35** (Michael Holford). Universitäts Bibliothek, Heidelberg: **244** T. University of Colorado Museum: **22** (Joe Ben Wheat).
Vatican Library: **124** (Scala); **218**; **255**; **309** T (Scala). Victoria & Albert Museum, London: **36**; **212** (Bridgeman Art Library). John Watney: **25** B. Weidenfeld & Nicolson: **241**. Wellcome Museum for the History of Medicine: **25**C (Angelo Hornak). Mike Wells/Aspect Picture Library: **122–3**. Henry Wilson: **60**. Xinhua News Agency: **70**.
ZEFA Picture Library: **43** R; **277** (David Thurston).

Illustrations by Giovanni Caselli: **10**; **15**; **30–1**; **40**; **104**; **131**; **136–7**; **141**; **150–1**; **158–9**; **173**; **206–7**; **220–1**; **264–5**; **294**.
Additional illustrations by David Ashby.
Cartography by Eugene Fleury.

Dorling Kindersley would like to thank the following for their special assistance: Lesley Gilbert, Professor Christopher Holdsworth, Dr Malcolm Lyons, and Nick Russell. Dorling Kindersley would also like to thank Pauline Faulks, Debra Lee, Jane Owen, and Steven Wooster for their design assistance; Julian Dorling, Jonathan Hilton, Cathy Meeus, Robin Widdowson, and Phil Wilkinson for their research assistance; and Susan Berry, Russell Chamberlin, Kathryn Coutu, Pauline Davidson, David Lambert, Donna Leigh, Paulette Pratt, Pippa Rubinstein, Robert Stewart, Mary Trewby, Eleanor van Zandt, and Catriona Warren for their help with the text.

Typesetting by Vantage Photosetting Co Ltd, Eastleigh and London.
Reproduction by Reprocolor, Milan.